THE ULTIMATE BOOK OF

MARCH MADNESS

The Player, Games, and Cinderellas that Captivated a Nation

TOM HAGER

MVP
BOOKS

First published in 2012 by MVP Books,
an imprint of MBI Publishing Company and the
Quayside Publishing Group, 400 First Avenue North,
Suite 300, Minneapolis, MN 55401 USA

The information in this book is true and complete
to the best of our knowledge. All recommendations
are made without any guarantee on the part of the
author or Publisher, who also disclaims any liability
incurred in connection with the use of this data or
specific details.

This publication has not been prepared, approved,
or licensed by the National Collegiate Athletics
Association.

We recognize, further, that some words, model names,
and designations mentioned herein are the property of
the trademark holder. We use them for identification
purposes only. This is not an official publication.

MVP Books titles are also available at discounts in
bulk quantity for industrial or sales-promotional use.
For details write to Special Sales Manager at
Quayside Publishing Group, 400 First Avenue North,
Suite 300, Minneapolis, MN 55401 USA.

To find out more about our books, visit us online at
www.mvpbooks.com.

LIBRARY OF CONGRESS CATALOGING-IN-PUBLICATION DATA

Hager, Tom, 1989-
  The ultimate book of March madness : the players,
games, and Cinderellas that captivated a nation / Tom
Hager.
    p. cm.
  Includes bibliographical references and index.
  ISBN 978-0-7603-4323-4 (hardback)
  1. NCAA Basketball Tournament—History.
2. Basketball—Tournaments—History. I. National
Collegiate Athletic Association. II. Title.
  GV885.49.N37H34 2012
  796.323'63—dc23
                                    2012020031

Editor: Adam Brunner
Design Manager: James Kegley
Book Designer: Mandy Kimlinger
Layout: Diana Boger
Cover Designer: Matt Simmons

Photo credits:
Cover photograph by Andrea Rugg Photography
Part I opener, William P. Straeter/AP Photo
Part II opener, Norfolk State Athletic Department

Printed in China

Contents

Preface

From the time I was a small child, the NCAA Tournament has held a special place in my heart. I clearly remember watching the 1996 Final Four between UMass and Kentucky. From that first introduction to college basketball, March Madness never ceased to amaze. I was nine years old when Gonzaga advanced all the way to the Elite Eight. It was love at first site, and they continue to be my favorite team to this day. But it wasn't until 2001 that I truly discovered just how special March Madness can be. During the first round I witnessed what I still consider to be the greatest sports moment in my lifetime—15th seeded Hampton upsetting Iowa State in the closing seconds. Hampton coach Steve Merfeld was hoisted in the air, an iconic image that will stay in my memory.

Shortly after that moment, I made up my mind that I was going to be a sports writer. I was never going to make the basketball team (I tried, but my initial theory proved to be correct) so I decided the next best thing was to write about basketball. But this project—my first book—is one that I actually stumbled into by accident. I wanted to buy a book on the history of the NCAA Tournament, and it quickly became apparent to me that no book truly captured everything the tournament is about. Some books had written about past championships and the Final Four, but no one had written a book on what makes the tournament truly special. I decided to write that book and to divide it into two sections: one to discuss each championship team and their journey to the title, and another to discuss all the incredible buzzer beaters that have become synonymous with March Madness.

For the year-by-year section, I look at what made each championship team special—the adversity they overcame, the characters on the team, and the games that helped them reach their goal. While the champions are usually the story of each year's tournament, a few years were special exceptions—for example, when a Cinderella team took the tournament by storm. In those rare circumstances, like Loyola Marymount's emotional journey to the Elite Eight in 1990 or VCU's improbable run to the Final Four in 2011, my focus for that chapter is on them. Of the 74 chapters (each two pages) in the first section, all but five focus on that year's champion.

To many fans out there, the tournament is less about the championship than about all the exciting games along the way. The buzzer beaters, bracket-busters, and unbelievable upsets keep these fans coming back year after year. These stories are chronicled in the second section of this book, ranking the 100 best games of all time. The games were ranked on the excitement of the finish, whether the game involved an upset or comeback, and any backdrop that made the game more intriguing.

To uncover all the great stories behind each of these moments, I interviewed more than 180 former athletes and coaches. Each person I interviewed was more than happy to talk with me: after all, it gave them an excuse to recall the biggest shot they ever made or the experience of winning a national championship. What I discovered along the way is that each person had an amazing story to tell, many of which have never been documented, until now.

One of my hopes for this book is that you can pick it up and turn to any page—at any year or any game—and begin a new story. I am extremely proud to present you *The Ultimate Book of March Madness,* and I hope you have as much fun reading it as I had writing it.

Thanks,
Tom Hager

PART I

A YEAR-BY-YEAR HISTORY OF THE NCAA TOURNAMENT

1939 Oregon

When the leaders of the National Association of Basketball Coaches gathered in the spring of 1938, they had no idea what they were creating. Back then there was no ESPN, much less an ESPN.com where nearly 6.5 million people filled out brackets each year. But even in the sport's infancy, a group of four coaches—Harold Olsen of Ohio State, Phog Allen of Kansas, John Bunn of Stanford, and William S. Chandler of Marquette—had a vision of just what the game could become. Along with one businessman from New York, the group decided to sit down and determine if a national basketball tournament was possible. They agreed to give it a shot, and while the first tournament would hardly qualify as a success story, it set in motion everything the NCAA Tournament would eventually become.

Before college basketball became a billion-dollar industry, before Final Fours were played in football arenas, and even before fans could watch games—or anything, for that matter—on television, the 1939 NCAA Tournament gave America its first taste of postseason basketball. Basketball had been gaining popularity since its inception in 1891, but for the first time the sport had a proper tournament to determine the nation's best team. A year earlier, the National Invitation Tournament had been created to pair teams from around the country, so in response the National Association of Basketball Coaches created its own tournament, one that included only the winners of each conference. But for all its ambitions, the first tournament hardly resembled anything that fans would recognize today.

For starters, only eight teams took part in the inaugural tournament, which was comprised only of East and West Regions. The West bracket's two games would be played at San Francisco's Treasure Island, in conjunction with the World's Fair exhibit. The games were merely a backdrop to the surrounding events, but that was far from the most notable difference from today's game. When Slim Wintermute and the Oregon Ducks arrived for the tournament, the local headlines read, "World Fair Displays Biggest Boy In Basketball Tonight." But compared with today's players, Wintermute would just be an oversized guard.

"He was tall—he was 6-foot-8. Of course, that isn't tall now," laughed roommate and guard Moon Mullen. "But in those days he usually had two bunks in the trains."

Wintermute may have been chastised for his extraordinary height, but he was the primary reason for the school's resurgence in basketball. The senior had his breakout year in 1939, earning All-American honors to deliver Oregon its first conference title in 20 years. In fact, the center had been so dominant that some of the sport's biggest names had proposed raising the basket to 12 feet. In the team's first-round match, Wintermute scored 14 of Oregon's 56 points in a blowout win over Texas. That total was an impressive achievement for the time, but the Ducks could have won with even a mediocre offensive night. With Wintermute leading the charge, they held Texas without a field goal for the first 11 minutes and followed up the performance with a 55–37 win over Oklahoma the following night.

For their efforts, the Ducks were awarded a silver trophy that resembled the NFL's Lombardi Trophy, but with a basketball at the top. On the line in the national championship game would be a vastly different masterpiece, one that shared more in common with a wedding cake than the regional award. Standing atop the tall trophy was a little figurine of a basketball player, sculpted as if it were preparing for a hook shot.

Claiming the title from Ohio State, however, would not be an easy task. The Ducks grabbed a 6–0 lead right out of the gate and took a 21–16 lead into halftime, but Oregon

Fans weren't exactly packing the stands at Northwestern's Patten Gymnasium for the championship game, but the Oregon Ducks found quite a different atmosphere upon their return to Eugene. *University of Oregon Athletic Department*

coach Howard Hobson wondered whether the team's starting lineup could hold on for the remainder of the game. Hobson's team had almost no depth, forcing him to play each of his starters for 39 minutes against the Buckeyes. And after 34 games, including a 22-day road trip during winter break, their legs were liable to wear down at the most inconvenient time. It certainly appeared to be the case as an energized Ohio State team trimmed the lead to 21–20 in the second half, but the Ducks weren't about to abandon their fast-paced offense. Hobson left his starters in as the team reeled off eight straight points to break open the game.

"We were in very good shape," said Mullen, one of just seven Ducks to play in the game. "Our practices were always intense."

Oregon now stood just minutes away from glory, but the Ducks' reckless style ended up costing them the trophy—in an odd way. The team continued to excel on the court, holding off Ohio State 46–33, but OU guard Bobby Anet, sprawling for a loose ball, tumbled into the trophy that was sitting at the edge of the floor. The collision sent the championship hardware crashing to the court, breaking off the figurine that had been so proudly crafted. The resulting championship ceremony was even less impressive than the now two-piece trophy.

"It was a two-handed trophy presentation that night, where the guy held the bottom of the trophy with one hand," guard John Dick

laughed, "and held the little man on top with the other."

The fans back home in Oregon decided they needed a proper memento to celebrate the title. In Dick's hometown of The Dalles, local residents gathered 25-cent donations to buy him a $75 gold watch—no small price in the years just following the Great Depression. Fans in the other players' hometowns followed suit, but the celebration did not end there. They knew the players were on a train back to campus, and they tried to organize a welcome home party in The Dalles on the way back. Railroad officials quickly nixed the idea, prompting the fans to give an ultimatum: The railroad company could either stop the train so the fans could embrace their heroes, or the fans would simply barricade the tracks and have the party anyway. The railroad president caved in, and the fans—at least those who were awake—were given the opportunity to welcome back the team as their train pulled in at 6:00 a.m.

The NABC leaders, despite the reaction from Oregon fans, were less than enthralled with their own tournament. They resolved to leave it as a one-time event unless somebody else could pick up the costs. The NCAA gladly paid for the first year's expenses in exchange for the rights to the tournament—and several decades and many memories later, fans are awfully glad they did. ●

1940 Indiana

Had it not been for an intervention by the NCAA, the 1939 tournament might have been the first and last of its kind. The NABC lost more than $2,500 while hosting the first tournament, and it was only because the NCAA stepped in to pay for the expenses that a second tournament became possible. In exchange for its kindness, the NCAA was given the rights for future tournaments—which also meant they, too, would lose money if history repeated itself. Fortunately for the NCAA, the 1940 tournament provided fans their first taste of March Madness. Kansas trailed USC 41–42 in the final moments of the West Regional final before Bob Allen stole the ball and fired a pass to Howard Engleman, whose shot from the corner sent the Jayhawks to the national championship game. The ticket sales were as pleasing as the action on the court, as the NCAA's profit of nearly $10,000 kept the tournament going for at least another year.

Regardless of how the season's final act would transpire, the Indiana Hoosiers knew they could walk away with their heads held high. They had beaten Purdue a day earlier, giving IU its first season sweep in the 40-year history of the rivalry. The Hoosiers did their part to try to win the Big Ten title when their 52–31 victory over Ohio State put them within a half game of the Boilermakers, who would be taking on Illinois in their season finale. An Illini win would give both Purdue and Indiana a share of the lead, and because the Hoosiers had won both head-to-head matchups, they would likely receive the conference's lone bid to the NCAA Tournament.

Both teams were deserving of a spot in the Big Dance, but the eight-team tournament could only accept one representative from each conference. Early on, it appeared that team might be Indiana after all. The Boilermakers had blown a seven-point lead and found themselves trailing by 10 points in the second half. Before the game ended, however, Purdue would mount an incredible comeback to take home a 34–31 victory and, most importantly, the Big Ten title.

But in this, just the second tournament and the first under the control of the NCAA, things were not as clear-cut as they are today. The NCAA surprisingly decided to give the Big Ten's bid to the second-place Hoosiers, on the strength of their two victories over Purdue. It was a completely unexpected gift—one they were almost not allowed to take.

The athletics committee at IU was not so keen on sending their basketball players across the country for more games, knowing that a successful run in the tournament could mean a few more missed classes. Indiana coach Branch McCracken had to argue his case before his team could head off for its opening game, and still the committee wasn't budging. Reluctantly, after hours of persuading from McCracken, the committee let the Hoosiers go. McCracken quickly went back to preparing his team, for in a few days his team would be playing Springfield University.

The players responded well, and by halftime they had jumped out to a 30–11 lead. Their eventual 48–24 victory gave them a meeting the next night with Duquesne, where the Hoosiers picked up where they left off. The Hoosiers raced off to a 7–0 lead and cruised to a 25–13 lead at halftime, after which McCracken took out his starters. He hoped to give his first team fresh legs heading into the championship game, but the Dukes pulled to within 33–29. McCracken knew it was time to put the starting five back in, and they held on to give Indiana the 39–30 final edge.

Indiana was now heading to Kansas City for the national championship game, but they'd be facing the Kansas Jayhawks, who would clearly have the crowd on their side. McCracken knew his players would need every advantage they could get, and he wanted his players to rest up before the title game. So it must have come as quite a shock to McCracken when he discovered that his wife had taken the players out to see a movie, which he believed would drain their eyes. Perhaps the only tired eyes were those of his wife, Mary Jo, who cried during most of the team's viewing of *Gone with the Wind*. The players, too tough for emotions, spent the entire time laughing.

Kansas got a quick sense of that toughness when Indiana's Curly Armstrong ran into Bob Allen, the son of KU coach Phog Allen. Armstrong reached over to Bob and said with a grin, "Maybe you better sit with daddy." Opposing coaches often accused McCracken of promoting aggressive play, and while the IU coach always replied that it was something he never encouraged, he slyly added that he didn't exactly discourage it, either. That sort of comment was nothing new for McCracken, who marched to the beat of his own drum. Months before, McCracken had gone on the court to challenge an official's call, only to have the referee tell him his next step would result in a technical foul. The coach responded by calling on his assistants to carry him off the court.

But at the start of the game, it was the Jayhawks who appeared to be the aggressors, holding Indiana without a field goal for the first eight minutes of the contest. IU guard Marv Huffman called a timeout to gather the team's composure, but no words were necessary. They knew what they had to do—not that they would have been able to hear each other over the crowd of 10,000 fans.

The Hoosiers came out of the timeout with a new sense of purpose and proceeded to play the rest of the half flawlessly. By the time the first period came to a close, Indiana had finished a 28–9 run. When the final seconds of their 60–42 victory ticked away, McCracken was once again carried off the court—only this time it was by his players. ●

1941 Wisconsin

Over 48,000 people, more than three times the number who saw the tournament in 1939, filled the stands in 1941. What they saw was a tournament of extremes. Washington State broke the tournament record for points in a game with 64 against Arkansas in the regional finals, then shot just 21.5 percent against Wisconsin in the finals, a record that would stand for 70 years. North Carolina set a record for futility that still stands today, scoring just 20 points against Pittsburgh. And while their third-place game in the East Regional was meaningless, UNC's George Glamack scored 31 points against Dartmouth, a record that would last until 1950.

On March 4, 1940, Wisconsin basketball hit its low point. The Badgers took on the University of Chicago that night to decide who would take last place in the Big Ten that year. Only 5,000 people showed up to watch the 4–15 Badgers play, which would have been understandable had Gene Englund not been vying for the school's all-time scoring record. The junior started the day just 10 points away from breaking the mark, and he played well early on. But, in a fitting end to the season, Englund fouled out just three minutes into the second half—with nine points.

The program appeared to be on its way back to respectability the following season, but a national championship was the farthest thing from coach Bud Foster's mind. He simply hoped his team could finish in the top half of the Big Ten. Of course, it's hard to outshine the competition with a roster comprised of second-hand recruits. Fred Rehm, a sophomore on the 1941 squad, had originally intended to play for UW's cross-state rival.

"He actually tried out at Marquette," his son Fred Jr. remembered. "And the Marquette coach told him, 'You're not going to be good enough to play college basketball.'"

Rehm had a much easier time making the team at Wisconsin, and once he cracked the starting lineup in the middle of the season, the Badgers were unstoppable. They won their last 12 games of the season to win the Big Ten title and qualify for the NCAA Tournament. To top it all off, the NCAA selected the Badgers to play their first two games in Madison, allowing the Wisconsin fans to support their local team. What those fans witnessed were two of the most thrilling games of the season.

In their first-round game against Dartmouth, the Badgers continued one of their few bad habits throughout the year and found themselves down at halftime. Wisconsin continued to trail throughout the second half until Gene Englund put UW up 46–44 with just a few minutes to spare. Englund later hit a hook shot, and sophomore John Kotz followed with a pair of free throws to give the Badgers a seemingly safe 51–46 lead. Dartmouth's Stan Skaug brought the Indians within 51–48 on a deep shot, and Wisconsin failed to hold onto the ball on the ensuing possession. At the last second, Bill Parmer heaved a shot from half-court that actually went in just as the buzzer sounded. Today, that shot would have tied the game, but with no three-point line at the time, Wisconsin escaped with a 51–50 win.

By this point, the local fans had realized what a special group they had on their hands. A sellout crowd of more than 13,000 fans, some of whom had paid nearly five times the face value just to snag a ticket, packed the Wisconsin Fieldhouse to watch their Badgers take on Pittsburgh. At stake was a trip to the national championship game, but again Foster's team came out flat as the Panthers grabbed an 18–14 halftime lead. Pitt coach Henry Carlson tried to run out the clock as the second half got underway, a rather brave decision considering 20 minutes still remained. Wisconsin decided to pound the ball inside, and Englund led the team as they raced back to take a 29–25 lead, sending the crowd into a frenzy.

Fred Rehm (No. 30) hardly factored into Washington State's defensive gameplan, but his effort—along with 13 points from teammate Gene Englund (No. 31)—paved the way for Wisconsin's 39–34 victory over the Cougars. *University of Wisconsin Athletics*

"I absolutely loved the Fieldhouse, and I think it was the absolutely greatest atmosphere to ever play or watch a game," Rehm said. "It would be so loud and the building was so old, it probably didn't meet the fire codes. And literally if things got going wild you couldn't hear the person sitting next to you talking to you, and all the sound would be held into the building by those walls."

Thanks to some clutch free throw shooting by the Badgers, the 36–30 win clinched their ticket to Kansas City for the national championship game. The fans went to Chicago to see the team off, yelling out their wishes of good luck. Ed Scheiwe quipped back, "Heck, we've forgotten how to lose." It was the sort of comment people had become accustomed to hearing from the junior. Early in the season, after sinking a toss from halfcourt, Scheiwe snapped his fingers and griped, "I'm still getting some rim on those shots."

Perhaps the Badgers had indeed forgotten how to lose. It was up to Washington State, fresh off a victory over undefeated Arkansas in the semifinals, to refresh their memories. Rehm, still far from being the primary option on offense, took it upon himself to deliver the championship. The sophomore made two shots early on and decided to try and keep firing away, much to the chagrin of his teammates.

"At the first stoppage of play Gene Englund, who was one of the All-Americans on the team, basically cornered him and said, 'Enough of that—you know, let's stick to the game plan,'" laughed Rehm. "What do you think you're going to try to do, all of a sudden come on and be a hero here?"

Perhaps the strategy backfired, as Washington State rallied from an early 6–0 deficit to take a 10–8 lead. The Cougars led 23–18 when Englund and star sophomore Johnny Kotz finally found their rhythm. The Badgers reeled off 10 straight points to take the lead and led 34–32 in the final minutes, when they made one last push to put the game out of reach. When news of the 39–34 victory reached Madison, the students ran onto the streets and started a campaign to cancel the following day's classes. The demonstration failed to persuade the school president, but the enthusiasm on campus made at least one lasting impression. Instead of spending the night in Kansas City, the team ventured back to Madison, arriving in the middle of the night, only to see 15,000 people still going wild to greet them. It may have taken some help from the basketball team, but Badger fans had quickly cemented their status as some of the best in the game. ●

1942 Stanford

In March 1942, just three months after Pearl Harbor and three months before the Battle of Midway, few Americans had basketball on their minds. A total of only 24,373 people showed up to watch the NCAA Tournament, the lowest total in the 70 years that would follow. Nevertheless, the small crowds were rewarded with excellent basketball. None of the four opening-round games was decided by more than six points, including a 46–44 squeaker for Colorado over Kansas. That would bring CU's record to 16–1, but not even the Buffaloes could stop Stanford's unprecedented lineup.

When Stanford coach Everett Dean set out to find the players who could deliver his first national championship, he did not have to search very far—he found five Bay Area players in his own backyard. They stood an average of 6-foot-4, and they would revolutionize the game. Each player started at center for his high school team, yet could run faster than most guards in the country. Dean converted Howie Dallmar into one of the nation's top guards, but the most athletic of the quintet was 6-foot-5 Jim Pollard, who was dunking from the free throw line before *dunk* was even part of the sport's vocabulary.

At a time when most teams worked the ball around for the perfect two-handed set shot, Dean let his players roam free to fly up the court and fire as many one-handed shots as they pleased. With a lineup that looked like the Harlem Globetrotters, many thought Stanford was well on its way to a national championship, including Dean himself.

Everything seemed to be going according to plan as Stanford, known as the Indians back then, cruised through the regular season to set up a meeting with Oregon State for the Pacific-8 title. Dean's squad won the first game in the best-of-three series, but after a 42–33 OSU victory in the second match, the Indians stood one loss away from missing the NCAA Tournament altogether. That possibility seemed even more likely when the Beavers took a 26–25 lead in the second half of the rubber match, and with a few minutes remaining the score was still tied at 33. Dallmar tossed in the go-ahead basket, and teammate Ed Voss added another field goal moments later to give Stanford a four-point

cushion. After escaping with a 40–35 victory, they set their sights on the much loftier goal of winning the national championship.

The Indians carried their momentum into the tournament, taking an early 33–21 lead against Rice in the opening round. But instead of blowing the game open, Stanford allowed the Owls to get right back into the game with a 20–4 run in the second half. Twelve minutes still remained, but the team knew it would be taking an early trip back to Palo Alto unless something changed. Luckily, Voss answered the call, converting a pair of free throws and adding two clutch shots to put the Indians back in front with five minutes to go. Thanks to a 26-point effort from Pollard, Stanford held off Rice 53–47. Pollard also led the team with 17 points as they powered past Colorado 46–35 to reach the championship game—but then disaster struck.

Pollard suddenly got the flu, forcing him to sit out the title game. Don Burness, another All-American, would also be watching the game from the sidelines with a sprained ankle. After suffering the injury against Oregon State, he sat out the first two rounds in hopes that he would be ready to play against Dartmouth for the championship. But two minutes into the game, it was obvious the ankle hadn't improved, and Dean was forced to take him out. To no one's surprise, Dean replaced Pollard with Jack Dana, yet another 6-foot-4 player, but stepping in for Burness was Fred Linari, a 5-foot-9 guard who didn't exactly fit their normal game plan.

Perhaps sympathizing with their poor luck, the championship crowd in Kansas City heartily pulled for Dean's club. Dean would need

Stanford's starting lineup (from left to right): Bill Cowden, Howard Dallmar, Ed Voss, Jim Pollard, Don Burness, and head coach Everett S. Dean, each of whom stood at over 6-foot-4. *Stanford University Athletic Department*

all the help he could get against Dartmouth, winner of 88 percent of its games under coach Osborne Cowles. A former pupil of Dean's back at Carleton College, Cowles knew exactly what type of game plan his mentor would bring. This became quickly apparent as Dartmouth took an early six-point lead and dominated much of the first half. Resilient, Stanford refused to cave in. Dana nailed a shot at the buzzer and the Indians took a 24–22 lead at halftime, their first of the game.

Dartmouth fought back to take a 27–26 lead, but Dallmar answered with a basket of his own, and when Linari knifed through the defense for a layup, Dean knew the title was his to lose. By the end of the game, the previously unheralded Linari had contributed six points and Stanford's 53–38 victory gave the school its first national championship in any sport. As Linari showed, perhaps height wasn't as important as heart. ●

1943 Wyoming

At first look, the 1943 tournament appeared unusually weak. Five of the top six teams in the country didn't play, including the Whiz Kids of Illinois, who had capped off their 17–1 season days earlier with a 92–25 victory over Big Ten rival Chicago. Fourth-ranked St. John's opted for the NIT, while 18–2 Notre Dame played in neither because of the school's ban on postseason play. Even if they had all played, however, the title would have likely gone to the same team, which finished with 14 more wins than the Illini. Perhaps the selection committee got it right after all—four of the first six games were decided by four points or less, including Texas's 59–55 victory over Washington, in which John Hargis scored more than half of the Longhorns' points.

Before Wyoming coach Ev Shelton could even contemplate a national championship, his first task was to make sure that freshman Kenny Sailors went out for the basketball team. When word reached Shelton that the undersized Sailors was considering going out for the football team, the coach quickly put an end to that endeavor.

"If you're dumb enough to go out for football weighing 138 pounds, to try to play left end at the college level, just don't come out for basketball," Shelton warned, perhaps only half-jokingly. "You won't be worth a nickel to me after the first game."

Usually, 138-pound athletes don't fare much better in basketball than they would in football, but Sailors was far from the average player. While growing up in a town of just 30 people, Sailors had learned the game from his brother, who was not only older but seven inches taller.

"He got a kick out of slamming that ball down my face every time I'd try to shoot it," Sailors joked. "He'd kid me a little. 'You'd better pick another sport, Kenny,' he said. 'You're just not tall enough, you're not big enough yet.'"

In order to counter the obvious size advantage, Sailors invented something nobody had ever seen before—a jump shot.

"I don't know how I came about it. I just thought, 'How the devil am I going to get up high enough to shoot a ball over him?'" Sailors said. "I just jumped in the air, and I got up pretty high and I got that ball over him. That thing went in."

Sensing he had just stumbled upon something completely innovative, Sailors practiced the move almost every day for years. By the time he reached campus in Laramie, his shot was the hardest to block in the country. Sailors continued to work on the shot in college, and as a junior his team was nearly unstoppable, achieving a 33–2 record despite playing only six home games.

Winning on the road was easy, but when the Cowboys arrived at the NCAA Tournament, they ran into some much stiffer competition. In their first game against Oklahoma, they found themselves down 14–4 thanks to the play of OU's 6-foot-6 Jerry Tucker. Shelton knew the score would get out of control if Tucker maintained his pace, so he instructed his players to lure the Oklahoma star into foul trouble. The plan worked to perfection, as Tucker fouled out before the first half was even over. Center Milo Komenich—who actually lived in Shelton's basement—took full advantage of Tucker's absence, scoring 16 points in the second half to give the team a 53–50 win.

Their second-round matchup wasn't any easier, as the Texas Longhorns grabbed a 26–13 lead at the start of the game and still led 33–27 when Shelton gave one of the most unconventional halftime speeches in tournament history. After the horn sounded to end the first half, the players gathered in the locker room, but their coach was nowhere to be found. After half of the intermission had passed, Shelton opened the door just enough to peer into the room and drop a bombshell on his players. "Boys, I hate to do it, but it looks like it's going to be that way. I'm going to go back to the hotel and start packing to go home," he said. "Sailors, you and Komenich have got to get the show going in the second half. I'll try to get back if I can."

As the Cowboys attempted to make their comeback, Shelton was indeed missing from the bench. The psychological ploy turned out to be as effective as it was unusual, and the Cowboys slowly began to turn the tide. Seven minutes into the half, Floyd Volker gave Wyoming its first lead at 37–36. Jack Fitzgerald and Buck Overall countered to put Texas back in front 39–37, but Jim Weir added a hook shot to tie the game. The score was still tied when Sailors and teammate Jimmy Collins hit two quick baskets, finally giving the team some breathing room. And true to his word, Shelton arrived back on the bench, just in time to watch his team pull out a 58–54 victory.

Not only did Kenny Sailors invent the jumpshot, he also scored 16 points in Wyoming's 46–34 victory over Georgetown in the national title game.
University of Wyoming Athletic Department

Now his players were just one win away from the national championship. Standing in their way was Georgetown, which featured one of the most formidable offenses in the country. The Hoyas held even with Wyoming, and the only difference in the first half was a Sailors basket in the closing moments to give UW an 18–16 lead. Georgetown's offense, which had lit up one opponent for 105 points earlier in the year, woke up after halftime. They grabbed a 28–24 lead midway through the second half, pushing the lead to 31–26 with 6:30 remaining. The Cowboys came back to tie the game at 31, leaving just 4:30 to decide the title. Komenich added a free throw and Collins tipped in two missed shots to put Wyoming in front 36–31. Georgetown made one last push to cut the lead to 37–34, but a slew of big plays by Sailors gave Wyoming a 46–34 win for the national championship.

Even with three impressive comebacks, fans remained unsure of the honors bestowed upon the Cowboys, insisting that the NIT was still the premier postseason tournament. Shelton decided to approach basketball promoter Ned Irish with a Red Cross Charity game against the NIT winner to truly determine the best team in the country.

Over 18,000 people—more than twice the entire population of Laramie—crammed into New York's Madison Square Garden to cheer on hometown St. John's University. They witnessed the best game of the season as the Redmen stormed back from a 46–38 deficit in the last two minutes, tying the game on a hook shot with 10 seconds left. Sailors came back to score at the buzzer, only to have it called off because he released the ball after the clock struck zero. St. John's carried all the momentum heading into overtime, but Wyoming guard Jim Weir converted three consecutive baskets to put the game out of reach—this time for good.

The Cowboys had convinced the nation: not only were they the best team in America, but the NCAA Tournament was the premier basketball tournament. Seven decades later, the tournament's magic and prestige remain undeniable. ●

1944 Utah

It wasn't until 1944 that World War II truly wreaked havoc on college basketball, with many of the country's best players sent off to war. Defending champion Wyoming as well as runner-up Georgetown both failed to put together a team. In fact, so many teams were faced with the same dilemma that Notre Dame cracked the final top 25 poll with a 10–9 record. But in a fitting moment given the climate of the country, Army topped the rankings at 15–0. Although the Cadets did not play in the tournament, they would have their moment—nine months later, their football team went 9–0 and won the national championship. As it turned out, the basketball title would go to an equally worthy champion.

The mood among the Utah players was understandably somber. The Utes had barely arrived in New York to play in the NIT when their season was cut short, courtesy of a 38–46 first-round loss to Kentucky. The team would already have to start packing for a trip back home.

But when team manager Keith Brown and assistant coach Pete Crouch took a walk downtown and found a Bible hidden beneath the snow, they thought perhaps it was a sign of better things to come. Their good luck arrived in mere minutes, as they returned to their hotel to find a telegram from the NCAA. The Arkansas team bus had crashed on the way to the tournament, and the NCAA was offering their invitation to the Utes. The season wasn't over after all. Or at least that was the initial reaction of the players, until coach Vadal Peterson voiced his opinion about traveling to Kansas City for the NCAA Tournament.

"He felt like we couldn't really do better. I think he felt like we'd had a good showing; I don't think he felt like we had a real championship team," guard Wat Misaka said. "'If we go back to Kansas City and lose there,' he warned, 'we're going home and you guys haven't seen New York—and most of you have never been here before; you may never come back again. You think about that.'"

That assessment, of course, didn't sit well with the players, who unanimously voted to ship out to Kansas City the next day.

"We were disappointed that we had lost to Kentucky because we kind of had it in our minds that we could have beaten these guys if

we had just played a little harder, or worked a little more together," forward Herb Wilkinson said. "We thought, 'What a gift this is to have a second chance to play,' and we were really eager to do it."

The confident Utes asked an employee at the Belvedere, the hotel at which they were staying in New York, to reserve some rooms for their return the following week, knowing that the NCAA championship game was to be held in Madison Square Garden. To get back to New York, however, they would first need to win a pair of games against higher-ranked teams, and the NCAA was not quite as accommodating as their Big Apple counterparts. After the Utes defeated Missouri in their first game, the NCAA decided to book only one room at the hotel for the two remaining teams out west, Utah and Iowa State.

"For economy reasons they asked the team that was going to lose to put their baggage in one room, so after the game they could get their baggage, get on the train, and they wouldn't have to pay for extra hotel rooms," said forward Arnie Ferrin, whose team was given little chance against the Cyclones. "And so they asked us to put our luggage in the hotel room because we'd be departing."

After dumping their belongings in what was meant to be Iowa State's room, Utah pulled off another shocker to give Iowa State an early return home. The next morning, following a good night's rest, the team departed for New York, and received an unusually warm welcome. The reason the applause at Madison Square Garden was so unexpected was because

Misaka was Japanese. And this was 1944, when America was still at war.

"I think that's typical of the New York fans, because if you go out and play hard they'll respond to that," Ferrin said. "Not how big you are, how small you are, or your ethnicity."

The reception for Misaka had not always been so pleasant, but teammate Dick Smuin made sure his Japanese teammate felt like he was part of the team.

"He was one of those guys that felt like any bad treatment of Japanese was not right and he was going to see to it that I was all right. He didn't actually come out and say that, but I found out later on that he felt like it was up to him to make sure that things were going to be okay with me," Misaka said. "Most of the pictures that we had taken when we were all on trips and so on . . . well, Dick would be with me wherever I went. He's kind of like my guardian angel. He wasn't going to allow me to ever get into any trouble."

The fact that Misaka even made the team was a miracle itself. From the age of 15 when his father passed away, he had to help raise his family on one of the most dangerous streets in America. Growing up on 25th Street in Ogden, Utah, where drugs, prostitution, and violence were the norm, Misaka spent much of his time making sure his younger brothers avoided the negativity surrounding them. With little income, the family was forced to live in the upstairs of a brothel. The location actually turned out to be a blessing, as it was outside the jurisdiction of the Japanese internment law, allowing Misaka to attend college. The guard grew to be only 5-foot-6, but nevertheless he made the team, where he quickly befriended Smuin. And thanks in large part to the duo, the Utes pulled off one of the most unbelievable upsets in NCAA history to win the championship (see page 348).

By the end of the year, many of the Utah players were fighting in World War II, including Misaka, who served for the United States. Fittingly, his job was to interview victims of the atomic bombings of Japan in an attempt to improve relations between the two countries. As for Smuin, his Good Samaritan attitude was rewarded a few months later when he was at war.

"While he was in the Pacific in the Navy, their ship was bombed and a bomb came through the deck into their compartment down below," Misaka said of his teammate. "But it didn't explode, and he said, 'See there, Wat's taking care of me.' He felt like I was looking after him."

And even if Wat didn't know it, perhaps he was. Kindness has a way of coming around. ●

1945 Oklahoma A&M

The 1944–45 season marked the birth of modern basketball. The three-second rule was implemented, as was the five-foul limit, goaltending, and unlimited substitutions. Fans got a taste of that new style when Arkansas and Oregon set the tournament record for points in a game in their 79–76 thriller. Their combined total of 155 points obliterated the old mark of 119. Equally dramatic was the 70–65 overtime game between NYU and Ohio State. The Violets faced a 10-point deficit with just two minutes to go, but 16-year-old Dolph Schayes led an NYU comeback and Don Forman's set shot with two seconds left tied the game at 62. The Violets' eventual 70–65 win sent them to the championship game, but awaiting them was the greatest player college basketball had ever seen.

Henry Iba was hoping he would not regret the decision he had just made. The Oklahoma A&M coach had just offered a scholarship to Bob Kurland, a young center from St. Louis, with no anticipation of what the seven-footer could bring to the team. Sure, Kurland was taller than everybody else, but how effective could he be? Nobody of Kurland's size had attempted to play major college basketball before, and Iba was putting his reputation on the line when he decided to offer him a scholarship.

"I've never seen a young man like you before," Iba remarked as he invited Kurland to step into his office. "I don't know whether you can play college basketball or not, but if you'll come to Oklahoma A&M—and you stay eligible, study, and do the job which will be assigned to you—I'll give you a scholarship at Oklahoma A&M."

It wasn't long before Kurland turned Iba into a genius. To say the young man ate, slept, and breathed basketball was not far from the truth. When Kurland wasn't playing with the team, he was earning money by sweeping the gym floors before every game and practice. And when Kurland was ready to call it a night, he returned to Gallagher Hall, site of the Aggies' basketball arena, where he slept. His love for the game and work ethic soon translated onto the court, where he would swat away every ball that came near the hoop. Kurland became so dominant that the NCAA decided to implement the goaltending rule.

"It was bad for the game for a guy to work real hard to get open and take a shot and then Bob would jump up and either slap it away from the basket or jump up and catch it and come down and throw it to one of his teammates. It was not good for the game of basketball, but it was good for Oklahoma A&M," said Aggies guard Weldon Kearns. "He never did like the goaltending part. I think he felt guilty. I think he felt like it made him kind of a villain—and he'd rather just play the game of basketball like it's supposed to be played."

The new rules were designed to prevent him from ever taking over a game by himself, but the now-liberated Kurland picked up right where he left off. Instead of camping his star player under the basket to block incoming shots, Iba instructed his players to return to the man-to-man defense they had played before Kurland's arrival. After defeating Utah 62–37 in the first round of the NCAA Tournament, the team faced an Arkansas team that was fresh off a 79-point performance against Oregon. The Aggies' man-to-man defense turned out to be even more effective than their old strategy, as they forced the Razorbacks to reluctantly shoot from the perimeter. The result was a 68–41 victory and a spot in the national championship game.

Facing them in Madison Square Garden would be New York University, which anticipated a big home-crowd advantage. A record 18,779 fans packed the arena to cheer on the Violets, but once the game started it became apparent the fans had fallen in love with Kurland's hustle and Iba's style of play. NYU decided to take their frustration out on the

Henry Iba (holding the championship trophy) owed much of his first title to center Bob Kurland (third from left in the back row). *Oklahoma State University Athletics*

Aggies; they played an extremely aggressive game, eventually sending guard J. L. Parks flying to the bench on a foul. They were also determined not to let Kurland touch the ball, and minutes before halftime the teams found themselves tied at 19–19. Even against the double team, however, Kurland managed to lead the Aggies on a late run as they took a 26–21 lead at the break. The Violets decided to increase their pressure on Kurland, almost to the point of neglecting the rest of his teammates; he was to be stopped at all costs. If the Violets were going to lose the national championship, it would not be at the hands of Kurland.

Cecil Hankins stepped up to score 15 points and push A&M's lead to 39–28 with 10 minutes to go, but the Violets were not finished. They reduced their deficit to just four points and had the ball heading into the last minute. The Violets took shot after shot but couldn't get any to fall, and moments later the exhausted Madison Square Garden crowd was applauding the Aggies' first national championship.

They had conquered the Violets and the fans, but the Aggies were not finished. They agreed to meet NIT champion DePaul in a charity game to benefit the Red Cross. In this game, known as the "mythical national championship," the NCAA winner had won the last two meetings, but experts had their doubts about Oklahoma A&M's chances against the vaunted Blue Demons. They were led by 6-foot-9 George Mikan, who many considered to be the best big man in the country, above even Kurland. The DePaul center had averaged 40 points per game in the NIT, but Kurland wasn't going to back down from anybody.

Although the Blue Demons grabbed an early 21–14 lead, Kurland continued to lure Mikan into foul trouble, and with six minutes still remaining in the *first half,* Kurland had fooled his opponent into his fifth and final foul. Oklahoma A&M recovered from the 26–21 halftime deficit to score the first nine points of the second period, and by the end of the match the Aggies had earned a 52–44 victory. Now there was no debating it—Kurland was the best center in basketball, and the NCAA Tournament was the grandest stage in basketball. And with Kurland back for another year, it was a stage they hoped to grace once more. ●

1946 Oklahoma A&M

It was official: The NCAA Tournament was steadily becoming one of the most popular sporting events in America. For the first time, the championship game was broadcast on television, and although it was only shown in New York, it still attracted an audience of 500,000. Perhaps the network should have broadcast the semifinals as well, because the East Regional final between Ohio State and North Carolina became an instant classic. Trailing 54–52 with 10 seconds to go, UNC's Bob Paxton sent the game into overtime with a 35-footer, and the Tar Heels won 60–57 to advance to an equally intense championship game against the defending champion Aggies of Oklahoma A&M.

To put it mildly, expectations were high for the 1946 Oklahoma A&M Aggies. Nearly everyone was back from their 1945 championship team, and there was no reason to believe a repeat was far away.

"We had been there before and knew we could do it, so it was a little more natural," guard Weldon Kearns said. "I really believed the '46 team was better than the '45 team because of the returning veterans."

In this case, veterans meant more than upperclassmen. Also returning to the team was Sam Aubrey, fresh from his tour of duty in World War II. Aubrey had deployed in the spring of 1943, just weeks after his junior season, but he was now back in Stillwater to finish his college degree. Originally, basketball was not to be part of those plans. A year earlier, Aubrey had earned a Purple Heart, a Silver Star, and a shattered hip after being shot while fighting courageously in Italy.

"It bothered one of his legs and he was almost a one-legged basketball player," Kearns said. "He hadn't fully recovered, and it was just kind of hard for him to get around."

His doctors warned that any additional stress on his knee could render his legs useless by age 35, but Aubrey refused to accept a life without basketball. For four months before his return to Oklahoma A&M, he had received therapy in El Paso, where he made incredible strides just to get off crutches. But that hardly meant he was ready to play competitive basketball, and Iba told him the sad but obvious truth: Unless something drastic changed, he could not put Aubrey on the team.

Aubrey couldn't even run down the length of the floor during his first attempts at a comeback, but he refused to give in. Finally, as fall gave way to winter, Aubrey started to show signs of the player he once had been. When it came time for Iba to finalize his roster selections, Aubrey not only made the team, he was in the starting lineup. A 13-inch scar was the only remnant of the injury, and the guard helped lead Oklahoma A&M to a 28–2 regular-season record. So dominant were the Aggies that each starter was named to the Missouri Valley Conference's first team.

They were the most talented team in the country—and often played like it—but their spot in the NCAA Tournament was hardly guaranteed. The Kansas Jayhawks, who also played in the Missouri Valley, were 19–2, and in 1946 only one team from each conference was invited to the Big Dance. A late-season bout between the two rivals would decide the league's lone bid, and Kansas coach Phog Allen didn't do his team any favors by taunting Aggies center Bob Kurland. Allen referred to the sport's only seven-footer as a "glandular mezzanine-peeping goon," a comment that only further motivated Kurland to humiliate the Jayhawks. The senior scored 28 points in a 49–38 win, and after two equally easy victories over Baylor and Cal in the tournament, the Aggies were back in New York once again for the national title game. Their worthy opponent, North Carolina, brought a 30–4 record into the game.

The Tar Heels knew their best chance relied on stopping Kurland, and that assignment went to Horace "Bones" McKinney. Despite the gritty nickname, Bones was six inches shorter than Kurland—but that didn't intimidate the undersized McKinney, who told the All-American Kurland that he wasn't even "All-Madison Square Garden." Kurland shrugged off the slight and let his game do the talking. Led by the big man, the Aggies took a 23–17 lead, and five minutes into the second half the margin had swelled to 31–18. Iba told his players to stall in an effort to run out the clock, but the plan backfired when UNC cut the lead to just 36–33 with 10 minutes left. Iba scrapped the delay strategy, opting instead to go back to a heavy dose of Kurland.

Moments later, McKinney recorded his fifth foul, and Kurland responded by scoring his team's last nine points as the Aggies grabbed a commanding 43–34 lead. The Tar Heels, even without McKinney, managed to cut the lead to just three heading into the last minute. Kurland responded once again, coming up with a steal and quickly whipping the ball to a teammate for the decisive layup. The Aggies were the first team to win back-to-back national championships, and Kurland, who made nine of A&M's 16 field goals and assisted on three others, was awarded the tournament's Most Outstanding Player Award. But to him, the real hero was Aubrey, who had shown just how far a little determination can take somebody.

"He had more guts than any guy I've ever seen," Kurland said. "And I suspect that I got more satisfaction out of associating myself with him than anybody else I ever played with. He's quite a guy." ●

Bob Kurland deservedly received all the praise and adoration after Oklahoma A&M's second consecutive national title, but it was Sam Aubrey (not pictured) who became the source of inspiration for the team. *OSU Athletics*

1947 Holy Cross

Though normally football schools, Texas and Oklahoma provided more than their fair share of excitement on the hardwood at the 1947 NCAA Tournament. The Sooners blew a 14-point lead against Oregon State in their opener but held on for the 56–54 victory. The Longhorns, on the other hand, had to come from behind in their opener against Wyoming to keep their 24–1 season alive. The Cowboys had a chance to put the game away with a 40–39 lead but chose instead to run out the clock, a move that backfired as Texas guard Slater Martin hit a shot in the closing seconds. UT's 42–40 win set up an even more exciting game against Oklahoma the following day. The Sooners trailed 54–53 late in the game until Ken Pryor, a seldom-used backup, hit a halfcourt shot with just 10 seconds left. His shot catapulted the Sooners into the championship game, where they ran into perhaps the most improbable champion of all time.

When Alvin "Doggie" Julian became the head coach at Holy Cross College in 1945, the Crusaders looked to be the most unlikely team ever to have a winning season, much less make an NCAA Tournament. Julian, who had originally been hired as a football coach, was taking over after Albert Riopel went 11–22 over the previous three seasons. In fact, the heavily academic school hadn't won 10 games in a season in 20 years, and it would be up to the oddly named newcomer to lure recruits to a place that had little interest in basketball.

"Basketball was absolutely nothing in New England," said George Kaftan, one of Julian's first commitments. "When you drove around New England, you never saw a basketball hoop."

They also would never see an arena, because Holy Cross had to play its home games 40 minutes away at the Boston Garden. The court in the converted barn that they used as their practice facility wasn't even regulation size. When recruits would come to look at the facility, Julian would suggest they grab a meal instead.

For the incoming players, however, everything seemed great. "It's not like today where kids expect everything on a golden platter. We had nothing, and that's the way it was," Kaftan laughed. "And we didn't have anything better, so we didn't really know."

The 1946–47 campaign didn't get off to a great start, as the Crusaders dropped three of their first seven games. Then, out of nowhere, the team started winning—and kept winning.

The players started rubbing Doggie's nose for good luck before the games and, for whatever reason, it worked. By the time the Crusaders reached the NCAA Tournament, their winning streak had reached 20 games.

It appeared that their luck had run out, however, when they faced Navy, a team that had lost just one game all year. Holy Cross trailed 23–15 with 5:35 left in the second quarter when, looking for a swing in momentum, the team's comeback came from an unlikely hero. Not wanting his star player to spend his energy on defense, Navy coach Ben Carnevale instructed Kenny Shugart to guard Dave Mullaney instead of Kaftan. Mullaney was rarely a threat to score for the Crusaders, but the overlooked sophomore took advantage of Shugart's lackadaisical effort, leading Holy Cross to a 29–27 halftime lead. By the game's end, he had tallied 18 points in a 55–47 victory.

Their next opponent would be the City College of New York (CCNY), whose coach, Nat Holman, had seen little of Holy Cross. Naturally, Holman assumed Mullaney was their go-to player as he prepared for the second-round match, and he put his top defender on him—a mistake that allowed Mullaney's teammates to feast on the weaker CCNY defenders. This lack of scouting knowledge was typical of the era, and for Holy Cross—which usually got its scouting reports from cab drivers on the way to the arena—it was a matter of pure luck.

"It wasn't like today with the television and the Internet and Facebook and all these things—iPads and Blackberries and the raspberries and the other berries," Kaftan joked. "We didn't have any of that stuff."

Holman's plan initially worked, as the Beavers held Holy Cross without a field goal for nearly eight minutes to start the game and cruised out to a 23–14 lead in the second quarter. But with CCNY's best defender on Mullaney, it was only a matter of time before Kaftan, the team's real star, began to pick apart the defense. Holy Cross went on a 13–0 run, and by the end of the first half Kaftan had tallied 19 points. Ironically, it was Mullaney's hook shot that gave the Crusaders a 27–25 lead at halftime. The score was knotted at 38–38 in the second half, but Holy Cross slowly pulled away to set up a title game with Oklahoma.

Despite a 22-game winning streak, fans were still not convinced that Holy Cross could win a championship. No team from the East Coast had ever won the tournament, and with the 6-foot-2 Kaftan serving as HC's tallest player, they were heavily undersized. They were also dealing with an inexperienced coach who was clearly letting his nerves get the best of him. When Julian tried to announce the starting lineup, the only players who knew their fate were Dermot O'Connell and Kaftan, whose parents had immigrated from Greece years before.

"The starting team is Dermie, George, O'Connell, Kaftan, and the Greek," Julian said to some bewildered faces in the locker room.

The speech continued to deteriorate from there, and eventually it was up to Kaftan to put the coach out of his misery.

"Doggie got so excited in the pregame talk, so excited. So in order to stop his ranting and get down to normal, there was a trash can just hanging there," Kaftan laughed. "So I grab the trash can, I roll it down, I said, 'Come on, let's go out and play now.'"

But before the game began, Kaftan had to engage in a little banter with Jerry Tucker, Oklahoma's 25-year-old All-American who had returned from a few years in the service. Standing in front of Kaftan as they waited for tip-off, Tucker said, "You're the young guy I've been hearing about all this time," to which the Holy Cross center smiled and replied, "This is a young man's game; you're too old for this."

Tucker held his own, however, scoring 14 points as the Sooners raced out to a 31–28 halftime lead. Julian knew he needed to make a change, and he told Bob Curran to shut down Tucker. Curran chased the OU star everywhere on the court, limiting the veteran to just one shot the rest of the game. Kaftan led the team on a 9–2 run to start the second half, and with the championship still hanging in the balance at 48–45, the Crusaders scored 10 of the game's final 12 points to take home the title. Kaftan was named Most Outstanding Player—not bad for someone who hadn't started playing until his junior year in high school.

With their twenty-third straight win, the Crusaders wrapped up one of the most unexpected title runs in NCAA history. "What happened then would never happen again in a million years," Kaftan said. "We were probably the original Cinderella."

While many Cinderellas have left their mark on the tournament since then, Holy Cross was the first—and perhaps the greatest of all. ●

1948 Kentucky

For the 1948 tournament, the NCAA deemed it fair to give 50 percent of the proceeds to the participating teams. And while it may not have been the most nail-biting tournament of all time, it left little doubt as to who was most deserving of that money. Blowouts were the theme of the tournament, but the one close game did its best to make up for it. In its first-round game against Washington, Baylor trailed 34–17 before crawling its way back. By halftime the Bears had cut the lead to 37–36, and midway through the second half they had tied the game at 44. Don Heathington's shot with two minutes left was the game-winner during the Bears' 64–62 victory.

Kentucky guard Ralph Beard had already won the NIT title as a freshman in 1946, and he didn't see his team slowing down anytime soon as the 1947 season got underway. Joining him in a repeat bid were teammate Wallace Jones and elder statesmen Cliff Barker and Kenny Rollins, fresh from World War II duty. Beard had scored nearly 10 points a game as a freshman, but he was anxious to improve his game. When asked what the sophomore could improve upon, coach Adolph Rupp suggested his pupil work on free throws and left-handed dribbling, in addition to developing an outside jump shot. "If you can correct those few weaknesses," Rupp told him, "you will not only be a great basketball player, but you will be almost a perfect basketball player."

Beard returned the following season in the best shape of his life, and the Wildcats ran out to a 34–3 record, but the team fell one game short by losing the NIT title game to Utah. The Wildcats were determined to come back even stronger the following year, and it didn't take fans long to realize this was the best UK team yet. They won their first game by 39 points, and soon enough the starters had earned the nickname "The Fabulous Five," a moniker they had definitely earned. For the third straight year, the Wildcats ran through the SEC season undefeated, winning by an astounding 28 points per game. If opponents needed any indication that UK wasn't satisfied with a regular-season crown, the team made a statement with a 56-point victory over Florida in the SEC Tournament. Beard was named

the Player of the Year, but just like the team's regular-season success, that honor would ring hollow without championship hardware to accompany it.

This year, however, Rupp wasn't messing around with the NIT—he was going straight after the NCAA crown. The first test would be against a Columbia squad that had gone 21–1 during the regular season, but the Wildcats stormed out to a 38–25 halftime lead and never looked back. Their 76–53 victory earned UK the right to face Holy Cross, the defending national champions and winners of 19 straight games. Kentucky took a quick 14-point lead, but the Crusaders would soon reel off nine straight points to bridge the gap to just 36–32 early in the second half. Rupp called a timeout while one Holy Cross fan voiced his pleasure in UK's misfortune.

"I got a foul called on me and some guy sitting behind the bench, he was just giving Kentucky and Rupp hell all the time," Jones said. "I'd get another foul and I couldn't listen to him."

Jones responded by scoring five quick points as the Wildcats went on a 7–0 run, and although Holy Cross kept it close, the UK defense was too much to overcome. Rollins had limited Holy Cross All-American George Kaftan to just one free throw as the Wildcats held on for a 60–52 victory.

"Coach Rupp stressed defense as much as he did offense—he was really tough on that," Jones said. "And Rollins was very good in staying on his man and keeping him in the position to shoot."

But the win had not stopped the crowd from heckling the Wildcats, and the last taunt at Jones was one too many. The junior, who was helping the team pack up after the game, shot back with a comment about the scoreboard, which only aggravated his adversary even more.

"He threw his program at me," Jones said with a smile. "And I had to drop my equipment and knock him down plain into the seats."

The Wildcats had already survived their toughest test, and when they faced Baylor in the championship game, it was over as soon as the ball was tipped. Kentucky held the Bears scoreless for nearly eight minutes to start the game, and by the time the Baylor shooters had found their touch they had already spotted UK a 13–1 lead. The lead quickly grew to 24–7, and although the Wildcats shot just 28 percent from the floor, the game was rarely close. Kentucky finished the game on cruise control and walked away with a 58–42 victory. For their efforts, all five starters for Kentucky were named to the Olympic team, where they picked up right where they had left off, winning each of their eight games to take the gold medal. As great as an NCAA title was, "best team in the world" had an even better ring to it.

"They're both special, but when you're standing in front of the King and Queen of England and get your medal, it's a real surprise and a real thing to happen for you," Jones said. "For a 20-year-old boy from the coal fields of Kentucky, standing in front of the King and Queen of England, it's a big honor."

But the accolades didn't stop there, as Beard would later find out. Years after the championship, Beard was attending a Wildcats football game when he introduced himself to the spectator sitting next to him. The new acquaintance looked on in amazement as he shook his hand and introduced himself—as Ralph Beard. It turned out that his parents had named him after their favorite UK star. In the 1990s, Michigan's Fab Five would also take their name after Kentucky's quintet—but as they would later find out, nothing is quite as good as the original. ●

1949 Kentucky

Close contests were again few and far between in the 1949 NCAA Tournament. The tourney was riddled with one blowout after another, which made the sole buzzer-beater even more exciting. After taking a 25–22 lead over Oklahoma A&M at halftime, Wyoming extended its lead to 10 points and seemed poised for a spot in the Final Four. A&M's Jack Shelton sank a hook shot with 1:40 left to bring them within three, and he scooted in for another score just moments later. His dunk with three seconds left proved to be the game-winner, sending the Aggies to the Final Four. They eventually reached the championship game, where they vied for their third national title in five years. But, as they would soon find out, their dynasty was giving way to another.

Like most kids growing up in the Bluegrass State, Wallace Jones had always dreamed of being a Kentucky Wildcat. Even before his brother had enrolled at UK, Jones would travel with his friends to the top of a local mountain to hear the Kentucky games on the radio. By the time Jones finished high school, he appeared well on his way toward landing a spot with the team. But in order for the Wildcats to land the prized recruit, they would have to lure him away from a Tennessee program that was willing to break the rules.

"I was kind of deep into Kentucky, but I had some people wanting me to go other places and they took me down to Knoxville. I had a friend of mine that played on the basketball team with me, and he and I went over to Knoxville in somebody else's car," Jones said. "And they wanted to keep me over there and kept saying that, and I kept saying I got to do something, and they said, 'We can take care of it.' And I said, 'Well, I got to talk to my mother,' so they brought out a new car and gave it to us to drive."

Jones was now faced with one of the biggest decisions of his young life—take the car and become a Volunteer or follow his dream of playing for Kentucky. He still had time to ponder his choice, and in the meantime he made sure to at least get some use out of the flashy new ride. But when Jones brought the car to the birthday party of his future brother-in-law, the reception was not exactly what he had planned.

"They all saw the car, and I said I was going to Tennessee and it was all through the house. Her dad went back to the private room and got on the phone and called Lexington and told them what was happening," Jones recalled. "So when I got home in Harlan, next morning I woke up and they were waiting on me to take me back to Lexington. And the team manager got a four-year scholarship for taking that car back to Tennessee."

Joining the student manager on the scholarship list would be Jones, who concluded that he couldn't play for anyone but Big Blue. In all likelihood, Jones was the difference maker between the two programs, as the Volunteers never lost more than five games in a season for eight consecutive years in the 1940s but made only one postseason appearance thanks to nearly flawless basketball from the Wildcats. Due in no small part to Jones, Kentucky took home the national title in 1948 and looked to do the same a year later. Four starters returned to improve upon their 36–3 record from a year before, as they ran through the SEC undefeated for a fourth consecutive season and tallied just two losses overall. That honor gave UK the dubious distinction of playing against Paul Arizin and Villanova in the first round. Led by Arizin, a future 10-time NBA All-Star, Villanova was considered a legitimate threat to take down Kentucky.

In the opening minutes, Villanova proved to be a worthy opponent, taking a quick lead before UK forced a tie at 15–15 midway through the first half. Arizin notched 11 points in the first

Going into the title game, Oklahoma A&M's Henry Iba was considered the greatest coach in basketball. But it was Kentucky coach Adolph Rupp who outsmarted his adversary en route to the 46–36 win. *University of Kentucky Athletic Department*

half, but the forward was just getting started. As the second half wore on and Villanova tried to keep pace with Kentucky, he scored 16 straight points for his team, and he would finish with 30 on the night. But Kentucky center Alex Groza, who had been guarding him, countered with 30 points of his own to help the Wildcats hold on for an 85–72 victory.

A blowout win over Illinois set the stage for a title match against Oklahoma A&M, a team that had won the national championship in 1945 and 1946 and was looking to add another trophy to its collection. Aggies coach Henry Iba instructed his team to disregard the zone defense that they had used the whole year, opting instead to play a man-to-man defense designed to slow the game down. The reasoning, of course, was obvious. Iba was afraid to play at Kentucky's breakneck speed.

"We played together as a team, passed the ball to the open guy, and we moved down the floor at a fast pace," Jones said. "A fast-breaking team in college was something else at that time because most were set-play deals."

Kentucky coach Adolph Rupp knew that the easiest way to counter the new defense was to have Jones drive to the hoop and draw a crowd of defenders before dishing off to Alex Groza at the last second. It was a bold proposition, considering that Jones had been rejected from the military years earlier on the grounds that his ankle wouldn't endure tour of duty. On top of it, Jones was still trying to recover from injuries to those same ankles, suffered during his All-American football season. But Rupp nevertheless counted on Jones to be swift enough to lure defenders away from Groza, a plan that worked to perfection as the big man made five layups on the night, in addition to four easy hook shots.

The game was relatively close at 25–20 heading into the break, but UK held the Aggies without a field goal for 12 minutes in the second half, and the championship was theirs for the taking. Even though Groza missed 13 minutes in the second half with foul trouble, it hardly mattered—the title was heading back to Lexington. ●

1950 CCNY

After two subpar postseasons, the NCAA Tournament rebounded nicely in 1950. In the first round, Baylor and Brigham Young University (BYU) played one of the best games fans had ever seen. The Bears trailed 54–50 in the final minute, but Don Heathington made a shot to cut the lead to 54–52. After a steal by Baylor, Gerald Cobb converted a three-point play with 18 seconds left to give his team a 55–54 lead. Although BYU tied it with nine seconds left, Heathington sank the game-winning free throw with just seven seconds on the clock for a 56–55 win. Baylor's second-round opponent, Bradley, had a first-round comeback of its own against UCLA, reeling off 15 of the final 16 points to secure the win. The Bears nearly pulled the same miracle against Bradley when they trailed by eight with just 3:30 to play before their potential game-tying shot at the buzzer rimmed out. The only noncompetitive game of the tournament, N.C. State's 87–74 win over Holy Cross, also featured plenty of excitement when the Wolfpack's Sam Ranzino broke the tournament scoring record with 32 points.

When Nat Holman first came to City College of New York, the 23-year-old coach knew he would be faced with a distinct disadvantage against his coaching peers. CCNY, better known as "City College" back then, was an apt symbol of the city of New York. As the Statue of Liberty stated on its base, the city opened itself with welcome arms to nearly anyone who had come for the American Dream. "Give me your tired, your poor, your huddled masses yearning to breathe free," the statue's poem read, a message that CCNY took to heart.

Following the same mantra, City College was a one-of-a-kind public institution. The college was funded by the taxpayers, meaning that anyone eligible to gain entrance would enjoy a free college education, regardless of his or her ethnic or economic background. But the school's greatest trait also meant that Holman had a huge mountain to climb to stay competitive on the court. The coach did not have the option of recruiting players; instead, he had to make due with whatever students made their way into the school.

The 1950 squad that Holman had to work with was a perfect snapshot of the school and the city it represented. Joining Holman that year was a mixture of whites, blacks, and Jews— some poor, some rich, some middle-class. Despite their differences, they could all play basketball, and they could play it quite well. The team surprised many fans by finishing the

regular season with a 21–5 record. That solid résumé, however, was barely enough to impress NIT officials, who selected the Beavers as the last representative in the tournament. Little was expected of the Beavers once they began play, but they shocked everybody by sweeping through the field to take home the NIT crown. That performance was enough to convince the NCAA selection committee to invite the team into their tournament as well, once again as one of the final entrants in the field.

In the first round, they faced Ohio State, Big Ten champion and owner of a 22–3 record. In a game that never featured a lead of more than five points for either team, both clubs went into the locker room at halftime having surrendered 40 points. Once the Beavers edged out to a three-point advantage early in the second half, they began to stall the game, forcing the Buckeyes to stage a comeback on their own. With no three-point line or shot clock at the time, Holman figured the strategy would entice Ohio State to come out and play defense 30 feet from the hoop, eventually opening up some lanes down by the basket. He did not expect the Buckeyes to employ a little gamesmanship of their own.

Ohio State stayed firm down low, letting nearly five minutes expire before baiting CCNY into an outside shot they didn't need. OSU would eventually cut the lead to two, and when the Beavers tried to run down the clock once more, they were again unsuccessful. They tried to take advantage of an experimental and long-since-abolished rule: If a team was fouled in the final two minutes, it could hold onto the ball, regardless of whether it made its free throws or not. The rule had been implemented to prevent what often occurs at the end of today's games—intentional fouls designed to stop the clock and get the ball back. At the time, it meant CCNY's lead would be safe unless disaster struck—which is exactly what happened.

Holding onto a 56–54 lead with a minute to go, the Beavers worked the ball around until they found an open Ed Warner underneath the basket by himself. Warner had the option of putting in the easy layup to give the team an insurmountable four-point lead or bringing the ball back out to waste more time off the clock. He did neither. The conundrum was too much for the sophomore to process in time, and moments later the referees whistled Warner for a lane violation. The ball was now going back to the Buckeyes, with plenty of time remaining for an equalizing shot.

The Buckeyes failed to convert the golden opportunity, but they were given yet another chance just seconds later. Sophomore Ed Roman decided to drive in for what would have been the decisive layup, but as he approached the hoop he ran into OSU senior Bob Burkholder. The referees ruled that Burkholder had established position first, meaning that Roman had committed a charge. Not only would the Buckeyes now get to shoot a free throw, as

the rules indicated at the time, they would also get the ball back after the shot. For many in the crowd, the mental collapse by the Beavers indicated one thing: The fix was in. A point-shaving scandal had been sweeping across the nation, one that would eventually implicate many of the CCNY players. Some college players would later admit to fixing-regular season games, but were Holman's players trading their chance at an NCAA title for a few more dollars?

Burkholder made the free throw to cut the lead to 56–55. On the ensuing possession, Ohio State worked the ball to junior Jim Remington for the final shot. As poorly as CCNY's players had handled the game's final moments on offense, they stepped up when they needed to, refusing to let Remington get a good look at the basket. Finally, with time winding down, Remington was forced to throw up a shot that clanged off the rim just before time expired. The Beavers had escaped with the victory, but it was hardly a confidence-building finish.

Two nights later, with a spot in the national championship on the line, the team found itself in a similar situation. Playing N.C. State, the Beavers were clinging to a three-point lead as the final minutes approached. This time, the Beavers left no doubt as to who was the best team. Warner sank a pair of crucial layups to seal a 78–73 victory and a spot in the title game against Bradley. As heart-stopping as the Beavers had made their first two games, nothing would compare to the drama that would ensue in the championship game (see page 232). ●

1951 Kentucky

The 1950 tournament was undoubtedly a tough act to follow, but the task for the 1951 tournament got a lot easier when the NCAA doubled the tournament from 8 to 16 teams. The field now included winners from 10 conferences and 6 at-large teams, most of which came from independent schools. Still, the tournament had no room for Bill Mlkvy's 12–13 Temple squad. Mlkvy was not only the best player in college basketball, leading the country in scoring and finishing second in rebounds and assists, he also had the best nickname basketball has ever seen: "The Owl Without a Vowel." Despite his absence, the tournament produced a plethora of great games, including Illinois' 79–71 upset over 21–0 Columbia. The Illini rallied from seven points down in that game, but the comeback of the tournament nearly belonged to Arizona, which trailed Kansas State by 21 in the first round when KSU removed its starters. Arizona cut the lead to just one point late in the game before Kansas State escaped with a 61–59 victory.

Simply put, Bobby Watson was meant to be a Kentucky Wildcat. As a kid, Watson idolized the UK players and dreamed of one day playing for Kentucky himself. Teaming up with future Wildcat star Cliff Hagan, Watson was an all-state basketball player at Owensboro High School, where he was coached by former Wildcat guard Lawrence McGinnis. So when Watson discovered he had failed to land a scholarship at UK, it was no stretch to say that he was crushed. Although Alabama coach Floyd Burdette offered him a roster spot, facing Kentucky twice a year was not exactly something he relished. And when Burdette started to wane on his scholarship offer, Watson made the easiest decision of his life.

"The coach at Alabama had made me an offer, and I had taken a train to UA and I was there two days, and coach didn't act like he knew me very well," Watson said. "So I caught a train back to Lexington and I entered Kentucky."

That didn't mean that the Kentucky staff was about to offer him a scholarship. Watson was put on the freshman team, and he paid his own tuition in the hopes that if he one day made the varsity team, he could finally have his tuition waved. It was a big risk for Watson; in addition to giving up a full ride to Alabama, he had also passed on a football scholarship from Murray State. The decision turned out to be a wise one, as Watson easily made the varsity team and eventually became the best guard in the conference.

"I was very happy that that's the way it ended up for me, because that's really where I wanted to go the whole time," Watson said. "It was an honor to be playing at UK."

By the time Watson reached his senior year, the Wildcats were 28–2 and looking to win a third title in four years. But before they could ever worry about championships, they would first have to beat in-state rival Louisville in the opening round. UK received quite a scare from the Cardinals, who led 64–60 late in the game, but a late rally put Kentucky in the second round to face St. John's. Again the Wildcats would need a late comeback, as they let a 42–34 lead slip as the New Yorkers tied the game at 43 with five minutes left. Kentucky ended the game on a 16–0 run, setting up a date in Minneapolis with the University of Illinois. Closing out the Illini, however, would not be as easy.

The Wildcats, who were quickly making a habit of slow starts, trailed Illinois 39–32 at halftime. After tying it up at the beginning of the second period, Kentucky was unable to pull away as both Hagan and Bill Spivey fouled out. While Hagan was only 3-of-9 from the floor when he left, Spivey had scored 28 points, leaving the team to cling to a 70–69 lead without its best player. Taking his place was Shelby Linville, a transfer from Miami University in Ohio. Linville quickly added a layup to give UK a 72–69 lead, but an Illini free throw cut the lead to 72–70. After a stop on the defensive end, UI's Irv Bemoras tied the game on a long set shot with 50 seconds to go.

With no shot clock, Kentucky could have held the ball for the last shot, but Linville got the look he wanted with 38 seconds to go and fired away. His shot sailed through, but Illinois wasted no time in setting up its offense. The Illini's Don Sunderlage took the early shot, tying the game at 74 with 29 seconds to go. UK sophomore Frank Ramsey then held onto the ball, waiting for the seconds to tick by, when he inexplicably found Linville alone underneath the basket. Ramsey fired it to Linville, who easily put away the shot for a 76–74 lead. Incredibly, 17 seconds still remained.

After calling a timeout with 12 seconds to go, the Illini attempted to go right back to Sunderlage. The Wildcat defenders stood their ground, refusing to let him within 10 feet of the basket. Unable to get a better look, Sunderlage was forced to cast off a long hook shot that bounced off the rim. The Wildcats were back in the finals, thanks in no small part to the Adolph Rupp's excellent coaching.

"He had a system of plays, and if you ran the plays like you should, then you should win the game," Ramsey said. "And if you didn't run the plays like he wanted you to, you heard about it. And when we practiced, there was no talking or joking around. It was all business."

Given his demeanor, it must have come as quite a shock to the coach when he saw how his opponent was approaching the championship game that night.

"We were playing Kansas State in the NCAA Tournament and we were at the gym and the other team was coming in. They hadn't dressed or anything, but they were coming in to get ready for the game and coach Rupp was standing there," Watson said. "Coach Rupp said they were laughing and cutting up, the other team was, and that they were whistling in the graveyard."

The indication, of course, was that the KSU players were trying to stay positive despite their impending beating. It was a confident prediction considering that many people thought Kentucky was going to lose. Not only would Kansas State win, Oklahoma A&M coach Henry Iba told Rupp before the game, but KSU was also the greatest team ever put together. It didn't help matters when Hagan came down with the flu before the game. The rest of the team wasn't much better off, as Spivey had a cold and Rupp was battling a cornea ulcer, in addition to back pain, high blood pressure, and swelling in his right leg that required a cast. In fact, by tip-off, the Wildcats had only six healthy players. The undermanned Wildcats found themselves down 20–13 in the first half when Rupp overrode the doctor's orders, sending in the sickly Hagan.

As soon as he was put in the game, Hagan tipped in a missed free throw to cut the lead to five, and by the time the first half ended, KSU's lead was down to 29–27. Kentucky stormed out to a 54–39 lead by the midpoint of the second half, and thanks to Hagan's solid play down the stretch, they held off Kansas State for the 68–58 win and the national championship. Perhaps the only player who performed better than Hagan was his other ill counterpart, Spivey, whose 50 points in the Final Four earned him Most Outstanding Player honors. Not bad for somebody who had arrived in Lexington as a 7-foot, 160-pound freshman. It was only thanks to a ridiculous diet of four malt shakes per day that Spivey bulked up to become a force down low.

The team returned home to find a parade being thrown in their honor. For many of the rural-born players, there were more people lined in the streets than they had ever seen at one time.

"You've got to realize all of us were from small towns—I came from a town of 5,000; Bobby and Cliff came from a town of 10,000," Ramsey said. "We were kind of overwhelmed by everything. We were just plain old country boys."

The scene may have been too much to handle for the players, but it was a small price to pay for a national title. And they were more than champions—they were basketball's first dynasty. ●

1952 Kansas

The Final Four made its official debut in 1952, as the four remaining teams traveled to a neutral site to determine a national champion. At that time, those four teams weren't the winners of four regions but rather the two finalists from both the West and East Regions. The one team that seemed guaranteed to make a spot in the Final Four was Kentucky, the top-ranked team in the country at 28–2. After an 82–54 victory over Penn State in the tournament opener, all the Wildcats had to do was beat St. John's—a team they had beaten 81–40 earlier in the year. But Bob Zawoluk scored 23 points in the rematch, ending UK's 23-game winning streak with a 64–57 upset. The Redmen followed that up with an upset over second-ranked Illinois, but the biggest shocker came from the Santa Clara Broncos, who entered the tournament with just a 15–10 record but also clinched a spot in the first true Final Four.

As one of the first pupils of Dr. James Naismith, the inventor of basketball, Forrest "Phog" Allen had seen his fair share of basketball games. Allen had played for Naismith at Kansas from 1905 to '07 and had been coaching the Jayhawks since 1919. But despite a career that consisted of nearly 600 wins, Phog had yet to win a national championship when he came across Clyde Lovellette, a high schooler whom Allen was convinced would help capture that elusive title. The only problem was that Lovellette was a native of Indiana, which likely meant he was going to become a Hoosier.

"It's sort of like a given fact the first thing you're going to do is go to Indiana," said Lovellette, who had received the standard recruiting treatment from IU coach Branch McCracken. "He talked to me a couple of times, but it was just a given fact that's where you were going to go."

Lovellette registered at Indiana before any KU coaches had a chance to meet him, but Phog refused to give up. He made the trek to Lovellette's hometown of Terre Haute, where the recruit was spending his final months of high school.

"At that time I was ready to go to Indiana, so I didn't want to talk to Phog very much and I tried to hide," recalled Lovellette of the day Allen showed up at the door. "I told Dad, 'I'm going to go leave,' so I went out the house and Phog came in. My mom was there, and she's very polite, and she said, 'He's out back.'"

Now with the youngster all to himself, Allen told Lovellette that he envisioned the big man leading Kansas to a national championship in 1952 and winning an Olympic gold medal the same year. Lovellette bought the story, and he took a trip out to Lawrence for a week. Still, he was not convinced. Lovellette decided to stick with the Hoosiers, prompting another visit from Phog.

"He reappeared on my doorstep and he reassured me that this is what was going to happen," Lovellette said. "I thought, 'Well, okay,' so I packed my bags and went to Lawrence."

And the dream was still alive by Lovellette's senior year, as his 28 points per game led the Jayhawks to a birth in the NCAA Tournament. Their first match was against Southwest Conference champion TCU, which was led by star center George McLeod. The contest looked to be over when McLeod unbelievably fouled out before the first quarter was even over, but the Horned Frogs nearly overcame a 34–24 halftime deficit. It wasn't until a few late plays by Lovellette that the Jayhawks escaped with a 68–64 win.

"That was the hardest game," captain Bill Lienhard said. "We were ahead the whole time, but they were pesky and they just stayed around the whole game and stayed with us."

The next game was much easier, as Lovellette broke the tournament record with 44 points to send the Jayhawks to Seattle, where the Final

Four was being held. Actually getting there, however, was another matter. Their propeller plane hit an air pocket and suffered a serious drop in elevation, leaving the players in a state of fear—except for Lovellette, who still kept his sense of humor.

"They had artificial flowers and Phog was over there sleeping—the turbulence didn't bother him," Lovellette said. "Anyway, I took up one of those bouquets of flowers, and I walked over and I stuck them into his hands. He woke up and I said, 'Phog, I just wanted to be sure you were ready if it did go down.'"

The plane would land safely after all, allowing Allen to focus his attention on the game. But for all the time he spent on developing his game plan, perhaps he could have spent a little more time on his pre-game speech.

"If you screw up, if you don't play like you're supposed to play, you'll have the outcome of losing that game," Allen told his players. "And I'm going to tell the press that you guys didn't do what you were supposed to do like we talked about the week before, and therefore it's going to be your fault."

Kansas avoided the negative publicity for at least one more night, running over Santa Clara 74–55 to send the team to the championship. Lovellette decided to celebrate with an old fraternity friend, who had a boat anchored just off the coast, but first he needed permission from Allen. That would be fine, the coach told Lovellette, as long as he got back in time to get plenty of rest for the big game. But while out at sea, some thick clouds rolled in and engulfed the entire area, blocking all visibility. Lovellette and his companion would not be able to dock until the weather passed, leaving Lovellette to worry not only about the fog but about the Phog, who had set a 10 p.m. curfew.

Lovellette finally made his way back to the hotel in the wee hours of the morning, hoping his late-night adventure would not turn into any headlines. But that possibility looked to be over as soon as he opened the door.

"There was a newspaperman sitting there in the lobby, and he looked up and saw me," Lovellette smiled. "I got up in the morning and didn't have as much sleep as they did, but got up, went down, and had breakfast just like nothing happened."

If Phog Allen looked at the morning papers that day, he was none the wiser for it. Gerry Barker, the man who witnessed Lovellette's secret return, kept the story to himself. In the end, he had plenty to write about. His new confidant scored 33 points in the championship, leaving him with a new record of 141 for the tournament. More importantly, his Jayhawks won the national championship with an 80–63 victory. Barker's counterparts in the media were not so friendly, as *Look* magazine left Lovellette off their first-team All-American roster. The KU fans voiced their displeasure, burning copies of the magazine at the victory celebration.

"I couldn't imagine he wouldn't have been an All-American—he was the leading scorer in the country and led us to a national championship," Lienhard said. "Of course, *Look* magazine is out of business. Maybe that's why—nobody knew what they were doing."

As for the gold medal, Lovellette would again prove up to the task. Perhaps *Look* was right after all—Lovellette wasn't the best player in the country. He was the best in the world. ●

Kansas coach Phog Allen, thanks to Clyde Lovellette's 40 points, had plenty of reason to be happy, as the Jayhawks took home the national championship. *AP Photo/Matty Zimmerman*

1953 Indiana

The NCAA added six more teams to the 1953 tournament, just enough to let Lebanon Valley sneak into the field. Even then, the little school from Pennsylvania needed some help. Both La Salle and Seton Hall turned down the bid, and Temple refused to play Lebanon Valley for the spot, so the Flying Dutchmen—with a student population of 425—became the smallest school ever to play in the tournament. Of course, having such a small school also meant the basketball team had little to work with. In its first-round game against Fordham, Lebanon Valley played only its five starters—none of whom were taller than 6-foot-1—yet still managed to beat the Rams 80–67. The tournament also marked a milestone for the NCAA, as teams had to choose between the NCAA Tournament and NIT. When four of the top five teams opted for the NCAA, the debate between the tournaments was essentially over.

By the time Branch McCracken began his twelfth season as the Indiana basketball coach, he had just about had it with finishing in second place. Through his first 10 seasons at the helm, McCracken had finished in second place in the Big Ten an incredible seven times. In the days when each conference sent only one team to the NCAA Tournament, this meant plenty of unwanted free time during March. Even when the Hoosiers grabbed the national title in 1940, they didn't enter the tournament as Big Ten champions but rather on a judgment call by the selection committee. In 1952, his squad had fallen to fourth place in the Big Ten, but he wasn't about to start cutting corners to reach that elusive title. McCracken sold his recruits on playing for "the glory of IU," an ethical stance that put him at quite a disadvantage.

"I don't remember all the offers, but I do know that there were some schools—not so much the schools, but the business people in the communities—that offered various things a couple of times," forward Charlie Kraak said. "I had a girlfriend at that time in Collinsville, Illinois, and Branch knew that the coaches down in Louisiana at that time figured I'd want to go back home every so often, and came up and offered a car."

But McCracken had one thing at his disposal that almost no other coach did—a deep culture of basketball to rely upon. The 1953 roster was comprised almost entirely of Indiana

natives, and Kraak, one of the few players from out of state, had declined other lucrative offers to play in Bloomington. In order to make the extra push toward the Big Ten title, McCracken moved Kraak from guard to forward and replaced him with the speedy Bobby Leonard. It was a move that worked to perfection as Leonard became an All-American guard, leading IU to a 17–1 record in the Big Ten and their first-ever conference crown.

"Our nickname was the 'Hurrying Hoosiers,' and I was very proud of that," Leonard said. "McCracken had very simple philosophies: first of all defense, which is one of the staples of the game. Pressure defense all over the floor—we worked on that constantly."

With the rare blend of speed and tenacious defense, the Hoosiers ran their way to the top ranking in the country, but the NCAA did them no favors by sending them to Chicago to play hometown favorite DePaul in the first round. The Hoosiers led 74–66 with just three minutes to go when the Blue Demons went on a desperation run, bringing the crowd to a frenzy.

"You talk about a wild place," Leonard exclaimed. "Ray Meyer was coaching DePaul—boy, they were a big Catholic school. And you know those Catholics, boy they get into a weekend like that and get to drinking beer and all that stuff—I mean, it was wild."

The fans watched as DePaul cut the lead to 82–80 in the final seconds, but Indiana held on for the unnerving victory. Unfortunately for McCracken's club, the crowd didn't get any easier as the Hoosiers next faced Notre Dame, another Catholic school that had plenty of Chicago ties. The Fighting Irish, who had beaten IU in the second game of the season, decided to up the ante by sending a telegram before the game, reminding their opponents that while the Hoosiers may have been the top team in the country, Notre Dame was still the best team in Indiana.

"I don't think we paid any attention to that," Kraak said. "We were worried about the big enchilada, not worried about who beat who during the season."

The Hoosiers decided to let their play do the talking, and it was sophomore Don Schlundt who had the last word. The forward scored 30 points in the first half, and by the end of the game he had finished with a school-record 41 as the Hoosiers eased to a 79–66 win.

"I enjoyed just feeding him, just to watch him make moves and score—he was that good a ballplayer," Kraak said. "I can't recall anybody else, either all the way up the line, high school through college, either playing with or against, that would have been equal to that. That's why I say he had the greatest shooting touch of a big guy. I haven't seen a better one yet even today."

The win sent the Hoosiers to Kansas City for the Final Four, where they quickly defeated LSU to advance to the title game. Once again the Hoosiers would have to face a hostile crowd, as they would take on the Kansas Jayhawks, the defending national champions who hailed from Lawrence—just 40 miles down the road. They hoped to find at least one supporter when they visited the office of Harry Truman, who had just finished his term as president that January and was now based in Kansas City. Perhaps more than anything, the visit by the players was for the simple purpose of riling up McCracken, who was an adamant critic of Truman. But what they discovered upon their visit was that despite being a native of Missouri, which had a deep rivalry with the Jayhawks, Truman would be heartily supporting Kansas the following day.

"Well, he probably wanted to get votes from out there in Kansas, too," Leonard said with a laugh. "You know, when you're president you need everybody going for you."

That confrontation, of course, did not sit well with McCracken, who had passed on the team trip to Truman's office. The team still brought back a picture taken with Truman, just to get a laugh at McCracken's expense, but it was McCracken who would get the last laugh.

"Back home in Monrovia," McCracken quipped upon looking at the photo, "we'd have hung this in the outhouse to scare the rats away."

In front of more than 10,000 Kansas fans, the Hoosiers pulled off one of the most thrilling title wins in NCAA history, bringing McCracken something much more meaningful than a conference title (see page 340). The Hoosiers were now NCAA champions, and when the team returned home the IU faithful made sure to atone for their absence in Chicago and Kansas City.

"When we came back, we had to land in Indianapolis and meet our team bus. By the time we got to Martinsville, Indiana, which was about 18 miles from Bloomington, the highways were lined with cars all the way home," Leonard recalled. "And when the bus finally got into Bloomington, the streets were just jammed with people. I mean, it was a big deal." ●

IU coach Branch McCracken, center, is shown with Bobby Leonard, Jim Schooley, Don Schlundt, and Lou Scott. *AP Photo*

1954 La Salle

For first time, the finals were broadcast across the country, and while the championship may not have been a close contest, the rest of the tournament certainly was. Idaho State survived a 77–75 overtime thriller to end Seattle's 26-game winning streak, and Notre Dame's Dick Rosenthal—despite collapsing moments earlier from an illness—sank a free throw with 15 seconds left to defeat second-ranked Indiana 65–64. With the defending champions gone, the tournament was nothing short of chaos. Unranked Navy advanced to the Elite Eight when Ken McCally's shot with three seconds left beat Cornell 69–67. The Final Four also welcomed two other Cinderellas in Bradley and USC, who came in with a combined 24 losses. Their semifinal matchup was perhaps the best of the tournament, as Bob Carney scored five points in the last 1:05 to help Bradley overcome a seven-point fourth-quarter deficit. Their 74–72 victory sent them to their second national championship game in just five years.

For a team that had gone 49–8 over the previous two years, expectations were quite low for the 1954 La Salle Explorers. The team appeared to boast a formidable roster before the year started, but the loss of two players to eligibility issues, followed by another who joined the military, left fans wondering just what the season held in store. Perhaps nobody had lower expectations than coach Ken Loeffler, who scrambled just to field a 10-man roster, even though 12 players were allowed on a team. The end result was a lineup that consisted of eight sophomores, one junior, and one senior. Freshmen weren't allowed to play back then, so with eight of the players having a combined zero minutes of collegiate experience, the weight appeared to be squarely on the shoulders of All-American Tom Gola to salvage the season. Loeffler announced to the press that "our team this year consists of Tom Gola and eight garbage men," a statement that didn't sit too well with the newcomers on the team.

"He was controversial. Obviously, I take issue with that," said Frank Blatcher, one of the team's sophomores. "He did a head job on a lot of people with that stuff."

To the surprise of everyone, except maybe the players on the team, La Salle ran off to a 21–4 start, good enough to earn a spot in the NCAA Tournament. Though happy about the regular-season success, the Explorers were actually disappointed by the outcome, as 1954 marked the first year that conference champions were required to play in the NCAA Tournament. As an eastern team that enjoyed the Madison Square Garden atmosphere of the NIT, most of the players were less than enthused about traveling to Kansas City, which is probably why the uninspired Explorers almost lost their first-round game to Fordham.

The vastly inferior Rams actually held a 66–64 lead with just four seconds to go when La Salle called a timeout to give the team one last chance. Thanks to the quick thinking of Charlie Greenberg, another sophomore, the team was going to make it a good one. As soon as he saw Francis O'Hara step to the baseline to inbound the ball, Greenberg saw that the plan was destined to fail.

"The play we were going to run before that was to throw it the length of the court," Greenberg said. "And I said to O'Hara, 'This isn't going to work,' because we were all the way down at the other end, so I said, 'Let's call another timeout.'"

The extra huddle not only gave the team a chance to reorganize, it also brought the ball up to halfcourt. The instinctive decision by Greenberg allowed the Explorers to run a much better option—feeding the ball down to Gola. That choice was equally obvious to Fordham, which triple-teamed the forward as soon as he caught the ball. That left Fran O'Malley wide open, and Gola fed the sophomore as he broke to the basket. O'Malley caught the ball in stride and laid it in just before the buzzer to send the game into overtime. Five minutes later, La Salle had escaped with a 76–74 victory. Even when Gola was trying to let somebody else enjoy the spotlight, he was still the hero of the game.

"He had magnificent peripheral vision and spotted that, then created a play. It was really all Gola doing what he had to do, and he did it. And it was not that he made a spectacular shot at all; it was that he made a spectacular play," Blatcher said. "He was not only a great player but an unselfish player and a team player."

The celebration came to an abrupt ending when the team returned to campus to hear the news that Blatcher's father had passed away. Even for somebody who had lived with his dad, the two were exceptionally close. Frank's father, despite being 70 years old, would walk several miles each day to pick up the one newspaper that carried every La Salle game, just so he could cut out each article. But while meeting with his family to make arrangements for the funeral, Frank got an unexpected message from his siblings.

"I had five sisters and I'm the youngest of 13 children, so we got kind of huddled together and all my sisters are saying, 'You know, Dad would want you to play, the team needs you,'" Blatcher said. "That was a very emotional time in my life."

After making sure his family would be all right, Blatcher returned to the team. In the week that he was gone, however, he had lost his starting position. Unfair as it may have been, Blatcher now had things in proper perspective. Not only did he take the benching with stride, he led the team in points the last two games to give La Salle the 1954 national championship.

"I basically dedicated those games to my father," Blatcher said. "The game is less important, but you know it's important for other people and consequently you go in and you just do what you have to do."

Blatcher was snubbed by not winning the Most Outstanding Player Award, but he received a much nicer gift from the city of Philadelphia.

"The mayor at the time honored us by giving us our graduation rings," Blatcher said, "which was quite interesting, because eight of us were sophomores. Graduation was kind of presumptive."

The early gesture turned out to be just fine, as each of the sophomores would earn his degree. Not bad for a bunch of garbage men.

"As I said later on to someone, the garbage began to smell pretty good after a while," Greenberg joked.

At least Blatcher's dad didn't have to trek across town to read about the garbage men's championship. He got to watch it from a much better place. ●

1955 San Francisco

If fans thought Bradley's run to the 1954 Final Four was a surprise, they were in for quite a shock in 1955. A year earlier, the Braves had made the Final Four despite entering the tournament with a 19–13 record, a run that was good enough to get head coach Forddy Anderson the coaching position at Michigan State. Anderson had won 72 percent of his games in his six seasons at Bradley, but his successor appeared to have no such luck. Bob Vanatta went 7–19 in 1954–55, but somehow the Braves snagged what had to be the final bid in the tournament. And after a 69–65 win over Oklahoma City University and a hard-earned 81–79 victory over SMU, the Braves were in the Elite Eight. The team to emerge out of the West, however, was a much more deserving 29–1 San Francisco squad.

Long before Bill Russell was the greatest champion in basketball history, he was just a scrawny student at McClymonds High School in Oakland. Standing at just 6-foot-2 and 128 pounds, Russell was not exactly a force to be reckoned with on the court. Russell had already failed to make the football team and cheerleading—yes, cheerleading—squad, and his venture into basketball was no different. The sophomore did not make the 15-man junior varsity roster, but coach Jim Powles bent the rules by adding a sixteenth member to the squad, which allowed Russell to join the team. After a year of sitting on the bench and continuing to grow, the now 6-foot-5 Russell tried his luck on the varsity team, where he was promptly cut.

The following season Powles was promoted to head coach of the varsity team, just in time for Russell's senior year. Once again Powles allowed his eager but untalented player to gain a roster spot, but it came with little playing time. He failed to break the 10-point barrier all season long, but University of San Francisco scout Hal DeJulio decided to stop by McClymonds for Russell's last game to see if the now 6-foot-6 Russell had any potential. What DeJulio saw was a complete misrepresentation of Russell's high school career, as Russell had the game of his life with 14 points.

A few weeks later, DeJulio called his new recruit to see if there was any chance Russell would be interested in attending USF. After Russell responded by asking what he was referring to, a perplexed DeJulio responded by simply saying "The University." "You mean

San Francisco State?" Russell asked DeJulio, who was now offended. "No," he retorted, "the University of San Francisco." The conversation was uncomfortable for both parties, but Russell was hardly to blame for his lack of familiarity with the program. In the team's 28-year history, they had never once even qualified for the NCAA Tournament. Nevertheless, Russell signed up, and history was about to be made.

He arrived on campus as a 6-foot-7, 158-pound freshman, but by Russell's junior year he was a 6-foot-10 All-American center. Thanks in large part to Russell, the Dons breezed through the competition with a 23–1 record and a spot in the NCAA Tournament. But had it not been for some intervention from the school, it may have been a bid they were willing to decline. The players had taken a vote on whether to participate in the NCAA Tournament or NIT, a vote that was split 7–7. The school stepped in to tell the players they would be playing in the NCAA Tournament, a decision that they started to regret when they took the floor for their first-round contest against West Texas State. Just three minutes into the game, one of his opponents sent Russell flying to the ground with a low hit, and two minutes later a different player knocked Russell in the back of his head, once again sending him sprawling to the floor. Russell could deal with a little pain, scoring 29 points in the 89–66 win, but he was hardly prepared for what he faced next.

In the following game against Utah, Russell—who vomited before almost every game out of nervousness—realized he was not just experiencing his typical pre-game jitters. In the locker room at halftime, Russell started coughing up what he believed was blood, prompting a quick decision from coach Phil Woolpert to leave him out of the second half. It wasn't a hard decision to make, as the Dons were already up 41–20, but when the Utes cut the deficit to eight in Russell's absence, it was decision time once again for Woolpert.

The team did not travel with a doctor, but the coaching staff sought the advice of Ed Duggan, a USF alum and doctor who happened to be sitting in the bleachers. Duggan discovered that Russell had not actually thrown up blood, but in fact had devoured some undercooked steak before the game. The junior may not have been feeling great, but Duggan cleared him for action, and within minutes Russell had pushed the lead back to 15 points. They would need a healthy Russell in time for their next game against Oregon State, which would be their toughest test yet.

Russell paved the way with 18 points in the first half as the Dons took a 30–27 lead, and they eventually stretched the margin to eight points with less than two minutes remaining, but Oregon State was far from finished. The Beavers cut the lead to 56–55 when they sent USF's Jerry Mullen to the line. The senior missed the first free throw, so even after he converted his second opportunity the door was still open for OSU. Woolpert inserted defensive specialist K. C. Jones for the final shot, but before play resumed the coach brought him back over to the bench for one quick piece of advice. Jones continued to chat over his shoulder with Woolpert as he jogged back on the court, completely oblivious to his immediate surroundings. Oregon State senior Bill O'Toole jumped directly into the path of the oncoming Jones, who bowled him over seconds later. The result was a technical foul on Jones, and when OSU captain Reggie Halligan sank the impending free throw, USF's lead was down to just 57–56.

This time it was OSU coach Slats Gill who brought his team over to the sideline, instructing Ron Robins to take the final shot. Robins missed a shot from the corner, but the rebound came to OSU center Swede Halbrook. Jones made up for his previous transgression by tying up Halbrook to force a jump ball, which

Bill Russell celebrates alongside USF supporters after his 23-point performance against La Salle led the Dons to a 77–63 victory in the national championship. *University of San Francisco Athletic Department*

in those days actually meant the two would jump for the ball as if it were an opening tip. Standing a full 14 inches shorter than the 7-foot-3 Halbrook, Jones knew his only chance to win the tip was to hit the ball on the way up. It was an illegal move, but when the ball went to USF guard Hal Perry without a call, Jones knew the Dons were on their way to the Final Four.

A win over Colorado put the Dons in the title game against La Salle, the defending national champion and owner of the top player in basketball, Tom Gola. But the star of the game turned out to be Jones, who held the 6-foot-7 Gola to just nine points in the first half as his team nearly went scoreless for the last 10 minutes of the period. By the game's end, Jones had tallied 24 points while Russell chipped in with 23 points and 25 rebounds of his own. Gola may have been the best player in the country, but the Dons had the best team. Fortunately for them, their work wasn't finished quite yet. ●

1956 San Francisco

The NCAA went back to its roots by hosting the finals in Evanston, Illinois, in 1956. But unlike the first tournament that produced only 15,025 fans and lost money, this one made more than $300,000 from its crowd of 132,000. The fans certainly got what they paid for, as Dartmouth upset West Virginia on a last-second jumper and Temple produced one of the most memorable Final Four runs in history. The Owls nearly lost their tournament opener to Holy Cross when the Crusaders held for the last shot with the score tied, but Temple came away with a steal, and Fred Cohen's shot with 10 seconds remaining sent them into the second round against the University of Connecticut. Their 65–59 victory over the Huskies was slightly easier, thanks to a ridiculous 34-rebound performance from Fred Cohen and a 40-point effort from Hal Lear. In his team's following game against Canisius, Lear sank a pair of free throws with two seconds left to give the Owls a 60–58 win, and although they lost their next game to Iowa, Lear's 48 points in the consolation game earned him the Most Outstanding Player Award. Lear was the first player to win the award without taking home the championship, but his performance began a period of 11 years in which eight of the MOP winners failed to win the tournament. With a record 160 points in five games, however, no one could argue with Lear's selection.

Like Bill Russell, K. C. Jones had never intended to play basketball for the University of San Francisco. His high school career may have been a bit more illustrious than Russell's, but his scholarship prospects looked just as bleak as he was finishing his senior year. USF coach Phil Woolpert had no intention of signing Jones, and it was only after a well-intentioned lie by *San Francisco Examiner* writer Al Corona that Jones had any offers at all. Corona asked the senior how many schools were pursuing him, and Jones replied that he had no takers. The writer smiled and said, "Read my column tomorrow." An article in the following day's paper claimed that Jones was being recruited by several major schools, and Woolpert, not wanting to let a highly touted prospect slip through his fingers, went to sign Jones.

But once Jones finally did get his scholarship offer, it was one he almost declined to take. With his family in desperate financial trouble, Jones felt the need to enter the work force and get the family off welfare. It was only after encouragement from both his mother and Woolpert that he agreed to attend USF. It turned out to be the right decision, as Jones helped lead the Dons to a national championship in 1955.

With both Russell and Jones back for their senior years, expectations were high for the team, and they delivered with an undefeated regular season. Rarely were the Dons ever challenged, and after they broke the NCAA record with their thirty-ninth straight victory, they just kept going. By season's end, the Dons stood at 28–0 and appeared primed to take home a second national championship. Disaster struck, however, when the NCAA ruled that Jones would be ineligible for postseason play. Jones had played one game as a sophomore before a burst appendix quickly ended his season. He regained his eligibility and was able to play three more seasons, but the NCAA had now ruled it was one game too many.

This wasn't the first time the sport's governing body had attempted to interfere in USF's quest for basketball immortality. No team had ever finished a season undefeated before, and the NCAA didn't anticipate the Dons would be the first. Before the start of the season, the NCAA had implemented changes that became known as "the Russell rules." They widened the free throw lane from six feet to 12 feet to prevent a player from camping under the basket. Players also had just three seconds to remain in the lane, making any extended stay by the hoop nearly impossible. Russell simply adjusted his game to keep up, but without Jones feeding him the ball, it would be up to Russell to carry the burden on his own.

The Dons' bid for a second straight title got off to a rather precarious start when they missed their first eight shots of their opening-round game against UCLA. The Bruins were the last team to defeat USF, and if anybody knew what it would take to defeat them, it would be UCLA coach John Wooden. Thanks to some stingy defense, the Dons doubled up the Bruins at 24–12 and pushed that margin to 39–21 at the break. They never looked back as they cruised to an easy victory.

Things didn't get any easier in the second round when the Dons faced the University of Utah, a team that would be looking to avenge its loss to USF in the previous year's tournament. Through the first 20 minutes, the Dons only found themselves up 44–41, and midway through the second half the lead stood at just 56–55. Russell had picked up his fourth foul, but Woolpert had no choice but to leave him in—without Russell in the game, San Francisco had little chance of pulling away. The senior avoided picking up the deadly fifth foul, and after a 15–2 run the Dons were on their way back to the Final Four.

Meeting them would be Southern Methodist, which had won 25 of its last 27 contests. The Mustangs faced a 41–19 deficit early in the game, but they slowly began to chip away at the lead. By the early second half SMU had scored 21 of the last 25 points to pull within 46–40. San Francisco recovered to make another late run, putting them just one victory away from history, but standing in their way would be Iowa, who at 26–5 would be no pushover. The Hawkeyes sent a message early on, running up a 15–4 lead as Carl Cain, who would eventually marry Jones' sister, seemed to be scoring at will. Jones, standing on the bench in street clothes, lit into his teammates when play stopped.

"You're choking, really swallowing the olive," Jones lectured. "You lose this one, and the winning streak you're gloating about won't mean a thing."

Jones also warned his teammates to watch out for Cain's shot fakes, something they quickly put an end to when play resumed. The Dons went on a 20–8 run, and by the end of the first half they had grabbed a 38–33 lead. Iowa still trailed by only seven points with four minutes to go, but another late spurt from USF wiped away any chance of a comeback. By the end of the game, Russell had tallied 26 points and 27 rebounds, but even more impressive were his 12 blocks, a record that would not be approached any time soon.

Neither would their winning streak, which eventually reached an incredible 60 games. In one way, the NCAA officials got their wish as Russell finally stopped terrorizing the competition. But that was only because Russell had moved on to the NBA level, where opponents found him equally impossible to stop. When the dust settled, he walked away with 13 championship rings—too many to even wear on his fingers. But of all those teams, perhaps none would be as dominant as the 1956 Dons. ●

Bill Russell and Carl Boldt showcase a little hardware upon their return from their second consecutive championship. *University of San Francisco Athletic Department*

41

1957 North Carolina

The 1957 tournament would begin nearly as exciting as it would end. In the first round, Pittsburgh's John Laneve, who hadn't scored all day, hit a shot in the final minute to give the Panthers an 86–85 victory over Morehead State. Equally surprising was San Francisco's run to the Final Four for a third straight year. In mid-December, the Dons were ranked second in the country at 5–0, but they saw their 60-game winning streak snapped when they lost two straight games, and by January the team was unranked. But USF managed to find its way to the tournament, and despite not having K. C. Jones or Bill Russell anymore, they defeated Idaho State and then pulled off a 50–46 upset over former Dons coach Pete Newell and his 21–5 Cal team. Even though San Francisco failed to win the whole tournament, they could at least say they took part in the most exciting Final Four in the history of college basketball.

Of the hundreds of players to don North Carolina jerseys, a select few stand in a class of their own, having become almost synonymous with Tar Heel basketball. Phil Ford. Tyler Hansbrough. James Worthy. Michael Jordan. But perhaps the greatest Tar Heel of them all never even wanted to play for North Carolina. In fact, he had wanted to do just the opposite.

Despite having his senior year of high school wiped out in a coaches' strike, Lennie Rosenbluth had garnered nationwide attention for his basketball skills. The lean center had played only six or seven games in his career, but it didn't matter. With his showcase of size and agility, he could play anywhere he wanted. And unfortunately for Tar Heel fans, that place turned out to be rival N.C. State.

Fortunately for Rosenbluth, his admiration for State coach Everett Case appeared to be mutual. In fact, when he went to visit the campus in April of his senior year, it appeared to be just a formality to adjust the young man for what was to come. But before concluding the tour, Case dropped one final piece of information. "By the way," Case added, "we're having big workouts at Thompson Gymnasium. We'd like you to come work out."

But for Rosenbluth, his lack of a senior season meant it had been over a year since his last day of real competition. "Well, Coach, I never brought my sneakers and of course I'm out of shape—I haven't played basketball for months!" replied Rosenbluth, who reluctantly

agreed to head over to the gym after more pleading from Case. "When I got down to the gym, there must have been 50 or 75 guys out there. A lot of high school kids trying out. I said I felt I had a scholarship—I thought you didn't sign papers or anything back then."

To Case, however, this was more of a tryout than a workout. And after watching Rosenbluth take the court, he didn't like what he saw. Calling the young man and his father into his office, Case uttered the harshest critique Rosenbluth had ever heard of his game. He only had one scholarship left, Case declared, and he wasn't about to waste it on Rosenbluth.

Now only a few weeks before his high school graduation and without a college, Rosenbluth scrambled to find another taker. As it turned out, he had one just 25 miles away in Chapel Hill. Unlike Case, UNC coach Frank McGuire understood Rosenbluth's predicament. As a New Yorker himself, McGuire was not only aware of the strike, he was more than tolerant of its consequences. Joining Rosenbluth on the North Carolina roster would be six others from the New York area. In fact, of the seven main players in McGuire's rotation, each would hail from the Big Apple.

To the folks in North Carolina, it must have been odd to watch this band of city slickers represent the state's flagship school. But the more the Tar Heels began to win, the less anybody mentioned where they came from. Their 1957 season started with a 10-game winning streak, which quickly turned into 15, and after Rosenbluth helped UNC stomp over Case's squad 83–57, he began to notice what was going on.

"I didn't think we were going to go undefeated, of course, but I did feel that we could win it all. Everybody bought into it. Once the season got going, I said, 'Hey, who should we lose to? We can win them all, Coach—don't worry about it,'" Rosenbluth laughed. "As we kept on winning, he didn't want to hear it. I would be taking a shower and yell, 'Hey, Coach, we got 16 more games to go! Don't worry about it!'"

By their sixteenth victory, the Tar Heels had finally taken over the top ranking in the polls, but against Maryland it appeared their ranking, along with their winning streak, would quickly be coming to an end. Down by two points late in the game, McGuire called a timeout to advise his players that if they were going to lose, to do so graciously. That, of course, didn't sit well with the team, who tied the game at 53 with a little over a minute to go and came up with a stop at the other end to force overtime. Five minutes later they came up with another defensive stop to force a second overtime, where they eventually won 65–61. The team was now officially on a course with destiny.

As the season went on, fans began to give McGuire their lucky coins, rabbit feet, or anything that they felt would help the team stay undefeated. But the worst superstition of all came from junior Pete Brennan, whose father had given him an old used car at the beginning of his sophomore year. Throughout the 1955–56 season the car continued to deteriorate, prompting Brennan to put up a sign before leaving for the summer: "Please do not move, am going to fix in September." But thanks to a case of laziness, as well as the superstitious nature plaguing the campus, the car was still there as fall gave way to winter, and once February rolled around McGuire decided to take matters into his own hands.

"The police wanted to move it and they left notes in it. Pete left it there, so they finally called coach McGuire, and he calls Pete into the office and he says, 'Pete, they got to move the car,'" Rosenbluth smiled. "Well, Pete didn't have enough money to move the car, he didn't know what to do, so he tells Coach, 'I'm going to tell you something—you know that car has been a good-luck piece for us. All the students walk by and they hit the car for good luck. You're not really going to move it,' he said. 'That car has to stay there till the end of the season.'"

Moments later, McGuire made a call to the local police department. The car was staying put. And as they continued through the regular season with a 24–0 record, it was hard to argue with their logic. Unfortunately, with the way the ACC was set up back then, their chase of perfection would all be in vain if they didn't win the conference tournament. The conference sent only one team to the NCAA Tournament each year, and as they trailed 59–58 in the semifinals against Wake Forest, it appeared that the Tar Heels might not be that team.

With the clock ticking down in the last minute, they had a final chance to save their season. It wasn't difficult to decide who would get the shot.

"When you have a guy that's scoring 28 points a game and you get to a tight spot, you want him to touch the ball," center Joe Quigg explained. "It's just like you got a tremendous backfield in football so you give it to the guy who's bound to do it a lot of times. Lennie would be in there, so we knew what to do."

And fortunately for the Tar Heels, Rosenbluth came through, delivering a three-point play to help UNC escape with a 61–59 win. After their ACC championship win over South Carolina, Rosenbluth had just five more games to count off. It had been a trying season—over a quarter of their games had been decided by five points or fewer—but if they thought the drama was over, they were in for a real surprise (see page 342). ●

1958 Kentucky

West Virginia was clearly the team to beat as the 1958 tournament began. Led by Jerry West, the Mountaineers piled up a 26–1 record en route to their top ranking, but in the first round of the tournament they had to face Manhattan College at Madison Square Garden. The 15–9 Jaspers pulled off an 89–84 upset, prompting the home crowd to storm the court. Second-ranked Cincinnati also bowed out in its first game, falling 83–80 to Kansas State in overtime. Oscar Robertson, the leading scorer in the country, had a chance to win the game at the end of regulation, but he missed a free throw to open the door for the Wildcats. He would take his anger out in the consolation game, where he nearly outscored Arkansas by himself, setting the tournament record with 56 points in a 97–62 win. The 1958 season featured three of basketball's all-time greats in West, Robertson, and Wilt Chamberlain, but the title would belong to a Kentucky team with virtually no stars.

For Vernon Hatton, becoming a Kentucky Wildcat was never a consideration—not because he wasn't good enough to play at UK, but because he had no desire to do so. Thousands of young men in the Bluegrass State envied Hatton's position, but the high school all-star had set his mind on attending Eastern Kentucky. UK assistant coach Harry Lancaster tried to visit Hatton to change his mind, but Hatton was certain he would never don the Kentucky uniform. Hatton began to avoid Lancaster, often going to great lengths to do so, but Lancaster was either very poor at taking hints or extremely persistent.

"I played in two or three all-star games that summer and he came to all of them, and so pretty soon I'd stay in the shower," laughed Hatton, who would remain in the locker rooms for hours to hide from Lancaster—often to no avail. "Everybody else would leave and I'd come out and there Harry would be, sitting there waiting on me and said, 'Boy, you like to get clean, don't you?'"

With nowhere to hide, Hatton reluctantly agreed to let Lancaster meet with his family for an official recruiting visit. Before long, Lancaster had done the impossible by getting Hatton. Soon after his arrival, Hatton found himself being kicked out of practice by head coach Adolph Rupp. Hatton had been assigned to guard someone nearly half a foot shorter than him, and when the youngster compared

the task to an elephant guarding an ant, Rupp put a quick halt to practice.

"Look Hatton, no one has ever quit on me before," Rupp screamed. "Get in the dressing room, and take all of your things out of your locker and get your butt out of here!"

For someone who had never wanted to play at Kentucky until a few months before, Hatton was quite heartbroken. "I was in there halfway crying and pouting and getting my stuff," Hatton recalled. "And an assistant coach came in and said, 'Vern, why don't you go on home and just leave your things in the locker and come back tomorrow, and we'll just act like nothing ever happened.'"

It would turn out to be the right move, as Hatton would lead Kentucky to three straight NCAA Tournament appearances, the last of which, in 1958, appeared to be set up perfectly for a run at the national championship. Not only would the Wildcats play the first two rounds on their home court, but the Final Four would be played just 90 minutes away in Louisville. The team would indeed win its set of home games, but winning at Louisville's Freedom Hall would prove to be a much more difficult task. Facing Kentucky in the semifinals would be Temple, the fifth-ranked team in the country and owner of a 25-game winning streak.

Led by All-American Guy Rodgers, the Owls were considered to be a stronger team, but Kentucky had an answer for every Temple basket. The teams left halftime tied at 33, and the outcome was still up in the air in the second half when Rodgers tried to pull a fast one on his opponents. Perhaps looking for a breather, or perhaps hoping to mess with UK's psyche, Rodgers went down to the floor, claiming he had injured his back. Nobody on the Kentucky bench was buying the routine, and the crowd didn't like the act, either. But Rupp was not about to be outsmarted by some youngster, especially in front of his own fans.

"Coach Rupp wanted me to act like I had a bad ankle or a bad arm," Hatton recalled. "And I said, 'No, Coach, I won't do that,' and so he got Johnny Cox to act like he had a bad leg so we'd kind of equal out Guy Rodgers."

It was Rodgers who appeared to have the last laugh, however, as his four outside jumpers gave the Owls a 59–55 lead with less than three minutes to go. Temple coach Harry Litwack instructed his players to slow down and run out the clock, but Kentucky got a huge defensive stop to keep the season alive. UK's Adrian Smith knocked down a pair of free throws with 1:30 left to cut the lead to 59–57, and although Temple forward Dan Fleming hit a free throw with 55 seconds to go, the comeback was still alive. Smith converted two more free throws, this time with 29 seconds remaining, to close the gap to 60–59. Kentucky quickly fouled Rodgers, sending him to the line for a one-and-one.

Rodgers had torched the UK defense all night, but on the easiest shot of the day, his free throw bounced off the rim and into the hands of Kentucky forward Ed Beck, who tipped it over to Smith to secure the final possession. Rupp called a timeout with 23 seconds left, instructing Hatton to take the final shot. It was Hatton who had beaten Temple earlier in the year on a halfcourt shot at the buzzer, and Rupp hoped

this time would be no different. Using a screen from Beck, Hatton drove toward the baseline and tried to cut back toward the basket. The Temple defense anticipated the layup, however, so Hatton kept right on going, and when he emerged on the other side of the basket, he was open for a reverse layup that gave Kentucky a 61–60 lead, and after the Owls threw a pass out of bounds moments later, the crowd of nearly 19,000 went crazy.

The mission, however, was not yet complete, and when Seattle University grabbed a 29–18 lead in the championship game, it appeared that UK's title aspirations were in jeopardy. The Chieftains still led 44–38 in the second half when one of their players decided to stray from the game plan, giving Kentucky a huge break.

"They had this guard, Sweet Charley Brown, and he was a fancy ball dribbler and he wouldn't slow down," Hatton said. "They could have frozen the ball with an 11-point lead . . . but he wouldn't do it. So while maybe they don't blame it on Sweet Charley Brown, we thank God for him being fancy and wanting to shoot the ball."

The Wildcats fought back to take a 61–60 lead and never looked back as they ran away with an 84–72 victory. Hatton, the tournament's hero, was immediately tackled by a group of cheerleaders, who were trying to pelt him with kisses. Underneath the pile, however, Hatton heard a voice calling out, "Verny! Come out from under there!" It happened to be that of his newly wed wife, who was not exactly pleased with what she was seeing. Hatton, of course, didn't need any love from the cheerleaders; he already had the girl. Now he had the national championship to go along with it. Whether he spent that night on the couch or not, well, that was his own problem. ●

1959 California

West Virginia entered the 1959 tournament with some unfinished business to attend to. The Mountaineers had lost their tournament opener in 1958 after being ranked No. 1, and they were back to redeem themselves. The Mountaineers won their first game this time to set up a second-round encounter with St. Joseph's. It appeared their season would again end prematurely when the Mountaineers fell down by 18, but thanks to 34 points from Jerry West, they managed to come back for a 95–92 victory. The Mountaineer fans celebrated the win, which was also the third-highest scoring contest in tournament history, by storming the court and carrying West off the floor. West Virginia eventually advanced to the title game, and while they would lose one of the most exciting games in tournament history, it was a much better showing than the year before.

To put it mildly, the 1959 Cal Bears were not your average team. In fact, nothing about their team resembled a college squad. The team had more talent than most, but the Bears were unique for their sheer quirkiness. Perhaps they developed it from their coach, Pete Newell, who enjoyed a steady diet of 15 cups of coffee per day yet refused to let his players quench their thirst.

"He would never let us drink any water. In today's scientific world, I think you're absolutely nuts, but there was no drinking fountain," forward Bob Dalton said. "And they used to feed us steak and eggs before the game, too. Worst thing you could eat is a steak before a game."

Newell, on the other hand, was often unable to eat anything before a game, resulting in severe weight loss each season. Sophomore Bill McClintock also lost substantial weight during the winter, but for entirely different reasons.

"One thing I did was quit drinking beer from September to March that year. I lost that excessive 20 pounds that I had," McClintock laughed. "I went from 245 to about 220. And that was my playing weight at Cal."

The antics were hardly limited to off-the-court behavior. The players developed their own language of saying words backwards, almost like Pig Latin. And before long, they were using it during games, and using it effectively.

"Basically what it was, my name is Darrall and they call me Lared. Yug—that was a guy," junior Darrall Imhoff said. "When we're out there on the floor, 'cabrood the yug'—that means 'backdoor the guy.'"

Of course, opposing teams had no idea what was happening, allowing the Golden Bears to set up a play whenever they desired. The only problem was that even their own coach was oblivious to the new language. Even when Newell finally did match the plays to the unique words, he didn't realize how the naming system worked. It wasn't until his wife informed him that some of the defensive plays were named after parts of the female anatomy that he understood what he was calling out.

"The fans and Pete's wife picked up on it. Finally she said you'd better name that pressing something else," McClintock laughed. "In that day, this was 1958 or 1959, you didn't say anything in public."

The plays, more humorous than vulgar, were actually quite effective, leading the Bears all the way to the Final Four. But standing in their way of the title game was Cincinnati, led by first-team All-American and future NBA Hall of Famer Oscar Robertson. Dalton, the player assigned to guard Robertson, received some advice from a sportswriter traveling with the team.

"We were talking and he says, 'What are you going to do with him?' I said, 'I'm going to try and nullify him physically; hopefully we can make him start to think a little bit mentally about it,'" Dalton remembered. "And he says,

'Well, you know you ought to go out and say something to him that throws him off.'"

Taking the advice to heart, the senior walked up to Robertson before the game, stuck his hand out, and said, "Hi, my name's Dalton. What's yours?" Robertson, who had been on the cover of every magazine and newspaper that year, was flabbergasted. The only people who missed the encounter were Cal's band and cheerleaders, who showed up right before tip-off. After facing a four-hour plane delay in Chicago, they had decided to drive to the Final Four by bus.

"We did notice that because that's one thing you couldn't miss," Dalton recalled. "They made a big hit coming in at that late time."

What the band witnessed was history in the making, as Dalton played the defensive game of his life. Cincinnati assistant Ed Jucker had boasted before the game about how his team would pick apart the Golden Bears, but on this night Dalton held Robertson to just 5–16 shooting, giving Cal a shot at the national championship.

"You got to a level that it didn't matter whether the guy was four or five inches taller than you and weighed 100 pounds more," Dalton said. "We always had this inner deep belief that we were so much better prepared than anybody we were playing against that we never got the feeling that we were going to be intimidated by anybody."

That is not to say the Bears advanced without any casualties. Oski the Bear, the mascot who arrived with the Cal contingent, broke his collarbone during the game. But because of the shape of his costume, nobody took notice.

"Well, the way Oski walks around, it looks like he's got both collar bones broken all the time," Imhoff laughed. "He walks around all slumped over. I think Oski should have been a grizzly bear with great big claws. I think that's been Cal's problem."

With or without Oski, the Bears had to face West Virginia, and in one of the most shocking title games in NCAA history, the Bears pulled off the upset to win the national championship (see page 312). Perhaps *title* pronounced backwards is *elite*, which might just be the best way to describe the nation's new best team. ●

1960 Ohio State

While the teams at the 1960 Final Four had a combined record of 99–8, the best ever to that point, the Elite Eight was filled with some of the unlikeliest teams ever. Duke had achieved a very pedestrian 12–10 record during the regular season but found its way into the tournament on the strength of three wins in the ACC Tournament. The Blue Devils then upset both Princeton and St. Joe's to clinch their spot among the elite of college basketball. Oregon and Kansas were also unranked, but the Ducks upset 25–2 Utah while the Jayhawks rolled past Texas also to find their way into the Elite Eight. But all three teams would lose their next games, setting up one of the most anticipated Final Fours in years.

Larry Siegfried had scored more than 40 points nearly every time he stepped on the high school court, but he had never given college basketball a thought until he was recruited by Ohio State coach Fred Stahl. Thanks to some persuading from his coach, Siegfried decided to give college a try, a decision that looked to be disastrous as soon as he set foot on campus. Stahl unexpectedly resigned, and while Siegfried averaged nearly 20 points per game, the team struggled to just 11 wins under new coach Fred Taylor.

Fortunately, joining Siegfried just one year later would be perhaps the best recruiting class of all time. These players, who had traveled to watch Siegfried play when he was dominating the high school competition, would now be joining their idol to form an unstoppable lineup. The team featured five future pros in Siegfried, Joe Roberts, Mel Nowell, Jerry Lucas, and John Havlicek. In fact, Lucas and Havlicek would both go on to become NBA Hall of Famers. The only player in OSU's regular rotation who failed to turn pro was a guard named Bob Knight, who would quickly show he had a basketball IQ that made up for any lack in talent. But if this team was to be more successful than the previous year, it would need Siegfried to be a role player for the first time in his career.

"Tom Landry said, 'Good leadership is getting people to do what they don't want to do so they can become all they want to be,'" Siegfried recalled. "The only thing I cared about was my responsibilities as a player."

And the main responsibility for the remainder of Siegfried's career was to get the ball to Jerry Lucas, who shared little in common with most basketball players. When Lucas wasn't on the court earning one of his three All-American selections, or taking care of his pet alligator that he hid in his dorm room, he was using his photographic memory to record straight As in the classroom. But perhaps the most unusual thing about Lucas was his 20–10 vision, which he used to find an open player the moment he broke free.

"It just was like a series of matches made in heaven because it was great chemistry on that floor," Nowell said. "We were all exceptional. We could see a play develop even before it actually developed."

The results were pretty obvious, as the Buckeyes cruised to a 21–3 record and qualified for the NCAA Tournament for the first time in 10 years. They got a scare in the first round when Western Kentucky raced out to a 43–37 lead at halftime, but 36 points from Lucas paved the way for the 98–79 victory. After a pair of easy wins over Georgia Tech and NYU, the Buckeyes had a chance to win the first national championship in school history.

Winning that title, however, would not be so easy. Facing them would be 28–1 Cal, winner of 19 straight games and the defending national champion. In addition, the game was to be played in San Francisco's Cow Palace, just across the Bay from Cal's campus. As if Taylor didn't have enough to worry about, he was also unsure if he would be able to play Havlicek, who had cut his hand on—of all things—a paper towel dispenser.

But the one thing Ohio State had in its favor was Cal's game plan. During the previous offseason, Cal coach Pete Newell had decided to give the struggling Taylor a few pointers on the game. Newell, however, took it a step further, showing Taylor exactly how the Bears operated their offense and defense. The pupil wasted no time in the title game showing just what he had learned. OSU started converting layup after layup, and no matter how Newell tried to counter defensively, Taylor's squad always found a way to get another open look. The Buckeyes made 15 of their first 16 shots, and by the end of the first half, they were still shooting over 84 percent from the field.

"At halftime we had a substantial lead," Nowell said. "And our goal was simply to come back out in that second half and not lose any of that lead as best we could."

Meanwhile in the Cal locker room, Newell implored his team to grab more defensive rebounds, which drew some odd looks in the locker room.

"Coach," center Darrall Imhoff responded. "There have only been three, and I've gotten all of them!"

OSU had an answer for every tactic by Newell in the second half, and as the game drew to a close, Taylor took his starters out.

"Over on the sidelines, the rest of them had gotten in during the last few minutes. I was beginning to let myself feel the overwhelming feeling of happiness, sweet happiness," Nowell said. "It's the only time in my life that all that had happened up until then—and I had had a lot of individual success—did I actually feel what elation felt like."

When the buzzer sounded, Nowell ran on court to celebrate with his teammates, only to appear as if he had missed a high-five attempt—one of his few misses on the night. He probably would have been able to live that down had he not fallen on the court as a result.

"I don't know that I was trying so much to give a five as much as I was just so happy I wanted to jump around, and when I jumped around, I jumped down toward the ground," Nowell laughed. "I kicked back up and I actually kicked one of the guys that I admire and love most, Dave Barker."

Barker would turn out to be fine—national titles have a funny way of curing all ailments—but celebrating off the court would turn out to be a harder task. The team tried to go celebrate downtown, only to be turned away because most of them were still under 21.

"What do you mean we can't come in?" Siegfried asked. "We just won the national championship!"

That, of course, did not go over well with the bouncer, who retorted, "I don't give a s--- what you won—you're not coming in!"

Siegfried, however, would finally get his revenge when the team flew back to campus.

"I remember coming into Columbus and the pilot, when we came in, told us to look out the window, and there were about 75,000 at the airport," Siegfried said. "You should have seen it."

And based on his word, it sounds as though the entire city of Columbus had. ●

1961 Cincinnati

Before the Ohio State Buckeyes could worry about defending their national championship, they first needed to focus on winning the opening game in the 1961 tournament. The longer their game against Louisville went on, the more likely it appeared that the Buckeyes would be taking an early trip back home. John Havlicek put Ohio State in front 56–54 when he connected on a shot with six seconds left, but the game was still in doubt when UL's John Turner went to the line with just a second to go. He made the first shot to bring the Cardinals within one, and it was only when his second free throw rimmed out that the Buckeyes could breathe a sigh of relief. Seattle University wasn't so lucky, as the Redhawks lost their opener to Arizona State in the most exciting game of the tournament. ASU's Jerry Hahn not only hit a free throw to tie the game with 16 seconds left, but as time expired he hit the game-winning shot in one of the tournament's first true buzzer-beaters.

For a team that had just been to consecutive Final Fours, expectations for the 1961 Cincinnati Bearcats seemed shockingly low. Departing from the program was Oscar Robertson, one of the game's all-time greatest players, as well as his coach, George Smith. In his place would be Ed Jucker, a man with no head coaching experience, a trait that quickly showed when he overhauled the team's offensive game plan. Smith's up-and-down style had led the Bearcats to a 79–9 record over the previous three seasons, but Jucker insisted on slowing down the team's pace, a move that confused fans and players alike.

"First of all, I had no idea that someone played that slow—only people in wheelchairs or 65-and-older people play that game that way," laughed sophomore Tom Thacker. "We had never in my life played a basketball game that slow, that deliberate."

Jucker's offensive philosophy did little to sway his critics when the Bearcats lost three of their first eight games, more than they had lost the entire season in Smith's last year. Jucker hoped his team would just pull out 15 victories to salvage a winning record, but once he inserted Thacker as his starting point guard, the Bearcats reeled off 18 straight victories to land a spot in the NCAA Tournament. The team kept on going, cruising through the tournament to land a spot in the championship game, but most experts were convinced it would be their last victory of the year. The reason: Ohio State, a team that had won the national title in 1960 and hadn't lost since, stood in their way. Led by Jerry Lucas, the Buckeyes took a 27–0 record into the title game, and win number 28 appeared to be just a formality.

"Oh man, you read the papers, I mean we were some fluke," Thacker said. "That's all you heard was Ohio State, and the national news said Ohio State was going to run over little Cincinnati."

The Bearcats had long played the role of little brother to Ohio State. Not only had the Buckeyes refused to play their in-state rivals for the previous 39 years, but the state's governor, Michael DiSalle, had publicly stated he would be pulling for OSU.

"Ohio was all endorsing The Ohio State, Fred Taylor, and all of them," Thacker said. "And they practically gave the governor trophy to Ohio State already before the game started."

One of the UC fraternities responded by hanging up signs with the phrase "DiSalle and State are second rate," which only fueled the fire even more. OSU students snuck onto the Cincinnati campus and decided to do a little artwork of their own. They painted on the windows, stating just how they felt about the Bearcats, none of which was exactly flattering. Neither side could wait for the game to start, and on the day of the championship they would have to wait a little while longer, as the third-place consolation game played before them went into an agonizing four overtimes. The players were periodically peeking at the scoreboard in between their constant warming up and rewarming up, but finally, after hours of waiting, the game was finally underway.

As predicted, Lucas dominated the early going, scoring 18 of the team's 39 points in the first half. But the Bearcats were content to let Lucas get his points as long as they held the rest of the team in check, which is precisely what happened. They trailed by only one point at halftime and evened the game at 48 early in the second half. The Buckeyes regained the lead at 59–55, but Cincinnati surged to a 61–59 lead with just a minute to go. OSU forward Bob Knight made a layup to even the score, prompting Cincinnati to hold the ball for the last shot. Thacker's jumper would ultimately fall short, but given the talent disparity between the teams, the Bearcats felt they had all the momentum heading into the extra period.

"Hell, we were just happy to be that close to Ohio State in overtime," Thacker laughed. "When you jump on a bucking bull, you just want to hang on for your dear life, and as the seconds and minutes tick off, the longer you ride, the more confident you get."

That confidence would continue to grow, as the Bearcats built up a 65–62 lead midway through the overtime period. Lucas would hit a short jump shot to bring the Buckeyes within one, but UC forward Tony Yates would answer with a free throw to extend the lead to 66–64. Ohio State's Larry Siegfried had a chance to even the game when he was sent to the free throw line, but he went only 1-for-2 from the charity stripe, opening the door for Cincinnati to put the game away. The Buckeyes fouled Yates, who converted both shots, and when Thacker nailed a jump shot in the closing seconds, the championship was theirs. With the 70–65 victory, Cincinnati had knocked off what many fans had considered the greatest team of all time. It was a monumental victory, and the Bearcats reacted appropriately.

"Like a cow jumping over the moon, we jumped as high as we could. We later celebrated everything, and I think everything was just a daze. Imagine you ever get in the situation where you cannot believe you're so elated and joyful that you're just jumping and running, and you're shouting all at the same time," Thacker said. "After you play a long overtime game, a nerve-wracking game, you got enough energy to do all that?"

They would need to save some of that energy, because the rivalry between the two teams was just beginning. ●

Ed Jucker suffered a tumultuous start to his tenure as UC's head coach but found redemption by winning the national championship the same year. *University of Cincinnati Sports Communications*

1962 Cincinnati

Long before Billy Packer spent decades calling some of the tournament's most exciting games, he was playing in them. His Wake Forest team entered the 1962 tournament with only an 18–8 record, but managed to survive one classic after another en route to the only Final Four appearance in Deacons history. They were on the verge of dropping their first-round game when Yale's Dave Schumacher stepped to the free throw line with the game tied and only two seconds left on the clock, but the Deacons were given a second chance when Schumacher's free throw was off the mark. Wake Forest would survive that game 92–82, only to see their season come to an apparent end when they trailed 74–72 in the waning moments of their second-round game against St. Joseph's. But Packer nailed a 21-footer with four seconds left and then helped his team score 22 points in overtime to put the Hawks away 96–85. And just as the Demon Deacons were bested by Ohio State in the semifinals, the Buckeyes would fall short in one of the most hyped championship games in history.

If Cincinnati needed any motivation to defend its 1961 title, it would come a year before they even had the chance to do so. Even though the Bearcats had just defeated previously unbeaten Ohio State in the title game, fans were still not convinced the better team had won.

"It was a fluke. Ohio State should have never lost that game," point guard Tom Thacker read after the match. "They said we were lucky, so we were really mad at that and didn't need any speech to boost us up. All we needed was the fact that we wanted to beat them convincingly to show we were the best in Ohio."

Ohio State would do its part to ensure a rematch, cruising to a 26–1 record on the way to another title game appearance. For the Bearcats, getting to the championship game would not be so easy. They would win 27 of their first 29 matches, but in the semifinals they would run into a UCLA team that would soon embark on a run to 10 championships in 12 years. Cincinnati would get off to an 18–4 start five minutes into the game, having scored on every single possession. That changed when UCLA sophomore Gary Cunningham began hitting a barrage of long jumpers, and just before halftime the Bruins tied the game at 35. They continued their pace right through the second half, and as time began to wind down, they led 70–68.

"I guess we were overlooking UCLA, and we just had a flat tire," Thacker recalled. "I

couldn't hit a shot to save my soul. I shot the ball six times and it didn't even touch the rim."

Fortunately for the Bearcats, Paul Hogue picked up the slack, hitting the equalizer for Cincinnati. The score was still tied at 70 with 10 seconds left when coach Ed Jucker called a timeout, instructing his players to get the ball to Hogue, who had scored the last 14 points for the Bearcats. But when it came time to inbound the ball, Hogue was completely smothered by the defense, forcing Thacker to take the inbounds. Thacker drove to his right side, but the closest opening he could find was from 25 feet with just four seconds left. Considering Thacker was not known as a good outside shooter and had done nothing on this day to prove otherwise, it seemed as if the game was headed for overtime.

"I had to take the shot—the clock was ticking down. I know the coach said I'm the last person in the world they want taking the shot," Thacker laughed. "Well, I was young and dumb. I didn't ever think I was going to miss a shot—I just had too much confidence."

And when Thacker pulled up, he sank the game-winner to make everyone's dream rematch a reality. Having already faced the Buckeyes in the title game a year earlier, Jucker had no need to scout his opponent, but that didn't stop him from trying anyway. The only problem was that when Jucker showed up in

Columbus, the local police knew exactly what he was up to and were determined to stop it. When Jucker made an illegal turn on his way to campus, the police decided to arrest him, preventing their rival coach from getting a second look at the Buckeyes. The next time he would see his opponent would be on the night of the championship.

But even before the two would face each other, the Bearcats were hearing excuses about their upcoming game. Jerry Lucas, the Buckeyes' All-American forward, had hurt his left knee a few days earlier, rendering the upcoming match unfair in the eyes of OSU fans. Even if Jucker's club was to repeat, they chimed, it wouldn't be a fair contest. Ohio State's standout guard, John Havlicek, would now be the team's main offensive threat, and drawing that unfortunate task would be sophomore George Wilson.

"When they told me I got to guard John Havlicek, now you might want to get nervous, but I didn't. I realized, hey, I got to do the job, and these coaches back in those days, they literally prepared you to go out there and do your job," Wilson said. "I didn't have to score anything, but my job was wherever Havlicek went, that's where I went."

Wilson would hold his man to just 5-of-14 shooting, while teammate Paul Hogue would limit Lucas to just 5-of-17 from the floor, quickly putting the game out of reach. The Bearcats went on a 16–2 run to end the first half with a 37–29 lead, and by the second half that lead would expand to 18 points. Ohio State went to a full-court press, but to no avail as Cincinnati hung on for a 71–59 victory. As for the injury to Lucas, the final score seemed to indicate that OSU would have lost regardless of how healthy Lucas was.

"The way big Paul played him, it wouldn't have mattered if he was healthy or sick," Wilson said. "You know we had planned to take care of business."

And for all the people who had claimed that the first title was not legitimate, vindication felt awfully sweet.

"The coolest part in winning any championship—and especially that one—is when they call a timeout with about a minute or something to go and it's about 50 seconds, 40 seconds, 20 seconds, you're running down

It was the Cincinnati vs. Ohio State rematch that everybody looked forward to, but first, the Bearcats needed a miraculous finish against UCLA in the semifinals. *University of Cincinnati Sports Communications*

the floor and you look up at the clock. 15 seconds—you're up by 12 points and the clock hits zero, and hello, that's when you release all that pressure that you've been in all that year," Wilson recalled. "It felt like Christmas and New Year's and birthday and everything rolled into one." ●

1963 Loyola Chicago

Even if the title game hadn't produced one of the most thrilling finishes in history, the 1963 tournament would have been worth watching. St. Joseph's rallied from a 12-point deficit to overcome 40 points and 16-of-16 free throw shooting by Princeton's Bill Bradley. But the Hawks' 82–81 overtime victory was a mild affair compared with Colorado's victory over Oklahoma City in the second round. Colorado's Eric Lee was pushed as he went for a layup, and the benches cleared. Fans rushed the floor in the chaos, and Big Eight Player of the Year Ken Charlton was twice thrown to the floor. After the dust settled, the Buffaloes escaped with a 78–72 win. Also worth noting is that UCLA lost its opener and subsequent third-place game in the West Regional, giving John Wooden a 3–9 record in tournament play. It wouldn't stay like that for very long.

In March 1963, America still suffered from the racism that had plagued the country for decades. Months away from Martin Luther King's "I Have a Dream" speech and over a year away from the Civil Rights Act, the nation was looking for a sign that equality was on the way. The answer came, of all places, from a basketball team.

At a time when it was considered taboo to have more than two African American players on a team, Loyola Chicago coach George Ireland had the audacity not only to include four black players on the roster but to start each of them. The move paid off as the team cruised to a 24–2 regular-season record and led the nation in scoring.

Although the players knew they were representing something larger than their school, race was never an issue for them.

"It was a bunch of guys that came together to play," said John Egan, the team's lone white starter. "It didn't have to do with whether they were black or white."

The same could not be said, however, for the rest of the country. As the Ramblers started to gain more notoriety, they began receiving letters from the KKK—so many that eventually all hate mail was forwarded directly to coach Ireland. And when Loyola was paired with Mississippi State in the second round of the tournament, many fans feared the game would not even take place. The Bulldogs had decided to end a pair of 24–1 seasons in 1959 and 1962 because of an unwritten rule at the university that prevented them from playing any team with African Americans, thus keeping them out of the NCAA Tournament. Now facing the prospect of their team playing a school with *four* black players, Mississippi Governor Ross Barnett and Senator Billy Mitts tried to create an official injunction preventing the team from playing in the game.

When word got to MSU coach Babe McCarthy and Athletic Director Wade Walker, they decided to drive across the state line to Tennessee, where they would be out of Mississippi jurisdiction. The next morning, the reserves on the basketball team drove to a private airport near campus to see if any authorities were awaiting the team. With the police chief assigned to serve the injunction on coffee break, the starters quickly joined their teammates and left town before any trouble ensued.

Once the team, now in one piece, made it to East Lansing, Michigan, for the game, they could put the chaos in Mississippi behind them. But before the tip-off, MSU captain Joe Dan Gold did what many in his home state would consider unthinkable—he walked over to Loyola captain Jerry Harkness and shook his hand.

"That game as of now in my mind was more important to me than winning the NCAA title because it changed America," Harkness said. "That's when I said to myself this is really more than a game."

Once the actual game started, the Ramblers found themselves in trouble. Loyola was held scoreless for nearly the first six minutes of the game, and the Ramblers found themselves in a 7–0 hole. However, it wasn't long before Harkness made a pair of three-point plays, and in a matter of minutes, the score was tied at 12. Loyola eventually worked to a 15-point lead before settling for a 61–51 victory. After the game, Gold and his teammates congratulated Loyola and patted them on the back.

"It was a learning experience," Harkness said. "We found out that not all Mississippians were that bad."

The Ramblers then waltzed over Illinois and Duke to set up a matchup with the University of Cincinnati for the national championship. The Bearcats, who had lost just one game in the regular season, had won the previous two championships and were trying to become the first team in history to win three consecutive titles. Three years earlier, while UC was in the midst of five consecutive runs to the Final Four, Ireland was hung in effigy by his own supporters for leading Loyola to a losing season. With history on Cincinnati's side, the Bearcats were a large favorite heading into the game.

"They were a very good team. They deserved to be No. 1 all year," Loyola junior Ron Miller said. "They had the big reputation, and we were the new kids on the block."

Nobody was newer than Harkness, who had never even played basketball until his senior year in high school. It wasn't until a stranger saw him shooting at a local gym that Harkness decided to try out for the team. Convinced by the new acquaintance that he could get a scholarship if he continued to improve, Harkness decided to commit himself to basketball.

His change of heart paid big dividends for Loyola, as Harkness helped lead one of the greatest comebacks in the history of the NCAA Tournament (see page 356). Down by 15 points with about 10 minutes left, Loyola staged a miraculous comeback to win in overtime. In the process, the Ramblers laid to rest a stereotype that African Americans were not mentally strong enough to be successful at sports. Conventional wisdom held that despite having an abundance of talent, blacks would crack under pressure. Ironically, all the abuse that the Loyola players had taken during the regular season actually helped them in the title game.

"Mentally, we had gone through so much in the South, we had kept our composure," Harkness said. "We had gone through all that and gotten through it, so we were mentally tough."

As if the team needed any more validation of its mental strength, all five starters from the team ended up with degrees. Vic Rouse, who was the hero of the game, ended up getting his degree in something quite fitting—social relations. His game-winning shot not only gave pride to Loyola Chicago, it also helped pave the way for the 1966 Texas Western team, which won a national championship with an all-black starting lineup.

For Harkness, who had grown up on welfare and was often forced to skip meals as a child, the victory was extra meaningful. And the gentleman who first spotted Harkness and encouraged him to give basketball a shot?

Jackie Robinson. ●

Loyola Chicago's four black starters, along with the rest of their teammates, show off their national championship trophy following their historic run to the title. *Loyola University Chicago Athletics*

1964 UCLA

If you were a college basketball team, 1964 was a good year to make the tournament. Of the eight teams that advanced to the regional finals, an incredible six of them enjoyed their best season in school history to that point. Most notable among them were unranked Ohio and Connecticut. The Bobcats snuck past Louisville 71–69 in the opening round and then blew by All-American Cotton Nash's fourth-ranked Kentucky team, 85–69. Despite a paltry 14–10 record, UConn made the tournament by winning the little-known six-team Yankee Conference. The Huskies had been just 1–9 in the tournament in their school's history, but they defeated Temple 53–48 in the first round and then beat Princeton 52–50 on Dom Perno's free throws with 32 seconds left. His steal moments later sealed the Huskies' first trip to the Elite Eight.

Long before John Wooden made national championships look routine, he was a 53-year-old coach without a title to his name. For 15 years, Wooden had been coaching UCLA, but all he had to show for it was a 3–9 NCAA Tournament record and an unfulfilled dream. By 1964, Wooden had assembled a team that he thought could deliver UCLA its first championship. Sophomore Doug McIntosh would be joining a team that was returning three budding stars in Keith Erickson, Walt Hazzard, and Gail Goodrich. The team had no championships to speak of, but the championship atmosphere was already in place for the dynasty that was to come. Some players, however, caught on later than others.

"I didn't think of us as a championship-caliber team going into the season. Maybe I should have," laughed McIntosh. "Goodrich told me categorically that he knew going into the season that we were going to win it all. He knew that without a question in his mind."

That confidence would be necessary to bring home the title, but not even Goodrich could have expected just what his team would accomplish that season. The Bruins not only rolled through the schedule undefeated, but they ran nearly every opponent into the ground. Few teams even dared to keep the games competitive, but UCLA finally found a worthy challenger in its tournament opener against the University of Seattle. The Bruins had stormed out to a 48–39 lead, but as the game wore on the Chieftains brought their game to another level. They took their first lead

of the game at 75–73 with 7:53 remaining, and at the five-minute mark they still only trailed 81–80.

Goodrich responded by firing a pass to freshman Kenny Washington, who promptly laid the ball in despite being fouled. Washington's free throw put the Bruins up four, and when Goodrich made a layup of his own moments later, the Bruins were back up 86–80. Seattle cut the lead to 95–90, but UCLA looked to Hazzard to finish off the game. The guard weaved his way through the defense, avoiding each foul attempt, as the Bruins ran off the clock to survive. It wasn't the most impressive of their wins, but they were moving on.

If the Seattle game was supposed to be a wake-up call, the Bruins had apparently slept through their alarm. In their next game against the University of San Francisco, the Bruins failed to make a basket for the first six minutes as they handed the Dons a 20–7 head start. By the end of the half, UCLA had shot just 31 percent from the floor and still trailed 36–28. Even Goodrich wasn't immune to the horrific shooting, making just one field goal as Wooden sent him to the bench in the closing minutes. Luckily for the Bruins, Goodrich was never one to lose his confidence, and when he sank a jump shot early in the second half, his team had grabbed its first lead at 45–44. His rebound in the closing seconds helped preserve a 96–90 win, but people started having their doubts on how good this 28–0 team really was.

"It seems like no matter who we played, people expected us to lose," McIntosh said. "It was really just routine. I mean, we had been underdogs in just about every game we played."

If the Bruins were hoping to convince their critics, they had an interesting way of showing it during their Final Four bout against Kansas State. The Wildcats took a 69–63 lead midway through the second half and still led 75–70 with 7:20 to go, but some unexpected help turned the tide back to UCLA.

"I got up in the morning after getting some sleep that night and pick up the Kansas City paper and found out we had won the game because the cheerleaders had arrived late," McIntosh recalled. "Their plane had been delayed and they weren't there at the start of the game, and suddenly late in the second half they arrived and cheered us on to victory. And I had to confess, I didn't know they were missing. So the writers were having a field day with that being the cause of the victory."

Now with the cheerleaders—as well as the press—on their side, the Bruins scored the next 11 points as they cruised to a 90–84 victory. The only team that stood in the way of a 30–0 record was Duke. The Blue Devils had posted 26–4 record, and they showed up ready to play. After Duke took a 30–27 lead, Wooden knew it was time to make a change—senior Fred Slaughter was pulled from the game.

"He was a good leaper, but he had this tendency to stand out at the top of the free throw circle and shoot fall-away jump shots, and you know Coach was all over him about that," McIntosh said. "And they came down the floor early in the ball game against Duke and threw the ball in the middle, and Fred turned and took a fall-away jump shot, and I think his feet hadn't touched the floor before Coach was yelling my name."

McIntosh was the sixth man of the team, but he played the game of his life, helping the Bruins go on a 16–0 run in the closing minutes of the half to go up 43–30. Wooden, who had started the same five players at the beginning of every half that season, went with his gut instinct—McIntosh was staying in the game. It was a smart move, as the role player guided the Bruins to a 98–83 victory and the national championship. Needless to say, McIntosh was still hyped up well after the game.

"Kenny and I were rooming together in the hotel in Kansas City, and we went upstairs and got in bed, turned the lights out, were in bed for about an hour, and at about one o'clock in the morning I said, 'Wash, are you awake?' And he said yeah, so I said, 'Let's go back downstairs,'" McIntosh remembered. "We got completely dressed, went downstairs, and the whole team is down there at one in the morning. None of us could sleep."

Wooden, on the other hand, slept just fine. Perhaps he knew his time atop the NCAA Tournament was only just beginning. ●

1965 UCLA

To say that Bill Bradley was a success story might be the understatement of the century. Bradley, who turned down 75 scholarship offers to play for scholarship-less Princeton, went on to study at Oxford and joined the Air Force before beginning his Hall of Fame NBA career. In 1965, he dominated the NCAA Tournament as few others ever have. His Princeton team was unranked going into the tournament, but the two-time All-American had higher expectations that most. He scored 13 of his team's last 18 points to help Princeton sneak by Penn State 60–58, and he followed that performance with a 27-point effort against N.C. State in a 66–48 victory. Bradley scored 41 more over 22–1 Providence to send the Tigers to the Final Four, and although they would lose to Michigan, Bradley wasn't done. In the final game of his career, the national third-place game, Bradley made 22 of his 29 shots and 14 of his 15 free throws for an incredible 58 points, a new tournament record.

It didn't take fans very long to realize that the 1965 UCLA Bruins shared little in common with their predecessors. Gone were Walt Hazzard and Fred Slaughter, two starters from the year before, and their departures were quite evident as the season began. The Bruins, who finished the previous campaign 30–0, dropped their season opener to the University of Illinois 110–83. "Illinois beat our heads on the ground," junior Doug McIntosh said. "I mean, they just crushed us."

The undefeated season was no longer a possibility, but the goal was still the same—UCLA fully intended to bring home another national championship. With every passing game, that goal appeared more and more attainable. The Bruins won 24 of their next 25 games to win the Pac-8 Conference and earn a spot in the NCAA Tournament. The NCAA, however, did the Bruins no favors by sending them to Provo to face BYU. The Cougars hadn't lost a home game in over a year, but thanks in large part to 40 points from UCLA senior Gail Goodrich, the crowd never became a factor. BYU trailed 51–40 at the break, and Goodrich scored 16 of UCLA's next 18 points as they prevailed 100–76.

UCLA scored a pair of easy wins over San Francisco and Wichita State to advance to the championship game against Michigan, but for the first time all season the experts were hesitant to side with the Bruins. Michigan had three losses as opposed to UCLA's two, but the Wolverines played in the more competitive Big Ten, and one of UM's defeats had come without their star, Cazzie Russell. Had Russell not been sidelined with a fever during their loss to Ohio State, his team would have likely finished their conference schedule undefeated.

"The thing that I was concerned about was I knew Michigan was a really good team, but I knew also that we could play with them and that we were underdogs again," said McIntosh, whose UCLA team had defeated Duke in the title the game the year before. "We were the No. 2 team in the nation, they were the No. 1, so we were supposed to lose. And just the fact that we were supposed to lose to them was, I think, all the motivation I needed to go out and play well."

The only problem for UCLA was that senior Keith Erickson had pulled a muscle in his leg the night before, and the Wolverines were not the least bit sympathetic. Michigan raced out to a 20–13 lead before UCLA coach John Wooden called a timeout and subbed in junior Kenny Washington for the injured Erickson. He would not become the last casualty of Wooden's substitutions, however, as McIntosh was taken out for sophomore Mike Lynn. Ironically, it was McIntosh who had come off the bench to save the 1964 championship game. Now, one year later, Wooden was asking him to return the favor by allowing Lynn to receive the bulk of the playing time.

"Mike Lynn was having the game of his life, and so when I came out Coach said, 'Sit here—I'm going to put you in for Keith in a few minutes,' but he never did," said McIntosh, who spent much of the game sitting by Erickson on the sidelines. "I wasn't going to argue with that as long as we had a lead."

And due in no small part to Lynn, the Bruins would do just that, outscoring Michigan by 20 points over the rest of the first half to take a 47–34 lead into the break. UCLA had unleashed its vaunted full-court press, and the Wolverines were completely unable to cope with the attack.

"Michigan was totally exhausted by the middle of the first half," McIntosh said. "And that was nothing unusual. We played a tremendous pace, and not many teams could play at that pace."

Lynn had put in a solid performance, but the real hero of the game was Goodrich, who scored 42 points to set an NCAA championship game record. The Bruins would need nearly all of them, too, as they hung on for a 91–80 victory.

"Gail is arguably the greatest competitor that I have ever been around," McIntosh said. "I didn't really realize that he was on a record pace or anything like that, but Gail was the sort of guy where the bigger the stakes, the better he played."

The real moment of truth would come when the team got back to the locker room. When Fred Slaughter had been taken out for McIntosh the year before, he approached Wooden after the game to share his agreement about the substitution. Wooden called it one of the greatest moments of his career, and he hoped McIntosh would do the same. He wouldn't have to wait very long, as the junior walked up to his mentor and expressed the same feelings. It wasn't hard for McIntosh to feel happy—after all, he had just won a second straight national championship—but Wooden wouldn't forget the conversation any time soon. After Wooden retired, having coached hundreds of players and 10 championship teams, he said he was never more proud of a player than McIntosh.

"The thought of having that sort of commendation is certainly a pleasant thing. If you can't have talent, I guess it's nice to have potential," McIntosh laughed. "It was very satisfying. You know, Coach's good opinion of me was very important."

Wooden, never one to focus solely on wins and losses, had just reached the pinnacle of his career—he had created a team full of selfless players who shared his mentality. And to Wooden, that was greater than a championship could ever be. ●

1966 Texas Western

The NCAA Tournament did not include UCLA in 1966—the last year before a stretch of 15 consecutive appearances for the Bruins—but there was no shortage of memorable moments. In the regional semifinals, Western Kentucky fell victim to perhaps the worst officiating in tournament history. The Hilltoppers led Michigan 79–78 with just seconds on the clock when the officials called a jump ball, sending WKU's Greg Smith to take the toss against Michigan forward Cazzie Russell. But when the referee's wayward throw headed toward Russell, Smith tried to lean in to get a piece of the ball. His foul sent Russell to the line, where he knocked down both shots to give Michigan the improbable 80–79 victory.

Don Haskins was by no means a saint. Included among his most beloved hobbies as a young man were drinking, skipping school, and gambling. But one thing Haskins always had was a sense of right and wrong, something that far too many people chose to ignore during the Jim Crow era. All across the South, blacks and whites grew up in separate schools, drank from separate water fountains, and were forbidden to marry each other by law. The basketball court was a slightly more tolerant place, at least at Texas Western College, but even school president Joseph Ray had his limits. When Haskins arrived in 1961 to coach the Miners, he was told that no more than three African Americans could be on the team—an order that Haskins completely ignored. Not only was his starting lineup in 1966 all black, but his seven-man rotation was comprised entirely of African Americans.

"I started my five best players," Haskins recalled. "That they were all black and it was the first time five black players had started in an NCAA championship game meant nothing to me."

That fact, however, was not lost on Kentucky coach Adolph Rupp, whose Wildcats would be facing Texas Western in the finals. Rupp, who hadn't hesitated to use the N word on multiple occasions, had never had a black player on any of his 36 Kentucky squads. The 64-year-old Rupp had claimed that he had tried to recruit African Americans to Lexington, but after nearly four decades without integrating, people started to question the sincerity of those attempts. According to author Alexander

Wolff, Rupp had actually asked Jimmy Breslin, a young sportswriter out of New York, to "kindly indicate 'colored' high school players with asterisks so Rupp would know where not to bother to send his recruiters."

Unfortunately, Rupp was less of an exception than an example of the norm. The stereotypes surrounding African Americans were abound. They were considered unintelligent, undisciplined, and, to many in Rupp's profession, uncoachable. In a comment that would be deemed completely unacceptable today, former West Virginia star Rod Hundley made the joke of the tournament when he gave his analysis of the Miners. "They can do everything with the basketball," he observed, "but autograph it."

In reality, however, the Miners played a structured style of basketball, giving up only 62 points a game en route to their 27–1 record. But Rupp, whose team was also 27–1, had won each of his other four championship games and was a heavy favorite to win his fifth. Perhaps the most vocal prognosticator was Rupp himself, who declared that no team of five blacks would ever defeat his Wildcats.

Haskins, rather than being offended, took full advantage of the situation by sharing the information with his players before the game.

"I heard him say it, and I couldn't believe he said it. It's up to you to do something about it," said Haskins, who before concluding his speech grabbed the arm of David Lattin, his powerful center. "The first chance you get, flush it," he said. "Flush it as hard as you can."

Haskins wanted to send a powerful message: The Miners were not going to be intimidated by anybody, especially an old man sitting on the Kentucky bench.

"From that point on," senior Harry Flournoy said, "Kentucky had as much chance of winning that game as a snowball had of surviving in hell."

After Pat Riley sank a free throw to give Kentucky a 1–0 lead, Lattin prepared to follow his coach's orders. Catching the ball underneath the basket, the 6-foot-6, 240-pound center rose up and slammed the ball right over Riley, who also committed a foul on the play. Lattin converted the free throw, giving the Miners a 3–1 lead and a huge psychological advantage.

Texas Western still led 10–9 when Bobby Joe Hill sent a message of his own. As UK senior Tommy Kron brought the ball up the floor, he was met by Miners guard Orsten Artis. Kron turned to his left to escape the reach of Artis but was met by Hill, who stripped the ball and raced down for a layup. The Wildcats had Louie Dampier bring the ball up the floor on the ensuing possession, but it made little difference as once again Hill stole the ball and laid it in to give Texas Western a 14–9 lead. When Lattin delivered another thunderous dunk to make it 16–11, Rupp had just about seen enough. Getting up out of his seat, Rupp called a time-out and lashed into his players. The mood on the other side of the court was quite different.

"You probably couldn't see it," Artis said with a grin, "but after we'd score a basket we made a habit of deliberately going down the Kentucky sideline. We'd wave, point, and smile at Rupp."

By halftime the Miners still led 34–31, leading Rupp to spew a level of hatred that few of his players had ever seen before. They would never be able to show their faces in Lexington ever again, he warned his players, if this team of five blacks beat them. "You've got to beat those coons!" Rupp screamed, embarrassing the group of young men who couldn't care less what players were wearing the opposing jersey. For the players wearing the Kentucky uniform that day, their only thoughts were on winning a basketball game. And as the second half began, that's exactly what they set out to do.

Twice the Wildcats would get to within a point, closing within 37–36 at the start of the second half, and once again at 46–45 with 12 minutes to go. The Miners, however, would not be denied. Artis buried a jumper and added a free throw to bring the lead back up to 49–45, and after Willie Worsley hit three free throws, Texas Western led by a comfortable seven points.

Riley and Dampier helped narrow the gap to 54–51, but the supposed "undisciplined" Miners would make 28 of their 34 foul shots, including one stretch in which they made 26 of 27, to seal the victory. The final box score would show that Texas Western had held Rupp's team to just 27-of-70 from the field, and as it turned out, UK's 1–0 lead would be their only of the game. Rupp, who had admonished Haskins earlier by asking "What does TWC stand for . . . two white coaches?" would now have to accept a new meaning for the acronym: The World Champions. ●

Of all the games Willie Cager and his teammates would play in, none would ever mean more than their 1966 championship against Kentucky. Cager's eight points, two of which came on this layup, helped the Miners come away with the historic 72–65 victory. *UTEP Athletics*

1967 UCLA

If 1967 wasn't the best tournament fans had ever seen, it was certainly in the running. Dayton became just the second team in history to make the championship game as an unranked team. Along the way, they survived one incredible finish after another. The Flyers won their opener against Western Kentucky 69–67 when Bobby Joe Hooper sank a shot with just a second to play and then survived a 53–52 squeaker against Tennessee in the Sweet 16. In the next round, Dayton met Virginia Tech—also unranked—and stormed back from a late 10-point deficit before finally emerging with a 71–66 overtime victory. Dayton then upset fourth-ranked North Carolina 76–62 thanks to 13 consecutive field goals from Don May. Southern Methodist, another unranked team, advanced to the Elite Eight by upsetting second-ranked Louisville with an incredible comeback win. The Cardinals led 77–69 in the closing minutes only to see the Mustangs catch up and take the lead on a Denny Holman layup with four seconds left.

With each passing day in Lew Alcindor's high school career, the pile of letters from college coaches seemed to grow even higher. He had always been tall as a child, but Alcindor just continued to grow, as did his basketball skills. By the time he had reached his final growth spurt, the 7-foot Alcindor had led his high school to 72 consecutive victories and three New York City Catholic championships. Fans and coaches alike flocked to Alcindor, hoping to lure him to one destination or another, but the man who ended up getting him made almost no effort to do so.

John Wooden, who had played back in the 1920s and 30s, seemed to be clinging to ideals that no longer existed. Never one to get sucked into the dirty world of recruiting, Wooden refused to pander to high school players. If a youngster wanted to attend UCLA, he would have to make the first contact. And luckily for Wooden, that is exactly what Alcindor did.

It didn't take fans very long to see just how dominant Alcindor would become. In the days before freshmen were eligible to play varsity basketball, the first glimpse of the young center would come in the junior varsity's preseason scrimmage against the varsity at Pauley Pavilion. The varsity team had won the last two national championships, but thanks to 31 points from Alcindor the JV squad easily won, 75–60. The Bruins were the No. 1 team in the country, fans started to say, but they were No. 2 on their own campus.

"At that point, it dawned on me what I was getting into," said Lynn Shackelford, Alcindor's teammate on the junior varsity squad. "This is going to be something unusual in the history of basketball, and I was going to be a part of it."

A year later Shackelford and Alcindor, along with two of their freshman teammates, would move up to the varsity to comprise one of the youngest teams in the nation. The starting lineup would include four sophomores and one junior, but expectations were still high. Fortunately, Alcindor was up to the challenge, and in his real debut the sophomore amazed the crowd with 56 points as the Bruins defeated crosstown rival USC 105–90. The rest of the season would be a similar story, as UCLA was rarely challenged during its 26–0 regular season. The Bruins didn't miss a beat once the tournament started, defeating Wyoming by 49 points in the first round to set up an Elite Eight matchup with Pacific. The Tigers put up a tougher challenge, trailing just 63–56 with 7:30 to go, but UCLA pulled away for an 80–64 victory, once again clinching a spot in the Final Four.

Awaiting the Bruins in the semifinals would be Houston, which featured All-American forward Elvin Hayes. Many fans perceived Hayes to be the only player who could challenge Alcindor, but Houston coach Guy Lewis went a step further, saying Hayes was the greatest player he had ever seen. But the most confident person in Hayes' abilities, it turned out, was Hayes himself.

"This will be a game," Hayes warned, "the UCLA players will remember for the rest of their lives."

As it turned out, Hayes was right, though they weren't the kind of memories he wanted UCLA to create. After the game, Hayes took time to remind people how much he had outplayed Alcindor, outrebounding him 24–20 and outscoring him 25–19. What he neglected, however, was that it took him 31 shots to do so, while Alcindor shot 55 percent from the field in UCLA's 73–58 win. That victory set up a title match with Dayton's Flyers, who at 25–6 had as good a chance to upset the Bruins as any other team. But any visions of an upset were short-lived, as the Bruins held their opponent without a basket for the first 5:44, and midway through the half their lead stood at 20–4. Thanks to four blocks by Alcindor, the Flyers would shoot just 23.8 percent in the first half, allowing UCLA to cruise to a 79–64 victory.

Just three days after the title game, the NCAA enacted the "no dunk" rule, specifically designed to prevent Alcindor from taking over the game. But as the NCAA would quickly discover, nothing—not even a rule—could hold him back. The greatest career in college basketball history was only just beginning. ●

1968 UCLA

Ohio State has never been much of an underdog, but there was no question the Buckeyes were the Cinderella of the 1968 tournament. After finishing the regular season unranked with a 19–7 record, OSU beat East Tennessee State 79–72 before taking on Kentucky, a seemingly sure bet for an Elite Eight victory. UK had made "California here we come" buttons in preparation for the team's trip to Los Angeles for the Final Four, but thanks to David Sorenson's short jumper with three seconds left, it was the Buckeyes who were California bound. That was certainly the game of the tourney, but Davidson's second-round game against Columbia wasn't far behind. With the game tied at 55 and just two seconds to go, Columbia's Bruce Metz had a chance to win the game at the free throw line. Davidson coach Lefty Driesell called a pair of timeouts to get inside his head, and Metz responded by missing the front end of the one-and-one, allowing the Wildcats to come away with a 61–59 victory in overtime.

In January 1968, Houston and UCLA met in a rematch of the previous year's Final Four, and both teams appeared to be just as strong early in the new season. Played in Houston's Astrodome, the game was the biggest spectacle college basketball had ever seen. Nearly 53,000 people crammed into the dome to witness the battle of unbeaten teams, and they would not leave disappointed.

Elvin Hayes, Houston's All-American forward, scored 29 points as the Cougars took a 46–43 lead into the break. Hayes would tack on another 10 points in the second half, but none were bigger than his two free throws with 28 seconds remaining, which put his team up 71–69. The Bruins came back looking for the equalizer, but when they tossed the ball out of bounds in the game's final seconds, the Cougars had pulled off an upset for the ages. Gone was UCLA's 47-game winning streak, and Hayes was instantly thrust ahead of UCLA's Lew Alcindor as the nation's premier player. *Sports Illustrated* placed Hayes on its cover the following week, a gesture that didn't sit well with Alcindor, who would later change his name to Kareem Abdul-Jabbar.

"I remember Kareem putting that picture inside his locker," UCLA forward Mike Warren recalled. "So that every day when he opened up his locker, he saw that picture."

Few people seemed to care that Alcindor had been severely limited by an eye injury that he had sustained a week earlier against Cal. The junior played the Houston game with a patch over his left eye, and the effects were obvious as he scored just 15 points against the Cougars. Alcindor made no excuses for his performance, repeating "never again" to himself as he pondered his first loss in a Bruins uniform. UCLA coach John Wooden hardly shared the same sentiment after the loss, stepping into the locker room with a big smile across his face. He knew the loss would serve as motivation, and that come March he was going to see the best that his team had to offer. As fate would have it, both teams ran the table the rest of the year to set up the much anticipated matchup between the 27–1 Bruins and 31–0 Cougars.

Hayes felt compelled to remind people just how great his Houston team was, claiming that the Bruins once again would be unable to keep up with the Cougars. In hindsight, it turned out to be a terrible idea.

"Well, he really didn't know what he was talking about. He claimed that my eye injury didn't affect my ability to play, and he had no way of knowing that," Alcindor said. "They won the game. There was no need to go shooting your mouth off about things that you really didn't know what you were talking about, but that was his decision and I guess he felt he had to say what he had to say."

UCLA assistant coach Jerry Norman devised a scheme to shut down Hayes in their rematter, but he would have to wait to see just how effective his idea would be. His plan was to play a "diamond-and-one" defense, with four guys playing a zone defense and one player stuck on Hayes wherever he went. When he approached Wooden with the strategy, the head coach suggested they try the defense in their regular-season finale for practice. Norman nixed that idea, pointing out that Houston would be scouting UCLA for any sort of advantage. So in the biggest game of the season, the Bruins were about to unveil a defense they had never played before. It was a big risk, but one Norman felt worth taking.

Unlike last time, the Bruins would now be playing in their own backyard at the Los Angeles Sports Arena. More than 15,000 people, the largest college basketball crowd the city had ever seen, were on hand to witness the greatest performance in UCLA history. Norman's zone defense completely shut down Hayes, preventing him from even taking a shot until the seven-minute mark. When Hayes finally made a shot 11 minutes into the game to cut the lead to 20–19, UCLA put on the burners, outscoring Houston 21–5 over the next five minutes. The Bruins pushed the lead to 22 at halftime and didn't stop there. The lead reached 44 points before Wooden took out his starters, who watched as the Bruins capped off the 101–69 win.

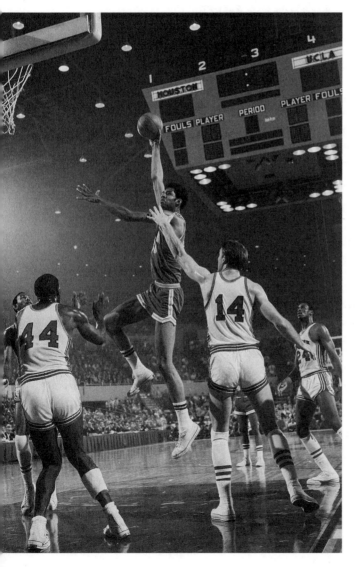

"Oh, it was very sweet revenge. That game in Houston kind of wore on my mind because I felt that we were a better team," Alcindor said. "You know, we weren't able to do anything about it till we met them again."

The mission was accomplished, but still remaining was a game against North Carolina, Final Four participants just a year earlier. The Tar Heels had scored 80 points in 15 of their previous 16 games, but on this night the UCLA defense stepped up once again, holding them to just 55 points. Alcindor chipped in 34 points on the offensive end as the Bruins safely cruised to the national championship.

"Alcindor is the greatest player who ever played the game," said UNC coach Dean Smith, who was just as impressed with his teammates. "They are by far the greatest basketball team I've ever seen."

More than four decades later, few can argue with Smith's sentiment. ●

Thanks to 19 points from Lew Alcindor, the Bruins had little trouble avenging their regular season loss to Houston, where the Cougars won "The Game of the Century," 71–69. *Sports Illustrated/Getty Images*

1969 UCLA

While they wouldn't win the tournament, North Carolina made the Final Four in 1969 for the third consecutive year. Getting there, however, wasn't so easy. The Tar Heels led Duquesne 67–53 with just four minutes to go, but they let the Dukes get to within a point before Lee Dedmon caught a full-court pass and scored with 30 seconds left to seal the victory. Their next game against Davidson was tied at 85 in the final moments when coach Dean Smith called a timeout. Smith instructed Charles Scott to drive to the lane and draw a crowd of defenders before passing to a teammate, but with three seconds left Scott took the shot himself. It turned out to be the right decision, as his jump shot sailed through for the 87–85 victory. Purdue would defeat UNC in the Final Four and also needed a buzzer-beater to get there. Rick Mount, who had become the first high school athlete to grace the cover of *Sports Illustrated* three years earlier, sank a 20-foot shot as time expired to defeat Marquette in the Mideast Regional final. Mount would score over 2,300 points in his three-year career, but he would call that shot the biggest of his life.

John Wooden entered the 1969 tournament hoping for history to repeat itself. His Bruins had won four of the previous five national championships, and with superstar Lew Alcindor back for another year, Wooden wanted more of the same. What he encountered was the most turbulent year his school—and his country—had ever seen.

Riots, protests, and unrest were commonplace across the country, and UCLA was no exception. The movement was gaining ground on campus until a January gunfight involving the Black Panthers and a rival group shut down the school for a semester.

"Unbelievable. Crazy time. If you think we got crazy times economically now, you got to realize when I arrived on campus just a few months before Martin Luther King was shot, civil unrest was unbelievable in regard to racial issues," guard John Vallely said. "People were as upset as they could be about this long-running war in Vietnam, and so everybody was upset about civil rights, everybody was upset about the war in Vietnam. And then you had all these hippies that were stoned at the time. College campuses were full of drugs—it was a crazy time and, most of the players will tell you, the UCLA Pauley Pavilion practice place was a refuge from the street. You got away from all that stuff."

The school may not have been functioning at the time, but Wooden still had a basketball team to run, and despite all the outside distractions, for Wooden it was business as usual. As he had in every year of his career, Wooden began the season not with an intense practice but with a lecture on proper foot apparel.

"As a junior college transfer going into UCLA, I will never forget the first time I sat in that room and coach Wooden told me how to put on a pair of socks. He wanted to make sure we knew how to do that properly. It was teaching us the basic fundamentals and I'll never forget Kareem," Vallely recalled of Alcindor. "He said, 'Come on, Coach, not the socks story again.' It was Kareem's fourth time to learn how to put on his socks properly. It was my first time. So I looked at this old guy and I thought he was nuts. I thought he's lost his marbles. I'm sitting there with Lew Alcindor, Sidney Wicks, Curtis Rowe, Lynn Shackleford, Ken Heitz—all the biggest players in college basketball at the time, and this guy's telling us how to put on a pair of socks."

With Wooden at the helm, UCLA maintained the level of play that fans had been accustomed to seeing. The Bruins won their first 25 games, dropping only their final game of the regular season to USC, 46–44. It was the first loss at Pauley Pavilion, made worse by the fact that it came at the hands of their archrival, yet it may have been a blessing in disguise.

Lew Alcindor was all smiles after wrapping up the greatest career in college basketball history. *Sports Illustrated/Getty Images*

Perhaps the two-time defending champions weren't invincible after all. More than 800 students, as animated about their basketball team as anything else, signed a 25-foot roll of paper in the equipment room that said, "Streaks may end, but champions go on."

A 15-point victory over New Mexico State in the opening round, followed by a 38-point thrashing of Santa Clara, proved that the Bruins were once again ready to defend their national title. Meeting them in the semifinals was Drake, a team that was lightly regarded coming into the game and did nothing to change their reputation when they made just one of their first 10 field goals. That slow start helped UCLA gain a quick 11–2 lead, but the Bulldogs actually fought their way back to cut the deficit to 41–39 at halftime. Drake would even grab the lead in the second half, but thanks to a career night from Vallely, the Bruins took a 10-point lead with just 4:11 remaining. Then disaster struck.

"So I fouled out with about four or five minutes to go and having scored 29 points in the game," Vallely said. "So I'm just sitting there watching and they got real close. Drake was getting ready to knock us off."

UCLA still led 83–74 with 1:12 to play, but the lead was far from safe. The Bulldogs soon cut the lead to five, and after Wicks accidentally threw the inbounds to Drake's Willie McCarter, the senior quickly swished a jumper to make the score 83–80. His team fouled UCLA sophomore Terry Schofield, but he missed the front end of a one-and-one free throw, and after Dolph Pulliam put in a shot at the other end, all of a sudden the lead was down to 83–82. Shackelford would hit a pair of free throws to put the game out of reach, but it was hardly a convincing victory. Drake finished with 33 more shots than the Bruins.

With the win, the Bruins moved within one game of a repeat. All they needed to do was beat Purdue, which was also John Wooden's alma mater. The Purdue fans, confident after their thrashing of UNC, had chanted "We Want Lew!" at the end of their semifinal game. Alcindor gave them exactly what they wanted, although by the end they may have regretted their wishes. He went off for 37 points and 20 rebounds as the Bruins raced out to a 67–47 advantage. Meanwhile, Heitz held Purdue's Rick Mount, the supposed answer to Alcindor, to just 2-of-16 shooting in the early going. With Mount out of the picture, the Bruins easily held on for a 92–72 victory. Wooden took out Alcindor with 1:10 to go, a mini coronation for basketball's first three-time champion and, as he would find out minutes later, basketball's first three-time tournament MOP.

"Lewis Ferdinand Alcindor Jr., was, in my opinion, the finest truly big man ever to play basketball up to his time," Wooden said. "He could do anything you asked of him, and do it almost to perfection." ●

1970 UCLA

The 1970 NCAA Tournament was as notable for its missing teams as its participants. South Carolina had sailed through its regular-season ACC schedule undefeated en route to a 25–2 record, but the Gamecocks lost the title game of the conference tournament. Five years later, the NCAA would allow conferences to send two teams to the tournament, but the Gamecocks had no such luck in 1970—they watched as ACC tournament champ N.C. State lost 80–68 in the first round of the Big Dance. The 22–3 Marquette Warriors were admitted as an independent, but when the NCAA selection committee sent them to play in the Midwest Region instead of the Mideast, coach Al McGuire chose the NIT in protest. Nevertheless, the tournament featured plenty of great games. Utah State defeated Santa Clara on a 15-foot jumper by Ed Epps in the final seconds, and Notre Dame's Austin Carr set the tournament record with 61 points against Ohio. Two nights later, Carr scored 52 against Kentucky. When his college career ended, he would own three of the five highest-scoring games in tournament history.

UCLA's hopes of a sixth title in seven years were almost over before they began. With Lew Alcindor headed to the NBA, John Wooden had already lost his best player from the year before, and now he was about to lose another. On the first day of practice, senior Sidney Wicks showed up in an afro and beard, in clear violation of Wooden's hair rules. The "Wizard of Westwood" had gone 22 years without any insubordination, and now his players were on the brink of mutiny. "Sidney, you know my rules about facial hair," Wooden lectured, but Wicks would have none of it. "Yeah, I know that, Coach, but this is going to be my year," he said. "And you're going to need me."

Wooden, not to be outdone, calmly walked up to his star. "You know what? There's 15 minutes till practice starts. You got 15 minutes to get up into that training room and get that facial hair cut off," Wooden warned, "or you won't be part of the Bruins."

This was a standoff that Wooden was not going to lose.

"I'm sitting there watching this go on, and I'm saying we might be losing our best player here and now," senior John Vallely said. "Next thing you saw was this 6-foot-9 guy running up the steps of Pauley Pavilion with his big old afro sticking out and he's running up the steps to go to the training room, and he showed up

next practice just a couple of minutes late with the facial hair all cut off."

Wooden was smart enough to let Wicks' tardy return slide. With he and Vallely leading the way, the Bruins were back where they belonged, finishing the regular season with a 28–2 record and another tournament bid. Three wins later, and the team was in yet another championship game, this time against the Jacksonville Dolphins. But unlike any other year in UCLA's dynasty, it appeared they had met their match in Jacksonville. Led by Artis Gilmore and Rex Morgan, also known as Batman and Robin, the Dolphins had achieved a 28–1 record and looked unstoppable. And although Wicks was back to join Vallely, they no longer had the greatest college player of all time in Lew Alcindor.

"We were now 'The Team Without,' they called us," Vallely said. "We weren't expected to win."

The Bruins had won five of the previous six championships, but without Alcindor, they were hardly a lock to win the title. They were on a mission to prove their doubters wrong, and they treated their task seriously, but for JU coach Joe Williams—who was half of Wooden's age—such was not the case. Williams let his players grow their hair however they pleased, refused to implement a curfew, and let his players create their own warm-up routines. Never was this

UCLA coach John Wooden receives congratulations from Jacksonville coach Joe Williams after the Bruins' 80–69 victory. *AP Photo*

contrast more apparent than when the two teams finally met for practice at the Final Four.

"They got to practice before us, and so Jacksonville goes out on the court, and they've got their boom boxes. They got crazy music going on, and this is their way of staying loose. So they're out there like these renegades running around having a good time, and it's wild and crazy," Vallely said. "We went through about a half-hour workout that was absolutely precise. There was no screwing around. There was no music, no nothing, no jive whatsoever. It was just serious business."

But just as they had done all year, the relaxed JU squad came out on fire. Gilmore torched the UCLA defense early, and when Wooden finally called a timeout, his team faced a 22–9 deficit.

"We went through some changes that we had to go through there," Vallely said. "Sidney

was fronting Artis and they were throwing the ball over the top, and Artis was getting a couple of easy shots early on. During a timeout, Sidney said, 'Why don't you put me behind Artis?'"

Together with Steve Patterson, who fronted Gilmore, the duo managed to completely neutralize the JU star. Even when Gilmore was lucky enough to get the ball, the tandem started swatting his shots left and right. The Bruins cut the lead to 24–15 midway through the first half, and by the break they had pulled ahead 41–36. By the end of UCLA's 80–69 victory, Wicks—who was six inches shorter than Gilmore—had blocked five shots and was named Most Outstanding Player of the tournament. He may have lost his hair and beard, but he gained something much more important— a national championship. That was one thing Wooden would let him keep. ●

1971 UCLA

Surprisingly, two teams entered the 1971 NCAA Tournament undefeated, and neither was UCLA. Both Marquette and Penn took 27–0 records into the tournament, yet it was 25–1 UCLA who came in with the top ranking. Unfortunately, the Warriors and Quakers failed to prove their doubters wrong as they both lost in the second round. Marquette's 90–89 loss to Ohio State wasn't as painful as Penn's 90–47 loss to crosstown rival Villanova, but Western Kentucky stepped in as another team looking for its first appearance in the Final Four. In the first round, WKU came back from 18 points down to tie Jacksonville and then won on the strangest of plays. While awaiting the inbounds pass with five seconds to go, the Hilltoppers' Clarence Glover pretended to tie his shoelace, then sprang up to take the pass and sink the game-winner. WKU then eliminated rival Kentucky 107–83 and overcame a 14-point deficit against Ohio State to send the game into overtime. Lightning struck twice for Glover, who hit the game-winning shot with 53 seconds to go to send Western Kentucky to the Final Four.

In six of the previous seven seasons, the Long Beach 49ers had to sit and watch as UCLA took home the national title, and it was a story they did not wish to see again. A rivalry between the two teams was brewing, enhanced by the fact that Long Beach coach Jerry Tarkanian was being investigated for NCAA violations, while he claimed that it was in fact the Bruins who were breaking the rules. Add on top a 23-point loss to UCLA in the previous year's tournament, and one of the nation's fiercest rivalries was born.

They met again in the 1971 tournament, with a Final Four spot on the line, but this time Tarkanian had a new strategy. Instead of using his standard 1–2–2 zone, he threw a 2–3 zone at the Bruins, one they were clearly not expecting. Unable to get any looks inside, the Bruins were forced to take outside jumpers, few of which fell down. By the end of the first half, three of their starters—Henry Bibby, Kenny Booker, and Steve Patterson—were a combined 0-for-17 as they trailed 31–27. They would tie the game at 31 early in the second period, but Long Beach pushed the lead back to 44–33 with 14:40 remaining. Bibby and Patterson atoned for their first-half performances by scoring the next nine points to cut the lead to 44–42, but once again the 49ers pushed back, taking a 49–42 lead as the game's final stretch approached.

They still led 52–51 with just over five minutes to go when forward Ed Ratleff committed his fifth foul. It would be the only time Ratleff would foul out in his college career, but his absence gave UCLA a big edge in the paint. It took only 10 seconds for the Bruins to take advantage, as Curtis Rowe hit a pair of free throws to put the Bruins up 54–53. Dwight Taylor hit a free throw to tie the score at 53, setting up one of the most anxious finishes in recent memory. Following a defensive stop at the other end, it appeared that the 49ers would survive after all when Bernard Williams found an open crease and darted toward the basket.

"I had actually gotten beat back door, and in my mind I thought I just cost us a chance to go to the national championship," said UCLA sophomore Larry Farmer, who was defending Williams on the play. "And there was that uncomfortable split-second where I didn't know if I should even try to chase the guy down because I had gotten beat back door. I mean, he set me up and cut back door; he was going one way and I was going another. And the only thing that saved the play was I decided I should chase him down."

Farmer looked for help as he chased down Williams, but no one was in sight. If somebody was going to save the season, it was going to be him. And luckily for UCLA, that's exactly what happened.

"Instead of just striding one, two and shooting a layup," Farmer said, "he came to a hop, and when he came to a hop it allowed me to make up some ground. So when he shot it, I got a piece of it and blocked it. So I went from goat to hero in about a split-second."

UCLA took the possession back, but Bibby missed a jump shot, handing the ball right back to Long Beach. Tarkanian called a timeout, instructing his players to hold the ball for the final shot, but apparently Taylor didn't get the message. Taylor was a defensive specialist whom Tarkanian allowed to play only under one condition: that he never shoot. But when he got the ball in the corner with 45 seconds left, he was completely open. He was open for a reason—the Bruins didn't think he would shoot the ball, either—but against his coach's wishes, Taylor fired away.

"If I had known he was going to shoot it," Tarkanian joked later, "I would have gotten a gun and shot him first."

Just as Tarkanian had feared, Taylor's shot was off the mark, and 20 seconds later Wicks knocked down a pair of free throws to put UCLA up 55–53. George Trapp missed the equalizer at the other end, and once again Wicks came up big, snatching the crucial rebound. His free throws gave the Bruins a 57–53 lead, and despite Trapp's buzzer-beating jumper, UCLA had survived.

Their journey would not get any easier, as the Bruins struggled to a 68–60 victory over Kansas in the semifinals to set up a championship match with Villanova. The Wildcats weren't the strongest opponent in the world, but most of the 31,000 people in attendance—the largest crowd the tournament had ever seen—would be pulling for the underdogs. The game was played at the Astrodome, where UCLA was not exactly a welcome guest. Perhaps the only team that hated UCLA more than Long Beach was Houston.

"I had played in a high school state championship game as a senior in high school, but it was certainly nothing like this. And it was just on a mega stage," said Farmer, who was in his first season with the Bruins. "And you quickly learned at UCLA, at least at that time, that this was business as usual, this is what was expected."

The Bruins may have experienced the Astrodome crowd before, but the last time they played there, they lost to the University of Houston 71–69. It was a loss none of the players would soon forget, and center Steve Patterson was determined not to let that happen again. The senior, who had struggled in the tournament to that point, responded with 20 points in the first half as UCLA took a 45–37 lead. Villanova would get to within 63–60 in the closing minutes, but a trio of free throws from Bibby, followed by a layup from Patterson, clinched the championship.

"I might as well die tonight," Patterson laughed. "I can never do something like this again."

With their seventh title in eight years, people started to wonder if UCLA would ever lose. It would happen, but not anytime soon. ●

1972 UCLA

Had it not been for a sudden departure by Marquette center Jim Chones, 1972 may have belonged to the Warriors. Although UCLA was cruising to a 20–0 record, Marquette was 22–0 until Chones left for the NBA just weeks before the end of the season. His $1.5 million contract with the Nets was enough to lure him away, all but handing the title to the Bruins. Marquette bowed out in the second round to Kentucky, but the title game still had enough intrigue to become the highest-rated basketball game ever at that time. Seven years would pass before another game drew such interest.

When UCLA assistant coach Denny Crum traveled down to San Diego to see a high school prospect named Bill Walton, he couldn't believe his eyes. Playing before him was a 6-foot-11 center who could score from anywhere on the court. In fact, Walton would make an astounding 82 percent of his shots his senior season, as his team frequently won games by 50 points or more. Crum raced back to Westwood to share the news with head coach John Wooden, feeling he had just witnessed the second coming of Lew Alcindor.

"Coach, I think he's the best high school player I've ever seen," Crum said. "He's so much better than Tom McMillen, it isn't even funny."

Unlike Walton, McMillen had just appeared on the cover of *Sports Illustrated*, and he was widely considered the greatest high school player in the country. Upon hearing this analysis from his assistant, Wooden got up out of his chair and closed the door to his office.

"Don't ever make a stupid statement like that," Wooden responded. "There's no red-headed, freckle-faced kid from San Diego who is the best high school player you've ever seen. People will think you're an idiot if you say things like that. It just isn't logical."

But Crum felt so strongly about his recruit that Wooden caved in. He went down to get a look for himself, and by the time he left, Wooden had come to the same conclusion as Crum. Walton was the real deal. Luckily for Wooden, Walton wanted UCLA just as badly as the team wanted him. Like Alcindor five years before him, as soon as Walton put on a Bruins uniform it was obvious that the national

title was going to stay in Westwood for a few more years. To the rest of the college basketball world, it seemed like another case of the rich just getting richer.

Alcindor's debut season saw the Bruins go 30–0, but the quickly dubbed "Walton Gang" one-upped their predecessors by also going undefeated and winning each game by an average of over 30 points. They didn't slow down once the tournament rolled around, defeating Weber State 90–58 in their opening-round game. Even more discouraging to opponents was the fact that only four of UCLA's points came from Walton, who hadn't slept the previous night. The team's hotel had no beds to accommodate Walton, and only when the Bruins threatened to leave did their hotel staff scrounge up an extra-long bed the following night. Walton would need it, too, as his team would be facing Long Beach, a team that was hungrier than ever to dethrone the Bruins.

The 49ers had taken UCLA to the brink in their 57–55 defeat the previous season, and now they would be meeting in the tournament for the third consecutive year. This time it would be Long Beach's turn to go sleepless before the game. The UCLA band played outside their hotel until three in the morning, making for some angry 49ers the following day. The contest was rarely close, but the intensity far exceeded any UCLA game in recent memory. UCLA would complain after the contest about the over-aggressive tactics of Long Beach, but 49ers coach Jerry Tarkanian countered, saying one of his players was cut in the lip while another was hit above the eye. But as physical as the game was, the Bruins advanced relatively unscathed, with a 73–57 victory.

With the victory, UCLA had eliminated one of its most hated rivals, but the Bruins' next opponent, Louisville, had a little score to settle as well. Coaching the Cardinals would be none other than Crum, who had left after Walton's freshman year. Fans felt Crum's departure was a reaction to his spat with Wooden at the previous year's Final Four. That season, in the team's 68–60 victory over Kansas, Crum had tried to insert guard Terry Schofield without Wooden's permission, and when the head coach overruled the substitution, the two got into a debate on the sideline. Junior Henry Bibby helped ease the tension, but when Crum took the new position at UL, people assumed it was Wooden who forced Crum out of Westwood.

"I've heard that, but I don't believe that. I think Denny was ready to be a head coach, and certainly that got proven out. I know that when Denny took that job, he and Coach were the best of friends and remained that way," UCLA forward Larry Farmer said. "And when Denny went into the Hall of Fame, Coach was the guy that took him."

In the first matchup of master vs. apprentice, it was Wooden who emerged victorious, as Walton scored 33 points in a 96–77 win. That victory set up a title clash with Florida State, a team that had cheated its way toward a spot in the finals. FSU coach Hugh Durham had twice been leveled with major NCAA infractions as he recruited the players who became his class of 1972. The school was placed on probation for three seasons, during which none of their games were televised. But by the time the recruiting class reached senior status, they were off the hook. Wooden, on the other hand, never offered his recruits more than a free education.

"There was no two sides or two faces to him. What you hear and what you read about him being kind and giving of his time," Farmer said. "The person, the humility—all of those things are true."

Wooden tried to downplay the good vs. evil angle, but few in attendance at the Los Angeles Sports Arena felt much sympathy for the Seminoles. The partisan crowd was silenced, however, when FSU raced out to a 21–14 lead. It was the largest deficit the Bruins had faced all year, but a late run before the half gave UCLA a 50–39 lead at the break. Florida State got within 77–68 while Walton sat on the bench with his fourth foul, but he returned to keep the Seminoles at bay. His 24 points and 20 rebounds turned out to be too much to overcome, and for the eighth time in nine years, UCLA was on top once again. ●

1973 UCLA

Perhaps the Bruins weren't the villains of college basketball after all. UCLA had made plenty of enemies because of its inability to lose, but Wooden's squad made way for another team in 1973—Providence. The Friars made their first Final Four, but during the year they had made headlines for entirely different reasons. During one practice before the season, Larry Ketvirtis accidentally struck Marvin Barnes, knocking out some of his teeth. Barnes would retaliate later on by striking his teammate with a tire iron, fracturing his cheekbone. For some reason coach David Gavitt kept Barnes on the team, but the guard would face some poetic justice when he dislocated his kneecap in their 98–85 loss to Memphis in the semifinals. The tournament wasn't nearly that bad, though. Austin Peay senior Fly Williams sank a jumper with four seconds to play to beat Jacksonville, keeping the best chant in college basketball alive for one more game. Alas, the team's season—along with the calls of "The Fly is open—let's go Peay!"—ended in a 106–100 loss to Kentucky in overtime.

Following a championship is never easy. Following an undefeated season is even more difficult. But for the 1973 Bruins, that is exactly what they faced as they tried to follow in the footsteps of a team that had outscored opponents by a record 30.3 points per game en route to a 30–0 season. Fortunately for coach John Wooden and the rest of the team, All-American Bill Walton hadn't gone anywhere. While the anti-establishment Walton often clashed with his coach, there was no denying that he was one of the greatest players ever to pick up a basketball. With Walton leading the charge, the Bruins once again cruised through the regular season undefeated.

They didn't stomp over opponents as they had the previous year, but the 1973 season was equally fun. One of the local television stations decided to broadcast the games on delay, which allowed the players to race back to their rooms and relive their artistry all over again. They placed bets to see how often their play would inspire announcer Dick Enberg's signature "Oh my!" call, and thanks to Walton the calls came early and often. For teammate Ralph Drollinger, whose high school team had lost to Walton's 104–48, the dominating performances were nothing new.

"He had not only the size and the agility but more importantly he had the attitude and the love for the game," Drollinger said. "He just had a phenomenal appetite for basketball."

The Bruins needed 28 points from Walton to get by Arizona State in the first round, and it would take an equally marvelous performance from the big man to get by USF in the second round. San Francisco coach Bob Gaillard told his team to slow the pace down in an effort to limit Walton's shot attempts, and the result was USF's best game of the year. Despite having to play in Pauley Pavilion, UCLA's home arena, the Dons grabbed an early 16–9 lead, and thanks to a 55-percent shooting performance in the first half, they trailed just 23–22 at the break. Eight minutes into the second half, the Bruins still only led 31–28, but with the crowd encouraging them they hung on to advance 54–39.

UCLA's Final Four match against Indiana and coach Bobby Knight, then a 32-year-old upstart, would prove to be the Bruins' toughest challenge yet. The Hoosiers grabbed a quick 20–17 lead, which prompted a frustrated Walton to throw his towel toward the end of the bench. The sweat-filled cloth accidentally hit Wooden in the face, but Walton would immediately make up for it. His Bruins went on an 18–0 run to take what seemed to be an insurmountable 40–22 lead at halftime. Wooden took the starters out, a move that made the game much more interesting. Knight's team went on a run of its own, scoring 17 straight points in a four-minute stretch to cut UCLA's lead to 54–51.

"Coach got real upset and put the starters back in. And then down the stretch it was a much closer and harder game to win than it needed to be," senior Larry Farmer said.

With just over nine minutes to go in the game, Walton took a pass in the paint, and when he turned to face the hoop, he collided with Indiana forward Steve Downing. The whistle blew and everyone looked to see who would be assessed with the foul. A blocking call would hand Downing his fourth foul, but a charge would send Walton to the bench for the remainder of the game with his fifth foul. Fortunately for the Bruins, the call went against Downing, and just over a minute later he recorded his fifth foul. Now the game was Walton's to lose, and he guided UCLA to a 70–59 victory to put the Bruins in the title game once again.

Unfortunately for Walton, on the night before the biggest game of his life, he couldn't sleep. A record 42 million people would tune into the championship match between UCLA and Memphis State, but that was hardly the reason for his long night. A day earlier, Walton had told Athletic Director J. D. Morgan that his bed was too short, and Morgan generously offered to trade his king-size bed for Walton's.

"Everything was fine until about 3 a.m. when I heard somebody trying to get into the room," Walton recalled. "I was so scared, I thought my heart was going to burst. Then just as I was settling down the phone rang. I didn't know what to do. I answered it, but there was no one on the other end. A few minutes after that, someone started knocking hard on the door. As I dialed Morgan's number at my old hotel, someone started yelling, 'police!'"

As it turned out, a member of the hotel staff had seen Morgan hauling his luggage and assumed that the athletic director was departing. He then offered Morgan's room—which now belonged to Walton—to another guest at the hotel. The police, who were unaware of the swap, hauled Walton out and kept him in the lobby until Morgan corroborated the story. It wasn't until 4 a.m. that Walton finally got back to sleep, but as the championship game got underway, it was obvious that a little sleep deprivation wasn't going to stop Walton.

"I remember actually, when we came out to warm up, Bill was in the warmup lane behind me and he was—I had never seen him that pumped up for a basketball game, and almost like he was screaming, 'Let's get this game going, I'm ready,'" forward Pete Trgovich said. "It was like he didn't even want to warm up."

Walton started the game perfect from the floor, but when he started to pick up some early foul calls, he could sense the Indiana game was repeating itself all over again. He decided to engage Larry Kenon, his defender, in a brief mid-game conversation.

"Hey Larry, why don't we back down a little bit?" Walton implored. "Or we'll both be watching this game from the bench."

Kenon was less shocked by the question than the fact that Walton had just referred to him by his name.

"What did you call me?" Kenon shot back. "You don't call me Larry; you call me Dr. K!"

Kenon, who was not, in fact, a doctor, had just made a big mistake. Walton may not have been a doctor either, but on this night he played the role of surgeon as he picked apart the Tigers defense. And his team needed the performance, because at halftime the game was still tied at 39–39. The Tigers actually took a lead early in the second half, and when Walton picked up his fourth foul, it appeared he might be taking an early trip to the sidelines after all. Still, the junior continued his relentless attack on Dr. K. Despite playing the last 9:27 with no fouls to give, he finished the night 21-of-22 from the floor en route to a championship-game record 44 points. In fact, he rebounded the only shot he missed and promptly put it back in.

"I never saw anybody that tall move like he did. I never saw a 6-foot-11 guy move as fluidly, and he just had the bounce that he had," Trgovich said. "With maybe not the first jump but the second jump, he had that explosiveness. Obviously I hadn't been around it, but I don't think many people had either."

Late in the game, teammate Greg Lee asked Wooden if the team could run a play for somebody else, to which Wooden half-jokingly responded back, "Why?" Walton's performance was as close to perfection as one could get, as was his college career. With the 87–66 win, he was now 60–0. The Bruins had not only met the impossible expectations, they had actually surpassed them. ●

1974 N.C. State

In 1974, the UCLA Bruins got a taste for just how much the rest of college basketball had caught up with them when they needed three overtimes to win their second-round game against Dayton. The Bruins would eventually win 111–100, but the tide in basketball was certainly shifting. That was never more obvious than when Oral Roberts, which had played varsity basketball for only eight years—including just three under the NCAA—made the Elite Eight. The Titans won their opener 86–82 over Syracuse in overtime, and although head coach Ken Trickey suspended himself after a DWI charge, assistant coach Jack Sutter led the team to a 96–93 win over Louisville in the Sweet 16. In their next game against NCAA powerhouse Kansas, ORU grabbed a nine-point lead with just four minutes to play, but the Jayhawks tied the game late at 81 and survived to steal the Final Four bid.

The Reynolds Coliseum crowd in Raleigh, North Carolina, watched in silence as N.C. State star David Thompson lay motionless on the floor. Moments earlier, as he soared above the rim to block a shot, Thompson's foot clipped the shoulder of teammate Phil Spence, immediately flipping him back toward the court. The thud that echoed through the arena was the sound of Thompson falling directly on his neck. Fans feared that the impact could paralyze Thompson, but as puddles of blood and urine formed underneath his jersey, it became clear that something much more was at stake. David Thompson, one of the greatest players college basketball had ever seen, would be lucky to still be alive.

But Thompson had come too far to see the journey end there. Just minutes after being carried off on a stretcher, he regained consciousness, and even though he still needed to be rushed to the hospital to receive stitches, he had the presence of mind to deliver a message to his doctors: "Tell the team to win." In fact, Thompson would recover in time to watch the ending in person as his teammates defeated Pittsburgh 100–72 to advance to the Final Four. Only two victories remained until the team could taste redemption.

Just weeks before the 1973 season began, the NCAA banned the Wolfpack from any postseason appearance for a supposed violation involving the recruitment of Thompson. The ACC had already investigated the issue in

1971 and opted to not penalize N.C. State, but NCAA officials had their minds made up. At issue were two points: that Thompson did not pay an $8 weekly housing fee while attending a Wolfpack basketball camp, and that Thompson participated in a tryout, illegal at the time, for N.C. State coach Norm Sloan. What they failed to see, however, was that Thompson—who grew up dirt poor—had slept on the floor of a dormitory during the camp, while the other attendees who paid the fee slept in beds, and that his supposed tryout had come from just playing some pickup basketball with his new teammates after he had already signed with State. ACC Commissioner Robert James criticized the NCAA for the seemingly unwarranted punishment, but it didn't matter. The damage was already done. The Wolfpack finished the 1973 season at 23–0, leaving fans and players alike pondering what could have been. And now that they had their second chance, Thompson was determined to see it out.

But that hardly meant they couldn't have a little fun along the way. During Thompson's first practice back, he decided to pull a little prank on Sloan, who had already kept Thompson out of the team's first practice following the accident and was cautious to put him in for the second. Sloan had warned his star to take it easy that day, but Thompson gave him much more than he bargained for.

"That's when *The Exorcist* had come out, so at some point after David had fallen on his head we [went] over to the movie, and I think we sat through it two or three times as a team, so we pretty much had every word, every action down by the time it was done," smiled Tim Stoddard, a senior on the team. "Thursday, we're going through our layups. David is now finally going through warmups—remember, dunking was illegal at this point—he comes up and he goes under. He's dribbling the ball, stops right underneath the basket, grabs his head, and does like Linda Blair did in the movies. Starts moaning, and you could see everybody kind of stand up like they're saying, 'Here goes any shot we have to win.'"

Sloan nearly began to convulse himself before a laugh from David, followed by a double-pump dunk, put any worries to rest. The 6,000 fans who had come to watch State's practice roared in approval. Fortunately for Thompson and his teammates, they would find equally friendly confines in the Greensboro Coliseum, just 80 miles away from their campus in Raleigh. And before a packed arena, the Wolfpack became the first team in eight years to eliminate UCLA from the NCAA Tournament (see page 284). It left them just one victory away from the national championship, but as the Wolfpack had just proved, nothing was impossible in the world of college basketball.

"You knew you had one more game to play, and Marquette wasn't anything to take lightly," Stoddard said. "Realistically, that was a lot of the speeches that you're getting all the time: Just because you beat UCLA, don't think you've won this already—this is a very good ball club. If you think you've accomplished anything and you go lose this game, you haven't done anything yet."

Thanks to some hot shooting from Stoddard and Thompson, N.C. State grabbed an early 10–2 advantage, but Marquette quieted the crowd of nearly 16,000 by tying the game at 12 and pulling ahead 19–18. The Warriors still led 28–27 when the Wolfpack finally got their act together, scoring 26 of the next 31 points. Thanks to seven blocks from 7-foot-3 center Tom Burleson, their lead never dipped below nine points. Burleson celebrated the 76–64 victory by sitting on the shoulders of a teammate—not that he needed to do so—to cut down the net.

Thompson would finish his career with three All-American honors and two National Player of the Year awards, but nothing would come close to a national championship. And had it not been for the NCAA, he might have even had two of them. ●

David Thompson (holding the trophy) was lucky to still be alive, much less play for a national championship, but it was his 21 points that paved the way for N.C. State's 76–64 victory. *North Carolina State University Athletic Department. Photograph by Ed Caram*

1975 UCLA

The tournament did away with the seven first-round byes in 1975, instead expanding the field 32 teams and making each team play a first-round game. The extra first-round games brought plenty of excitement, as Georgetown and Central Michigan played in one of the oddest tournament games of all time. With the game tied at 75, Georgetown's John Smith sank what appeared to be the game-winner with three seconds left—until the referees called a charge on him for running into CMU's Leonard Drake. The sophomore was sent to the line with no time on the clock, and he made both free throws for the 77–75 victory. The second round didn't disappoint either, as Arizona State went on a 15–2 run over the final five minutes to beat UNLV 84–81, and Syracuse beat North Carolina 78–76 on Jim Lee's 15-footer with three seconds left. The tournament also marked the first time that more than one team per conference could participate: Maryland won the ACC regular season, lost in the conference tournament, and managed to make the Elite Eight.

John Wooden was never meant to be standing in the UCLA locker room. Decades before, while serving in the Navy during World War II, Wooden suffered an injury that required him to spend a month in rehabilitation back home. He was replaced by Freddie Stalcup, an old friend of his from their college days at Purdue, only to have a kamikaze pilot gun down Stalcup and the post Wooden was meant to be holding. He lived to tell that tale, but it was never meant to be told to UCLA players.

In 1948, Wooden was supposed to accept the head coaching job at Minnesota when Athletic Director Frank McCormick would call him at 6:00 p.m. An hour later he would be receiving a phone call from UCLA, during which he planned to let them know he would be coaching the Gophers instead. But due to a freak snowstorm, McCormick couldn't reach a working telephone in time, and when UCLA Athletic Director Wilbur Johns gave the call right on time, Wooden gladly accepted. When McCormick phoned a few hours later, Wooden let him know that he was in fact moving to Los Angeles.

But here Wooden was, standing in the UCLA locker room after their semifinal win over Louisville. Having just completed one of the greatest games of all time (see page 282), Wooden told his team he would be retiring. After nine championships in eleven seasons,

the following day's championship would mark his last game—win or lose.

"It got quiet, it got real quiet because you didn't think he was going to do it at that time," senior Pete Trgovich said. "You thought maybe after the last game he would say I'm done. But he made that decision before the game."

The Bruins were now faced with the responsibility of sending out America's greatest coach as a winner, but that was a burden they were glad to carry. Like Wooden, they were never meant to be in this position either. Gone from the previous season were four starters, including legend Bill Walton. The team was losing the player not only responsible for two national championships but two undefeated seasons. For the first time in over a decade, the Bruins had doubters.

"Most of the Walton Gang graduated, and now we've got the Cinderella team. We've got a bunch of guys that aren't expected, especially by the eastern media, we're not expected to win or rate high," center Ralph Drollinger said. "It's almost like we had a liberty card so to speak of not having all the pressure because we're just a bunch of second-stringers behind the Walton Gang that are now coming into our own, and that's why it was deemed appropriately the Cinderella team."

Indiana, with its undefeated record, and Louisville, not far behind at 25–2, were considered favorites to win the title. The predictions seemed to be only confirmed when both teams cruised through the first two rounds, while UCLA needed some last-minute magic just to advance over Michigan and Montana. The Bruins were up 37–28 in the first half before the Wolverines tied the game at 44 just before halftime. Even when the Bruins built the lead back to 83–77 in the final minutes, Michigan managed to tie the game once again, and the Wolverines actually had a chance to win the game at the end of regulation. UCLA managed to escape in overtime, but it was hardly a convincing performance.

The Bruins appeared to have an easier finish against Montana when they grabbed a 57–48 lead with just seven minutes to go, but Trgovich rolled his ankle, forcing Wooden to take him out of the game. Eric Hays quickly made a three-point play for the Grizzlies, and when he made a layup moments later the lead was down to 57–53. Wooden decided to bring Trgovich back in, and the senior scored five points in less than a minute to give the Bruins some breathing room. Hays refused to quit, and Montana got as close as 64–62 in the final minute, but thanks to some clutch rebounding by Trgovich the team was still alive.

"I think it was our whole attitude that we weren't going to lose. We never thought about losing—we never went into a game thinking that you know we might lose this game," Trgovich said. "At UCLA at that time, we just didn't ever think we were going to lose, so when the game got close I don't think we felt any pressure."

After defeating Arizona State and surviving the epic match against Louisville, the team would face Kentucky for the national championship. As if Drollinger didn't have enough to contemplate already, the game would be played in his hometown of San Diego, where dozens of his old friends and family would be in attendance.

"That will be a memory I will never forget," Drollinger said. "It couldn't have been more focused; it couldn't have been more surreal; it couldn't have been more pressure. The whole stage is set here for coach Wooden to have just a fairy tale ending to his career, as a Cinderella team rises from the ashes of no expectations and wins it for the coach, and it's in my own backyard."

The Wildcats, however, were not going to make it easy, and midway through the second half the momentum was clearly on their side. They had just cut the lead from 74–67 to 76–75 and had a chance to take the lead moments later, but on this night UCLA was not to be denied. Drollinger, who usually played in a backup role, had the game of his life, shutting down UK star Ricky Robey. UCLA pushed the lead to 80–77, and even after Kentucky continued to answer each basket, the Bruins made three huge shots in the final minutes to push the lead back to five. When the clock struck zero, Wooden has his tenth championship in 12 years—a record that will never be touched in college basketball. The usually reserved coach, known for his reluctance to compare teams or players, said this was the most satisfying group he ever had the privilege of coaching.

"It was a great compliment coach Wooden has given that team and myself," Trgovich said. "You got to understand, I'm a big John Wooden fan, I defend him all the time. A lot of people come in and they say, 'Well, you know it's easy when you have Lew Alcindor and Bill Walton to win championships.' Well, take those five championships away and coach Wooden's still got five, so now what are you going to say?"

Simply, that John Wooden was the greatest man ever to coach the game of basketball. Perhaps Wooden was actually meant to be there all along. ●

1976 Indiana

Undefeated Indiana garnered all the attention in 1976, but the Hoosiers were not the only team to bring a perfect mark into tournament play. Rutgers had never made the tournament before the previous year and finished the regular season 28–0—and almost lost in the first round against unranked Princeton. The Tigers had a chance to win the game when Peter Molloy stepped to the line with four seconds left. Molloy had only made 9 of his 16 free throws on the year, and Rutgers coach Tom Young called a timeout, hoping to remind the freshman of his struggles from the line. Molloy indeed missed the free throw, and the Scarlet Knights made the Final Four, marking the only time that two undefeated teams advanced that far. Rutgers had beaten VMI in the Elite Eight. The Keydets were an embarrassing 1–25 in 1971 and hadn't had a winning season since 1921, but they came just one victory short of making a little history of their own.

Indiana coach Bob Knight had watched his team's undefeated season slip away due to some serious misfortune in 1975, and he was not about to let it happen again. In that season, star forward Scott May had broken his wrist just weeks before the NCAA Tournament, and although he came back in time to face Kentucky in the regional final, he was clearly not at his best. Kentucky pulled away from the 31–0 Hoosiers, and a late comeback bid fell just short as IU lost a 92–90 heartbreaker. Before the following season began, Knight made it clear that his players were going to finish the journey they had started 12 months earlier.

"The day before practice in that '75–76 season, I had our team sit down and I told them this: 'All right, there's a team that can win the Big Ten, there's a team that will win the NCAA—neither one of those is our goal,'" Knight recalled. "Our goal this year is to play this season completely undefeated from our opening game through the championship of the NCAA Tournament. That's what this team is capable of doing, and I expect it to do just that."

Going undefeated, however, was easier said than done. During one eight-game stretch in Big Ten play, the Hoosiers had to survive five halftime deficits, including a miracle finish against Michigan. Indiana had overcome a 2-for-22 shooting performance from three of its starters to keep the game competitive, but still trailed by four points in the final minute

when junior Quinn Buckner sank a shot with 22 seconds left to cut the lead to two. The Hoosiers fouled Michigan guard Steve Grote, who missed the front end of a one-and-one, and when Indiana got the rebound they had a chance to keep the undefeated season alive. IU missed the equalizer, but Kent Benson was there for the game-tying tip at the buzzer to send it into overtime. The Hoosiers would emerge victorious, and they would win their following eight games to cap off the spotless regular season. Unfortunately, that achievement was not rewarded by the NCAA, as they placed IU in the same region as Marquette, the second best team in the country with a 26–1 record.

Before they could even meet Marquette, they would first have to get by sixth-ranked Alabama. The Crimson Tide rallied from 12 points down to take a 69–68 lead in the final two minutes before May nailed a long jumper to put IU back on top. Knight assumed the Tide would go to their star forward Leon Douglas, and he told Benson not to let his man get a shot off.

"Now, Bennie, I don't want Douglas to get the ball," Knight warned. "In fact, Bennie, if Douglas so much as touches the ball this trip, just start running through that door down there, because I'm going to run your butt all the way back to Bloomington."

The defense would indeed step up to the task, as Indiana escaped with a 74–69 win. The Hoosiers faced an equally tough challenge against Marquette, as the Warriors stormed back from a 10-point deficit in the closing stretch. They held IU scoreless for six minutes, and they got to within 55–52 before May came to the rescue once again. His shot gave the Hoosiers some much needed breathing room as they held on for a 65–56 victory.

In the semifinals, Indiana faced UCLA, winners of 10 of the last 12 NCAA championships. All five Bruins starters would play in the NBA, as would IU's top five, but gone from the equation was UCLA coach John Wooden. Once the Hoosiers took a 34–26 lead, they never looked back, cruising out to a 65–51 victory. Now the only thing standing in Knight's way of an undefeated season was Michigan, a team the Hoosiers had beaten twice during the year. Neither of those victories had come with ease, but that didn't stop Knight from upping the stakes against counterpart Johnny Orr. Knight called the Michigan coach early on Sunday morning after the Wolverines' semifinal victory, pretending to be the president of the United States, Michigan graduate Gerald Ford. As legend goes, it was Mrs. Orr who received the phone call.

"She got John on right away and I was sailing along, pretending to be President Ford, congratulating him on winning the regional and telling him how proud he had made 'M' men all over the world," Knight said. "I went on too long. If I had just stuck with short sentences, I think I'd have had him."

But when Knight oversold the impersonation, Orr had his chance to get back at Knight, who was an alumnus of Michigan's archrival. "President, hell," Orr replied. "How could any dumb bastard from Ohio State get to be the president?"

But once the game started, it seemed that perhaps Knight's undefeated season wasn't meant to be. With the game tied at 4, IU forward Bobby Wilkerson jumped in the air to defend a Wayman Britt fast break. Brit would convert the layup, but more importantly Wilkerson had landed on his head and was not quick to get up. He was diagnosed with a concussion, and now for the second straight year, Knight would be without one of his big stars. Michigan quickly took advantage by grabbing a 10–4 lead and eventually pushed its edge to 18–10. The Hoosiers responded with nine straight points, but by halftime they still trailed 35–29. The Wolverines had shot 61 percent from the field, and it would take a massive effort for Indiana to crawl back without Wilkerson.

They would quickly even up the score in the second half, but Michigan wasn't willing to hand over the title just yet. Both teams battled to six ties in the second half before the Hoosiers finally pulled away. The lead was still only 73–69 before a 10–0 run put any of Knight's doubts to rest. The Hoosiers finished the season undefeated—something no team has accomplished since. ●

The mood in the locker room would be slightly more upbeat after Indiana wrapped up their 74–69 victory over Alabama in the second round. Fortunately for the Hoosiers, that was as close as anybody would get the rest of the tournament. *Rich Clarkson/Sports Illustrated/Getty Images*

1977 Marquette

It didn't take long for the intensity to pick up at the 1977 tournament, as 29–2 San Francisco and 29–3 UNLV squared off in the first round. The Rebels, who featured a record six NBA draft picks, would win 121–95 and advance to the Final Four. Ironically, none of UNLV's players were first- or second-team All-Americans. UNLV's run came to an end against North Carolina, thanks to a pair of John Kuester free throws with seven seconds left. The Tar Heels also used some clutch free throw shooting to beat Notre Dame, when Phil Ford sank a pair from the line for a 79–77 victory. Free throws proved to be the difference as well during Idaho State's 76–75 upset of UCLA, whose second-round loss marked its earliest since 1963.

Jim Boylan was in his dorm room just before Christmas when his phone rang. You need to come downtown, the voice on the other end said, and meet at a restaurant called "The Clock." There would be a pretty huge announcement coming from head coach Al McGuire. The Marquette senior made his way across the snow-covered streets to the restaurant, where he got the surprise of a lifetime.

"We went down there and there were a lot of people kind of upset. I remember walking in, and as soon as I walked in I saw these people and I could see that there was something wrong. Then one of the players came and said Coach is going to retire," Boylan said. "It was very strange, a very kind of surreal setting and a surreal moment, and a lot of thoughts going through your head."

The first thought, to many people in the restaurant, was why. McGuire was only 48 and in the midst of an excellent run at Marquette. The Warriors had been close to a national championship for much of the past decade, and with a No. 1 preseason ranking, he had his best chance yet.

"We didn't know what was going on. Retiring? Retiring from what?" senior Butch Lee remembered. "When he gave us that news, it was like we were at a funeral. Everybody was there all crying."

But before McGuire could ride off into the sunset, there was still work to do. He wasn't going to retire until the season was over, leaving his team with one last opportunity to give him a national title. The Warriors found themselves back in the NCAA Tournament after a contentious regular season, but the frustrations didn't end once the team grabbed one of the last spots in the Big Dance. In fact, McGuire almost came to blows with his team during their first-round game against Cincinnati.

"We were down at halftime and there was a little bit of a confrontation between coach and Bernard Toone at halftime, and it got a little crazy in the locker room," Boylan said. "So we didn't really get a chance to talk about anything regarding the game."

And although the team trailed by three points at halftime, perhaps no plan was the best plan, as Marquette surged ahead for a 66–51 win. And after the victory, McGuire and Toone were back to being friends.

"Nowadays they're going to fire a coach just for some of the stuff that happened with us," Lee joked. "But Al was good because he was a pro, he didn't hold that against you. Just because you argue with him doesn't mean you're not the best point guard or you're not the best player."

With that mess now behind them, Marquette squeaked past Kansas State and Wake Forest to arrive at the Final Four. A buzzer-beater by Jerome Whitehead against UNC-Charlotte (see page 274) put the Warriors into the championship game against North Carolina; win or lose, McGuire would be coaching in his last game. But that didn't mean he was sweating out the countdown to tip-off. Actually, his mind was completely elsewhere, as he decided to take a pre-game ride on his motorcycle. McGuire got lost and arrived at the stadium just 45 minutes before tip-off, plenty early for his unconventional schedule. In fact, he had frequently skipped his own practices back in Milwaukee.

"Al would come walking in and everybody would be shooting around and he'd walk to the right, would make a circle, and would walk right back out the building," Lee laughed. "And we wouldn't even see him anymore, so we were accustomed to different things like that."

The players had too much on their minds to worry about McGuire's absence, especially Boylan. The Jersey City native would be playing against his childhood friend in forward Mike O'Koren. Boylan and O'Koren played evenly in the first half, but the Warriors used a late run to take a 39–27 lead at halftime. McGuire warned his team not to get overconfident, as the Tar Heels would surely make a run, but not even McGuire could have predicted it would happen so quickly.

O'Koren nailed four quick shots at the start of the second half, and by the time Walter Davis tied the game

Marquette coach Al McGuire watches as his Marquette team wins his final game, the national championship over North Carolina. *Rich Clarkson/Sports Illustrated/Getty Images*

at 41–41, almost all of the second half still remained. The game was tied again at 45 when UNC coach Dean Smith directed his team to go into a stall, hoping to lure the Marquette defenders into an easy basket. If his Tar Heels could hold onto the ball long enough, Smith hoped the defense would become impatient and take some risks to get a steal. But the strategy backfired two minutes later, when Bo Ellis rose up for a huge block.

"We needed to get the lead back, so making that stop was absolutely essential for us," Boylan said. "A lot of people questioned coach Smith about the fact that he did that and maybe took

their momentum, but they had done that all year and they had gotten to the championship game playing that way."

The block allowed the Warriors to play their style of play the rest of the game, and with just over a minute left they had taken a 57–51 lead. North Carolina refused to give in, but thanks to some clutch free throw shooting Marquette held on for a 67–59 win. As the final seconds ticked away, McGuire covered his face in his hands while the tears streamed down.

"That was an incredible story," Lee said. "And like they say, sometimes the truth is stranger than the fiction." ●

1978 Kentucky

An unfamiliar guest nearly snuck into the 1978 Final Four, as Cal State Fullerton—which hadn't been to the tournament in its 17-year history and wouldn't be back for another 30—upset twelfth-ranked New Mexico in the opening round and followed it up with a 75–72 win over USF in the Sweet 16. Fullerton trailed the eleventh-ranked Dons by 12 at halftime but won on a Keith Anderson 20-footer with just two seconds to go. Their run eventually came to an end in the regional finals against Arkansas. The Titans led 58–57 late in the game, but Ron Brewer's shot with 1:24 left paved the way for the Razorbacks' 61–58 victory. The tournament's wildest ending came when Western Kentucky defeated Syracuse 87–86 in overtime. SU's Mark Byrnes hit what he believed to be the game-winner with three seconds to go, but the officials ruled that he had been fouled before the shot, and his ensuing free throw rimmed out to determine a one-point deficit for the Orangemen.

The honeymoon was officially over. Just five years earlier, Joe B. Hall had become Kentucky's first new coach since the start of the Great Depression. Hall was taking over for Adolph Rupp, the winningest coach in NCAA history and owner of four national championships. The successor had filled in Rupp's shoes admirably, but three SEC championships and one Final Four appearance later, Hall was going through a depression of his own. Expectations were always high for Kentucky fans, but when his team was ranked atop the nation's preseason polls, Hall knew the only way to avoid a catastrophic disappointment would be to win the title. He was stuck in a bind: If he did manage to deliver a championship, it was just business as usual. If, heaven forbid, the dream fell short, the inevitable questions would arise: Couldn't Rupp have taken the team all the way?

The Wildcats hung onto the top ranking virtually the entire year, only relinquishing the spot for a brief period in February before reclaiming their stake as the best team in the country. By the time the regular season had reached its conclusion, Kentucky was the top team in the nation at 25–2 and in great position to finish what the team had set its sights on before the season started. However, that did not guarantee UK an easy path to the championship. Due to a new bracket that NCAA officials were testing out, a method they scrapped after its trial run, Kentucky was forced to play its first-round game against twelfth-ranked Florida State.

The Seminoles quickly showed why they were a dangerous team, taking a 20–18 lead on a long jumper by Mickey Dillard. FSU widened the gap to 37–27 with 3:54 before the break, and thanks to 55 percent shooting from the field, they still led 39–32 at halftime. The first-half performance was unacceptable to Hall, who sent star players Rick Robey, Truman Claytor, and Jack Givens to the bench for the start of the second half. One of their replacements, sophomore Lavon Williams, cut the deficit to 45–44 on a dunk with 12:52 to go, but when the Seminoles pushed the lead back to 51–46, Hall looked to his stars to keep the season alive. Claytor helped lead the team to a 14–0 run, and when Macy nailed a jumper with 8:38 to go, The Wildcats grabbed a lead they would not relinquish.

UK would go on to defeat Miami of Ohio in its second game, but Hall's squad was nowhere near midseason form. Sophomore Kyle Macy, who had come into the Miami game averaging 13 points per contest, chipped in just two points on just 1-of-3 shooting. Hall played the role of psychologist, taking the opportunity to build Macy's confidence.

"Kyle hasn't even showed up yet," Hall said. "But Michigan State will know he's there on Saturday."

Unfortunately for the Wildcats, Macy seemed to be absent against the Spartans as well, as MSU shot 58 percent in the first half to take a 29–24 lead. The Wildcats, who had averaged more than 85 points per game, were making just 40 percent of their shots, none of which had come from Macy. The guard was shut down by Michigan State's 2-3 zone, and unless something changed the Wildcats were going to be sent home earlier than expected.

In an effort to limit the damage at the other end, Kentucky went into a zone defense as well, a strategy that worked early on as the team went on an 11–4 run to tie the game at 35 with 10:42 remaining. The game was still tied at 41 with 6:16 to go when Macy found his touch. His three-point play gave UK a 44–41 advantage, and during the final stretch Macy delivered with 16 crucial points. The Spartans twice pulled within one point during the final minute, but the Wildcats made sure they got the ball to Macy. Michigan State was forced to foul Macy to stop the clock and tried to call timeouts to ice his touch, but Macy nailed all four free throws to send Kentucky to the Final Four. Only two games remained until the dream was complete.

As good as Kentucky had been during the season, the best record in the country belonged to 31–2 Arkansas, UK's opponent in the semi-finals. Neither team backed down from the other, rarely allowing the lead to reach more than a few points before making a run. The Wildcats thought they had finally broken free when Claytor gave the team a 59–53 lead late in the game, only to have the Razorbacks storm back to trim the lead to just 59–58 with 3:31 to play. Lee gave his team a much needed breather when his shot sent the lead back to 61–58, and after Givens followed with a layup of his own just under the two-minute mark, Kentucky knew they were heading to the championship game.

Unlike the Wildcats, who by this point were dealing with as much pressure on the court as they were off, the Duke Blue Devils were having the time of their lives. After finishing last in the ACC for four straight years, little was expected of the Blue Devils, who had one junior, two sophomores, and two freshmen on the starting roster. But they had shocked the country by winning the league's tournament to grab an automatic bid, and thanks to three wins by a total of nine points, as well as one easier victory, they were somehow in the championship game.

Kentucky's senior-heavy lineup had already tasted the defeat of losing the 1975 title game, but they were not about to blow their second opportunity. A few weeks earlier, Hall had criticized Givens for not wanting the ball in the clutch, but now when it counted the most, the senior had the best game of his career. Givens scored 16 of the team's last 18 points as they closed the first half with a 45–38 lead. The Blue Devils weren't about to go away, but 18 more points in the second half from Givens was too much to overcome. When the clock struck zero, Hall took a deep breath, and more importantly, flashed a smile. He had managed to meet impossible expectations, and for that his predecessor would have been awfully proud. ●

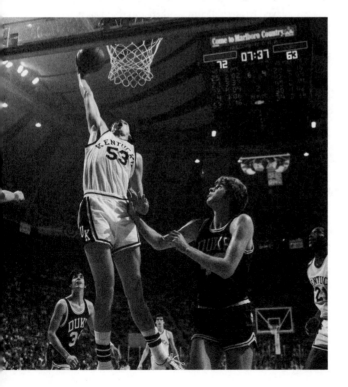

Kentucky's Rick Robey puts the finishing touches on Kentucky's first national title in 20 years. *Rich Clarkson/Sports Illustrated/Getty Images*

1979 Indiana State— Michigan State

The 1979 tournament will always be remembered for the two teams that played in its championship game, and rightfully so. Magic Johnson's Michigan State squad matched up against Larry Bird's Indiana State Sycamores in a preview of future Lakers-Celtics battles. But the most surprising team in the Final Four that year was Pennsylvania. In the first tournament to feature 40 teams, each seeded 1 to 10, the Quakers entered the field as a nine seed. After a 73–69 victory over the Iona Gaels, Penn upset top-seeded North Carolina 72–71, despite having to play the game before 12,400 hostile fans in Raleigh. In what became known as Black Sunday in the state, second-seeded Duke lost hours later to St. John's on a Reggie Carter jumper with five seconds left. The real kicker was that both teams would have gotten to play their next two games in Greensboro.

When Bill Hodges first tried to recruit Larry Bird in 1975, the Indiana State coach spent no time explaining why Bird should play for his school. That part was irrelevant. His main concern was whether he could get Bird to consider attending college at all. The last guy to try was Louisville coach Denny Crum, who had challenged Bird to a game of HORSE. If Crum won the game, Bird would agree to become a Cardinal. Eight shots later, Crum was walking out of the gym empty-handed.

Bird had actually tried his hand at college once before. A year earlier, he tried to play at Indiana, but that experiment ended after a few weeks when Bird packed his bags one day and went back to his home in French Lick. Bird got a job with the street department picking up garbage, a lifestyle that suited him just fine.

"You got to consider the fact that he's from French Lick—that and West Bend put together its 3,000 souls. You go to IU and it's 45,000 on campus. I think he felt lost," Hodges said. "And when he came home everybody really gave him a hard time. I mean, they kind of ostracized him—everybody except the people that gave

him a job at the street department. I think he had just kind of withdrawn from society and just played basketball and worked and that was it."

It wasn't the homecoming Bird had hoped for, but it was only because everybody knew what kind of opportunity he had squandered. He, of course, didn't see it that way, until Hodges decided to use some psychology on Bird to make him reconsider college.

"He was talking about his teammate that was playing AAU ball with him and his name was Kevin Carnes," Hodges remembered. "Larry was telling me how good he was—he said he's a heck of a point guard—problem is he got married. If he had gone to college, he would have been really good. And I looked at him and I said, 'Larry, one of these days they're going to say that about you.'"

Bird, who always looked at the ground during conversations, tilted his head and looked Hodges in the eye. The young coach knew he had just recruited Bird to play at Indiana State. What he didn't know was just how incredible he would be. Luckily for Hodges and his team, it didn't take them long to find out.

Larry Bird scored 19 points in the title game, but it was Magic Johnson's 24 points that helped Michigan State win the most-watched championship in history. *James Drake/Sports Illustrated/Getty Images*

"We would play together in the summers and it was hot in that arena and he would just drill them from 25 feet, and I thought, man, this guy, he's a freak," junior Bob Heaton said. "He just doesn't quit, he doesn't miss."

When the season started, Bird somehow managed to elevate his game even more, and the team started winning. And kept winning. By the end of the regular season, the Sycamores—who had only become a Division I team 10 years earlier—were 33–0. Playing in the Missouri Valley Conference, Indiana State was able achieve the top ranking in relative obscurity. Even less was known about Bird, who refused to grant interviews in an effort to not outshine his teammates.

"I had a couple of friends out there in Denver who would call me when they saw Larry on TV, shocked that he was white," laughed Heaton. "It was something where the country was mystified a little bit by this Larry Bird. And Indiana State going undefeated—and who is Indiana State?"

Emerging at the same time was sophomore Earvin "Magic" Johnson, who had almost nothing in common with Bird—except talent. Anybody who had followed college basketball that year knew of Johnson, the outgoing 6-foot-9 point guard who thrived in the spotlight. Johnson appeared on the cover of *Sports Illustrated* before the season began, and it wasn't long before his Michigan State Spartans were the No. 1-ranked team in the country. But as the season progressed, a future meeting with Bird looked more like a wish than a reality. The Spartans soon lost four games by a combined six points, and responded by getting blown out by Northwestern, a team that was 4–12 and winless in the Big Ten. Had the tournament not expanded to 40 teams that year, Michigan State's season could have been over with that loss. As it was, they would need to go nearly undefeated just to sneak into the tournament.

But with Johnson at the helm, they did just that, cruising through the rest of the schedule to qualify for the Big Dance. The Spartans didn't stop there, as they breezed through the NCAA Tournament to land a spot in the title game. Indiana State's path was not quite so easy. The Sycamores needed a miracle finish just to make it to the Final Four (see page 214) and then a last-minute comeback to beat DePaul 76–74.

"We were never cocky, but we just felt confident that we can go out and if we play hard and execute that we were going to pull it out in the end," Heaton said. "I guess just having the peace of mind knowing you've got the best college player in America on your team, that was a bit of a comfort having that."

Although the program may have said that the battle would be between Michigan State and Indiana State, most people recognized the game as a matchup between the two best players in college basketball. Nearly a quarter of all televisions were tuned in that night to watch Johnson's squad emerge on top 75–64, a television rating that has yet to be touched by any other basketball game.

"Larry might have been a conservative, quiet, shy kid and Magic an outgoing city kid, but they played the game in a similar fashion. They played the game to make the guys around them better," Hodges said. "I think that's why this particular game is everlasting."

Bird and Magic would continue their duels in the NBA, saving the struggling professional league. But more importantly, the duo helped America realize why March Madness is so special. And all these years later, they haven't forgotten. ●

1980 Louisville

For the second consecutive year, the tournament expanded the field by eight teams. The new 48-team tournament forced the fifth and sixth seeds to play in the opening round, as opposed to the previous year when the top six teams in each bracket got a first-round bye. Despite their head start on everyone else, only one team seeded in the top four advanced to the Final Four. In fact, none of the top seeds would make the semifinals, something that wouldn't occur again for another 26 years. Iowa, which did reach the Final Four as a five seed, had to overcome a 14-point deficit to Georgetown in the finals of the East Region. The Hawkeyes shot 71 percent in the second half to get within 80–78, and when Steve Wait converted a three-point play with five seconds left, they advanced to their first Final Four since 1956.

When Darrell Griffith walked into a room to announce where he would be attending college, the entire basketball world stopped to listen. Griffith, the prodigy with the 48-inch vertical leap, had just about every institute of higher learning begging for his services. The school with the most at stake was the University of Louisville, the town Griffith had lived in his entire life and the team that had come up just short of a national title the year before, losing in the Final Four by a single point. While landing Griffith would not guarantee a championship, it would drastically improve Louisville's odds, and when Griffith announced to a crowded room of friends and reporters that he would indeed be attending UL, he took care of the speculation himself.

"I plan on winning several national championships," Griffith declared, much to the delight of the Cardinal faithful. Griffith wasn't usually the kind of person to make bold predictions, but it was something his new head coach didn't mind one bit.

"That's what he wanted to do and that's what he *expected* to do. And I can only tell you that he was good enough that there weren't many people that could stop him," Louisville coach Denny Crum recalled. "He was good enough to do that. So I wasn't upset about that—as a matter of fact, it pleased me. You're thinking in terms of winning and you kind of want that word to get out that he's promising it. And what I would say was come along and help. Help us get there and do that."

Griffith lived up to his billing as one of the sport's emerging stars, but by the time his senior year came around, he had yet to win a national championship. His promise of several titles was now thrown out the window, but he still had one more chance to salvage at least one title. The only problem was that to do so, he was going to have to win alongside three sophomores and a freshman. With Griffith's help, the Cardinals managed to qualify for the tournament and win their opening-round game in dramatic fashion (see page 254). But they still had four games before Griffith could fulfill his promise, and when they took on Texas A&M in their next contest, it looked as if the run could end there. Thanks to 10 early points from Griffith, the Cardinals took a 12–2 lead, but the Aggies would tie the game at 35 and go on to take a 47–43 lead with 11:49 to play.

Fortunately for Louisville, forward Wiley Brown sank a pair of shots to knot the score, which would still be the case when regulation came to a close with the score locked at 53–53. The Cardinals, who had shot just 32 percent in the second half, were lucky to still be around, but they would score the last 10 points to survive their second consecutive overtime game. It hadn't been easy, but the dream was still alive.

The Cardinals raced off to another 12–2 lead in their following contest against LSU, but just like Texas A&M, the Tigers came roaring back, scoring 16 straight points while Griffith sat on the bench with three early fouls. Risking a fourth foul was not something Crum wanted to do to his star player, but when LSU pushed its lead all the way to 29–21, he had little choice. Griffith was going back in. With 3:21 still to play in the first half, the senior came in and helped Louisville score the final 10 points to take a 31–29 lead at the break.

The Cardinals would carry that momentum with them all the way to the title game, where they were set to face UCLA, the same team that had ruined Louisville's title aspirations in 1975. The Cardinals had been one free throw from advancing to the championship that year, but Terry Howard—who hadn't missed a foul shot all year—missed the free throw in the closing seconds, and UCLA's Richard Washington made him pay by sinking a shot at the buzzer. It was a devastating loss for the Cardinals, especially Crum, who had graduated from UCLA and coached the Bruins for four years as an assistant to John Wooden. This time Crum was determined to emerge victorious, but before he could focus on the task at hand, he had to take care of something completely different.

Wiley Brown, one of the heroes of Louisville's victory over Texas A&M, had lost—of all things—his right thumb. Brown, who had his thumb amputated when he was four, had played all season long with a prosthetic thumb that Crum had ordered for him. The prosthetic had given Brown a tighter grip and more control of the ball, but now just hours before the biggest game of his life, Brown had left it at the Hilton Hotel, where the team had eaten a pre-game meal. As soon as the sophomore realized his error, the team raced back to the hotel, where everyone naturally assumed the thumb had been thrown in the trash along with their food. When UL junior Randy Bufford asked where the staff had put the garbage, he heard the last words he wanted to hear—they had thrown it into the dumpster. Neglecting all concern about his appearance, or smell, Bufford hopped into the giant green dumpster behind the hotel. But after digging around the filth for a while, Bufford gave up. The thumb was nowhere to be found.

Now desperate to find the thumb, Bufford went back into the hotel kitchen and asked if anybody had seen a thumb, which drew puzzled looks from the workers. They were of no help, but finally, after a lengthy search, Bufford found it in the kitchen under a pile of syrup-soaked eggs, sausages, and pancakes. It was finally time to play some basketball.

Finding the thumb was supposed to be a much more difficult challenge than defeating the UCLA Bruins, who had ended the regular season at just 17–9 and had finished fourth in the Pac-10. But after grabbing a 14–12 lead, the Cardinals proceeded to miss their next eight shots from the field, along with missing three free throws and committing two turnovers. By halftime the Cardinals still trailed 28–26, and Crum was not about to let his team blow it for a second time.

"I told them it was a shame that they played so well getting there to the championship, that it was a shame they were playing the way they were playing, because UCLA was certainly not any better than we were," Crum said. "But we just weren't playing together and playing like we could, and that we needed to get everything in gear and do the right things and just play like you did all year."

But with less than four minutes to play, it was the Bruins who still led 54–50, and when UCLA senior Kiki Vandeweghe intercepted a pass at midcourt, it appeared as though the Bruins were about to deliver the final blow. Vandeweghe strode toward the Louisville basket with no one in his path, but just before he laid it in, he was caught by UL's Jerry Eaves, who got just enough of the ball to keep it from falling in the basket. Brown grabbed the rebound and fired it back to Eaves, who dropped in a 16-footer to cut the lead to 54–52 with 3:26 to go. Following another UCLA miss, Eaves raced down for a layup to tie the game at 54, which was followed moments later by a jumper from Griffith. His shot, which put Louisville up 56–54, turned out to be the game-winner, as his team held on for a 59–54 victory.

And for living up to just part of his promise, Griffith was about the most beloved person the city of Louisville had ever seen. ●

1981 Indiana

The 1981 tournament is considered one of the greatest in history—an incredible seven games would be won in the final seconds, a mark that has yet to be touched. Oregon State and DePaul, who entered the tournament with a combined 53–2 record, both lost their opening games at the buzzer. A 16-footer with two seconds left by Kansas State's Rolando Blackman eliminated the Beavers 50–48, while the Blue Demons lost 49–48 to St. Joe's on a John Smith layup with three seconds to play after DePaul had led for the entire second half. Northeastern defeated Fresno State 55–53 thanks to Chip Rucker's layup with four seconds left, while Pitt's Dwayne Wallace defeated Idaho 70–69 on a bank shot with three seconds left in overtime. The most impressive buzzer-beater of all came from Wichita State's Mike Jones, who defeated cross-state rival Kansas on a shot from well beyond NBA three-point range. It was worth only two points in college, but when it sank through with two seconds left, it sent the aptly named Shockers to the Elite Eight.

When Indiana coach Bob Knight first saw a young Isiah Thomas play, he knew right away he would have to do everything in his power to land the recruit—even if it meant venturing into one of Chicago's worst neighborhoods to visit the home of Thomas. The atmosphere inside the home was as rough as the streets outside, as Knight faced a berating from one of Thomas' nine older brothers. The coach did not want to cause a stir in front of the prized recruit, but one can only mess with Bob Knight for so long before there are consequences. Knight shouted right back at his newfound adversary as the scene quickly grew tense. Under most circumstances, a coach can kiss a recruiting opportunity goodbye with an altercation like that, but Knight's toughness made him an unexpected ally.

"You know it definitely was a unique thing," Thomas recalled, "the fact that Coach stood up for himself. How can I say, it uplifted him and the family and uplifted him definitely in my mom's eyes. I mean, they bonded in a way that was very unique."

And once Knight promised to bring that same demeanor and toughness to help Isiah get his college degree, mother Mary Thomas was sold.

"Sometimes when you're a gifted athlete as I was, you're allowed to kind of cut corners and do things that you can get away with. And I was lucky that I had my mom and coach

Knight, my dad and everybody else, who didn't let me take short cuts, didn't let me cut corners, and they had the courage to be confrontational with me and not let me get away with it," Thomas said.

The pair would have their share of fights during Isiah's freshman year, but by the start of the 1980–81 season, the Hoosiers looked prime to make a run deep in the tournament. *Sports Illustrated* listed IU seventh in the preseason rankings, but three losses in its first eight games sent a shock to the team. The Hoosiers traveled to Hawaii for a Christmas tournament, where they hoped to leave their slow start, as well as the cold weather, behind them. Instead, the Hoosiers lost a 58–57 heartbreaker against Clemson, and in the consolation game against lowly Texas-Pan American, they lost again to drop to 7–5. By the time their record fell to 10–7, Knight had just about reached his boiling point. With each accumulating loss, junior Landon Turner was receiving less and less playing time, to the point where he was entering games for one-minute stints.

"Oh yeah, we knew how close he was to not playing—that was made loud and clear," Thomas remembered. "But you know what you didn't understand was the internal growth and strife that Landon was having with himself."

The reality was that Turner was stuck in a cycle—the worse he played, the more he felt the blame for the disappointing season, which only further shrunk his confidence, resulting in even more disastrous performances. The situation came to a head on January 24 against Northwestern. Coming off two losses in Indiana's last three games, Turner continued with another lackluster performance against the Wildcats, resulting in a quick removal by Knight. It looked to be the last minutes of Turner's season, until later in the game Knight decided to give him one last chance to redeem himself. The junior found his game just in time, scoring nine points in his second appearance of the night to salvage his season.

"This is where great coaching comes in, because Coach Knight didn't give up on us," Thomas said. "It could have been very easy for him to say, 'Well, this team's not good enough, they're not going to make it.' I mean, our record was not that good going into the start of the Big Ten season. But he kept working and he kept pushing and he kept prodding and he kept tinkering and then he found the right mix, and once he found it and we became together, we became really good really fast."

Turner had failed to produce for much of the season but still had the courage to ask his teammates for more looks at the ball, and his teammates obliged. Their decision gave Turner the confidence he had been missing, and he rewarded their faith by helping the team win 11 of its last 13 games to qualify for the NCAA Tournament. The icing on the cake for the Hoosiers was that after a first-round win over Maryland, they would be playing their next two games on their home court.

"It was crazy, but crazy good....There's nothing like playing basketball at Indiana University," Thomas said. "The way the students are, the way the fans are, the way the community embraces you, there is nothing like it. It's an indescribable feeling the way Assembly Hall makes you feel."

In front of the home crowd, Thomas scored 27 points to lead the Hoosiers to a victory over UAB. With a Final Four appearance on the line against St. Joe's, Turner put in a masterpiece, making seven of his eight shots to help give IU a 78–46 win. The team now stood just two

wins away from a national championship, but its momentum was quickly halted as the LSU Tigers stormed out to a 30–27 halftime lead in their semifinal match. Instead of laying into his team as he usually would, Knight told his players to relax. The Hoosiers didn't need any adjustments—they already knew what needed to be done. Knight's steady attitude paid off as Indiana outscored the Tigers 40–19 over the final 20 minutes to earn a spot in the title game.

However, it was a game that almost was not played, as President Ronald Reagan was shot just hours before the contest. It was only 20 minutes before tip-off that the NCAA, after hearing reports that Reagan was in stable condition, decided that the game against North Carolina would go on as scheduled.

"We said our prayers for the President and we knew what the situation was, but the rest was out of our control," Thomas said. "The job at hand was to try and win a basketball game."

Thomas would shoot 1-of-7 in the first half as Indiana struggled to a 27–26 lead at halftime. Fortunately for Thomas, he recovered to drain 7 of his 10 shots in the second half as the Hoosiers started to pull away. Turner chipped in with 12 points of his own to give IU the 63–50 win and the national championship. It was the second title in just six years for the Hoosiers, but for Thomas it was a bittersweet moment.

"Even though we had won the championship game, that didn't change our living situation," Thomas said. "So yeah, you won the championship but you're still going back home and the situation was the lights were out and you didn't have a phone and there was no food in the house."

The situation for his family back in Chicago was getting desperate, so Thomas, a sophomore, applied for the NBA's financial-hardship rule and declared for the draft. It was not how Mary Thomas had envisioned her son ending his IU career, but it was a move that needed to be made. Years later, after 11 all-star appearances and an NBA title, Thomas finished the degree he had promised to his mother. Only now when he showed her the diploma, she didn't have to hang it up in a rundown house. ●

1982 North Carolina

It took 43 years, but finally the NCAA eliminated the useless third-place game, which had been detested almost universally by coaches and players. Fans would have plenty of other exciting basketball to watch in 1982, as top-seeded DePaul was eliminated in its opening game for the third consecutive year. This time it was Boston College that knocked off the Blue Demons, 82–75, thanks to 21 points from Michael Adams. Adams had averaged just 3.9 points a game and had never scored more than 13 points, but he and John Bagley scored 47 of BC's 82 points. The Eagles would eventually make it to the Elite Eight, but perhaps the biggest surprise of the tournament was the University of Alabama-Birmingham. The Blazers had played basketball for only four years, but took out defending champion Indiana in front of their own fans in Birmingham and then eliminated top-ranked Virginia 68–66.

As Dean Smith watched the final seconds tick away during the 1981 NCAA championship game, one had to wonder if a national title was ever meant to happen for the North Carolina coach. The 63–50 loss marked the sixth time in Smith's career that he had reached the sport's grandest stage—the Final Four—and returned to Chapel Hill empty-handed. Perhaps even more painful, three of those six losses had come in the national championship game. Some fans unfairly started questioning Smith's tactics and coaching ability, but perhaps the one thing Smith was better at than coaching was keeping things in perspective.

"Even if you lose both games in the Final Four, I think it's a compliment to your program," Smith said. "I think every program would like to be in the Final Four every year and never win it."

Fortunately, Smith's outlook was not limited to the coaching staff.

"I love the game, but there's a whole lot of worse problems in the world right now," senior Al Wood said after the 1981 loss. "I'm just thankful for the opportunity to play basketball.

And while Smith knew there was more to life than a championship, that hardly meant he didn't want a ring. Unfortunately, it appeared he would have to wait a few years before another opportunity came his way. Not only were few people picking the Tar Heels to win the tournament the following year, but few even believed the Tar Heels had what it took to win the ACC. Led by 7-foot-4 Ralph Sampson, it was the Virginia Cavaliers who were the front runner heading into the season. The Tar Heels had lost to Virginia in February, but a few weeks later point guard Jimmy Black called a players-only meeting in his dorm room to come up with a way to turn the season around. For Black and fellow senior Matt Doherty, this would be their last chance to get the monkey off their coach's back.

"As players I think if we had anything that motivated us, it was to win for him, because he had gotten there so many times and hadn't won it, and that was the only criticism people had of him," Doherty said. "And he realized how much luck goes into winning the national championship, so that was probably the biggest driving force for us, was to win it for coach Smith."

After the meeting, UNC swept through the rest of the regular season to finish with a 27–2 record and arrive back in the NCAA Tournament. And for the first time in Smith's tenure, his team was actually the favorite heading into the Big Dance. The tournament was custom-built for a Tar Heels championship, as all of their games leading up to the Final Four would be played in North Carolina.

But had it not been for some heroics, that dream would have been over before it really started. The team faced James Madison in the first round, a school that appeared to be little trouble for the Tar Heels, especially when Kyle Campanelli—son of JMU coach Lou

Campanelli—approached Smith before the game to ask for his autograph. But the Dukes came ready to play, and the longer the game went on, the more it appeared they were going to pull off the upset of the century. UNC got down by five in the first half, and they led only 47–46 in the last minute before James Worthy's three-point play put the game out of reach. It was only Worthy's second shot of the half, but it was a big one as the Tar Heels hung on for a 52–50 win. Perhaps the team's journey back to the Final Four would not be so easy after all.

"Sometimes it's a kiss of death," Doherty said of the expectations. "We almost lost the first game to James Madison. You play in those games, and you think we're playing at home, we're playing against a school that no one has ever heard of before, and it's going to be easy. And we end up sweating it out."

Smith's players were a little more prepared to play their next game, as all five starters scored in double figures to earn a 74–69 victory over Alabama. Next up was Villanova, with a chance to go to the Final Four on the line. This time North Carolina left little room for doubt, shooting 15-for-20 in the second half en route to a 70–60 win. Smith, who graduated nearly all of his players during his career, made the team attend classes during the tournament run, which was quite all right with them.

"Actually it was fun to go to class," Doherty said, "because you get people patting you on the back. So we definitely went to class, no question."

As if they hadn't set the bar high enough already, the Tar Heels dropped the hammer from the moment they arrived at the Final Four. Before the University of Houston knew what hit them, North Carolina had torched them for 7-of-9 shooting to gain an early 14–0 lead. Larry Micheaux pulled the Cougars back, tying the game at 29 just before halftime, but some more clutch play from the Tar Heels gave them a final margin of 68–63.

Once again, Smith was in the championship game. He was going to have to earn it against the Georgetown Hoyas, one of the most talented teams ever to play the game, but thanks to a last-minute shot by a little-known freshman named Michael Jordan, the Tar Heels won 63–62 (see page 288). At long last, Smith had his national championship. The always modest Smith claimed he was no better of a coach after the game than he was three hours before, and he may have had a point. It's hard to improve upon perfection.

"I agree totally," said Doherty, who took over the program three years after Smith's retirement. "Some of the best coaches I know never won a national championship. All it does is validate his greatness in the eyes of the public, but anybody who knows basketball and anybody who played for him or worked with him knew he was one of the best coaches in all of team sports."

No matter what the win did for Smith's legacy, it sure felt good. For the first time in 35 years, the trophy was back in Chapel Hill. ●

It took 21 years, but in his seventh trip to the Final Four, Dean Smith finally had his first national championship.
Heinz Kluetmeier/Sports Illustrated/ Getty Images

1983 N.C. State

The nail-biting conclusion of the 1983 tournament will never be forgotten, and fans were treated to plenty of other thrills along the way. With his team trailing Chattanooga 51–50 in the final moments of its opening-round game, Maryland coach Lefty Driesell drew up a play for star Adrian Branch to take the final shot. The plan fell apart on the court, but Len Bias hit a 17-foot jumper with two seconds to go for the victory. In Purdue's 55–53 victory over Robert Morris, Steve Reid emerged as the hero when his 22-footer went in with five seconds to go, but RMU's Forrest Griffin nearly stole the show when his halfcourt shot bounced off the back of the rim. The tournament was also noteworthy because it marked Louisville's emergence as arguably the premier program in the state of Kentucky, at least for the time being. Thanks to a Scooter McCray tip-in with a second left, the Cardinals beat Arkansas 65–63 to advance to the Elite Eight, where they met Kentucky for the first time in 24 years. UL emerged with an 80–68 victory in overtime, but the Wildcats would get their revenge a year later by knocking them out in the Sweet 16.

Before Jim Valvano could ever set his eyes on a national championship, his first priority at N.C. State was merely to keep his team together. When Valvano arrived in Raleigh in 1980, he inherited a group of young men who were there to play for Norm Sloan, the architect of one undefeated season at N.C. State and champion in another. Convincing the players not to transfer would not be an easy task, one that only became tougher when Valvano's team went just 14–13 in his first year, far from the 20–8 mark set a year earlier by Sloan. The Wolfpack failed even to qualify for the NIT that year, but Valvano had a vision that was simply too vivid for his players to walk away from.

"When Jim Valvano became our coach, he made it clear to that particular team that year that his goal was to win a national championship," recalled Thurl Bailey, a sophomore on the 1981 team. "As a matter of fact, he was pretty emphatic about the fact he knew he was going to win one. And he didn't say this year, but he said, 'I'm going to win a national championship—I know it, I've dreamt about it.' His goal was to help us to visualize what he had dreamt about and for us to add to that masterpiece, so to speak, that picture he was starting to paint in his mind."

That vision seemed to be right on schedule by Valvano's third season, when N.C. State started 7–1—but as the year wore on that dream began to turn into a nightmare. The Wolfpack dropped their next two games, and in their following contest against Virginia, the team lost one of its leaders. Senior Dereck Whittenburg, who had scored 27 points in the first half to give the Wolfpack a 50–34 lead, broke the same foot he had injured in high school. Whittenburg initially feared his career might be over, and when his foot snapped, so did the aspirations of a championship.

"All of us, when it happened, our first thought was we could write our season off, because when you lose a player like that, as important as Derrick was to us at that time, that's the first thing that comes to mind. We've just lost a huge piece of the puzzle that we need to get to that next level," Bailey said. "At the time, I mean, it's just total devastation because you wonder, well, how can we achieve what we set out to achieve when all of a sudden we get this moment that could possibly take us out of it?"

Without Whittenburg in the lineup, N.C. State went just 9–7, including a 2–6 stretch that included a loss to unranked Wake Forest by 18 points.

"Coach V would test us quite a bit," Bailey said with a smile. "He would come in and say things like 'You know, maybe we could win the NIT' just to tick us off and see how we would react."

Whittenburg managed to return for the regular-season finale and help the Wolfpack avenge their earlier loss to Wake Forest with a 41-point victory, but it was hardly enough to save their season. If the Wolfpack wanted to guarantee themselves a spot in the Big Dance, they were going to have to win the ACC Tournament. Their first assignment? A highly motivated and freshly wounded Wake Forest team.

This time, the Demon Deacons played more like the team that had won the opening contest back in January, as they grabbed a 70–68 lead late in the second half. N.C. State point guard Sidney Lowe hit a pair of free throws to tie the game with 4:20 to play, but Wake Forest decided to stall the game and play for the final shot. The Deacons managed to take nearly four minutes off the clock, but with just 20 seconds to play Lowe turned the table by stealing the ball. The Wolfpack called timeout to set up a final play, and when Lorenzo Charles went up for the game-winning layup with three seconds

to go, he was fouled—leaving the fate of N.C. State's season to be decided by his free throws. His first shot rimmed out, but on his second attempt, Charles sank the free throw to put the Wolfpack in the ACC semifinals.

Their journey appeared to come to an end a night later against North Carolina, but again the Wolfpack refused to give in. Trailing 82–76 with just two minutes to play in overtime, Whittenburg scored 11 of the team's final 15 points as they closed the game on a 15–2 run. That 91–84 victory set the Wolfpack up for an ACC title clash against Virginia and three-time National Player of the Year Ralph Sampson. N.C. State would score 12 of the first 13 points, but the Cavaliers stormed back to claim a 59–51 lead in the second half. By this point in the season, however, N.C. State had a date with destiny. Bailey hit a jumper to cut the lead to six, and Lowe added a three-pointer to bring the Pack to within 59–56.

Although the Cavaliers answered back with a shot of their own, N.C. State kept right on going. Terry Gannon drained a three-pointer to cut the lead to just 61–59, and when Bailey hit another three-pointer with 7:02 left, the Wolfpack had finally grabbed the lead back at 67–65. They would extend the lead to 75–66 with just 4:20 to go before the Cavaliers would mount a comeback of their own to cut the deficit to 79–78 in the final minute. They eventually fouled Whittenburg to try and grab the ball back, but with six seconds to go the senior nailed both free throws, sealing his team's 81–78 victory. Against all odds, the Wolfpack had found their way into the NCAA Tournament after all. But as strenuous as their journey to the tournament had been, the drama was only beginning. ●

If the N.C. State Wolfpack felt on top of the world after their last-second victory over Virginia in the Elite Eight, they were in for quite a surprise. *North Carolina State Athletic Department. Photograph by Clayton Brinkley*

1984 Georgetown

In its first season without three-time Player of the Year Ralph Sampson, seventh-seeded Virginia managed to make the Final Four anyway. Along the way, the Cavaliers provided fans with plenty of entertainment. They won their opening game 58–57 over Iona thanks to an Othell Wilson runner with five seconds left, and upset Arkansas 53–51 in their next game on Rick Carlisle's shot with four seconds to go. They squeaked by Indiana 50–48 before ultimately losing to "Phi Slama Jama"—Houston's dynamic squad featuring future Hall of Famers Clyde Drexler and Hakeem Olajuwon. Olajuwon sent the game into overtime with a game-saving block and then made another block in the final moments of the extra session to preserve Houston's 49–47 lead. One of the tournament's most exciting games, however, came from a different Virginia school. Trailing Northeastern 69–68 with just two seconds to play, Virginia Commonwealth inbounded the ball to Rolando Lamb, who drained a turnaround shot as time expired to send the Rams to the second round.

Of all the perks that come with winning a national championship, coaches quickly learn that the biggest benefit comes in the months ahead. When they go on recruiting visits wearing a freshly polished championship ring, it's rather hard for a recruit to say no. But for Georgetown coach John Thompson, losing the 1982 national championship game in heartbreaking fashion was the best thing that ever happened to his recruiting ability. Millions of people watched that night as sophomore Fred Brown had a lapse in judgment and accidentally tossed the ball to the wrong team in the final seconds, effectively eliminating the Hoyas' chances of winning a championship. Thompson, instead of chastising the young man for his error, engulfed him in a bear hug. The image was not lost on Reggie Williams or Horace Broadnax, both of whom signed up to play for Thompson.

"That all played a big picture in me deciding Georgetown at the last minute, because I mean you've seen the moment with coach Thompson and Fred Brown," Broadnax said. "It was just an indelible mark that was on my father's mind and my mind."

With both Williams and Broadnax in the lineup in 1984, the Hoyas instantly improved and set their eyes on the school's first national championship. It would also be Brown's senior year and last chance to avenge the mistake that was burned into his memory. The Hoyas

looked to be the sentimental favorite to bring the title home, but when Thompson added freshman Michael Graham to the lineup, the team instantly lost its connection with most of the country. Graham's aggressive play helped popularize the phrase "Hoya Paranoia," a phrase that branded the players as thugs. For a team comprised entirely of African Americans, the label bordered on racism, but the players hardly seemed bothered.

"I think the brilliance of coach Thompson was that he didn't allow it to distract us from what we were trying to accomplish on the basketball court and in the classroom, so I think he used a lot of that," Broadnax said. "He looked at it and said let me use this as an opportunity to motivate these players to play at a high level."

Instead of taking their frustrations out on the media, the Hoyas let their play do all the talking as they ran out to a 29–3 regular-season record. Win No. 30 would not be so easy, however, as the Hoyas took on ninth-seeded SMU in their tournament opener. Georgetown got an early impression of what the game would be like when SMU's John Koncak dunked right over Georgetown's All-American center, Patrick Ewing. The vastly inferior Mustangs knew their best chance to win would be to work the clock and only shoot when a clean look presented itself. The plan worked beyond their best hopes, and when the first half came to a close SMU enjoyed an eight-point lead.

The Hoyas, who preferred to score 80 points a game, had been held to 16 points. They turned the tide on the Mustangs in the second half, yielding just one basket through the first 13:48, but after the Hoyas grabbed a 32–26 lead Thompson inexplicably brought the game to a halt. Instead of trying to pad the lead, Thompson instructed his players to run out the clock, a decision that backfired severely. Junior Larry Davis sank a trio of shots to go along with a shot by Koncak, and with 2:46 to play the game was knotted once again at 34–34.

"I was surprised. We played like that all year, and to come into the tournament and change our persona was a little different," Williams said. "So it was more like a chess game—you're going back and forth, back and forth."

The Hoyas would get their chance to retake the lead when Gene Smith stepped to the foul line with 51 seconds left, but before he fired away Ewing decided to switch spots in the lane. The center usually lined up on the low block, but during a discussion with Thompson he concluded that a position change could catch SMU off guard. And when Ewing tipped in Smith's missed free throw moments later, he had become a visionary.

"That's the type of individual that he is, a competitive individual trying to create an edge, and I think that coach Thompson sensed that," Broadnax said. "And sometimes that's what coaches do. They have a sixth sense to say if you feel strongly about that, then go with it."

The Hoyas would go on to escape with a 37–36 victory, and after victories over UNLV and Dayton they were back in the Final Four. Meeting them in the semifinals would be Kentucky, a popular pick to win the tournament. And after grabbing a 29–22 lead at halftime, the Wildcats gave no reason to think otherwise.

"The media had basically given Kentucky the championship," Broadnax said. "We realized that they were an excellent basketball team but not a team that couldn't be overcome, and that's where our momentum in the second half and our energy level went to a whole new level."

With a renewed sense of purpose, the Hoyas relentlessly harassed the UK offense, and for 13 minutes they held Kentucky without a point. The Wildcats struggled even to get shots off against Georgetown's press, and by the time UK broke the spell the Hoyas were well on their way to a blowout victory.

"We were determined to shut them down," Williams said of the defense. "They got caught up in it, and they couldn't do anything."

The only team that stood between them and the title was the Houston Cougars, who were looking for a bit of redemption of their own after losing the 1983 title game. Houston came out hitting its first seven shots, but the Hoyas had come too far to end the dream now. They proceeded to shoot 55 percent from the floor, and by the final minute Georgetown had taken a commanding 72–65 lead. Thompson called for Brown to come out of the game, and he received a standing ovation from the fans. Once again, Thompson gave his player a huge hug. Only this time, Brown was a national champion. ●

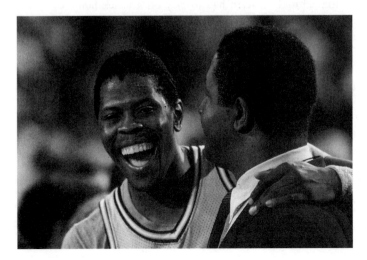

Patrick Ewing is all smiles as he and coach John Thompson celebrate their victory over Houston. *Rich Clarkson/Sports Illustrated/ Getty Images*

1985 Villanova

The tournament expanded once again in 1985, but the new 64-team field lasted for the next 25 years. Instead of a first-round bye, the top four seeds in each region now had to play like everyone else, and it didn't take long for the new rule to claim its first upset victim, as thirteenth-seeded Navy toppled LSU 78–55. The tournament just got better from there. North Carolina used a late steal and Kenny Smith dunk to defeat Notre Dame 60-58 in the second round, and a day later Memphis guard Andre Turner buried a shot with six seconds left to defeat Alabama-Birmingham 67–66 in overtime. He followed it up by winning their next game against Boston College on a 17-footer in the closing seconds, officially putting an end to the nickname his critics had given him—Andre Turnover.

While every team in the country dreams of making the NCAA Tournament at the start of the season, that hope often fades as losses accumulate. In late January, the Villanova Wildcats were still clinging on to their dream of competing in the Big Dance after earning a 13–3 record against tough competition. But within a matter of weeks, the entire season unraveled before their eyes, as five losses in seven games posed a serious threat to their tournament chances. Three straight wins gave the Wildcats a chance possibly to save their season if they could beat Pitt in the regular-season finale.

"We really needed that game, we felt, in order to go to the NCAA Tournament. That was an important game for us, that was a nationally televised CBS game," Villanova coach Rollie Massimino said. "And what happened was we were down 15 at halftime. I told the players, 'You got five minutes to play, and if you don't play you're all coming out whether it means us going to the NCAA Tournament or not.' And what happened was we didn't play, and I took them all out and put the second team in and we got beat by 23."

That loss dropped Villanova's record to 18–9, which seemed to be one loss too many.

"We didn't think we were getting in, we honestly did not," senior Ed Pinckney said. "We had gotten our twentieth win in the Big East tournament, and typically 20 wins may or may not get you in."

Luckily for the Wildcats, that season also marked the first time the NCAA was expanding the tournament to 64 teams, a decision that still gave Villanova a glimmer of hope. The Wildcats waited anxiously on Selection Sunday as they saw other names pop up on the screen. And when "Villanova" flashed across the television, the players acted like they had just won the lottery. What they had really been given was a second chance.

"We all decided, look, we've got to really focus on what we're doing," Pinckney said. "I think we had parts of the season that became successful when we would focus in, but we weren't truly 100 percent focused in until we got blown out by Pitt. That was an eye-opener for us."

The Wildcats didn't get much of a chance to refocus, as a few days later they would be taking on the Dayton Flyers—at Dayton's arena.

"I can't think of another time when another team had to play on a team's home court in the tournament—it just doesn't happen very often," Pinckney said. "We know it's going to be tough, but we have a chance, and in every game we felt that way. We just have been down that road so many times in terms of difficult situations, it didn't faze us. In fact, if you talk to other guys, there were times when we were actually having fun on the court."

The game may not have been as fun when the score was tied and Dayton was holding the ball for the last shot, but junior Harold Pressley knocked the ball away to give Villanova the final possession. Guard Harold Jensen also tried to run the clock down, but when a crease opened up in the Flyers defense with 1:15

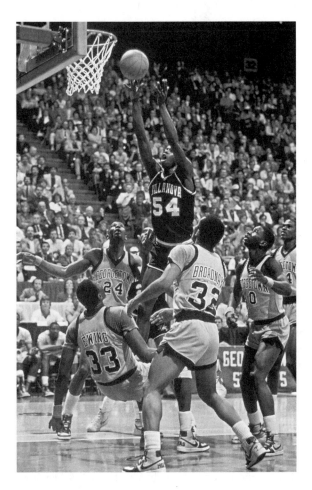

Ed Pinckney takes a shot amidst a swarm of Georgetown defenders, with Patrick Ewing falling to the floor under the basket. *Carl Skalak/Sports Illustrated/Getty Images*

have never been on the same mindset as four other guys when you're playing on the court as we were then."

By this point in their season, Pinckney, Jensen, Pressley, and twins Dwayne and Gary McClain could communicate on the court without even verbalizing anything. One glance of eye contact was all they needed, and against heavily favored North Carolina the Wildcats put their relationship to good use as they rolled to the 56–44 victory. The team that wasn't supposed to make the tournament was now in the Final Four.

Accompanying the team would be Jake Nevin, Villanova's long-time athletic trainer who months before had fallen victim to Lou Gehrig's Disease. Having worked for the university since 1929, Nevin was as much a part of Villanova basketball as any player or coach in the school's history. But after 56 years on the job, these would be Nevin's final two games, and the team wanted to make sure they sent him off with a bang.

Things got off to a good start as Villanova defeated Memphis State to reach the championship game. But standing in the way was Georgetown, a team considered by nearly everybody to be unbeatable. The Wildcats had tried and failed twice during the regular season, but on one magical night in 1985, they pulled off the biggest upset in championship history to give the program, and Nevin, their first national title (see page 320).

"It was obviously a very important moment in my athletic career," Massimino remembered. "It was something that was very special not only for me but for the university, the fans, all the other athletes at Villanova, and it was something that we could all celebrate as a family."

But now they were more than just family. They were champions. ●

to play, Jensen broke for the basket and gave Villanova a 51–49 lead. After another defensive stop, the Wildcats were heading to the second round. Unfortunately, their opponent would be Michigan, winner of 17 straight games.

But once again, the Wildcats willed themselves to the victory, holding the Wolverines to their lowest point total of the season. The 59–55 shocker sent the team to the Sweet 16 to face Maryland. Yet again, Villanova would not be denied, as they pulled out a 46–43 win over the Terrapins.

"I think this is pretty indicative of any senior class in the NCAA Tournament—I mean, you want to leave your mark. You want to feel as though the guys came and did something special," Pinckney said. "When it's your last go-around, you want things to go around in the best fashion. And we had everything go our way. It's just unbelievable. I have never— I've played 12 years of NBA basketball—I

1986 Louisville

The first 47 years of the NCAA Tournament had been nothing short of great, but March Madness truly came alive in 1986. Not only did a 14 seed win for the first time, but the 1986 tournament produced two of them. Arkansas-Little Rock upset Notre Dame 90–83, and Cleveland State did one better, shocking Indiana and then defeating St Joseph's to advance to the Sweet 16. Twelfth seeded DePaul also made the Sweet 16, and David Robinson led seventh-seeded Navy to the Elite Eight, but there was no bigger Cinderella story than LSU. After a 10–0 start to the season, the Tigers dropped 11 of their final 19 games to limp into the tournament as an 11 seed. But thanks to Anthony Wilson's last-second putback to beat Memphis State and Ricky Blanton's layup with 17 seconds left to beat Kentucky, the Tigers became the first 11 seed to advance to the Final Four.

If there was one thing Louisville coach Denny Crum was known for, it was his bravery. Concerned less about his regular-season record than how his teams were performing in March, Crum would run his teams through the gauntlet during the regular season. The Cardinals often sacrificed a few wins along the way, but three trips to the Final Four in just four years more than proved his theory correct. But in the 1985–86 season, Crum's peers started to wonder if he had even taken it a little too far. After scheduling what seemed to be every top team for their out-of-conference schedule, the Cardinals stood at just 11–6.

"If you look at the numbers, we were a very mediocre team right around Christmas and New Year's," senior Jeff Hall said. "I know some people made some comments, along with myself, after we played N.C. State in Raleigh. They beat us on national TV, and there were basically some words said after the game in a team meeting that some people have to get their acts together or we are going to have a very mediocre year."

Crum knew his team would have to be nearly perfect just to steal one of the tournament's final bids, and his team responded by winning 15 of its last 16 games to make the tournament. A win over Memphis in the conference tournament gave the Cardinals an automatic berth, but they were hardly a favorite to return to the Final Four. Of course, history said otherwise.

"By the time we go into the tournament, we already had seven losses on the season, which, when you have that many losses, you know usually you're not good enough to win, but our team just got better and better," Crum said. "Their attitude and the effort that they gave, we just kept working on the fundamentals and the things that we thought we needed to be able to do to win, and they just got better and better at it."

But early in the tournament, it appeared as though the Cardinals were regressing when they found themselves tied at 42–42 against fifteenth-seeded Drexel in the first round. Louisville recovered to pull away, but two nights later Crum's squad was tied once again at 59–59 against Bradley. The Cardinals would pull out that victory as well, and in their following game against North Carolina, they were determined not to be plagued by another slow start. They raced out to a 59–47 lead, only to have the Tar Heels pull in front 74–73 with 4:31 to play. Some clutch free throw shooting helped UL escape, but even after defeating Auburn 84–76 to advance to the Final Four, they knew they had plenty of room for improvement. For a team that had just won its nineteenth game in 20 tries, the plane ride back home felt awfully somber.

"We had won the regional," Crum recalled, "and I was sitting there reading, I was on the aisle, and I noticed there was somebody set down on the aisle right next to me, actually just kneeled down, and it was Herbert Crook. And he came up and said, 'Coach, I owe you an apology.' And I said, 'For what, Herbert?' And he said, 'For my play. I played like a dog, but I want you to know the real Herb Crook will step up and you'll like the way I play the rest of this tournament.' And he did."

Along with Billy Thompson, who sank 10 of his 11 shots, Crook shot 8-of-13 from the field to give UL an 88–77 victory over LSU. Their reward was the Duke Blue Devils, who had won 21 games in a row and 37 for the year, which had broken the single-season NCAA record. For Crum, it was just another opportunity to shock the world.

"I can just tell you those kids were really tough mentally, all of them were. They just didn't think that there was anything that they couldn't accomplish," Crum said. "They just felt like they could do anything they wanted to do and that they would be successful at it, and I think that they had a lot of trust and confidence in me. And I had the same amount in them."

Beating the Blue Devils, however, wouldn't be so simple, as they were led by Johnny Dawkins, a two-time All-American who would

be playing in his last game. From the opening minutes, Dawkins made it clear it was a game he did not intend to lose, as he started 5-of-6 from the field to give Duke a 15–8 lead. By halftime, Dawkins had already tallied 20 points, and Crum was livid. Just minutes into the second half, Milt Wagner, who had been guarding Dawkins, picked up his fourth foul. While Crum brainstormed for the proper substitute, Hall was relishing the chance of facing Dawkins. Besides, how much worse could he do?

"All of a sudden, during a timeout, I guess, Crum and the assistant coaches got together and said, 'Hey, put Jeff on him. What's it going to hurt?'" recalled Hall. "'He's burned everybody else up, so let's see if Jeff's drive and determination can maybe be a factor on him.'"

The senior responded by holding Dawkins without a field goal for the rest of the game. The Cardinals stormed back from a 61–55 deficit to pull ahead 64–63 with just 3:20 remaining. The lead was still just one point when UL had the ball with a minute to go, needing a basket to clinch the game. With no three-point line in effect, the Cardinals knew that a shot would likely give them the championship. But the Blue Devils, playing with a sense of urgency, prevented any looks inside the basket, forcing Hall to put up a desperation shot just seconds before the shot clock expired. The ball failed to hit the rim, but it landed mercifully in the hands of freshman Pervis Ellison, who put it back just as the shot clock hit zero.

"It wasn't a pass. I used to joke around about it and say it was a pass, not a shot," laughed Hall. "But to be truthful, it was a shot and it ended up being short, but with Pervis being there and able to get it and lay it in, it ended up being the best air ball I ever shot."

One minute later, the Cardinals were national champions, and Crum now had a new reputation. He wasn't just the bravest coach in the country, he was also the best. ●

With his 25-point performance against Duke, "Never Nervous" Pervis Ellison became the first freshman ever to win Most Outstanding Player honors. *Manny Millan/Sports Illustrated/ Getty Images*

1987 Indiana

The 1987 tournament gave fans everything they could ask for and more. Not only would sixth-seeded Providence emerge as a Cinderella, but there was no shortage of upsets or buzzer-beaters. The Friars, coached by one future legend in Rick Pitino and led by another in point guard Billy Donovan, opened their tournament by playing on UAB's home court, but they won that game 90–68 to face Austin Peay in the second round. The fourteenth-seeded Governors were supposed to be blown away by Illinois in the opening round, but Tony Raye hit a pair of free throws with two seconds left to upset the Illini 68–67. No one was more surprised than Dick Vitale—who had promised to stand on his head during ESPN's tournament coverage if the Governors won. He fulfilled his promise, and it appeared that Austin Peay was on its way to the Sweet 16 when Providence trailed 75–65 with less than six minutes to play. But the Friars stormed back as Donovan hit a late jumper to force overtime. They prevailed 90–87, and their run wouldn't end until the Final Four.

The 1987 Indiana Hoosiers could hardly be considered an underdog. Not only was the No. 1 seed gunning for its fifth title, the NCAA had just implemented the three-point line—perfectly suited for long-range shooter Steve Alford. Alford, like nearly every other young man recruited by Bob Knight, had been a superstar in high school. For Keith Smart, however, such was not the case.

As a 5-foot-3 guard entering high school, Smart was nowhere near Indiana's recruiting radar. After little physical growth playing on the freshman and JV squads, Smart tried out for the varsity team, and he was promptly cut. By the time Smart was a senior, he grew to 5-foot-6 and made the team, only to break his wrist in the third game of the year.

"That was the end of my high school career," said Smart, who struggled to regain his shooting touch for months. "Once the season started in high school, once my casts came off and I'm ready to go play basketball, well, I couldn't play. All my friends were on the team, so I couldn't play anywhere."

The solution came in the form of Lester Roberts, a local youth center director, who recommended junior college to the frustrated athlete. He might be able to land a scholarship, Roberts told Smart, but only after a year of paying through school as a regular student. Nevertheless, Smart took the risk and moved out to Garden City Community College in Kansas, joining the intramural basketball team to stay in shape as he waited to become eligible. But just as things seemed to be heading in the right direction, disaster struck again.

"I got a motorcycle for graduation from high school, and then I got into an accident, so I broke my wrist again," Smart said. "I fell off the bike, broke my wrist, and separated my shoulder—it was really banged up a little bit."

Smart was just lucky to survive, but he managed to make a full recovery and land a spot on the JC team. He was still no closer to becoming a Hoosier, however, and it was only by pure luck that Smart had a chance to make an impression on the Indiana staff. Assistant coach Jodi Wright traveled from Bloomington—not to see Smart but to watch the opposing team, which featured two future Hoosiers in Todd Jadlow and Andre Harris. On this particular night, Smart decided to have the game of his life, scoring 34 points and grabbing 12 rebounds to catch the eye of Wright. Even that performance was almost too pedestrian to persuade head coach Bobby Knight, who had never taken a junior college transfer, but Knight ignored his gut instinct and gave him a chance. The move paid off, as Smart helped the Hoosiers earn a top seed for the 1987 tournament.

Their dream of a championship almost vanished at Cincinnati's Riverfront Coliseum, where the Hoosiers found themselves in a battle with LSU. The Tigers shot 59 percent in the first half and just continued to torch the nets as the second half began. LSU was enjoying a 59–51 lead when IU forward Ricky Calloway, who had already hurt his knee earlier in the season, aggravated the injury, forcing him to leave the floor. Calloway eventually found the strength to come back, only to find the doors to the court locked. After pounding on the door, he eventually found his way back on the court, just in time to miss a dunk. And with IU already down nine and less than five minutes to play, things did not look good.

"I don't remember any panic," senior Steve Alford said. "We had done a good job of making plays in the last five minutes all year long, and that was another game where we made more plays than our opponent the last five minutes."

Indiana held the Tigers without a field goal for the final stretch, but even after Smart hit two free throws with 30 seconds to go, the Hoosiers still trailed 76–75. They decided to foul LSU's Fess Irvin, who, despite being an 80 percent free throw shooter, was just a freshman. Irvin could not have picked a more inopportune time to miss a free throw, as Indiana's Darryl Thomas quickly snatched the rebound and drove to the lane. With six seconds to go, Thomas tossed up a floater that landed short of the rim, but Calloway rose up for the rebound and dunked it in just moments before the buzzer to give the Hoosiers a 77–76 victory.

After upsetting UNLV, the top-ranked team in the country, the Hoosiers found themselves paired against Syracuse in the national championship game. In one of the most thrilling games in NCAA history, Smart hit a shot just before the buzzer to win the title (see page 344). For a player who used to be too afraid to even have the ball in his hands, much less take a potential game-winning shot, Smart had come a long way.

"When you come out of a situation in Baton Rouge where you weren't supposed to make it, so to speak, all of a sudden you're not sure about who you are," Smart said. "Everyone practiced every day and night and wants to make a championship-winning shot. And here you were, the guy that actually did it—you made a shot to win the national championship game. Not a game, but *the* game."

The win was also extra special for Alford, whose seven three-pointers helped give Knight his third national championship. After letting his players celebrate, Knight waved Alford over, and the normally tough coach said that he had never been prouder of a player.

"It means a great deal. That is why he is a mentor of mine and a dear friend," Alford said. "It was a very special time and just a dream come true that I got to play for him."

As for Smart, who had watched from the bleachers as his high school team won the state title, he now had a championship of his own. Smart may still have been the smallest guy on the court, but for the moment he was on top of the world. ●

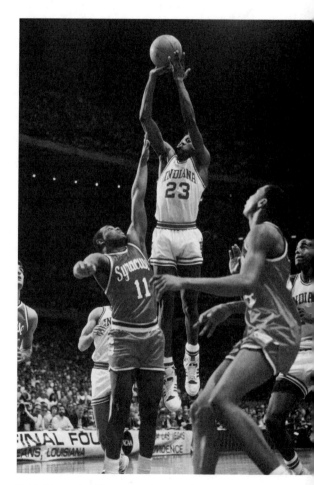

Keith Smart, seen here shooting over Greg Monroe, became just the fourth player in history to win the national championship with a last-second shot. *Rich Clarkson/Sports Illustrated/ Getty Images*

1988 Kansas

It didn't take fans long to realize that the 1988 tournament would be a special one. Not only was defending champion Indiana defeated in its opening game, runner-up Syracuse was eliminated one round later. Richmond eliminated Indiana and Rhode Island eliminated Syracuse, and both advanced to the Sweet 16. One former champion who did find success was Mark Plansky, the last remnant of Villanova's 1985 championship team. With his team trailing Illinois 60–53 with less than two minutes remaining of their second-round matchup, Plansky hit a three-pointer to bring the Wildcats within four, and his free throws with four seconds left won the game. The tournament concluded on an equally memorable note, as it marked the final time two teams from the same conference—Kansas and Oklahoma—played for the championship.

Since their first national title in 1952, the University of Kansas had maintained its tradition as one of the premier programs in college basketball. The school that was home to the father of the sport, James Naismith, had made it back to the Final Four a total of five times in that span, but heading into the 1988 season Kansas still held just one NCAA basketball championship. Few were more aware of KU's tournament disappointments than Danny Manning, a Lawrence native who was also a senior on the 1988 squad.

The pieces were in place for a run to the title in Manning's final year, but by Christmas it appeared that fans would have to wait at least another season to see championship No. 2. Kansas suffered a slew of injuries, which was naturally followed by a slew of losses. KU coach Larry Brown juggled the starting lineup as the injuries accumulated, and by season's end he had gone through 13 different lineups, including one stint in which he was forced to bring in two members from the football team. But little that Brown tried seemed to work, as Kansas stumbled to a record of 12–8. The Jayhawks had lost five of six games, and unless something changed soon, they would fail to even land a spot in the NIT. What they needed was a miracle. Luckily for them, that's exactly what they got.

Led by Manning, the Jayhawks rallied to win nine of their last 11 games to earn an NCAA Tournament bid. A first-round win over Xavier gave the team a second-round bout against Murray State. That is when the miracle really began to kick in. After trailing by five at halftime, the Racers rallied to take a lead late in the second half. Manning, determined that this would not be his final game in a KU uniform, put the team on his back. He scored 8 of their final 10 points, and his hook shot with 38 seconds left gave Kansas a 59–58 lead. When MSU's Don Mann missed a hook shot at the other end, Manning was there for the rebound, and his ensuing free throws gave the Jayhawks a 61–58 lead, one they would hold until the final buzzer.

By this point, the term "Danny and the Miracles" was well underway. Manning would follow his 25-point performance against the Racers with 38 against Vanderbilt to put the Jayhawks into the Elite Eight. The only problem now was that the three teams standing in their way—Kansas State, Duke, and Oklahoma—also happened to be the last three teams to beat the Jayhawks.

The in-state rivals had played a total of 213 times in their history, but none would be bigger than this. With a spot in the Final Four on the line, Kansas State gave one of its best performances of the season, shooting 55 percent in the first half and holding a seven-point advantage early in the second period. That lead would only be temporary, however, as Kansas reeled in the Wildcats to get within 42–41, and after a pair of steals the lead was back in the hands of KU, 45–44. The Jayhawks would ride away with a 71–58 win to land a spot in the Final Four, which was to be hosted in Kansas City.

Using the crowd to their advantage, Kansas blew right out of the gate against Duke, taking a 14–0 lead before the Blue Devils even knew what hit them. But only six weeks prior, Duke had stormed back from an early 23–8 deficit to defeat the Jayhawks in Lawrence, and this time they still had more than 35 minutes to make up the difference. A 55 percent shooting performance by the Jayhawks in the first half prevented any quick comeback, and after Manning sank a pair of shots early in the second period, the lead was up to 46–28. The gap was still 49–33 when the Blue Devils came alive. They went on an 8–0 run to cut the lead in half, and they continued to chip away at the gap, as Quin Snyder's shot with 2:20 remaining put the Blue Devils to within 57–54. But once again Manning was there for the rescue, as his putback moments later, for his twenty-fifth point of the night, sealed the deal once more. The only team remaining between them and the title was Oklahoma, the top-scoring team in the country with 103.4 points per game.

Before tip-off, Brown brought his starters together. "Guys, we know Oklahoma loves to run," he said. "We can't get caught up in that. If we do, we're going to lose."

Brown walked away moments later, giving Manning time to counter. "Forget that crap," Manning said. "Let's run and show them we're not afraid of them."

Manning kept up his end of the bargain, scoring 14 first-half points as the Jayhawks traded punch for punch. By halftime, the score was 50–50, and neither team looked willing to budge. In a game that featured 10 ties and 13 lead changes, the score was still tied at 71 with less than six minutes left before Kansas found some breathing room at 77–71 with two minutes to go. The Sooners, who were 35–3, were not done quite yet. They cut the lead to 78–75 with 58 seconds to go, and after KU missed a free throw, Oklahoma came back to score again on a Mookie Blaylock jumper with 40 seconds remaining.

Now with the lead down to 78–77, the Sooners took their time to commit the right foul, sending Scooter Barry to the free throw line with 16 ticks on the clock. He swished the first attempt, but just as the Sooners hoped, he missed the second. With a rebound, Oklahoma could have a chance to win the game or send it into overtime. But Manning's miracles were not over yet, as he dove for the rebound, an effort that drew another Oklahoma foul call. He would make the most of his opportunity, nailing both shots to put the game out of reach. A few seconds later, when the final horn sounded, the Jayhawks' 36 years of frustration were finally over. ●

Danny Manning's free throws with just four seconds left secured KU's first national title since the Truman administration. *Manny Millan/Sports Illustrated/Getty Images*

1989 Michigan

For the first time in regular-season history, the team atop the national rankings changed for five consecutive weeks. That unpredictability was a sign of things to come in the 1989 NCAA Tournament. In their opening-round games, both Georgetown and Oklahoma nearly became the first teams to lose to a 16 seed, and the Sooners needed a Mookie Blaylock layup with 1:21 left to escape with a 72–71 victory over East Tennessee State. Fellow No. 1 seed Arizona lost its third-round game to UNLV when Anderson Hunt buried a three-pointer with two seconds to play. Three of the four 11 seeds would win their opening-round games, including Evansville. The Aces upset Oregon State 94–90 in overtime, thanks to Reed Crafton's three-pointer in the final seconds. The 11 seeds were not the only party crashers, as DePaul (12), Middle Tennessee State (13), and Siena (14) all made the second round.

Just two days before his team was set to embark on the 1989 NCAA Tournament, Michigan coach Bill Frieder delivered an announcement that appeared to be as cruel as it was untimely. Not only would Frieder be leaving the program to coach at sunny Arizona State the following season, but he had the nerve to mention that he would coach the Wolverines for the remainder of the year. The statement, right before the team was to play its biggest game of the season, struck a nerve with everyone in Ann Arbor, especially football coach and athletic director Bo Schembechler, who promptly fired Frieder. Claiming that "a Michigan man will coach Michigan," Schembechler ousted Frieder and replaced him with assistant coach Steve Fisher. It was a brave decision, considering that Fisher had no head coaching experience at the college level and that no interim coach had ever reached the Final Four. But Fisher, whose Wolverines were seeded third as the tournament began, felt his team had as good a chance as any.

"I had been there since 1982," Fisher said. "I had the good fortune of having been given a lot of responsibility. I was very involved in practice, I was very involved in game planning. I would speak to the team in a lot of different ways, so for me to stand up and talk to the team was not the first time. Even though it was the first time with the interim head coach label, I think that was very good for me that I already had credibility with the players, and I think there was mutual respect."

Fisher's plan for his players was to break the bracket into two-game mini tournaments. If the Wolverines could win their first two mini tournaments, they would be in the Final Four, and if they could win the remaining mini tournament, the national championship would be theirs. But before he would have a chance to put his theory to use, he first had to worry about getting his players in a state of mind to play basketball, which was not going to be so easy after the departure of their head coach. Luckily, he got some assistance from Schembechler. Their old coach was gone, Schembechler pointed out, so it was time to get on board with Fisher or get out of the way.

"I think he probably started off with Sean Higgins because Sean was talking about transferring at the time," said forward Terry Mills. "And he said, 'Sean, if I hear one more word out of your mouth that you want to transfer—as a matter of fact, I got the papers right here in my pocket,' he said. 'If you're ready to go, then let's go.' Then he came to me and he's like, 'Mills, I'm tired of hearing excuses, you're an All-American in high school, and all this. You're at Michigan now, we're in college. I don't want to hear anything else about that.' He took every individual and he challenged them, and we moved on from there."

Schembechler's tone was normally reserved for the football field, but it was something the basketball team needed to hear. And as the Wolverines got set to take on Xavier in their first game, it was now up to Fisher to deliver an equally inspiring message. But coming from a guy with 224 fewer wins than Schembechler, it was a daunting task.

"If a guy wasn't nervous, he had no pulse. I was scared to death before the game," Fisher admitted. "We talked about circling the wagons and making sure that we believed in one another and we were good. We just need to go out and not worry about anything for 40 minutes other than doing whatever we had to do to win that game against Xavier."

For much of the game, that appeared to be in doubt, as the Musketeers led by as many as six points in the second half, but a late run in the final minutes allowed Michigan to pull out a 92–87 victory. It wasn't a convincing statement against a 14 seed, but Fisher's team had advanced to the title game of their first mini tournament. A 91–82 victory over South Alabama brought the Wolverines to the Sweet 16, where they would square off against North Carolina in a highly anticipated matchup.

Both teams had national title aspirations, and to no one's surprise the score was still tied at 83 with less than five minutes to go. The game was still up for grabs in the final minute when the Wolverines, clinging to a two-point lead, found Glen Rice behind the three-point line. Rice stepped up and delivered the critical shot, which gave Michigan a five-point lead, one they would ultimately keep as they disposed of the Tar Heels 92–87.

"We played North Carolina in the round of 16 each of the last two years and we had lost," Fisher said. "So when we beat Carolina to get to the Elite Eight, I do believe that that was a watershed game that had all of us saying we can accomplish something truly remarkable."

Their fourth-round game against Virginia proved to be much easier. The Cavaliers were fresh off an upset over top-ranked Oklahoma, but 13-of-16 shooting from Rice prevented the Wolverines from suffering a similar fate. The eventual 102–65 victory came just one day after Fisher's forty-fourth birthday, and his players gave him a belated present by reserving the final strand of the net for their coach. But the celebration was only beginning, as his team not only toppled Illinois (see page 182) but Seton Hall as well (page 294) to claim the school's first national championship in basketball. For Fisher, it was almost too much to take in.

"I went from the non-descriptive assistant coach to a phone call from President Bush to a visit to the White House with my wife. We stayed all night at the White House. We went to one of the state dinners with Yitzhak Shamir, the prime minister of Israel at the time, and I sat between Bob Hope and Audrey Hepburn and both of them knew who I was. And three weeks before, half the people in Ann Arbor didn't know who I was," Fisher said. "Usually when crazy-good things happen and hit the lottery, they happen to somebody else, and this time it happened to me." ●

Glen Rice comes down with one of his 11 rebounds during Michigan's win over Seton Hall. *John W. McDonough/Sports Illustrated/Getty Images*

1990 Loyola Marymount

Of all the tournaments in the NCAA's illustrious history, none has matched the emotion, intensity, and drama of 1990. Not only did the tournament provide one of the most touching stories of all time in Loyola Marymount, it also gave fans one thrilling finish after another. Of the 63 games in the tournament, an incredible 29 were decided by four points or fewer, and more than a handful came down to the final seconds. Paris McCurdy capped a three-point play with no time remaining to give twelfth-seeded Ball State a 54–53 upset over Oregon State. Georgia Tech overcame a four-point deficit to Michigan State in the final 13 seconds of regulation, thanks to Kenny Anderson. The guard raced down for a quick layup, then buried a jumper after a missed MSU free throw to send the game into overtime, where the Yellow Jackets won 81–80. Arkansas guard Todd Day tipped in his own miss with four seconds left to beat Dayton 86–84, and eighth-seeded North Carolina upset top-ranked Oklahoma 79–77 on a Rick Fox layup at the buzzer. The madness would finally come to an end when UNLV won the national championship 103–73 over Duke.

The Hank and Bo show could simply not be separated. Not now, not after a decade of playing with each other. Hank Gathers was passing on millions of dollars to stay in school for his senior year at Loyola Marymount, but playing one more season with Bo Kimble was worth much more than any paycheck. Ironically, when the best friends first played with each other in eighth grade, Hank seemed to be about the last person with hopes of an NBA career.

"But Hank was very determined," Kimble recalled. "Hank was determined to be successful, and he wouldn't let anything stop him from achieving that."

Yet the heart that made him such a great player was also what ultimately betrayed him. On the night of March 4, just days before the Loyola Marymount Lions were to play in the NCAA Tournament, Gathers collapsed on the court in the West Coast Conference Tournament. Some in the crowd initially thought Hank was playing around. After all, this was the same player who, a year earlier,

amid all the NBA speculation, said he was giving up basketball entirely—to pursue a career in boxing. But there was no laughter on this occasion, and when Gathers didn't move, it was quite clear something was seriously wrong. Although the team prayed on the court while he was taken away in an ambulance, minutes later Hank Gathers was pronounced dead.

"I believe in the Lord and I believe everything happens for a reason," senior Jeff Fryer said. "I believe it was Hank's time."

Kimble, who never missed a day of church, also looked for a greater purpose in what had just transpired.

"You know, God takes some of the greatest people first, as I hear," Kimble said. "So that was the thing. When your faith is strong no matter what happens, you know that God will find a way."

WCC officials canceled the tournament, handing their automatic bid to the Lions, who were now faced with the impossible task of playing just days after the tragedy.

The NCAA gave Loyola Marymount an 11 seed and picked the Lions to play their first two games at the Long Beach Arena, just miles from their Los Angeles campus. The outpouring of support was obvious, and nothing was going to please the crowd more than to see Kimble step to the free throw line. As a tribute to his fallen friend, Kimble planned on shooting his first free throw left-handed, just like Gathers had during his playing days.

"I told everyone that I didn't care about the shot going in, and I also told people it's really about honoring him by taking the shot, not making the shot," Kimble said. "But that went in one ear and out the other of everybody that was ever watching, because everybody that really knew what the left-handed free throw was about wanted me to make it."

But Kimble almost never got that chance in the first-round game against New Mexico State, as he picked up four fouls at the beginning of the game. Although one more foul would have ended Kimble's day on the court, Paul Westhead left him in the game, and minutes later Kimble stepped to the line for his first free throw attempt. Despite airballing the shot in practice days earlier, Kimble nailed the free throw, bringing a standing ovation from the fans. As for Westhead, his faith in Kimble paid huge dividends, as the senior finished the game with 45 points to give LMU a 111–92 win.

"I just felt that first game and all throughout the tournament I literally felt like I had the power of two," Kimble said. "Because all the letters I read on the way to the game, just emotionally made me feel like I was Superman."

That win set up a match with the Michigan Wolverines, the defending national champions who appeared to be well on their way to repeating. Loyola Marymount was facing so much pressure and so many emotions that Westhead felt it was time to throw his players a curveball.

"I was trying to relax them as best I could. We'd kind of laugh and giggle about how many three-point shots we were going to take and spread the wealth around," Westhead said. "'Bo, you could shoot threes, and Fryer, you could shoot threes,' and when we get to Tom Peabody, I say, 'Tom, I don't think you should shoot a three yet.'"

The much-needed humor loosened up his players, but Fryer took the message to heart. With free rein to shoot, Fryer started to drain three-pointers and continued to do so relentlessly. His third shot from behind the arc put LMU up 24–19, and the senior soon extended the lead to 33–24 and 60–48 with more deep shots. And this was all in the first half.

"It just felt like after the first four shots that I made I just had it going," said Fryer, who had 21 points in the opening period. "A lot of the players stepped up in that situation as well and were able to play to the best of our abilities."

When the Wolverines got within seven points in the second half, Fryer pushed the margin back to 70–60, and minutes later he increased the lead to 89–76. By the time he drained his eleventh three-pointer of the night, the Lions were up by 30 points and well on their way to a 149–115 victory. The performance, which set the tournament record for most points in a game, sent the Lions to the Sweet 16.

"I think everyone felt that they were performing well, but it wasn't the normal, like, if you win everybody celebrates," Westhead said. "It was like we won and we'd like to keep this going, because the alternative of not playing they didn't like, because this was a way to kind of avoid the reality of Hank's death."

And win they did, upsetting Alabama in the last minute to advance to the Elite Eight (see page 240). The journey stopped there, but that was only the beginning of their legacy. Kimble started 44 For Life, named after Hank's number, an organization that continues to promote cardiac awareness and honor the legend that was Hank Gathers.

"Hank was such an extraordinary person off the court and he was a great athlete on the court, so at least if you're going to be associated with someone, you want to be associated with someone you love and respect," Kimble said. "I can't think of a better person I would want to be linked with, and when people are linking us, they're not linking us in a bad way. They're linking me to an amazing person on and off the court with a legacy and a heart bigger than mine." ●

1991 Duke

CBS made history in 1991 by broadcasting all 63 tournament games for the first time, much to the delight of fans across the country. Fourteenth-seeded Xavier pulled the upset of the tournament by beating Nebraska 89–84, while tenth-seeded Temple came within three points of reaching the Final Four. On the other end of that 75–72 decision was North Carolina and coach Dean Smith, who tied John Wooden for the most tournament wins in a career. Fans watching at home were also treated to Villanova's 50–48 victory over Princeton when Lance Miller swooped in for a layup with a second to go, as well as Utah's 85–84 win over Michigan State in double overtime. Down 75–73 in the final moments of the first overtime, MSU's Mike Peplowski intentionally missed his free throw, which Jon Zulauf put in to tie the game. But thanks to a 29-point effort from Josh Grant, the Utes hung on.

His Duke team was less than 24 hours removed from the biggest win in school history, yet the last thing coach Mike Krzyzewski felt like doing was celebrating. The Blue Devils were fresh off an upset of previously undefeated UNLV, a team many considered to be among the greatest of all time, but with one more game on the horizon it was no time to be living in the past. When his players strutted in for practice the day before their championship game against Kansas, Coach K reminded them just how far they still had to go.

"I don't like the way you're walking, the way you're talking, or the way you're dressing," Krzyzewski snapped. "You guys are acting like you're big-time, and right now, you haven't done anything big-time yet."

It was a harsh response to be sure, but it was most likely a necessary one. This was Krzyzewski's fifth appearance at the Final Four in the last six years, and each of his earlier trips had ended painfully short of the title. Staying satisfied with a semifinal victory was not an option. Fortunately, his players got the message.

"We knew the significance of beating UNLV, the type of game that it was," point guard Bobby Hurley said. "It was probably the most well-played game that I've ever been in just in terms of us executing at a very high level, not making any mistakes. We couldn't afford to make any mistakes against them—they were that good. But you had to put it past you. People would have called that a fluke, beating UNLV, if we didn't come out and win the whole thing."

Hurley had played all 40 minutes of that game, but he still had enough energy at the end to run around and jump on the back of teammate Clay Buckley as they headed off the court. Krzyzewski's attempts of calming his players by motioning his hands toward the ground went unnoticed. But by the time tip-off against Kansas had arrived, it was obvious that his sharp words at practice had done the trick. The Blue Devils ran off to a 7–1 lead at the start of the game, highlighted by a halfcourt alley-oop from Hurley to Grant Hill. They would keep their lead through halftime, when they led 42–34.

The Jayhawks tried to pull their way back, but some impressive three-point shooting by Duke kept the comeback bid from ever gaining momentum. They hit six of their first eight shots from beyond the arc, and as the 10-minute mark approached the lead had swelled to 61–47. The Jayhawks eventually crept to within 70–65 in the last minute, and they nearly had a chance to really give the Blue Devils a scare before Duke sophomore Thomas Hill made the smartest play of the season. The Jayhawks had applied full-court pressure to try and force a turnover, and nine seconds into Duke's possession, it appeared they were about to get one.

The Blue Devils had yet to cross the half-court line, and with just one second to spare before his team committed a 10-second violation, Hill had the presence of mind to spend his team's final timeout. When the

Thanks in part to Grant Hill's 10 points, 2 of which came on this first-half dunk, Duke never trailed in their championship game against Kansas. *John W. McDonough/Sports Illustrated/Getty Images*

Blue Devils inbounded the ball moments later, Brian Davis easily broke away from the Jayhawk defense and sealed the championship with a slam dunk. The Blue Devils had not only won their first national title, they had done so by leading the entire game. Coach K would win more than 900 games in his career, more than anybody else in college basketball history, but few would ever feel as satisfying as this one.

"The thing I am most proud of about the 1991 team is that they developed throughout the season and that they won what is arguably one of the biggest games in the history of the NCAA Tournament in the semifinals by defeating UNLV, stopping their 45-game winning streak," Krzyzewski said. "To then come back, 48 hours later, after having such a high of beating UNLV is one of the best things any of my teams has ever done. It was amazing winning that game, and to get over that elation in order

to get on to the next play was really remarkable. That is the thing I'll always remember about that team."

Duke hadn't just played well during its final two games. They shot over 50 percent from the field in all six tournament games, a feat that has never been repeated and most likely never will be. The Blue Devils rolled over their first four opponents—Louisiana-Monroe, Iowa, UConn, and St. John's—by an average margin of victory of almost 19 points.

"For us, I had a tremendous experience," Hurley said. "Up until that point, being a sophomore, I couldn't have asked to have had a more enjoyable college experience. I just respected Coach K tremendously. I felt like we deserved it, and I felt we were happy to get that NCAA title."

And with the kind of performances his team had strung together, a little celebrating was in order. ●

1992 Duke

Twenty-six years after making history, UTEP coach Don Haskins showed he still had it in 1992. His last-minute decision to use the "four corners" defense paid off when his Miners upset top-seeded Kansas 66–60 in the second round. It was the first pair of tournament wins for Haskins since 1966, when the school was known as Texas Western, but the shock of the tournament belonged to fourteenth-seeded East Tennessee State. Thanks to a 13-of-25 shooting performance from beyond the arc, the Pirates knocked off third-seeded Arizona. It was the first of three upsets the Wildcats would suffer in four years.

Duke point guard Bobby Hurley had barely had time to enjoy his first national championship, and already he was back in the gym working toward a second title. Hurley, the son of perhaps the greatest high school coach ever (Bob Hurley, winner of more than two dozen state championships with St. Anthony's in New Jersey), had too much respect for the game to sit idly by as other teams prepared to knock the Blue Devils off their perch. Hurley and his teammates had a chance to make history—nobody had repeated as champions since the 1972–73 UCLA Bruins—and all the pieces were back for Duke to make it happen. But, as high as expectations were for the Blue Devils, coach Mike Krzyzewski made sure to alleviate any pressure his team might be feeling.

"We are pursuing a national championship, not defending one," Krzyzewski asserted. *Defending* is a word to use when someone is trying to take something from you, he explained, and nobody could ever take away their 1991 title. That pursuit, however, nearly came to an end in the 1992 regional finals when they faced Kentucky. An accidental bank shot by UK's Sean Woods put the Wildcats in front 103–102 which just 2.1 seconds to play. The Blue Devils had 90 feet to go, but fortunately for them all of Kentucky's big men had fouled out of the game, leaving 6-foot-6 Deron Feldhaus as the tallest defender on the court. After discussing the situation with his assistants, Kentucky coach Rick Pitino decided to put all five defenders on the far end of the court to cover the pass. It left Grant Hill open to heave the ball downcourt, but it was the best option Pitino had. He just hoped it wouldn't

be a repeat of three weeks earlier, when Georgia Tech won its first-round game with an impossible shot at the buzzer (see page 252).

"We watched the end of the Georgia Tech vs. USC game together," Pitino recalled. "When James Forrest hit a miracle three-pointer with 0.8 seconds remaining, I said I'd kill myself if that ever happened to us."

Hill delivered a perfect strike to Christian Laettner near the free throw line, and all that was left was the shot—after a quick fake to his right, Laettner turned toward his left and fired the winner as time ran out. The Duke senior had already hit a game-winner against UConn in 1990, and he followed it up with a pair of game-winning free throws against UNLV in 1991, but this was the shot of a lifetime.

Laettner ran down the court and was mobbed by his teammates, but Krzyzewski had the grace and presence of mind to find Kentucky senior Richie Farmer. "You guys are not losers," he said. "Keep your head up because tonight there were no losers."

Then, before he walked off the floor, he made his way over to the press row, where Cawood Ledford was calling his last Wildcat game after 39 years on the job.

"I wanted to seek you guys out because all the Kentucky fans would be listening," Krzyzewski said, "and just to say how much empathy we have as a staff and team for the Kentucky kids—they were absolutely sensational."

His words resonated with UK fans and garnered him respect throughout the country, but seven days later his team faced a major challenge once again. Coaching from the opposing sidelines would be Indiana coach Bob Knight, who had taught Krzyzewski all the tricks of the trade when the protégé was a point guard at West Point. Just 10 minutes into their semi-final game, the Hoosiers found themselves up 27–19 and shooting an incredible 12-of-15 from the floor. As the first half started to wind down, the Blue Devils still trailed 39–27.

"We haven't played well," Krzyzewski told his club. "We're going to lose unless you pick your level of play up to Hurley's."

The team responded by matching the intensity of their point guard, and a 10–3 run to end the half, followed by a 13–0 run to start the second period, put Duke in front 50–42. The Blue Devils eventually pushed the lead to 60–47, and still led 73–64 after Hurley hit a pair of free throws with 1:16 to go, but Knight's club was not done yet. Indiana guard Todd Leary hit a three-pointer to cut the lead to 73–67, and after Duke hit a pair of free throws to bring the lead back to eight, Leary came right back and knocked down another trey to bring IU within 75–70.

Duke's Marty Clark converted two more free throws, but Leary struck once again—hitting a three-pointer with 26.8 seconds to go to close the gap to just 77–73. Clark made yet another free throw to put Duke up by five, but his second free throw was off the mark, and during the scramble Laettner fouled IU's Matt Nover. His foul not only stopped the clock, it sent Nover to the line, where he promptly cut the lead to 78–75. On the ensuing inbounds pass, Hurley stepped out of bounds, and all of a sudden the Hoosiers appeared to be duplicating

Duke's miracle against Kentucky. But it was not meant to be: Jamal Meeks missed the equalizer from the right corner, and the Blue Devils went on to survive 81–78.

The last team to conquer was Michigan, perhaps better known as the "Fab Five." Michigan's starting lineup of five freshmen, four of whom would play in the NBA, were hungry to avenge their 88–85 loss to Duke earlier in the year, and for much of the first half it appeared as if they would get their wish. Laettner, who a day earlier had been named Player of the Year, finished the first half with five points and seven turnovers as the Blue Devils trailed 31–30. Even worse, Laettner was walking up and down the court—hardly the effort expected of basketball's greatest player. Krzyzewski walked into the locker room, turned to his senior, and went off.

"Christian, you suck. You don't give a s---. It's incomprehensible for me," he screamed. "We're playing for the god---- national championship. You're supposed to be the leader of the team, and you have seven turnovers. It's bulls---!"

Krzyzewski smashed a blackboard and exited the room but Laettner's lecture was hardly over. Now it was Hurley's turn.

"Thomas Hill and I decided to really get after him at halftime to try and shake him up to get him to come out and play the way we expected him to play—the way he played for us his whole four years," Hurley said. "We got after Christian, and he responded and had a great second half."

Laettner's layup to start the second half put Duke back in front 32–31, and before long he would add two more buckets to put his team up 46–39. In case the Wolverines still had any thoughts of a comeback, Duke scored on 12 of its final 13 possessions, and by game's end Laettner had led all scorers with 19 points to finish his NCAA Tournament career with 407, a record total that may never be touched. With their 71–51 over Michigan, the Blue Devils had won their second straight national championship, and as Krzyzewski was sure to point out, they wouldn't have to defend this one either. ●

Bobby Hurley leads a fast break during the 1992 championship game.
Manny Millan/Sports Illustrated/Getty Images

1993 North Carolina

For fans hoping to see a bit of March Madness, the 1993 West Regional provided more than enough chaos. Seventh-seeded Temple advanced all the way to the Elite Eight and George Washington made the Sweet 16 as a 12 seed, but it was Southern University that provided the best story of the tournament. Before Georgia Tech's opening-round game against the thirteenth-seeded Jaguars, Yellow Jackets forward Malcolm Mackey asked Southern's Jervaughn Scales if they were actually a Division 1 school. Mackey scored 27 points in the game, but Scales tallied 27 of his own to help the Jaguars overcome a 14-point deficit in their 93–78 victory. The West Region would ultimately belong to Michigan, but not before the Wolverines overcame a 19-point deficit to UCLA in the second round, winning on Jimmy King's putback with two seconds left.

If there is anything possibly worse than losing in the NCAA Tournament, it would have to be watching your rival go on to win the national championship. And for UNC players, the only thing worse than watching Duke win a national title was to see the Blue Devils do it for two years in a row. But heading into the 1993 season, that was exactly what the Tar Heels faced after having to stomach back-to-back championships for Duke in 1991 and 1992. Needless to say, they were not interested in watching a three-peat.

"They were our rivals, like 15 minutes away, and to see them win it back-to-back really motivated us," guard Donald Williams said. "We felt like we were on their level, and we felt like we could win a national championship too."

To drive that point home, coach Dean Smith put a picture of the Superdome, the site of that year's Final Four, in the locker of each player before the year started. Underneath each photo, the caption read "North Carolina: 1993 national champions." A bold prediction, yes, but if his players gave everything they had, Smith knew it would be an accurate one as well.

Everything went according to plan as the Tar Heels earned a No. 1 seed in the NCAA Tournament, but the dream appeared to be in serious jeopardy in the Elite Eight against Cincinnati. The Bearcats grabbed a 15-point lead in the first half, but UNC refused to give in and came back to send the game into overtime. The team actually had a chance to win it in regulation, as Smith called a timeout

with 0.8 seconds remaining and conjured what appeared to be the perfect play for junior Brian Reese.

"To tell you the truth I remember in the huddle Coach Smith said to Brian, he drew up the play and said, 'Brian, you're going to be open right here. All you have to do is catch the ball, and just drop it in the basket.' He said, 'But please don't try to dunk the ball because you might not have enough time,'" guard Derrick Phelps said. "I recall that like it was yesterday, and of course the play worked. Brian happened to be open—I threw the pass for Brian, nice little lob touch pass to catch him right close to the rim, and of course Brian goes to try and dunk it."

Reese missed the dunk at the buzzer, forcing Carolina to play another five minutes, but in overtime the Tar Heels would capitalize on their opportunity. They ran away with a 75–68 victory and followed it up with a win over Kansas to lock up a spot in the national championship game. Williams, who was still in the zone from his 25-point performance against the Jayhawks, elected not to attend the shoot-around the day before the game. Instead, the sophomore spent his time pondering the matchups in his hotel room. Had he turned on the TV for any insight, he would have seen just how little of a chance people were giving his team against Michigan's Fab Five, a quintet led by future NBA all-stars Jalen Rose, Chris Webber, and Juwan Howard.

"You hear all the stuff on the news, Michigan was going to do this, and Chris Webber this, and it was like, oh man, I can't wait for the ball to go up," Phelps said. "We felt that we could play just as well as they were."

Early on that was the case, as the Tar Heels grabbed a quick five-point lead and took a 42–36 lead at halftime. UNC still led 61–60 after a Williams three-pointer with just over seven minutes to play, but a bucket by Howard and a three-pointer from Rose put the Wolverines in front 65–61 with five minutes to go. UNC was 26–0 when leading at halftime, but the Wolverines were 30–0 when leading in the last five minutes of a game. Something was going to give. And Smith made sure it wasn't going to be UNC.

"He was the coolest guy ever when it comes to being under pressure. He just never let us panic, no matter what the time and score is in a basketball game," Williams said. "He always kept that confidence in us that we were going to win that game."

Williams knocked down a jumper to bring the Tar Heels to within two, and moments later he nailed a huge three to bring UNC within 67–66.

"I knew that if I made my shots, we were going to be a tough team to beat," Williams said. "It all starts with your coaches and your teammates. I think they had so much confidence in me shooting the ball and scoring that they did everything they could do to get me the ball and to get me open."

Phelps converted a layup to put Carolina back in front, and after center Eric Montross added a dunk with a minute to go, the team was up 72–67. But the Wolverines were not quite done yet. Ray Jackson's long jumper put Michigan within three, and after Reese stepped out of bounds on the next possession, the Wolverines had a chance to tie. Webber put in a missed shot with 36 seconds on the clock, and all of a sudden the lead was down to one.

Michigan elected to foul Pat Sullivan, and the junior responded by hitting the first free throw. But his second was long and Webber grabbed the board with 18 ticks to go. Phelps, ever alert, darted in front of Rose and Jimmy King, UM's primary ball-handlers. Now only 15 seconds remained, and Webber had no choice but to bring the ball up himself. Phelps and teammate George Lynch pressured him into the corner, where Webber called a time-out with 11 seconds left. Under any normal circumstance, Webber's decision would have been the right call, but unfortunately for the sophomore this was not one of those times. The Wolverines had no timeouts to use, resulting in a technical foul. Two free throws later, the game was all but over. Although Webber took the blame for the loss, it couldn't have been further from the truth.

"He knew, as badly as he felt, as much as he said 'I lost the game,' he didn't lose the game," Michigan coach Steve Fisher said. "He was the reason we got there."

Just as Webber received too much blame for the loss, Phelps didn't get enough credit for the heads-up play.

"People always just think if Chris Webber didn't call that timeout that we would have lost that game, which is not true because we were up at that moment," Phelps said. "They had to make a basket for them to get a chance to win that game."

Weeks later, Webber became the No. 1 overall pick, the first of many accomplishments for the five-time NBA all-star. But on this night, the Tar Heels were the better team, and for the third straight year the championship was staying in North Carolina. This time, however, it belonged in Chapel Hill. ●

1994 Arkansas

North Carolina's streak of 13 consecutive Sweet 16 appearances—a run no team has ever come close to matching in the modern tournament era—came to an end at the hands of Boston College in 1994. North Carolina looked poised to defend its national championship, but the ninth-seeded Eagles—who had gone 8–20 just four years earlier—had destiny on their side. In their next game against Indiana, BC closed out the last five minutes on an 18–4 run to advance to the Elite Eight. Also fitting Cinderella's slipper was twelfth-seeded Tulsa—The Golden Hurricane upset UCLA in the first round and then defeated fourth-seeded Oklahoma State on a Lou Dawkins three-pointer with 8.6 seconds left.

When Nolan Richardson implemented the "40 Minutes of Hell" defense years earlier, it shook the basketball world upside-down. Opposing coaches watched as Richardson's teams employed a system that seemed to defy all logic. Not only would they trap opponents anywhere on the court, but they would attempt to do so from tip-off until the game's conclusion. It was a system that required a certain level of anger, which for Richardson was quite easy to find.

In addition to Richardson facing his fair share of critics as the SEC's first African American coach, his first teams struggled mightily to implement his system, leaving many people to question his competency as a coach. By 1994, however, his system had come full circle, and channeling that anger was proving to be a much harder task. Richardson insisted that the Razorbacks were still underdogs, despite the fact that they were ranked No. 1 for most of the year and had lost only two conference games by a total of three points. To top it all off, they played in a brand new arena, one that was frequently visited by President and former Arkansas Governor Bill Clinton.

"That was probably one of the most memorable moments of all, the chance to spend time with him," junior Scotty Thurman said. "He came to several of our games that year, and it was always kind of a huge deal when he came to town. So we really felt like at that time, Arkansas was at its best because we had not only the best team in the country but we had the guy from our own state running the country, so we were pretty much on top of the world."

The Razorbacks would finish the year 16–0 at the new arena, but along with the President's support came hoards of Secret Service throughout the building. It wasn't ideal for a college atmosphere, but if Bud Walton Arena wasn't the rowdiest place to watch a game, it was quickly turning into the safest.

"We would see them all the time," Thurman said. "When we came into the arena, we had to go through metal detectors and different things before the game and they'd be strategically placed. And he'd always come into the locker room and visit with us and he had 11 guys with him. They never really wanted him to interact with us the way that he always chose to, which I thought was awesome."

Richardson appreciated the enthusiasm from Clinton, but it still wasn't the mentality he was going for. He wanted his teams to have PhDs—meaning to play Poor, Hungry, and Desperate. He continued to hammer that it was his team against the world. The message sounded hollow as they quickly defeated North Carolina A&T, Georgetown, Tulsa, and Michigan, but Richardson finally found the edge he had been searching for as his team prepared to take on Arizona in the Final Four. Tournament officials neglected to inform Arkansas that the time of their pre-game shootaround had been altered, rendering their practice useless.

"We didn't get a chance to shoot around but maybe two minutes. You know, they give you 45 minutes on the clock and once it starts

Razorbacks forward Corliss Williamson finishes a dunk against Arizona in the Final Four. *Doug Pensinger/ Getty Images*

and ticks off, that's it. Well, we didn't get our time," Thurman said. "Coach Richardson was extremely upset, and he was walking around the coliseum, you could just hear him going around the carousel just barking and upset, saying it's us against the world and nobody wants us to win."

The Razorbacks went into the game a little underprepared, but it may have been a blessing in disguise. Arizona took a 67–62 lead with just 8:23 to play, but if the Razorbacks were ever going to play with hunger and desperation, this was it. Richardson's club ran off the next 12 points to take a 74–67 lead and would go on to emerge victorious, 91–82. No one was enjoying the victory more than Alex Dillard, who had made a pair of crucial three-pointers to spark the win.

Of all of Richardson's players, none better fit his mantra more than Dillard, who had arrived in Fayetteville as a 25-year-old freshman. The shooting guard had worked for three years in a grocery store and fast food restaurant before getting his GED and then attended junior college in order to become eligible at the Division I level. Finally, after biding his time, Dillard was able to enroll at Arkansas and play on the team. His three-pointers helped put Arkansas within a victory of the national championship, but their last game would have to come against Duke.

The Blue Devils had won two of the previous three national titles, but in a game for the ages the Razorbacks held on for a 76–72 victory (see page 276). There was no denying it now—Arkansas had garnered the respect and admiration of the country. With the championship came one more meeting with the President—this time with the Razorbacks as the guests of honor. ●

1995 UCLA

Arkansas would ultimately advance to the national championship in 1995, but the journey there was anything but easy. After beating Texas Southern by 66 points a year earlier, the Razorbacks only survived the rematch 79–78 when Tigers freshman Randy Bolden missed a free throw with 6.1 seconds left. Their season should have come to an end in their next round against Syracuse, but once again fate was on the side of the Razorbacks. Syracuse forward Lucious Jackson appeared to preserve the 82–81 victory when he stole the ball in the final seconds, but teammate Lawrence Moten called a timeout the Orangemen didn't have, allowing Scotty Thurman to tie the game at 82–82 on a free throw. Thanks to a steal of their own near the end of overtime, the Razorbacks escaped with a 96–94 victory. Their third-round opponent, Memphis, also squeaked into the Sweet 16 with a last-second tip-in by David Vaught to defeat Purdue.

UCLA coach Jim Harrick stood in the locker room before the 1995 championship game, pleading for someone to get him a basketball. He had been trying to convince himself the previous three days that somehow his senior guard, Tyus Edney, would be able to play by tip-off. Edney had badly sprained his wrist during the Saturday semifinal win over Oklahoma State, and although team doctors had told Harrick on Sunday that the wrist was not looking good, Harrick was still holding out hope. But now it was Monday night, and it was decision time. Harrick had seen Edney airball a shot in warmups—a shot that was taken five feet from the basket—and knew in the back of his mind that Edney was not going to be able to play. But before keeping his best player out of the title game, Harrick had to be convinced one more time. Now with the ball in his hand, Harrick tossed it over to Edney, hoping his senior would pull out some last-second magic, as he had done two weeks earlier against Missouri (see page 250). But when Edney raised his arm to catch the ball, he did so with his opposite hand. Not a good sign.

"He tries to dribble it, and the ball just pitty-pats weakly down there close to the floor, where my spirits have dropped as well," Harrick recalled. "Seeing Edney so, I am absolutely devastated."

Making the situation worse was the fact that UCLA's lineup was extremely thin. Harrick often relied on only seven players, and now with Edney hurt, it would be up to six players to carry the burden. As it would turn out, the six Bruins would play 197 of their team's 200 minutes that night.

"Fellas, you've got to go out there and play the greatest game you've ever played in your lives. That's all it is. The greatest effort you've ever given," Harrick said. "Leave nothing to come back in here with."

Harrick tried to use Edney in the opening minutes, almost as a decoy, as Edney brought up the ball with his left hand. The move would also ease the load on his other six players, but when Arkansas guard Elmer Martin stripped the ball from Edney, leading to a Razorbacks layup, Harrick could no longer afford to keep him in. Just over two minutes into the game, Harrick brought in sophomore Cameron Dollar.

"Cameron, you know why you're on scholarship, don't you?" Harrick asked, bringing a puzzled look to his guard's face. "To get the ball to Ed O'Bannon."

Dollar beamed a big smile, but in reality Harrick probably intended to have O'Bannon, the team's All-American, take more than his fair share of shots. But for O'Bannon to have any looks, he would first need Dollar to get him the ball, which didn't look so promising after Dollar's first possession in the game. Just four seconds after receiving the inbounds pass, Dollar had the ball swiped by Arkansas guard Clint McDaniel, who quickly laid it in for a 12–5 Razorbacks lead. It was the tenth straight point for Arkansas, and they showed no sign of slowing down.

"It was the greatest thing that could have happened to me at that point," Dollar said. "Because at that moment, when I lost the ball, I looked at him laying it up and all the anxiety and tension I had just left. I knew right then it was just a game and I was just going to have some fun."

The following possession, Dollar came back down and fired a no-look pass to O'Bannon for a quick layup. In fact, Dollar would turn the ball over just two other times the rest of the game, and thanks to his sharp play the Bruins fought back to take a 40–39 lead at halftime. UCLA would go on to push the lead to 65–53 midway through the second half before a 10–2 run by the Razorbacks brought them to within just four. The under-8:00 TV timeout came just in time, as Harrick gave his troops one last speech before the final stretch began.

"Don't you dare get tired on me now!" Harrick implored. "There is no getting tired in this game!"

The Razorbacks would trim the gap to just 67–64, but O'Bannon hit a turnaround jumper to put his team back up by five. They pushed the margin to 71–65 before Dollar delivered the crucial blow, blocking an Arkansas shot from behind and hitting a pair of free throws seconds later to put UCLA up by eight points. Before long, the Bruins were counting down the final seconds of their 89–78 victory. O'Bannon was named the tournament's Most Outstanding Player, but Edney would have his recognition after all. During the team's celebration back at Pauley Pavilion, O'Bannon made sure to let everybody know that his teammate was the true MOP, and the subsequent roars indicated just how much the fans agreed. ●

Freshman Cameron Dollar, who started the title game as a last-second replacement, filled in admirably for the injured Tyus Edney. *Stephen Dunn/ Getty Images*

1996 Kentucky

The Final Four welcomed a pair of newcomers in 1996—UMass and Mississippi State—and while the tournament saw no massive upsets, it provided plenty of entertaining close calls. Texas Tech entered the tournament with a 28–1 record, but needed two late free throws to preserve a 74–73 victory over fourteenth-seeded Northern Illinois. The sixth-seeded Iowa Hawkeyes dug themselves a 17-point hole against George Washington, but they escaped with an 81–79 win after a pair of Russ Millard free throws with three seconds to go. Fellow six seed Louisville squeaked out an 82–80 overtime win over Tulsa after trailing by 12 points in the final four minutes of regulation, but the biggest scare came to top-seeded Purdue. No team had ever lost to a 16 seed in the tournament's history, but the Boilermakers needed a putback by Brandon Brantley with 1:29 left to emerge with a 73–71 victory over Western Carolina.

Kentucky coach Rick Pitino needed no reminder before the 1996 season that he had yet to win an NCAA title. Nevertheless, he got one—from the Pope. The summer before the season, Pitino's group had visited Italy and had a chance to meet John Paul II. After Pitino leaned over to kiss his rings, the pope attempted to return the favor before saying, "Oh, you don't have a ring." The Pope may not have been aware of the Wildcats, but most sports fans knew that if Kentucky was going to win its first championship since 1978, this was the year to do it. Even more problematic, most people *expected* them to win the title.

With an arsenal of 10 future NBA draft picks at their disposal, Kentucky appeared unbeatable. But all of the lofty praise came crashing down after the Wildcats lost their the second game of the season to UMass.

"We knew we had a good team, but that gave us a little bit of a reality check," junior Anthony Epps said. "We all just decided we're going to be as good as we are capable of being, and we all need to get on the same page."

The results were pretty obvious the next time Kentucky took the floor. The Wildcats won their next 27 games, by over 24 points per contest, including an 86–42 first-half performance against LSU. Even though UK had achieved a 28–1 record heading into the SEC championship game, Pitino made sure their players stayed grounded.

"A lot of teams when they get criticized they take it the wrong way, but he wants you to get better," Epps said of Pitino. "Whether you were a McDonald's all-american or you were just a walk-on, he treated everybody the same and he never showed anybody any favoritism."

Never was this more apparent than when Pitino sat future NBA all-star Antoine Walker for the majority of their next game against Mississippi State for lack of team play. The win would have given the Wildcats a 19–0 record in the SEC for the year, but the 84–73 loss taught the much larger lesson of teamwork.

The Wildcats found their stride once again, and if anything, they actually made winning look even easier once the tournament started. Kentucky outscored its first four opponents by an average of 28 points to set up a Final Four rematch with none other than UMass.

"Everybody hoped we'd see UMass again— that's all we were waiting on," shooting guard Derek Anderson said. "We knew we were a better team. We were just so mad that we slipped up so early."

Their rematch would be quite a different story. The Wildcats built up a 15-point lead and still led by 10 with less than three minutes to play. But UMass put together a flurry of shots, and after Edgar Padilla nailed a three-pointer with a minute to go, Kentucky's lead had been cut to three.

"A lot of times what happens is when teams get down in a game, an individual will try to do things that they don't normally do," sophomore Jeff Sheppard said. "And we had the uncanny ability to just stay the course and continue to play."

Despite not having a timeout to regroup, the Wildcats responded with their most impressive run of the season. Five different players scored the last 10 points for Kentucky as they cruised into the national championship game. Their opponent, albeit one with less bad blood, would be Syracuse.

The Wildcats never actually got a chance to watch any film of the Orangemen before their title bout, but they still managed to take a nine-point lead as the first half came to a close. That lead would grow to 13 midway through the second half before the Orangemen began to find their stride. They knifed right through the UK defense for four dunks and a layup over the next three minutes, and by the time John Wallace converted a pair of free throws with five minutes left, the lead was down to just 64–62.

Kentucky desperately needed an answer, and got one as Walter McCarty responded with a tip-in and Anderson added a three to push the lead back to seven. When the buzzer sounded, Kentucky had scored 12 of the last 17 points to win the sixth national championship in school history. And in a testament to the teamwork Pitino had strived for, Kentucky's bench outscored Syracuse's 26–0.

Of all the people in the stadium that night, perhaps none was prouder than Anderson's uncle, George, who had changed Derek's life around. Growing up without a father and with an alcoholic mother, Derek ended up attending a boot camp after his mom left him to fend for himself as a 12-year-old.

"I had to go to a homeless shelter because nobody signed for me out of boot camp. Nobody knew I was there," Anderson said. "My mom did drugs and all this other stuff so I had to wait on my uncle to find out where I was at and come get me. So I was sitting in the homeless shelter, and once I found out he gave me—my uncle is a kind of a strict guy—and once he gave me that second opportunity in life, I made the most of it by playing basketball."

Derek and his family weren't the only people who appreciated his accomplishments. Two years after the title, he ran into a family who had named their son after him—first and middle name. The younger Derek Anderson still keeps in touch with his predecessor, and he is turning into a fine basketball player himself.

"That's something that you cherish because that's a person who looked up to you and you've done something in your life that affected a family and another child," Anderson said. "I felt privileged, and I felt like, you know, it's not about basketball anymore. It becomes a friendship."

By the time his apprentice started picking up basketball, Anderson had signed a $45 million contract with the Portland Trail Blazers, using a sizable portion of the money to start the Derek Anderson Foundation. The charity helps provide assistance to at-risk kids, and helps people from similar backgrounds attend college. The team may go down in history as the untouchables, but they have touched more lives than they can imagine. ●

Derek Anderson, who came to Kentucky to be part of Rick Pitino's fast break offense, had a chance to showcase some of his skills during UK's 76–67 victory over Syracuse. *Doug Pensinger/Allsport/ Getty Images*

1997 Arizona

It didn't take very long for the brackets to be busted in 1997, as Tennessee-Chattanooga became just the second team to make the Sweet 16 as a 14 seed. In their 73–70 win over Georgia in the opening round, the Mocs raced off to a 20–2 start before watching their lead dwindle to 70–69. They managed to pull out the win, and then defeated sixth-seeded Illinois 75–63 to make the tournament's second week. Before the game, the Illini were celebrating Providence's upset over Duke, which made Illinois' path to the Final Four that much easier, but five players on Chattanooga scored in double figures for the upset. However, the real shocker of the tournament came when fifteenth-seeded Coppin State pulled off perhaps the biggest upset in NCAA history with their 78–65 victory over second-seeded South Carolina. The Eagles, who were 30-point underdogs, beat the spread by a ridiculous 43 points.

Of all the problems that Lute Olson faced when he arrived in Tucson in 1983, meeting impossible expectations was certainly not among them. Olson, the third coach in three years for the Wildcats, was following up a pair of predecessors that had gone 13–42 over the previous two seasons, including just 1–17 in the Pac-10 the year before his arrival. Fans were shocked when Olson had left a budding Iowa program to take what many considered to be the worst coaching job in the country, but U of A was an ideal place for the 48-year-old. In Tucson, Olson found a place where he could escape the fishbowl experience of Iowa City, as well as the cold weather. It just so happened that Arizona was a national power waiting to be tapped into, and the minute that Olson stepped foot on campus, the perception of what Arizona basketball could become forever changed.

"I think it was a very successful tenure. We went form a losing program to a winning program in one year," said Olson, whose team led the Pac-10 in attendance each of his 24 years at the helm. "We established Arizona as a national basketball power and it established Tucson as a basketball town, and I think that still stands."

The community wholeheartedly embraced the Wildcats, and Olson's team responded by giving them something to cheer about. From 1987 to 1997, Arizona had the best record of any team in the country, winning more than 81 percent of its games. The only thing missing from the trophy case was a national championship, and after suffering a trio of unthinkable upsets in 1992, 1993, and 1995, fans started to wonder if it would ever happen.

"I didn't feel that I needed to win the national championship for my career to have been a success," Olson said. "I understood other people felt differently—that's the world of sports—but it wasn't the scale I used to measure my career."

A national championship would by no means define Olson, but it would officially complete the greatest turnaround in college basketball history. But before his players could ever worry about getting rings fitted, they had some maturing to do. Gone for the team's first 11 games would be senior Miles Simon, who was paying the price for academic troubles from the year before. His absence left the team with just one returning starter from the previous season, forcing Olson to rely on a group of inexperienced players to survive the first 11 games until Simon's return. The team passed the test with a 9–2 record, and although Simon could not take part in team activities, he managed to show some leadership by attending each of the team's road games, at his own expense. With Simon joining a now proven batch of youngsters, hopes for a national title began to grow once more, but his addition did not translate into wins. The Wildcats won just 10 of their last 17 games, leaving fans wondering just how good this team really was.

Nevertheless, Arizona found its way into the NCAA Tournament, and the mission started in earnest with a tightly-contested 65–57 victory over South Alabama. An equally scary 73–69 victory over College of Charleston in the second round put the Wildcats back in the Sweet 16, but that was as far as most experts had them going. Facing them next would be the Kansas Jayhawks, who were 34–1 and had returned everybody from the squad that had beaten Arizona 83–80 in the tournament the year before.

"When we were going to play Kansas in the Sweet 16 that following year, our players were confident that we could beat them even though they had been No. 1 all year long," Olson said. "We were on a roll at that point—that's the key to winning the NCAA Tournament."

The Wildcats would go on a late 11–0 run to seemingly put the game out of reach at 75–62 with 3:25 to play, but the Jayhawks quickly showed why they were the top-ranked team in the country. KU coach Roy Williams substituted in four guards to improve their outside shooting, and his players responded by closing the gap to just 83–82 with 19 seconds to play. Moments later, Arizona freshman Mike Bibby sank a pair of free throws to bring the lead back to three, and although the team had yielded 20 points in just over three minutes of action, they came up with their best defensive possession of the year when it mattered most. Kansas would get three looks at the basket in the final seconds, none of which were open, as the Wildcats held on for the 85–82 upset. For the first time in ages, Arizona found out what it was like to be on the other end of a tournament upset.

Olson's club followed up the win with another excruciatingly close victory, this one over Providence. The Friars overcame a huge deficit in the final minutes to force overtime, but the Wildcats' eventual 96–92 win sent them to the Final Four against North Carolina. For Simon, who had been told five years earlier that he wasn't good enough to be a Tar Heel, this would be his shot at redemption. Simon had held onto the rejection letter as motivation, which clearly worked as his 15 first-half points, and 22 overall, paved the way to a 66–58 win.

"He's one of those guys you would say was a born leader," Olson said. "He was demanding of his teammates, yet did it in such a way to build confidence. That's the key ingredient in the leader."

They would need that confidence in the championship game against Kentucky, perhaps the only team in the country that could make a case for being stronger than Kansas. The Wildcats from the Bluegrass State had won the national title in 1996, and they would do so again in 1998, but in between would be a championship game for the ages. No team would ever lead by more than six points, and Arizona led by just a point at halftime. The game continued to seesaw back and forth, as the teams remained tied on 20 different occasions and exchanged leads on 18 others. It was Kentucky that led 68–67 when Arizona seemed to deliver the knockout punch.

Simon, already with 23 points, hit a floater to put UA back up 69–68, then followed it up with another free throw that gave his team a two-point lead. Bibby then hit a pair of free throws to push the lead to 72–68 with just 1:01 left, but this game was too fantastic to end that early. UK's Ron Mercer, despite facing double teams all day, drained a three-pointer with 51 seconds remaining. And although UA guard Bennett Davidson hit a bank shot with 18.6 seconds on the clock, the game was still far from over. Kentucky guard Anthony Epps dribbled down the court and quickly faked a shot once he got to the three-point line. The fake got Bibby to leave his feet, and Epps seized the opportunity by hitting the game-tying three. After Simon missed an answer, the season's final game needed at least five more minutes to decide a champion. Olson, sensing his opponent had all the momentum, pulled the team together.

"Did you guys come this far to lose now? Are you going to finish the job?" Olson asked. "The toughest team is going to win this game. Are they tougher than we are?"

Olson found out soon enough, as his team hit an incredible 10 free throws in the extra session to give Arizona an 84–79 victory. Davidson ran over to mess up Olson's always-perfect hair. The coach, who fittingly descended from King Harold "The Fair Haired" of Norway, finally had a crown of his own. ●

1998 Kentucky

The 1998 tournament was like no other. Six games made this book's top 100 list, and several more were strong contenders. Washington's Deon Luton sank a long jumper with 10 seconds left to beat Xavier, giving the Huskies their first tournament win in 14 years. A few hours later, Cincinnati forward D'Juan Baker buried a three-pointer with just 3.5 seconds left to beat Northern Arizona 65–62, and a battle between Tennessee and Illinois State capped off the wild opening night. Tennessee's C. J. Black hit a layup with 15 seconds remaining to give the Volunteers an 81–80 lead, but with two seconds to go Dan Muller returned the favor by converting a layup of his own to give the Redbirds the victory. Perhaps the game most deserving of making the top 100 list was Syracuse's first-round win over Iona, when Marius Janulis hit a three-pointer with just 1.2 seconds on the clock for the 63–61 victory. Even the noncompetitive games provided some excitement, as Kansas set a new record for largest margin of victory with a 110–52 win over Prairie View A&M.

When Rick Pitino left for the NBA before the 1998 season, it looked like the end of an era for Kentucky basketball. Gone was the larger-than-life coach who had assembled the 1996 national champions and the 1997 national runners-up. Stepping into his place was Tubby Smith, the first African American coach at Kentucky, who made sure his players believed they could win a championship, even when nobody else did.

After a Saturday afternoon loss to Ole Miss near the end of the regular season, Smith called his players up at 5:00 a.m. on Sunday morning to alert them that he would be holding an extra practice in an hour. The next day, he called his players at the same time to hold another pre-dawn practice, and after a third session the following day, Smith proceeded to tell his players why they would be holding two-a-days for the rest of the season.

"You all think that because you got a new coach and a new coaching staff that you guys are like 'You know what? This is a rebuilding year.' Well, you all need to know that your coaches—this isn't a rebuilding year for us," senior guard Cameron Mills recalled of the speech. "There is a banner that we're planning on hanging at the end of this year, and you guys either need to get on board with us or we're going to forfeit the rest of these games. But we're not going to go out and play like you did Saturday."

The team responded by running off three consecutive victories, but their momentum came to a screeching halt when the mother of senior Allen Edwards passed away. Mills, a future minister, led the team in prayer for the Edwards family as Allen briefly left the team for the funeral.

"Compared to this, basketball is just silly. This is real life," Mills said. "It all kind of reminded us—you know what—there's something more important than basketball. And as odd as it sounds, that sort of attitude drew us all closer together as a family."

Edwards' absence would be the team's biggest challenge yet, but adversity was nothing new for the Wildcats. Junior Scott Padgett, one of the biggest contributors on the team, had watched from his parents' house when the 1996 team won the championship, because of academic trouble.

"It was probably the toughest night of my life other than the meeting that coach told me I flunked out of school," Padgett said. "If you're dreaming of playing at Kentucky, you're dreaming of a national championship, and it's not like they grow on trees."

Luckily for Padgett, he would get a second shot at a national title after Pitino allowed him back on the team the next year—if, and only if, he paid his own way back to school. Balancing three jobs, Padgett worked from 6 in the morning until 9 at night every day until he got the money to pay tuition. Instead of wearing down Padgett, the hard labor actually served as a blessing in disguise.

"I realized real quick how much I was making, which wasn't much, and I knew that wasn't the route I wanted to go in life, so it gave me a wakeup call," Padgett said. "When I came back, it made me appreciate everything—working hard, getting better, doing the little things. When it's a tough day, you look back and say this hard day isn't anywhere near the hard day I had this fall."

The path to putting on a Wildcats uniform was slightly more complicated for Mills, who turned down a scholarship from Georgia to walk on at Kentucky—the team his father, Terry, had played for decades before. Before his son signed the letter of intent to play for the Bulldogs, Terry called Pitino's staff to see if Cameron would ever have a shot at playing for his alma mater.

"He says to me, 'They want you to walk on,'" Mills said. "Of course, I only hear those first few words: 'they want you.' That's all I hear."

The gamble paid off, as Cameron, wearing his dad's No. 21 jersey, guided Kentucky to the Final Four after one of the greatest comebacks in NCAA history against Duke (see page 280). Never a team to take the easy road, the Wildcats found themselves in a 13–3 hole against Stanford in the opening minutes of their semifinal matchup, and they trailed for the first 30 minutes of the game. Padgett's free throws gave the team its first lead at 54–53, but the Cardinal battled back to take a 68–66 lead with a little over three minutes to go. Jeff Sheppard, Kentucky's most reliable player the whole season, took it upon himself to will the team to victory. Back-to-back threes by Sheppard gave Kentucky a four-point lead with just over a minute left.

"It goes back to our whole career at Kentucky," Sheppard said. "Every preseason

workout, every film session, every 6 a.m. practice we had. You go back to your training. That's what you train for, that's what you work for."

Stanford's Arthur Lee drained a three with 30 seconds to go to force overtime, but Sheppard's third straight shot from behind the arc gave the Wildcats an 82–78 lead, one they would not relinquish on the way to an 86–85 win. The victory pitted the Wildcats against Utah for the third consecutive year. And true to form, Kentucky decided to make it interesting.

After being outrebounded 24–6 in the first half, Kentucky went into the locker room facing a 41–31 deficit. But after everything else the team had overcome, this would be the easiest wall to climb.

"If you just watch the Utah team and the Kentucky team exit the floor at halftime, you see a really interesting dynamic. You see one team that's winning by 10 points that actually looks like they're losing by 10 points," Sheppard said. "We look like we have the momentum by the way we carry ourselves. That picture says a lot about what happened in the second half. It says a whole lot about our team that year."

Normally one to let his play do the talking, Sheppard fired up his team at halftime and came out hitting five clutch shots. His last shot, a steal and dunk with 7:15 left, gave Kentucky a 60–58 lead, its first since the beginning of the game. And after his free throws with four seconds left sealed the 78-69 victory, the emotions started to pour out for the team.

"I'm just kind of overwhelmed with 'Oh my gosh, that is my last college game ever,'" Mills said. "I fall on my face in the middle of the floor and I just start weeping."

So the 1998 Kentucky team would forever be remembered as the "Comeback Cats," but their nickname applied to so much more than basketball. And in a run that defied all odds, they also became perhaps the most likeable team of all time. ●

1999 Gonzaga

After watching three seasons dissolve in the Elite Eight, UConn coach Jim Calhoun finally advanced to his first Final Four in 1999, then carried that momentum all the way to the national championship game, where the Huskies defeated Duke 77–74. The Blue Devils came into the game riding a 32-game winning streak, but UConn point guard Khalid El-Amin promised viewers before the game that his team would shock the world, and he backed it up by sinking two huge free throws with five seconds to play to preserve the win. El-Amin was not the only player that year to shock the world, as Miami of Ohio's Wally Szczerbiak scored an incredible 73 percent of his team's points in a 59–58 win over Washington. He added 24 two nights later as the tenth-seeded RedHawks upset second seed Utah. The unlikeliest team in the Sweet 16, however, was twelfth-seeded Southwest Missouri State—the Bears won their opening game despite scoring just 43 points. In that same contest, however, they held Wisconsin to just 32 points and then destroyed fourth-seeded Tennessee by 30 points in the second round for their first-ever Sweet 16 berth.

When Gonzaga University tried to pursue Matt Santangelo out of high school, the odds were certainly stacked against them. As a program with no NCAA Tournament wins in its history, Gonzaga hardly appeared to be a promising option for Santangelo, who was being coveted by colleges across the country.

"To be honest with you I had no idea, when Gonzaga began recruiting me, I didn't know who Gonzaga was," Santangelo said. "They weren't even really on my radar."

Landing recruits like Santangelo was no easy task for assistant coach Dan Monson, and it was only made tougher given the financial situation of the athletic department. Money was hard to come by for the small Catholic school, and if Monson was going to persuade any players to come to Spokane, it wasn't going to be due to any lavish presentations.

"I know our recruiting budget was $15,000, and we weren't spending it on recruiting because we slept on other coaches' floors," laughed Monson, who used the funds to rebuild other parts of the basketball program. "But personally for me, I was so thrilled to be a full-time assistant coach that I didn't care."

But once Santangelo had his first taste of Gonzaga, he knew it was home, and when fellow guard Richie Frahm followed suit, the young assistant had just landed the best recruiting class of his life. Within a few years, the Spokane native became head coach, and his team was actually competitive. But with the lack of resources, getting to the NCAA Tournament still seemed like a lofty goal.

"Basically, it was like a fancy high school. We went there, we got recycled athletic gear, we got one pair of Nike shoes per season. That was pretty special," Frahm laughed. "At the time, I think we could compete because we felt like we were underdogs. That was our niche, and we felt like we could go in and we had nothing to lose."

With that mindset, the Bulldogs went out and dominated the West Coast Conference en route to a 25–6 record, good enough to land them a spot in the NCAA Tournament. The icing on the cake was that they were a 10 seed, which meant they would play just down the road in Seattle. Their first-round opponent was Minnesota, who just hours before tip-off had five players declared ineligible for the game due to an academic scandal. For the first time, it appeared that Gonzaga had lost their under-dog status—until Monson decided to turn the tables in his pre-game speech.

"I told them they're still going to send out five kids that got Big Ten scholarships on the floor, and none of you guys were recruited at that level," Monson said. "So we still have our hands full."

And the Zags did, as they let a 45–26 half-time lead slip to just 65–63 with 1:22 remaining. But before the Gophers could pull any closer, Frahm put the game out of reach with a crucial three-pointer, and Gonzaga won 75–63. That victory set up a second-round clash with Stanford, the second seed in the region and a squad that had returned nearly everyone from its Final Four team the year before.

"That game right there was one where a lot of Gonzaga faithful thought that it was over. . . . It's Stanford; they're not expected to lose," Santangelo said. "We were definitely a Cinderella, but at the time it was a little belittling to hear somebody say that about us, because we felt just as much of a man as the next team."

Giving Santangelo extra motivation was the fact that Stanford had recruited him three years earlier, but opted to give its last scholarship offer to guard Arthur Lee. Although Lee did become an All-American for the Cardinal, when the two faced off it was Santangelo who played the role of hero, scoring 22 points to give Gonzaga an 82–74 upset. Stanford, despite being considered the top rebounding team in the country, was outrebounded 47–33 by the vastly undersized Bulldogs. Cinderella had emerged, and the local crowd knew it.

"You would see that the whole state was on your shoulders," Monson said. "But at the time, it was your first time on that stage, and you didn't realize till after that game was over that hey, Seattle loves us here. The bus pulled out of town and people were lining the street yelling and waving."

But before Monson and his squad headed back to Spokane, he had to treat himself to a celebratory beer, which became an impromptu pep rally.

"I remember walking through downtown after the Stanford game at the end of it when it was all over, and the mob scene when I walked into a bar," Monson laughed. "The whole bar had me stand up on the counter to try to speak to them, and Richie Frahm came through and I pulled him off the street and the place went crazy."

The emotions for Santangelo were equally happy, but perhaps a little more heartfelt. After the game he ran into his father, who had made his way into the tunnel below to celebrate with his son. No sooner had Santangelo left the locker room than he saw his father sitting by the door, overcome with emotion.

"He's sitting there and he's doing what I'm doing now, he's half laughing, half crying and he didn't know what to do. He was completely speechless after what we just accomplished," Santangelo said. "I just remember coming out and all he can do, he's speechless, he was crying, he was laughing, all he can do is give me a big bear hug, and that will stay with me forever."

Gonzaga was hardly done, however. Days later, the Bulldogs produced another miracle by upsetting Florida in the final seconds to advance to the Elite Eight (see page 278). The school that couldn't afford to provide hotel rooms for their coaches, or new clothes to their athletes, was now America's team. And although their run stopped there, the effects of Gonzaga's journey were only beginning. The exposure from the tournament brought in more students, more donations, and, best of all, more wins. Gonzaga has found a way to make the tournament every season since that first magical run, but in the hearts of many, they will always be Cinderella. ●

2000 Michigan State

The 2000 NCAA Tournament had fans all across the country tearing up their brackets after both North Carolina and Wisconsin made the Final Four as eight seeds. Tenth-seeded Seton Hall made a run of its own, advancing to the Sweet 16 on a pair of thrilling finishes. In the opening round, Shaheen Holloway put in a bank shot with 1.9 seconds left, lifting the Pirates to a 72–71 overtime victory against Oregon. Holloway would be injured for the next game, but sophomore Ty Shine filled his shoes by sinking a three-pointer with 18.9 seconds left to give his team a 67–65 win over Temple. But the shot of the tournament came from Florida sophomore Mike Miller, who buried an off-balance jumper to seal a 69–68 victory over Butler as overtime expired.

As the 2000 tournament approached, Mateen Cleaves knew this would be his last chance to cement his legacy at Michigan State. As a sophomore, the point guard had told Final Four announcer Jim Nantz that someday he wanted CBS to play their "One Shining Moment" montage to clips of a Spartan championship. Unfortunately for Cleaves, his team was beaten soundly by North Carolina in the 1998 tournament and was ousted the following March by Duke. It took Cleaves a matter of minutes after the Duke loss to announce he was coming back for a final shot at a national championship.

"I wanted that to be my ultimate goal, to be listening to 'One Shining Moment,'" Cleaves said of the tournament anthem, played for each champion. "We always watched the Final Four and gathered around the TV, and as a kid I just took a liking to that song."

Cleaves wasn't the only kid from Flint, Michigan, with lofty dreams. He and Morris Peterson had played against each other since elementary school, and the pair had discussed winning a national championship together nearly a decade before they even got the chance. Along with junior Charlie Bell, who also hailed from Flint, the trio became known as the "Flintstones."

But before any Flintstone could step foot on the Michigan State campus, they would have to escape their tough surroundings. They also knew that basketball could be their ticket out.

"I remember everything that I went through in my life just coming up as a kid,

losing friends to violence, drug violence, killings, all that stuff," Cleaves said. "It's easy to say, 'I want to be successful, I want to make it,' but come every day it's a challenge to make it to that goal. So whenever someone asks you to do drugs or run with gangs or do something that isn't right, just think about that ultimate goal."

Their goal was almost cut short, however, when the team arrived in nearby Detroit for the second weekend of play. In their Sweet 16 matchup against Syracuse, the Spartans played their worst opening half of the season, going nearly the last eight minutes without a bucket. Cleaves was held scoreless, and their early 11–3 lead evaporated into a 32–19 deficit. When the team arrived in the locker room, the senior let everybody know that they would need to play with more ferocity if they were to have any chance of coming back.

"We just knew if we stuck to our core business and stuck to our goal of what he had to accomplish, we would be all right," senior A. J. Granger said. "And we had a game plan that was strong enough to allow us to do that."

The Orangemen actually went on an early 6–0 run to stretch the lead to 40–26, but a barrage of three-pointers by Peterson, Cleaves, and Granger allowed the Spartans to edge in front 58–56 with 6:10 remaining. After a bucket by Syracuse, Michigan State scored the last 17 points of the game for the 75–58 victory.

Their following game against Iowa State looked equally desperate, as the Cyclones went right at MSU's biggest strength. Despite leading the country in rebounding, the Spartans were dominated on the glass 38–27, and they faced an eight-point deficit with 11:45 to go. The situation looked increasingly desperate when Iowa State led 59–52 with less than six minutes remaining, but again the Spartans refused to panic. After a pair of three-pointers by Granger and Peterson, the home crowd was roaring. In fact, the arena got so loud that it almost began to backfire.

"We couldn't verbally dialogue with each other because it was so stinking loud," Granger said. "I remember walking down the floor and it was so loud in there, it was shaking the fluid in my ears to the point where I couldn't see straight."

The team relied on hand motions to communicate, but the relationship between Cleaves and Peterson also proved to be the difference. With no prior indication, Peterson broke to the basket just as Cleaves lofted the ball for an alley-oop, giving them a three-point lead with two minutes to play. Their 11–3 run in the closing minutes put the game out of reach and set up a Final Four date with Wisconsin, their fourth encounter of the year.

The two defensive-oriented teams perhaps knew each other too well, as fans were treated to one of the ugliest opening periods in Final Four history. Michigan State failed to make a shot for the final 11:42, a feat nearly equaled by the Badgers, who trailed 19–17 as the half came to a close. The Spartans eventually pulled away for a 53–41 victory, but one game still stood in the way of their dream.

Their final test would come against Florida, and while the Spartans got off to the fast start they had been looking for all tournament, it appeared to be all in vain. With the Spartans clinging to a 50–44 lead early in the second half, Cleaves severely sprained his left ankle, forcing head coach Tom Izzo to look toward his bench and ask, "Who's going to step up?" Transfer Mike Chappell answered the call by hitting two clutch baskets, and Granger soon followed with a three-pointer to put the team up 58–49. Granger, who was the team's fifth-leading scorer during the season, scored a career-high 19 points on 7-of-11 shooting. Moments after the shot, Cleaves returned to put the nail in the coffin.

"Nothing was ever going to keep me out of that game," Cleaves said. "I knew I wasn't going to be able to go out and score a bunch of points. I knew I wasn't going to be able to go out and play great defense because I barely could move. But one thing I knew I could bring to the table was just my leadership."

Cleaves didn't make another basket, but he didn't need to, as the entire team rallied to hold off the Gators for its first national title in 21 years. And as Cleaves hobbled toward his teammates at the buzzer, the emotions of realizing his dream came true.

"I was crying, and it was like tears are flowing, but it was the best feeling in the world," Cleaves said. "That was the best feeling I ever had in my life." ●

"When that horn went off I just thought about all the hard times, the work we put in," said Mateen Cleaves, who felt the same emotion as coach Tom Izzo, but expressed it in a different way. "We all had one common goal, and for that to come down and formulate and come to just winning a championship, that was the best feeling in the world."
Getty Images

2001 Duke

March Madness got started early in 2001 when eventual 16 seed UNC-Greensboro advanced to the tournament on an unbelievable play. Down by a point with 2.6 seconds to go in the Southern Conference Tournament championship, UNCG's Jay Joseph hurled a pass 75 feet to David Schuck, who hit the game-winner—a la Christian Laettner—to send the Spartans to the Big Dance. The fun was just getting started, as Missouri's Clarence Gilbert sank a jumper with 0.9 seconds left to beat Georgia, and Georgetown's Nat Burton became a hero later that night when he ignored the instructions of coach Craig Esherick. The ball was supposed to go to Kevin Braswell for the final shot, but Burton held onto the ball and delivered the layup as time expired to beat Arkansas 63–61. In a scene reminiscent of 1999, Casey Calvary put in a missed shot in the final seconds to give Gonzaga an 86–85 win over Virginia. Their second-round opponent was an unexpected one, as Indiana State's Kelyn Block suffered three chipped teeth in the final moments of regulation, only to score five points in overtime as the thirteenth-seeded Sycamores upset Oklahoma 70–68. The ensuing contest would go to the Zags, who advanced to the Sweet 16 for the third straight year.

Duke coach Mike Krzyzewski heard a knock on the door. Standing outside his house were three of his players: Chris Carrawell, Nate James, and Shane Battier. The trio had come over to share some good news with their coach, something he hadn't heard in quite some time. All three men would be returning to Durham for the 1999–2000 season, which was music to Krzyzewski's ears. Following his team's loss to UConn in the 1999 title game, an unprecedented seven players left the program, either to the NBA, graduation, or to another school. Among those leaving were three-time All-American Trajan Langdon and reigning Player of the Year Elton Brand, leaving the trio standing before Krzyzewski as the only returning players in Duke's rotation. The task before them was monumental, but in Carrawell, James, and Battier, Coach K knew he had three players willing to help rebuild the program.

Led by Battier and freshman Jason Williams, the Blue Devils won the 2000 ACC regular season and backed it up with a title in the conference tournament. Their journey would ultimately end at the Sweet 16, but the season was undoubtedly a success. And with Battier back for one final year, a national championship in 2001 was certainly within their grasp.

Battier and Williams led the team to a 29–3 record en route to All-American honors

for both players, but on senior night they got a reminder of just how beatable they really were. During his final game at Cameron Indoor Stadium, where his No. 31 jersey had already been hung in the rafters, Battier and his teammates fell 91–80 at the hands of Maryland. The Terrapins weren't Duke's oldest rival, but by this time they might have become their most hated. That rivalry further intensified when they faced off for the third time in the ACC Tournament. James tipped in a shot in the final second to give Duke the victory, but that battle would not be their last.

Maryland did its part to ensure another rematch by cruising to the Final Four, but Duke's journey was not so easy. The Blue Devils' Sweet 16 game against UCLA was still in doubt in the second half until Williams took his game to a completely new level. With his team clinging to a 40–37 margin, Williams scored 19 consecutive points as Duke pushed the lead to 59–51, and while the game wasn't out of reach, his performance was enough to help the Blue Devils hold on for a 76–63 victory. If it was any consolation to the Bruins, Williams then ripped apart UCLA's crosstown rival, USC, two nights later with 16 points in the first half. The Blue Devils would need each of them as they led only 43–38 at half, but the sophomore added another dozen points over the final period to bring the much anticipated rematch with Maryland to fruition.

Duke had led nearly every minute of their first four games, but round No. 4 against Maryland was quite a different story. Before the first half had even reached its conclusion, the Terrapins had grabbed a 22-point lead, a margin no team in Final Four history had ever overcome. Krzyzewski assured his players they were not going to lose by 40 points, and told them just to play the rest of the game without any set plays in mind. It was certainly a bold strategy, but as it turned out it was also an effective one. By halftime his players had cut the deficit in half, and with seven minutes left they grabbed their first lead.

Duke's 95–84 win was not only the largest comeback in Final Four history, it also put the Blue Devils in the championship game against Arizona. But with the victory, they instantly went from the role of heroes to villains. Nearly everybody outside the Duke contingent would be pulling for Arizona coach Lute Olson, whose wife, Bobbi, had died on New Year's Day. In fact, Olson even had a fan in Krzyzewski.

"Heck, if I didn't have to coach against him," Krzyzewski noted, "I would have been rooting for Lute, too."

To get the team in the right frame of mind to play, Krzyzewski brought in members from the 1991 team, who had captured America's heart during their run to Duke's first national championship. That squad had played the role of underdogs to perfection, and now with the "favorite" label slapped on their successors, the '91 team made sure that Battier and Co. were prepared for what they would encounter later that night. Not only would the crowd be pulling for their opponent, but the Wildcats were not exactly a bunch of scrubs, despite what their Cinderella status might have indicated.

From the opening tip, the Wildcats made it clear that Duke was going to be in for a long night. No team led by more than five points in the first half, and by the time the first 20 minutes came to a close, Duke's lead was a meager 37–35. The gap was still only 40–37 when a hero emerged for Duke in the form of Mike Dunleavy. The sophomore hit back-to-back three-pointers to give his team a 46–39 lead, and when Arizona's Jason Gardner tried to answer back with a layup, Battier raised his play to that of Dunleavy's.

Before the ball could even leave Gardner's hand, a streaking Battier ripped it away, and before falling out of bounds, he tossed it behind his back to keep the play alive. Seconds later, Dunleavy hit another three-pointer, and just like that the lead was 10. The Wildcats closed the gap to just 75–72 in the final minutes, but Battier, despite having played every second of the championship, found enough energy to seal the title with an emphatic dunk. With the 82–72 win, Krzyzewski became just the third coach in history to win at least three championships, an honor he did not take lightly.

"First of all, you thank God that things worked out. For instance, you avoided injuries. There's usually just a few plays—one shot, a steal, a rebound, or a loose ball—that could stop you from being there," Krzyzewski said. "You thank the basketball gods for putting everything in motion to allow things to happen. There's certainly some luck involved. It is a humbling experience to look back and see how close we were to not doing it. I think that drives you forward to try to be even better as you try to do it again."

And luckily for Krzyzewski, he would get another chance nine years later (see page 328). ●

2002 Maryland

The NCAA Tournament went to the pod system in 2002, which was designed to reduce travel for the top teams. Even more appreciative were the fans, who bested the previous year's attendance mark by 110,000. They got to see a plethora of incredible games, as Southern Illinois came back from a 19-point deficit to defeat Georgia 77–75, and Oregon defeated Texas 72–70 on a Fred Jones scoop shot with 2.8 seconds to go. But the story of the tournament was the Elite Eight, when twelfth-seeded Missouri and tenth-seeded Kent State crashed the party. The Golden Flashes, who started the year at just 4–4 and then reeled off 21 consecutive victories, were led by none other than Antonio Gates. The power forward would turn some heads by choosing to play in the NFL, but eight Pro Bowls later it's safe to say he made the right decision.

After their 2001 season came to a painful close, the Maryland Terrapins were determined to end things differently if they ever got a second chance. Never again would they become complacent as they did when they blew a 22-point lead against Duke in the 2001 Final Four. Fortunately, everybody who had endured that heart-crushing loss returned to make amends the following year, and within weeks the path toward redemption was underway. Players started returning to the court after practice for some midnight basketball, a habit that caught on quickly with everybody on the team.

"Once you get a couple of guys doing it, it's funny how all of a sudden it just starts translating throughout the whole team," junior Drew Nicholas said. "Because then everybody doesn't want to be looked at as an outcast, so then everybody starts doing it."

For most players on the team, meeting a challenge was nothing new. Nicholas, a 6-foot-3 guard generously listed at 160 pounds, was told by almost every college that he was too skinny to play Division I basketball. Center Lonny Baxter, on the other hand, was considered to be too heavy, and the Maryland native took the only scholarship offer he was given, which happened to be from UM coach Gary Williams.

"I guess he just knew how much I wanted to be there. And he just took a chance with me, and everything happened to work out," Baxter said. "I was just working, you know, happy to be a Maryland student, a player—just to put on a uniform every night and just to represent the Terrapins."

Juan Dixon, another senior from Maryland, had to overcome more adversity than perhaps any player in history. Dixon's parents, both heroin addicts, had died of AIDS when he was a teenager. He spent the rest of high school under the care of his grandparents, but when it came time to qualify to attend a college, his 840 SAT score prevented him from enrolling at Maryland. During his first year out of high school, Dixon worked for minimum wage at a shipping dock while spending his free time studying for his next SAT test. Dixon earned a 1060, only to have the College Board question the validity of his score. But the persistent Dixon took the SAT for a third time and aced it, allowing him finally to join his teammates.

"Coming up from the Baltimore area, losing both of his parents, he's just a tough kid just going through those life struggles. And to be able to do what he did and to make it to the NBA and play as long as he did, that just shows the type of character he has," Baxter said. "Juan's a great competitor. You could see it in him just what type of person he is, always wanting to win, just wanting to give it his all every shot every time on the floor. And you could see that early from one of the first times I was at Maryland."

Thanks to more than 20 points a game from Dixon, the Terrapins earned a top seed for the tournament and looked prepared for one last shot at the national championship.

Three wins later, they were in the Elite Eight, needing just a win over Connecticut to reach the Final Four once again. But in a game that featured 21 ties and 24 lead changes, the Terps got all they could handle from UConn. Caron Butler's free throws gave the Huskies a 77–74 lead in the final minutes, but some clutch shooting by Dixon and Baxter put Maryland back in front 83–79. After a Connecticut free throw trimmed the lead to 83–80, Williams called a timeout with 34 seconds left and told point guard Steve Blake, also a senior, to get the ball to Dixon or Nicholas—an instruction that Blake overruled. Blake knew that UConn would be looking for his teammates to take the last shot, and he told his coach that he would take it himself. Or so the story goes.

"That story's close, there's a lot of urban legends out there," laughed Williams. "They weren't worried about him shooting, and the thing he said to me on the way out of the huddle was, 'If they go underneath the screen and I'm open, I've got to take it.'"

Just as Blake predicted, the Connecticut defense left him open, and when he nailed the crucial shot from the right wing the Terps led 86–80 with 25.4 seconds to go.

"Steve, he's a gusty guy. He's not afraid of anything," Baxter said. "If he says he has it, then you know he has it. Nobody is going to change his mind. He's kind of stubborn, but he's a great leader, a great point guard, and a guy I love to play with."

The win put Maryland back in the Final Four, but a 13–2 run by Kansas to start the semifinal match left the Terps' championship aspirations in serious doubt. Williams, sensing that the team was feeling shades of their 2001 loss, huddled the team over.

"We were nervous going into that game because we had lost in the semifinals the year before. We just had to snap out of it," Williams said. "Juan Dixon was the big catalyst in the

timeout. He grabbed Baxter and [Chris] Wilcox and said they got to be tougher defensively. We went out and this is how Juan Dixon was. It's one thing to say something like that in the huddle, but he hits back-to-back threes."

Dixon actually sandwiched a steal and layup between the two three-pointers, and when he scored his tenth consecutive point for his team, they had cut the deficit to 17–15. Dixon's three-pointer minutes later gave Maryland its first lead at 26–25, and by halftime the lead had stretched to 44–37. The Terps didn't stop there, as Byron Mouton's jumper with 6:38 to play gave them a seemingly insurmountable 80–63 advantage. But the Jayhawks would storm back, cutting the margin to 87–82 with two minutes remaining when Williams called a timeout.

"Kansas is a strong team. Of course they're going to make a run because they're hungry for that championship, too," Baxter said. "But we were able to keep the focus and just keep the lead and take the game."

Unlike the previous year's collapse, the team held on for the victory to reach the title game. And against Indiana, the Terps played their best defensive game of the season in a 64–52 victory. Williams found his daughter, with whom he had finally reconnected after years of estrangement, and gave her a huge hug. His team, the first ever to win a title with no high school All-Americans, had proven everybody wrong.

"I think what made it so sweet was also knowing that we brought the first one to the University of Maryland, doing something that a Maryland team has never done before," Nicholas said. "And for so much of the team, all the guys were playing with chips on their shoulders because everybody said when we were coming to Maryland we weren't good enough. But to be able to do it with that group of guys was really special." ●

2003 Syracuse

Two years after the death of legendary coach Al McGuire, Marquette reached the Final Four for the first time since his retirement in 1977. Dwyane Wade's performance propelled him to become the fifth overall pick in the NBA draft that year, and two of the players chosen before him—LeBron James and Chris Bosh— would eventually become his teammates. Butler couldn't quite match the talent level of the Miami Heat's "big three," but the twelfth-seeded Bulldogs became the darlings of the tournament. Brandon Miller made a runner with six seconds left to beat Mississippi State, and the Bulldogs followed that with an upset over Louisville. Nobody enjoyed the run more than Butler junior Mike Monserez, who leaped on top of the press table three years before George Mason did so, to celebrate their 47–46 victory over MSU.

Ever since Jim Boeheim arrived in Syracuse as a student in 1962, he had eagerly striven toward a national championship. His years as a player were rather pedestrian—which was still a huge accomplishment considering the team had started the season 0–22 the year before he arrived—but three years after graduation Boeheim returned back to Syracuse, intent on bringing that title to his alma mater. He was only a graduate assistant at the time, but within seven years Boeheim was promoted to head coach, a position he was still holding by the start of the 2003 season. During that span, Boeheim had nearly reached that goal on several occasions, but each time his Orangemen had come up just short, leaving fans wondering if Boeheim would ever get his elusive national title. And judging by the looks of his 2002–03 roster, he would have to wait at least one year more.

"We really didn't expect to win halfway through the year. We didn't expect to be in the hunt for a national championship. We just thought we were too young and there were too many veteran teams out there," Boeheim said. "And you know, we just thought that we had a good team, we can make a run in the tournament, but we really didn't think we were going to win the national championship two quarters of the way through the season."

The problem had little to do with the players' abilities; the talent on the team was there. The experience, however, was not. Led by a pair of newcomers in Carmelo Anthony and Gerry McNamara, as well as sophomore Hakim

Warrick, the Orangemen boasted one of the youngest teams in the nation. Boeheim only had one senior on the team, and seven of the players in his nine-man rotation were underclassmen. A title run in 2005 looked like a definite possibility. But in 2003, the Orangemen, who were unranked at the beginning of the year, had some ground to make up.

"Texas and Kansas and Kentucky had a lot of guys back, so there were lot of veteran players on their teams, so you weren't thinking that much of winning a national championship. But as the season went on, as the end of the year came, we did start to play better," Boeheim said. "We had two road wins—one at Notre Dame, one at Michigan State—that kind of gave us an indication, you know, we could be a good team. So we thought we had a team that could get in the tournament and win some games, get to certainly the Sweet 16 and maybe a regional final. But there were probably five or six teams better than us going into the tournament, so we knew we had a hard task, a long way to win a national championship."

Their first test would come in the tournament's second round against Oklahoma State. Just 12 minutes into the game, the Orangemen found themselves down 25–8, prompting Boeheim to call timeout. By halftime, Syracuse had cut the deficit to 31–25, and five minutes into the second period they grabbed a 40–39 lead on a three-pointer by McNamara. The Orangemen would eventually hang on for a 68–56 victory, but an even

The Orangemen's Josh Pace (No. 5) in action against Kansas' Kirk Hinrich (No. 10) and Nick Collison (No. 4). *John Biever/Sports Illustrated/Getty Images*

tougher challenge would come the following game against Auburn. Much like the Cowboys five days earlier, the Orangemen grabbed an early 33–16 lead, only to see the Tigers storm back to get within 41–37 early in the second half. It appeared they would hang on after all when Anthony tipped in a shot with 39 seconds left, putting them up 73–67, but the Tigers were not done quite yet. They scored 11 points over the final 30 seconds, and it was only thanks to some clutch shooting from the foul line that Syracuse escaped with a 79–78 win.

Next up was Oklahoma, another team like Syracuse that featured only one senior. The only difference, however, was that OU's senior came in the form of Big 12 Player of the Year Hollis Price. The Sooners were awarded the top seed in the East Region, a ranking that appeared justified as they took an early 17–16 lead over Syracuse despite an unwelcoming crowd in Albany. But Boeheim, whose 2-3 zone defense had become the stuff of legend, stuck to the game plan, and by the opening minutes of the second half his team had taken a commanding 38–20 lead. The Sooners, who had made seven of their first 14 shots, had now hit just one of their last 18. As for Price, he would finish with 3-of-17 shooting and his team would end up with more turnovers than shots. With the 63–47 win, the hometown fans bid the Orangemen farewell as they departed for New Orleans to take on Texas in the Final Four.

If there was a player more celebrated than Hollis Price in college basketball, it was Longhorns point guard T. J. Ford. Price had been awarded the conference's Player of the Year award, but it was Ford who won National Player of the Year honors. McNamara would actually hold Ford to just 3-of-8 shooting, but all the focus on Ford opened the door for Texas forward Brandon Mouton to step up in his place. Mouton's 20 points kept UT within 48–45 heading into the break, and it was his three-pointer with 12:13 left that gave the team a 61–59 lead. Once again, however, the Syracuse defense recovered to come away with a 95–84 victory. The only team that stood between the Orangemen and the championship was yet another Big 12 powerhouse—Kansas. The Jayhawks would certainly make them earn it, but after 41 years of waiting, Jim Boeheim finally had his national championship (see page 326). As for the eight freshmen on the roster, they had waited all of five months.

"A bunch of young guys did something that was almost impossible I think to overcome," Boeheim said. "Kansas, with the veteran players they had, the overall team they had, how they just demolished Marquette in the semifinals, I mean, they had all the momentum in the world going in. And I just felt they would be a very difficult team to beat, and for our young guys to do that—no team's won with a team dominated by freshmen. Our *two* best players were freshmen." ●

2004 Connecticut

The 2004 season started and ended with Connecticut at the top of the basketball rankings, but along the way it was little-known St. Joseph's that captured the attention of the basketball world. Behind future NBA star Jameer Nelson, the Hawks ran off a 27–0 record on their way to the No. 1 ranking. Their magical season would come to an end in the Elite Eight, however, when Oklahoma State's John Lucas drained a three-pointer with just eight seconds left to give the Cowboys a 64–62 victory. For fans heartbroken over their loss, there were still plenty of entertaining games to ease the pain, and few matched the drama of the second-round matchup between Vanderbilt and N.C. State. Down 67–56 with less than 3:30 to play, Vanderbilt's Matt Freije scored 11 of his team's next 16 points as they took a 72–71 lead. N.C. State came back to take the lead, but Corey Smith's three-point play with 21 seconds left proved to be the difference-maker for the Commodores.

Emeka Okafor turned around and headed for his own basket, knowing his team's season was in serious peril. Moments earlier, the UConn center had bricked the front end of a one-and-one free throw. It was the last thing the Huskies needed, as they already faced a 75–68 deficit to Duke in the semifinals with 3:15 to go. It had not been a pleasant day at the office for Okafor, who sat for much of the first half with foul trouble and didn't score a point until the game's thirty-fourth minute. And now it was his missed free throw that still left the Huskies three possessions down, without the ball and little time to do anything about it. Okafor and his teammates made their way back to their end of the court, knowing they were about to get the biggest character test of their careers.

For UConn, this was unfamiliar territory. Thanks to a slew of upsets in their region, the Huskies never had to play higher than a six seed on their way to the Final Four. The easy schedule had allowed them to win their first four tournament games by an average of 17.5 points, but a challenge could have done them some good. Now they were going to learn how to swim by being thrown in the water.

The first order of business was to get a stop on the defensive end. They would get exactly what they were looking for when Luol Deng missed a three-pointer, leading to a UConn fast break. If the Huskies were going to make up some ground, they were going to have to

do so in a hurry. Within three seconds after grabbing Deng's miss, Taliek Brown had raced past midcourt and fired a pass to teammate Rashad Anderson, who was standing alone in the right corner. Anderson immediately hoisted up a three-pointer, which rattled in with 2:39 remaining to trim the lead to 75–70. They still had a long way to go to catch up with the Blue Devils, but they were now at least one step closer. Again the Husky defense held strong, forcing Duke guard Daniel Ewing into a difficult fadeaway shot from just inside the three-point line. Ewing's shot was well short, and UConn quickly went on the attack once more. This time it took only four seconds for the Huskies to get a shot off.

Ben Gordon didn't make his layup attempt, but the UConn guard did the next best thing: He drew a foul. Gordon, already 5-of-6 from the line, stepped up and nailed both shots to put Connecticut within 75–72. The Blue Devils tried to answer back with a drive to the basket, but the Huskies would have none of it. Ewing was stripped on his way to the basket, and although the ball ended up in the hands of Duke forward Nick Horvath, he, too, had the ball slapped away. Blue Devils guard Chris Duhon eventually picked up the ball, but now the shot clock was winding down. Duhon also tried to take the ball into the paint, but like Ewing and Horvath before him, he was unable to get a shot off before the ball was knocked out of his hands. The ball rolled toward the

Emeka Okafor going up for a block against Georgia Tech's Clarence Moore during UConn's easy victory.
Rich Clarkson/Sports Illustrated/Getty Images

baseline, but before reaching the end line it was snatched up by a sprawling Josh Boone. The UConn center called a timeout with 1:35 left, and 16 seconds later Okafor drained a hook shot to bring the Huskies within 75–74.

The Blue Devils went back to Deng, but his shot bounced off the rim and over the backboard with 44.5 seconds to go. Connecticut had trailed for the last 30 minutes, but now had a chance to take the lead. It was partly thanks to Okafor that the Huskies had trailed for so long, but now during the biggest possession of the game his teammates relied on him to take the crucial shot. Okafor actually missed a jumper from 10 feet away, but as Boone tried to tip it in from underneath the basket, his putback hit the bottom of the rim and ricocheted back toward Okafor. This time Okafor delivered, and his bank shot with 25.9 seconds left put the Huskies within one stop of the national championship game. Duke coach Mike Krzyzewski called a timeout to try and draw up a final shot, but for the fifth straight time, UConn was up to the challenge. Blue Devils sophomore J. J. Redick drove toward the basket, but before he could even get a shot off Anderson had swiped the ball away, writing UConn's ticket to the title game.

The win seemed to seal coach Jim Calhoun's spot in the Hall of Fame, voting for which would take place on the day of the championship game. It was the 703rd victory of Calhoun's career, and his 453rd at UConn, which had one of the most lackluster programs in NCAA history before his arrival. Nevertheless, hours before his team would take on Georgia Tech, the HOF selection committee declined to enshrine him. As it turned out, Calhoun had been one vote short. If Calhoun didn't want to leave San Antonio completely empty-handed, he was going to have to defeat a Georgia Tech squad that had blown out his team earlier in the year. In that late-November game, Calhoun's squad missed 20 free throws in a 77–61 loss, but on this night the Huskies were ready to play.

Okafor, ready to avenge his first-half performance against the Blue Devils, scored 10 points in the early going as UConn built a 41–26 halftime lead, the largest for a title game in 37 years. The Huskies eventually pushed the lead to 60–35, leaving no doubt as to who was the best team in college basketball. A year later, Calhoun would deservedly be inducted into the Hall of Fame, but on this night he celebrated something much more meaningful. ●

2005 North Carolina

After a relatively quiet opening night, the 2005 tournament quickly exploded into one of the most exciting in history, and it just kept getting better as it progressed. Fans thought they had seen the game of the tournament when Arizona's Salim Stoudamire defeated Oklahoma State on a last-second jumper, but Louisville overcame a 20-point deficit to defeat West Virginia in overtime just two days later. A day after that, Kentucky and Michigan State battled to a double-overtime classic. With time winding down in regulation and his team trailing 75–72, Kentucky's Patrick Sparks hoisted up a three-pointer that rested on the rim, the season hanging in the balance. The ball dropped in, but Michigan State eventually emerged with a 94–88 victory.

After grinding out an 88–82 victory over Wisconsin to reach the 2005 Final Four, the North Carolina players were enjoying what seemed to be a well-earned celebration. It was a huge accomplishment for a squad that had gone 8–20 just three years earlier and finished the following season with a loss in the NIT. Watching this all unfold, head coach Roy Williams knew it was time to step in. If they defended against their next opponent like they did tonight, he warned, the team would be taking an early exit home.

With that comment, any buzz still lingering from their victory was instantly killed. But if anybody knew that national championships didn't come easy, it was Williams. In 17 seasons as a head coach (15 with Kansas), he had reached the Final Four a remarkable five times, including two trips to the championship game, only to fall short each time.

"I think it's hard, those years coming so close, and a couple of years I actually thought we had the best team. If it had been a best of five or a best of seven, I think we would have won it," Williams said. "I said we're going to keep knocking on the door and one of these days we're going to knock the sucker down, and I strongly believed that."

The team arrived back at Chapel Hill to practice, only to find that Williams had removed the rims from every backboard. True to his word, Williams was not going to allow his players to defend Michigan State with the same effort they had against Wisconsin. Practice was going to be completely about defense. Although it was a little out of the ordinary, the plan worked perfectly, as the Tar Heels held Michigan State to 33.8 percent shooting and cruised to an 87–71 victory. Next would be Illinois, owner of a 37–1 record and the top spot in the national polls.

"At that point in the season, we were so confident as individuals," forward Marvin Williams said. "And as a team, we felt like we could really play with anybody in the country."

But confidence wouldn't be enough to calm the nerves of their coach, who took the whole team out to a bridge over the Mississippi River and instructed them to spit in the water for good luck. His Tar Heels would need all the luck they could get, as the Illini would be enjoying a huge home-crowd advantage because the game would be played in nearby St. Louis. In the locker room before the game, away from the thunderous Illinois fans, Williams gave one of the most powerful speeches of his career.

"The whole theme was Illinois is such a great team and North Carolina is talented but they are not as good of a team, so that was the focus," Williams said. "We didn't have the respect, and I said, 'Hey, everybody is talking about talent versus team. Let's show them that we can be a team, too, and that we're all in this together.'"

UNC distributed the ball to perfection, as Sean May and Raymond Felton each scored 12 points, while Rashad McCants chipped in with 14 of his own to give UNC a 47–32 lead early in the second half. But the good-luck charm was starting to wear out as Illinois guards Deron Williams and Luther Head combined for six quick buckets, and in a matter of minutes the lead had dwindled to 52–50.

"I said, 'Hey guys, it's not easy to win a national championship. That team down there has won 37 games,'" Williams said. "I expected them to come back. So now they've made their run. Let's just play."

The plan was to feed the ball to Sean May, who appeared to have the hot hand. May responded with a three-point play and a layup, giving UNC a 57–50 lead. By the time May added another three-point play and two more free throws, he was 10-of-11 from the field. More importantly, the lead was back up to 10.

But the matchup between the nation's two best teams was destined to go down to the wire. Once again Head answered the call, hitting another three-pointer to tie the game at 70–70 with just 2:39 left. Staring directly at a third championship loss, Williams called a timeout and delivered a simple message.

"I don't have anything to tell you," Williams said. "I just wanted to give you one last breather before we go out and finish this game better than we finished all year."

The unlikely hero ended up being Marvin Williams, a freshman who had struggled throughout the game. After McCants' reverse layup was off the mark, Williams was right there to tip in the crucial basket.

"I really feel like champions find ways to win," Williams said. "We just knew we had to bring our 'A game' to beat them."

The Illini understandably went right back to Head, but this time Felton was there for a crucial steal. His free throw put UNC up 73–70, and after another defensive stop, the Tar Heels had just earned Williams his long-awaited championship. But after waiting all this time for the moment to happen, the coach was nowhere to be found. Williams, who admired Illinois coach Bruce Weber so much that he often showed his team clips of the Illini as examples of how to play, needed to find his friend.

"At the end of the game, gosh, everybody is jumping around and hugging you and all of a sudden I realized I hadn't had an opportunity to shake hands with Bruce. He had stood there off to the side waiting on me, and then I realized that he had gone off, so that's when I made that run off to the end of the court to try to catch him before he got to his locker room," Williams said. "I told him I'd been there, I had lost two national championship games, and knew exactly how he was feeling. Bruce is just one of those quality guys in coaching that I really do enjoy. I have a great deal of respect for him. I just didn't want him to get off the court without me sharing that moment and telling him what a great job he had done."

As it turned out, that conversation meant just as much to Weber as it did to Williams.

"If you're going to lose to somebody, you want to lose to somebody you respect and who has done it the right way," Weber said. "For Roy and Carolina, you couldn't feel better for them."

The championship was great for Williams, but it didn't make his players or fans like him any more than they already did—that wasn't possible.

"You know what? The thing I love most about him is that he cares about us as people and he makes that very clear," Marvin Williams said. "Just having a coach like that who cares so much about you as a person really means a lot to me."

Of course, this isn't to say that the championship didn't mean anything. For the first time in 12 years, the Tar Heels could say that they not only had the most talent, they also had the best team. ●

2006 George Mason

While Duke's J. J. Redick and Gonzaga's Adam Morrison dazzled crowds during the 2005–06 regular season, and George Mason captured America's heart in the tournament, the Florida Gators quietly put together an incredible championship run. On the verge of elimination in the third round, Florida's Corey Brewer delivered a three-point play to put the Gators up 55–53 over Georgetown. In the title game, the Gators held UCLA to just 36 percent from the floor during a 73–57 victory. Fellow SEC member LSU also made the Final Four, but had it not been for Darrel Mitchell's deep three with 3.9 seconds left against Texas A&M, their season would have come to an end in the second round. Considering that Florida's 2006 football team also won the national championship, it was an incredibly successful year for the school and the SEC.

Life at the mid-major level can often be a difficult one. Because they face schools with more money, more students, and more exposure, the mountain they must climb to become an elite program can seem impossibly high. But for all the challenges these programs are up against, perhaps the biggest obstacle is their mindset. In 2006, before Butler and VCU made their trips to the sport's biggest stage, most mid-major schools considered an NCAA berth, with possibly one victory in the tournament, a successful season. No one knew this better than George Mason coach Jim Larranaga, who brought a sports psychologist into the team's inner circle before the start of the season.

"At that meeting, he asked them to close their eyes and dream about the best season they thought they could have. Then he asked them to open their eyes and asked one of them to offer what they envisioned," Larranaga said. "Lamar Butler raised his hand and said, 'I dreamt that we got to the Final Four.' Dr. Rotella asked the players, 'How many of you buy into that dream, that believe you guys can make it to the Final Four?' And all of the guys raised their hands."

But before they could worry about making a run in the tournament, the Patriots would first have to worry about getting there. The players seemed to slip farther away from their goal with each passing game, as they started the season 7–4. They recovered to end the regular season with a 22–6 record, but when they lost to Hofstra in the conference tournament, an at-large berth appeared highly unlikely. For seven straight days before Selection Sunday, Larranaga listened to experts rail on George Mason and their prospects of getting into the Big Dance. Fortunately, the selection committee did not agree. The Patriots were in as an eleven seed, though not to everyone's liking.

"Actually the team was at my house on Selection Sunday, and we had a chance to listen and watch the selection show together and listen to Billy Packer and Jim Nantz talk about the selection process and basically say that George Mason didn't belong and that we would get crushed by Michigan State in the first round," Larranaga said. "When I turned the TV off to address the team, I repeated what I had told them before the show began, and that was they had never seen us play before, they don't know how good we are. We do—you are the best team in George Mason history. You are the best team I ever coached, and you are going to be able to show the world what we're capable of doing when we play Michigan State."

Larranaga asked his players to dream once more, this time about what it would be like to play their best basketball against the Spartans. And just like the first time, things did not exactly go according to plan.

"The next day after practice, Jai Lewis picked up the Gatorade jug full of ice water and poured it over my head, and when I turned around the whole team was on the floor laughing," said Larranaga, who of course asked his senior what he was doing.

"Visualizing," Lewis said.

"Visualizing what?" his coach retorted.

"Visualizing the celebration when we beat Michigan State on Saturday night!"

And although it looked doubtful when the Spartans took the lead with 6:44 to play, a 10–0 run in the final minutes propelled George Mason to the second round. But whatever momentum they had clearly did not carry over into their second game against North Carolina. Five minutes into the game, the Patriots were shooting 1-of-7 from the floor and the Tar Heels had grabbed a 16–2 lead, prompting Larranaga to regroup the team.

"I told the team to look me in the eye. Everybody was gathered around me, and I said, 'Look, we've got these guys right where we want them,'" Larranaga remembered. "And they all just looked at each other and one of them said, 'We do?' And I said, 'Yeah, look down at the North Carolina bench—look, they are celebrating like the game is over, like they've already won. The game has just begun, and we haven't even started to play yet. We need to start playing George Mason basketball.'"

The only problem was they couldn't play George Mason basketball, at least for the time being. Larranaga's son had called him the night before, at 4 a.m. in Italy where he was stationed, and told his father that Carolina's weakness was their freshman point guard. But knowing that UNC coach Roy Williams was one of the best in the business, the Patriots would have to wait until after halftime, when Williams was done making adjustments, to unleash the press.

"So we switched into a 1-2-2 zone, a defense that we had never played the entire season, but we put it in," Larranaga said. "Teams would not be prepared for it, and we were going to use the 1-2-2 zone as a curveball to see how they reacted."

Slowly but surely, the Patriots clawed their way back into the game, and after 24 minutes of action they had their first lead at 32–30. George Mason was still holding onto a 54–51 lead when UNC senior David Noel drained a shot from the left corner, tying the game with just three minutes to go. Larranaga called a timeout, and when the Patriots emerged back on the floor, it was obvious who they wanted to have the ball. Butler, the team's leading scorer, sank a pair of free throws to give his team a 56–54 lead, and he then sliced through the UNC defense with a minute left to put the team up by four. George Mason held on for a 65–60 victory, and the team that was never supposed to be in the tournament was now in the Sweet 16. *Sports Illustrated* decided to reward Butler by making him their cover boy.

"It was crazy. I still remember that day. We were shooting—practice was over—and I just heard coach scream, 'Oh, my God!' I just turn around. There's a huddle of players around me, and he had something in his hand, so I just walked over there and I saw it," Butler said. "I just knew at that point we had reached the national level. We knew we had notoriety. For me personally, it's something I could show my grandkids: 'Hey your grandpa was on *Sports Illustrated.*'"

The win also marked the first time that Patriots memorabilia had become valuable collector's items, as kids lined up to grab their autographs. And when the team defeated Wichita State to advance to the Elite Eight, those demands increased only further.

"Later you saw those same things on eBay," laughed Butler. "Of course, as a player you're not going to say no to a kid or person, but the same things you signed you saw on eBay—like I remember that. It was crazy prices. We would check every day to see what would be on there, and we just looked at the prices and we were like, that's it, we're not signing any more autographs. But of course we did."

Butler was now one victory away from achieving his preseason dream, but in order to get there his team would have to defeat Connecticut, considered by analysts to be one of the best teams ever assembled. But these were the same experts who had said that the Patriots had no business in the tournament, and after one of the greatest upsets of all time, the dream was complete (see page 300). Their 86–84 victory over UConn sent George Mason to the Final Four—but the game meant so much more than that. Even though George Mason would lose its following game to Florida, teams could wear the "mid-major" badge with pride for the first time ever. The CBS analysts came over and apologized, admitting their mistake. The players were more than happy to forgive, but if their critics wanted to snag an autograph, well, they could go find one on eBay. Only now they might cost a bit more. ●

2007 Florida

Ohio State's run to the 2007 national championship would end just one game short, but the Buckeyes provided plenty of drama along the way. They trailed 59–50 with just three minutes to play in their second-round game against Xavier, but fought back to tie the game on a Ron Lewis three-pointer with four seconds left. OSU prevailed in overtime 78–71, only to fall behind by 20 points in the next game to Tennessee. Once again they came storming back, and Mike Conley Jr.'s free throw with six seconds to go broke the 84–84 tie. Virginia Tech also needed some last-minute magic, as the Hokies scored the last 12 points of their opening-round game to beat Illinois 54–52 for their first tournament win in 11 years. At the other end of the spectrum, Duke ended an 11-year streak by losing its first-round game against VCU. Rams guard Eric Maynor hit three crucial shots over the final 90 seconds, including a jumper with 1.9 seconds to go to seal a 79–77 victory.

For the 2007 Florida Gators, the journey toward a second national title began before they ever even had a chance to play for their first. Just days removed from their victory over Villanova, which sent them to the 2006 Final Four, Florida coach Billy Donovan sat in a golf cart with center Joakim Noah and forward Al Horford. The trio was driving toward an interview session with the media, but before they reached their destination, the 40-year-old coach had a few words of wisdom for his sophomores.

"You guys can do something real special, you know. You win a national championship and you're able to come back and do it back-to-back," Donovan said. "If you guys keep working, keep getting better, you can make history."

The Gators still had plenty of work to do before claiming their first national championship, but the seed had already been planted.

"He said it then, and me and Joakim kind of nodded, and we were like, yeah. And I don't want to say that we were sure we were going to win that first one, but Coach D just basically put that in our minds," Horford said. "And that was the thing that strongly drove us to return and try to make us something special."

The team would indeed win its first national title a few days later as they defeated UCLA 73–57. Thanks to their stellar play in the tournament, Noah and Horford, along with fellow sophomore Corey Brewer, were all assured of becoming first-round NBA draft picks. Financial security and stardom were within their grasp, but each chose to return to Gainesville. The NBA could wait; history needed to be made first. But before they could begin their quest for repeat titles, Donovan shared some more words of advice for his three superstars.

"Listen, I don't need anyone coming out here trying to score 20 points a game and doing all this other stuff," Donovan said. "I need five guys to score between 10 and 14 points a game. If we do it like that and we defend, we give ourselves a chance to be good and we'll see how good we can be."

Not only would the Gators have five players in double figures, but Horford and Noah would become the third- and fourth-leading scorers on the most balanced team in the country. With other teammates sharing the burden, the duo would combine to make 61 percent of their shots on the year, leaving opponents unsure of who to guard as the Gators compiled a 24–2 record by mid-February.

"The group, the team that we had, we were very unselfish, and I think that at the end of the day we were just focused on winning and being the best team that we could be," Horford said. "And the best thing about it was the guys really didn't mind. Being part of a team like that, it's rare where everybody just focused on the bigger picture, not necessarily about numbers."

Fans and experts alike appeared ready to hand the Gators a second title, but Noah knew that a repeat title was no guarantee. As the team was practicing late in the season, Noah decided to speak up about the team's current situation. It was Donovan's inspiring words that had gotten them this far. Now it was time for Noah to return the favor. While the team was contemplating the upcoming tournament, Noah cautioned them, "Well, first we have to make the NCAA Tournament," a statement that turned some heads.

"People looked at us crazy, like what are you talking about?" Horford laughed. "And I think that once he said that, it got everybody thinking, and we were like okay, you know, if we're doing this all over again, we have to be focused."

That focus would soon be put to the test, as the Gators, who did manage to make the field of 65, faced Butler in the tournament's third round. The Bulldogs took a 54–53 lead with just 3:30 to play before Florida went on a 10–2 run to preserve the season. Their next opponent, Oregon, was equally up to the task, playing to a 45–45 score early in the second half. The Gators would go on to take a 67–57 lead with eight minutes to go, but the Ducks hung tough, trimming the lead to just 78–74 in the closing moments. Once again the Gators met their challenge head-on, making seven of their nine free throws as they survived 85–77.

There would be no need for last-minute heroics in the semifinals, as the Gators played the defensive game of their lives against UCLA. The game was more than 10 minutes old before the Bruins scored their seventh point of the game, and with less than 10 minutes to go UCLA had still only put 32 points on the scoreboard. At that point in the game, Florida had held UCLA's star duo, Darren Collison and Arron Afflalo, to a combined 0-of-14 from the field. That performance would send the Gators into the title game to play the Buckeyes, who would surely present a tougher challenge. OSU had lost by 30 points in their regular-season match, but with 23 consecutive wins under their belts, the Ohio State players felt confident enough to talk a little trash before the game.

But just like the football team had done to Ohio State in the BCS title game three months earlier, the Gators left no doubt as to who was the better team. Donovan's club grabbed the lead with 12 minutes left to play in the first half and never looked back, as the Gators cruised to an 84–75 victory. As for the school's quest for history, the three basketball/football championships in two years was not only the first time a school had ever achieved that feat, it just might be the last. ●

Florida's Al Horford (No. 42), Taurean Green (No. 11), Joakim Noah (No. 13), Lee Humphrey (No. 12), and Corey Brewer (No. 2) celebrate their championship. *Streeter Lecka/Getty Images*

2008 Kansas

For a tournament that saw all four No. 1 seeds reach the Final Four, the 2008 tournament was quite a wild one. UConn suffered its first opening-round loss since 1979, courtesy of a fadeaway from San Diego's De'Jon Jackson with 1.2 seconds left. And had it not been for a Gerald Henderson layup in the closing seconds, Duke would have been just the fifth team in history to fall to a No. 15 seed. But without question, the story of the tournament was Stephen Curry and Davidson. Curry quickly made a name for himself by scoring 40 points against Gonzaga in the first round—and followed it up by scoring 25 points in a 17-point comeback win over second-seeded Georgetown. In the Sweet 16, Curry scored 33 points against defensive specialist Michael Flowers to upset third-seeded Wisconsin. It also marked the last tournament for NCAA announcer Billy Packer. In his 35 consecutive years behind the mic, few games were more exciting than the last one he called, pitting Kansas against Memphis.

For years, Bill Self had been synonymous with the phrase "best coach to have never been to a Final Four." It was certainly intended to be a compliment, but it wasn't exactly one that the Kansas coach wanted to hear the rest of his career. In nearly each of the previous 10 years, his teams had shown promise of breaking that barrier before falling short. Self's 2008 squad once again brought promise, as the team raced out to a 20–0 record. This only served to increase the pressure to play into the tournament's third week. If Self would be unable to reach the Final Four with the abundance of talent at his disposal, his name would be unfairly synonymous with another word—*choke*.

The Jayhawks closed out the regular season with a 31–3 record, and after blowout wins over Portland State, UNLV, and Villanova, Self's team stood just one win away from the next level. All they needed to do was defeat 10th-seeded Davidson, the easiest matchup Kansas could hope to find at this stage of the tournament. Prior to 2008, Davidson, a school with a student enrollment of 1,700, hadn't won an NCAA Tournament game since 1969. But the Wildcats had a weapon that no other team in the tournament could lay claim to: Stephen Curry, son of NBA star Dell Curry. Just a sophomore, Curry had led the Wildcats to 25 straight wins and the brink of college basketball immortality.

Not only did nearly all of the Davidson students travel to the Midwest Regional by bus, but the Detroit crowd also adopted the Wildcats as their native sons. It wasn't long before the Jayhawks realized they were going to have to earn their spot in the Final Four. Nearly 10 minutes into the game, Kansas had scored only six points, and junior Russell Robinson had gone to Self and reported he was having trouble breathing.

"That's usually not a good sign," Self said. "It just didn't feel like a natural game, or natural circumstances."

The Jayhawks were keeping Curry in check to stay close, but Curry was known to heat up as games wore on, and this night would be no different. Once the shooting guard sank his first shot at the 9:44 mark, he lit up KU for eight points in just 59 seconds. All of a sudden, the Wildcats were up 17–13, and early in the second half they still led 33–30, thanks to 20 points from Curry. Even though the Jayhawks would soon pull ahead after an 8–0 run, Davidson refused to quit. They trailed 59–53 at the one-minute mark and hadn't made a field goal in over five minutes—but they woke up just in time to give the Jayhawks the scare of their lives.

Forward Thomas Sanders, catching the KU defense asleep for a split-second, took advantage by breaking to the hoop for an open layup. Kansas junior Mario Chalmers chose to foul Sanders, sending the 55 percent free throw shooter to the line. And although Sanders made his first free throw, it appeared to be the right decision after all when his second shot rimmed out with 58 seconds to play. The only problem, however, was that a massive scramble ensued for the rebound, and the ball was knocked out of bounds by KU guard Brandon Rush. On the followimg inbounds, Curry retrieved the ball at the left wing and immediately nailed a three-pointer to cut the lead to 59–57. In just a handful of seconds, KU's six-point lead had nearly vanished.

Self noticed that his team was slow to set up its offense, and called a timeout with 17 seconds left on the shot clock. Only 36 seconds remained in the game, and Self wanted his

team's last shot to be a good one. Unfortunately, his message failed to get through as Sherron Collins was forced to fire a guarded jumper before the shot clock expired. His shot clanged off the rim and rolled out of bounds with 16.8 seconds to play.

"That was a crap possession," Self recalled. "That was bad all the way around."

While Davidson coach Bob McKillop called a timeout to set up the game's final play, Self had a message of his own. Calling his players back over to the bench, Self made it clear that they were to stop Curry at all costs.

"It's going to come down to whether we get a stop or not," he implored, "if we're tough enough to get it."

The Jayhawks would indeed double-team Curry as he entered the Kansas zone, but as Curry cut to the left wing, Rush tripped on his feet and went sprawling to the floor. For the moment, it was five on four.

Curry tried to cross over to the right side of the court, but Chalmers—Rush's backup on the play—was still there to defend. By the time Curry had made it to the right wing for a potential game-winning three-pointer, Rush was right next to Chalmers to prevent any look. With three seconds left, Curry had no choice but to dish the ball off to Jason Richards, who was standing 35 feet from the hoop. Richards was open, but from that distance even Curry was out of range. As the ball flew off the backboard, the normally stoic Self fell to his knees.

It wasn't easy, but for the first time in his career, the Jayhawks were moving on to the Final Four. Luckily for KU fans, they weren't done just yet (see page 346). ●

Bill Self, seen coaching his team in the first round, finally put all the demons of tournament past behind him with the 2008 National Championship. *Shane Keyser/Kansas City Star/ MCT via Getty Images*

2009 North Carolina

Though the 2009 tournament saw few upsets, it certainly did not lack excitement. Trevon Hughes made a layup with just two seconds left in overtime as Wisconsin beat Florida State 61–59, and Villanova's Scottie Reynolds made a layup of his own to beat Pitt in the Elite Eight. In a play that looked remarkably similar to Danny Ainge's game-winner in 1981, Reynolds traveled the length of the floor to lay it in with just 0.5 seconds on the clock. And while this tournament had no Cinderella, twelfth-seeded Arizona nearly missed its first tournament in 25 years before peaking late in the season to reach the Sweet 16.

Exactly one day had passed since the final game of his junior year, and Tyler Hansbrough was already in the weight room. Working with the team's trainer, Hansbrough pushed himself as hard as he had done for every practice and game throughout his career. The North Carolina center was determined never to relive the way he felt during his team's 84–66 loss to Kansas a day earlier. In actuality, the final score was not indicative of how thoroughly the Tar Heels had been beaten. At one point late in the first half, North Carolina trailed 40–12.

"We played perhaps the worst I've ever had a team play in a big game in the Final Four when we lost to Kansas," UNC coach Roy Williams said. "I was sick during the game— I'm throwing up in the towel kind of thing— and I made the statement to one of our alums that I was sick during the game. And he said 'so was I'—and he was just talking about how we were playing."

It was a loss that Hansbrough had all but erased from his memory, yet still stored deep in his competitive spirit. Though he never watched the tape of the game, it was one of the driving forces in his return to Chapel Hill. Hansbrough, the only player in history to be a first-team All-American since his freshman year, was passing up on millions of guaranteed dollars in the NBA to come back for another year. The money could wait one more season. First he had some hardware to bring to North Carolina.

"I thought from day one he was really going to be a special player," Williams said of Hansbrough, who was also an All-American at the high school level. "He was an incredible young man and an incredible player. The most focused, most driven college player I've ever seen in my life."

In an era in which many of college basketball's upper classmen were seen as players unable to make the early jump to the NBA, Hansbrough's loyalty to his coach and school hardly went unnoticed. A few weeks after his decision to stay in Carolina, fellow teammates Ty Lawson, Danny Green, and Wayne Ellington followed suit. With all four back in Chapel Hill, the Tar Heels had everything in place for a run at the 2009 national championship. And for the next six months, they would prove just how good they truly were.

Their 28–4 record would earn them a top seed in the NCAA Tournament, where they would win their opening game by 43 points. A second-round bout with LSU would prove slightly more competitive, but with their 84–70 victory the Tar Heels were packing off to Memphis for the Sweet 16. Facing them would be Gonzaga, one of the tournament's most notorious giant killers over the past decade. In fact, the Bulldogs, coached by the level-headed Mark Few, had upset the Tar Heels just two years earlier. It was perhaps the most anticipated game of the tournament's second weekend, but Williams and his assistant coaches still found a way to keep their sense of humor, albeit at Few's expense.

"The Gonzaga staff and my staff went down to Tunica to shoot craps together. As we're coming back, I was stopped by a patrolman. And I don't know if I was talking too much and he thought I was driving recklessly," Williams grinned, "but I tried to get him to look out for the other car with the Gonzaga staff coming about behind us. I asked him if there was any possible way that you could pull them over—that would be a great situation."

The request was all in fun, but their ensuing game was no laughing matter for Gonzaga. Thanks to no turnovers and 6-of-9 shooting from beyond the arc, the Tar Heels cruised out to a 43–30 lead late in the first half, a lead they eventually expanded to 66–45. As soon as the Zags had clawed their way back to get within reach at 68–57, UNC scored 12 points in the next 79 seconds to drown out any hopes of a comeback. The lead would soon reach 28 before they eased their way to a 98–77 victory. It marked the ninety-ninth tournament win in UNC history, the most of any program. Victory No. 100 would come more easily than anyone expected.

Standing in their way was Oklahoma and 2009 Player of the Year Blake Griffin. The Oklahoma sophomore had taken the title from Hansbrough, who had claimed the prize the previous year. With their matchup, it marked the first time in 41 years that two reigning POYs had faced off against each other in the tournament. The game, however, would not be competitive for long. Less than six minutes into the game, North Carolina had taken a 13–2 lead, and by the time the lead had expanded to 61–40 in the second half, Griffin's team was shooting 0-of-15 from beyond the arc.

UNC's semifinal game against Villanova wasn't much closer. This time it took less than 8:30 for the Tar Heels to build a 26–12 lead, and a little over four minutes later, that margin had ballooned to 40–23. Their eventual 83–69 victory left them just one game shy of avenging their embarrassing loss from a year earlier.

But winning that final game against Michigan State would not be so easy. With the game being played in Detroit, many were beginning to believe that the Spartans were the team of destiny.

That theory would be quickly debunked as the Tar Heels stormed out to a 34–11 lead midway through the first half. They had more than tripled MSU's total, and they did not let up anytime soon. Thanks to seven steals from point guard Ty Lawson, North Carolina scored a championship-record 55 points in the first half. Hansbrough eventually finished with 18 points as his team ran away with the title. When Williams took his star out with 1:03 left, to a standing ovation, the first thing he did was give Hansbrough a huge bear hug.

"I'm corny, I'm one of those guys who thinks things should happen just because it's the right thing," Williams said. "And I really thought it was the right thing for Tyler Hansbrough to win a national championship, to be the picture of college basketball—that you could stay in school for four years and enjoy your experience and still win a national championship and still be a No. 1 draft choice. That was the first thought in my mind—I can tell you that."

While defeating their opponents by 20.2 points per game, the Tar Heels trailed for less than 10 minutes during the entire tournament, a statistic that will likely become as rare as players of Hansbrough's character.

"It was the best decision I ever made," said Hansbrough of his return. "All the hard work I put in, all the tough practices, all the weight room, that was what this was about."

And now he didn't just win the national championship, he was part of one of the best teams to ever do so. ●

2010 Butler

Just before the 2010 regular season concluded, NCAA officials sparked instant outrage by proposing that the tournament expand from 65 to 96 teams. Fans across the country protested the move, claiming it would render the regular season useless, but reports came in that the expansion was already a done deal. March Madness had its finest hour in what many thought would be the last tournament of its kind. Over a third of the games were still up for grabs in the last minute of regulation, and upsets abounded as Northern Iowa (9 seed), St. Mary's (10), Washington (11), and Cornell (12) all made the Sweet 16. The biggest upset of all came when fourteenth-seeded Ohio nearly broke the century mark in a 97–83 thrashing of third-seeded Georgetown. In the aftermath of the perfect tournament, the NCAA revised its proposed expansion to just 68 teams.

Brad Stevens was faced with the biggest decision of his life. The 23-year-old had two very distinct options on what to do with his future—continue the promising career he had started for himself with pharmaceutical company Eli Lilly, or drop everything and try to fulfill his lifelong goal of becoming a coach. The choice seemed to be obvious: one was a high-paying job with room for advancement through the company; the other was an unpaid assistant position at a mid-major program. And like anybody who has ever chased a dream, Stevens opted for the latter.

"I was fortunate to have saved some in working at my first job; I didn't need money. I didn't have any immediate family of my own . . . it was the right time to take a leap," Stevens said. "I just knew that I wanted to try it, and so my point in trying it was let's see if I can find a place that has good people where you can learn and grow as a coach."

The young coach landed a job at Applebee's to make ends meet, but as luck would have it, one of the paid assistant coaching jobs at Butler opened up just as Stevens arrived, allowing him to focus full-time on basketball. By 2007, Stevens had ascended to the head coaching position, and although he was the second youngest coach of nearly 400 in Division I basketball, the Bulldogs went 56–10 in his first two seasons. The Associated Press rewarded his efforts by ranking the Bulldogs eleventh in its 2010 preseason poll, instantly sparking discussion of whether the Bulldogs could advance to the Final

Four, which would be held just 5.7 miles away at Lucas Oil Stadium in Indianapolis. Those talks quickly stopped, however, when the Bulldogs stumbled to an 8–4 record. Before their next game, Stevens addressed his players, reminding them that they could still be a dangerous basketball team. All it would take was each player discovering what he needed to do to improve.

"I was fortunate to have guys that really not only bought on," Stevens recalled, "but continued to get better as the season progressed."

After the talk, the team began to win. And then win some more. And by the time they won the Horizon League tournament, the Bulldogs had won 20 consecutive games and were right back where they started at eleventh in the country. And thanks to a last-minute shot by sophomore Ronald Nored to beat Murray State, Butler was still alive as the tournament's opening weekend came to a close. But as great as their run had been, most experts predicted it would come to an end in their next game against top-seeded Syracuse, the nation's top offensive team.

The Orangemen had shot 52 percent on the year, but seven minutes into their game it was the Bulldogs who led 12–1. Syracuse, for all its offensive prowess, was 0-of-4 from the field with five turnovers. The eventual 35–25 halftime deficit was twice as high as any Syracuse had faced all season long. Butler still led 48–43 midway through the second half when the Orange finally made the run everyone had been anticipating. An 11–2 spurt, capped off by a Kris Joseph dunk, gave the Orangemen a 54–50 advantage with 5:19 to go.

The score was still the same with just over three minutes remaining when once again Nored came to the rescue. His three-pointer just before the shot clock expired—Butler's first shot in over six minutes—pulled the Bulldogs within one. Moments later, Matt Howard converted a layup to put Butler in and front, and after Nored came up with a steal at the other end, they had a chance to put the Orange away for good. Again the Bulldogs were forced to fire up a three-pointer at the end of the shot clock, this one from Willie Veasley. The ball rolled around the rim and popped out, only to drop back into the hoop to seal the victory.

"I felt like *one* of these is going to go in," said Stevens of their three-point shooting. "We were 6-of-24 in that game—that made up for a few that rimmed in and out."

The victory left the Bulldogs just one game away from the Final Four, but Stevens made sure to keep the team relaxed. They were going to Indianapolis one way or another, he joked; it was just a matter of whether or not they would still be playing. They would find out soon enough as they took on second-seeded Kansas State.

And just as they did against Syracuse, the Bulldogs put the Wildcats in an early hole as they raced out to a 20–10 lead. Butler still led 49–39 after Shelvin Mack drained a three-pointer with 7:35 to go, but KSU stormed back, and when Denis Clemente nailed three-pointer with 4:51 remaining, the Wildcats had their first lead of the game. They only led 52–51, but it appeared Butler's dream season was slipping through their fingers.

"We know that the game is not 35 minutes or whenever they took the lead—we know it's a 40-minute game," senior Willie Veasley said. "We didn't get rattled, and we just stayed the course and just played our game. This team, we knew that we could do it."

On the next trip down the court, forward Gordon Hayward sank a pair of free throws to put Butler back in front, and Matt Howard added a free throw of his own a minute later to put Butler up 54–52. Clemente answered back, hitting a runner to knot the score at 54–54, leaving just three minutes to decide a spot in the Final Four.

And of those three minutes, just about every second belonged to the Bulldogs. They scored 12 of the final 14 points, including four layups, to secure a 63–56 victory. The Bulldogs piled on top of each other at midcourt while Stevens lifted his four-year-old son up on his shoulders. The Bulldogs were going back home. And fortunately for the fans in Indianapolis, the drama in the early rounds was just a sign of what was to come (see page 328). ●

Brad Stevens, coaching in the championship game against Duke, won 89 games in his first three years, 8 more than any other coach in history.
Butler University

2011 VCU

The 2010 tournament would be nearly impossible to top, but 2011 gave it a run for its money when four consecutive games were decided in the final seconds on opening day. Butler nearly missed the tournament after starting the season 14–9, but beat Old Dominion on a last-second tip by Matt Howard. Shortly after Howard's bucket, Kentucky freshman Brandon Knight hit a layup with two seconds left to beat Princeton in the first round, and two games later he followed it up by eliminating top-seeded Ohio State on a jumper with 5.4 seconds to go. The Wildcats made the Final Four, but Knight was bested by tournament MOP Kemba Walker, who led the UConn Huskies to their third championship in just 13 seasons.

Shaka Smart needed to send a message, and he needed to send one loud and clear. His VCU squad had just completed a wretched month of February with a 3–5 record, placing the Rams squarely on the tournament bubble. If the team was going to salvage the season, Smart knew something was going to have to change—and quick. So before the start of the conference tournament, Smart whipped out a calendar with the month of February and burned it before his team.

"We just weren't quite playing our best basketball, but I wanted the guys to understand that with the end of the regular season and the start of the conference tournament comes new life," Smart said. "And it just so happens that it was March 1st because our tournament begins in early March, and so I thought that was something that at least would catch their eye and get their attention. With players these days—it's something I learned from Billy Donovan—the more you can do visually the better you can send a message, and I thought that was a pretty strong visual message."

If Smart was trying to catch the attention of his players, he certainly achieved his goal—especially when the basketball floor accidentally became part of the act.

"Yeah, he kind of just . . . he had a big, huge lighter and then he started lighting it," point guard Joey Rodriguez recalled with a laugh. "It kind of caught on fire on the court a little bit; they had to start stomping it out."

The court would survive, as would the Rams, who won a pair of critical games to wind up in the conference tournament championship

game. It was just enough to persuade the selection committee, which added VCU as one of the last teams in the field. The experts in the media, however, were not so impressed. ESPN selection guru Joe Lunardi claimed that the Rams couldn't play defense, while basketball analyst Jay Bilas decided to go a step further.

"When he said this doesn't pass the laughing test, I'll never forget him saying that," Rodriguez recalled. "We were like, whoa, come on, man. We're still Division I college basketball players, you know. We beat some good teams this year. Don't act like we can't play basketball or we're not good enough to play with these teams. And once he said that, it was like a fuse lit in everybody and we were just like, all right, let's go."

Ever the psychologist, Smart made sure to take full advantage of the criticism laid upon his team.

"I did think that in our players' minds starting with the selection, they felt like there were members of the media that had crossed the line, in terms of it's one thing to give your opinion but it's another thing to belittle the accomplishments of a team and its student athletes," Smart said. "And they really felt like some of that was going on, so we seized upon that and showed it in videos and used it to galvanize our team and motivate our team."

If the Rams were going to silence their critics, they were going to have to do it on the basketball court. Their first assignment was the USC Trojans, who like VCU had to play in the tournament's new preliminary round, designed to eliminate some of the tournament's

"The biggest thing I wanted to do was just to make sure we set a foundation for setting our players as people, and I really feel like that development is intimately tied to the basketball," said Shaka Smart, who became the second-youngest coach to reach the Final Four. "But it also is what our job is, and that's to make these guys better and help them be in the right position to be successful after college." *Virginia Commonwealth University Athletic Department*

most undeserving candidates. Despite their supposed inability to play defense, the Rams held USC to just 46 points as they advanced to the tournament's real first round, against sixth-seeded Georgetown. VCU stepped up its defense even further, as the Hoyas shot just 38.5 percent from the field, including 19 percent from beyond the arc. By this point, critics were starting to take back what they had said, but the Rams weren't about to let go of their biggest motivator, especially the comments about their defense.

"We used that specific clip, and our video guy was able to find a picture of Joe Lunardi sitting on a couch, and it's just kind of a—I'm not trying to make fun of the guy—but it's just kind of a picture that gave the guys a little bit of a rise," Smart said. "And so we had a picture on the screen, and then it had his comments about defense. I think what he said was, 'VCU can't guard me.' And so what the guys

are seeing is this picture of him on the couch and it's saying he can't guard me. And we kept repeating it over and over again on the video. So stuff like that was great in that it just added fuel to the fire."

Playing as though they still had something to prove, the Rams went out and smoked third-seeded Purdue. The Boilermakers would put up 76 points, but VCU torched their defense for 94. The win sent VCU to the Sweet 16, but their journey was far from over (see pages 216 and 218). By the time VCU reached the Final Four, they had defeated teams from the Pac-10, Big East, Big Ten, ACC, and Big 12. And although UConn would ultimately take home the national title, VCU was America's new favorite team. ESPN now wanted a piece of the Rams, calling back like an ex-girlfriend looking for a date. The Rams chose the high road and graciously accepted the requests, and this time ESPN had nothing to say but "sorry." ●

2012 Kentucky

From the NCAA's "First Four," it quickly became apparent that no lead was safe in the 2012 tournament. With President Obama watching, Western Kentucky rallied from 16 points down in the last five minutes to beat Mississippi Valley State, and in the second game of the double-header, BYU overcame a 25-point deficit to beat Iona. The second round was more of the same, as Indiana held VCU to just 4 points over the last 12:20, and pulled ahead on Will Sheehey's jumper with 11 seconds to go. The craziest comeback of the tournament, however, was Kansas' last minute miracle over Purdue. The Jayhawks trailed for nearly 39 minutes in the contest, but won on Elijah Johnson's layup with 25 seconds to play. They would carry that momentum all the way to the championship game.

With just two minutes to play in the 2008 National Championship game, Memphis coach John Calipari looked on from the sidelines, seemingly destined for his first national title. His team's nine-point margin appeared safe, but before regulation came to a close, the Tigers had found a way to squander that lead. Their eventual 75–68 loss was one of the most heartbreaking in NCAA history, but Calipari's tournament nightmares were just beginning.

Two years later Calipari became the head coach of Kentucky, where he led the Wildcats to the top ranking in the polls, only to be upset by West Virginia in the Elite Eight. The following season Calipari led his team to the Final Four, but once again his season came to a disappointing finish, losing to UConn in the semifinals. It was his third trip to the Final Four, and people started to question if a national championship was ever going to happen for the 52-year-old coach. He had won over 500 games in his career, more than 78 percent of the games he coached, but the one win missing from his resume was the most important of all.

"I didn't know," Calipari said about his odds of winning a title. "You know you just do the best you can every year, and what I kept saying was if you're up at bat enough, you'll back into one."

If Calipari planned on taking home the championship the next year, he would have to give one of the best coaching performances of his career. With a roster full of freshmen and sophomores, Kentucky presented one of the youngest lineups in the history of the game. Not since 1944 had a team so young won a championship, and despite the abundance of talent on the UK roster, people still had their doubts.

Those critics were silenced when the Wildcats raced out to an 8–0 record, but their undefeated season came to an end in December, when Indiana sank a three-pointer at the buzzer to upset the top ranked UK team. Instead of letting the loss shake their confidence, Calipari's band of youngsters reeled off 24 straight wins and took their momentum to the Sweet Sixteen, where they met up with Indiana once again. The Hoosiers enjoyed a 43–39 lead in the closing minutes of the first half, but the Wildcats were not quite ready for history to repeat itself. They went on an 11–4 run before halftime to take a 50–47 lead into the break, and never looked back as they held on for a 102–90 victory. It was a big win, but paled in comparison to the hype they would encounter two games later when they faced off against cross-state rival Louisville in the Final Four—with a trip to the championship on the line. Despite being massive underdogs, the Cardinals held their own, evening the score at 49 midway through the second half. Just when an upset appeared to be brewing, however, the Wildcats went on another quick run, scoring 11 of the next 13 points to put the game out of reach. With a 69–61 victory, Calipari was back in the championship, ready to erase the pains of four years earlier. And in a script that only Hollywood could write, his opponent for the championship would be none other than Kansas. Calipari would certainly do his homework on the Jayhawks, but there was one piece of film he was not going to watch anytime soon. "I have never looked at that tape," Calipari said of the 2008 title game. "That tape was flung out the door of the bus as we were going to the plane."

This time, his team raced out to a lead that nobody, not even his Memphis team, could have blown. With less than three minutes to go in the first half, the Wildcats grabbed a 39–21 lead. The question did not seem to be if Kentucky would win, but if they would double their opponent's score. But as Calipari had already learned, no championship comes easily. Kansas went on a 9–2 run—a step in the right direction, but the Jayhawks still trailed 41–30. KU continued to fight but couldn't seem to cut Kentucky's lead to single digits, and when

Anthony Davis nailed a jumper with just over five minutes to play, the margin was back to 15. It appeared to be the nail in the coffin, but Kansas guard Tyshawn Taylor knew that his team had one final run left in them. He quickly nailed a three-pointer to cut the lead to 59–47, and after a three-point play moments later, his team was within nine. Kentucky freshman Marquis Teague nailed a critical three-pointer with 2:50 left to bring the lead back to 10, but Jayhawks answered right back. Elijah Johnson made a three of his own, and after Thomas Robinson converted a pair of free throws with 97 seconds to play, they had cut the lead to 62–57. Shades of 2008 began to creep back, especially after Davis hit just one free throw at the other end of the floor, but Calipari was not going to let another championship slip through his fingers. He called a timeout to regroup his players, and a minute later Davis atoned for his missed free throw by altering Johnson's three-pointer at the other end of the floor. With a seemingly open look that could have brought the lead down to three, Johnson rose up, only to find Davis flying at him. Johnson tried to plant his feet and take a dribble, but by that point his momentum had carried him off the floor, and the resulting travel call cemented Calipari's first national title. For Kentucky, however, it was the opposite story. It was the eighth national championship in the program's history, and one they'll never forget.

"What a lesson for these young people, that if you share, you give up some of yourself for everyone around you, if you care more about your teammates than yourself, it's amazing what you can accomplish," Calipari said. "It doesn't matter your age. That's the lesson in this."

And unlike the previous trip, this was one game Calipari would never get tired of seeing. ●

Kentucky's Anthony Davis goes up strong for a dunk against the Jayhawks' Jeff Withey. *Chris Steppig/Pool/Getty Images*

PART II

THE 100 GREATEST GAMES
IN TOURNAMENT HISTORY

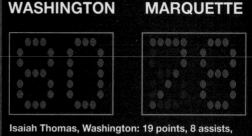

#100

2010: WASHINGTON vs. MARQUETTE

For a conference that had produced 16 national champions over decades of continued excellence, it didn't take very long for the Pac-10 to ruin its reputation. The conference had sent 18 teams to the NCAA Tournament in the previous three years, but when the teams got off to a slow start in 2010, experts were quick to jump ship. They predicted the Pac-10 would be the first major conference to send just one representative since the tournament expanded to 64 teams.

"We had heard those comments and remarks the majority of the year," UW coach Lorenzo Romar said. "I think it was unfair, in that early on there were some key injuries to teams who lost some nonconference games as a result. And I think people made a judgment at that point and never looked back to check back again. 'Hey, how's the Pac-10 doing?' I think teams got better as the conference went on."

The Cal Bears would play solid throughout the year, eventually earning an eight seed, but the experts' prediction nearly came to fruition as the rest of the teams continued to hand out losses to each other. Romar's Huskies saved the conference from an infamous spot in the record books by sweeping through their last seven games, including the Pac-10 Tournament, to ensure themselves an automatic bid. That late run failed to convince their skeptics, however, as the Huskies were handed an 11 seed. Facing them in the first round would be Marquette, the top-shooting three-point team in the country.

Washington would overcome the hot-shooting Golden Eagles, who made six of their first nine three-point attempts, to grab a 41–36 lead in the closing minutes of the first half. The Huskies were beating Marquette at its own game, and it was a strategy that would work as long as they continued to make all their shots. But when the Dawgs went 1-of-7 from the floor over the next eight minutes, the game plan started to fall apart. The Golden Eagles continued their pace, sinking four of their next five three-pointers to take a commanding 60–45 lead with less than 14 minutes remaining. The gunslinging approach was quickly scrapped, but the Huskies still had their resolve.

"I've always told my teammates to keep faith and things can happen," junior Isaiah Thomas said. "I'm always in my teammates' ear, every second of the game, that we're not out of it, we're never out of it, and just keep faith and play defense and we can come out with wins."

Romar implored the team to tighten up the defense, and he watched as his team forced four critical turnovers on Marquette. The Huskies would match their inspired defense at the other end, as they shot 12-of-14 from the floor over the next nine minutes, capped off by Elston Turner's three-pointer with 5:23 left that gave the Huskies a 72–71 lead.

"We showed a lot of grit and heart being able to come back from that," Romar said. "We had to really climb a mountain to get back in that game."

The crowd anxiously awaits the outcome of Quincy Pondexter's last-second shot against Marquette. *AP Photo/Paul Sakuma*

The game would be tied at 74, 76, and 78 as the teams battled into the last minute still knotted up. Thomas missed a go-ahead three-pointer with 39 seconds to play, but the ball came to UW forward Quincy Pondexter, who brought the ball back near midcourt as the seconds ticked by.

"I looked at the clock and immediately started to think—should we call timeout? I wanted to get a feel for how we were playing," Romar said. "If we looked very indecisive, we would have called timeout. But our guys start to get in that alignment with Quincy with the ball at the top, and as I saw that come together, we've done this one before—we understand what to do here."

Pondexter, who had played in more games than any other player in Washington history, had earned the respect from Romar and his teammates to take the final shot. Earlier in the season, Romar had designed a play with the specific purpose of isolating his senior. Pondexter had delivered on that night, and as he continued to hit clutch shots the rest of the season, his teammates knew who to get the ball to at the end of a game. And despite his 6-of-16 performance so far against Marquette, this situation would be no different.

"As a senior, you don't want that to be your last game, you don't want to end on a sour note," Pondexter said. "I know my teammates didn't want to go home—I definitely didn't want to go home—and I had to step up. I didn't want to let these guys down."

Pondexter bided his time to strike, watching as the clock ticked all the way down to six seconds. His coach glanced from the sidelines, waiting as his senior was about to take the biggest shot of his life. Romar, who had hit a few clutch shots of his own during his days as a UW player, knew exactly what Pondexter was going through.

"Let me put it to you this way," Romar said. "If you were fighting for your life and you're in a scrap or you're in the war, you're not nervous. You're thinking, 'What do we do? How do we get this done?' Your mind is racing 100 miles a second trying to come up with the best way to do this, and whatever happens happens at that point."

Pondexter drove to his left, splitting a pair of defenders before stopping eight feet from the hoop. A crowd of defenders was waiting for him by the basket, and a pull-up jumper could be blocked from behind, so he chose the only option he had left—he leaned in and shot the ball off the glass. And with just 1.2 seconds left on the clock, the ball caromed back into the net for the game-winner.

"It's something you dream of as a kid, and it's one of those storybook shots," Pondexter said after the game. "I'm just so happy right now, I don't know what to say."

Luckily for Pondexter, he let his game do all the talking. And what beautiful words they were. ●

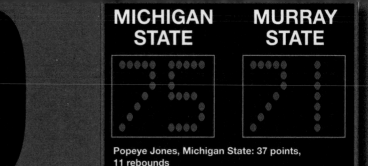

#99

MICHIGAN STATE **MURRAY STATE**

75 71

Popeye Jones, Michigan State: 37 points, 11 rebounds

1990: MICHIGAN STATE vs. MURRAY STATE

Although most players at Murray State would never admit it, becoming Racers had not been their lifelong dream. Like most others at the mid-major level, the 1990 Murray State team was comprised of rejects from the sport's top tier. But for Popeye Jones, even getting interest from the mid-majors seemed impossible. In fact, Division II Tennessee-Martin, whom Jones watched numerous times as a kid, had no intention of signing the local prospect. Jones, of course, had no one to blame but himself—he was 315 pounds coming out of high school—but he finally found one taker in MSU coach Steve Newton. But Newton had one condition. Jones was going to have to shed a massive amount of weight.

Jones responded by dropping 40 pounds, leading the Racers to the 1990 NCAA Tournament and a 21–8 record to end the regular season. The NCAA selection committee was not exactly enthused, handing the team what many felt was an execution sentence as a 16 seed. No school had ever won a game as the tournament's lowest seed, and this year looked to be no different.

"There was still that same 'Hey, you're a 16 seed; you know it's never happened. You're going to go and play your game, and then you know you're going to go home.'" Jones said. "'And hey, good for coming but you know you can't compete against a No. 1 seed.'"

But if Jones could lose 40 pounds in a few months, upsetting top-seeded Michigan

State was not out of the realm of possibility. The plan was to double-team All-American forward Steve Smith and hope his teammates would miss some open looks. Smith was indeed held in check, but Spartans guard Kirk Manns filled in by scoring 11 of his team's 16 points as they took an early 22–12 lead. Jones then put together a little run of his own, but unlike Manns, he didn't stop. And the more he drained shots from all over the court, the more his teammates wanted to get him the ball.

"When you get caught up, you don't realize what you're doing. You don't realize how many points you got, you're just out there trying to win the game," said Jones, who accounted for over half of his team's points with 37 on the night. "I think it was one of those things where people say, 'Well, they're in the zone.' I didn't notice anybody in the crowd. I could feel the crowd but I didn't really notice anybody, and the thing that mattered was that game, and that was the only thing that I could see."

Despite the unworldly performance from Jones, the Racers still trailed by eight points as the final minutes approached. Something needed to change, and quick. The answer came just in time, as Jones somehow found a way to take his game to another level, making four consecutive baskets as Murray State cut the lead to 65–62 in the last minute. Following an empty trip down the floor by the Spartans, the Racers had a chance to send the game into overtime. Everybody in the arena was certain that Jones would take the deciding shot, but what they didn't know was that the game's star was feeling severe cramps in his calves. Jones, who had played every minute of the game, would be in the game merely as a decoy.

The ball would ultimately end up in the hands of teammate Greg Coble, who was perhaps the best alternative to take a three-pointer. Coble had broken free of his defender's grasp, but the form wasn't exactly pure. The shot was off-balance as Coble fired it just before the buzzer, but what mattered was where the ball ended up. And as the clock expired, Coble's shot hit nothing but net to send the Racers where no 16 seed had ever gone before.

Smith had watched Jones steal the show for 40 minutes; now it was his turn to take over the game. The junior hit a jumper to start the overtime period, but Jones wasn't quite done, either. Following a free throw by teammate Paul King, Jones hit a jump shot with 2:52 to

go to put the Racers up 68–67. Not to be outdone, Smith hit a pair of huge shots to put the Spartans back up by three before Murray State came back once more. Frank Allen, a freshman guard, nailed a three-pointer with 1:07 left to tie the score at 71.

Ironically, the most important shot of overtime would come from neither Smith nor Jones. On the ensuing possession, the ball ended up in the hands of Manns, whose specialty was firing those jump shots left open by Smith's presence. On this occasion, Manns decided to take it straight to the hole, a decision he soon regretted when he was met by a group of defenders. Left with few options, Manns kept right on going, dipping underneath the basket before blindly tossing up a wild shot behind his head. This shot made Coble's three-pointer from minutes earlier look like a work of art. But with 43 seconds to go, Mann's shot sank through to put Michigan State up 73–71.

"You know he can sit up there and chuck threes," Jones said, "so one of the adjustments that we tried to make was, hey, he's a stand-still shooter. Even though we're focusing on Steve Smith, when he gets the ball we want to make him dribble. And it took some air out of us for a stand-still shooter like him to drive and make a wild reverse."

The Racers called a timeout to set up their next possession, but Jones missed a hook shot with 26 seconds left, and when Michigan State guard Dwayne Stephens rang in a layup 13 seconds later, the game was essentially over. The Spartans had survived, and although Smith's 22 points had saved their season, he knew who the real star of the game had been. Smith walked over to his counterpart and let Jones know just what he thought about his game.

"I'll see you in 'The League,'" Smith said with a smile as the pair walked off the floor. And for nine years in the NBA, they indeed would. ●

"When we got back to school it was still pandemonium," Popeye Jones recalled after his 37-point performance against Michigan State. "As a sophomore I didn't realize that all of America was watching this game. I was a kid at 19 years old and just wanting to play the game that I could play and I remember coming back on campus and I was a star." *Murray State Archives*

1998: RICHMOND vs. SOUTH CAROLINA

John Beilein was ready to go. In one day his Richmond Spiders would be taking on third-seeded South Carolina in the NCAA Tournament, and the head coach liked his chances. Not only had the Gamecocks dropped their tournament opener as a two seed a year earlier, but Richmond already had a reputation as a giant killer. The program had recorded upsets as an 11, a 12, a 13, and a 15 seed in years past, and if Beilein could watch a little game tape on South Carolina, he felt he could get another upset as seed No. 14. There was just one problem.

"We forgot to bring the TV with us and the remote control," recalled Beilein, who asked the hotel staff if they could lend the missing equipment. "They were going to charge us $400 a day to have a VCR. So we sent the managers back to get a VCR, to go back and get the remote so we could watch tape."

The ordeal was certainly frustrating, but compared with the other obstacles Beilein had overcome, a few hours without film was nothing. When he arrived at the school a year earlier, the team was coming off a three-year stretch in which it had gone just 29-55.

"He said 'We are going to win 20 games this year,'" guard Marseilles Brown recalled when Beilein first arrived. "That's what he told us, and he made us believe it. Oh, my God, the way we worked was ridiculous. You weren't on the team unless you could run the mile in 5:15 for guards, so he told us you will run a mile in

5 minutes, 15 seconds, and the big guys would run it in 5:40, and we're looking at each other like, 'What? I've never run a mile under 6:30!'"

Thanks to Beilein's conditioning standards, the Spiders surpassed their goal by winning 22 games and were looking to add a few more come tournament time. But for all the positive energy Beilein had brought to the program, he knew there was another coach who needed to talk with the players before the game. Sharing his wisdom would be Dick Tarrant, the former Spiders coach who had orchestrated each of the school's monumental upsets over the previous decade. Tarrant had earned a reputation as a fiery coach, and Beilein made sure to use a similar approach before his team took the floor.

"He said 'We're not backing down, we're going to hit them in the mouth,' and I think that was obvious because the first play we ran was a lob," Brown said. "I threw Jarrod Stevenson a lob, and he dunked it. When you play a game like that and you come out and throw a lob, that's a statement like, 'We're here.'"

The Spiders would continue to attack the South Carolina defense, and thanks to a 14–4 run to end the first half, they took a 34–29 lead into the break. Leading the charge was Brown, who hit an unbelievable five three-pointers. His first had come on an open look in the early going, but when he swished his second shot from beyond the arc—a 27-footer with the shot clock winding down—he knew it was going to be a good day.

"I was like, okay, I'm hot now, and I had done that a couple times that year," Brown said. "I would go for like 15, 18 in a half. And so our guys were used to [that], they could tell, and coach Beilein would kind of let go of the reins a little bit when he saw that happening. I was like I'm going to get at least 25 at this rate, and I was like I know one thing, I'm not going to stop shooting, and coach Beilein said that during the timeout—you keep shooting."

Richmond eventually pushed the lead to nine points, but the Gamecocks weren't ready for history to repeat itself just yet. They held the Spiders scoreless for a seven-minute stretch in the second half, and by the final minute they actually had a chance to take the lead. Richmond didn't need to watch any game tape to know who USC was going to. BJ McKie had already scored 24 points, connecting on six of his first seven shots from the floor. Beilein tabbed sophomore Jonathan Baker as the man responsible for McKie, but he also reminded his players that they had a foul to give. With just five team fouls, they could commit a non-shooting foul, forcing the Gamecocks to start their offense all over again. The later they could commit the foul, the better.

The key for the Spiders was to foul before South Carolina attempted a shot; otherwise, the Gamecocks would go to the free throw line with a chance to win. The foul came with 11.4 seconds left, which was much earlier than Beilein would have preferred, but now the stage was set. Richmond had to play clean defense, especially Baker, who knew that his man would be taking the final shot. And as McKie caught the inbounds at midcourt, he took advantage of the foul situation by driving right past the sophomore. Stopping at the top of the key, McKie pulled up for the go-ahead jumper. But his shot sailed long, and as the ball hit off the back of the rim, a massive battle ensued for the crucial rebound.

"We were like wolves going for that rebound at the end," Richmond coach John Beilein said. "All we wanted to do was hang onto the ball."

The ball would ultimately end up in the hands of South Carolina's LeRon Williams, but by the time he grabbed it underneath the hoop, just tenths of a second remained. Williams frantically tossed the ball back before time expired, but the ball innocently clanged off the front of the rim, setting off a wild celebration among the Spider faithful. Back in the Richmond locker room, the team continued its season-long chant of "Uh-oh, they don't know!" But after a fourth major upset in 14 years, most of America did. The Spiders were for real. ●

"Richmond had four seniors and they were so hungry to win. I was lucky enough to walk into that situation," recalled Spiders coach John Beilein. "Whatever we said, they were going to do. They just willed it, and we were very good." *Doug Pensinger/Getty Images*

Artis Gilmore, Jacksonville: 30 points, 17 rebounds

1970: JACKSONVILLE vs. IOWA

Rex Morgan's introduction to Jacksonville basketball was not exactly glamorous. When the University of Evansville sophomore signed his papers to transfer to JU, his new team made headlines by losing to Florida State by 65 points.

"It was in *Sports Illustrated*, and all my friends were going, and *that's* where you're going?" laughed Morgan, whose second impression of the team didn't get any better when he visited the campus. "It's a tie ballgame, the Jacksonville guard thinks he's ahead by one, and the New Orleans guard thinks he's behind by one. And it's a tie game, and he knocks the Jacksonville guy down, steals the ball, lays it up, and they win."

The new recruit decided to go ahead and approach head coach Joe Williams, just to see how he was handling the adversity. "That's why we're recruiting you," Williams said. "When those things happen, we'll give you the ball and that won't happen anymore."

But Williams was hardly the only one facing some adversity. Evansville wouldn't grant Morgan his release, forcing him to transfer to a junior college for a year before he was free to attend whatever school he wanted. Once he arrived on campus, however, he realized just how easy life had been compared with some of his teammates. Center Artis Gilmore had grown up in dire poverty in Florida's panhandle, sharing a bed with two of his brothers until he was 16. Gilmore, who was just one of nine children, never received a Christmas present while growing up. The fact that Gilmore somehow excelled at athletics was simply remarkable, considering he had to play barefooted.

"We were unable to afford any kind of shoe for me growing up as an athlete," said Gilmore, who suffered from blisters on his feet as a result. When his family was able to purchase his first shoes, it hardly resembled the Chuck Taylor shoes that had become so popular.

"They were made just of the cheapest possible piece of equipment that you could possibly even dream of," Gilmore said. "And they were even ripped up and had holes in the bottom, and we put paper within that to try and provide some comfort."

Needless to say, when Gilmore discovered that JU didn't even have a weight room, requiring him to work out across the street at a local gym, it was hardly a problem. In fact, now that basketball was their only concern, Morgan and Gilmore responded by leading the Dolphins to their first NCAA Tournament appearance in school history. The 23–1 Dolphins became the first team to average 100 points per game in an era with no three-point line and no shot clock. They seemed unbeatable until they met Iowa in the tournament's second round.

The Hawkeyes, who had won 17 consecutive games, trailed virtually the entire contest but always stayed within striking distance. They trailed only 50–49 at halftime, and even when Jacksonville pushed the margin back to 79–75 with 11:29 to play, the lead was hardly safe. Minutes later, Gilmore, the only player in basketball to average 20 points and 20 rebounds a game, received his fifth foul. If the big man was to play another game that season, it would be at the hands of his teammates.

"Sitting on the bench for that extended period—now that's not fun," Gilmore said. "Very quickly you're certainly watching from a different perspective."

Gilmore watched as the Dolphins blew a 97–89 lead in the last five minutes of the game. Iowa stormed back to tie the game at 100 and, moments later, took the lead on a free throw. JU answered with a basket to go back up 102–101, but Iowa had the opportunity for the last shot. The Hawkeyes worked the ball to Fred Brown, who had already scored 25 points on the night. Brown would have preferred to shoot just before the buzzer, but when he saw an opening with 20 seconds left, he decided to take it. His shot was off the mark, but he put back his own miss, and with 17 seconds to play the Hawkeyes were back on top 103–102.

Just as Williams had promised years earlier, Morgan took the inbounds pass. But instead of looking to cement his growing legacy, Morgan dished off to teammate Vaughn Wedeking. "I had it on the left side and I was faking to shoot," Morgan said. "And I saw Wedeking open and hit him."

Wedeking fired away, but from the moment it left his fingers the shot looked off. JU forward Pembrook Burrows, along with Morgan and junior Greg Nelson, raced toward the basket anticipating a rebound opportunity.

"One of the facts of that is if you look at the tape we were the only ones underneath the rim," Morgan said. "Everybody else on Iowa when the shot went up, they just turned and watched."

But time still remained, and after the ball bounced off the rim, it landed in the hands of Burrows, who had already made 10 of his 11 shots. The junior tipped the ball in just as time expired, and he ran around the court as his teammates chased him down. The team that had started out with nothing had finally run into its fair share of luck. ●

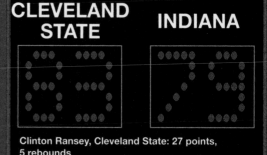

Clinton Ransey, Cleveland State: 27 points, 5 rebounds

1986: CLEVELAND STATE vs. INDIANA

Clinton Ransey's future in basketball was looking bleaker by the day. The senior had just finished an illustrious high school career that concluded with no takers at the Division I level. From all accounts, Ransey was too small and unskilled to play forward but too large to be a guard. Desperately needing a miracle to resuscitate his chances at major college basketball, Ransey took a trip with his AAU squad to a tournament in Toledo. Ransey put on a clinic, delivering a 22-point, 17-rebound performance in the first game and backing it up with a 42-point and 23-rebound explosion in the second contest. Still, no college coach was willing to offer a scholarship, with the exception of Cleveland State coach Kevin Mackey, who hadn't exactly thrived since his arrival.

"I got there, the first thing I noticed is they are coming off an 8–20 record," Ransey said. "So my thought process with that is that if I come here, I can be a part of something that can be ready to blow up."

Explosive was actually a fitting word to describe the Vikings, who played at a speed that few teams dared to even try. Most coaches claim that defense wins championships, but Mackey always countered that with the obvious but overlooked fact: the team with the most points wins the game.

"Basically, it was controlled chaos if you can call it that, where you had your number, you had your position, you know where you were

going each and every time up and down the court, but we were running out there like mad men," Ransey joked. "We had practices where we ran an hour and a half straight—full-court pressing and trapping. Coming out of no time-outs, no breaks, the first year was very brutal. Understanding that, we had times where we would be running up and down the court and a guy would fall over or sprain an ankle and fall down. He said, 'Okay, the next person in, just pick him off to the side.' Here the next guy comes, and fills in for him. Again we were running at full speed for that entire practice."

The result was the nation's top offense at over 100 points per game and, more importantly, a 27–3 record. The Vikings boasted the fifth-best record in the country, but their conference, known as the AMCU-8, did not receive an automatic bid from the NCAA. If they were going to play in the NCAA Tournament, it would be as an at-large seed. Most of the players felt confident about their selection, but when the brackets were revealed the Vikings were the last team in.

"As the selection was going down and down and down, after our name was called it was an eruption in the press room," Ransey laughed. "We didn't even see who we were playing. It was just Cleveland State, 14 seed, and that's all we heard…I don't think we actually found out who we played until after things calmed down or even, maybe, some of us the next day in practice."

Their opponent was third-seeded Indiana, a team that shared little in common with the Vikings. The Hoosiers were led by Bobby Knight, a defensive-minded coach known for strictly controlling his offense. His team was also a heavy favorite to advance in the tournament, but perhaps they were paying a little too much attention to what the media was saying. "Just get me to the Final Four," coach Bobby Knight told his team, "and I'll do the rest." History was on Knight's side, as the Hoosiers had won NCAA titles in 1976 and 1981 (they'd win another in 1987). Moreover, a 14 seed had never won a game in the NCAA Tournament.

Ransey, however, was intent on becoming the first. He scored the first six points for the Vikings as they took an early 6–2 lead, and even after IU pulled ahead 22–18, his team answered right back. Led by Ransey, they went on a 19–6 spurt and led 45–41 when the half ended. Leading all scorers was the junior, with 14 points.

"The person guarding me just didn't understand how I played," Ransey said. "And I used that to my advantage."

CSU scored the first six points of the second half, and when Paul Stewart drained a jumper minutes later, the Vikings enjoyed their largest lead of the game at 64–53. Most teams would have started to slow the pace, but Mackey had no interest in looking at the clock. He was looking at the scoreboard. Mackey continued to rotate players in and out of the lineup, which allowed his team to attack the Hoosier defense without wearing down. Knight, hardly one to agree, kept his starters in as they attempted to rein in the Vikings.

"They couldn't—they didn't have the energy, they didn't have the wind to make that run that everybody else was expecting them to make," Ransey said. "I mean, we were getting layups like the whole game."

And so with just over a minute remaining, CSU still led by 10. That would soon change, as IU's Andre Harris sank a shot, which was followed by a turnover by Ransey. Indiana junior Todd Meier added another shot with 50 seconds to go, and when CSU forward Eric Mudd clanged a free throw off the back of the rim, the Hoosiers had possession once again. Indiana guard Steve Alford banked in another jumper, and with 30 seconds still remaining the lead stood at just 81–77. But just when the Vikings appeared on the verge of a collapse, CSU center Clinton Smith hit a pair of clutch free throws to seal the deal. Cleveland State had just pulled off the impossible. The press literally couldn't wait to talk to the Vikings, as they invaded the team's hotel to join in the celebration.

"It was funny, my brother Kelvin was playing a camp that night, and as I'm sitting there in the Jacuzzi here comes the news camera and I'm doing a live interview from the Jacuzzi for the news back in Cleveland," Ransey laughed. "So my brother calls me after that, and I'm talking to him and he's like, 'Yeah, I just saw you in the Jacuzzi, live in Cleveland!' It was really strange."

If Ransey's goal was to continue flying under the radar, that chapter had come to a close. When you're doing live interviews from poolside, you've officially made it big. ●

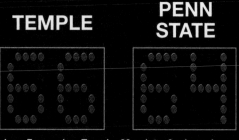

Juan Fernandez, Temple: 23 points, 3 rebounds, 3 assists

2011: TEMPLE vs. PENN STATE

Seventeen years had come and gone, and still Fran Dunphy wondered when he would taste NCAA glory again. The coach pulled off an upset in just his second year at the University of Pennsylvania, and made 10 more trips back to the Big Dance, only to leave after the first round each year. Many of the losses had come at the hands of perennial favorites, but nevertheless, each loss started to sting a little more. Dunphy moved from Penn to Temple in 2006, and let a great chance slip by in 2010. The fifth-seeded Owls had posted a 29–5 record and had shown promise of a possible run to the Final Four, only to see another early exit—this time at the hands of Cornell. Four of the starters from that squad returned the following season, vowing to finally get their coach over the hump.

To do that, however, they would need a drastic change from Juan Fernandez. The junior had shined the previous season, averaging nearly 13 points a game as the Owls claimed the Atlantic 10 title, but with the heightened expectations came more pressure. The burden appeared to be too much for Fernandez, who saw his numbers dip to just 9.7 points a game. Fernandez started pressing to force the issue, but to no avail, as the team failed to win the conference tournament for the first time in four years.

"I've tried everything. I'm talking to my dad, who knows a lot about this," Fernandez remarked near the end of the regular season.

"I'm talking to a sports psychologist to try to make the best out of the situation, because come playoff time I'm going to need to bring the 'A' game to help this team get to where we want to."

The Owls would undoubtedly need his best effort in the first round as they faced Penn State and scoring extraordinaire Talor Battle. Unlike Fernandez, Battle had followed his stellar 2010 campaign with an equally impressive senior season, scoring more than 20 points a game. Battle came ready to play against the Owls, torching the intrastate rivals for nine points as his team took an early 20–11 lead. Fortunately for Dunphy and his Temple squad, Fernandez was equally up to the challenge.

The junior almost single-handedly led the comeback, scoring 17 of the team's 30 points as they grabbed a one-point lead with 3:25 to play in the first half. Just two points would separate the teams at halftime, and as the second period wore on it was clear that the game was heading for a dramatic finish. Neither team would take a lead of more than four points, and over the last four minutes the lead changed hands five times. Trailing 57–55, Temple's Ramone Moore nailed a three-pointer to put the Owls back on top, only to have Battle swoop in for a layup with 2:39 left that gave Penn State the 59–58 lead. Temple forward Lavoy Allen came back with a layup of his own 15 seconds later, and it was the Owls who were once again in command.

Juan Fernandez is the center of attention as he puts up an off-balance jumper at the end of Temple's first-round game against Penn State. *John W. McDonough/Sports Illustrated/Getty Images*

The teams would trade jumpers on the next two possessions, and with a minute to play, Temple still had the lead at 62–61.

The Owls appeared finally to catch a break when Battle had a rare miss with 39 seconds to play. Fernandez was there for the rebound, and his free throws moments later gave Temple a 64–61 edge with 28 seconds left. Dunphy warned his club that Battle would likely try to take the last shot, but when Battle received a pass nearly 30 feet from the hoop, the defense was reluctant to chase him. There was no possible way he was going to shoot the ball from that distance. But did Battle have any doubts as to who would take the team's final shot?

"No, heck no," he said. "I was going to shoot it from halfcourt if I had to. I just kept backing up to wherever I was open, and I swear I was open. When I caught it, I could care less where I was at."

Sure enough, Battle let it fly from the left wing near the scorer's table. And just like it had so many times throughout his career, the shot was pure. The lengthy jumper was enough to impress Reggie Miller, one of the game's all-time great shooters, who was calling the game for TNT. Battle glanced over at Miller and grinned. Dunphy was not as pleased.

"We never should have left Talor Battle and never should have left him open behind the three, no matter how far away he was," Dunphy said. "We fell down on that defensive possession, and Talor Battle made us pay."

Still, plenty of time remained for the Owls to come up with an answer, and when Dunphy called a timeout moments later, 11 seconds still remained. History may have said otherwise, but there was no question who the team wanted to take the final shot.

"The coaches got together and we all had pretty much the same idea—we were going to get the ball to Juan," Dunphy said. "What happened when we got in the huddle was Khalif Wyatt had said let's give the ball to Juan, and I think it just reaffirmed how everybody felt—not only the coaches but the players as well."

Fernandez took the ball at the far end of the court and jogged toward the Penn State zone, biding his time to strike. He found his moment with five seconds to go, as a pair of Nittany Lion defenders came out to guard him at the top of the key. The junior drove to the right side, instantly dropping one of his opponents. But his other defender managed to stick to him, and even when Fernandez went for a pump fake, his opponent wasn't budging. Now with just two seconds to play, Fernandez leaned to his left to try to create some separation and fired up an off-balance jumper. It wasn't the prettiest shot, but just before time expired the ball sailed in, giving Dunphy the tournament win he had been striving after for so long. With just one shot, Dunphy had found redemption. And thanks to the confidence his coaches and teammates displayed in him, so had Fernandez. ●

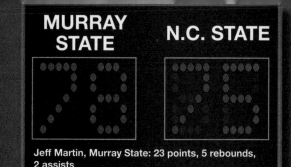

Jeff Martin, Murray State: 23 points, 5 rebounds, 2 assists

1988: MURRAY STATE vs. N.C. STATE

Before the Murray State Racers ever stepped on the floor to take on N.C. State, they were already at a distinct disadvantage. While NCAA officials put the Wolfpack in one of Lincoln's finest hotels, they decided to stick the fourteenth-seeded Racers in the dorm rooms at the University of Nebraska. With the students on spring break, the dorms were suddenly vacant, and the NCAA decided to take full advantage of the situation. The rooms were uncomfortable enough for normal students, but now they were about to be occupied by some rather lanky basketball players.

"The dorm room was so small—we were two to a room," 6-foot-5 junior Jeff Martin said. "And we were on top of each other, literally."

The motives behind the NCAA's decision were obvious. Murray State, listed as a 250,000-to-1 shot to win the NCAA Tournament, was not expected to have a long stay in Lincoln. In fact, the oddsmakers may have been a little generous, considering the Racers hadn't been to the tournament in 19 years and had never won a tournament game in school history. And with eight losses already under their belt, this year's squad did not appear ready to deliver the first.

Things were going according to plan in the early going, as the Wolfpack took an eight-point lead in the first half behind 10 points from Vinny Del Negro and eight from teammate Rodney Moore. That lead would not last long, however, as Murray State junior Don Mann sparked the Racers to a 9–0 run.

Mann, who at 5-foot-8 was perhaps one of the few players enjoying a good night's sleep in the dorms, soon hit four straight three-pointers as his team took a 41–36 lead into the break.

"That was definitely one of his specialties," Martin said of his teammate. "I mean, he can definitely shoot the three. He could shoot from anywhere on the floor. We had a lot of guys that could shoot and we encouraged it—if you're open, shoot it."

Even more encouraging was that the Racers had done much of this without Martin, who had sat on the bench with three fouls in the first half. When Martin returned in the second period, he scored 9 of the team's first 12 points as they started to pull away from N.C. State. The increasingly desperate Wolfpack tried to put on a press, but the Racers broke it with ease as they pushed the lead to 11 points. Behind 13 second-half points from Martin, Murray State still led 69–63 when N.C. State made one final push. The Wolfpack trimmed the lead to four, and when Del Negro made another shot with 1:37 remaining, the lead was down to just 73–71. Moments later, N.C. State committed a foul, which stopped the clock and sent the underdogs to the line for some pressure free throws. If the Racers were going to pull off the unthinkable, they were going to have to earn it.

The Wolfpack got exactly what they were looking for as MSU missed the ensuing free throw, but freshman Chris Ogden was there for the putback to give the Racers a two-possession lead. N.C. State missed each of its next two shots, and Mann, the smallest player on the floor, skied up for the rebound both times. Unfortunately, he missed each of his free throws to keep the score at 75–71, and when NCSU's Chucky Brown drove in for a layup with 21 seconds left, the gap was back down to just two points.

The Wolfpack knew exactly what they were going to do next—foul Mann once more. This time, Mann sank both free throws to push the lead back to four with 19 seconds left, but the game was hardly over. N.C. State's Charles Shackleford hit a shot 10 seconds later, and when MSU freshman Paul King made just one of his free throws, the Wolfpack had a legitimate chance to send the game into overtime. They worked the ball to Del Negro, who had already scored 16 points on the night, but when his three-point shot clanged off the side of the rim in the game's final second, the dream was complete. The Racers had just pulled off the unthinkable.

"It was a great feeling. I do remember that I distinctly went to shake coach Valvano's hand—that's the first thing I did," Martin said. "Win or lose, I would have done that, but maybe not as quick as I did it when we won."

For their efforts, NCAA officials awarded the team with a slightly nicer stay the following night. But their belated generosity was not overlooked by the Racers, who only then realized they had been the only team to spend the previous night in the dorms.

"It didn't bother us until we realized that everybody, after we won, went to a Marriott," laughed Martin. "Hey, everybody stayed in a nice hotel—why didn't you put us where you put them? We knew why; it was because we were a low seed. Now we're staying where all the other kids were staying. We had arrived." ●

SIENA   STANFORD

Marc Brown, Siena: 32 points, 6 assists

#93

1989: SIENA vs. STANFORD

When a friend of Siena forward Tom Huerter decided to take a trip to Puerto Rico over winter break, nobody apparently gave him the memo that what happens there doesn't necessarily stay there. The vacationer returned to campus, unaware that he had brought a highly contagious case of the measles with him. Dozens of Siena students fell victim to the illness, forcing the school to cancel classes and vaccinate everyone on campus. Not even the basketball team was immune, as guard Mike Brown had to miss several practices while being treated. But instead of surrendering the season, the team was allowed to continue playing under one condition: no fans could attend the games.

"It's one of those things where now that you look back you say wow, we were lucky it wasn't worse than it was. We were fortunate we were able to play some of those games," Huerter said. "If anything, it probably brought us closer together. It definitely toughened us up."

The call was made in order to prevent any further spread of the disease, but luckily the shots on campus weren't confined to the vaccination room, as the Saints won 16 of their last 19 games. Of course, that didn't mean it was easy.

"The biggest part of it that I didn't like was that we had to play the conference championship at the Hartford Civic Center in front of an empty arena that was a 12-to-13,000-seat arena," said sophomore Marc Brown, whose

team won at the buzzer to advance to the NCAA Tournament. "And to play that championship on ESPN with no fans was pretty difficult."

The win also gave the newly healed fans a chance to see the team again, and they wasted no time in making up for their two-month absence. When the team bus pulled into the parking lot of the Greensboro Coliseum for their first-round match against Stanford, the players realized just what they had been missing.

"When we got off the bus, there had to be hundreds of Siena fans in the parking lot, and when they saw the bus pull in they ran over to the fence and started cheering for us. And it wasn't five or ten people—I'm literally talking hundreds of people," Huerter said. "I just remember Steve Downey, my roommate and teammate, saying this is probably as close as we'll get to feeling like rock stars. It was truly a weird feeling, but a great feeling."

With all the hotels in Greensboro booked, the hordes of Saints fans decided to get buses of their own and just sleep there. Six buses full of supporters made the trek to Greensboro, and the team did not let them down. Early in the first half, Siena battled even with the Cardinal, trailing just 17–16 with about 10 minutes to go, when all of a sudden Marc Brown went on a 9–0 run of his own. Stanford simply couldn't keep up with the point guard, and with 6:40 to go in the first half, Brown's team was up 25–17.

"I think mentally the biggest hurdle that you have to overcome when you're the underdog is believing in your own mind, after actually playing, that you can win," Huerter said. "I thought we could upset them, and I think it was a matter of us playing confident—and we did play confident the rest of the game."

The partisan crowd could feel the upset brewing as well, but third-seeded Stanford scored 12 of the next 14 points to grab a two-point lead, and at halftime the score was all tied at 37. Howard Wright's bucket gave the Cardinal a 43–40 lead early in the second half, but Siena guard Jeff Robinson decided it was time to elevate his game as well. Robinson knocked down three shots from behind the arc, and when teammate Steve Downey converted a three-point play, the Saints led 61–45 with just 12 minutes to go.

"We knew it was going to be a 40-minute game," Huerter said. "I think you're hoping that the seconds can tick away, but you're also realizing that Stanford's a very good team and you're expecting them to come back. You know, I think you have to expect that."

Not to be outdone, the Cardinal went on a 13-point run of their own in less than three minutes, and when Todd Lichti stole the ball and dunked at the other end, they had tied up the game at 66 with 6:28 to play. The game was still tied with just over a minute remaining when Brown curled around a screen to nail a jumper to put Siena up 78–76. Lichti missed a three-pointer moments later, and Siena appeared to have the game wrapped up when Brown was fouled with 54 seconds to go, but he missed the front end of a one-and-one to give Stanford another chance.

Siena's defense stepped up again, as Eric Fleury made a crucial steal to seal the win. Or so he thought. With just 36 seconds remaining, Brown stepped to the line once more with a chance to give the Saints a four-point lead, but again his first free throw clanged off the back of the rim. This time the consequences were much more dire. Fleury committed a foul while trying to grab the rebound, sending Stanford center Adam Keefe to the line. Keefe completed the four-point swing by converting both of his free throws, tying the game at 78 with 34 seconds on the clock.

The Saints, who had the last possession, gave Brown a chance to atone for his missed free throws by feeding him the ball. He drove to the hoop as the clock wound down, but for the third time in less than a minute he was fouled. Now, with just three seconds remaining, there was no room for error.

"If I had made my foul shots toward the end, we would have won by about six or eight. I made it exciting at the end—believe me, I didn't try to do that—it just happened that way," Brown joked. "I was pretty nervous, to be honest with you."

Before Brown took his shots, Keefe decided to provide some unexpected commentary. Huerter, who was standing next to Keefe in the lane, was concentrating on getting a rebound when Keefe caught him off guard.

"He looks at me and he just said, 'I don't know about you, but this is the greatest game I've ever been in,'" Huerter recalled. "I just remember saying—I didn't know what to say—I was like 'yeah.' Because I'm kind of in the moment, hoping that Marc wins the game."

And this time, with the game on the line, Brown did just that, sinking both shots to give Siena the unbelievable win.

"It was a big deal. It was the biggest win in the history of the program," Brown said. "It was icing on the cake to an unbelievably weird but successful season."

Despite having no contact with the fans for much of the year, Brown jumped right into the student section to hug everybody in sight.

"We weren't afraid because the small school environment that we had at Siena College, those faces in the crowd that had the Siena T-shirts, we knew them personally," Huerter said. "If you ask any Siena student that happened to make that trip, the greatest experience of their four years at Siena College was making that trip and living and being a part of that experience, and you know that's special."

And fortunately, everybody with the measles lived to tell about it. ●

#92

N.C. STATE   **UNLV**

Thurl Bailey, N.C. State: 25 points, 9 rebounds

1983: N.C. STATE VS. NEVADA-LAS VEGAS

As one of the prominent members of UNLV's 28–2 team, Sidney Green had felt he had earned the right to speak his mind. The 6-foot-9 senior, who was leading the team with 22.1 points per game, was correct—his play had certainly earned him some privileges that could only come with excellence on the court. However, just because he had that power did not mean it was necessarily wise to exercise it.

Before his team's second-round contest against N.C. State, Green had spoken freely about his thoughts on the Wolfpack, who were lucky to still be playing with a 21–10 record. More specifically, he had mentioned just what he thought about the man he'd be facing that night, Thurl Bailey.

"Sidney Green, who was UNLV's power player at that time, he had come out and said some things in the press about Bailey not showing him much in some previous games that he had watched," Bailey said. "And so when you hear things like that, the press starts to bring it up for me. Coach [Jim] Valvano was very good about just telling us not to respond, just to show that team some respect, which in itself is a lesson for anybody. But internally it's just something that ticks you off. It's something that you want to go out—you want to prove a point. It doesn't even have to be talked about among the team. Everybody knows it."

Besides, a little criticism was nothing new for Bailey. The forward had not only failed to make his seventh grade roster, he followed it up by getting cut from his eighth grade team as well. By the time Bailey was a senior at N.C. State, he had developed into to one of the premier forwards in the conference. He just wasn't up to Green's standards.

It didn't take long for Bailey to make his presence known, as the Wolfpack raced out to an early 12–4 lead. The Rebels managed to take a 33–27 edge at halftime, and they even pushed the gap out to 52–40 with 11:40 to go, but with Bailey on top of his game, the contest was far from over.

After Valvano called a timeout to reenergize the team, Bailey went to work, scoring eight of his team's next 14 points to bring them within 56–54. All of a sudden, Green wasn't so confident about his assessment.

"He didn't talk trash during the game at all," Bailey smiled. "I think there was a certain point in the game where he understood my goal was to show him something, and it wasn't to do it in a way that took away from our team goal."

The Rebels still led 70–67 in the final minute when Bailey made one last push. With 36 seconds to go, he knocked down a jumper to bring N.C. State within a point, and when UNLV's Eldridge Hudson missed the front end of a one-and-one just four seconds later, the Wolfpack actually had a chance to win the game. The only problem was that they had no timeouts, a fact that quickly became obvious when they couldn't find an open look.

Finally, with the clock down to eight seconds, Dereck Whittenburg fired a well-defended jumper from 18 feet out. His shot clanged off the back of the rim, right into a crowd of players standing in the paint. Bailey skied up to redirect the ball back toward the hoop, but it hit right off the front of the rim and back toward the throng of fans. All the UNLV players jumped up for the rebound, but the ball had bounced back so quickly that it landed back in the arms of Bailey, who was still following through on his first attempt.

"If you look at that play when Derrick got the ball on the outside, I was just constantly moving around underneath with the expectations that hopefully the ball would come off at least close to me so I can have a chance to get a hand on it," Bailey said. "And when it first did, I tipped it to myself and grabbed it and quickly shot it off the glass."

And with just three seconds to go, Bailey's shot caromed off the backboard and through the net, giving N.C. State a 71–70 victory. For Bailey, his final shot gave him 25 points on the night, a far cry from Green's pre-game expectations. Green would finish with 27 points, but it was Bailey who emerged with the win.

"It really ended up being poetic justice for me at least, that I was the one with the winning basket and had a great game against a great player like Sid Green. And there are a few lessons to be learned on both sides of that," Bailey said. "He's a great player, no question—I think everybody knew that—and maybe the consensus was that Sidney Green is going to eat Thurl Bailey's lunch. I don't know whether he was embarrassed or not. What I do know is that it ended their season and I had ended his career in college basketball on that game."

Bailey would have only three more games left himself, but his career would end on a slightly different note (see page 353). ●

OHIO   ILLINOIS STATE

Vic Alexander, Ohio: 14 points, 7 rebounds

1983: OHIO
vs. ILLINOIS STATE

As the oldest university in Ohio, and the school with the state's name attached to it, one would assume that Ohio University would dominate the athletic landscape in its area. But somewhere along the line, a newer, prettier face named Ohio State decided to claim its stake on the region—and athletics at OU seemed to be swept away for good.

While the Buckeyes enjoyed the friendlier confines of the Big Ten, their counterparts to the southeast were relegated to the Mid-America Conference. By 1983, nine years had passed since their last NCAA Tournament appearance, and the team hadn't won a game in the tournament since 1960, the same year that Ohio State took home the national title. And with tournament wins coming few and far between, money wasn't exactly pouring in. The university made the men's and women's teams travel together to save a few extra dollars—on a bus that had no bathroom.

"Anytime somebody on the women's team or the men's team had to go to a restroom, we had to stop the bus and go to a rest area or a restaurant," laughed Billy Hahn, an assistant on the men's team. "The women's team played before us when we traveled that year. In those years, that budget was so small."

But the dark days of Ohio basketball must have seemed like paradise to head coach Danny Nee, who two decades earlier was fighting in the swamps of Vietnam. To Nee, the school's lack of resources was less of an

obstacle than a challenge that most knew he would overcome.

"Danny just came in with a brand new attitude, and he came in and he was a very strong disciplinarian type guy," Hahn said. "I don't think a lot of players in the past were held accountable for anything, and he just came in and changed the whole mental attitude of doing things the right way and being held accountable for your actions."

And in just his third year at the helm, Nee turned the program around from just seven wins in his first season to 23 wins and a berth in the NCAA Tournament. Ohio basketball was relevant once again.

"It was like catching lightning in a bottle. It was a dang miracle," Nee said. "It was really cool; the town embraced us. It was just a really special time in my life, in all of the coaches' lives, when all the things come together like a perfect storm."

The Bobcats earned the right to play Illinois State in the first round, a team that boasted a 24–6 record and played a defense so fierce that they became known as the "Bruise Brothers." Thanks to solid work on the defensive end, the Redbirds grabbed a 43–37 lead with only 6:28 to play. Hank Cornley stepped to the free throw line a minute later to try and give ISU an eight-point lead, a nearly insurmountable figure for the defensive-oriented Bobcats. But the junior ended up missing both free throws, and Ohio's Vic Alexander made him pay by cutting the lead to four on the ensuing possession. After a travel on Cornley, Alexander hit another shot to put Ohio within 43–41, and when Rick Lamb committed a charge on the other end, the Bobcats had a chance to even the score.

"Our philosophy was work hard and never give up, keep chopping, keep working and let's not worry about the score," Nee said. "Because if we work hard and we play defense and rebound, everything else will take care of itself."

The team did tie it up at 43, but heading into the last minute the Redbirds had possession with the score knotted at 47. Illinois State tried to run out the clock for the final shot, but a hero emerged for Ohio in the unlikely form of Robert Tatum, a freshman who had averaged only 4.4 points per game on the year. Tatum was making just his third start in place of the injured Eric Hilton, but he saw an opportunity to make a play when ISU's Michael McKenny carelessly held onto the ball. Tatum knocked it loose from McKenny and converted a layup with just 14 seconds left to give Ohio a 49–47 lead.

The Redbirds took their time to set up the perfect shot, and they got it when Raynard Malaine drained a deep jumper from the baseline with just three seconds left. The Bobcats called a timeout a second later, but it appeared that both teams were headed for overtime. Nee instructed his team to run "Hawks," a play designed to quickly cover the length of the floor. Jeff Thomas would take the ball under his own basket and throw it to John Devereaux, who would try to create a scoring opportunity before the buzzer. The team practiced the play before every game, and more often than not, the play would work.

"It did," Nee said with a smile, "because we would call a foul—because we'd always want the offensive team to win."

But when the team tried to run it against the Redbirds, it was another matter altogether.

"It was scramble city. Devereaux went up and he got cremated and then he kind of pushed, shoved it over," said Nee, who watched him get the ball to Tatum. "And Tatum through his quickness, he got cremated. I mean, there were two fouls and they didn't call either one of them. The referees weren't going to call a foul at that portion of the game."

By the time Tatum threw up a shot just before the buzzer, he was in midair with his body completely contorted. While trying to recover from the first foul and hoping to create some space from an oncoming defender, Tatum had his body nearly parallel to the court. But when he managed to release the unorthodox shot, it found its way through the basket. Tatum jumped into the arms of his teammates, who were in shock. After all, none of them had experienced the tournament before, and now they were in the thick of the madness. And while Ohio may not have been the richest program, on that day they were certainly the kings of college basketball. ●

Illinois State's Rickie Johnson would grab 10 rebounds on the day, but the biggest loose ball of the night found its way into the hands of Ohio's Robert Tatum. Fortunately for the Bobcats, he would make the most of it. *Illinois State Athletic Department*

#90

NOTRE DAME   **CINCINNATI**

Adrian Dantley, Notre Dame: 27 points, 8 rebounds

1976: NOTRE DAME vs. CINCINNATI

For the Notre Dame Fighting Irish, luck wasn't a small advantage to be taken lightly—it was a serious business. For decades, the school channeled its Irish roots to bestow good fortune upon the football team. Luck did not come so naturally to the basketball team, however, and it wasn't until years later that they discovered they would have to earn their luck. They introduced the leprechaun as the official mascot in 1965, and when Digger Phelps became head coach six years later, he implemented the green jerseys for important games. No exceptions. The plan worked, as they ended UCLA's 88-game winning streak in 1974, the first of eight seasons in which they made the NCAA Tournament. But in the 1976 tournament, it almost seemed like their luck had run out.

When the Irish faced Cincinnati in their first-round matchup, the Bearcats stormed out to a 39–33 lead, an edge they would not relinquish virtually the entire game. Even when Notre Dame made a run to get within two points at halftime, Cincinnati came right back in the second half to take a 55–49 lead. With just 8:42 remaining, the gap widened to 61–53.

"We always talked about believing and never giving up," said Notre Dame sophomore Duck Williams. "I always believe in that never-die attitude. You know, if there's time on the clock, you've still got a chance to win this game. Some teams stop playing and some teams play to the end, and our thing was as long as there's time on the clock, we still got a chance at this."

The team had battled back from a 12-point deficit in the final two minutes to snap UCLA's streak, but this was different. If the Bearcats blew this lead, their season would be over. Everybody on Notre Dame knew that if they were to come back, it would have to be on the back of Williams, who had developed a reputation throughout the season for stepping up in crunch time. The sophomore had guided the team to victories over Maryland and San Francisco with last-minute shots, and today would have to be no different.

"Like I say, some people want the ball when the game is on the line, and that's what I pride myself at doing," Williams said. "And it's just something that I was used to doing, and when it came down to it, when the bright lights were on, I wasn't afraid. You know, you can't be afraid to fail, and that's the way I looked at it. I'd rather take the tough shot."

Thanks in large part to Williams, the Fighting Irish cut the lead to 69–66, and when Adrian Dantley sank a jumper with 3:56 to go, the lead was down to just a point. Notre Dame was still trailing by one when UC's Harry Yoder drove in for a layup to give his team a 74–71 lead with 1:45 to go. Williams came back to answer with a 25-footer to make the score 74–73, and the team went into a full-court press to try and come up with a steal. With no three-point line in effect, the Irish would need to get at least one defensive stop to have a chance to come back.

176

Dantley fouled Hal Ward to send him to the line, but the senior sank both shots to bring the lead back to the critical three-point plateau. Notre Dame raced down the floor and found Williams open in the left corner six seconds later. The shot hit nothing but net with 57 seconds to go, and moments later it appeared that the Irish had finally gotten the stop they were looking for. Junior Toby Knight intercepted a lengthy pass near the left sideline and tossed it back to a teammate before running into the crowd. But just as the fans started to enjoy the critical turning point, an audible groan rang through the arena. The referees had ruled that Knight's toe had crossed the out-of-bounds line before he made the pass. Cincinnati ball.

During the following possession, it looked as though the Irish had once again gotten the crucial stop, only to have their hearts ripped out. The Bearcats tried to waste as much time as possible before Mike Jones took a shot from just six feet away that clanged off the back rim. During the mad scramble for the rebound, UC's Brian Williams picked it up and banked it in for what appeared to be the dagger. "That should do it" play-by-play announcer Dick Enberg called as the Bearcats took a 78–75 lead with just 20 seconds to go. But once again, the Irish found Williams in the corner. This time, he faked the shot before nailing a jumper to cut the lead to 78–77 with 12 seconds remaining.

"My shot was just flowing really good that day, and I was just in a groove and, you know, it was like you win or go home. And we didn't want to go home, so we just kept fighting," said Williams, who had just scored his team's third straight bucket. "When you're in the zone you feel like the basket is as big as the ocean. You know you're not going to miss, and that's the way I felt at the time."

Phelps called a timeout to devise a new plan. This would be their last chance to make a defensive stand.

"Digger was a really good defensive coach. He really was good at preparing us for games, knowing situations," Knight said. "When we put our defensive pressure on, I mean, there's a good chance that they can't get the ball in."

And just as Phelps had hoped, the players responded by swarming around the Bearcats as they tried to inbound the ball. Ward tried to call a timeout, but it was too late—the Irish had forced a five-second violation to reclaim possession and a have chance to win. The plan, of course, was to find Williams. The Bearcats knew better by now, taking away his chance at a game-winning shot, but nobody else on the team was open, either. Finally, with time winding down, it was up to Bill Paterno, who had been only 2-of-7 on the day, to fire away a prayer from 18 feet out. The ball was heading straight for the rim, but it was also headed for the most determined player on the floor—Toby Knight. The junior had failed to crack the starting lineup until well into his senior year, but at this moment he was on the court with the opportunity of a lifetime.

"I felt like if I went in there and got an offensive rebound that I was going to put it back up. I was like, that's my ball," Knight said. "I know that desire and effort, you can become a good college player with those two things, and on that last play I had a lot of that. I knew that Billy was taking the shot, and looking at the ball come off, I saw where it was going to go."

The ball banked off the backboard and straight to Knight, who tipped in the winning basket just before time expired. Knight and his teammates raced back into the locker room to celebrate, but the effects of the shot were felt long after the game. Knight, who now operates a basketball equipment company, recently had to make a sales pitch to an old adversary.

"I was on a sales call with the coach from Cincinnati," Knight laughed. "And he was pretending that he was all pissed off at me because I made the shot and now you want me to buy your hoops?"

Knight was guilty as charged, but that shot was easily worth the price of a missed sale. He actually went on to make the deal, but needless to say, he may have had a little luck helping him out as well. ●

#89

2005: WEST VIRGINIA vs. CREIGHTON

For a player who already knew his team was safely in the NCAA Tournament, Mike Gansey was abnormally nervous on Selection Sunday. Cleveland State University, which was located a few miles from his hometown and happened to be where his younger brother played, would be hosting some games, and the West Virginia guard knew his team had a shot of being selected to play there. Sure enough, when WVU was selected to play Creighton in Cleveland's Wolstein Arena, newspapers estimated that 300 people would be there to watch Gansey play.

"Three hundred is on the low end," Gansey joked. "The day before, they have an open practice for the public and I swear, I saw all my teachers from high school, my friends from middle school—there were probably 300 at practice, let alone the game."

The next day, the junior got a taste of what the atmosphere would be like when he tried to catch some of the Wake Forest game, which was being played before WVU tipped off.

"I remember I walked out of the tunnel real quick, just to take a peek at the game. I literally saw six or seven people I hadn't seen since middle school or maybe my freshman, sophomore year of high school," Gansey said. "Of course I acknowledge them, but then I'm like I got to go back in there—there are too many people I know. It's a good thing, but at the same time I got to play good here and we got to win. I don't want to be one of the worst players to come to Cleveland and not play well."

Unfortunately, that is exactly what happened to the team, as Creighton nailed its first four shots and took a 10–0 lead less than three minutes into the game. Mountaineers coach John Beilein called a timeout and made sure his players calmed down.

"Hey, guys, it's the NCAA Tournament. Just go out and have some fun," Beilein said. "Get these cobwebs off. It's only ten-to-nothing. It's early."

West Virginia's Kevin Pittsnogle came out and hit a three-pointer, and three minutes later the Mountaineers had tied the game at 10. They didn't stop there, as the team stormed out to a commanding 31–19 lead.

The Missouri Valley champions would push back, however, holding West Virginia to one shot in the last five minutes of the half to pull within 33–31, and when Nate Funk hit a pair of three-pointers in the second half, the Bluejays surged ahead 40–36. Creighton was able to hold off the Mountaineers until Tyrone Sally, who had only two points in the first half, put the team on his back. His three-pointer tied the game at 53, and on the next play, he dove for a loose ball and threw it behind his head to Gansey for the go-ahead dunk.

"We hustled so much as a team, and it just seemed liked that was a play that helped us get some momentum," Gansey said. "I was just like maybe this is our night. We've got to keep going and keep fighting and something good is going to happen."

Creighton managed to take a two-point lead late in the game, but when the team needed him, Sally was still there, sinking two free throws to tie the game at 61 with 42 seconds to go.

Hoping to just get a stop and send the game into overtime, Beilein directed his team to switch to a 1-3-1 zone. It was a last-ditch effort to try and stop the Bluejays, who had already won four games on the final possession during the regular season. The strategy worked, as Creighton worked the entire shot

clock trying to get a clean look. Unable to find anything inside, the Bluejays swung the ball to Nate Funk, who jumped for what he thought was an open look with four seconds to go. Out of nowhere came Sally, who got just enough of the ball to leave it well short of the basket. It fell in the hands of Pittsnogle, who recognized that the situation resembled something the team ran in practice.

"It's a drill we do called 'perfection,'" Beilein said, "where the ball has to go from end to end without it ever hitting the ground."

Also picking up on the opportunity were Gansey and Sally, who both raced down the floor as soon as the ball was tipped. Pittsnogle fired it toward the left side to Gansey, who, without even needing a dribble, fed Sally for an open dunk with just 2.9 seconds to play.

Creighton threw the ball down the floor and called a timeout with just over a second remaining. Now inbounding from midcourt, the Bluejays once again went to Funk, who had scored 23 points on the night and was 4-of-7 from beyond the arc. Catching the ball on the right wing, Funk knew there was enough time to throw off the defense with one of the oldest tricks in the book.

"I was right on him and he shot-faked me," Gansey remembered. "At the time, I went for every shot fake, and for whatever reason, they put some glue on the floor, but I didn't go for it."

With Gansey's hands in his face, Funk was forced to throw up a prayer, which sailed long. Not only were the Mountaineers advancing to the second round, they had also just notched win number 500 for their coach, who likely won the game with the late defensive tactic.

"Everything coach Beilein drew up, it was just unbelievable," Gansey said. "It was like clockwork. I mean everything worked well." It was a perfect play, and a perfect ending for West Virginia. As for Gansey, the fun was just beginning (see page 212). ●

In a span of three games, Tyrone Sally made two of the biggest plays in West Virginia history. Seven days after making this game-winning dunk against Creighton, Sally would make the game-saving block against Texas Tech to send the Mountaineers to the Elite Eight. *Lisa Blumenfeld/Getty Images*

LEHIGH   **DUKE**

C. J. McCollum, Lehigh: 30 points, 6 assists, 6 rebounds, 2 steals

2012: LEHIGH
vs. DUKE

After four upsets between 1991 and 2001, over a decade had passed since the last time a 15 seed won a game in the NCAA Tournament. Finally, after years of heartache and close calls, fans were once again able to relive the magic when Norfolk State upset Missouri in the opening round of the 2012 tournament (see page 256). Before they could even finish celebrating the historic upset, however, the volcano known as March Madness erupted again. Less than two hours after NSU's victory, Lehigh gave fans a second helping.

Just before his team was set to take on Duke, Lehigh coach Brett Reed became aware of the historic upset just pulled by Norfolk State. Rather than share the result with his players, however, Reed decided to keep the score to himself. "We did talk about belief and that being such a key word to our journey here," Reed said. "There's so many people that fill out so many brackets and we hear so many things, whether it's on radio or television or so on and so forth, that it was very important for us to suspend disbelief and not listen to that repeated thing that Lehigh wasn't going to win, but rather believe in ourselves, believe in each other, believe in our system."

One thing that Reed also ignored, however, was that everybody had picked Duke for a reason. The Blue Devils had dropped just one tournament opener over the past 15 years, winning the others by an average of 27 points, and it didn't look like this would be the time for

loss number two. The game would be played in nearby Greensboro, where they were 12-0 in tournament history. Lehigh had some history coming into the game as well, none of which was good. The Mountain Hawks had never won a tournament game, and the last time they played the Blue Devils, in 1996, they lost by a staggering 52 points.

It appeared that this game was headed for a similar finish when Duke began its first possession. Catching the ball beyond the three point line, junior Mason Plumlee faked out his defender before driving to the basket. From just a few feet inside the free throw line, he soared to the rim to deliver one of the best dunks of the entire season. Plumlee didn't slow down from there, making seven of his team's first eight field goals as he finished the game a perfect 9-of-9 from the field. But as unstoppable as Plumlee was, his performance hardly put the Mountain Hawks away. Choosing to focus instead on Duke's vaunted three-point shooting, Lehigh allowed Plumlee to tally 19 points while limiting his teammates to 15-49 shooting. Although the Blue Devils would finish the first half with a 30-28 lead, they made just one three-pointer before the break.

"One of our major keys was to try to defend that three-point line to the very best of our ability, to do it with a unified team defensive effort," Reed said. "One of the strengths of our defense is its unity, and when we have five guys in the rights spots, doing the right thing and playing with that type of energy and passion, it ultimately makes us a much stronger unit."

Not only did they take away Duke's main strength, but Plumlee was nearly negated by his counterpart Gabe Knutson, who finished with an equally impressive 5-of-5 from the field and 6-of-7 from the line. The real star of the game, however, was Lehigh point guard C. J. McCollum, who scored 18 of his 30 points in the second half. After Duke pushed their lead to 37–32 early in the second period, McCollum scored nine quick points as the Mountain Hawks took a 47–42 lead. McCollum, who had considered quitting the game as a struggling 5-foot-6 high school player, was starting to show why he was the fifth leading scorer in the county.

"We had all the confidence in the world coming in. We knew Duke was a great team but at the same time we didn't have anything to lose as a 15 seed," McCollum said. "We just played as hard as we could and left everything on the court."

Lehigh was holding onto a 56–54 lead when McCollum made the biggest shot of the game, a three pointer from the top of the key that brought the lead back to five points. When senior John Adams raced in for a dunk with just two minutes to play, the lead was up to 61-54. The Blue Devils made a push, cutting the lead to 65–59 in the last minute when they threw a full court press at McCollum. Instead of looking to safely inbound the ball, however, McCollum spotted Knutson breaking all the way down court towards the other basket, and caught him in stride for the easy dunk. Even after Duke answered back with a three pointer and a pair of free throws, cutting the lead to just 67–64, McCollum had one last dagger to deliver. The Blue Devils nearly had a chance to tie it up, as Lehigh sophomore Mackey McKnight fumbled the inbounds pass, but McCollum was there to save the day. Not only did he snatch the ball, he then darted around the defense before finding an open Jordan Hamilton underneath the basket. His dunk, with just 23 seconds to play, sealed an upset for the ages.

"I told my teammates all year," McCollum said, "whenever in doubt, get me the ball and I'll make a play for us."

Reed, who at 37 was one of the youngest coaches in the country, couldn't have been

Lehigh's C. J. McCollum was instantly catapulted to superstar status after his 30-point effort against the Blue Devils sparked the 75–70 upset. *Lehigh University Athletic Department*

prouder of his star player. "C. J. is just a phenomenally talented individual—he has the ability to score the basketball, he can shoot from the perimeter, make plays off the dribble, but he's really embraced the opportunity to make players around him better," Reed said. "His leadership has improved this year, his playmaking has improved, he's just done a wonderful job not only making plays on the floor but giving our team a tremendous amount of confidence because he's so calm, cool, and collected."

In the same manner he taught McCollum, Reed instructed his players to remain calm and give the impression that they had experienced this before. The fans actually had experienced it before—just moments before Lehigh tipped off—but their reaction was not exactly the same. After 11 years of waiting, the fans were entitled to a little extra celebrating. ●

MICHIGAN   ILLINOIS

Glen Rice, Michigan: 28 points, 5 rebounds

1989: MICHIGAN vs. ILLINOIS

As great as the first four games under interim coach Steve Fisher had been (see page 106), the Michigan Wolverines were not satisfied with merely getting to the Final Four. With a game against Illinois looming on the horizon, the team had some unfinished business to attend to.

"We played them the last game of the regular season. It was the last home game for our seniors and they embarrassed us," Fisher said. "They beat us bloody at our place, and our kids remembered that."

Not only had the Illini blown out their rivals in Ann Arbor, they had also handily defeated the Wolverines at home two months earlier. The only thing more impressive than their 31–4 record was the fact that they had gone 8–4 while shooting guard Kendall Gill recovered from a broken foot, meaning they were a perfect 23–0 with him in the lineup. Gill had returned just in time to hand the Wolverines their 89–73 defeat in the regular-season finale, and with the way his team was playing, it was hard to believe their third match would go any differently.

"If you played a seven-game series," Fished conceded, "Illinois was probably the best team in the country."

The Wolverines may not have had much success against the Illini earlier in the year, but both losses had come under former Michigan coach Bill Frieder. The game plan hadn't worked for his predecessor, but Fisher decided not to alter his team's strategy, ultimately concluding that it was too late in the season to make any drastic changes. The Wolverines would indeed bring their best effort, but no matter what they threw at their opponent, it always seemed that the Illini had an answer.

Matching each other shot for shot, the teams battled to 33 lead changes, an unheard-of figure. No team would ever lead by double digits, and for most of the contest neither team would lead by more than two. The Wolverines were up 39–38 at halftime, and—to no one's surprise—the score was tied at 74 with less than four minutes remaining.

"You try to make sure that everybody remained composed in a close game. You want to have them unafraid," Fisher said. "And I thought that they all really did a good job of just saying, 'I'm going to do whatever is in the cards to help us get this next rebound, get this next defensive stop, set this next screen, make this next basket.' I think that good players play and win, and you need to make sure that you don't get in the way."

UM senior Mark Hughes threw down a dunk to put the team up 76–74, and when guard Rumeal Robinson came away with a steal moments later, leading to a Glen Rice dunk, it appeared that the Wolverines had finally gotten the separation they had been searching for all game. Illinois coach Lou Henson called a timeout with 2:56 to go, and Kenny Battle delivered with a three from the right corner to fittingly bring the Illini back to within a point.

Following a miss by Rice, UI's Lowell Hamilton hit a jump shot as the lead swapped hands one more time. Now it was Michigan's turn to dig in. Fisher called a timeout and put in Sean Higgins, a forward who had a tendency of wandering toward the three-point line. With Illinois ranking among the best rebounding teams in the country, Fisher knew he would need Higgins' presence down low. But before play resumed, he had one more message for the sophomore: Stay. Down. Low.

The final minute would give Fisher an indication about the character of Higgins, as well as the rest of his team. A day earlier, coaches across the country had predicted an Illini victory—not because of a talent gap, but because Michigan couldn't last for 40 minutes. And although the Wolverines had played well for 37 minutes, it was appearing as if Fisher's colleagues were right after all.

The Wolverines worked the ball to Terry Mills, who fired up a jumper from just inside the free throw line. His shot was off the mark, but following up on the miss was Hughes, who softly put it back as he was fouled. Hughes capped off the three-point play to give UM an 81–79 lead, one that did not last for very long. On the ensuing possession, Battle fired up a turnaround jumper that clanged off the back rim and generously bounced back in to tie the game at 81. Thirty-nine minutes and 26 seconds had passed, and neither team was any closer to victory than when the game started.

Fisher elected not to call a timeout, instead trusting his players to make the right decisions on the floor. The team wisely tried to get the ball in the hands of Rice, who was on his way toward breaking the single-tournament scoring record, but the Illini would have none of it. The Wolverines settled on Robinson, who bided his time, waiting for the clock to reach 10 seconds before making his move. Now with the stage set, Robinson drove down the left side of the lane, hoping for a crease to sneak through, but nothing ever opened. By the time he reached the baseline with eight seconds left, Robinson was stuck.

With the Illinois defense right in his face, Robinson jumped up and fired a cross-court pass to Mills, standing at the opposite corner.

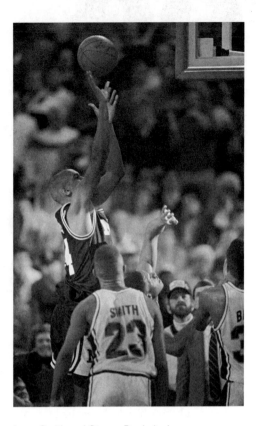

Larry Smith and Steven Bardo look on as Michigan's Sean Higgins puts in the game-winning putback with one second left, propelling the Wolverines into the national championship.
AP Photo/Susan Ragan

Mills hoisted up a shot with six seconds to go that hit off the front of the rim and bounced back toward the left end of the court—right were Higgins had planted himself. Higgins skied up over a trio of Illinois players to grab the rebound, and with one second left, softly put in the game-winner. With one shot, Higgins had not only sent the Wolverines to the national title game but he had turned Fisher into a genius.

"A shot like that always rebounds on that side unless it's short," Higgins declared after the game. "Coach is harping on that all the time. I knew I had to be over there or I'd be chewed out."

The game was considered an instant classic, but the drama that had unfolded in the semifinal would pale in comparison to what would take place two nights later in the national championship game (see page 294). ●

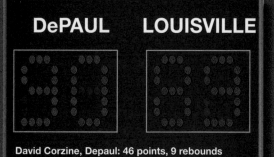

DePAUL   LOUISVILLE

David Corzine, Depaul: 46 points, 9 rebounds

1978: DePAUL
vs. LOUISVILLE

Dave Corzine knew this was his chance for revenge. It had been less than a year earlier that the DePaul star was benched at the World University Games by Team USA coach Denny Crum. What had irked Corzine more than the fact that he was benched was the sense of Crum's conflict of interest.

"We did well and won the gold medal and all that, and that was a nice thing, but I got in very little of the games, which was frustrating for me," Corzine said. "And on that team also was Ricky Gallon, who was the center for Denny Crum's team there at Louisville. And he got a lot of playing time, and I didn't agree with that necessarily. I thought I deserved to play more than I did. So I had a little bit of resentment from that situation, and then as it turned out it worked out well for me."

When the teams met in 1978 for a chance to go to the Elite Eight, Corzine was hoping to come out and prove a point. But even he didn't anticipate what he was about to do once the game started. Facing his old teammate Gallon underneath the basket, Corzine started scoring at will. The Louisville forward, too small to stop Corzine once he got the ball, tried instead to play in front of his opponent. The DePaul guards responded by simply throwing right over Gallon's outstretched hands on nearly every possession, allowing Corzine to lay in the ball for an easy bucket. By the time the first half had come to a close, the center had scored 20 of DePaul's

36 points, a streak that coach Ray Meyer thought was not likely to continue.

"See at halftime, even coach Ray says they're going to adjust on Corzine," DePaul point guard Randy Ramsey said. "Now we always waited for the weak-side help to come in to prevent us from being able to do that. It never happened."

Corzine continued right on through into the second half, and as he approached the 40-point plateau, his team enjoyed a 66–55 lead with eight minutes left. Meyer was shocked that Louisville didn't change up its defense, but he wasn't about to lend any advice on how to stop the big man from scoring layup after layup.

"I thought the funniest comment of all, when somebody asked David how come you didn't dunk those, he said, 'I was getting so many of them, I was getting tired,'" laughed Joey Meyer, Ray's son and an assistant coach on the team. "He said, 'I wanted to save my energy.'"

The Blue Demons still had a sizeable advantage when UL's Rick Wilson, who was held scoreless the entire first half, started to duplicate Corzine's performance. The senior made nine shots in the half, scoring 20 points to bring the Cardinals back in the game. After Darrell Griffith scored to cut the lead to four, Wilson hit another shot to bring UL within 74–72. They sent DePaul's Clyde Bradshaw to the free throw line with 47 seconds remaining to attempt a one-and-one, and his first attempt clanged off the front of the rim.

DePaul grabbed the ball back, but when the Cardinals fouled Ramsey, he also missed his first shot. This time Louisville cleared the rebound, and when Wilson buried a shot from the corner with two seconds to play, the Cardinals had new life. Meyer, who had just seen his team lose both its lead and momentum, made sure his players were ready for overtime.

"That game, Coach was the most focused that I probably saw him throughout the year. . . . He really thought that we were going to win this game, so that transcends into us, too," Ramsey said. "He had a tremendous amount of confidence, and in regards to winning that game I think that helped us tremendously."

Corzine chipped in four points in the extra session, but after Louisville junior Larry Williams drilled a shot near the end of overtime to give his team an 82–80 lead, it appeared to be the Cardinals' game to lose. The Blue Demons tried to work the ball into Corzine for their last shot, but Curtis Watkins saw an opening with 17 seconds left and decided to fire away. The shot was pure, and when the Cardinals failed to convert at the other end, the teams were heading to a second overtime.

DePaul managed to pull in front 89–88 before Wilson answered the call once again, hitting a baseline jumper to put the Cardinals back on top with just 20 seconds left. This time DePaul was going to try to get the ball to Corzine at all costs. Despite playing all 50 minutes, Corzine had gotten the Blue Devils to this point, and they were going to win or lose the game on his hands.

"Sometimes guys want to be heroes and stuff, but as I said to those seniors, hey, this is what we're going to do," Meyer said. "When you're young, you're stat-orientated a little bit sometimes. We always talk about in the NBA you see those older guys, all they talk about is rings."

Corzine didn't care about padding his already impressive totals, but it was hard to argue against his 17-of-27 performance from the field. Unless somebody on the team was completely open, he was going to take the final shot. As it turned out, somebody on the team was wide open, and to everyone's shock, it happened to be Corzine.

"Believe me, I want to get rid of the ball as quickly as I could," Ramsey laughed. "And when he came across, I couldn't believe how wide open he was."

Once Corzine found a crease across the middle of the court, he delivered once again, hitting a hook shot from a few feet away. His forty-sixth point of the night gave the team a 90-89 lead with just six seconds to go, and after one final stop, the Blue Demons were moving on to the Elite Eight.

"At that moment, I don't know that there's a better feeling in the world," Corzine said. "You're doing something that you love to do and you're doing it on as big a stage as a lot of other people have been on at that point. And to be in that situation and do the right thing and make the right play, or hit the big shot, that's what everybody lives for." ●

#85

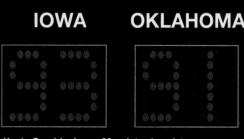

IOWA   OKLAHOMA

Kevin Gamble, Iowa: 26 points, 4 assists, 3 rebounds

1987: IOWA vs. OKLAHOMA

Perhaps the only thing tougher in sports than following a legend is following two of them, which is exactly what the University of Iowa faced after the departures of Lute Olson and George Raveling. Iowa needed to hire somebody who not only had the credentials to coach, but had an appreciation for the school's winning tradition. No one fit that category better than Tom Davis, who was actually an expert in sports history.

"That was my original idea, I was going to be a sports historian. I actually did do some teaching as an assistant coach," Davis said. "In those days, a professor would pay more than a basketball coach."

Davis had read a countless number of books about basketball's illustrious past. Little did he know that he was about to take part in a game people would be reading about for years to come.

Almost as soon as the game began, the 29–4 Hawkeyes found themselves in a hole. The sixth-seeded Oklahoma Sooners raced off to a 14–7 lead, and by the midway point of the opening period, that lead had ballooned to 37–21.

"We had been in that situation before," forward Kevin Gamble said. "That style of play, we can score 10, 15 points within a couple minutes, so we felt we were always in the whole game."

Iowa responded with 19 unanswered points near the end of the half, and by the time Gamble sank a three-pointer with seven

minutes left, the Hawkeyes had their largest lead at 78–72. But their style of play left them prone to give up points as quickly as they could score them, and the Sooners responded with a run of their own to go up 85–80 with just 2:17 to play. If the Hawkeyes wanted to keep their season alive, they were going to have to come up with one final run.

Fortunately for Iowa, they would do just that, scoring the last five points of regulation and the first five points of overtime to take a 90–85 lead. Now it was the Hawkeyes who remained just two minutes from a victory. But if they hadn't already figured it out, no lead was ever safe. David Johnson hit a pair of free throws to bring Oklahoma within 90–87, and when teammate Dave Sieger added a layup 15 seconds later, the lead was down to one. The game was still Iowa's to lose, but before the Hawkeyes could put up another shot OU's Kevin McCallister came up with a steal, leading to a Darryl Kennedy layup with 1:02 to play.

Davis, having just seen his lead slip away, wisely called a timeout to set up Iowa's final possession.

"You've got to kind of take what the defense gives you rather than force something at them," Davis said. "But we've all done that as coaches. We go and try to force something, and usually that doesn't work quite as well."

The only problem was that the Sooners didn't give them anything to work with, and as the time began to wind down, Iowa had little option but to force up a shot. The ball bricked off the rim, but the Hawkeyes, who were arguably the best rebounding team in the country, snagged the ball to give themselves a second chance. They kicked the ball out and tried to run the offense, but the Oklahoma defense was even stingier the second time through, forcing IU sophomore Roy Marble into an errant leaner with 14 seconds on the clock. The Hawkeyes didn't grab the rebound this time, but they got the next best thing: Oklahoma knocked the ball out of bounds while fighting for possession.

Iowa managed to inbound the ball to guard B. J. Armstrong, their best player, but to no one's surprise the Sooners held their ground. Armstrong tried to drive down the right sideline to find an open shot, but with five seconds to go he still had two defenders in his face, forcing him to dish the ball off to Gamble at the top of the key. A year earlier, during Gamble's freshman year, he would have been about the last option to take the final shot. Gamble rarely left the bench that season and averaged just two points a game, but by choosing hard work over complaining, he had worked his way into the starting rotation. And now he had a chance to send his team to the Elite Eight.

"He was the ultimate team player," Davis said. "He's got a very good personality, a very coachable personality, and he was willing to adjust."

And as staunch as the OU defense had been during the final minutes of overtime, Gamble was wide open. As a forward he wasn't used to shooting that far out, but this time he fired away.

"I was comfortable taking that shot," Gamble said. "I made my mind up after the first time I passed it to Roy [for Marble's leaner moments earlier]—if I'm open I'm going to take the shot."

Gamble's shot was on line to go in, as long as the distance was right. And as the ball grazed the back of the cylinder, the crowd anxiously waited to see where the ball would drop. Even if it bounced back onto the floor, Gamble could still be considered a hero. Not only had he already scored 23 points and made the game-saving block to send the game into overtime, he had overcome experiences that made his time on the bench seem like paradise. Born and raised in the projects of Springfield, Illinois, Gamble escaped from a neighborhood where drugs and violence were rampant.

"I just knew right from wrong, which sounds simple, but I didn't want to indulge in some of the other things that some of my friends and some of the other people in my neighborhood were doing," Gamble said. "My mom basically kept me on the straight and narrow."

His mom, a single parent, cleaned houses around the area to earn whatever money she could. But that still wasn't enough to keep the family off welfare, and before Gamble's senior year in high school, a college education wasn't something he had even considered. Fortunately, Davis had stepped in to provide him a basketball scholarship, and on this night Gamble made sure he had earned it. With just one tick on the clock, the ball glided off the rim and into the net, giving Iowa a 92–91 victory. And for Gamble, that was a feeling that no amount of money could buy. ●

Iowa guard Kevin Gamble, who shot an incredible 11-of-13 from the field, gets mobbed by his teammates after shot number 11 sent Iowa to the Elite Eight. *AP Photo*

Kenny Green, Wake Forest: 25 points, 13 rebounds

1984: WAKE FOREST
vs. DePAUL

After 42 years on the job, it had finally come down to this. Ray Meyer, who had been coaching since World War II, would be entering his final NCAA Tournament as head coach of DePaul. The 70-year-old Meyer had produced 37 winning seasons during his four decades at the Chicago institution, but an NCAA championship had eluded him. This season, however, with a 27–2 record and a star-studded lineup, he appeared to have his best chance yet. But before he could worry about national titles, he would first have to get by a Wake Forest team that many had overlooked.

"He was a legend. I mean, I grew up and just heard about Ray Meyer and DePaul Blue," said Wake Forest guard Delany Rudd. "That was a great coach who, if he had gone on to win it, we would have been happy for him. But in life, you get one chance to do something, to be in the record books, in the history books, and that was our moment, our chance."

With a 21–8 record, few believed the Demon Deacons posed a serious threat to DePaul's title chances. Those opinions seemed to be confirmed as the Blue Demons grabbed an early lead and never looked back. For nearly 40 consecutive minutes, Meyer's club imposed its will on Wake Forest, but the decisive blow had yet to be landed. With three minutes to go, the Demon Deacons trailed by eight points—a large chunk to be sure, but one they were certainly capable of overcoming. They cut the lead to six with two minutes left, but that pace

would leave their comeback bid just short, forcing the Demon Deacons to raise the intensity a step further.

"The last couple of minutes, we went with a 'What do we have to lose?' attitude, and we just started playing aggressive and picking them up full-court man to man," Rudd said. "I think that the whole strategy was to just to get aggressive and see if they would panic, and I think that that's what happened."

Coming back from a six-point deficit would become a much easier task just three years later when the three-point line was implemented, but in 1984 the Deacons would need several big stops if they were going to reel in their opponent two points at a time. Fortunately for Wake, the Blue Demons began to crack under the pressure. The Deacons cut the lead to 67–65 with a minute to go when DePaul went on a turnover rampage.

First it was Jerry McMillan, who was called for a backcourt violation with 56 seconds to go. Although the Deacons would come up empty on their next two possessions, they had no need to worry, as DePaul did its best to hand the ball right back. Blue Demons junior Kenny Patterson threw an alley-oop pass with 26 to go that sailed well over his intended target and right out of bounds. WFU freshman Mark Cline missed a shot with just 11 seconds to go, seemingly ending any shot of a comeback, but the Blue Demons had one final turnover left in them. They had the option of either running around the court in an effort to run out the clock, or waiting to get fouled and putting the game away with one free throw. What DePaul forward Dallas Comegys did was neither. The freshman tried to throw a pass down court to a teammate, a pass that was promptly intercepted by WFU's Kenny Green.

Green quickly turned around and fired a pass to Rudd, who was the team's primary scorer in the clutch.

"I was just never afraid to fail. I mean, I always wanted that opportunity and never ran away from it," Rudd said. "And it's just an attitude that you have and it's a confidence deep down. And I was never considered a superstar at any level, but a lot of superstars we see today can't make game-winning shots, so that's a lot of confidence and working on that stuff."

Rudd had practiced in his yard almost every day, pretending the seconds were ticking by as he put up the game-winning shot. Although he wouldn't always make the basket, he would continue shooting until he made the game-winner. This time, however, he would get only one shot. And if it fell off the mark, the season was over.

"You know, I had an incredible vision— I will say that for myself. I just believed that I was supposed to do those things," Rudd said. "So I think those things like that, it's an inner strength that you have to have to be able to deal with the fact that if you miss that shot, what people are going to say. I just was never one of those that worried about what people would say."

Fans would have plenty to say about Rudd following the game, but it would all be in adoration, as Rudd's shot right at the buzzer sent the game into overtime. Not only would the Demon Deacons be carrying all the momentum with them, but they were entering their seventh overtime of the season, where they were already 5–1. Now with a fresh slate to work from, Wake Forest coach Carl Tacy urged his players to keep up the desperation that they had played with for the last minutes of regulation.

"Guys, I told you so. All we wanted was this opportunity, and that's what we got," Tacy said. "This is what we came for—go take it!"

The Deacons would play admirably in the overtime period, but the game was still tied at 71 with 19 seconds left when Rudd fouled Patterson, sending him to the line to shoot a one-and-one. The junior had a chance to give DePaul a huge advantage heading into the final possession, but it was obvious his errant pass at the end of regulation was still haunting him.

"You could just see in his face when he was at the free throw line. I watched the videotape of it maybe a year ago, and I could see his face. He looked like, 'Man, I have to make these?'" Rudd said. "You could see that they were sitting there feeling like, 'Why are these country guys not going away? Why would they not quit?'"

The answer was simple: This game had proven that all Wake Forest had to do was make shots; DePaul would provide all the errors it would need on the other end to make a comeback possible. And this case would be no different, as Patterson's free throw bounced off the rim and right into the hands of Cline, who tossed it off to senior Danny Young. Contrary to his name, Young was the team's elder statesman, and he knew exactly who to look for.

"He kicked it to me at the top and they rotated over to help," Rudd recalled. "And I threw it right back to him."

Now with defense caught off guard, Young saw the opening he was looking for. With time running out, the senior dribbled in and fired a shot just before the last second ticked by. And just as Rudd had done five minutes earlier, Young sank the winning shot to send the Demon Deacons to the Elite Eight. As for Meyer, his 724 wins said it all. He could hold his head up high too. ●

WAKE FOREST   TEXAS

Al-Farouq Aminu, Wake Forest: 20 points, 15 rebounds

2010: WAKE FOREST vs. TEXAS

Ishmael Smith had enjoyed a career at Wake Forest that most other players could only dream of. During his four years as a starter for the Demon Deacons, Smith had made a habit of hitting last-second shots to win games. Perhaps the only downside to his career was that he never knew how responsible he was for his own success. As a religion major who prayed with his mom before every game and brought a Bible on each road trip, Smith may have been receiving some help from higher places. But whatever the reason for Smith's late-game heroics, it was a pattern he wasn't planning on breaking anytime soon.

"I loved wining. Everybody loves to win, but I think certain players, you do what it takes for you to win," Smith said. "I used to always tell people I'm just doing the easy part. My teammates have done all the work by getting us here. I'm just doing the easy part by making the last-second shot."

It was that type of attitude that had brought Wake Forest so much success early in the season, but as the tournament approached the team seemed to lose some of its magic. After an 18–5 start, the Deacons looked forward to receiving a three or four seed come tournament time, only to have several heartbreaking losses push them all the way down to a nine seed. The punishment for the late-season slump? A Texas team that had been ranked atop the national polls when they started the year 17–0. An equally disappointing finish gave the

Longhorns motivation to prove their doubters wrong as well.

Both teams had stumbled into the tournament, but one squad would walk away with a victory. Early on, that team appeared to be Wake Forest, as the Deacons grabbed an early 18–7 lead. The Longhorns trimmed the margin to just 38–37 at halftime, but 7-of-10 shooting by the Deacons to start the second half gave them a 54–42 lead with 13 minutes remaining.

"We were up 12, feeling good about ourselves," Smith said. "In our minds we're thinking like, okay, all we got to do is close this out—a few minutes to go and we go home. And we kind of relaxed, took our foot off the pedal."

Texas took a timeout and guard J'Covan Brown, who had been held scoreless the entire first half, found his touch just in time. Brown scored 10 points down the stretch to cut the lead to 65–64 with two minutes left, and when he nailed a three-pointer with 55 seconds to play, the Longhorns had evened the score at 67. Smith never got a chance to be a hero in regulation, and after 40 minutes of play the score remained tied. Due in large part to Smith's play, Wake Forest had won each of its four overtime games that season, but a fifth victory appeared highly unlikely after the Longhorns took a 76–68 lead with just 3:05 to play in the extra session. WF coach Dino Gaudio told his players not to panic, noting that plenty of time remained for a comeback.

"Some teams, maybe instead of winning the game in regulation, they let it slip through their fingers and all of a sudden they go to over-time with an improper mindset," Gaudio said. "But our mindset was, I would always go into the huddle and say, 'Boys, is this great or what? We play basketball—that's what we do, and we get to play five more minutes. It doesn't get better than that!'"

The speech worked wonders, as the team clawed its way back, and when Ari Stewart sank a three-pointer with 19 seconds to play, the Deacons were within 80–79.

"More than anything, I think you embody your coaches' personality," Smith said. "Our whole coaching staff kept holding us up and kept telling us guys we're still good, we're fine, stay in it."

Gaudio's final instruction was to immediately foul whomever received the inbounds pass to avoid any wasted time. But when the Longhorns inbounded the ball to Brown, an 88 percent free throw shooter, the players overrode Gaudio's orders. The Deacons pressured Brown into tossing the ball to Gary Johnson, who at 69 percent was a much better alternative.

"I'm thinking to myself, okay, we foul him, and even if he makes both of these, we're still somehow, someway going to win this game," Smith said. "And I think that's from my mother and my father. They instilled in me just this never-stop, never-lose attitude."

Smith's dreams appeared much more likely when Johnson bricked both free throws and Wake Forest sophomore Tony Woods grabbed the rebound with 10 seconds to go. Everybody on the Deacons sideline knew who the last shot was going to.

"You feel good when you got a guy like that, that you can put the ball in his hands," Gaudio said of Smith. "He took great pride in playing the position. I think he had a lot of confidence in taking the big shot."

Smith took the ball and raced down the right sideline, driving toward the basket before pulling up from 15 feet away. Avery Bradley was right there as Smith faded away, but it didn't matter as Smith still got the shot off, swishing it with just a second left to give the Deacons an 81–80 victory. Smith was instantly dubbed the hero of the game, but he had somebody else in mind.

"I'm really proud of him because that kid has just been an overachiever," Wake Forest coach Dino Gaudio said of Ishmael Smith, shown here celebrating his game-winner. "He has a great attitude, he works very hard. You'll never have a problem with him off the court. I'm just really happy for his success because he really deserved it." *Dave Martin/Getty Images.*

"I think all of us athletes, we know what we've been blessed to do. God has truly blessed us with the ability on and off the court to do some things," Smith said. "I don't know why it is that I thrive in those situations. It's something that I can't explain, but I'm blessed that I got it."

Perhaps somebody was guiding in that shot as the last seconds ticked by. Perhaps Smith's game-winner was all his own doing. But whatever the case, Smith was certainly singing the Lord's praises after the game. ●

#82

1995: GEORGETOWN vs. WEBER STATE

Don Reid flipped on the television as he tried to pass the time in his hotel room. The Georgetown forward was still hours away from tipping off against Weber State in their second-round matchup, so Reid did the only thing he could to take his mind off the upcoming game—he watched more college basketball. A special program happened to be on ESPN, one that relived all the tournament's great moments, including the 1983 N.C. State title game against Houston. Reid was only 10 years old when Lorenzo Charles redirected the game-winning shot as the last moment, but it was a moment that would stick in the memory of anyone who saw it. In fact, Reid would later practice that same move for 30 minutes every day, and in a few hours he would finally have a chance to put it to use.

By 1995, Reid was the captain and leader of the Hoyas, but when he had watched N.C. State win the title 12 years earlier, he actually had yet to pick up a basketball. It was only due to his tenacity and eagerness to learn that he managed to make the high school basketball team.

"It really started because I had no clue, and the first thing I could pick up was defense, because I couldn't shoot, couldn't dribble," Reid laughed. "The defensive part of the game was something I could lock in on pretty quick, and I tried to say I can never have an off day playing defense."

That same demeanor earned him a spot on the Georgetown roster, but the offensive woes were far from over. Five games into his freshman year, Reid was shooting just 10 percent from the floor, and he would average 1.6 points a game for both his freshman and sophomore seasons. Reid was periodically bounced from the starting lineup to the bench, until his junior year when the offensive touch began to click. He started to score more than seven points a game, and by his senior year the Hoyas looked primed to break their second-round curse. The Hoyas had not advanced past the second round since 1989, but with fourteenth-seeded Weber State slated as their second-round opponent, Reid and his teammates appeared bound for the Sweet 16.

The Wildcats did little to change anybody's mind at the start of the game, as Georgetown unleashed a press that led to 10 quick points before Weber State could even get on the scoreboard. In fact, the WSU offense would never get going, as the Wildcats would make just 18 of their 51 shots on the night. What the Hoyas didn't expect, though, is that their offense would quickly become just as bad. Their front line ran into foul trouble, removing the team's most effective shooters, and Georgetown's guards were equally unproductive. By the game's final minute the team was shooting an abysmal 18-of-49.

Perhaps it was because the Hoyas, who couldn't name any of the players on Weber State, were taking their opponent lightly. Perhaps it was because the rims happened to be strung a little too tight on that particular evening. But whatever the reason, with Georgetown's offense unable to break through, the score remained knotted at 51 as Weber State took its final possession.

Wildcats guard Ruben Nembhard, the conference Player of the Year, took it upon himself to deliver the game-winner, but Reid was there to swat it away with nine seconds left. Weber State went right back to Nembhard, and this time the senior drew a foul with just 7.4 seconds to play. Georgetown coach John Thompson called a timeout, hoping to ice Nembhard at the line while also giving him time to share final instructions with his players.

"The rebound will kill you more than the shot," Thompson warned, reminding his players to box out. It seemed like a useless reminder, considering that Nembhard was the game's leading scorer and a 77 percent free throw shooter, but Nembhard's shot bricked off the back of the rim, right into the hands of Georgetown forward Jerome Williams. The plan was obvious—get the ball over to lightning-quick guard Allen Iverson.

"He could probably get up the floor in two and a half seconds, so we knew we were going to get a shot up," Reid said. "My thoughts were just to get down to the other end of the court to keep up with Allen."

Iverson would be an All-American each of his two years in a Georgetown uniform, but this had not been his night. WSU's Lewis Lofton had limited him to just 6-of-20 shooting, and shot No. 21 would be the ugliest of them all. Iverson raced down the left side of the court, hoping to blow by Lofton, but the WSU sophomore stayed stride for stride with his man. Finally, with time running out, Iverson cast off a leaning, unnatural shot from the left wing that dropped well short of its intended target. Weber State forward Kirk Smith, anticipating a long rebound off the distant shot, readied himself well outside the area under the basket. But Iverson's shot

was so poor that it failed to hit the rim, leaving Reid wide open to try and toss it back in.

"Everybody just started looking at the ball after Iverson got it in his hands, and you get to the point where you don't want to foul anybody so everybody stood still," Reid said. "And I was just trying to get close enough to the basket."

Reid came in from the right baseline and caught the ball as if he were in the middle of a reverse layup. With only 0.4 on the clock, Reid did the only thing he could, which was to toss it over his shoulders. Before the ball even hit the backboard, the clock had already struck zero, as everybody in the arena waited to see where it would land. And just as Reid had watched on TV earlier in the day, his last-second putback went through as the Hoyas broke their curse. ●

Allen Iverson chases a loose ball during his team's second-round thriller against Weber State. *AP Photo/Dave Martin*

#81

2006: TENNESSEE vs. WINTHROP

For years, whenever people mentioned Tennessee basketball, the first thing that came to mind was the Lady Volunteers. Thanks to head coach Pat Summitt, the women's team had enjoyed eight national championships while becoming the most success team in women's basketball history. Coaching the men, on the other hand, was not an easy task. When Buzz Peterson was fired after four consecutive years without an NCAA Tournament appearance, the men's program had hit a low point.

"Tennessee basketball was basically the laughingstock of the SEC," guard Chris Lofton said. "We were second to last in the SEC, and it was just embarrassing for us."

Peterson was replaced by Bruce Pearl, an enthusiastic head coach who saw better things in UT's future.

"When coach Pearl came on board, it's like everything turned 360 degrees," senior Stanley Asumnu said. "He had the energy and the fire and spark as far as wanting to turn the program around and have it go in the right direction."

The change became apparent almost immediately, as the Volunteers went 22–6 in his first year and were rewarded with a two seed in the tournament. *Dealt* might actually be a more accurate term, as the selection committee saw fit to pair Tennessee with Winthrop, a team that was making its sixth tournament appearance in seven seasons.

The 23–7 Eagles probably should have been ranked higher than a 15 seed, and they decided to take their anger out on the Volunteers. Winthrop took an 18–15 lead early on and made a late run to trail just 36–34 at halftime.

"We knew up top it was going to be a tough game," Asumnu said. "It wasn't going to be one of those games where you're just going to come in there and walk over them just because we're from the SEC."

The Volunteers had a conference in the locker room at halftime about what they were doing wrong. There wasn't much they could do about Winthrop sinking all its shots, but being outhustled by the Eagles was a completely different matter. The team came back out with a renewed sense of purpose and surrendered just five points over the final ten minutes. The only problem was that the Eagles matched every steal and block with a stop of their own, and when James Shuler knocked down a three-pointer with 3:30 left, it was Winthrop who led 61–60. For the remainder of the game, neither team refused to budge on defense.

The game was tied at 61 when Winthrop inbounded the ball with 52 seconds left, and to no one's surprise the Vols stood firm, forcing the Eagles to take a hurried three-pointer before the shot clock expired. UT's Major Wingate snatched the rebound, and Pearl elected to let the players set up the game-winning shot on their own. C. J. Watson brought the ball up the floor, but he was hounded by Chris Gainer as soon as he crossed midcourt. Watching as the seconds ticked away, Pearl decided to take a timeout—right at the moment that Watson appeared to break free toward the basket. The timeout may have wiped out a golden opportunity to score, but Tennessee still had 21 seconds to get another look.

This time the Eagles weren't as generous, forcing Watson to clang a three off the back of the rim, resulting in a mad scramble for the ball that went past midcourt. Craig Bradshaw picked up the ball and drove toward the basket, but again Pearl called a timeout right before the shot, this time with only 2.9 seconds remaining. Pearl's nerves were not just limited to his timeouts.

"He drew up something and then he erased it; then he drew up something and then he erased it again; then he drew something else," Asumnu laughed. "So we're looking at the

board like, 'Okay, all right.' So when we left the huddle, we just said, 'All right, hey Chris, we're coming to you.'"

Chris Lofton, who had missed all of his shot attempts in the second half, was hardly the person most fans expected to take the last shot. But as a player who would beat cancer a year later, Lofton was the kind of person who could handle a little adversity.

"It was a great feeling to know that my coaching staff and my teammates had the confidence in me for me to take the last shot," Lofton said. "I was in a win-win situation. If I miss it, we go to overtime. If I make it, we win."

On the inbounds, Lofton circled around a screen and caught the ball in the right corner. Without hesitation, the sophomore turned and fired a fadeaway jumper from just inside the three-point line, which is not only the hardest shot in the game, but also the slowest.

"The ball is up in the air and you were watching it. It goes in slow motion and it's going and it's taking forever to come down," Asumnu joked. "It was like, come on—and everybody is just sitting there."

But when the ball finally did make its way toward the hoop, it went in just before the buzzer. Lofton naturally assumed the horn went off and started celebrating, and he was not the only one. But 0.4 seconds still remained when Winthrop took a timeout.

"People ran on the floor thinking the game was over, but it wasn't over yet and luckily they called timeout," Asumnu said. "Because if they didn't call timeout and they're all running on the floor, something could have happened. Technicals could have been thrown here and there."

Unbelievably, when Winthrop heaved the ball the length of the floor, it hit off the backboard and into the hands of one of its players, who just missed the game-tying shot at the buzzer. The Volunteers knew they had just escaped from a major scare. But more importantly, they knew that Tennessee was once again relevant in basketball. Men's basketball. ●

Tennessee's Major Wingate goes up for a dunk over Winthrop's Craig Bradshaw. *Streeter Lecka/ Getty Images*

#80

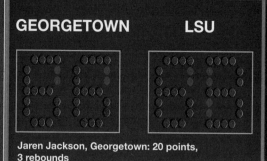

GEORGETOWN   **LSU**

Jaren Jackson, Georgetown: 20 points, 3 rebounds

1988: GEORGETOWN vs. LOUISIANA STATE

Georgetown guard Jaren Jackson knew there were going to be some angry fans in attendance at the Hartford Civic Center. Facing the Hoyas in the first round of the NCAA Tournament would be LSU, whom Jackson had grown up rooting for as a New Orleans native. Many fans in Louisiana expected him to sign with the Tigers, but as a valedictorian of his high school, Jackson knew that Georgetown would give him the best balance of basketball and academia. That didn't sit well with the LSU faithful, but making the situation worse was that three other New Orleans natives had also packed up and left for Washington, D.C.

"There was a lot of talk about all the New Orleans guys being at Georgetown and the fact that they did not go to LSU," Jackson said. "And there was a lot of hype about that, and it gave the game a little pre-game hype, a little buzz."

Jackson could take solace in the fact that Georgetown had a much better team. LSU was only 16–13 on the season and had just sneaked into the field of 64. But Christmas came early for the Tigers, who were generously awarded a nine seed—and on this night, they actually played like one. Even though Georgetown would go on a 13–0 run in the second half to build an 11-point lead, LSU would answer right back. The Tigers climbed to within 63–61, and when Wayne Sims buried a jumper with 45 seconds left, the score was tied once again.

The score was still the same when Georgetown inbounded the ball with nine seconds to play. Coach John Thompson had instructed his players to get the ball to junior Charles Smith, who was the Big East Player of the Year, but considering he was just 3-of-12 on the night, with no baskets in the second half, it was a risky decision to say the least—especially considering that Jackson led all scorers with 20 points.

"I think there have been times throughout my career where any player, especially a guard or a winning player, would just love to take the ball. You hear the clock coming down—three seconds, two, one—and just let it go and dream of hitting the winning shot," Jackson said. "And don't get me wrong, I was having a good game. I would have loved to take a last shot, too. But I have no problem at all at that time with Charles taking it because he was an integral part of our team."

In order to catch the defense off guard, Thompson had Jackson take the inbounds before delivering a pass to Smith. It was not Smith's best day on the court, but Thompson had taken something else into consideration— Smith owned the final seconds of a game. He had nailed a game-winner the previous year against Ohio State, and earlier in the season he made another to beat Syracuse.

"He was coming into his own as a college player, and Coach felt pretty comfortable putting the ball in his hands in last-second situations," Jackson said. "Charles at that time had previously done it before and he felt comfortable doing it, so I think the scouting report was out that Charles was probably going to be the one to get the opportunity to take the last shot. And that's exactly what happened."

Smith did indeed take the final shot, but it was not exactly a thing of beauty. The Tigers read the final play to perfection, forcing Smith to fire a shot from well beyond the three-point line. As the ball sailed in the air, it was clear that Smith had put way too much into the shot. In fact, the shot was so horrendous that it hit failed to even touch the rim. But what it hit was even better, as the ball caromed off the backboard and into the net to give the Hoyas an improbable 66–63 victory. Smith tried to play it off as cool, but his teammates weren't buying it.

"Anytime somebody banks a shot in for a winner or something like that from the top, you get the old tease—please call a bank, call glass," Jackson laughed. "Don't just shoot it and act like you meant to hit the glass. So I think he probably got a little teased, but I think at that time who cares, and that was it." ●

#79

Shane Battier, Duke: 25 points, 8 rebounds, 2 assists

2001: DUKE vs. MARYLAND

Duke senior Sean Battier made his way toward Maryland guard Juan Dixon, just moments after their third classic battle of the season. The Blue Devils had survived their ACC Tournament semifinal on a last-second tip by Nate James, and Battier wanted to let his opponent know just what he thought about the Terrapins.

"See you in the Final Four," Battier said with a smile before walking off the floor.

The comment was not meant to rub the victory in Dixon's face—it was a sign of mutual respect. The two teams were rivals, but each had learned a lot about the other's character over the course of the season. In January, the Blue Devils had defeated Maryland at Cole Fieldhouse, only to have the Terrapins return the favor on senior night at Cameron Indoor Stadium. It was Duke's only loss of the season that hadn't come at the buzzer, and now after this finish, Battier could sense that a fourth match was on the horizon.

Battier's prediction would come true, but a few minutes into the national semifinals game, he was probably wishing it hadn't. The Terrapins came out scoring the first seven points of the game, and although Duke managed to settle in and trail just 16–10, Maryland went on another run, this one of a much more devastating variety.

In just over one minute, the Terps reeled off another seven points to take a 23–10 lead, and they kept right on going. Dixon's three-pointer

midway through the half brought the lead to 28–13, and the Terrapins showed no signs of slowing down. Not only were they shooting 55 percent from the field, compared with Duke's 26 percent, but they had rebounded all but two of their misses. Dixon hit another three a minute later, and when point guard Steve Blake hit a three-pointer of his own with seven minutes left in the half, the lead had ballooned to a ridiculous 22 points. The game was only 13 minutes old, and it appeared the Terrapins had already delivered the knockout punch with a 39–17 lead.

It was the largest deficit the Blue Devils had faced in a long time, but they were not about to give up. Head coach Mike Krzyzewski, affectionately known as Coach K to his players, had trained them always to portray a look of determination, regardless of what the scoreboard said. If the Blue Devils were frustrated or anxious, Maryland would never know. The same went for the coach himself as he gathered his players together.

"We were too excited and we were not ourselves. When we got 22 points down, there was still a lot of the game left. I just told our players, 'Look, it's Saturday afternoon and I am not calling any plays anymore,'" Krzyzewski recalled. "'You guys just play basketball. Have fun playing basketball. You haven't had fun yet. Let's see what happens.'"

The situation looked bleak, but Krzyzewski had a reason to believe: his players had already pulled off one miracle against Maryland that season. During their win in College Park, in what became known as "The Miracle Minute," the Blue Devils had trailed by 10 points with less than a minute to go before pulling off the unthinkable. Their eventual 98–96 overtime win was proof that no lead was too insurmountable, and now it was time to put that theory to the test.

James quickly drilled a three-pointer to cut the lead to 39–20, and his lay-in minutes later narrowed the gap to 42–26. Battier joined the comeback with a three-pointer of his own, and when freshman Chris Duhon hit a pair of free throws near the end of the half, the Blue Devils had already cut 14 points out of their deficit. The Maryland lead was down to 46–38, but just before the buzzer Dixon unleashed a shot from beyond the NBA three-point line that sank through, putting the momentum right back in their hands as they headed into the locker room.

"When you're up against a team like Duke, you're so excited it's kind of like you've already won even though it's just halftime," Maryland center Lonny Baxter said. "We just

got a little relaxed and everybody thought we had the game."

The game wasn't won just yet, but the Blue Devils were certainly taking longer than they hoped to come back. With 16:51 left, the Terrapins still led by eight, and ten minutes into the second half the lead was still at seven. If the Blue Devils were going to complete the comeback, they would need to rediscover the spark that they had found near the end of the first half. That spark came in the form of Shane Battier, one of just two seniors in Duke's rotation. His shot from the left corner brought the Blue Devils within 69–65, and less than two minutes later he buried another triple to bring his team within 69–68. When Williams took a screen from Battier and buried a shot of his own with 6:51 left, Duke had its first lead at 73–72.

But that lead did not guarantee them a victory, and with less than five minutes to go Maryland had reclaimed the lead at 77–76. Duke would storm back in front 80–77, but it came with a heavy price. As Chris Duhon ran toward midcourt to intercept a Maryland pass, he viciously collided into Steve Blake. Duhon's face was met by Blake's shoulder, which instantly sent him hurling toward the floor. The sophomore landed directly on his back, but the real scare came when his head snapped back a second later and hit the court with a thud.

The Blue Devils had the lead, but they were going to try and keep it without their versatile guard, who was taken to the locker room for evaluation. Harking back to Krzyzewski's instructions, the team played on with a look that indicated business, and in Duhon's absence they outscored Maryland 11–5 to seal one of the greatest comebacks in NCAA history.

As for Duhon, he recovered to return in the final seconds, where he was greeted by Blake. Unlike the appreciation Battier had shown Dixon earlier, Blake leaned over to his opponent and smirked, "I knocked you out." Duhon, looking at the 93–84 score with 22 seconds left, looked back at Blake. "Actually," Duhon reminded him, "I knocked you out." ●

Shane Battier blocks Lonny Baxter's shot during the largest comeback in Final Four history. *Bob Rosato/Sports Illustrated/Getty Images*

#78

VERMONT   SYRACUSE

Germain Mopa Njila, Vermont: 20 points, 9 rebounds, 5 assists

2005: VERMONT vs. SYRACUSE

After 19 years at the University of Vermont, head coach Tom Brennan was ready to call it quits. With four consecutive conference titles and three straight NCAA Tournament appearances under his belt, Brennan had accomplished all of his goals at Vermont. Except win a tournament game.

With a collection of seniors also departing after the season, it was now or never for the Catamounts. Standing in their way was Syracuse, winner of the Big East and national champion just two seasons before. The Catamounts were a 13 seed, but with one of the oldest lineups in the country, they at least had a chance of pulling off the shocker.

"They knew they were playing for something real special, and this was kind of the last time because four of those guys were graduating," Brennan said. "And wouldn't this be an unbelievable way to cap it off?"

Leading the way for the seniors were conference Players of the Year Taylor Coppenrath and T. J. Sorrentine. And although their styles meshed well on the court, that was about the extent of their similarities. Coppenrath was a shy kid from rural Vermont—so rural, in fact, that his home didn't have an address. Sorrentine, meanwhile, was a hilarious, if brash, individual from Rhode Island. Not surprisingly, at Vermont's selection show party, when everybody else was disappointed to see the team paired against Syracuse, Sorrentine was thrilled.

"Everyone's like ahh, that's a terrible draw," Sorrentine said. "I'm saying man, I'm excited we're playing them. I can shoot 20 threes in the game."

Sorrentine did take 20 shots, but he connected on only five of them, and to make matters worse, Coppenrath was having an off night as well. Thanks to the poor shooting, the Catamounts let a 19–18 lead slip away and found themselves down 23–19 at halftime. The late run, however, turned fellow senior Alex Jensen's pre-game joke into a reality. Before tip-off, Sorrentine asked Jensen if the team had a chance, to which Jensen curiously responded, "If we're losing at the half by four."

"So we come in at the half and I tapped him, and I said, 'We're down four.' And he's like, 'I know. We're going to win,'" laughed Sorrentine. "I just smiled and kept it at that."

Now that the first part of Jensen's premonition had come true, it was up to the rest of the players to hold up their end of the bargain. Germain Mopa Njila, a forward from Cameroon who averaged a little over five points a game, decided to have the game of his life, making 9 of his 10 shots, including the equalizer with just over 90 seconds left.

Each team added another bucket before Syracuse walked the ball up the court with 55 seconds to go. The Orangemen got the ball to Hakim Warrick, who had scored the last eight points for Syracuse, but when he turned to the basket to make his move, he accidentally drilled UVM's Martin Klimes in the face with an elbow, and the charge gave Vermont a chance to win it in regulation.

Now it was Mopa Njila's turn. The senior made his move at the six-second mark, driving on the baseline and banking in what he thought was the game-winner. Before any celebrations began, however, the referees pointed to where Mopa Njila took off and waved off the basket. Out of bounds.

"I said to Njila, 'Aren't you an engineering major?'" Brennan joked. "You got to know where the lines are if you're going to be an engineer!"

Gerry McNamara's shot at the buzzer was long, and the game would head into overtime.

"The last thing I want to do is play five more minutes—really, I do not want to do that," Brennan said. "But as soon as the kids came over, I remember just saying to them, 'Hey, where else would you rather be? Five more! We'll stay all night—I don't care!'"

The Orangemen worked their way to a 55–53 lead and looked to pad the lead even further when Warrick took a pass with just over two minutes to go. Klimes came up with another big stop, this time tying up Warrick, with the possession arrow pointing toward Vermont. Njila found an opening behind the three-point line and delivered with a swish to put the Catamounts up 56–55 with 1:58 left. Moments later, he anticipated Syracuse's next pass and handed it off to Sorrentine to run the offense.

Assistant coach Jesse Agel told him to run "red," which called for Sorrentine to pass the ball to the wing and look to get open later in the shot clock. Trying to distract the opposition, Sorrentine yelled out "run the play." Except he didn't. With the crowd chanting "U-V-M," Sorrentine stood just shy of the midcourt logo, dribbling the ball as the shot clock wound down. Then with eight seconds left and plenty of time to set up a play, he decided to launch a shot from nearly 30 feet away.

"I really felt if I gave up the ball, if I passed the ball, I wasn't going to get it back," Sorrentine said. "I just wanted to get it off sure enough. I just made sure I got my legs into it, let it fly, and hoped for the best."

Brennan watched from the sidelines as Sorrentine ignored the orders from the coaching staff.

"I get honest to God, thousands—I'm not making this up—thousands of people in the last five years have told me where they were when T. J. made that shot," Vermont coach Tom Brennan said. *Sally McCray, UVM Photography*

"He said to me, 'If I didn't love you so much and respect you so much, I wouldn't have taken that shot,'" Brennan laughed. "Once it leaves his hand, you just got to root for it because there's nothing else you can do at that point. . . . When I saw it, I thought damn, that's got a chance."

Sure enough, Sorrentine's heave sailed straight through the net, and a minute later Vermont had pulled off the upset. Brennan waved to all the fans, none of whom wanted this to be his last game. Thanks to Sorrentine's heroics, it wasn't, but a party throughout all of New England was still in order.

"My favorite memory was sprinting off the court," Sorrentine said. "I was the only guy in the locker room for like two minutes. I'm like, where is everybody? They were all celebrating on the court. I had no idea what to do with myself."

The win was immortalized when Ben & Jerry's dedicated a new flavor of ice cream to their beloved coach, naming it Tom Brennan's Retiremint. It turns out that the taste of victory is sweet after all. ●

OLD DOMINION   **VILLANOVA**

Petey Sessoms, Old Dominion: 35 points, 8 rebounds, 2 assists,

1995: OLD DOMINION vs. VILLANOVA

The first round of the 1995 NCAA Tournament featured 32 games, and almost none of them appeared to be more of a sure thing than Villanova's matchup against Old Dominion. The third-seeded Wildcats came into the tournament as one of the hottest teams in the country, winning 17 of their last 19 games as well as the Big East championship. The team was led by future NBA lottery pick Kerry Kittles, a 6-foot-5 shooting guard who had emerged as one of the most talented players in the country.

Old Dominion had saved its season by winning the CAA tournament, but few considered the Monarchs a threat to Villanova's title aspirations. The Monarchs had challenged themselves in the regular season against several quality opponents, but the plan backfired when ODU emerged from the buzz saw with a 5–9 record. To top it all off, the Monarchs would be playing without their best player, center Odell Hodge. Nevertheless, head coach Jeff Capel gave the team an unusual amount of confidence heading into the game.

"Coach Capel was the master of the mind games, and he kept trying to preach to us that we're conference champions just like they're a conference champion, and we have just as much a right to be there as they did," senior Mike Jones said. "At some point we obviously started to believe that."

Without Hodge in the lineup, Capel had his undersized players use brooms in practice to simulate Villanova's trio of big men. The strategy seemed to work, as Old Dominion raced off to a 25–13 lead. Kittles, who had come into the game averaging more than 21 points a contest, was limited to just four points in the first half. But as the opening period drew to a close, the Wildcats made a late run to cut the lead to 29–24 before the break.

"The one thing I remember coach Capel really emphasizing to us was, 'You know what? We got their attention. They're going to come at us harder,'" Jones said. "'They're going to try to push us around.'"

The Monarchs held their ground, stretching the lead back to 49–40 midway through the second half, but as soon as Kittles started to find his rhythm, Villanova made the run that ODU was dreading. The Wildcats went on a 16–3 spurt that was capped off by a Jonathan Haynes steal and lay-in by Kittles with 3:00 left. Now facing their first deficit since the first two minutes of the game, it was up to the Monarchs to respond. They cut the lead to 58–55 and had a chance to tie the game when Petey Sessoms was blocked by Kittles with 1:50 left. Villanova looked to run off some time, letting the shot clock run down to five seconds before center Jason Lawson attempted a turnaround jumper. And although his shot missed off the side of the rim, the ball was tipped back out to give the Wildcats a fresh shot clock.

The season was now on the line for Old Dominion. Facing almost a sure defeat without a stop, Jones stepped up for ODU's biggest defensive play of the season. Kittles called for a screen from his teammates and got one, darting to his right on the way to the basket. But before he could attempt the knockout punch, Jones took a charge to give the Monarchs the ball with 46 seconds left. Moments later Sessoms dribbled to the corner for a three-pointer, and although Lawson was there to defend the shot, he committed the unthinkable—he fouled Sessoms.

"You see a guy coming at you and you may want to put your foot out a little bit to make it seem like they can hit your foot or anything," Sessoms said. "It was just one of those times where he did hit me and they had to call something."

Sessoms converted all three shots to knot the score with just 18.9 seconds to play. Lawson had a chance to redeem himself when he took a pass in the final seconds, but his bank shot from just three feet away was off the mark, as was his ensuing tip-in. When Lawson missed a third putback as time expired, the teams were heading to overtime. ODU found itself in a similar situation at the end of overtime, as Sessoms stepped up to the line with 25 seconds left and his team trailing 67–65. Sessoms came through once again, as would his teammates moments later. They tied up Villanova's Alvin Williams as he went for the game-winning shot, and with the possession arrow favoring the Monarchs, they actually had a chance to win the game. Unfortunately for them, with just 2.4 seconds to work with, they would need a miracle. As it turned out, they almost got one.

As soon as small forward Mario Mullen caught the ball near the left wing, he surprised everybody by whipping the ball behind his head. There to receive the pass was Jones, who was wide open underneath the basket. But with Kittles racing back toward the hoop, Jones missed the shot.

"I could have went up and dunked the ball, but I freaked out," Jones said. "It was the NCAA Tournament. I didn't really think; I just kind of reacted. Had I thought, it would have never made it to the third overtime."

Perhaps the only thing more impressive than Mullen's pass was the reaction from the bench after Jones' shot.

"They didn't even reference the fact that it happened, which I really appreciated," Jones said. "Obviously they could have been all over me because the game should have been over."

Both teams traded free throws in the double-overtime as fatigue started to set in. With a short bench, ODU fell behind by five points in the session, but a free throw by Jones tied the game once again with just 34 seconds left to play. Following the trend, the Wildcats responded to the tying free throws with an empty possession, sending the game into a third overtime.

The game seemed destined for a fourth extra session after ODU sophomore E. J. Sherod missed a free throw that would have put his team up by four with just 34 seconds to go. Villanova snatched the rebound and Haynes drove toward the basket, only to pass on the shot when he found a streaking Zeffy Penn in perfect position for a backdoor layup. But just before Penn could lay it in, Sessoms blocked the ball from behind, smacking it off the backboard and into the hands of Mullen.

Sessoms, who had the presence of mind to break down court, caught a pass from Mullen and raced toward the hoop. Villanova's Eric Eberz attempted to break up the play by committing a foul, but Sessoms emerged on the other side and sank the reverse layup for his thirty-fourth point of the night.

"You can call that the nail in the coffin," Sessoms smiled. "I knew he was going to foul me."

The ensuing free throw made it 87–81, and the party was on. Capel told his players to get the celebrating out of their system, because they would need to be in bed early that night. Nobody took that to heart more than Jones and his roommate, David Harvey. They called room service for some pizza, and before they knew what happened, it was the next morning.

"We were so exhausted emotionally after the game that we woke up the next morning . . . to go to practice and we both still had what we wore to the game on," Jones said.

So after three hours of action, the Monarchs got to enjoy the victory for all of a few minutes. The celebration may have been short-lived, but needless to say, the team slept quite well that night. ●

ARIZONA   GONZAGA

Channing Frye, Arizona: 22 points, 12 rebounds

2003: ARIZONA VS. GONZAGA

As the University of Arizona geared up to play Gonzaga in the second round of the 2003 NCAA Tournament, basketball was the last thing on many people's minds. Just days before, President George W. Bush had given the order to send troops into Iraq, reminding many of the players just how far removed sports were from the rest of the world.

"I remember in the locker room, all of us . . . just talked about it after practice. We talked about it for 20, 30 minutes, about Bush. A lot of guys had different ways they went with the war," said Arizona senior Rick Anderson. "We put it in perspective all the time."

Nevertheless, the top-seeded Wildcats still had a game to play, a game that head coach Lute Olson knew his team could lose. Arizona had recently fallen victim to fourteenth-seeded East Tennessee State and fifteenth-seeded Santa Clara, and Olson was not about to let that happen again, warning his team that the vastly underrated Bulldogs were actually deserving of a No. 1 or No. 2 seed.

"That was a very good Gonzaga team," Olson said of his opponent, who would make each NCAA Tournament since then. "Now that they've established themselves, they would not have been a nine seed."

Convincing his players of that sentiment, however, was easier said than done. After Anderson's reverse layup gave the Wildcats a 26–20 lead 10 minutes into the game, Gonzaga stormed back. Ronny Turiaf scored five straight

points for the Bulldogs, and when point guard Blake Stepp converted an easy layup with seven minutes remaining in the half, the underdogs had their first lead at 30–29. Arizona had shot 52 percent from the floor and held Stepp to just two field goals, but when Turiaf sank a shot in the closing seconds of the first half, it was the Zags who still led 44–41.

"We knew it was going to be a big game and that they had a ton of success that season, but we weren't intimidated and I felt like all of us sensed that we had a great opportunity," Gonzaga senior Rick Fox said.

The mood in the Wildcats' locker room wasn't so positive.

"Everybody is just like thinking to themselves, 'S---, we got to win this game,'" Anderson said. "It was like, this is going to be tougher than we expected."

The Wildcats grabbed the lead back and were still in front by four points when Stepp rediscovered his touch midway through the half. His three-pointer cut the margin to 56–55, and by the time he converted a four-point play with 7:11 left, he had scored Gonzaga's last 11 points. His layup with four minutes to go put the Zags within 74–71, and when he drove to the hoop on the next possession, he took the Arizona defense with him. At the last minute, Stepp swung the ball back out, and when Tony Skinner drained an open three-pointer, the game was tied once again. The Salt Lake City crowd rose to its feet, and it was obvious that the Wildcats would be receiving little support the rest of the way.

Arizona senior Luke Walton put his team in front with a free throw, and after two empty possessions from the Bulldogs, the lead still remained 75–74 heading into the final minute. The Wildcats attempted to use as much clock as possible, but that resulted in a desperation shot from Salim Stoudamire just before the shot clock ran out. The ball ricocheted off the rim and went all the way out to midcourt, where Walton grabbed the loose ball.

Now the Zags were forced to foul, and after the Wildcats made both free throws, the lead was back up to three with 25 seconds to go. Stepp missed a three-pointer at the other end, but Fox tipped in the miss with 13.5 seconds remaining to cut the lead to one. The Zags immediately fouled UA's Jason Gardner, who responded by making his first free throw. But his second rimmed out, and seconds later Stepp was firing again from the three-point line. This time the ball hit off the front of the rim, but there to snatch the rebound was Tony Skinner, who threw it back at the hoop just before time expired. Everybody in the arena waited for the outcome as the ball bounced around the rim, but the shot was almost compromised as Fox, instinctively jumping toward the basket, appeared to make contact with the ball as it lay on the cylinder.

"You know, I went up there thinking if he misses it and he misses it hard, I'm going to be able to tip this in quickly," Fox said. "It's funny, I had a buddy of mine tell me a story. He's watching that game at home in Denver, and when he saw it live he thought I touched it. And he was sitting down on his couch and he had a lamp next to him, and he grabbed the lamp and threw it across the room. He was so mad at me."

As it turned out, however, Fox had removed his hands just in time, and when the ball settled in the basket the score was tied once again. Overtime.

At this point Anderson was already starting to feel the effects of his asthma—a condition that was only heightened by the Utah altitude—but the team captain was hardly about to quit. He put back his own miss to give the Wildcats an 82–79 lead in overtime, and when he scored on a layup with 1:22 to go, the margin was 87–84.

"I literally was running down the court and I was so tired that my brain wasn't even working—I wasn't even thinking," said Anderson, who knew his opponents felt likewise. "They were just as dead. Whoever could survive mentally. I think it was more mentally than anything."

But Stepp found enough energy to bury a three-pointer from the top of the key, and after Walton threw the ball out of bounds, junior Cory Violette found a streaking Fox right underneath the basket for the easy lay-in. Now trailing 89–87 with just 14 seconds to go, Arizona needed a bucket, and quick. Walton delivered, backing down Violette before hitting a huge turnaround to send the game into a second overtime.

"He's so smart that he saw that opportunity and took advantage of it and scored," Anderson said. "We were shocked because Luke usually dishes it off, and that shows a lot of character and guts."

Arizona, despite using the same five players since the beginning of the second half, managed to grab a 96–95 lead as the final minute of double overtime approached. Stoudamire looked to deliver the knockout punch as he drove to the hoop with 22 seconds left, but Violette jarred the ball loose, causing Stoudamire to fumble it out of bounds.

Stepp brought the ball up for the game's final possession and tossed it to Fox, who swung the ball out to Skinner with five seconds to go. His shot hit off the back of the rim, but now Stepp was there to return the favor from regulation. He grabbed the ball just before the buzzer and fired it off the backboard. But as the clock struck zero, the ball hit off the rim and onto the court, giving the Wildcats a win they would never forget. Both Fox and Walton collapsed onto the floor, and instead of exchanging handshakes, both teams opted for hugs as a sign of mutual respect.

"Once that game was over, I felt that that it would go down as one of the classic games," Olson said. "You're under that kind of pressure of 'win or go home,' and I never saw either one of the teams react like 'win or go home.'"

And while the Zags would be heading back to Spokane, they could at least hold their heads high. They had given Arizona the fight of a lifetime. ●

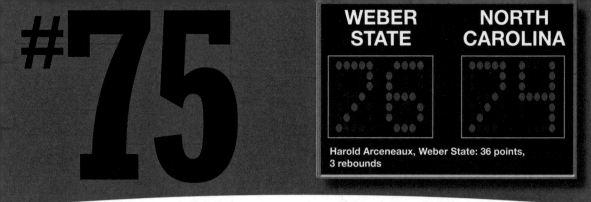

WEBER STATE **NORTH CAROLINA**

Harold Arceneaux, Weber State: 36 points, 3 rebounds

1999: WEBER STATE
vs. NORTH CAROLINA

When Andy Jensen saw that his Weber State Wildcats were going to be play UNC in the first round of the 1999 NCAA Tournament, he felt like the luckiest guy in the world. His team was about to play one of the most historic programs in basketball history, but his emotions had nothing to do with basketball. He had just become a dad.

"I remember my son came out and the doctor turned on the TV and handed me the scissors to cut the cord, and right then our region popped up and it said North Carolina. It was really surreal actually," Jensen said. "It was really cool. It was a flood of emotions all at once."

The newest member of the Jensen family would be in attendance to cheer on his dad. Unlike most other players, Jensen was 25 years old, making him the oldest American player in the tournament. And he would need to put all that experience to use, as his opponent would be none other than Brendan Haywood, a future NBA lottery pick who enjoyed a seven-inch height advantage. Conventional wisdom would say to devise a new strategy to neutralize Haywood, but then again, Ron Abegglen was not your average coach.

"Going into the game, we didn't really do any homework on North Carolina," forward Harold Arceneaux said. "The night we had to play, the coaching staff got together and figured out how we were going to approach the game."

Their conclusion was to do absolutely nothing different. Just because North Carolina

hadn't lost a first-round game in 19 years was no reason to change the game plan.

The Tar Heel players were equally unafraid of Weber State, and they made sure their feelings were known.

"The trash talking, the disrespect that we felt before the game, we felt that they looked down at us," Arceneaux said. "Let's be honest, you're Weber State, you're never supposed to compete with North Carolina."

And at the beginning of the game, it appeared that is exactly what would happen. Arceneaux, who was WSU's best offensive player, missed his first four shots of the game. But the team continued to feed him the ball, and once he nailed his first shot at the four-minute mark, the goal was to get him the ball on every trip down the floor. It turned out to be the right decision.

The junior, perhaps better known as Harold "The Show" Arceneaux, made a bank shot to tie the game at 10. He then nailed back-to-back threes, and still UNC did not guard him at the three-point line. Moments later he made them pay by sinking another shot from beyond the arc, giving the Wildcats a 19–15 lead. The UNC players, so confident just minutes before, were speechless.

"They didn't know how to approach it. They didn't know to talk trash to me or not," recalled Arceneaux, not that it would have mattered anyway. "Because I was basically in the zone, I didn't really hear anything."

By the time the half ended, Arceneaux had already lit up the Tar Heels for 16 points as they took a 35–33 lead into the break. UNC tried to get Haywood going in the second half, but Jensen would have none of it. When he drew a charge on Haywood early in the period, the Wildcats had pushed the lead to 41–35.

"At the press conference, I had one question. A guy from the *Salt Lake Tribune* said they had just interviewed Haywood and the other North Carolina players and asked them what I did, and all they could say was I reminded them of an old grandpa at a YMCA—that I was a dirty player," laughed Jensen, who limited Haywood to one free throw and one rebound. "My reply back was I said I'd probably say something like that, too, if I wore Carolina blue and just got my lunch handed to me by me."

Not to be outdone, Arceneaux was still putting on a show at the other end of the floor. He continued to drain three-pointers, and when the Tar Heels finally came out to the perimeter to guard him, he drove right by them for layups. The only person more shocked than the UNC players was Arceneaux himself.

"All year I was getting double-teamed," Arceneaux said. "And they just allowed me to go one-on-one."

Thanks to Jensen's defense, North Carolina started the second half shooting just 5-of-23, and Weber State stretched the lead to 57–46 with less than eight minutes to go. But once the Tar Heels caught fire, Arceneaux took it upon himself to carry the Wildcats. After UNC's Ademola Okulaja hit a three-pointer, Arceneaux answered with a jumper of his own. Ed Cota and Vasco Evitmov cut the lead to 59–54, only to have Arceneaux make a shot through a double-team and then follow it up with a guarded three-pointer from nearly 30 feet out.

"He is unconscious!" play-by-play announcer Kevin Harlan said, and Arceneaux countered yet another three-pointer from Okulaja with a baseline jumper at the other end. After converting a pair of free throws, UNC applied full-court pressure, only to have Arceneaux deliver with a bank shot, prompting Harlan to scream, "The bar for heroism has just been raised!"

"Carolina didn't do anything about it. They just kind of sat there and watched it happen, too," Jensen said. "I kept waiting for them to

Harold "The Show" Arceneaux's total of 36 points was nearly as much as the rest of his teammates' totals combined. *Weber State University Athletic Department*

do something, and it's almost like they were stunned. It was slow motion with Harold."

North Carolina continued to fire away and eventually cut the margin to 75–74 with four seconds left, but Arceneaux had one final retort left in him. WSU's Noel Jackson made only one of two free throws, leaving the door open for a three-pointer to win the game, but Arceneaux intercepted the inbounds pass, closing the curtain on one of the greatest individual performances in NCAA history. "The Show" instantly became a legend in Utah, as well as the most hated man in the Tar Heel State.

"To give you an idea, this is what Carolina is. Years later, I was an assistant on Weber State's staff," Jensen said. "We walked in to a restaurant where all the Carolina people were and we had our coaches' purple Weber State on and the whole place erupted in boos. And this was probably five or six years after the fact."

But as much as the UNC fans wouldn't let Weber State forget about the game, neither would the fans of Duke, North Carolina's most hated rival.

"They printed T-shirts that said 'Weber State 78, North Carolina 76,'" Jensen said. "Their tennis and golf teams wore those T-shirts when they played against North Carolina that spring." ●

1982: IDAHO VS. IOWA

Just a few years before Idaho's berth in the 1982 NCAA Tournament, the Vandals seemed to be the unlikeliest team to field a competitive squad, let alone ever make a postseason. The school had just handed over the reins to Don Monson, a former Idaho graduate who had never been a head coach at the college level. In fact, the 45-year-old Monson had never even desired to coach college basketball at all.

Monson had been coaching high school basketball for 18 years before Jud Heathcote, an old friend and newly hired Michigan State coach, asked Monson to join him in East Lansing. After two years at MSU, where he was coaching an emerging point guard by the name of Magic Johnson, Monson decided to take the vacant coaching job at Idaho.

"I was raised in Coeur d'Alene, Idaho, which is real close to here. This was the area I wanted to be," Monson said. "I look over to Michigan State, it was good. So why wouldn't this be good?"

For starters, he was inheriting a program that had never made the NCAA Tournament and had finished 4–22 the year before. While the Spartans were enjoying a national championship in 1979, Monson's first team went 11–15 and finished last in the Big Sky Conference. Still, Monson had no regrets about the move.

"I never really gave another thought of 'I wish I hadn't come' or 'How am I going to get out of this?' or anything else," Monson said. "I

was proud that I could take the university that I played at and come back and coach them."

His loyalty soon paid off as the 1982 Vandals cruised to a 27–2 record in the regular season to set up a date with Iowa in the NCAA Tournament. The best part was that the game was being played at Washington State University, just eight miles from the Idaho campus. Vandal fans came out in full force, breaking the arena attendance record and creating an intimidating home court advantage.

The Vandals decided to come out with a full-court press, and it worked to perfection as they stormed to an 8–0 lead. They continued to stay the aggressors and pushed the lead to 23–12 before taking a 33–23 lead at halftime.

"Right from the get-go, we came out and ran," Idaho senior Brian Kellerman said. "We played a style that was pretty much predicated on our defense, and from game to game we pretty much stayed true to who we were."

Idaho pushed the lead to 40–29 before the Hawkeyes found their stride. Bob Hansen tied the game at 42 on a jump shot with 13:42 to play, and they grabbed their first lead of the game with seven minutes left on a tip-in. If the Hawkeyes could get a defensive stop, head coach Lute Olson was likely going to instruct his players to stall, because several key players were in foul trouble. What happened next was a worst-case scenario for his team.

While trying to defend a drive to the hoop, Steve Carfino, who had been leading Iowa in scoring for much of the night, committed his fifth foul. After inbounding the ball, the Vandals fed the ball to Kelvin Smith, who made a turnaround jumper. While shooting, Smith was also fouled by Michael Payne—which was also his fifth foul. Smith's ensuing free throw gave Idaho a 55–52 lead.

Olson had no choice but to go to his bench, inserting Jerry Dennard into the game. The move immediately paid dividends as Dennard nailed a jump shot to put the Hawkeyes within a point. Following another free throw and defensive stop with 2:00 left, the Hawkeyes were finally able to run their stall offense to take the last shot. The game seemed destined to end on Iowa's final possession until Dennard was bumped while trying to chew up the clock. Dennard's front end of a one-and-one was long, and Idaho wasted no time in setting up its offense. Popping out near the elbow was Kellerman, who drained a shot with 1:11 left to give Iowa the 57–55 lead.

Instead of playing for the last shot to send the game into overtime, this time Iowa went for the quick score and got it. Hansen drove to the hoop and faded back for an open bank shot, which tied the game with 35 seconds to go. The Vandals worked the ball around until they found an open Kenny Owens in the corner. His jumper with three seconds left was short, but Smith managed to pick up the ball and toss in a turnaround shot as the buzzer sounded. The referees decided to check with the timer as the crowd went frantic. The meeting took only a matter of seconds before the referees decided that the shot didn't count, leaving the score tied at 57 as the teams prepared for overtime.

"It was a little loud, and we thought we'd won in regulation," Kellerman said. "We clearly didn't. It just kind of added to the drama of the whole thing."

It took only a few possessions before Idaho started running away with the game, and when Phil Hopson sank a pair of free throws with 1:50 left, Idaho held a commanding 65–59 lead. But the game was not over yet, as Iowa freshman Todd Berkenpas, who hadn't played since February but was forced into action because of his team's foul trouble, made a jumper to cut the lead to 65-61. Dennard then added a tip-in

and a pair of free throws to tie the game with one minute to go. Idaho's Pete Prigge converted two free throws to give the Vandals a two-point edge, but seconds later Hansen took a lob pass over two Idaho defenders and easily laid it in with 36 seconds on the clock.

The Vandals had five starters averaging more than 10 points a game, but Monson knew exactly who was going to take the last shot. The year before, in Idaho's first NCAA Tournament, Kellerman passed on a potential game-winning shot in regulation against Pitt, and the team eventually lost in overtime. This time the coach made sure Kellerman, a childhood friend of his son, would have the ball in his hands.

"Those kids would even play hearts or something, and Brian always won," Monson said. "He had to win whatever he was doing."

Kellerman worked the ball around to his teammates until he received the ball back with four seconds left. He was instantly met by two Iowa defenders, so he decided to elevate as high as he could and fire.

"The shot had to go higher than a normal shot," Kellerman said. "It seemed like it had a chance and it was going straight on."

But when the ball arrived at the front of the rim, it rolled to the back part of the iron and bounced up. Moments later it came down, only to hit the rim and bounce up in the air again. The ball was still in the cylinder the entire time, so all the players hoping to tip the ball in or out were forced to watch the ball carom around the basket.

"In the moment, it just slows down to a crawl," Kellerman said. "You play your whole life—whether it's in your backyard or practice—you play for those kinds of moments."

On this particular night, luck was on Kellerman's side, as the ball finally rolled in. The arena erupted in joy, while Monson ran into the stands to kiss his wife and hug his family, who had decided that the eight-mile trip was worth it.

"There was a lot of emotion," Monson said. "As I've always said, it was the greatest game that I've ever been in."

And for most of that record crowd, they couldn't agree more. ●

1998: WEST VIRGINIA vs. CINCINNATI

After five straight seasons without an NCAA Tournament appearance, West Virginia fans had come to terms with reality: Their runs deep into March were a thing of the past. Not since the days of Jerry West in the 1950s had the Mountaineers won more than a single game in a tournament, and fans were starting to act accordingly. The brother of WVU guard Jarrod West scheduled his wedding for March 14— the same day that the tournament's second round would take place. Jarrod was meant to be the best man, but thanks to his team's 82–52 thrashing of Temple in the first round, he was going to be absent from the wedding. He had other business to tend to.

Facing the Mountaineers in the second round was Cincinnati, the former team of WVU coach Gale Catlett and a trendy pick to win the national title as two seed. West Virginia, seeded tenth, turned some heads at the start of the game by going right after the Bearcats. WVU was sitting on a 14–13 edge before their 10–0 run, capped off by a three-pointer from West, blew the game open. But soon enough the Bearcats would respond with a 10–0 run of their own, and for the remainder of the game West Virginia could feel the heavy favorites breathing down their neck.

"We controlled most of the game, but for some reason we could never bunch it up to double figures," West said. "We were frustrated the whole game because we felt like we should have been up more than we were. And as a

coach with much experience, I could sense that coach Catlett kind of knew that the game was going to get closer, because we never really put them out the way we should have."

Catlett's prediction would eventually ring true, as UC's Ruben Patterson converted a pair of three throws to tie the game at 64 with just 3:43 remaining. West came back with a three-pointer, and the Mountaineers soon pushed the lead to 72–68 with 1:26 left. But with a minute to go, UC's D'Juan Baker answered with a three-pointer of his own to cut the lead to 72–71 at the one-minute mark.

"I knew what was going through everybody's mind—we had UMass at home as a freshman up 18 and lost in overtime. We had Georgetown at home with Allen Iverson, up 18 and lost. We had Georgetown with Victor Page and lost," West recalled. "So for three or four years, we've been on the bad end of some comebacks that we've let get away from us. And that was the first thing I thought about, that there is no way we can lose this game like that."

But that possibility appeared much more likely after West's shot at the other end was off the mark. The Bearcats grabbed the rebound and walked the ball up the floor as the seconds ticked down, biding their time to take a game-winning shot. West Virginia anticipated that Baker would take the last shot for Cincinnati—after all, it was his buzzer-beater against Northern Arizona that had propelled his team into the second round. But on this occasion Baker initially acted as if he was going to screen for a teammate, momentarily throwing the Mountaineer defense off guard. By the time they realized it was just a decoy, it was too late. Baker drained the three-pointer from the right wing with 7.1 seconds on the clock to put Cincinnati in front 74–72.

Just as the Mountaineers knew who would take Cincinnati's last shot, the Bearcats knew exactly where the ball was going for the final shot of the game. Time and again during his career, the ball had found West's hands during the final seconds of a game, and more often than not he had delivered.

"I relished that role of being the guy with the ball in my hands taking shots," West said. "If somebody is going to take the last shot, make it be you because you know you can deal with it, you can handle the pressure."

Catlett elected not to call a timeout, leaving it up to the players to improvise a game-winning play. West took the inbounds pass and dribbled down court, passing his first defender before pulling up at the three-point line, just in front of renowned shot-blocker Kenyon Martin. He knew he was far enough away to shoot over Martin's outstretched hands, but he was unaware of a streaking Patterson coming over from the left sideline. Only at the last second did West feel Patterson's presence, and by then it was too late, as Patterson got just enough of the ball to alter the shot. Fortunately for West, he had wildly overshot the ball, so Patterson's tip had actually prevented the ball from sailing over the backboard.

"When I released it, the ball was on line. That's all I remember, the ball being on line and I actually thought—*I knew*—it had a chance," West said. "The funny thing is, I tell people all the time, when I leapt for that shot all I can do is see the clock on the top of the scoreboard, and I mean everything just slowed down. And it might sound crazy or corny, but that was the longest one or two seconds—I mean ever—the ball moved so slow."

The West family, watching on a television back in Mississippi, had delayed the wedding to watch the ending of the game. And what they saw as the ball hung in the air was . . . nothing. The television had lost its signal right as the ball was on the way down. What they missed was a miracle, as West's shot banked off the backboard and into the bucket just before the buzzer expired. The television signal at the church came back on 30 seconds later, and the family members erupted as they saw teammates mobbing the best man.

"Once the buzzer went off, like I said, it was an out-of-body experience because you see it, especially me. I followed college sports my whole life, and you see it everywhere, the Cinderella or a buzzer shot," West said. "And you just always wish or hope that you would be in that situation. And for it to happen that way, it was a special moment."

It was one moment that few Mountaineers fans would ever forget. Cincinnati fans wouldn't forget it anytime soon either.

"Funny thing, I talked to Ruben probably two weeks later at the Indiana pre-draft camp, and he said, 'You know I touched that ball, don't you?'" West said. "And he said, 'The sad thing is if I don't touch it, it probably comes off the backboard hard,' so it was definitely divine intervention."

Fortunately, the wedding turned out to be a much smoother affair than West's last-second heave. Safe to say, it was a good day for the West family. ●

West Virginia teammates Carl Williams, Damian Owens, and Jarrod West celebrate a narrow victory over Cincinnati. *Brian Bahr/Getty Images*

WEST VIRGINIA **WAKE FOREST**

Mike Gansey, West Virgina: 29 points, 7 rebounds, 2 assists

2005: WEST VIRGINIA
vs. WAKE FOREST

As thrilled as the West Virginia Mountaineers felt after their last-second victory over Creighton (see page 178) in the first round, their celebration was short-lived. In just two days, the team would face the enormous task of playing Wake Forest, a team that many considered the most dangerous in the entire field. The Demon Deacons, who had returned every scholarship player from the previous season and set a school record for wins, actually felt disappointed when they received a two seed. The Mountaineers didn't blame them.

"We called them the fifth top seed in that tournament," West Virginia coach John Beilein said. "They could have very well been a top seed."

So when Beilein lost his ability to talk before the game, WVU's chances appeared even more unlikely. Beilein had managed to coach the opener against Creighton, but his voice failed to improve over the rest day, and by tip-off against the Demon Deacons, he was practically mute. So the man who guided the Mountaineers to their best season in years was forced to hand the reins to his assistant, Jeff Neubauer.

"Coach Neubauer was pretty much the coach that game," junior Mike Gansey said. "Obviously he was doing what Coach was saying, but it was tough. It was a little bit different not having coach Beilein being able to talk."

The initial prognosis looked as poor for the team as it did for Beilein, as the Demon Deacons made eight consecutive shots and ran off to a 25–12 lead. WVU attempted to cut into the lead, but as Wake began to receive some favorable officiating, Beilein had seen enough. Despite struggling to talk, he expressed his displeasure loud enough for the referees to hear, and he was assessed a technical foul. Adding insult to injury was Justin Gray's three-pointer at the buzzer, which matched Wake's largest lead at 40–27. Gansey, who was one of West Virginia's best players the entire season, finished the half with one field goal.

"I played pretty much the whole regulation, but I never feel like I got in rhythm," Gansey admitted. "It seemed like I was just out there—I didn't really do much. I didn't really have an impact on the game."

Fortunately for Gansey, his teammates picked up the slack. By the time Patrick Beilein—the coach's son—hit a three-pointer with 10:56 to play, the Mountaineers had closed the gap to 54–51. A few minutes later, Tyrone Sally chimed in with another three-point play to put the Mountaineers within a point, and the WVU bench implored the partisan crowd to get on their feet. The fans gladly obliged.

Both teams added a basket before West Virginia got a much-needed stop, and moments later Fischer found Sally on a backdoor cut to give the Mountaineers a 73–72 lead, their first since it was 6–4 in the opening minutes. They still led 76–74 with just 21 seconds remaining when Gansey stepped to the line with an opportunity to put the game away. His first shot brought the lead to three, but his second free throw rimmed out, giving Wake Forest a second chance. West Virginia expected future NBA star Chris Paul to take the final shot, but the Demon Deacons surprised everyone by swinging the ball to Taron Downey, who was open on the left side. His three-pointer sailed through with 13 seconds left, and overtime was on the way.

Gansey, perhaps motivated by his missed free throw, went off in overtime. With his team nursing an 81–80 edge, he drove in for a layup, and after Paul answered with a three-pointer to tie the game, Gansey went back for a layup once more. After Paul converted two free throws to put Wake Forest ahead 87–86 in the last minute, Sally drove down attempting to take Gansey's defender with him. By this point, the defenders had learned their lesson and stuck on Gansey, but it didn't matter.

"Once I hit my first shot, and then hit another one, I was like, man, keep giving me the ball. I don't care where it is, or when it is, it's going in," Gansey said. "It's an unbelievable feeling just to know every time you shot it, you know it's going to go in,"

Sure enough, Gansey nailed the contested three, and West Virginia had an 89–87 lead with 40 seconds to go. Paul eventually cut the lead to 91–90 on a layup with 24 seconds left before the Mountaineers went right back to Gansey. Although he had the hot hand, Wake Forest had no choice but to foul. Gansey hit both shots from the line, and once again the Demon Deacons were down by three with one last chance. Paul raced down the court, but instead of taking the shot, he once again deferred to Downey, who was circling behind him. And just as he had at the end of regulation, Downey nailed the clutch shot to tie the game at 93.

"It was the late game, so everybody was shutting down, and it kept going on," Beilein said. "They wouldn't stop making shots; we wouldn't stop making shots. It was a classic basketball game."

WVU raced down to get a shot off, and Gansey found teammate Joe Herber cutting

to the hoop with his man beat. Herber took the pass and went in for the layup before WFU center Eric Williams raced over from the side to swat the ball away. Despite playing in their sixth match in 11 days, the Mountaineers would have to continue on.

From the moment the second overtime started, Gansey would not be denied. His bank shot to start the period gave West Virginia a 95–93 lead, and moments later he followed it with another three to put the Mountaineers up 98–94. Paul committed a charge on the other end, forcing the Deacons to use a full-court press, but Gansey broke the press anyway and drove to the basket before drawing a foul. Gansey sank both shots, and the junior who ended regulation with just 10 points had now scored 17 of his team's last 19 points. The six-point margin turned out to be the difference, as WVU emerged with a 111–105 victory.

Growing up just 10 minutes from the Cleveland arena where the game was played, Gansey pulled an all-nighter celebrating with all his old friends. But nothing compared to the reaction he got when he arrived back in Morgantown.

"The next day I went to Panera Bread after class for lunch, and I'm in line just minding my own business. I mean, it was packed, lunchtime," said Gansey, who was trying to avoid making a big scene. "All of a sudden, everybody just starts clapping. 'Hey, Mike Gansey, he's a Mountaineer!' Everyone stood up clapping."

Another local establishment put up a sign saying, "Mike Gansey for President." Although he never reached that level of fame, Gansey did become quite recognizable—for of all things his fashion sense.

"Sometimes I would wear two or three shirts underneath my jersey. I don't know, I was just weird," Gansey laughed. "I wore that same T-shirt the whole Big East Tournament. It's probably my lucky T-shirt."

Call it luck or skill, but Gansey's performance elevated him to legendary status. And for many Mountaineer fans, that label has never left. ●

1979: INDIANA STATE vs. ARKANSAS

Indiana State coach Bill King knew what he was doing when he handed the program over to Bill Hodges in 1978. When King suffered a brain aneurism before the season, he quickly appointed the 35-year-old Hodges as his successor, which came as a shock to many who doubted the abilities of the first-year head coach. But it didn't take long before Hodges proved why he was the man for the job.

Predicted to finish fourth in the Missouri Valley Conference, the Sycamores came out of nowhere to roll through the regular season undefeated. Their record was still unblemished when they ran into Arkansas in the Elite Eight. With All-American Sidney Moncrief leading the way, many felt the Razorbacks would be a tough matchup for anyone, let alone a team that had faced such little competition all season. In a move that few other coaches would ever try, Hodges essentially yielded the first half to Arkansas by playing without his effective full-court press. If the Sycamores could just survive the first 20 minutes without digging too large of a hole, their chances to come back in the second half were great.

"I knew they could be pressed, but if I would have pressed in the first half they would have had time at halftime to adjust," Hodges said. "They probably hadn't gotten film of us pressing, and so I felt like they didn't know much about us."

As it turned out, ISU went into the locker room down by only two points, allowing Hodges to unleash the defense when the second half started. Minutes later, Brad Miley gave the Sycamores their first lead at 55–53 with a tip-in, and when Carl Nicks scored with 7:25 remaining, they had pushed the lead to six.

Now it was up to Arkansas coach Eddie Sutton to match Hodge's savvy, and he decided to put Moncrief on ISU All-American Larry Bird. The Razorbacks fought back, and with just under five minutes to play, they had tied the game at 65. Moncrief's bank shot with 2:46 left gave Arkansas a 69–67 lead, and although Bird managed to tie the game at 71 with 1:31 to play, the Razorbacks had the option of draining the clock for the last shot.

Sutton called a timeout to organize his team, but when play resumed Arkansas guard U. S. Reed tripped over the foot of Nicks, resulting in a traveling violation with 1:02 to play. Now it was Indiana State's turn to run out the clock, and Hodges called a timeout of his own with 18 seconds left.

"See, I have plays that are timed at the end of the game, and it takes 17 seconds to run this one play, and so I said we're going to run this and if they double-team Larry, then I want you to reverse the ball and whoever gets the shot takes it," Hodges remembered. "And sure enough, they double Larry."

But of course, rarely does a play lasting 17 seconds actually go according to plan. "It would've taken 17 if they hadn't doubled him,"

Hodges smiled. "It's like any set play. You have alternative things you do, and when you do it all the time kids learn how and they see what's happening and they just run the alternate play."

With Bird out of the equation, the Sycamores worked the ball to Nicks, who couldn't find an opening either. Nicks swung the ball over to guard Steve Reed, but the Arkansas defense smothered him as well, forcing Reed to dump the ball off to Bob Heaton, the sixth man on the team. Now there was no time left for passing the ball around, and Heaton drove straight to the lane, only to see 6-foot-10 Scott Hastings standing in his path.

"I thought if he's there, I'm going to have to put my body between him and the ball, so

that's why I went up left-handed," Heaton said. "And I was okay left-handed. I didn't practice it a lot, but I worked on some close shots left-handed."

Heaton's opposite-handed toss hit the rim with three seconds left, bounced around the rim, and continued to roll around the iron until just before the buzzer, when it softly rolled in. Pandemonium ensued, as fans stormed the court, including one Arkansas fan who charged straight at Bird. The ISU senior was forced to throw a punch in self-defense, but few people noticed as everybody was wrapped up in the moment.

"With all the excitement, I forgot to shake Eddie's hand. I think he's still mad at me about that," laughed Hodges. "I apologized later, but you just get excited, especially when we were as young and naive as we were."

Ironically, Heaton had almost lost the left hand that sent ISU to the Final Four. Two days after Christmas in 1967, an 11-year-old Heaton was working on a farm when his coat sleeve got caught in some heavy machinery used to hike corn.

"It broke my arm and it really chewed me up, so to speak, but I was very fortunate my grandfather was there and he immediately shut the tractor off. If he wasn't there, I probably would have lost my left arm," Heaton said. "Another three or four seconds, if my grandfather didn't turn it off in time, I would have lost my left arm totally."

Thanks to Heaton's grandfather, Indiana State's dream season was still alive. The finish thrilled the entire country, with the exception of one very powerful man.

"One of my good friends was Bill Clinton's lawyer, and they were talking about that," Hodges remembered of the controversial last minute. "And Clinton said, 'You just tell coach Hodges one thing—U. S. Reed got fouled.'"

Perhaps he was, but it's hard to feel too bad for Clinton. His days of fame would come. But on this night, the Sycamores were on top of the world. ●

Larry Bird scored 31 points on the night for the Sycamores, but the real hero of the game was teammate Bob Heaton. *AP Photo*

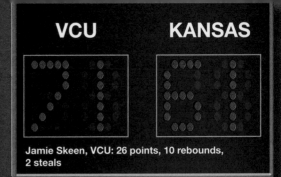

VCU   KANSAS

Jamie Skeen, VCU: 26 points, 10 rebounds, 2 steals

2011: VCU
vs. KANSAS

As the Kansas and Virginia Commonwealth players went to shake hands and exchange pleasantries before their Elite Eight matchup, the Jayhawks had some choice words for VCU point guard Joey Rodriguez. "The run ends here," they warned Rodriguez, whose eleventh-seeded Rams were never supposed to reach the fourth round.

"Yeah, you know usually we'd really say something back and just start talking, but we were just so focused we were like, all right, we will just play," Rodriguez said. "We didn't really say that much—just like good luck, and that was it. We were expecting things like that, and we kind of knew they didn't respect us, so we just let our game do the talking."

The pre-game comments reeked of arrogance, but Kansas at least had the results to back up the prediction. The 35–2 Jayhawks, who were the top-shooting team in the nation, had only trailed for 3:29 during the entire tournament—and never by more than two points.

"We kind of sat there as coaches and we said these guys have no flaws. I mean, they really have a phenomenal team," VCU coach Shaka Smart said. "And they were extremely formidable as an opponent. But make no mistake about it, I mean, we were confident and we believed we were going to win. That's the only chance you have to win is if you have that belief."

The Kansas players had tried similar antics two days earlier against VCU's crosstown neighbor, Richmond, as they ran into the Spiders' pre-game huddle. The poor sportsmanship sparked a tussle between the two squads, but KU responded by running off to a 37–14 lead. Against the Rams, it appeared the Jayhawks were heading for a similar finish as they grabbed a quick 6–0 lead, but VCU answered back with a 20–4 run. They kept on the attack, pushing the lead to 33–17, and by the time Brandon Rozzell sank his fourth three-pointer of the half, and the ninth for his team, the Rams were up by an unfathomable 18 points. VCU was on the verge of not only upsetting Kansas, but blowing them out.

"It showed just a confident guy to be able to stand up to those guys and shoot the ball. And some of those shots, some people might not label as the greatest shots, but that's how we play," Smart conceded. "We want those guys to play with confidence and shoot the ball when they feel it's a good look and when they're in rhythm."

That style of play came back to haunt the Rams as they missed their next eight shots, which was only compounded by four turnovers. Less than five minutes into the second half, the Jayhawks had cut the lead to 44–39.

"We all knew that they were going to make a run," Rodriguez said. "Adversity was going to hit and things weren't going to go our way. We just didn't know it was going to be that drastic."

The situation came to a boiling point when Smart was whistled for a technical foul for trying to talk things over with the officials. The technical, which was the first all year for Smart, may have been a blessing in disguise.

"Well, I think the technical came at a great time in retrospect just because the game was slipping out of our hands to some extent at that point and there were some calls that had gone their way that we didn't necessarily agree with," Smart said. "But much more importantly than that, we weren't playing the same type of aggressive basketball that we had played earlier in the game. So I think what it did was it refocused us. Brad Burgess showed a great level of leadership when that technical occurred. He pulled the team together and he said, 'I don't care what happens, we're staying together, we're not losing our head, we're going to be the aggressors.' And you know, player leadership is

a thousand times stronger than any leadership that can come from a coach."

The Jayhawks soon cut the lead to just 46–44, and on the next possession Rodriguez fired an airball, but the Rams held their ground. Even after Rodriguez had his next shot swatted away, he responded with a critical three-pointer with 4:57 left that put the Rams up 60–52. Kansas tried to make one last push, trimming the lead to 63–57, and was about to force a shot clock violation on VCU when Rodriguez found Burgess cutting to the basket. He lofted up a pass, which Burgess banked in with one second on the shot clock to seal the win.

"It was kind of back and forth, and you know they kind of guarded well that whole possession," Rodriguez said. "And for us to score on that possession took the last breath out of them, and we kind of knew after that."

Two minutes later, the Rams were heading to the Final Four. When the players arrived back in the locker room, they saw the pictures that fans back home had texted to them. Their team was responsible for the biggest party Richmond had ever seen. The Rams had not only shocked the college basketball world, they may have even shocked themselves. Before the season, the goal was to reach the Sweet 16, and now they were at the pinnacle of college basketball. For a team that had few believers outside its locker room, this was a dream come true.

"The great thing about sports is it really doesn't matter what anybody else says," Smart said. "If we would have dwelled on that then we wouldn't have won, because now you start thinking maybe we don't belong here, maybe we can't win. But our players did a phenomenal job of understanding, hey, it's the five of us against the five of them. We're just as talented, we're just as capable. We're playing better than anybody and shooting better than anybody and we got a great chance, and then they went out and did it." ●

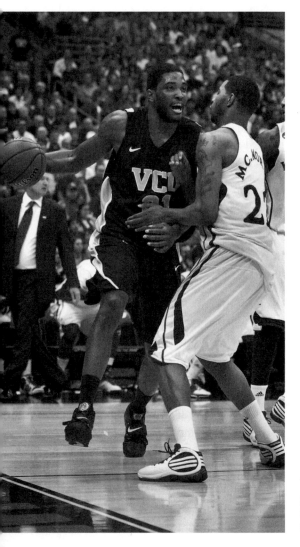

Thanks to 26 points from Jamie Skeen, the Rams pulled off one of the biggest upsets in NCAA history with their 71–61 victory over Kansas. *Virginia Commonwealth University Athletic Department*

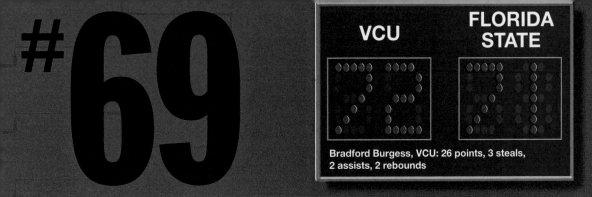

#69

2011: VCU vs. FLORIDA STATE

Before the VCU Rams could ever worry about taking on Florida State, and even before they could think about making their first Sweet 16 appearance in school history, their main concern was just getting to the tournament. And after finishing the season with a very pedestrian 23–11 record, that was certainly no guarantee.

"It was probably the most nervous day ever to me, being a senior and me just wanting to be in March Madness," point guard Joey Rodriguez said. "It was crazy because everything fell in place. Everything that we needed to happen happened, so I knew we had a chance."

When bubble teams like Virginia Tech and Georgia lost in their conference tournaments, the door remained open for VCU to snag one of the final bids. And when the NCAA selection committee released its field days later, that is exactly what happened.

"Oh, we went nuts," Rodriguez said. "All the team lives right next to each other in these apartments. . . . Brad Burgess and I are the only two guys that really know what was going on, so we started screaming and yelling and banging on everybody's door."

The only problem was that Rodriguez got so excited that he injured himself as a result. While raising his arms in celebration, the senior clocked himself with an uppercut.

"And I really did punch myself in the face and started bleeding because I was going nuts, man," he said. "I almost started crying because I'm a big college basketball fan—I've been

watching college basketball my whole life—so I knew I wanted to have one more chance to get to the Final Four and just play in March Madness, so it was probably the happiest moment ever."

The Rams then pulled off a trio of upsets to advance to the Sweet 16, where they were met by Florida State. For Rodriguez, who hadn't received a scholarship offer from FSU despite being the best high school point guard in the state, it was a chance for payback. Early on he got his wish as VCU took a 34–25 lead, and although the Seminoles edged in front 49–48 midway through the second half, the Rams answered back with a run of their own. Senior Brandon Rozzell, who failed to score any points in the opening period, lit the Seminoles for 14 points as VCU took a 59–51 lead. The team would even push the margin to 62–53 with just over seven minutes to play, but six late free throws by Florida State cut the lead to just 65–62. And thanks to a pair of missed field goals by VCU, the Seminoles had a chance to tie the game with a minute to go.

The Rams knew that FSU needed a three-pointer to tie and naturally guarded the perimeter tightly. So Florida State forward Chris Singleton took the first option available, which was to fire up a shot from well beyond the three-point line. The shot rang through with 45 seconds left, and after the Seminoles blocked a final shot by Burgess, the teams were heading to overtime. Florida State had all the momentum, but VCU coach Shaka Smart greeted his team with a big smile.

"You know, right when we got into overtime in the huddle, coach Smart was like, 'We're going to win this game,'" Rodriguez said. "He's probably the easiest coach I ever communicated with. He just understands what's going on."

If anybody knew how the players were feeling, it had to be the 33-year-old Smart, who was just a decade removed from his own playing days. Thanks to the positive reinforcement, the Rams would recover to take a 70–67 lead with three minutes left. Unfortunately for VCU, the Seminoles had one last run left in them, and when Singleton sliced through the lane and slammed home a dunk with 29 seconds left, the lead was back in Florida State's hands, 71–70. Rodriguez took it upon himself to deliver the game-winner, but when his shot was slapped out of bounds, only 7.9 seconds remained on the clock. Smart called a timeout to set up the final shot, but as the players took their positions for the inbounds, it became increasingly obvious that the FSU bench had just as easy of a time relating to Smart as he did to his own team.

"We diagrammed a play, and it is a play that had been pretty successful for us throughout the year," Smart said. "And I think because of that, Florida State did a nice job once we came out of the timeout and went into the alignment we were in. They did a good job—we could hear their assistant coaches calling out what was going to happen."

FSU coach Leonard Hamilton called a timeout to instruct his players on how to handle the inbounds, and when they came back out on the floor it appeared as if they had sniffed out VCU's final play. The seconds were ticking by and nobody was getting open. Faced with a quickly approaching five-second count, Rodriguez was getting ready to throw the ball back out to midcourt, but at the last possible moment he spotted Burgess darting toward the basket. Rodriguez, who hadn't faced a five-second call all year, waited until just the perfect moment to deliver the pass to an open Burgess.

"Joey's a terrific passer and he's got a very good basketball IQ," Smart said. "He's always taken the ball out of bounds for us, and he's always had a clock in his head."

Burgess put in the go-ahead bucket, and the Seminoles raced down to try their hand at a game-winner. Derwin Kitchen drove to the baseline and fired a pass back to Singleton, whose final shot was swatted away by Rob Brandenburg as the VCU bench erupted.

"I absolutely lost control. I was like, I really don't remember it that well, that's how much control I lost," Rodriguez laughed. "I just absolutely went crazy—best college moment ever. I would take that moment over everything."

But once he arrived in the locker room, the laughter turned to tears of joy.

"Well, I think that's one of the great things about sports and about coaching is you get a chance to see how much the games and the victories and the different moments mean to your student athletes," Smart said. "These guys, they worked their butts off and there is so much blood, sweat, and tears that the average fan doesn't see. They see the games, they see the end result, but the sacrifice that these guys have made is extreme. And so when you're able to come up with a big win like that, sometimes it can be overwhelming emotionally because you think back to all the sacrifices you made."

The Rams had already surpassed their goal of making the Sweet 16, but now they had a chance to reach the Final Four. And what a game it would be (see page 216). ●

Bradford Burgess, who made a layup in the closing seconds, was the hero of VCU's 72–71 victory over Florida State. *Virginia Commonwealth University Athletic Department*

Morris Finley, Alabama-Birmingham: 17 points, 2 assists

2004: ALABAMA-BIRMINGHAM vs. KENTUCKY

UAB came into its second-round matchup against the University of Kentucky with plenty of reasons to play conservatively. Not only had the Blazers just finished an exhausting 102–100 barn-burner against Washington in the first round, but the game had ended well past midnight. Now facing the top overall team in the entire tournament, UAB coach Mike Anderson could have elected to slow the pace down, giving his team a much needed breather. But Anderson decided he wanted his team to go full throttle, playing at a pace few teams could handle for an entire game, let alone for a second time in three days.

"I wanted our guys to play with reckless abandon," Anderson said. "To get to this point to change the way we played, that's not who we are."

Not many experts believed that the 22–9 Blazers could trade punches with Kentucky, but after a little pre-game encouragement from his brother-in-law, guard Morris Finley was ready to play.

"I was talking to him, he's like, 'You're just as good as they are, so don't worry. It's not like you're playing [UK legend] Rex Chapman. Jamal Mashburn isn't going to be out there tomorrow,'" Finley joked. "We kind of laughed. I thought to myself, he's right. They're a good team, but I felt like we could beat them.'"

Anderson told the team that the pressure was going to be on Kentucky, so his players should relax and have fun. Perhaps the team was a little too relaxed, as senior Sidney Ball arrived on the court without a jersey on. Ball managed to get dressed before tip-off, however, and once the action started it was obvious that Anderson's strategy was working. After fighting their way to a 19–19 tie, the Blazers went on an 18–7 run, and they still led 42–33 as the first half came to a close.

"I went back to the locker room just to gather my thoughts a little bit, and he told me to have a little fun and use my pump fakes," Finley said of Anderson. "That was the thing that sticks out to me now."

The Blazers were still holding on to a 52–44 lead with 13:30 left when UAB's pair of identical twins, Ronell and Donell Taylor, came up with one of the most spectacular plays of all time. After a UAB miss, Kentucky grabbed the rebound and threw the ball up court to Antwain Barbour for a three-on-one fast break. Ronell anticipated that Barbour would throw the ball cross court to teammate Erik Daniels, and he spun in the air for the interception. Now facing the baseline, he heaved the ball—behind his head—50 feet to the Blazers' end of the court. The ball landed in the hands of a streaking Donell, who flushed it down seconds later.

"That's probably one of the more creative plays I've seen in person in a basketball game," Anderson said. "When we did that, you could sense that something special was going on."

Now playing with their backs against the wall, the Wildcats started playing with desperation, and they clawed their way to a 59–58 lead. UAB tried to fight through the run, but when Gerald Fitch made a three-pointer with five minutes remaining, the Blazers faced their largest deficit of the game at 69–63. Perhaps the up-and-down tempo was starting to take its toll.

The Wildcats still led 71–67 with two minutes remaining when momentum shifted once again. UAB's Carldell Johnson came up with a steal and found Demario Eddins right underneath the hoop, and he scored to trim the lead in half. Kentucky threw it down court to Kelenna Azubuike for a fast-break opportunity, but Gabe Kennedy, UAB's lone defender, held his position for the charge. Seconds later, Donell Taylor swung the ball to a wide-open Finley, and his jumper from the corner with 1:38 to go gave the Blazers an improbable 72–71 lead.

Both teams added another basket when Kentucky brought the ball up with 45 seconds to go, trailing 74–73. UK worked the ball to Daniels, who was positioned near the hoop. Turning to his left, Daniels missed the short jumper, but a trailing Chuck Hayes raced forward for the rebound. His attempt was too hard, but Azubuike soared over everybody to slam it back with 29 seconds remaining.

Anderson called a timeout, and the team tried to run the same play that Finley scored on moments earlier. This time, however, Kentucky was ready. Unable to find another opening in the corner, Finley circled back up to the top of the key and passed the ball off to freshman Squeaky Johnson at the right wing. Johnson attacked the hoop until the last moment, when he fired the ball back across his body. There to receive the pass was a wide-open Finley, standing just behind the three-point line.

"Sometimes it's easy to get outside yourself and think about the situation too much. You have to try to just relax and do what you've done a million times over," Finley said. "I got the ball right back, and I actually thought about what coach Anderson said."

Hayes saw Finley spotting up to take the shot and raced toward the perimeter. But just as he prepared to jump, Finley used the pump fake and Hayes went flying by. Now with plenty of time to spare, Finley took a step inside the three-point line and delivered the shot of the night.

Kentucky called a timeout to set up a last shot, and Anderson subbed his star out of the game. Finley wanted to support his teammates, but the gravity of the moment was too heavy to watch.

"I got onto my knees and I prayed. If you were in a plane and the plane was going down, you would say, 'God, save us,'" Finley said. "I didn't even see the last play. . . . I knew there were enough Kentucky fans in the crowd that if they scored, there would be an uproar."

There was certainly a buzz in the arena when UAB left Fitch wide open at the three-point line with three seconds left. But his shot hit the front of the rim, and Hayes missed a tip-in at the buzzer, giving UAB one of the biggest shockers in tournament history.

Now instead of praying for the victory, Finley was praying for a different reason.

"I'm 5-foot-10; I'm from nowhere Alabama. Nobody ever expected me to even be there," said Finley, who was passed up by virtually every college in America. "For me it was just a time of thanksgiving. I thanked God that he even allowed me to play."

Finley wasn't the only person appreciating the moment. Anderson had been an unpaid assistant coach for six years before he ever made a penny coaching basketball. Working a variety of side jobs to make ends meet, he had worked harder than anybody to reach this moment.

"You can know there were some lean years there. Very lean years," Anderson said. "There's always going to be a starting point, and it's not always peaches and cream."

It may have taken awhile to get there, but on this night it was certainly worth the wait. ●

#67

2002: CREIGHTON vs. FLORIDA

For Terrell Taylor, this was not just another game. As soon as the Michael Jordan fanatic realized that his Creighton team would be traveling to Chicago for the 2002 tournament, Taylor knew this was his pilgrimage to basketball's Mecca. Like nearly every product of the 1990s, Taylor wanted to be like Mike. But when it came to pure fandom, Taylor was truly in a class of his own. One had to look no further than his Jordan tattoo or one of his 60 pairs of Jordan shoes to realize he took things to an entirely different level.

"It started from before I can even remember—I was a Jordan fan and the reason I decided to play basketball. I just remember watching him as a kid and just being in awe, trying to mimic his moves once I started playing and wearing his sneakers all the time," said Taylor, who also donned the No. 23 jersey. "It came from him being such an influence and me wanting to play basketball and be so good in the first place."

Friends would occasionally drop hints that perhaps Taylor was obsessed with Jordan, but that failed to slow him down at all.

"For my eighth grade graduation, everybody wore suits and ties and everything. I had a whole Jordan uniform—the Chicago Bulls shorts, his jersey, his sneakers, his wristband on the left forearm, everything," Taylor said. "My mom asked me what I wanted for graduation, and that was it."

So when he arrived at the United Center, where the Bulls had won six titles in eight years, Taylor took a moment to reflect on where he was. Taylor stood next to Jordan's statue, sat at his locker, and got his ankles taped on the same table that Jordan had used so many times before. But when the game against Florida began, Taylor was anything but Jordan-esque, missing his first six shots as the Gators took a 38–31 halftime lead. For Taylor, who had wanted so desperately to shine, the emotions were taking their toll.

"The fact that it was on such a big stage made it even worse. Playing at the United Center and it being the first round of the tournament, it made it even worse. I was a little down on myself," Taylor said. "I can tell you, I will never forget how I felt walking into the locker room at halftime and the feeling of being there and people telling me it's all right, keep your head up, keep shooting."

If the Bluejays were to have any chance of coming back, they would need Taylor to channel his inner Jordan. Senior Kyle Korver was an NBA player in the making, but the forward would not be able to bring Creighton back by himself.

"The one thing that he was never losing was his confidence, and you know if you would say, 'Is there somebody on your team other than Kyle that's capable of having eight threes in a half and double overtime?' Nobody on that team would have hesitated to say that

Terrell was capable," sophomore Michael Lindeman said. "At the end of the day if you get good shots within your offense and they just don't go in, that's part of basketball. And fortunately after missing six in the first half, he obviously turned it around."

Taylor hit one shot early in the second half, and his confidence soared as if he hadn't missed all day. And for the rest of the game, that was nearly the case. The guard poured in 20 points in the second half, and thanks to a ridiculous 8-of-10 shooting from beyond the arc, the Bluejays mounted a miraculous comeback. Down 67–59 with just 2:42 remaining, Creighton eventually cut the lead to 69–63 before Taylor launched a critical three-pointer with 1:35 left. His shot sailed through, and 60 seconds later he drilled the equalizer to send the game into overtime. By this point Taylor was running on fumes.

"For people that are blessed enough to experience that, it's pretty indescribable," Taylor said. "But it's like a great shooter once told me, he never tried to make every shot. He tries to make every shot perfect, like all net, and coming up shooting with that mentality, it makes the margin of error that much smaller."

Overtime wasn't enough to decide a winner, so the teams went to a second extra period, where the Gators held the advantage. Lindeman hit a layup to trim the lead to

79–78, but Florida's Matt Bonner converted a three-point play to give his team an 82–78 lead with a minute to go. Taylor responded with another basket, this time inside the arc, and when the Gators received a five-second violation moments later, the stage was set for an epic conclusion. Creighton waited to take the last shot, but Florida guard Justin Hamilton knocked the ball out of bounds with just 4.5 seconds remaining, leaving the Bluejays with little time to run a play.

Coach Dana Altman instructed Taylor to take the last shot, and he offered to provide his star with a screen to get an open look. Taylor declined, knowing that everybody in the arena already knew the ball would end up in his hands, and having a teammate in the area would just put another defender in his way. Taylor took the inbounds pass, and taking a page out of Jordan's book, he crossed his defender up and let the shot fly as the final second ticked away.

"You know if you see the video, I'm standing right underneath the hoop when it goes up," Lindeman said. "So I had a pretty good view of the whole thing."

And just as his idol had done so many times, Taylor's shot rang through the net to give the Bluejays the unbelievable victory. Taylor may not have thought about it at the time, as his teammates mobbed him, but the shot was eerily similar to Jordan's final shot as a Chicago Bull, when he crossed over Byron Russell to win the 1998 NBA title.

"I had someone edit the shot against Florida, and it was almost the exact same move," Taylor smiled. "Almost from the same spot on the court and everything." For Taylor, who had ridden the bench for much of the season, it was a dream come true.

"People play their whole careers and don't do that—even some of the greats haven't had an opportunity to do things like that," Taylor said. "So it's definitely one of those things that makes your whole career and everything you're going through with basketball worthwhile." ●

The Creighton bench was in pandemonium after Terrell Taylor's last-second shot upset Florida 83–82. *Creighton University Athletic Department. Photograph by Dave Weaver*

WISCONSIN   TULSA

Michael Wilkinson, Wisconsin: 18 points, 8 rebounds

2003: WISCONSIN vs. TULSA

Tulsa coach John Phillips looked around the locker room before his players stepped on the floor for their second-round NCAA Tournament game.

"I'm telling you right now, Wisconsin doesn't respect you," Phillips declared. "They just don't respect you. They shouldn't—we play in the WAC. Nobody knows anything about Tulsa. You've got to earn your respect!"

That message, however, may have been better reserved for Bo Ryan and his Wisconsin Badgers. Many experts had predicted the team to bow out in the first round to twelfth-seeded Weber State, a game that only further convinced the critics that a UW loss was forthcoming. The Badgers had escaped that game, but guard Freddie Owens had rolled his ankle in the first half after coming down from a jump shot. With little depth to begin with, the now shorthanded Badgers would be taking on a Tulsa squad that had won 50 games over the last two years, and was receiving its fair share of publicity after an upset over fourth-seeded Dayton two days earlier.

"That's why you see things like upsets in the NCAA Tournament, because some teams might take a so-called smaller school for granted. Everybody has Division I players. Every team has great coaches who deserve to be where they're at," Owens said. "We prepared for every opponent like they were the No. 1 team in the country."

The junior decided to play with one healthy ankle, but even a completely healthy Owens would not have been able to stop Tulsa's offense. The Golden Hurricane drained half of their shots as they took an early 18–11 lead, and by the end of the first half they were still shooting 43 percent from the field. Guard Jason Parker had torched the Badgers for 15 points, while the Badgers were struggling through their worst offensive performance of the year. Owens had chipped in just one point, while Kirk Penny, UW's leading scorer, had been held to just three points. As a team, the Badgers had converted only 30 percent of their shots and were punished with a 32–25 halftime deficit.

What made a comeback even more daunting was that Penny never found his groove. He finished the game shooting just 2-of-12, and when Tulsa forward Kevin Johnson nailed a three-pointer with just 4:05 remaining, the Golden Hurricane had pushed the lead to 58–45. During the four-minute television timeout moments later, Ryan huddled his team together.

"This will be one that they'll talk about for a long time," Ryan declared. Wisconsin's slow-pace offense was not suited for a double-digit comeback, but Ryan knew his club had the will to win.

"He showed belief; he never panicked. I can't recall any game where he actually just panicked. He always just stayed in character, and he showed us that we can believe and take it one possession at a time and anything can happen," Owens said. "We all bought into that, and it worked."

Wisconsin sophomore Devin Harris nailed a three-pointer, and the team decided to go into a man-to-man defense in an attempt to pick up the pace. Ryan's club forced Johnson into an errant shot, and when freshman Alando Tucker was fouled going for a loose ball, UW had a chance to cut the lead to eight. Not only did he convert both free throws, he forced a jump ball moments later to get the ball back. His shot in traffic with 2:04 remaining cut the lead to just 58–52—but Tuckers still wasn't done, stealing the ball at the other end to reclaim possession once again. Forward Mike Wilkinson hit another pair of free throws to cut the lead to 58–54, and suddenly Ryan's vision was coming to fruition.

"You can't ever let any doubt or any negative thoughts take in because that's when they take hold," Owens said. "As you can see, three minutes is a very long time."

The Badgers came up with yet another steal, this one courtesy of Harris with 1:30 to play. At the other end, Harris swung the ball

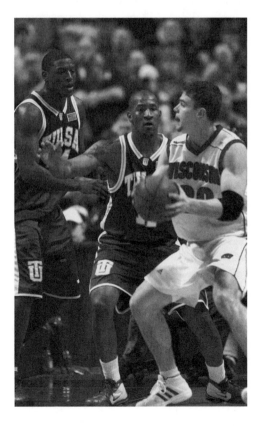

around to Wilkinson, who was standing wide open at the top of the key. His foot was on the line, but the big man swished the shot to trim the lead to 58–56. Johnson answered to give the Golden Hurricane a 62–58 lead with less than a minute to go, but it took Harris all of 10 seconds to race back down and score a layup to bring the Badgers back within 62–60.

Tulsa had the option of going for a quick shot, which could have given them two possessions before the end of the game, but the Golden Hurricane elected instead to work the clock for one shot. It was a move they would soon regret, as Wisconsin forced a shot clock violation with 12.1 seconds to go. Wisconsin had come back from the dead to have a chance to tie the game or take the lead.

"Coach drew up the play in the timeout. We all knew what the play consisted of," Owens said. "We worked on those types of situations every day at the end of practice, where we're up two or down two and so many seconds were left. It was nothing new to us."

Ryan instructed the team to get the ball in the hands of Harris, but Phillips read his mind and called for the Golden Hurricane to double-team the shooting guard. Harris received the inbounds, but he circled around the court looking for an open shooter. With time running down and no options opening up, Harris resorted to driving to the basket, despite the crowd of defenders hounding him step for step. But just before Harris forced up a shot, he found Owens, standing wide open in the left corner. The pain in his ankle had hardly gone away, and Owens was not typically a three-point shooter, but no time was left—he had to take the shot.

The Tulsa defense collapsed on Owens, but not in time, as the junior sank the shot just before the clock expired. It was hardly the way Ryan had drawn it up, but the shot couldn't have looked more poetic. The Badgers had finally earned the respect they deserved. ●

With leading scorer Kirk Penny stifled all night by the Tulsa defense, the Badgers had to look elsewhere for offensive production. And though it came 36 minutes later than Penny would have liked, his teammates stepped up when it counted most. *Walt Beazley, The University of Tulsa*

GONZAGA · WESTERN KENTUCKY

Matt Bouldin, Gonzaga: 20 points, 8 rebounds, 6 assists

2009: GONZAGA VS. WESTERN KENTUCKY

The 2009 matchup between Western Kentucky and Gonzaga figured to be a battle of two mid-majors heading in opposite directions. Gonzaga, long regarded as the cream of the crop when it came to small-program success, had failed to make the Sweet 16 since 2006, when they collapsed in heartbreaking fashion to UCLA. The Hilltoppers, on the other hand, were fresh off an upset of fifth-ranked Illinois, and they had pulled off the same feat a year earlier against Drake. And thanks to the shooting of Orlando Mendez-Valdez, it appeared that Western Kentucky was going for the trifecta against the fourth-seeded Zags.

The senior wasted little time in finding his rhythm, burying his first three shots of the game, and from there he continued to tear apart the Gonzaga defense without mercy. By the time he had drilled another three-pointer from the right wing with 10:47 to play, he was shooting 6-of-7 from the floor. More importantly, the Hilltoppers led 21–16.

"I remember after the game I wanted a Mendez-Valdez jersey. I looked online, me and my buddies looked online to see if we could find a Mendez-Valdez jersey, because he could play," Gonzaga guard Matt Bouldin said. "When he's shooting like that, he's one of the better guards in the tourney at that point. It was fun. You definitely can't guard a guy like that."

Gonzaga coach Mark Few switched up the defense, placing Demetri Goodson on Mendez-Valdez to limit the damage. But by putting all their focus on stopping him, the Bulldogs neglected to cover A. J. Slaughter, who picked up right where his teammate had left off. The shooting guard proceeded to score the next eight points for the Hilltoppers, and when he sliced through the defense to give Western Kentucky a 29–25 lead, he and Mendez-Valdez had combined for all but one of the team's points.

After Jeremy Evans sank a turnaround jumper to push the lead to 31–25, Few had seen enough. His defense, which was ranked second in the country during the season, was allowing the Hilltoppers to shoot well over 50 percent from the field. Rather than laying into his team, the ever-positive Few encouraged his players to step it up. The pep talk worked, as the Bulldogs went on a 14–3 run to grab a 46–40 lead. Thanks to the play of Bouldin, who led the team in scoring, rebounding, steals, and assists during the contest, the Zags pushed the lead to nine with just 2:14 to play.

"I never would consider myself a selfish player or anything like that, so I think one of the better things about me is a lot of my points come in the flow of the offense in the course of the game. You're not trying not to press it," Bouldin said. "There are certain times where you have to be more aggressive; there are certain times where you don't. I guess it's just a happy medium."

Bouldin would not be so happy, however, when the lead started to crumble slowly. Slaughter knocked down a pull-up jumper with

2:05 left to cut the lead to 81–74, and he followed it up with a steal moments later. The Hilltoppers rushed down the court and tossed the ball to Mendez-Valdez, who struck yet again. Standing near the top of the key with the ball and his back turned to the basket, Mendez-Valdez waited for a teammate to set a screen to his left. But the senior faked out both his teammate and his defender by spinning to the right for a wide-open shot, which cut the lead to 81–77 with 1:31 to go.

This time Gonzaga made sure to get the ball in the hands of Bouldin, who had been invincible the entire night. On this occasion, however, Bouldin tripped on his own feet. Not wanting to be called for traveling, the junior maintained his dribble on the ground, but before he could get up Mendez-Valdez jarred the ball loose. The shooting guard quickly tossed it over to Steffphon Pettigrew, whose dunk with 58.7 seconds to go pulled Western Kentucky within two points at 81-79.

Gonzaga gave Bouldin a chance to redeem himself, but his jumper with 30 seconds left was

Gonzaga's Matt Bouldin shoots over Steffphon Pettigrew of Western Kentucky. *Jonathan Ferrey/ Getty Images*

off the mark, and the Hilltoppers called timeout after grabbing the rebound. During the break, Few debated with his staff as to whom to put back on the court. Should they leave in center Josh Heytvelt for a potential rebound, or put Goodson back out there to stop Mendez-Valdez? After all, Goodson had been the only player able to contain him the entire night. They decided on Goodson, who was able to prevent Mendez-Valdez from any open looks. But when Slaughter fired up an errant three-pointer, Gonzaga had no big man for the rebound and Pettigrew tapped it back in with 7.2 seconds to play. Tie game.

Fortunately for the Zags, Goodson also happened to be the fastest player on the court. They quickly threw the ball in to the freshman, who raced down the court trying to beat the clock.

"We practice that a lot, and I was very comfortable with Meech having the ball in his hand," Few said. "He's a terrific finisher, and he has a real knack for splitting gaps and getting to the rim."

His teammates, though equally confident in his abilities, weren't as willing to give up the ball. "I looked up on the clock and saw like seven seconds. I started dribbling and [Jeremy] Pargo was calling for it, but I just kept going down," Goodson laughed. "The lane opened up, and I was able to drive in there and shoot the shot off the backboard."

Goodson was driving from the left side, yet shot the leaning, floating, impossible shot with his right hand. Despite the degree of difficulty, however, Goodson banked it in just as time expired. Gonzaga may have been back where it belonged, but the phrase "act like you've been there before" doesn't apply to buzzer-beaters.

"You know I don't ever remember being so happy," Bouldin smiled. "It's like you're so happy you don't even know really how to react. We went back and watched some of everybody's reaction probably 15 times just because they're hilarious, because people probably don't know what they're doing. Just hopping around. It really just takes you over—you can't even control it."

For the Bulldogs, who had been on the wrong end of more than a few heartbreakers since their first days as a Cinderella, it was nice to enjoy the madness once more. ●

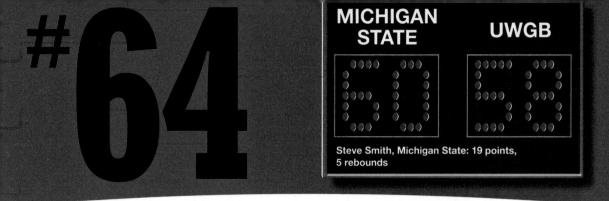

MICHIGAN STATE   **UWGB**

Steve Smith, Michigan State: 19 points, 5 rebounds

1991: MICHIGAN STATE vs. WISCONSIN-GREEN BAY

Dick Bennett was done playing games with his son. All of his other recruits had committed to play for him at the University of Wisconsin–Green Bay, but the lone holdout was his own son, Tony, who was still hoping to go on some exotic recruiting visits to a college in Hawaii or California. Tony was a highly recruited prospect and a bigger Dick Bennett fan than anybody else, but by Senior Day he had still failed to commit, forcing his old man to lay down the law: Either Tony would sign with the Phoenix, or Dick would have to look elsewhere for a point guard. Tony decided to take his frustration out on both his father and his final high school opponent.

"I remember every time I scored a basket, I would just look at him in the crowd and glare at him," Bennett laughed. "I scored 40-some points in that game—it was just, okay, we'll see about that. And then I committed the next day, so he put a power play on me, he played hardball with his son. Deep down inside, I knew I wanted to play for him and I was going to go there, but I had this notion that maybe I'll check out one other place. But he was smart. He got it done when he needed to."

It hadn't been easy, but coach Bennett had found somebody who was more than a playmaker. He had landed a charismatic person, one capable of filling up an arena night after night— someone a lot like Tony Bennett, the world-famous singer. The younger Tony not only had to deal with constant comparisons to the jazz crooner, but he also had to compete with the Green Bay Packers linebacker of the same name.

"It's funny, one time the singer came in to do a concert and he flew into the GB airport and the SID at Green Bay and the community guy for the Packers had both of us meet him at the airport. And all the news cameras were there, and he had a signed football and I had a signed basketball," Bennett recalled. "And he came off the plane, so we all got the picture and we all got to meet, and I remember that was pretty cool. But I get teased so much to this day: 'Sing a song for us!' I got more jokes about that than I can remember, but I got some good stories, too, so it's worth it."

It wasn't long before the freshman made a name for himself, and by the time Bennett had reached his junior season, the Phoenix were heading to the NCAA Tournament as a 12 seed. The team found an ideal draw in Michigan State, which a year before nearly became the first top seed ever to lose a first-round game. The Spartans would go on to survive that scare, but conditions for this year's game were perfect, as they would square off in Arizona.

"We knew the West was the place that all the upsets happened. Everybody knew the only twos ever getting beat by a 15 seed always happened in the West," senior Dean Vander Plas said. "So you felt like, hey, karma's going our way."

In the early going of the game, the Phoenix did nothing to dissuade that theory, getting a trio of three-pointers from Bennett as they took a 27–25 lead with 6:09 remaining in the opening period. His teammates followed suit, and by the end of the first half the Phoenix had made 8 of their 10 shots from the perimeter as they took a 35–30 lead. Although the game was played in Tucson, the Arizona crowd was certainly falling in love with the conveniently named Phoenix.

"You had 15,000 other people who, as the game started to go, they started to be Phoenix fans," Vander Plas said. "You know, everybody could sniff 'uh-oh, this little guy is going to knock off this big guy,' and it just kept building. And by the end of the game, it felt like the biggest home game we'd ever had."

The lead was still at five when Green Bay led 51–46 with 9:15 to go, and after GB forward Ben Johnson nailed a three-pointer with 4:01 to play, the lead was 56–52. The Phoenix implemented their victory zone defense, knowing they were a few stops from pulling off the shocker.

"During the game, I just felt momentum building like we were getting stops. And Steve Smith was by far their best player, and we were holding him, he wasn't going off on us," Vander Plas said. "And you could just feel it one possession at a time starting to build."

Smith, who would go on to play 15 years in the NBA, was not quite done yet. He nailed a deep three-pointer to trim the lead to 56–55, and even though Green Bay tacked on two more points, Smith tied the game with another shot from downtown. The victory zone was quickly scrapped, and when UWGB's John Martinez missed a shot with 22 seconds left, Michigan State actually had a chance to win the game in regulation. Green Bay assumed Smith was going to take the last shot and put defensive specialist Ben Johnson on the hot hand.

Smith had plenty of talented teammates to rely on, but Johnson knew his man wasn't about to give up the ball. Wherever Smith went, Johnson followed, and as the seconds ticked by the options were starting to run out for Smith. By the time Smith had traversed from the left wing out to midcourt and raced over to the right wing before coming back to the top of the key, just three seconds remained. Smith reluctantly fired up a jumper with Johnson's hand right in his face.

"He couldn't have defended him any better," Bennett recalled. "I mean, Ben was draped all over him."

Nevertheless, Smith got the shot off, and with just one second remaining on the clock the ball reached its intended destination. With no way to stop the clock, the last second innocently ticked by as Smith was embraced by teammates.

"I think a lot of people forgot the special performance Steve Smith had to end that game, to change it from a loss," Vander Plas said. "I mean they were down, it wasn't like it was back and forth. They were down, and he came back and got it done."

It was the last game Vander Plas would ever play, but he could take solace in the fact that his team was like Rocky. They had taken Apollo Creed the distance. ●

As great a coach as Dick Bennett was, perhaps his greatest skill was persuading his son Tony (25) to play for him at UWGB, where they took Michigan State down to the wire in the 1991 NCAA tournament. *Green Bay Athletic Department*

#63

2011: MOREHEAD STATE vs. LOUISVILLE

When Donnie Tyndall chose to come back and coach at his alma mater in 2006, friends warned him of what he was about to undertake. The Morehead State job is a graveyard for coaches, they warned. Nobody has ever been successful there. Tyndall would be inheriting a team that had gone just 4–23 the season before, but considering everything he had gone through to get there, turning around a dormant program was a piece of cake.

"I started my coaching career literally as an unpaid assistant coach at a junior college in Iowa and worked my way up, so no challenge or no obstacle is too big for me. And with that being said, I now completely and totally understand now just how hard it is to win at this level," said Tyndall, whose teams increased their win total every year since his arrival in 2006. "So I'm very humbled and proud of what we've been able to accomplish. But yeah, I think you do carry a little chip on your shoulder when you have people that maybe think of Morehead State as a lesser-known program that's never going to achieve success."

But before he could turn the MSU program around, Tyndall first had to figure out how he would pay the bills back in Iowa. When he wasn't working 12 hours a day as an assistant, he was working the graveyard shift.

"I did security in this little beaten-down old car at the junior college from 11:30 at night until 4:30 in the morning Sunday night through Thursday, and back then I think minimum wage was maybe like $5.25. So I did that five nights for $5.25 an hour just to make enough money," Tyndall said. "This is the truth: I had one pot in my dorm room—I stayed in the dorm—and in that pot I had one spoon and one fork. And for breakfast I'd buy those cheap bags of cereal. Like you know there's the brand name Froot Loops? Well, these would be called like Loops of Fruit, or something, in big plastic bags. So I'd eat out of that pan with my one spoon, and then at night I had a little one-burner deal I'd plug in my wall, and I'd use that same pot and I'd cook up either mac and cheese or ramen noodles."

But for Tyndall, the motto was always "no plan B," and by the time the 2011 regular season came to a close, his Eagles had earned the right to take on in-state power Louisville in the NCAA Tournament. Despite having lost to the Cardinals 13 straight times, Tyndall had some news for his players—this was going to be the best day of their basketball lives.

"In my mind, and I hope this will not come across as arrogant, but I think I can coach against [Louisville] coach [Rick] Pitino," Tyndall said. "And I think when your players truly watch their coach and they can feel that confidence, they can feel that swagger, they can see the path that you're taking with them and really feel that you truly believe, that it rubs off onto them."

And right from the start of the game, it was apparent that the pre-game speech had worked.

Only 4.5 percent of the brackets on ESPN.com had called for the Eagles to pull off the upset, but six minutes into the game Morehead State had raced off to a 10–0 lead. Minutes later, MSU's Terrance Hill drained a three-pointer to put the team up 15–2.

"See, men, I told you, I told you we were better than these guys," Tyndall said in the huddle. "Now they're going to make runs; we know how they play. We're going to turn it over here or there, but stay poised."

The Cardinals did in fact make a run, taking a 47–39 lead with 12:18 remaining, but the Eagles answered right back. A 13–3 spurt gave the lead back to Morehead State with five minutes to play, prompting a timeout by Pitino. The Cardinals again began to chip away at the deficit and eventually took a 61–57 lead with just 1:14 left—but the Eagles had one final push left in them. Senior Kenneth Faried knocked down a pair of free throws to cut the lead in half, and after Louisville's Elisha Justice missed the front end of a one-and-one, the Eagles had a shot to tie or take the lead. Tyndall, who called a timeout with 24 seconds on the clock, told his team he had dreamt of this same scenario the night before.

"You know I think that story gets a little exaggerated, I didn't actually dream it. I woke up about 2:30 and I couldn't get back to sleep, and so I'm thinking the rest of the morning. What am I going to do if we're up one, down one? Different scenarios," Tyndall said. "But when I went into the huddle, I actually did tell our team that I dreamt it. I said, 'Look, I dreamt about this s--- last night at 2:30 in the morning. Here's what we're going to do.' But it really wasn't a dream—I was just up thinking about it. And I'm telling you, when I called timeout, my coaches always come over to me, and I looked at them. I said, 'I got it. I don't want to hear anything.' I knew exactly what we're going to do."

The plan was for Demonte Harper to wait until the clock had run down before launching a three-pointer. Staying true to his word, Tyndall was going for the win. There was no plan B. For Harper, it was music to his ears. Throughout his career, Harper was constantly scolded for taking outside jumpers. But in the biggest moment of his career, that is exactly what Tyndall wanted him to do.

"He stepped up out of the huddle, he looked me dead in the eye, and he said, 'I got you, coach,'" Tyndall said. "And I know that sounds like a movie—you get a little emotional just talking about it—but that's just how it played out."

Harper, biding his time, dribbled motionless at halfcourt as the clock ran to eight seconds. The senior made his way to the three-point line, and there, without taking a screen or driving anywhere, Harper fired the game's deciding shot. And just as Tyndall predicted, the ball rang through with 4.2 seconds to play. The most excited person in the building? His daughter, who was jumping up and down on the bench as the final seconds ticked by. And after a block by Faried moments later, the Eagles ran around the court, knowing they had shocked the world. If Tyndall wasn't really dreaming before, he sure felt like he was now. ●

MSU coach Donnie Tyndall and guard Demonte Harper enjoy their time in the spotlight after Harper's three-pointer upset Louisville 62–61. *Morehead State University Athletic Department. Photograph by Guy Huffman*

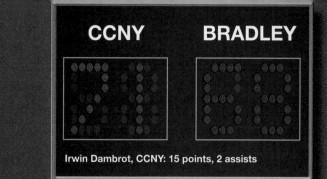

1950: CITY COLLEGE OF NEW YORK vs. BRADLEY

As the CCNY players prepared to take on Bradley for the national championship game, they knew that history was within their reach. No team had ever swept through both the NIT and the NCAA in the same year. Four schools had tried in the previous 10 years, and each had failed. This year, however, felt different. Not only would the Beavers be playing in front of their own fans at Madison Square Garden, but their opponent was also the same club they had defeated 10 days earlier to take home the NIT crown. In that game, Bradley had been a three-point favorite, but CCNY defeated the top-ranked Braves 69–61 to win the title. If the Beavers were to defeat Bradley once more, it would not come so easily.

In their first matchup, Bradley had employed a man-to-man defense, a strategy that had failed miserably. This time, the Braves opted for a zone defense, which early on countered CCNY's blazing speed. Midway through the first half, the Braves had taken a 15–14 lead, but it was newcomer Ed Roman who managed to conquer the defensive strategy.

Bradley had packed its defense down low, conceding any open looks on the perimeter. The team was banking on the assumption that Roman, who had never played basketball until four years earlier, would not be hitting any deep shots. Much to Bradley's surprise, however, Roman responded by nailing six shots in the first half to give his team a 39–32 lead at the break. The Braves scrapped the zone

defense for their old man-to-man strategy, but not before sending one of CCNY's best players to the locker room. Three minutes before the half came to a close, Bradley's Aaron Preece knocked into Norm Mager, a collision that resulted in a two-inch gash over Mager's left eye. The senior would eventually return, but his injury left onlookers squeamish and his teammates a little shorthanded.

Fortunately, his teammates picked up the slack in the second half, slicing through the man-to-man defense just as they had done in their first match. With just 10 minutes to play, CCNY had a 58–47 lead and six of Bradley's players had four fouls. The consensus was that unless the Braves wanted to finish the game with four players, they were going to have to play some pretty casual defense while mounting their comeback bid. But Bradley coach Forddy Anderson scrapped the textbook approach, instead instructing his players to play a full-court defense. What resulted was nothing short of miraculous.

The Braves cut the lead to 62–55 with nine minutes to play, and although All-American Paul Unruh would eventually succumb to foul trouble, his teammates still cut the lead to 66–61 with two minutes left. That's when the fun really began.

CCNY had possession of the ball, but Bradley senior Gene Melchiorre came up with a steal, and his subsequent layup cut the lead to 66–63. Even though the Beavers brought the lead back to 69–63 in the last minute, the Braves were determined to keep the season alive. Joe Stowell converted a free throw to trim the lead to 69–64, and Melchiorre followed with another steal seconds later. Once again, he penetrated to the basket and laid in the ball to bring the Braves within 69–66.

CCNY still seemed to be in control, but less than 20 seconds later Melchiorre came away with his third steal. The guard raced down and converted yet another layup—this one with 40 seconds left—to cut the lead to 69–68. CCNY had nearly blown a similar lead against Ohio State in the tournament's first round, but this collapse was beyond comprehension. Still,

with no shot clock in effect, if the Beavers could avoid making another monumental error in the remaining 40 seconds, the title would be theirs.

But this game was too epic to end without more drama. Despite calling a timeout to design a foolproof play, City College managed to make another huge error in judgment. The Braves were still pressing from end to end, and in the most important possession of the season, they forced CCNY into another wild pass. The ball sailed over its intended target and ended up in the hands of—who else—Melchiorre. His team was now just one field goal from pulling off the most improbable comeback in NCAA history.

To no one's surprise, Melchiorre lowered his shoulder and drove toward the basket for the game's decisive shot. But this time he sensed that the Beavers would be ready for a layup, so as the final seconds ticked by, the senior stopped and pulled up at the foul line for a jump shot. Melchiorre knew that penetrating any further would be risking a block, but what he didn't anticipate was the Beavers rising to the occasion for the jump shot. CCNY forward Irwin Dambrot rose up and tipped the ball, which fell back into his arms. He fired the ball down the court to Mager, who had recovered from his earlier cut to make the game's decisive play.

A layup would put the game out of reach at 71–68, but as Mager went in for the critical shot, a Bradley defender had caught up to him. It appeared that the Braves would have a block of their own to keep the game alive. Fortunately for City College, Mager felt the presence of his defender and dipped under the basket to attempt a reverse layup. His quick thinking fooled his opponent so much so that he was whacked as he released the ball, a foul that went unnoticed by the officials. Nevertheless, Mager's shot rolled in with just 10 seconds left to put the Beavers up for good. City College would be national champions after all. ●

CCNY coach Nat Holman is hoisted up by his players following their 71–68 victory over Bradley in the title game. *AP Photo*

2010: MURRAY STATE vs. VANDERBILT

Despite compiling an incredible 30–4 record in the regular season, Murray State was hardly a household name heading into the 2010 NCAA Tournament. That was the case, at least, until President Barack Obama touted the Racers as his Cinderella of the tournament. And when the President speaks, people usually start listening. After Obama penciled in Murray State on his bracket, the team suddenly became America's new sleeper.

"We know he follows college basketball," Murray State coach Billy Kennedy said. "So when the President of the United States picked us, we knew that was special."

The President may not have been as confident in his prediction had he known that the team's leading scorer, B. J. Jenkins, was battling an injury. While cutting the nets after winning the conference championship, Jenkins had sliced his index finger. But with six players averaging 10 points per game, the team hoped it could withstand an injury to one of its players, even to a star like Jenkins.

"That was just the makeup of our team— we had 12 guys on scholarship and literally 10 or 11 of them could have started for us," Kennedy said. "We had good team chemistry, and the strength of our whole team was the character of our guys."

Perhaps the most unselfish player was senior Danero Thomas, who was determined to cut into his personal statistics to make sure the team had more balance.

"I was telling them I was willing to sacrifice, whatever I have to do, even if I have to take less shots, so guys can get their share," Thomas said. "We came to an agreement and we made it work."

And early on against fourth-seeded Vanderbilt, it did work, as seven Racers combined to give Murray State a 36–32 lead at halftime. Even more encouraging, Jenkins was not only able to play, he led the team with nine points. As the second half wore on, MSU even stormed out to an eight-point lead.

Now facing their largest deficit of the game, the Commodores started to play with a sense of urgency. Lance Goulbourne responded with a basket, and a minute later John Jenkins (no relation to B. J.) added a three-pointer to cut the lead to three with 14:26 remaining. Vanderbilt inched its way back to a 52–52 tie, and after Jenkins nailed another shot from behind the arc, this one with 4:46 to go, the Commodores had their first lead in nearly 22 minutes. Facing a 58–56 deficit with no momentum, Kennedy looked to his players to see how they would respond.

"I didn't see anybody hang their heads or get frustrated," Kennedy said. "Our guys, they kept it even-keeled the whole time."

The Racers managed to cut the lead to 60–59 when VU's Brad Tinsley tried to deflate their spirits with an emphatic slam. Driving from the left baseline, Tinsley attacked to the hoop and went up for the dunk, only to see

Murray State forward Jeffrey McClain rise up and smack the ball off the backboard. McClain fired an outlet pass to start a fast break, and moments later Jenkins connected on a three-point shot to put the Racers back in front by two. Thomas then followed with another jumper to give MSU a 64–61 cushion with 1:13 on the clock.

On the ensuing possession, Vanderbilt found center A. J. Ogilvy streaking toward the basket. Ogilvy may not have been the most agile player on the court, but at 6-foot-11 he was nearly impossible to stop. By the time he went to lay it in, four Murray State defenders had converged on him, but it made little difference as Ogilvy powered in the layup to bring the Commodores within 64–63.

The normally disciplined Racers turned the ball over at the other end, and with 28 seconds to go, Vanderbilt had a chance to take the lead once again. Standing near the top of the key, Ogilvy looked as if he was going to pass the ball to Jermaine Beal, who had darted out to receive the pass. But when Beal couldn't find an opening on the perimeter, he instinctively cut back to the basket. Isaac Miles fell for the fake, and as he raced back to block Beal's layup, he also fouled him on the arm. Beal calmly sank both free throws to give VU a 65–64 lead with just 12.7 seconds to play.

Kennedy had a play set up for the final seconds, one that envisioned Jenkins coming off a screen and firing the game-winning shot from the top of the key. Everything went according to plan—except the shot barely grazed the rim. The ball landed by the baseline, and in a brief fight for the rebound, Vanderbilt's Andre Walker knocked it out of bounds with 4.2 seconds left.

Kennedy called a timeout and decided to draw up a new play, one his team had never seen before. In fact, his players had almost never seen Kennedy draw up a new play and immediately put it to use.

"He really didn't have to, because we were blowing everybody out," Thomas said. "But at that moment, he had to pull out his bag of tricks."

While diagramming a play for Isaac Miles, Kennedy reminded his players that there was no need to rush the shot. Miles caught the ball near the three-point line and tried to penetrate to his left, but it only took him one dribble into double coverage to realize the play was busted. He fired a pass back to Thomas, who was standing nearly four feet behind the arc with just 2.4 seconds remaining. Now it was time to improvise.

Thomas dribbled past his defender and found an opening about 18 feet from the basket. ESPN's Michael Wilbon, who was not blessed with Kennedy's sense of patience, was seated only a few feet from Thomas when he screamed, "Shoot the damn ball, kid!" And when Thomas finally did let it go, the ball rang through the net just as the horn went off.

The shot set off a massive dogpile at the other end of the court, which only some of the players could enjoy.

"I couldn't breathe, man. I was like, get off of me," Thomas laughed. "And then when everybody else got off of me, my other teammate, B. J. Jenkins, he *still* wouldn't let me get up."

As much as Thomas was enjoying the moment, nobody could have used a victory more than MSU junior Picasso Simmons, whose mother had passed away only days before in a car accident. A former track star at Murray State, she was actually working as a nurse at Vanderbilt when she learned that her son was going to face her employer. But three days before the game, a trailer got unhitched from a truck, setting off a massive pile-up. Looking out for both his real family and basketball family, Picasso flew home for the funeral and flew right back to be with his teammates at the game.

"That speaks volumes about the character he had," Kennedy said. "Our guys respected that and loved him for that."

And when Thomas was finally able to make it back to the locker room, he saw the team standing in a circle saying a prayer, taking time to remember what was really important. Even the other Picasso couldn't have painted a better ending. ●

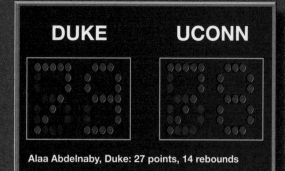

DUKE   UCONN

Alaa Abdelnaby, Duke: 27 points, 14 rebounds

1990: DUKE vs. CONNECTICUT

Two nights earlier, the University of Connecticut Huskies had blown a 19-point lead over the final 13 minutes against Clemson, resulting in a 70–69 deficit with just one second to play. Still 90 feet from the hoop, UConn's Scott Burrell hurled the ball down court, right into the hands of teammate Tate George. The Connecticut junior turned around and buried a shot at the buzzer to give the Huskies one of the most improbable wins in NCAA history. The play certainly left a bitter taste in the mouths of Clemson fans, and now it was time for the Huskies to get a taste of their own medicine.

Connecticut's opponent, with a trip to the Final Four on the line, would be none other than Duke. Even if their game wasn't going to go down to the wire, it was sure to be closer than the last time the teams played with as much at stake, when the Blue Devils won by 47 points. A quick start by the Huskies assured that the game would at least be competitive. Duke reeled off 10 straight points late in the first half to take a 31–23 lead, but in a tournament that featured 29 games decided in the final minute, it was a lead that was anything but safe. The Blue Devils made just one of their first nine field goals to start the second half, and thanks to a 16–3 run by the Huskies, it was UConn that led 46–42 with 16:30 to play.

"There wasn't such a thing as feeling like putting your head down," Duke point guard Bobby Hurley recalled. "Coach K was always like 'next play,' and that was something we always talked about whether we made a bad play or a great play."

With coach Mike Krzyzewski at the helm, the Blue Devils were rarely out of any game. Even when the Huskies led 69–64 with four minutes to play, thanks to just one Duke field goal over the previous nine minutes, Krzyzewski knew his players still had one last push left in the tank. If they couldn't hit any jump shots, they would just find other ways to score. Duke's Phil Henderson converted a pair of free throws to trim to lead to 69–66 with 3:41 to play, and even though Henderson would miss a tying three-pointer moments later, sophomore Brian Davis was there for the putback to bring the Blue Devils within 69–68.

Henderson would get another chance with just under a minute to go, and this time he delivered, draining a three-pointer to put the team up 71–69. Hurley even added a free throw to put the team up by three with 16.8 seconds left, but moments later UConn's Christopher Smith buried a three-pointer from the right wing to send the game to overtime. Fans had already gotten their money's worth through 40 minutes of action. The encore presentation, however, would be nothing short of legendary.

Connecticut took a 78–77 lead with just over a minute to go, a lead that appeared to be secure when Duke failed to convert at the other end of the floor. With 54 seconds remaining, however, Krzyzewski knew his team did not have to commit a foul. If his players could play solid defense for one final possession, they would get the ball back with enough time on the clock.

They got the stop they were looking for, as Tate George fired up an airball at the shot clock buzzer. But the Huskies had eaten up all 45 seconds, leaving the Blue Devils with just 10 ticks to work with. Alaa Abdelnaby, who snagged the miss, tossed it to Hurley to start the final possession. The freshman drove down the middle of the court and tried to fire a pass over to Henderson at the left wing, but just before Henderson could get his hands on the ball, George darted in to deflect the ball out of bounds. And although only 2.6 seconds now remained, considering how close George had come to an outright steal, it was a situation Hurley gladly took.

"I almost threw away our chance to get to a Final Four—it was close," Hurley said. "Tate George had his hands on the ball. Not a great decision, not a great play."

Had this game occurred a few years later, there would have been no question on how to

approach the final seconds. In 1991, Christian Laettner would sink a pair of free throws in the final seconds to upset undefeated UNLV, and he followed it up the next year with the most famous shot in college basketball history against Kentucky. But in 1990, Laettner's résumé was relatively bare. He had to start somewhere, of course, and Coach K was just about to give him his first chance.

Krzyzewski had originally called for Henderson to take the final shot, but just before his players took the floor, he had a change of heart. His gut instinct told him that Laettner would find a crease in the UConn defense, and he told the forward to relay the message to Brian Davis, who would be passing Laettner the ball. Laettner was just a sophomore at the time, but Krzyzewski felt comfortable putting the ball in his hands.

"First of all, Christian had great ability. He could influence a game in every way. He could do everything out on the court at a very high level," Krzyzewski said. "But the thing that separated him was that he had a great mind for the sport and he loved being in the arena. What people would call pressure, he called moments."

The plan was for Laettner and Davis to run "Special," a play that called for Laettner to inbound the ball to Davis, who would fire it right back. In order to make it work, however, Krzyzewski had to leave the other players out of the loop. If Hurley, Henderson, and Abdelnaby ran an entirely different play, it might be just enough to confuse the Husky defense.

As soon as Laettner tossed it in from the left sideline, his teammates scattered about the floor as he made his way toward Davis. The sophomore passed it back to a trailing Laettner, who took one dribble before leaning in for the game's ultimate shot. And just as he would do for the rest of his college career, Laettner delivered when it counted the most, hitting nothing but net to put Duke in the Final Four once again. For Laettner, it was only the start to one of the most illustrious careers in tournament history. ●

Christian Laettner leans in for the game-winning shot at the buzzer against Lyman DePriest of UConn. It would be just a sign of things to come. *David E. Klutho/Sports Illustrated/Getty Images*

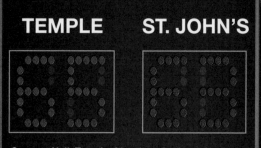

TEMPLE   **ST. JOHN'S**

Granger Hall, Temple: 20 points, 6 rebounds

1984: TEMPLE vs. ST. JOHN'S

As a high school senior, Terence Stansbury was one of the most sought-after recruits in the country. The point guard seemed capable of doing anything on the basketball court, but when he arrived on the Temple campus a year later, head coach Don Casey made it clear to his pupil that he had two responsibilities: passing the ball and playing defense. Stansbury quietly went about his duties, but when injuries decimated the team during his junior year, he was forced into the lead role.

Despite receiving two concussions of his own, Stansbury knew his team desperately needed his services and battled through the pain, missing just *seven minutes* the entire year as he led the team with 25 points a game. His efforts alone weren't enough, however, as the Owls struggled to a 14–15 record. Fortunately for Temple, forward Ed Coe and All-American Granger Hall returned after missing that season, and together with Stansbury the trio led Temple back to a 25–4 record and a spot in the 1984 NCAA Tournament.

Opposing them would be ninth-seeded St. John's, which at 18–11 was considered lucky to snatch a tournament bid. But once the game started, the Redmen showed just why they belonged, as guard Mike Moses picked the right time of year to have his best defensive effort.

"He was all over me," Stansbury said. "I hadn't faced a defensive player that was underneath my legs, under my shot that much in

years. Really, he was the best on-the-ball defensive player that I had faced in my four years at Temple, so I was struggling a little bit."

The Owls did have a 53–44 lead in the second half, but St. John's trimmed the margin to 57–50 with 10 minutes to go and then proceeded to hold Stansbury and his teammates scoreless for the next five minutes. Center Bill Wennington gave St. John's the lead at 59–57, and after a pair of Temple baskets put the Owls back in front, Wennington answered with two more shots of his own to give the Redmen a 63–61 advantage with just 2:03 to play. An empty possession at the other end gave St. John's the ball once again, but Coe came up with a crucial steal. The sophomore started a fast break, and when Hall sank a jump shot moments later, the game was knotted up with just a minute to go.

Both teams had already experienced their share of last-minute drama throughout the season, plenty of which had come with misery. Temple had lost a game to West Virginia just days before at the buzzer, while St. John's had seen an incredible 16 games decided in overtime or the last minute of regulation. Number 17 would top all of them.

The Redmen ran the clock down before working the ball to Chris Mullin, their All-American and leading scorer on the night with 21 points. Mullin drove toward the hoop, where he was greeted with a hard foul by Jim McLoughlin with eight seconds remaining.

Temple coach John Chaney, who had taken over for Casey the year before, decided to call a timeout in hopes of icing Mullin. The Owls would need all the help they could get, as Mullin was a 91.1 percent free throw shooter. The timeout may not have affected him, but it did serve one purpose: It gave Stansbury time to deal a major blow to his psyche.

"If you look at the video, you will see that I stand directly behind him at the top of the key, and if you can read my lips, I say to the guys, 'He did it before; he can do it again.' And I'll never forget that," Stansbury said. "I had seen a game with Georgetown a few months before—or Villanova, or one of those teams—he was there and he missed. I told the guys he did it before; he's going to do it again. And I never really talked when I played—I was so focused. But just at the moment, I felt something come back from the past."

Mullin refused to turn around, trying to focus on the ensuing free throw.

"He pretended like he didn't hear it," Stansbury grinned. "I'm sure he did—everybody heard it."

The nation's top free throw shooter proceeded to clang his shot off the back of the rim, right into the hands of the Owls, who called a timeout with four seconds to go. Although Chaney brought Stansbury to Temple to distribute the ball, there was nobody else he now wanted taking the last shot.

"You don't always have to make the shot," Chaney reminded him earlier in the season. "But the ball has to be in your hands to make the decision."

"Okay, I'm fine with that," Stansbury jokingly warned back. "But if it's in my hands, I'm going to take the shot most of the time."

And when Stansbury saw the play develop, he almost had no choice but to take the shot. Moses played off his man, anticipating that Stansbury would try to drive to the hoop. But when he pulled up from 25 feet away, Stansbury had his first clean look all day.

"I didn't see him anywhere near me. It was like Moses and the Red Sea opened up," Stansbury said. "I knew that I wasn't going to the basket because I was taught to have confidence in your shot. When this guy wasn't all over me, I knew I was going to shoot a jumper somewhere way behind the three-point line."

Stansbury had struggled all day against Moses, but he delivered when it counted, sinking the shot just as the clock expired. The senior had scored nearly 2,000 points in his career, but none would ever be sweeter than this. ●

LOYOLA MARYMOUNT   **ALABAMA**

Bo Kimble, Loyola Marymount: 19 points, 6 rebounds

1990: LOYOLA MARYMOUNT vs. ALABAMA

To put it mildly, the Loyola Marymount Lions were a collection of castoffs. Their head coach had been bounced from the Los Angeles Lakers years before, despite winning an NBA title with the team, and wound up at LMU. Bo Kimble and Hank Gathers were playing at USC when a new coach arrived and decided not to not renew their scholarships, more than happy to let them transfer across town. Corey Gaines was also a transfer, courtesy of UCLA, and Jeff Fryer was a lightly recruited guard who was told he would never get much playing time at the next level.

"I hadn't heard of Loyola Marymount before I was recruited by them, and they just happened to come to all my good games that I played in," Fryer joked. "I remember coach Westhead came to my school and was wearing an NBA championship ring and walked around campus with me and told me you would have the green light to shoot it."

That was music to Fryer's ears, and now with all the pieces together, Paul Westhead's vision of an unstoppable offense was now a reality. The Lions, who tried to shoot within the first two seconds of every possession, smashed the all-time scoring record with an average of 125 points per game.

"They were really focused on basketball, winning games, and tiring people out. They wanted to crack the opposition and make them feel spent, exhausted," Westhead said. "I wouldn't discount the value of defense, but at the end of the day the team that has the most points wins."

But in one instant, LMU's high-octane offense came to a screeching halt. Just days before its first-round game, Gathers collapsed on the court during the West Coast Conference Tournament, due to a heart condition he had been coping with for much of that season. Gathers was aware of the disorder and had been taking medication to treat it, until he realized that the pills were slowing him down on the court. And in Westhead's up-and-down strategy, *slow* wasn't part of the vocabulary. Afraid that he might hurt the team or his draft stock, Gathers quietly tried to cut back on his medication, a decision that cost him his life.

Faced with the option of ending the season or playing in honor of Hank, the Lions opted for the latter. Wearing a black patch with No. 44 in memory of Gathers, the players found their stride once again, scoring 260 points in their first two games (see page 108) to find themselves in the Sweet 16. Awaiting them was Alabama and coach Wimp Sanderson, who was not about to let his team fall into the same trap as LMU's first two victims.

"Wimp Sanderson did a good job of controlling the tempo," Westhead said. "He was hell-bent on not playing fast, and I think he probably made the right decision."

The Crimson Tide waited until five seconds remained on the shot clock before starting their offense, virtually eliminating LMU's game plan.

The decision did not sit well with the LMU-friendly crowd, but the tactic was as effective as it was unpopular. Alabama recovered from an early 9–2 deficit to get within 18–17, thanks to a 5:30 stretch in which they held the Lions without a field goal. Terrell Lowery ended the drought with a jumper, but by halftime the Crimson Tide were back within a point.

The 22 points scored by Loyola Marymount was not only well below their expectations, it was also the lowest first-half score of any team in the entire tournament. Westhead tried to lighten the mood by telling his players they needed only 103 more points to reach their average. But the reality was that Sanderson had sent Westhead and LMU a message about who was going to control the pace.

"Especially when they had three-on-one breaks and they pulled it out and didn't try to score, that's when we knew we were dealing with a different type of game," Fryer said. "We didn't know what to think, because they took us totally out of our game, and it was a game where we had to really just keep plugging away and keep trying."

The tension rose in the second half when Alabama's Melvin Cheatum committed a hard foul on Kimble that was not called, and the lack of officiating clearly got the best of Kimble. When the refs missed another obvious foul moments later, the LMU senior lost it. Kimble committed a hard foul in retaliation, only this time the refs were all too aware of the situation, handing him a technical foul. In perhaps the most inspirational moment of the tournament, teammate Chris Knight went over and pointed to the patch on Kimble's jersey, as if to remind him who they were playing for.

The Crimson Tide went on a 9–0 run to take a 49–41 lead with seven minutes to go, but the Lions were far from over. Gathers may not have been at the arena, but he was present in each of the players that day. And over the final stretch of the game, it showed.

"You had younger players who had horrible footwork through the regular season, all of a sudden overnight they just had Hank Gathers' footwork," Kimble said. "It's like, who are these people? But they weren't playing for themselves and they weren't worrying about their footwork. They were just doing the business because their hearts were thinking."

The Lions cut the lead to 52–45 before Tom Peabody, a reserve player who averaged just over four points a game, went on a tear. The Alabama players made it clear that their defense was going to focus on Peabody's teammates, and he made them pay by driving straight to the hoop for a layup. Peabody then forced a turnover at the other end of the floor, and when he made his second layup with 3:49 to go, Loyola Marymount was back on top 57–56.

Cheatum answered with a shot of his own, but the ever-clutch Fryer nailed a three-pointer to give Loyola Marymount a 60–58 lead. After Robert Horry buried a shot just before the one-minute mark to tie the game, Kimble tried to hit the go-ahead jumper with 45 seconds left. His shot was off the mark, but LMU kept the ball alive, and moments later Kimble was again taking matters into his own hands, driving straight toward the hoop. The ball was knocked out before Kimble could get the shot off, but there to scoop it up was LMU sophomore Terrell Lowery, who laid it in with just 33 seconds on the clock.

The Crimson Tide needed an answer to force overtime, and it appeared they had one when Cheatum found himself alone underneath the basket, but LMU's Per Stumer had raced back to knock the ball away before Cheatum could get the shot off. Lowery grabbed the loose ball seconds before the buzzer, and for the third time in a week, the Lions had honored their fallen teammate.

"I'm proud of the team because during a very tough time they stepped up and played well," Kimble said. "There's no getting over Hank—Hank was such an extraordinary person on and off the court, it was devastating to us. But the best therapy was each other, being there for each other."

And although Hank was not there, at least Kimble knew he had a cheering section in a higher place. ●

#57

NORTHERN IOWA — MISSOURI

Jason Reese, Northern Iowa: 18 points, 15 rebounds, 2 assists

1990: NORTHERN IOWA vs. MISSOURI

Of all the teams entering the 1990 NCAA Tournament, perhaps none came in with more momentum than the Northern Iowa Panthers. They probably weren't even among the top 50 teams in the field of 64, but considering what they had overcome, the team was flying high.

When coach Eldon Miller arrived in 1986, the Panthers had just four players and had never been relevant in college basketball. In just four years, Miller guided his team to the Mid-Continent Tournament semifinals, where they overcame an eight-point deficit in the final 2:10 to win at the buzzer. The team followed it up with a 53–45 victory over UW-Green Bay, wrapping up the first tournament bid in school history. It seemed like nothing could go wrong for Miller's club, and he knew his team had a great chance to pull off an upset against Missouri in the first round. But before the fourteenth-seeded Panthers could shock the world, they would first have to get to the game, which they soon discovered was no guarantee.

"You ever been on that amusement ride down at Disney World, The Tower of Terror? That's what it was like," laughed forward Troy Muilenburg. "The floor was dropping out of it and we dropped 20, 30 feet just with turbulence. It was quite the ride."

But to Miller, surviving the plane ride would be more difficult than surviving a game against the third-seeded Tigers.

"There are a lot of guys who can score, so it's going to be a challenge for us to guard them, but I can also tell you that they can't guard us," Miller told his team before the game. "It's going to be easier to get shots against this team than it was in our own league."

And once the game started, it quickly became apparent that his players had bought into the message. The Panthers, who made 39 percent of their three-pointers on the season, nailed seven of their first nine shots from beyond the arc, and when Muilenburg drained one from the top of the key, the Panthers led 25–11.

"At that time you're just thinking of how easy it was coming, and we knew at some point we couldn't continue to make all these shots," Muilenburg said. "But we're just going to ride this as long as possible."

Not only were the Panthers excelling on the offensive end, but they were shutting down Missouri star Anthony Peeler. For the entire game, forward Cedric McCullough would yield just one basket to Peeler, and thanks to his defensive effort the Panthers still led 63–53 with six minutes to go. That's when Muilenburg made the shot of the tournament. Muilenburg drove to the free throw line to take a pull-up jumper, but when a defender came over at the last instant to swat it away, he contorted his body in midair to get the shot off. It wasn't pretty, but it hit nothing but net to put UNI up 65–53 with just over five minutes to play.

"At that point we just wanted to finish it," Muilenburg said. "We overcame a ton of these 10, 12-point leads just to get into the tournament, so we knew how easy it was to blow a lead."

As if on cue, the Tigers reeled off 11 straight points, and although they had trailed almost the entire game, they were now within just one point. Northern Iowa pushed the lead back to 69–66 with 1:13 to go, but a layup by Chris Heller trimmed the gap to 69–68 with 48 seconds remaining. The Panthers knew Missouri would try to foul, and they got the ball inbounds to Jason Reese, who had made 77 percent of his free throws on the year. Reese knocked down both shots, but he offset his contribution by fouling UM's Nathan Buntin on a shot seconds later. Not only did Buntin's shot fall in, as did his game-tying free throw, but the foul happened to be the fifth on Reese, sending him to the bench. The Panthers still

The form of Maurice Newby's two-handed shot was less important than the result, which gave UNI the 74–71 win over third-seeded Missouri. *David E. Klutho/Sports Illustrated/Getty Images*

had 29 seconds left to win the game, but they would now be without their best player.

Reese's absence was noticeable right away, as Muilenburg found himself trapped on the left wing with 10 seconds to go. Facing a five-second call, the Panthers were forced to burn their final timeout. Miller decided to insert Maurice Newby, who had played with Reese since the third grade. Newby had been a quality shooter, but after sitting on the bench for the previous 10 minutes, it was a peculiar substitution to say the least.

"It wasn't like it was a mind-shattering decision—Maurice could flat out shoot the ball," Miller said. "Maurice is just an extremely solid human being, a very strong young man, and did a variety of things for us in the program. He was always called upon and a lot of times came off the bench."

The only thing stranger than Miller's substitution was the play that he subsequently called. Muilenburg, who had led the team in scoring on the night, would not be the shooter, but would instead be responsible for setting a screen. To top it off, it was a play that the Panthers had run time and again throughout the season, to the point where other teams could almost anticipate it.

"There wasn't any question of what we were going to do," Miller smiled. "We would run the same play, and we didn't care if they knew what was coming."

And as the final play developed, it quickly became obvious that the Tigers had read the scouting report. When guard Dale Turner drove around the perimeter and lateraled it back off to Newby, a defender was right there to greet him. But with just five seconds to go, passing the ball would have been risky.

"Once Newby got that shake going, we all knew the ball was going up," Muilenburg laughed. "That was kind of his trademark. When he started shaking those shoulders, you knew he was about ready to shoot it."

The shot could not have been any uglier—a two-handed heave that would never be found in a textbook. But the ball sailed through the net, and before the Tigers could even inbound the ball, the clock had struck zero. Miller was dubbed a genius—and even better, Newby was labeled a hero. ●

Luke Schenscher, Georgia Tech: 19 points, 12 rebounds

2004: GEORGIA TECH vs. OKLAHOMA STATE

Georgia Tech coach Paul Hewitt sat across the dinner table from Will Bynum, hoping to make amends for the junior's lack of playing time. The reserve guard had played just six minutes in the team's second-round victory over Boston College, and although the team had advanced to its first Sweet 16 in eight years, Bynum had not played a huge role in the team getting there.

"Look, we need you to stay ready," Hewitt pleaded. "You never know when you're time is going to come."

Bynum's chance would come soon enough, as leading scorer B. J. Elder went down with a sprained ankle just three minutes into the next game against Nevada. Whether by necessity or not, Hewitt had kept up his end of the bargain. Now it was time for Bynum to hold up his. Not only did Bynum score the game-winning bucket with just 1:04 to play, but he accomplished the same feat two days later against Kansas. With the score tied at 71 late in overtime, Bynum's three put the Yellow Jackets up for good. That shot put his team into the Final Four, where they would face an Oklahoma State team considered to be vastly more talented.

The Rambling Wreck, who had been picked to finish seventh in the ACC before the season started, were never even supposed to be at the Final Four. And Bynum, who had transferred from Arizona after his sophomore year, was never supposed to be in a Georgia Tech uniform at all. The Chicago native had originally tried

to transfer to Oklahoma State to play alongside high school teammate Tony Allen, but with no scholarships left in Stillwater, he packed up and headed for Atlanta. It turned out to be a great decision for Hewitt and the rest of the team, but OSU would be just fine without him. And with a vast majority of the crowd behind them in San Antonio, the Cowboys appeared to be heavy favorites to arrive at the title game.

"I remember when they introduced the Oklahoma State team—they definitely got a pretty strong ovation. We realized quickly you were closer to Oklahoma than you were to Atlanta," Hewitt said. "But again it's funny, that's part of why this team was successful— we were able to block all that stuff out and just go play."

Thanks to five three-pointers in the first half by senior Marvin Lewis, the Yellow Jackets stunned the 40,000 orange-clad fans in attendance. The team had gotten a combined two field goals from the hobbled Elder and the team's other superstar, Jarrett Jack, yet by halftime they still led 37–30.

In the second half, center Luke Schenscher picked up where Lewis left off, hitting five consecutive shots to give Georgia Tech a 63–57 lead with just 4:21 left. The Yellow Jackets still led by six points with less than three minutes remaining when OSU began to play with desperation. They started double-teaming the Yellow Jackets in an attempt to force turnovers, knowing that with All-American John Lucas shooting just 3-of-13 from the field, they would need as many looks as possible.

"One of the reasons why that team was very successful was the fact that they were really good at working together defensively—they were one unit," Hewitt said. "You really appreciate your guys working together. Those guys really understood the whole point of helping each other on defense."

What Hewitt didn't anticipate, however, was that it would be his offense that would nearly give the game away. Bynum missed the front end of a one-and-one with 2:01 to go, and in a moment of frustration he fouled Lucas eight seconds later. Lucas converted only one of his free throws to close the gap to just 65–62, leaving the door open for Georgia Tech to seal the win with a big shot. But Bynum would miss once again, this time on a layup with 1:25 to play.

"I was upset I missed that shot," Bynum said. "But the coaches and players told me to stick with it."

The team knew it would need Bynum's help to defend the last shot, but a screen helped Lucas get open momentarily, which was all the time he needed. The junior had hit just three of his 13 shots during the game, but his three-pointer from the right wing tied the game at 65 with 26.3 seconds to go, sending the crowd into a frenzy. Hewitt remained calm and brought his team over to talk about the game's final possession. It was really because of Lewis that Georgia Tech was in a position to win, but everybody knew who should take the last shot.

"I called a timeout, and as they were running over I was kind of curious to see what they thought, and I said, 'What do you guys think?' And I remember Marvin said, 'Give the ball to Will,'" Hewitt recalled. "It was a play that we had in mind, but I wanted to see what they said, and that's also what they suggested."

Bynum had contributed more than his fair share to the team's collapse, but his teammates were going to leave the season in his hands. It

Will Bynum drives to the bucket in the closing seconds, catapulting the Yellow Jackets to the championship game. *Georgia Tech Athletic Department. Photograph by Christopher Gooley*

was Bynum's late-game heroics that had gotten them to the Final Four, and if the team was to lose on this night, it would be with Bynum having at least one more shot to redeem himself.

Jack took the inbounds and raced past midcourt, where he patiently waited for Bynum to get open. Bynum took the ball with 10 seconds to go and slowly crept toward the three-point line, where Schenscher was setting a screen, before making his move. When Bynum curled around the screen, he hesitated as if to take a jump shot, throwing off the trio of defenders nearby. Now with no one to beat, Bynum drove to the basket and banked in the shot off the glass with just 1.5 seconds left to send the Yellow Jackets to the championship game. Bynum, for the third time in three games, was the reason why. ●

#55

2009: SIENA vs. OHIO STATE

When the NCAA Tournament bracket was revealed on Selection Sunday, the Siena Saints had every right to feel as if they had been given the worst draw in the entire field. They were fairly awarded a nine seed after a 26–7 regular season, but they were matched up against Ohio State—in Dayton. If at all possible, the ratio of Buckeye supporters to Siena fans was even more lopsided than the 55,000 to 3,000 ratio of their student bodies. The Saints, however, relished the challenge of playing a "neutral" game just 70 miles from the OSU campus.

"A lot of publicity was surrounding, 'Well, they gave you a nine but they sent you to Dayton to play Ohio State—that's really not fair.' I didn't look at it that way," Siena coach Fran McCaffery said. "For us, Dayton is not around the corner, but it's close enough that all of our parents could get there."

One parent that McCaffery could count on was the father of senior guard Kenny Hasbrouck. Kenny's dad, Jeffrey, had been confined to a wheelchair as the effects of multiple sclerosis set in, but he and his wife, Deborah, still made the eight-hour drive to each of Kenny's home games. Even as the disease started to take away the use of his legs and proceeded to strip Jeffrey's use of his arms, the disease couldn't take away his passion, and he quickly became a fan favorite.

"After the games, we always go over there and say hello to him because he was definitely one of our biggest fans," senior Ronald Moore said. "[Kenny] played for him all his life. For him to have that strength . . . it really showed how much heart and courage he had for the rest of the guys on the team."

On this particular night, however, the Siena star was having trouble finding his touch, and with 14 minutes left, the Saints trailed 41–30. Facing elimination if they didn't make a run, the Saints responded by scoring nine straight points, and Ryan Rossiter's layup at the three-minute mark tied the game at 49. But even with the fresh start, Siena allowed the Buckeyes to score on each of their next four possessions, and with just a minute left to play, the Saints found themselves four points down—and without the ball.

The Saints quickly sent OSU center B. J. Mullens to the line, and after the freshman missed both free throws, Hasbrouck promptly nailed a three-pointer at the other end of the court. The lead was now down to just one, and with 47 seconds still on the clock, the Saints could play out the next defensive possession without having to foul.

"Now you can see it in their eyes," McCaffery said. "We weren't going away—they were going to have to beat us."

Another Ohio State miss actually gave the underdogs a chance to win the game in regulation, as Hasbrouck got fouled with eight seconds remaining. The first free throw clanged off the back of the rim, but the second shot was pure, forcing overtime.

Hasbrouck started the extra session with a layup, giving Siena its first lead since the second minute of the game. The Saints still led 62–61 with a little over a minute to go when Mullens converted a layup, putting the Buckeyes back on top. Hasbrouck was unable to answer back, getting stripped with 55 seconds to play as the Buckeyes took over. The Saints defense held their ground, forcing OSU's Evan Turner into an errant jumper at the end of the shot clock, but their efforts were in vain. Mullens tracked down the ball in the corner, and just before falling out of bounds he tossed it over to teammate P. J. Hill. Siena had no choice but to foul, and Hill's free throws with nine seconds to go put the Buckeyes up 65–62.

Siena inbounded the ball to Moore, who was 0-for-4 from beyond the arc for the game, and had been unable to connect on any three-pointers over his last five games. But Ohio State coach Thad Matta didn't want to give Moore even a chance at tying the game and instructed his players to foul. For one reason or another, however, his players didn't get the message, leaving Moore with an opportunity to save Siena's season.

"Being a shooter, there are times when you're cold and you got to keep shooting, and that's something that coach has always told me," Moore said. "As my teammates know and my coaches know, I especially love the final minutes of any game and try to step up."

True to form, Moore faked out Hill on a cross-over and rose for the final shot. Fading slightly back as he released it, Moore nailed the shot to send the crowd into shock. Jon Diebler's last-second shot was long, and double overtime was on the horizon.

The Saints carried the momentum into the second overtime, taking a 68–65 lead midway through the period, but in a game that saw each team trading punches, OSU's Evan Turner tied up the game on a three-pointer. Moore added a free throw with a minute to go, but Turner, the leading scorer in the Big Ten, split four defenders on his way to the basket. His off-balance runner gave the Buckeyes a one-point lead with 17.9 seconds to go. Trusting his team to find a better shot with both teams in transition, McCaffery declined to call a timeout. Moore once again brought the ball up the court and quickly passed it to leading scorer Edwin Ubiles, who actually deferred the final shot.

"Now here you are at the top of the key, you're open, you're essentially a 2,000-point scorer. A lot of guys would let it rip right there," McCaffrey said of Ubiles. "He caught it, and it was one of the most instinctive plays I've ever seen. He read people coming to him to contest, so he faked shot and drove it right into the gap, and as soon as he ran into the gap three people came right to him. And as soon as they came, he banged it right to Ronald. Now Ronald had a year and a day to shoot that ball—there wasn't anybody near him."

Moore once again delivered with the biggest shot of his life. Standing exactly where he had made his previous shot, Moore's swish gave the Saints a 74–72 lead with just 3.9 seconds left. For Moore, who was playing in memory of his recently deceased aunt, the emotions immediately set in.

"My mom told me, 'She's with you in spirit,'" Moore said. "It was a lot going through my mind. Just for that to happen and for me to lift my team up, to win the game and go on to the next round in that manner was definitely a special moment for me, and I knew that right off the bat."

Ohio State called a timeout, and Moore pointed to the sky in honor of his aunt. McCaffery, who did not hear about the news until after the game, was furious over what he assumed was a premature celebration.

"Kenny and Alexander [Franklin] are hugging him like we just won the game, and he is in tears. So I am screaming at those three guys to compose themselves," McCaffery laughed. "I was like, do I have to take him out?"

Although unintentionally harsh, McCaffery's response served as a wake-up call, and Moore was kept in the game. And after Turner missed a running three-pointer, both Moore and McCaffery could enjoy the victory. As could his aunt. The team will never know if his aunt guided the last shot in, but having a name like the Saints certainly didn't hurt. ●

#54

1981: BRIGHAM YOUNG vs. NOTRE DAME

For a pair of religious institutions, Notre Dame and Brigham Young seemed to share little in common as they prepared to face each other in the 1981 NCAA Tournament. The Fighting Irish, rooted in Catholicism, preferred to take their time on each possession and stifle opponents with their defense. The "Stormin' Mormons," on the other hand, didn't care how many points they surrendered as long as the final scoreboard showed the Cougars on top. BYU's rivalry with Utah may have been called "The Holy War," but plenty of reputations were at stake against the Irish as well.

"It was a big deal for us. We felt like it was important—we wanted the Mormon guys to show well against these Catholic guys that we had always watched on TV," junior Fred Roberts said. "And I think it was important that we represent ourselves well and the school well across the nation."

Both teams would pray before their tip-off, but their means of doing so were not always the same.

"I never could get myself to pray for the other team," Roberts laughed. "They can pray for themselves."

He was kidding, of course, but Notre Dame probably didn't need any extra help to begin with. The 23–5 Irish were considered the favorite to win, and they played like it early on as they raced out to a 16–8 lead. They made it clear that the game was going to be played at their pace, and with just 7:30 remaining in the

first half BYU was still shooting just 20 percent from the floor. By the time the half reached its merciful close, the Cougars had tallied only 18 points, and All-American Danny Ainge had been limited to just two free throws. The Irish hadn't fared much better, putting only 28 points on the scoreboard—but that was exactly where they wanted to be.

"They were very deliberate in their offense, so it slowed the tempo for the game down," Roberts said. "And Danny's strength is actually getting the things going and getting up and down the floor, and it wasn't that kind of game."

Ainge had averaged over 24 points a game during the season, but if the Cougars were going to chip away at the deficit they would need help from some other players. Three early fouls on Roberts sent him to the bench, and BYU coach Frank Arnold looked to the team's sixth man, Greg Ballif, to bring the team back. But the pace wasn't to Ballif's liking either, and when Notre Dame's Kelly Tripucka rolled in an easy layup early in the second half, the lead had grown to 32–18.

"There was no question that it was a challenging game, that we were sluggish and not playing well," Ballif said. "It was frustrating to a degree that we weren't scoring at the rate that we were used to scoring at. I think people were just out there slugging it out."

The Cougars still trailed 40–29 when they finally found their scoring touch. A 7–0 run brought them back within four points, and moments later they had closed the gap to just 44–42. A three-point play by Ballif with 3:40 to play cut the lead to 48–47, and when he drained a jumper from 15 feet away, the Cougars had their first lead of the game with just one minute remaining. For Ballif, a Provo native whose father and grandfather both played football at BYU, it was a dream come true.

"What I remember most emotionally about the game was the elation that came from when I hit that shot," Ballif said. "It put us in a really good position to win the game, but you're smart enough to know that with that much time left anything can happen."

Sure enough, the Cougars played solid defense for 51 seconds, only to see Tripucka return the favor by draining a 15-footer of his own with just nine seconds remaining.

It was one of the worst games Danny Ainge ever had in a BYU uniform, but his last-second drive against Notre Dame made him a legend of March Madness. *Manny Millan/Sports Illustrated/Getty Images*

"We felt like we made them take a shot they didn't want to take, and Tripucka just made a great shot," Roberts said. "I thought, wow, that's it for us."

Ainge called a timeout as his team set up a final play. As a point guard and the best player on the floor, Ainge knew the ball was going to be in his hands. He had played one of the worst games of his career, but he now had one chance to redeem himself. But with 90 feet to go and little time remaining, it was a tall order.

"We only had one option. It was mainly get the ball in as fast as we could and spread the floor to try and get a shot," Roberts said. "It kind of worked out perfectly for us—they played where they ended up chasing Danny instead of just keeping him in front of them."

Ainge took the inbounds near his own baseline and delivered a behind-the-back pass to himself near midcourt to weave through a trio of Notre Dame defenders. He scooted by one other player as he made his way to the basket, but standing in front of the hoop was Irish center Orlando Woolridge. Just minutes earlier, Woolridge had swatted away a shot from Ainge at nearly the same spot on the floor, and a similar block would give Notre Dame the victory. But this time, Ainge floated the ball a little bit higher in the air just before the buzzer sounded.

"Woolridge probably blocks 9 out of 10 shots that are played out that way, and Ainge knew just how to get it over," Ballif said. "It was a combination of a lot of skill and no question a little bit of luck just getting it high enough to get over the top of his fingers."

The ball sailed over the outstretched hands of Woolridge, and as time expired it landed softly in the net to give BYU a 51–50 victory. Notre Dame may have had the luck of the Irish, but the Cougars had something much more important. They had Danny Ainge. ●

1995: UCLA vs. MISSOURI

Exactly one year earlier, the headlines across Southern California had blasted Jim Harrick in no subtle terms. The UCLA coach had dropped his first-round match a day earlier to Tulsa, and the fan base back home was not so pleased. "Following Latest Fiasco," the L.A. *Daily News* read, "Harrick Should Be Fired."

Compared with some of the boosters and alumni, the feelings from the newspaper were rather mild. Jim Harrick was not a well-liked man. The reasons were obvious—it was the same reason the program had gone through five coaches in a nine-year period. John Wooden had brought 10 championships to Westwood in 12 years, and in the two decades following his departure, the team had failed to win a single title. And fans weren't coping well.

Although it was never directly stated, Harrick knew his team would have to play well into March if he wanted to keep his job. His Bruins had lost only one game all year heading into the 1995 NCAA Tournament, but each win only raised the expectations further to win that elusive title. And for all intents and purposes, that journey started in the second round against Missouri.

The Tigers, who at 20–8 came into the game with nothing to lose, played fearless basketball. And for much of the first half it showed, as they ran off a 12–2 run to take a 42–34 lead into the locker room. It was the largest deficit the Bruins had faced all year. Harrick and his players kept a positive atmosphere in the locker room, focusing only on how they would claw their way back into the game. But when the Tigers pushed their lead to 52–43, the mood quickly changed.

"I look out, and, for the first time this season, I see our guys dropping their heads and their shoulders," Harrick recalled. "They've got that 'what are we going to do?' look on their faces."

If the Bruins were going to come back, they were going to have to find a way to stop Paul O'Liney, who had already scored 21 points. The senior had made eight of his nine shots from the field, including all five attempts from beyond the arc. Harrick called a timeout, and his players responded by holding O'Liney scoreless for the next 9 minutes. They also picked it up on the offensive end, scoring 15 straight points after the timeout to go up 58–52 midway through the second half. That lead appeared to be safe, but the Tigers came back with a run of their own, reeling off nine of the next 11 points to pull back in front with 6:16 to play. Missouri still led 72–69 with just over two minutes left when UCLA made one final push.

Senior Ed O'Bannon connected on a pair of free throws to cut the lead to one, and the Tigers naturally looked to O'Liney for an answer. By this point in the game, the Bruins were ready, and when O'Liney fired a shot just before the shot clock buzzer, he had two men in his face. The ball circled out of the rim, and there for the rebound was UCLA freshman Toby Bailey. The

Bruins went back to O'Bannon, and his pump fake with 58.9 seconds remaining sent Julian Winfield flying off the ground and into the side of the UCLA forward. O'Bannon sank both free throws to put UCLA back on top, 73–72.

With a minute still remaining, it seemed like the perfect opportunity for the Tigers to take a quick shot, assuring them another possession in the final seconds. Instead, they chose to take their time and spread the floor as the clock ticked by. The Bruins were content to have the final shot of the game, but that plan backfired when sophomore Cameron Dollar collided into UM's Jon Sutherland with 38.9 seconds to go. It didn't send Missouri to the line, but it awarded them something much greater—a fresh 35-second shot clock.

Now the Bruins would have only a few seconds to take the final shot, if they ever got the ball back at all. Once again, the Tigers let the clock run down until six seconds remained on the shot clock, when Kendrick Moore made his move at the top of the three-point key. The freshman lowered his head and drove toward the right wing, and with four seconds on the clock, he turned back toward the middle. Moore rose up, ready to fire a fadeaway jumper, but managed to find Winfield streaking toward the basket. Before Moore landed back on the ground, he delivered a strike right to Winfield, who banked in the shot with just 4.8 seconds left to put Missouri up 74–73.

Harrick called a timeout to set up a final play. The assistant coaches advised him to throw a long pass like Duke had done three years earlier with Christian Laettner, but Harrick's mind was already made up. Rather than risk an interception on a full-court inbounds, Harrick was going to rely on the speed of 5-foot-10 senior guard Tyus Edney.

"Edney, I want you to get the ball. Hopefully, you can get it around the foul line and push it down the floor like you always do," Harrick instructed. "And they're *not* going to foul you. Take it to the rim."

Harrick instructed his other players on where to set up for the final shot, but before his team went back out on the floor, he had some final words for his senior.

"Tyus, *you* shoot the ball. Make *sure* you shoot it," Harrick said. "It's your ball. Your rock. Your game. Just go on and make it happen."

Tyrus Edney took a page out of Danny Ainge's book when he went coast-to-coast for the game-winner against Missouri. *AP Photo/Jack Smith*

The season, as well as his coach's career, would be riding on Edney's. The guard took the ball near his own baseline and scurried up the left side of the floor, arriving at midcourt with three seconds remaining. Then, without breaking stride, Edney dribbled behind his back to change his direction and get to the right side of the court. Now only two seconds remained. Edney took a few more paces before rising up, holding out his right arm to ward off the Missouri defense. The ball left his hand with 0.5 seconds to go, and a moment after the buzzer sounded, it banked off the glass to give UCLA the victory. For Edney, it was the shot of a lifetime, but perhaps nobody in the arena was more thrilled than his coach.

"I felt like a guy who was facing a firing squad, heard the executioner yell 'fire!' and then all 12 guns failed to go off," said Harrick, who revised his analogy. "I didn't dodge a bullet. I dodged a 50-megaton bomb."

Not only would Harrick live to see another day, the victory gave the Bruins a chance to bring home the national championship. And sure enough, two weeks later, Harrick was the most popular man in Los Angeles. ●

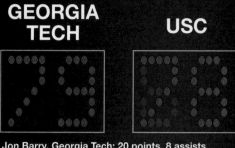

1992: GEORGIA TECH vs. USC

When the NCAA Tournament came to Milwaukee in 1992, it was finally a chance for Al McGuire to return home. The longtime Marquette coach, now retired from the sidelines, would be at the Bradley Center to call the action for CBS. Unfortunately for McGuire, he was so overwhelmed by the first round of games that his voice was shot. His broadcast partner and director concocted some blend of pills, honey, and castor oil to remedy McGuire's voice. The potion worked just in time, as the next day he was about to call one of the greatest games in tournament history.

McGuire awoke the next morning to prepare for the Memphis State vs. Arkansas game, the first contest in a double-header. The game turned out to be even more dramatic than the first day's action, as Memphis State won on a shot just seconds before the buzzer. McGuire was up to the challenge this time, and by the start of the second game his voice was still intact. The same could not be said for the crowd, however, which was eerily quiet when Georgia Tech and USC tipped off. McGuire said the fans just needed a little recovery time from the first contest before they got into the game, but few could blame them for being less than enchanted by the second matchup. Led by Harold "Baby Jordan" Miner, the second-seeded Trojans had set a school record for wins and were supposed to make quick work of the Yellow Jackets.

"You have certain guys who are just talented, and nothing else," Georgia Tech freshman James Forrest said. "And we knew with him as long as we made him a jump-shooter, as opposed to him getting to the cup and posterizing someone, we had a chance."

Never one to shy away from a challenge, Georgia Tech coach Bobby Cremins told his players to go right at Miner. Cremins, who inherited the program after the Yellow Jackets went 4–23 the year before his arrival, instructed his players to crowd the paint. The plan worked even better than expected, as they held Miner to just one shot in the first half. Nevertheless, his teammates picked up the slack as USC took a 39–38 lead into halftime.

Miner started to find his rhythm in the second half, and after a halfcourt alley-oop from Rodney Chatman to Lorenzo Orr, the Trojans had taken a commanding 62–51 lead. Perhaps even more disheartening was that Cremins' club was getting outhustled.

"We weren't playing Georgia Tech basketball, we weren't sharing the ball, we weren't making stops," Forrest said. "We were doing things out of the ordinary. And we needed to tidy it up if we wanted to move on."

Once the Yellow Jackets dug their heels in, they refused to let USC get any easy baskets. GT eventually tied the game at 69, and from there neither team could break free. The Yellow Jackets had a 74–72 lead when Miner, who had gone cold by missing his last six shots, spun his way to the hoop and tied the game with 1:43 to go. When Travis Best tried to answer at the other end with a jump shot, the ball slipped out of his hands, instantly starting a four-on-one fast break for the Trojans. Orr easily laid the ball in, putting USC back in front with 1:17 to play.

Now needing a shot to tie, Georgia Tech senior Jon Barry drove to the elbow before leaning in for a jumper. His shot was pure, but now the shot clock was turned off, leaving USC with the option of taking the last shot. Chatman stood just past midcourt, working the clock down until there was seven seconds to go. With the stage set, the junior drove to the baseline and faded away for a clear look. His shot sailed through with 2.2 seconds left, and Georgia Tech's chances looked slim. That is, it looked desperate to everybody else except the players.

"I was still hopeful. If you can see the video, no one's head is down," Forrest said. "Everybody is like, okay, we still got time. That was our mindset."

The plan, called "Home Run," was for Matt Geiger to stand at the baseline and inbound the ball to a streaking Barry. Geiger would indeed find Barry at midcourt, but Chatman knocked the ball out of bounds, leaving the Yellow Jackets with only 0.8 seconds to work with. Now inbounding at midcourt, the plan was still for Geiger to throw the ball into Barry, the best three-point shooter on the team. But USC coach George Raveling knew exactly what Cremins was thinking, and when Geiger looked to inbound the ball, Barry was smothered by the defense. Best, the second option on the play, was also nowhere to be found. Facing a five-second call, Geiger was forced to throw the ball into Forrest, who had missed all three of his attempts from beyond the arc that year.

"James truthfully was the last option. You know the play was not working," Cremins smiled. "So I thought it was over and I was walking down the bench to shake George Raveling's hand."

Forrest, who had a little more faith in himself, caught the ball well beyond the three-point line with his back to the basket. With no time to find a better shot, the freshman turned around and fired the ball toward the hoop. As the buzzer sounded, the ball sailed through the net, prompting McGuire to completely let loose. Although there were no words to go along with his screaming, his initial reaction ended up being the most famous call of his career. Accompanying the commentary were the images of Forrest and his team parading around the court. Cremins, who had been facing the other end of the court, turned around and ran to catch up with the hero.

"I'm so proud of you," Cremins said as he grabbed Forrest. "You deserve to get ACC Freshman of the Year."

Earlier that day, Forrest had been passed over for the honor. But he gladly traded a buzzer-beating shot in its place.

"What happened was a couple of the guys had already said whoever gets it, it's a catch and shoot," Forrest recalled. "It was just a prayer. It was just a catch and square and let it go with form. When you look at the shot again, it looks like I knew what I was doing, but it was a straight miracle."

McGuire concurred, dubbing the moment the "Miracle in Milwaukee." Cremins decided to take a little time to reflect on what had just transpired, declining the bus ride back to the team hotel.

"It was snowing and I decided to walk back to the hotel in the snow, and I'll always remember," Cremins said, "It didn't make any difference how cold it was. I was so high on that shot, I was floating back to my hotel."

So perhaps two miracles happened in Milwaukee that night. But even if he didn't float back to the hotel, Cremins could still enjoy one of the unlikeliest shots in the history of the game. ●

#51

LOUISVILLE | **KANSAS STATE**

71 | 69

Derek Smith, Lousville: 20 points, 7 rebounds

1980: LOUISVILLE vs. KANSAS STATE

When Tony Branch cracked open his door at the Hilton Hotel in Lincoln, few could blame the Louisville guard for what was racing through his mind. Two weeks earlier, teammate Marty Pulliam had purchased a water gun, and from that moment on, any teammate who thought he was out of harm's way was sorely mistaken. Before long the whole team had gotten in on the frenzy, soaking their teammates with a heavy dose of H_2O. By the time March had rolled around, however, Branch had come prepared. When the senior heard a knock on his door the day before UL's first-round game against Kansas State, he naturally assumed it was one of his teammates, getting ready to fire away once again.

But on this particular occasion, head coach Denny Crum had been making the rounds to pump up his team for the big game. Crum rarely made trips up to his players' rooms, and this time he found another reason why. After knocking on the door, Crum expected to see a fired-up Branch awaiting him. What he encountered instead was a bucketful of water, courtesy of his point guard. When Branch opened the door to see which would-be assailant he had defeated, he was petrified. It was a moment of incredibly poor luck for Branch, who seemed to be in the doghouse already.

Branch had started 22 games as a junior in 1979, but in what was supposed to be his best season, he was replaced by teammate Tony

Eaves, just a sophomore at the time. It wasn't so much that Branch was getting outplayed by his successor, but when they performed equally on the practice floor, Crum felt compelled to go with Eaves, who would only improve as the years went on. The thinking was that Branch had nearly reached his peak. And when Branch played only a total of 92 minutes during the 1980 season, it appeared he had.

The only thing that made the benching more difficult was that Branch was being punished for his positive attitude. Factoring into Crum's decision was that Branch could handle the demotion, whereas Eaves was more of an uncertainty.

"Naturally I was crushed," Branch said when he found out he had been placed on the second team. "The first week I was hurt, the second week angry, the third bitter and after about a month I was able to get myself back together. In that period I'd thought about quitting. I loved my teammates but thought mentally I'd be so negative I'd hurt them."

But staying true to his colors, Branch never complained about his playing time and became Eaves' biggest supporter.

"Well one thing about Tony, he was a class person," Crum recalled. "He had been a starter and ended up getting beat out, but he worked just as hard in practice and he was a great role model and a great team player."

Unfortunately for Branch, that work ethic didn't translate to success on the court. A year earlier, Branch had finished third on the team in assists and tops in free throw percentage, but in his final four games of the 1980 season he had averaged just 1.5 minutes a contest. And now with a fresh coat of water to Crum's attire, his season had perhaps hit a new low.

Crum wasn't as upset as Branch feared, but that didn't necessarily mean that he was anxious to give his guard more playing time. Louisville trailed nearly the entire first half with Branch on the sidelines, but when Darrell Griffith hit a late jumper to give the Cardinals a 39–37 lead at the break, it appeared that maybe Crum wouldn't need Branch's services at all. That lead would only continue to widen as the game went on, and by the time UL pushed the lead to 61–54 with just 7:39 to play, Branch still had yet to make an entrance.

Louisville was on the verge of putting the game away when Kansas State's Ed Nealy, who had shot just 1-of-5 in the first half, suddenly found his touch. An 11–6 run by the Wildcats put them within two points, and when Rolando Blackman sank a 10-footer in the final seconds, the teams headed to overtime tied at 67 apiece.

The Cardinals would recover to score the first two points of the extra session, but the game took a dramatic turn when, with just over two minutes to play, Griffith fouled Blackman. The Kansas State junior would sink both free throws to tie the game, but more importantly, the foul was the fifth and final for Griffith. For the remainder of the game, Louisville would be without its only senior, who happened to also be a first-team All-American and college basketball's Player of the Year.

"Darrell was a guy that everybody looked up to because he had such a great work ethic. He was such a great player and he had worked so hard through his career, and he was one of those guys all the other players idolized," said Crum. "He was always there when they needed him, and they just figured he would just kind of take over, which he was capable of doing. He always came through for them."

But now, in the biggest moment of the season, Griffith's teammates would no longer be able to rely on him as a crutch. To fill in for Griffith's enormous shoes, Crum turned to a player who hadn't even attempted a shot all day long: Tony Branch.

With the game tied at 69, Branch held onto the ball until only 14 seconds remained before calling a timeout. Crum had a specific plan in mind—Rodney McCray would inbound the ball to Branch, who would then either pass the ball off to one of the forwards or take the shot himself. And despite the fact that Branch had come in cold off the bench, it was a decision Crum felt quite comfortable with.

"We knew that he was capable," Crum said. "He'd done it every day in practice."

The only problem was that Kansas State had anticipated the inbounds pass to Branch, nearly forcing McCray to burn a timeout that, as he would later find out, they didn't have. That would have resulted in a technical foul, giving KSU a free trip to the line, but at the last moment he found small forward Wiley Brown. The ball eventually did get to Branch, but by the time he received it only seven seconds remained. That left him with little option but to take the shot over the 6-foot-6 Blackman, the three-time reigning Defensive Player of the Year in the Big Eight.

Branch dribbled to the free throw line, where KSU's Glen Marshall quickly joined Blackman for the double team.

"When I got trapped, my experience said to me I've got to get a shot up," recalled Branch, who split the double-team. "They weren't quite in front of me so there was a little gap. I didn't know if I could get the shot off or if Blackman could block me with his size. I leaned in because it was the only way I could get it off, but when I let it go I thought it was going in."

His off-balance jumper managed to clear the defense, but when it arrived at the rim with four seconds to play, it clanged off the right side and toward the brace connecting the rim to the backboard. From there it managed to spin back toward the left, bounce around twice, and, finally, with one second to play, settle in the basket.

For Branch, it was far more satisfying than the last shot he had taken—the one in the hotel room. And Crum would join in on the fun during practice the following week, calling Branch over for a quick word, only to drench the senior with his own bucket of water. Smiling at one another, both parties happily agreed to call it a draw. ●

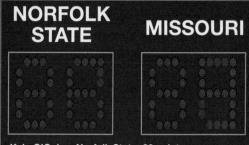

2012 NORFOLK STATE vs. MISSOURI

Five years ago, Kyle O'Quinn seemed like the last person who would ever play college basketball, much less in the NCAA Tournament. O'Quinn never played basketball until his junior year of high school, and most of his limited experience was gained on the bench—and that was fine by O'Quinn, who viewed the game as a means to stay in shape and have fun. It wasn't until his coach threatened to kick him off the team that O'Quinn began to show his potential. But even a stellar season in his final year wasn't enough to persuade college programs, which completely ignored him. That is, except for little known Norfolk State, who offered a scholarship just weeks before he graduated.

Unfortunately, NSU's basketball history was about as sparse as O'Quinn's. Since moving to Division 1 in 1997, the Spartans had never made the NCAA Tournament, and things didn't appear any different after O'Quinn arrived, as the team went 35–57 in his first three seasons. By his senior season, the Spartans had turned things around to snag the first tournament bid in school history, but as great as their comeback story had been, that appeared to be the final chapter. Facing them in the first round was Missouri, who despite earning a two seed was considered by many to be the frontrunner to win the championship. The Tigers started the season 14–0 and seemed to finish the season on an equally high note. Six days before taking on NSU, the Tigers defeated eventual Elite

Eight squad Baylor for the third time that season to claim the Big 12 Tournament title and the third spot in the national polls. No team came in with more momentum than the Tigers, and the odds-makers at Las Vegas took notice. After the pairings were announced on Selection Sunday, Missouri was listed as a 21.5 point favorite, the largest spread of any game the entire tournament.

"You look at that as someone's not on our side, someone's not believing in us," O'Quinn said. "Let's prove a couple people wrong."

Even if Norfolk State managed to cover the spread, it seemed doubtful that they could actually pull off a victory. A 15 seed hadn't won in 11 years, amassing a combined 4–105 record against second-seeded teams.

It wasn't long, however, before the Spartans made their presence felt. O'Quinn nailed three straight baskets in the opening minutes, and by the time Pendarvis Williams nailed a jumper just over six minutes into the game, Norfolk State led 15–7. Missouri responded with nine straight points to grab a 16–15 lead, but as the first half came to a close the score was tied at 38, shocking the largely pro-Missouri crowd in Omaha.

Even as the second half got underway, the Tigers struggled to break free. A 6–0 run gave Missouri a 61–59 lead with 11:24 to go, but O'Quinn made another trio of baskets to tie the game once again at 64. The score was still tied with eight minutes to play when the game took a drastic turn. Chasing down UM's Phil Pressey, O'Quinn appeared to make the play of the tournament when he blocked Pressey from behind, only to be called for a foul. After the replay showed a clean block, the fans erupted in boos. The Kansas contingent, waiting for the Jayhawks to play in the following game, started to empathize with the underdogs. Sensing the injustice, or perhaps wanting their Big 12 rivals to lose, the KU fans began to lustily cheer against the Tigers. They continued to voice their displeasure as Pressey made both free throws to put Missouri up 68–66, but as the next possession began, something changed in the tone of their cheering. Their frustration toward the officials suddenly turned into support and encouragement for the Spartans.

"Everybody likes to see the underdog survive—not only survive, they like to see the underdog win," O'Quinn said. "So that feels good to get the fan support, even if they're not our fans, any kind of support is good."

Using the energy from the crowd, Norfolk State soon went on a 12–2 run to take an 81–75 lead with just 2:17 left. It appeared history was theirs for the taking after all. But before they could celebrate, Missouri made one final push. Marcus Denmon made a pair of free throws to cut the lead to four, and after a miss by O'Quinn at the other end, Michael Dixon sank a jumper with 1:30 to go. Dixon then followed it up with a steal, forcing NSU's Rodney McCauley to commit a foul before Dixon could break free for a dunk. It made no difference, however, as the junior sank the ensuing free throws to tie the game at 81 with just 50 seconds to play. All of a sudden, the game was slipping through their fingers.

Things didn't look any better as NSU forward Chris McEachin missed a baseline jumper with 35 seconds to go. Before Missouri could snag another rebound, however, O'Quinn was there to save the day. Not only did he catch the ball as it sailed well beyond the basket, he banked in the putback while being fouled.

"It came off without hitting the rim. I jumped—if it would have hit the rim, I might have mistimed it, but thank God it hit no rim," O'Quinn recalled with a smile.

He would sink the ensuing free throw to put the Spartans up 84-81, but the Tigers were not done yet. Although Denmon missed a three at the other end and O'Quinn added another free throw with 17 seconds left, Pressey responded by nailing a three just seven seconds later. Now down just 85-84, Missouri sent McCauley to the line with 8.2 seconds to play, and while he would make his first free throw, his second caromed off the back of the rim. A Missouri rebound would give them a chance to tie or take the lead, but O'Quinn—who already had 26 points and 14 rebounds—had one more miracle left in him. He tipped the ball in the air as he fought with UM's Ricardo Ratliffe for the rebound. Neither was able to come up with the board, and both hands sent the ball flying in the air. The two continued to struggle for the rebound, and the ball was tipped in the air four times before Pressey and O'Quinn found themselves simultaneously locked on. The officials ruled a jump-ball, with the possession arrow pointing toward Norfolk State.

"When you see the possibility of a win is so close, it's anybody's ball," O'Quinn said. "Whoever wants it more is going to get it."

The Tigers sent O'Quinn to the line, and although he would miss both shots, by the time Missouri grabbed the rebound and called timeout, just 2.9 seconds remained. Pressey's desperation three-pointer clanged off the rim, and the Spartans had pulled off one of the biggest upsets in NCAA Tournament history. Missouri had not given the game away—they had shot an incredible 53 percent from the floor—but the Spartans managed to play even better. Despite no points from their bench, Norfolk State made 54 percent of their shots, including 63 percent in the second half as they held on for the 86–84 victory.

As O'Quinn proudly declared after the game, he had busted everyone's bracket— including his own. He may have been kidding about his own bracket, but as for everybody else, well, that was another matter altogether. ●

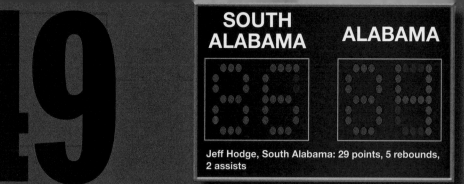

Jeff Hodge, South Alabama: 29 points, 5 rebounds, 2 assists

1989: SOUTH ALABAMA vs. ALABAMA

As hard as it is to keep a strong rivalry when one team always wins, it's even harder to maintain a rivalry when the two teams don't play each other. Alabama may not have considered its first-round matchup in the 1989 NCAA Tournament a rivalry game, but much more was at stake for South Alabama, which was playing the Crimson Tide for the first time. The Jaguars, especially head coach Ronnie Arrow, wanted to prove they were just as good as their northern counterparts.

"Coach Arrow, he brought it to our attention as a team that they tried to get a tournament going with UAB, Auburn, Alabama, and South Alabama. But Wimp Sanderson, who was coaching Alabama then, said he had no reason to play us, he had nothing to gain," senior Junie Lewis said. "They threw us right under the bus by telling us we're not even in their class, so let's get at them."

The Jaguars tried to come out as the aggressors, but some hot shooting by Alabama quickly put an end to their momentum. Less than five minutes into the game, the Tide had made six of their nine shots to take an 18–8 lead. Alabama never let up as the game wore on, and after Alvin Lee made his sixth shot in seven attempts, the gap stood at 15 points. Even worse, the neutral crowd, normally a supporter of the underdogs, had turned on the Jaguars.

"I never pay attention to the crowd when we're playing, but after the game and over the years it's funny to watch," Arrow said. "Because as you watch the game, it was very visible that Alabama had three-quarters of the crowd."

The fans roared even louder when the Crimson Tide converted consecutive layups to stretch the lead to 45–28, prompting a time-out by Arrow. UA's lead would eventually grow to 19 before the Tide took a 49–33 lead into the break. The Jaguars, not known as a team to come back from big deficits, were dejected when they arrived in the locker room.

"Now reality was setting in that we were representing the Sun Belt, we were playing the SEC, and I even made a statement maybe we didn't belong playing the SEC," Arrow said. "Maybe we didn't belong playing Alabama in the first round, because we sure didn't show up ready to do it."

The reasons for South Alabama's deficit were obvious. Guards Junie Lewis and Jeff Hodge, known more affectionately as "Peanut Butter and Jelly," had been completely ineffective in the first half. Hodge got the second half started the right way with a tip-in, and a minute later Lewis added a jumper of his own. After another jump shot from Lewis and putback by Hodge, the difference was only 12 points. Two more baskets from Hodge put USA within 57–49, and now the crowd was starting to change its opinion of the Jaguars.

South Alabama's Gabe Estaba soon converted a three-point play, and after Lewis hit another jumper, the lead was down to just five with 12 minutes to go.

"Even if inside I felt like, man, we're in trouble, I didn't show anybody. I said, 'Listen, we're going to get back in this, man, just a few points at a time, come on,'" Lewis recalled. "Jeff and myself, we knew no matter what, that at any time both of us could heat up or one of us could really get some motivation going to get back in the game."

The Crimson Tide continued to cling to their lead, but they could hold off the momentum for only so long. When Estaba converted another three-point play with just 91 seconds to go, the Jaguars had their first lead at 83–81. Even though the Tide would answer back with a three-pointer of their own, South Alabama had the option of holding out for the last shot. Arrow called a timeout with 34 seconds left, but when nobody could get open he was forced to burn another with 10 seconds to go. Now with no remaining timeouts, it was up to his players to win the game on their own.

John Jimmerson tried to inbound the ball to Lewis, who was camped under the basket, but the defense anticipated the pass and knocked it away. Lewis chased the ball down at the baseline, but by now the final seconds were rapidly ticking by. He twisted around and jumped in the air, ready to cast a desperation fadeaway in front of his own bench, but at the last second he saw Hodge out of the corner of his eye.

"That was a blessing from God because that ball was on its way out of bounds and I tiptoed—I was a hair away from the sidelines," Lewis said. "I got it and I took a dribble and I just jumped. I turned my body around toward the basket, and while I was going up I heard a 'Yo!' It was Jeff, and I tossed it right to him."

The defense had already collapsed around Lewis, leaving Hodge wide open behind the three-point line. Hodge calmly rose up and swished the shot with four seconds left. Fans watching at home heard the announcers scream "South Alabama wins it!" as the Jaguars bench started celebrating, but plenty of time was still on the clock.

"After he made the shot, if you look at the tape, our freshmen are jumping up and down like it's over with," Arrow laughed. "What people don't understand is that they got a pretty dog-gone good shot at the buzzer."

Alabama heaved the ball the length of the court, right toward a streaking Askins near the free throw line. But his jump shot bounced off the front of the rim, and when time expired Arrow ran toward the middle of the court and jumped on his players.

"You saw my vertical," joked Arrow. "There have been great games in the NCAA Tournament, but none better than rivalries through excitement, through the little guy beating the so-called big guy. If you lived in the state of Alabama, they said there were hardly any cars on the streets. And it was one of those deals if you were in Alabama, you knew what a big thing it was."

It would be safe to assume that Alabama wouldn't want to play the Jaguars again anytime soon. But now it was for an entirely different reason. ●

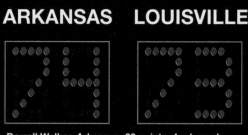

Darrell Walker, Arkansas: 23 points, 4 rebounds, 3 assists

1981: ARKANSAS vs. LOUISVILLE

To the dedicated fans who showed up early enough to catch warmups, it appeared that Razorbacks guard U. S. Reed was not taking the upcoming contest against Louisville very seriously. While his teammates were lining up for some last-minute preparations, Reed was firing long-range bombs, something he had never done before—and something that would instantly put him on the bench were he to try it during a game. But the more bewildered his teammates became, the farther away Reed began to shoot.

"They were so long, the guys in the line were saying, 'What are you doing?' I was saying I may have to hit a long shot at the end of the game. You never know," Reed laughed. "It's kind of a heave-from-the-chest jump shot. When you've practiced something before you do it, it's almost like you've already done it."

Arkansas coach Eddie Sutton put an end to the pre-game theatrics. If his players were going to knock off the defending national champions, a team that had started off 2–7 but had now won 15 straight games, they were going to need all the practice they could get. The Cardinals were three-point favorites heading into the game, and everything seemed to be going according to plan as they took an early 25–21 lead. Arkansas, however, responded with an 8–0 run, prompting an order from Sutton to stall the game. The tactic worked as his team still maintained a 37–33 edge when the first half came to a close. And thanks to

10 first-half points, Reed avoided any halftime lectures about his questionable preparation.

Arkansas would continue to lead for most of the second half, but the Cardinals were never in danger of getting blown away, and heading into the game's final minute they only trailed 72–69. UL junior Poncho Wright knocked down a pair of huge free throws to close the gap to just one, and after an empty Arkansas possession, the Cardinals had a chance to win the game on their final shot. Wright took it upon himself to fire the game-winner, and although his fadeaway was off the mark, the ball caromed off the backboard and into the hands of teammate Derek Smith, who sank a falling jump shot to put Louisville on top 73–72. Arkansas called a timeout, but with just five seconds remaining it seemed that a win just wasn't meant to be.

"When it got down to the final few seconds, to be honest with you, we were pretty down," Reed said. "The momentum had changed, and we were on the verge of collapsing."

Fortunately for the Razorbacks, Sutton was holding out a little bit more hope.

"U. S., you're going to get the ball," Sutton instructed, unaware that his star was nearly despondent. "Get as close as you can, and you're going to have a shot or kick it to Scott [Hastings]."

But Louisville coach Denny Crum had read Sutton's mind, and he inserted a 2-2-1 press that would prevent Reed from getting any decent look at the basket.

"Well, we knew that he was going to be the one that shot," Crum said. "They always put the ball in his hands at the end of tight games, and so we double-teamed him."

When Arkansas freshman Darrell Walker tried to inbound the ball, the Louisville press seemed ready to pounce on any pass farther than five feet away. Reluctantly, Walker tossed the inbounds to Reed, who was standing nearly 85 feet from the other hoop. The Louisville defense had also managed to shut off any looks at Hastings, so Reed would have to create an open look on his own. From the moment Reed headed up court, it was apparent the final play was turning into a disaster. Reed wasted the last five seconds trying to weave between his two defenders, spending as much time bouncing from side to side as he did dribbling up the floor. Finally, with one second remaining and 45 feet to go, Reed had no choice but to cast off the same shot he had been practicing during warmups.

"When I let it go, it felt good. It almost seemed like—I don't want to sound crazy—everything stopped, and everything was quiet," Reed said. "It was like a *Twilight Zone* kind of thing. You're focused. It was like you were in another realm."

Whether it was an alternate reality or divine intervention, there were definitely some larger forces at work as the ball sailed through the air. Reed, a future pastor, said a quick prayer. And on this particular day, his calls were answered, as the ball dropped in to give the Razorbacks the most unbelievable buzzer-beater of all time.

Reed's teammates ran over to pile on top of him, but this time he knew better. He had gone through that ordeal when he beat Texas earlier in the year, and this time he decided to run over to the sidelines and jump on top of the scorer's table.

Reed would manage to leave the scene unscathed, but the Louisville fans were not going to let him forget the shot that easily. After Reed was drafted by the CBA's Louisville Catbirds, fans made sure to treat him to a nice chorus of boos every time he entered the game. But compared with the mugging he was going to take from his teammates after the shot, perhaps a few boos weren't so bad after all. ●

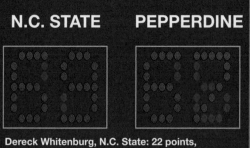

N.C. STATE PEPPERDINE

Dereck Whitenburg, N.C. State: 22 points,
4 assists, 1 rebound

1983: N.C. STATE vs. PEPPERDINE

For three consecutive games, the Wolfpack had made a habit of living on the edge. Needing to win the ACC Tournament to secure a spot in the NCAA Tournament, they had survived a trio of nail-biting finishes to arrive in the Big Dance. Their style of play had earned them the nickname "The Cardiac Kids," but in their first-round game against Pepperdine it appeared their dangerous play had finally caught up with them.

The Wolfpack missed their first 11 shots from the field, and when Dane Suttle hit a baseline jumper five minutes into the game, the Waves had taken an early 10–2 lead.

"I know that Pepperdine was favored, but sometimes it takes you a little bit when you're in that tournament," senior Thurl Bailey said. "It's a whole different ballgame from playing in your conference or the regular season. You don't get to see teams a lot and your preparation isn't as thorough."

N.C. State would actually go on a 19–5 run to grab a 21–15 lead late in the first half, but before long the lead was back in the hands of Pepperdine. And as the game headed into crunch time, it was the Waves who led 47–45. True to their billing, the Cardiac Kids managed to stave off defeat once again, tying the game late on a jumper by Terry Gannon, but minutes later their efforts appeared to be in vain. The teams went into overtime still tied at 47, but just as they had at the beginning of the game, the Wolfpack couldn't buy a basket. More than

three minutes of action had passed and still they had yet to score. Even worse, Pepperdine had pulled out to a 53–47 lead, and with no three-point line or shot clock in effect, a comeback seemed nearly impossible.

N.C. State coach Jim Valvano called a timeout to reorganize his players, who quickly found their touch from the floor. The only problem was that Pepperdine couldn't miss from the free throw line, and with a minute to go the gap was still six points. When Whittenburg missed the ensuing shot, the Waves not only had the 57–51 lead, they also had possession of the ball.

"We were trained as a collective team that as long as you're in a position to win, you're still in the game, so that was our overall mindset," Bailey said. "No matter what the time is, no matter what the score is, that you're in a position to win."

The Wolfpack took care of the first step by stealing the inbounds pass, which quickly led to a pair of free throws by Gannon. Pepperdine's Victor Anger added a free throw of his own to bring the score to 58–53, but when he missed his second attempt, N.C. State raced down for a fast-break layup. All of a sudden, with 48 seconds to go, the lead was down to just 58–55.

This time the Wolfpack chose to send Pepperdine's Mark Wilson to the line. Wilson hit one free throw to bring the lead back up to four, and even though Gannon missed the following shot to hand the ball right back, the Waves were still within reach. The Wolfpack didn't have the three-point line to work with, but they did have one big advantage at their disposal: There was also no double bonus. In 1983, the Waves had to shoot one-and-one free throws for the remainder of the game. It was a rule that would prove to be quite costly.

After Gannon's shot rimmed out, they were forced to foul the first person they could. Unfortunately for the Wolfpack, it happened to be Dane Suttle, one of the best free throw shooters in the country at 84 percent. But, as Bailey pointed out, "The tournament is a very intense time, even for decent free throw shooters."

Suttle, who had averaged more than 23 points per game, was the reigning WCC Player of the Year. But on this night, under this pressure, his first attempt was woefully short. As soon as his ball clanged off the front of the rim, the Wolfpack pushed the ball up the floor, and within five seconds they had another basket, this one courtesy of a Bailey dunk.

Now with the lead down to just 59–57, N.C. State was actually in the game. Pepperdine did the smart thing by inbounding the ball to Suttle. He had just missed his last free throw,

but if there was anybody the Waves wanted at the line, it was him. And with 20 seconds to go, the Wolfpack obliged.

One free throw would have likely put the game away. Two free throws would have certainly sealed the game. But when the sweet-shooting Suttle stepped to the line, his shot found everything but the net. The ball spun in and out of the basket, giving N.C. State one last chance. The Cardiac Kids were still alive.

They quickly got the ball to Dereck Whittenburg, who took it right at the most vulnerable man on the court. Suttle had made two critical errors to give the Wolfpack a chance, and now with the game on the line, he committed a third. With nine seconds to go, Suttle fouled Whittenburg, sending him to the line to try and do what Suttle could not. Just like Suttle, Whittenburg was his team's best free throw shooter. There was only one problem: He hadn't attempted a free throw all day.

Valvano, keenly aware of the dilemma, brought in Cozell McQueen and demanded that he switch sides with Lorenzo Charles, who was lined up on the left side of the free throw lane. Charles didn't think anything of it, but Valvano was adamant—he wanted McQueen, who was left-handed, to be on the left side of the lane for a potential putback. Sure enough, Whittenburg's free throw bounced off the rim and right into the hands of McQueen, who softly put it in with six seconds to go.

Suttle's last-second shot bounced off the rim, and after cheating death twice, the Cardiac Kids were exactly where they wanted to be. Now in double overtime, they eventually worked a 69–67 lead in the final minute, leaving them just one defensive stop away from a victory. Pepperdine worked the ball to Wilson, but his shot sailed wide, completing one of the most implausible comebacks in NCAA history. The Wolfpack had now survived four incredible finishes, and as it would turn out, game number five would be every bit as thrilling (see page 353). ●

Pepperdine's Orlando Phillips (34) faces some tough defense from Lorenzo Charles as he goes in for a layup. *Oregon State University Athletic Department. Photograph by Mike Shields.*

UNC WILMINGTON   **MARYLAND**

Drew Nicholas, Maryland: 22 points, 4 rebounds, 3 assists

2003: UNC-WILMINGTON VS. MARYLAND

If the Maryland Terrapins were looking for a sign of good things heading their way before the 2003 NCAA Tournament, they certainly would have been hard-pressed to find one. NCAA officials handed the Terps a six seed after they had spent most of the year ranked among the top 15 teams. As a result the team was forced to play UNC-Wilmington, a notorious bracket buster, in the first round. The Terrapins ventured out to Nashville to take on the Seahawks, but before they could even take the floor they had to call an audible. Somebody had stolen their jerseys.

"I know the equipment manager was real nervous telling me," Maryland coach Gary Williams laughed. "It's one of those things you can't make any excuses because of the color jersey you wore. You have to go play."

The Terrapins were scheduled to wear their white jerseys, but thankfully they had brought their red uniforms as well. UNCW had also packed both jerseys, so the game was allowed to continue without a further delay. All distractions aside, the game plan was still the same for Maryland. Williams told his players that Brett Blizzard, who had averaged more than 21 points per game for UNCW, needed to be stopped at all costs. The Terps knew they would have to leave somebody open to double-team Blizzard, and John Goldsberry seemed like the safest risk. The freshman had averaged fewer than five points per game and was considered more of a passer than a shooter.

And initially he didn't blame the Terps for thinking that way.

"To be honest with you, I've just never been a 20-point guy, really," Goldsberry said. "I've never had that mentality."

Of course, a player can only be left open for so long before he takes the shot. And when Goldsberry did decide to let a shot fly, it was pure. The Seahawks gave him another chance, and he delivered again. And again. And again.

"Once you make a few like I did in the game, it is a confidence booster. And from then on, it just felt good so I kept on doing it," Goldsberry said. "You're not thinking about if I'm going to be long or short or left or right. You're just shooting it because it feels good."

Goldsberry set an NCAA record by going 8-of-8 from the three-point line, one of which came just before halftime to put UNCW within three points of the Terrapins.

"That's always dangerous right before halftime if a team makes a run because they go in very positive into the locker room, ready to go to start the second half," Williams said. "When that happens to you, you have to get the players to understand that we can get it back."

The defense shifted its focus toward Goldsberry, giving Blizzard the one-on-one matchup he had been craving. Now it was his turn to shine. His three-pointer from the corner tied the game at 62 with six minutes left, and his triple from the left wing gave the Seahawks a 68–63 lead with 3:38 to play.

UNCW still led 71–69 in the last minute when Maryland point guard Steve Blake penetrated to the basket in hopes of kicking it back to an open teammate. The defense anticipated the pass and knocked it loose, but the ball trickled out to UM's Nik-Caner Medley. By this point Blake, who had been running along the baseline after losing the ball, was wide open. After he received a pass in the corner, the senior nailed the three-pointer to put Maryland in front 72–71.

The Seahawks held for the final shot, but Maryland gave them a huge break by violating the cardinal rule of last-minute defense— they committed a foul. Even worse, it came with only five seconds left on the clock. Aaron Coombs sank both shots, leaving the Terps 90 feet from the basket and needing a prayer to stay alive. Williams drew up a play to get the ball to Blake, but Nicholas knew the Seahawks were going to be as determined to stop Blake as the Terps had been to stop Blizzard.

"I specifically remember coming out of the timeout telling Tahj Holden, who was taking the ball out, I said 'Tahj, I'm going to be coming back to the ball, so if Blake's not open I'll be there,'" Nicholas said. "I didn't want to go home that night thinking about, well, what if, what if. If anything, I'm going to go out by something I did. At least I can live up to that responsibility."

Sure enough, Blake was smothered and Holden fired the pass to Nicholas near his own three-point line. With no time to spare, Nicholas made a beeline for the right wing, and just before the buzzer went off, he turned his body around and threw up a fadeaway shot from his left leg. But despite the low percentage, his biggest fan was also his biggest believer.

"Drew is as good a shooter as I've coached when he can get open and he can get a shot," Williams said. "He wasn't real open, but his shoulders were square. It was right in front of the bench, so I was right on line with the shot and it looked good all the way."

Yet the player taking the shot didn't exactly agree.

"To be honest, this is something that I tell everybody when they ask me about it, I thought it was an airball," Nicholas laughed. "I thought that my college career was over."

But as the shot sailed in the air as the horn sounded, it found its way toward the basket and dropped perfectly through the net. Nicholas sprinted into the locker room, as if the court couldn't contain his joy. Perhaps the only person happier than Nicholas was his brother, who was celebrating his thirtieth birthday.

"I told him I was going to get him 30 points and a win," Nicholas joked. "And it ended up being 22 and the game-winner."

Nicholas may have fell short of his mark, but it was a present his brother would take any day. ●

UNCW's John Goldsberry shot a record 8-of-8 from the three-point line, but his performance would be outshined by one magical shot by Maryland's Drew Nicholas. *UNCW Athletic Department. Photograph by John Domoney*

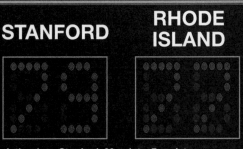

STANFORD **RHODE ISLAND**

Arthur Lee, Stanford: 26 points, 7 assists, 4 rebounds

1998: STANFORD
vs. RHODE ISLAND

To say that Stanford center Mark Madsen was having a rough start to his second week of the NCAA Tournament would be quite an understatement. NCAA officials scheduled Madsen and his teammates to play Rhode Island on a Sunday, despite knowing it conflicted with his Mormon beliefs. As if Madsen didn't have enough on his mind, Stanford's quarterly academic system required the basketball players to take their finals in the days leading up to their Elite Eight showdown. Studying wasn't normally an issue for Madsen, an economics major whose pre-game routine included reading *The Economist* and the *Wall Street Journal*. But with the biggest game of his life upon him, all of the pressure was overwhelming.

"I distinctly remember having a lot of academic work to do, and I remember studying in the bus going to and from practice and remember being so tired from practice, so tired of studying, I almost threw up," Madsen said. "I almost felt sick to my stomach. Everybody on the team was going through it."

If the outside distractions were an issue for the team, it certainly didn't show in the first half, as Stanford went into the locker room tied at 38–38. The second period was a different story altogether, as the Cardinal started ice cold to find themselves in a 60–49 hole with just 8:43 to go. They were able to cut the deficit to four points as the half continued, but when URI's Preston Murphy hit a pair of free throws, the gap widened to 66–60 with two minutes to play.

"There are times when you take timeouts, you think geez, what do you say? Anybody looking at it would have said they're done," Stanford coach Mike Montgomery said. "But at that stage, you've got two minutes to go to the Final Four, so what have you got to lose? So let's go for it!"

The message clearly resonated with point guard Arthur Lee, who laid in a shot to cut the lead to 66–62. And although Rhode Island guard Preston Murphy answered back with a jump shot of his own with just 1:34 to play, Lee was not to be denied. The junior raced down the floor and drained a three-pointer with 1:23 left to put Stanford within 68–65. Unfortunately for the Cardinal, their momentum seemed to stop there. Murphy came back with a free throw, and after junior Kris Weems missed a three-pointer on the other end, Stanford was forced to foul. Cuttino Mobley made both free throws for the Rams, and what had looked like a promising comeback was back to a six-point deficit with 59 seconds to play.

Stanford needed a bucket, and the plan was simple: get Arthur Lee the basketball. Sure enough, seconds later Lee sank another three-pointer to bring his team within 71–68.

"Arthur Lee basically went out there and almost single-handedly got us within striking distance. Once you get in striking distance, everyone's body language changes, everyone starts believing again," Madsen said. "You start saying to yourself, this is really doable."

The Cardinal once again sent Mobley to the line, and when the senior made just one of his free throws, Madsen took advantage by quickly laying in a bucket at the other end of the court. His basket cut the lead to just 72–70, and although Murphy would convert both of his free throw attempts to bring the lead back to four, the Cardinal weren't done yet.

Lee delivered with another three-pointer, this one coming the old-fashioned way. The junior was hammered by URI's Luther Clay on his way to the basket, but Lee still managed to put in the layup, as well as the ensuing free throw, to put Stanford within a point. The shot clock was turned off with just 32 seconds remaining, but Montgomery instructed the team to go for the steal or 10-second count. A foul was to be committed only as a last resort.

Arthur Lee's three-point play in the final minute sent the Cardinal to their first Final Four in 56 years. *Jonathan Daniel/Getty Images*

"I don't know that you give up the first two options with that amount of time left without giving yourself a chance," Montgomery said. "You never foul just to be fouling. You always try to get the steal first."

Montgomery made the smart decision of placing Lee on Mobley, who received the inbounds. While CBS broadcaster Al McGuire screamed, "You've got to foul, you've got to foul right away!" Lee followed his coach's orders and waited for the perfect moment to strike. As soon as he saw Mobley start to dribble with his left hand, Lee jabbed with his right hand and popped the ball loose. Madsen picked it up and soared toward the rim, where he was greeted hard by URI's Antonio Reynolds-Dean, who had inbounded the ball. Despite being fouled, Madsen powered right through Dean and slammed the ball with 26 seconds to go, giving Stanford an unbelievable 75–74 lead.

"That was one of those crazy comebacks where you can try 30 times and duplicate it and it probably isn't going to happen," Madsen said. "You have to give Arthur Lee a lot of credit. People like to focus on what he did offensively, but it was really a defensive thing that turned things around at the end."

As it turned out, Madsen's go-ahead basket came about by accident.

"After the game, Mike Montgomery said to me, 'Hey, you were in the wrong spot,' and I think I was. I don't know why I was in that spot," Madsen laughed. "I don't know if I was meant to be there or not, but I'm glad I made that mistake."

Madsen finished the play by converting the free throw to give Stanford a 76–74 lead, and after another defensive stop the Cardinal were headed to the Final Four.

Though the team had been relatively anonymous before the season began, it didn't take long for the players to realize they were suddenly a big deal. They went out to celebrate at a restaurant afterward, where they spotted Academy Award–winning actor Kevin Costner sitting unnoticed at his table. The Stanford players, on the other hand, were the center of attention. After all, people win Oscars every year. Scoring 19 points in the last two minutes of a game? That is something we may never see again. ●

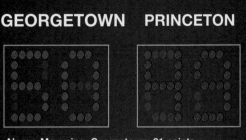

Alonzo Mourning, Georgetown: 21 points, 13 rebounds

1989: GEORGETOWN vs. PRINCETON

When the NCAA bracket came out on Selection Sunday, John Thompson III felt his heart pulling from two sides. The recent Princeton graduate saw that his alma mater would be matched up against Georgetown, where his dad was coaching. Most people had a much easier time deciding who to root for, as the similarities between the teams stopped there. The top-seeded Hoyas had four future NBA players in their starting lineup, while none of the Princeton players even dreamed of playing in the NBA, which may not have been the worst thing in the world. The basketball team was already ostracized enough to begin with.

"It's very different at the Ivy League schools, where I think there's kind of a division, at least in my experience, there's a division between the students that were there for academics purely and the athletes," said guard Bob Scrabis. "A lot of the professors had the feeling that the athletes were taking up a seat that should belong to somebody who is more gifted academically."

Unlike the Hoyas, who were worshiped during their brief stay on campus before heading to the NBA, the Tigers had to pay their own tuition and sat at the bottom of the social totem pole. Apparently, an Ivy League title wasn't good enough for their student body. Neither was it good enough for NCAA officials, who were considering restructuring their tournament.

"I remember in the press conference the night before the game, talking about removing the automatic bids from the smaller conferences—the Ivy League being one of them—and I remember getting very angered at that," Scrabis said. "To me, that is the true essence of the tournament. The first round of the NCAA Tournament is why people watch, in my opinion."

Even for a first-round game, this matchup garnered extra buzz, as it became the highest-rated college basketball game in ESPN's history. And what viewers saw was Dick Vitale showing up to the pre-game show in a Princeton sweater, promising to attend their next game in a cheerleading uniform if they pulled off the upset. As 25-point underdogs, it didn't appear to be a likely scenario, but for Princeton and coach Pete Carril, the odds were of no concern.

"As a team we just weren't intimidated, and Carril made it clear that we were playing to win," junior Matt Lapin said. "It didn't matter what everybody else thought as far as what our chances were."

And early on in the game, it was apparent that the Tigers had come to play. When Lapin hit a midrange jumper with 7:51 left in the first half, Princeton enjoyed a 15–10 lead. Lapin then added a three-pointer, and by the time he drove in for a layup minutes later, the lead had grown to 24–16.

The Tigers were not only scoring with incredible consistency, they were using the full shot clock almost every time, controlling the pace of the game. When Princeton went into the locker room with a 29–21 lead, 10 of its 13 field goals had come from layups. To top it all off, the Tigers had held Charles Smith, the Big East Player of the Year, completely scoreless. Scrabis reminded his teammates that there was plenty of time remaining, but the emotions could only be held in for so long.

"I think the key moment was coming out of halftime. Georgetown scored to start the second half, and we came back and answered it immediately and scored," Scrabis said. "You could hear it in the crowd as soon as we made that first basket in the second half. It was like we were right back in the game and people were like, 'Oh my God, this is happening.'"

Princeton was still clinging to a 37–30 lead midway through the second half when the Hoyas scored the next nine points to take their first lead of the game. But the Tigers continued to hang around, despite being outrebounded 17–1 in the half, and when Lapin nailed another three-pointer, his team was back in front 43–41.

The game was tied with a minute left when freshman Alonzo Mourning came up with a huge steal to give Georgetown possession. Junior Mark Tillmon misfired on a jump shot, creating a huge fight for the rebound, and on his fourth attempt to tip the ball in, Mourning was fouled. He converted the first free throw, but his second attempt hit off the rim and

right into the hands of Scrabis with 21 seconds remaining. Now Princeton had a chance to win the game, and Carill called a timeout with 15 seconds left to set up the perfect play.

The Tigers worked the ball to Scrabis, who circled around the three-point line, waiting for teammate Kit Mueller to run behind him. As soon as Scrabis felt Mueller's presence, he turned around to use Mueller as a screen, setting up what he thought was the game-winning shot. But once again Mourning found himself in the right place at the right time, swatting the ball away with just one second left.

"You got to hand it to him as a freshman for stepping up and doing what he did. He came out of nowhere," Scrabis said. "How many times do you sit in your backyard or you're on the playground and you don't leave until that shot goes in? But you don't have 6-foot-10 guys jumping out of the bushes coming to block your shot."

Time was not on Princeton's side, but the team looked as though it had one miracle left when Lapin got ready to inbound the ball. And had the officials given him the ball sooner, that miracle would have likely become a reality.

"I was trying to get the ref to give me the ball. I kept thinking give me the ball, let's get this going," said Lapin, who noticed that Mourning had left Mueller open underneath the basket. "Because I could have just lobbed it over and Kit would have had a layup."

While Lapin waited for the referee's signal to start the play, the Georgetown bench screamed over to Mourning to get back, and by the time Mueller caught the inbounds pass, Mourning was there for the game-saving block. The crowd, feeling Mueller had been fouled, responded with a loud chorus of boos. But as the Princeton players made their way off the court, the fans rose to their feet to applaud the Tigers, who had just saved the NCAA Tournament. No longer would mid-major teams worry about getting their shot in the Big Dance. They were now there to stay. ●

Alonzo Mourning made two blocks in the final eight seconds, including this one against Kit Mueller at the buzzer, to preserve Georgetown's 50–49 victory. *Manny Milan/Sports Illustrated/ Getty Images*

#43

DUKE **UNLV**

Christian Laettner, Duke: 28 points, 7 rebounds, 2 assists

1991: DUKE vs. UNLV

Several months had passed since his team's loss to UNLV in the 1990 title game, and still Bobby Hurley could not shake the images from his mind. The Duke point guard had not been solely responsible for his team's 103–73 drubbing at the hands of the Rebels, but he had certainly played his part. The freshman had missed all of his shot attempts, but what really haunted him long after the game had passed were his five turnovers.

"You felt humiliated," Hurley said. "I can't remember a loss that I personally took harder than that one, just because of the setting, what was at stake, and to have that type of performance—even to this day I'm not happy with the effort I had there."

The loss so affected Hurley that he began having nightmares on a regular basis. The main culprit of the night terrors seemed to be none other than UNLV coach Jerry "Tark the Shark" Tarkanian.

"I would be in some type of water, even pools, and there were sharks coming after me," Hurley recalled. "I never got analyzed on that, why I was having those, but I was for a while."

Hurley was probably not the only victim of Tarkanian and his squad. Heading into their 1991 rematch against the Blue Devils, UNLV had won 45 straight games, few of which had ever been in doubt. The Rebels boasted college basketball's Player of the Year in forward Larry Johnson, and they showed no indication that anybody could stop them from repeating.

"There were about 30 people in the whole world who thought we had a chance to win," Duke forward Christian Laettner said. "The players, the coaches, and the people who work with the team."

In the days before the game, Duke coach Mike Krzyzewski took each individual aside and showed him clips from the previous year's game. It wasn't easy, but Krzyzewski had managed to find the few highlights as proof that the team was indeed capable of playing with the Rebels. Only this time they would have to give that kind of performance for 40 minutes. Coach K wasn't guaranteeing that would translate into a victory, but they would at least give themselves a chance. And considering the Rebels had rarely faced any close games over the previous two years, the Blue Devils would have a huge advantage heading down the stretch

"Externally, we approached it like we were the underdog and didn't have a chance. I don't usually do that. But internally, it was just the opposite. We felt like we were going to win and we had a lot of time to prepare," Krzyzewski said. "We were really wired for that game. What a lot of people don't realize, we also had Grant Hill, who was the most talented player on the court. Nobody knew that yet."

Duke was playing 600 miles away from Cameron Indoor Stadium, but there was little question whom the Indianapolis crowd would be pulling for. UNLV had developed a reputation for being a bully on and off the court, something the players did little to dissuade. Tarkanian's players refused to sign any autographs during their stay, while the Blue Devils, on the other hand, staged a dunk contest during their Final Four practice, much to the delight of the local fans.

And when it actually counted, the fans still had plenty to cheer about as Duke raced out to a 15–6 lead. The Rebels were only three possessions behind, but it was a start the Blue Devils would take any day. UNLV would fight back to take a 43–41 lead at halftime, but Krzyzewski's players were still hanging around, and just one minute into the second half they snatched the lead right back.

Even if the Blue Devils eventually surrendered their lead, it was the best fight any UNLV opponent had given in well over a year. The Rebels had faced only three deficits that season, and had only trailed for 80 seconds in the second half. Now they were fighting just to keep pace with Duke. The first order of business for Tarkanian was to get the ball to guard Anderson Hunt, who had scored 29 points on the Blue Devils a year earlier. This night Hunt would again tally 29 points, and the more he continued to make shots, the more his teammates wanted to feed him the ball.

By the time Hunt completed a three-point play with just over 13 minutes left, he had scored all 14 of his team's second-half points, and the Rebels' backcourt was outscoring Duke's by a ridiculous 40–16 margin. Nevertheless, the score was still tied at 57, and two minutes later, the Blue Devils pulled back in front 64–59. Tarkanian entered the game with 599 career victories, but if he was going to get win No. 600, he had some work to do.

The Rebels would eventually grab the lead back at 76–71, but not without a price. With 3:51 to go, UNLV point guard Greg Anthony collided into Duke's Brian Davis, resulting in a charge. Anthony, who had scored 16 points in the first half, would be watching the rest of the game from the sidelines.

"When Greg Anthony fouled out, that was a real turning point in that game. He was their leader," Hurley said. "When he was out of the game, it was different. They weren't as organized. Anderson had to slide over and play point guard. They weren't the same team without him on the floor."

Hurley quickly nailed a three-pointer to bring the Blue Devils within 76–74, and on the next possession, his team found out just how crucial Anthony's departure would be. For the first time all year, the Rebels failed to beat the shot clock buzzer, handing the ball right back to Duke. With just over a minute to go, Grant Hill, Krzyzewski's secret weapon, drove in toward the basket before dishing the ball off to Davis at the last minute. Hill's drive had done just enough to draw George Ackles out of position, and Davis easily blew past him as he went in for the game-tying layup. Nevertheless, as Davis released the ball Ackles tried to swipe at it from behind. What he actually caught was the arm of Davis, who still managed to make the shot despite the foul. With the ensuing free throw, the Blue Devils took a 77–76 lead with just 57 seconds remaining.

Larry Johnson had a chance to put UNLV back in front when he stepped to the free throw line with 49.9 seconds to go, but both of his shots fell short. Fortunately for him, Duke sophomore Thomas Hill stepped into the lane during the second free throw, giving Johnson a third attempt from the line. This time he rattled it home to tie the game for the seventeenth time.

Hill (no relation to Grant) tried to make up for his mental error by driving in for the game-winning shot. His jumper from 10 feet away rimmed in and out, but teammate Christian Laettner was there for the rebound. Laettner was fouled as soon as he caught the ball, sending him to the line with 12.7 seconds to go. Tarkanian called a timeout to try to ice Laettner, which seemed to be a good idea, considering two years earlier Laettner had missed a pair of free throws in the final seconds to lose a game against Arizona. But what it also did was give Laettner, who had played every second of the contest, a moment to catch his breath. As he came over to the bench, he smiled at Krzyzewski and simply said, "I got 'em, Coach."

True to his word, the junior swished both to put Duke up 79–77, and when Hunt's desperation shot clanged off the back of the rim moments later, Duke had done the impossible. Goliath was defeated. ●

SANTA CLARA   ARIZONA

Pete Eisenrich, Santa Clara: 19 points

#42

1993: SANTA CLARA vs. ARIZONA

When a team shows up to a game as a 25-point underdog, people are usually a little hesitant to put any faith in its chances. Such was the case in 1993, when Santa Clara showed up to take on second-seeded Arizona, which had won 22 of its last 23 games. Fans in Salt Lake City hoped for the best, but the game appeared to be a foregone conclusion.

What is more surprising, however, is that NCAA officials had even less faith in the Broncos than anybody else. They arranged for the team to stay downtown at the Red Lion Inn, fully aware that a convention taking place the following day would prevent any extended stay for the team. But with oddsmakers considering a 24-point blowout a success for Santa Clara, such matters were of little concern to the tournament's governing body. Fortunately, the team had at least one believer in coach Dick Davey.

"I sat them down one day and said, 'Hey listen, you can play with anybody. I don't care who it is we're going to play, I know you can play with anybody,'" Davey said. "It's not who you play, it's how you play, and I think that's important."

The message sank in, and right from the start of the game the Broncos were ready to go. Arizona had an early 7–4 lead, but Santa Clara scored the next seven points, and before long the Broncos had built up a 33–21 lead.

"I hate to say this but I think they took us for granted. I think they thought, okay, we'll put them away, we'll put them away, our time

will come," senior John Woolery said. "You could tell they were playing harder and they were fighting for it, they were competing for it. I think they thought we'd go away, and we weren't going to go away."

If the Wildcats needed any confirmation that the Broncos weren't backing down, all it took was a little trash talking from Arizona's Damon Stoudamire, a decision that made him look quite foolish.

"I stole it from Stoudamire once early, and he told me that will never happen again," said Woolery, who smiled minutes later after repeating the same feat. "To be honest, I was thinking it can't be this easy. I just thought we were getting everything we wanted."

The team knew that Arizona was going to make a run, but nobody anticipated just how severe it would be. Over the last five minutes of the first half, the Wildcats went on a 14–0 run to take a 35–33 lead into the break. But instead of recuperating at halftime, the Broncos went on another five-minute scoreless streak, and by the time Mark Schmitz finally ended the drought, Arizona had scored the last 25 points of the game. Yet Davey, the eternal optimist, still believed his team was in a good position to win the game, despite the 46–33 deficit.

"I knew I had to do something so I called a timeout. And I sat along the bench for two minutes and 15 seconds, about how long a timeout lasts in the NCAA, and never said a word. And they looked at me and I looked at them and never said a word, and then my genius came into play and I said, 'Gentlemen, we have to score,'" laughed Davey. "So you just see how important coaching is. You have to really be astute at the game."

Soon after the huddle, forward Pete Eisenrich came alive, scoring 9 of Santa Clara's 13 points as they battled back from a 50–41 hole to take a 54–53 lead with just over two minutes left to play. The offensive production was matched by their defense, as the Broncos held Arizona to just 1-of-15 shooting during the stretch. Santa Clara pushed the lead to 58–55 with a minute to go, and after another Arizona miss, the Wildcats resorted to fouling. The man they chose was Steve Nash, who would go on to become the best free throw shooter in NBA history. But in 1993, Nash was just a freshman, and at times he struggled to find his touch.

"When he was a freshman, about a month into his freshman year, we sat down in the bleachers one day and he told me, 'I don't know if I can play college basketball,'" Davey said. "John Woolery was eating him up defensively, causing all kinds of problems for him."

Fortunately for Santa Clara, Nash stuck with it, coming in after practice and working out until 1 o'clock each morning. And as he stepped to the line, Nash would finally be able to see if all that hard work would pay off.

"We kind of looked at him and he said, 'I'll make these free throws,'" Woolery recalled. "He would have literally floored me if he had missed any of those."

Six free throws later, after six attempts, Woolery was still standing. However, thanks to some late magic from Arizona, the Wildcats still had a chance to tie the game when they inbounded the ball with five seconds remaining. Stoudamire, who caught the entry pass, managed to race all the way to Santa Clara's three-point line before hoisting a shot just before the buzzer.

"We just said no fouls, that was it. And it looked like he was going to make it," Woolery said. "I remember that feeling, thinking holy crap, he's going to make this thing."

But fortunately for the Broncos, the ball bounced off the rim, sending the arena into absolute pandemonium. Pulling off the perhaps biggest upset in tournament history?

Check. Acting like they had been there before? That was a different story. Despite the rough treatment from the NCAA, the players were more than happy to pick up everything that tournament organizers were tossing after the game, preferring to call them souvenirs.

"There's all this stuff they're throwing away, the banners, and I remember our guys are like, 'Hey, can I have that?'" Woolery laughed. "The banner of the regional and the year, the water bottles, and the guy's like, 'Yeah, it's all trash anyways.' We go back and we got a guy who's got the logo and the big banners up in their dorm."

The NCAA may have been trying to discard all reminders of the game, but the fact still remained that Santa Clara needed a place to stay, which was more than a little problem.

"At six in the morning I started getting phone calls from press people in New York and all over the country. Obviously it was a pretty big story that next day, and one of the calls was from the hotel saying that we were going to have to move out," Davey said. "And I got with our assistant athletic director and told her, 'Hey, we're not going anywhere.'"

The NCAA caught a huge break when all the Arizona fans went home early, leaving more than enough space at their hotel for the Santa Clara contingent. Needless to say, when Nash led the Broncos back to the tournament his junior and senior years, the NCAA had plenty of rooms to spare. ●

Mark Schmitz and Steve Nash enjoy what is arguably the biggest upset in tournament history.
Robert Borea/AP Photo

#41

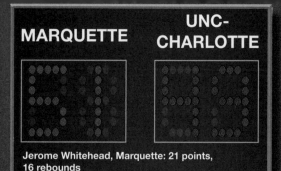
1977: MARQUETTE vs. UNC-CHARLOTTE

For a team that had competed in Division I for only five years, UNC-Charlotte's appearance in the 1977 Final Four was nothing short of remarkable. The team had never been to the NCAA Tournament before, but thanks to the play of Cedric Maxwell, the 49ers swept through their opponents to reach the sport's biggest stage. Facing them would be Marquette, a team that was considered by many to be the title favorite heading into the season. Yet by the time Marquette arrived at the Final Four, it was the Warriors who had become America's most improbable team.

Everything had gone according to plan at the start of the season, as MU raced out to a 14–2 record. But after suffering a one-point heartbreak at the hands of Cincinnati, the Warriors then registered their fourth loss of the season against DePaul. And when the Warriors lost yet another one-point game, this one on a last-second shot to Detroit, coach Al McGuire told his players that they would probably miss the NCAA Tournament.

"We were losing to teams that we had no business losing to, and we were kind of falling apart at the seams," sophomore Jim Boylan said. "Midway through the season, we were on no one's radar and kind of just limping along and trying to figure out a way we could make it into the tournament. So we scrapped and fought and came together."

But team bonding does not always equal success, and in their next game, the last home game for the retiring McGuire, the Warriors lost by 11 points to unranked Wichita State. Both McGuire and senior Bo Ellis were thrown out of the game, and the team was showered with a chorus of boos.

"We were in quite a bad way at that time as a team," Boylan said. "We had five games at the end of the season, all on the road. And we felt like if we wanted to even get in the tournament—because at the time it was not as big as it is now—we felt like if we even wanted to have a chance to get in, we needed to win all five games, and they were on the road against good teams."

The Warriors recovered to win the first four games, resulting in a phone call from the NCAA. At halftime of their final game against Michigan, McGuire alerted his team that Marquette had been invited to the NCAA Tournament. As if NCAA officials needed any further skepticism in what was likely their last selection, the Warriors went back out and lost their finale to the Wolverines, again by one point.

But Marquette proved everybody wrong by pulling off one upset after another to set up a meeting with the 49ers. Still riding the momentum from their recent success, the Warriors held UNC-Charlotte to just three field goals for much of the first half, resulting in a 23–9 lead. UNCC's Lew Massey decided it was time to put an end to the run, and his three shots at the end of the first half helped bring the 49ers within three points. After the break, Massey hit another trio of baskets to give UNCC its first lead at 30–28, and when Ellis recorded his fourth foul minutes later, they had pushed the lead to five.

"To this day, that's the hardest game I ever remember in my life," Marquette guard Butch Lee said. "I was thinking that we were going to win the national championship, and they just kept running through my mind, like this cannot be happening. How are we going to win the championship if we don't win this game?"

Jerome Whitehead was able to match Massey's effort, hitting four big shots to put Marquette back in front 44–39, but Charlotte came right back once again. Eight straight points by the 49ers put them up 47–44 with just 1:41 remaining.

The Warriors had proven their inability to close out games all year long, but they picked the right time to change their habits. Lee connected on a jumper to put the team within a point, and after a defensive stop, he nailed another jump shot to give Marquette the lead with 30 seconds to go. A crucial stop on the other end gave Marquette junior Gary Rosenberger a chance to ice the game with two free throws, but the senior missed the second shot with 13 seconds left to give Charlotte one last chance. This time Cedric "Cornbread" Maxwell made the Warriors pay, as his shot from 10 feet out tied the game at 49 with just three seconds to spare.

The normally fiery McGuire calmly asked for a timeout to stop the clock and see if Lee could throw the ball the length of the court. After getting confirmation from the senior that he could, McGuire simply replied, "Butch, just let it go."

Standing underneath his own hoop, Lee took a step and hurled the ball toward Ellis at the top of the key, but the pass sailed over his outstretched hands and toward Maxwell, who had been guarding Ellis from behind. Cornbread managed to get a finger on the ball, but his deflection tipped it right to Whitehead, the closest player to the basket. Whitehead, who like everyone else had been facing the pass, took a dribble while he turned his body toward the basket and went up to dunk the ball. Once again Maxwell got a piece of it, this time just enough to knock the ball out of Whitehead's hands and send it flying toward the backboard.

The play only got more chaotic once the ball bounced off the glass and back toward the rim. Whitehead was still holding onto the rim as the ball rolled off his hand and into the hoop as the clock struck zero. Both coaches immediately made their way over to the scorer's table to see what the ruling would be.

"We fouled them, Jerome got fouled on the shot, Jerome could have been called for offensive goaltending—all those things happened," Boylan laughed. "It happened in the blink of an eye, and I think the referees, they weren't worried about what had happened. They were just concerned about whether or not the ball had gone in the basket before the buzzer sounded."

Even that part is debatable, but there is no argument that the play was one of the most exciting in NCAA history. "When I see that pass, that's incredible that we were able to make that happen. We never practiced anything like that, and I don't know if you can," Lee said. "I just tried to make the best pass that I could, getting it close to the basket."

McGuire, who helped popularize the term "March Madness," had now seen just how crazy March could be. ●

Butch Lee, seen here celebrating with coach Al McGuire, threw the full-court pass that set up the game-winning shot. *AP Photo*

ARKANSAS   DUKE

76   72

Corliss Williamson, Arkansas: 23 points

1994: ARKANSAS vs. DUKE

Scotty Thurman was 12 years old when he watched Indiana's Keith Smart take one of the biggest shots in basketball history. With his team trailing 73–72 in the final moments of the 1987 championship game, Smart hit a baseline jumper, instantly catapulting him into basketball lore. With one shot, Smart had not only became a hero in the eyes of IU fans, he had instantly become a national celebrity. No one would ever have a chance to make a bigger shot than Smart, but seven years later Thurman would have a chance to come awfully close.

Unlike Smart, who was returning to his hometown of New Orleans to play in the title game, Thurman and his Arkansas teammates had few allies in the Charlotte Coliseum. Facing them in the title game were the Duke Blue Devils, who not only hailed from nearby Durham, but had also won the national championship in 1991 and 1992. Thurman knew that the crowd would be hostile. What he didn't expect was that the refs would be just as bad. After trying to reason with one of the officials over a call in the opening minutes, the referee made it clear he was not in the mood for a discussion.

"I think I was arguing about a call or something or complaining about some of the rules and he just told me, 'Don't say anything else,'" Thurman said. "And I told him that was fine, I'll let my game do the talking. That was kind of that."

That sort of remark by a referee would normally turn coaches livid, but Arkansas coach Nolan Richardson was not about to let a motivational opportunity slip by. Richardson had been the driving force behind Arkansas' season, reminding his players that they never received the respect they deserved. The goal was to take their anger out on their opponents, and this night would be no different.

"You felt like it was us against the world anyway, so when we were playing the game we felt like the referees didn't want to see us do well either," Thurman said. "We still wanted to come out and prove everybody wrong."

Richardson's feelings toward the officiating would turn out to be worse than he feared. The Razorbacks wouldn't step to the free throw line until nearly six minutes had expired in the second half. Thurman used the unbalanced officiating as more fuel, tallying seven points in the opening period as the Razorbacks kept pace with Duke. The sophomore would hit a three-pointer near the end of the half to give Arkansas a 34–33 lead going into the break. It would be a sign of things to come.

But early in the second half, it appeared that Thurman would never have a chance to make history. The Blue Devils came out of the locker room with a renewed sense of purpose, scoring 15 of the first 19 points to take a commanding 48–38 lead. Richardson called a timeout and gathered his players as he tried to yell over the buzzing Duke crowd.

"Calm down," Richardson implored. "We're going to get back in it. Don't panic."

Thurman responded with a short jumper to bring the lead back down to eight, and he knocked down a three-pointer minutes later to cut the lead to 50–45. Arkansas didn't slow down, scoring 14 of the next 18 points to take the lead back at 59–54. The lead was still five with just over three minutes to play when the Blue Devils began to close in. Antonio Lang came back down to hit a pair of free throws for Duke, and after three straight empty possessions by Arkansas, Duke senior Grant Hill knotted the game at 70 with a three-pointer from the top of the key.

Richardson again called timeout, hoping to set up a better shot than what he had been seeing as of late. But when his team took the floor, what Richardson saw was a catastrophe playing out before his eyes. The shot clock continued to tick down as the Razorbacks failed to establish anything resembling an open look. Finally, with six seconds remaining, junior Corey Beck attempted to slash into the lane, where he was greeted by a swarm of Blue Devils. Beck tossed the ball back out to Dwight Stewart, who would have had an open look had he not fumbled the pass. But by the time Stewart retrieved the ball, he was met with a hand in his face,

forcing him to shuffle the ball to Thurman at the last possible second.

"Actually, I saw Dwight Stewart catch the pass and I thought that he was going to shoot it, but when he fumbled the ball I just kind of popped back out to the wing in a split-second," Thurman said. "And he threw it to me, and when I caught it, I had already looked at the shot clock so I knew I had to shoot it. I just caught it and let it go."

Thurman's look was no better than Stewart's would have been. Lang was standing just inches away, forcing Thurman into a high-arching three just to get the ball out of Lang's reach. The shot clock had expired long before the ball ever reached its destination. But when it finally did, it sailed through to give Arkansas a 73–70 lead with just 50 seconds remaining. And after a pair of huge defensive stops, the Razorbacks were national champions for the first time in school history.

"Believe it or not, I've lived in Arkansas now for 15, 16 years and not a day goes by it doesn't come up at least once throughout the day, at least multiple times," Thurman said. "And walking into the people that you see on the street or in the grocery store or in a restaurant, just knowing how many lives that you've touched by just playing a game of basketball, that's probably the biggest thing." ●

Scotty Thurman's three-pointer with 50 seconds left proved to be the game-winner in Arkansas' 76–72 victory. *John Biever/Sports Illustrated/Getty Images*

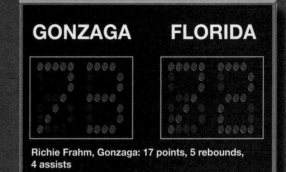

GONZAGA **FLORIDA**

Richie Frahm, Gonzaga: 17 points, 5 rebounds, 4 assists

#39

1999: GONZAGA vs. FLORIDA

When Gonzaga coach Dan Monson brought his players together to watch the NCAA Tournament selection show in 1998, he knew that the team's chances of getting into the Big Dance were slim. The team had won 23 games and most likely deserved a bid, but it was doubtful the selection committee would see eye-to-eye with his club. Sure enough, when the show ended, the bracket had been filled and the Zags were nowhere to be seen. It was not something they were going to let happen again.

"That summer is when we decided to dedicate ourselves to get to the NCAA Tournament because we realized that it was actually a reality," junior Richie Frahm said. "I think we took it more as a job, and we all had a chip on our shoulder knowing we all have to work a little bit harder than those other schools if we wanted to beat them."

It didn't take long for the new attitude to take form, as the Zags cruised through the conference schedule and arrived back at the conference championship game. The Bulldogs had lost only six games on the year, but a repeat of the previous season was not something they were willing to risk.

"There's no way that we're going to be sitting there on Selection Sunday where we think we're a bubble team and watch ourselves not make the NCAA Tournament," said guard Matt Santangelo, who led the Bulldogs to a 91–66 win in the conference title game.

"And then once we got there, it was like wait a second, let's go make some noise. This isn't good enough, this group's better than that."

And a week later, the Bulldogs were still alive after upsets over Minnesota and Stanford. Their next game against Florida would be for a spot in the Elite Eight, but Monson was going to make sure his players stayed grounded. Sure, their early tournament success had made them the talk of the tournament. But before leaving for their first-round game, the Zags had made a mess of the brand new locker room, an infraction that Monson had not forgotten.

"They had hair in the shower and hadn't cleaned it up. I told them that you didn't do that, and you guys are going to lose privileges in the locker room," Monson remembered. "I said you guys better hope you don't win both these games this week, because you don't have a locker room when you get back."

But now that the team was still alive, Monson needed to stick by his word.

"So we got back and we won both of those games, and I locked them out and we had media everywhere," Monson laughed. "And of course a guy like Casey Calvary is making a big scene. He's changing his shorts in the bleachers with all this media before we went to Phoenix."

When the Zags arrived, they were even less intimidated by the Gators than they were of changing in front of the cameras. Gonzaga grabbed an early 18–10 lead, and by the time Florida coach Billy Donovan called a timeout with 5:30 left in the first half, the gap had widened to 26–13.

The Gators came out of the timeout fired up, tying the game at 27, but as the second half got underway the Bulldogs managed to pull away once again. For the first eight minutes, they shot 70 percent from the field to take a 52–44 lead, while holding the Gators to just 1-of-16 from the three-point line. The Gators finally found their touch as senior Greg Stolt hit a three-pointer to cut the lead to five, and when teammate Major Parker hit another three, they had tied the game at 56. It was appearing that Gonzaga's one weakness might be coming back to haunt them.

"One thing that the coaching staff was kind of worried about with our group was they thought we were all too nice," said Santangelo, who put himself through humiliation each day in practice by playing against ex-Zag John Stockton. The NBA Hall of Famer won the majority of the battles, but the losses helped improve Santangelo's thirst for winning. "What it instilled in us was okay, great, you can be gentlemen, you can be friends, but you got to find ways to win ballgames."

So even when Stolt hit another three-pointer with 46 seconds left to put Florida up 72–69, the Zags refused to quit. Frahm fired a pass to Jeremy Eaton underneath the basket with 20 seconds left, and his layup cut the lead to one. Monson instructed guard Quentin Hall to foul only if he would be unable to come up with a turnover, a decision that worked to perfection.

"We had the one trap and Quentin just hesitated before he fouled and we were yelling from the bench, 'Get him, Quentin!'" Monson remembered as he watched Hall apply the pressure to Florida's Brent Wright. "Quentin had an instinct there—that the kid was a little hesitant and a little bit rattled."

Wright tried to stop as he picked up his dribble, but he dragged his left foot, resulting in a travel and Gonzaga possession with 17 seconds to play. When Hall received a pass with eight seconds left, he decided to attack to the hoop, letting a runner fly from just inside the free throw line. From the moment it left his hands, however, the shot looked way long.

"But one of the things we always instructed in those situations is when a shot goes up, you have to assume the miss and you have to have the rebound or foul trying," said Monson, as the ball caromed off the backboard and straight to Casey Calvary. "And that's where Casey's at his best, as an offensive rebounder. He's so athletic, and when Quentin missed that shot he went up there and got a piece of it."

His tip-in gave the Zags a 73–72 lead with four seconds to play, but Eddie Shannon weaved through the defense to give himself a look from the three-point line as time expired.

"We just held our breath that whole possession. He made an amazing play to get the ball down court," Frahm said. "It was just one of those things where I've lost games at the buzzer before when guys hit shots in high school and college. It's one of those moments where you're like, oh gosh, this could be another one of those."

But thankfully for Gonzaga, the ball rimmed out, and as announcer Gus Johnson proclaimed of the Cinderella story, "The Slipper Still Fits!" Assistant coach Billy Grier jumped on Monson's back, while the players piled on Calvary.

"It was just overwhelming emotionally for us," laughed Frahm, who kissed Calvary on the head in the dogpile. "I still hold my breath every time I watch that play just because you think Eddie Shannon's shot is going to miraculously go in."

As soon as the players got back to the hotel room, they all headed straight for the pool and jumped in with their uniforms still on, another moment that was captured by television cameras. One brave reporter asked for an interview, and the Zags gladly obliged on one condition—she had to jump in the pool just like they did. So the country watched as Fox's Angie Arlati, still in formal clothing, conducted a poolside interview with a team that looked equally unfit to be in the water. Awkward? Yes. Hilarious? Absolutely. ●

#38

1998: KENTUCKY vs. DUKE

Six years had passed since Christian Laettner destroyed Kentucky's dream season in 1992, but the wounds from the game had not exactly healed quickly. The Wildcats never got a chance to face the Blue Devils after that game, so for the better part of the '90s, Duke had the last laugh.

"Every person who's ever worn a Kentucky jersey can say without a doubt, if you ask them, the most annoying part about March every year during March Madness is how many times they show that shot," junior Scott Padgett said. "Even though it's not a natural rivalry because we don't play each other that often, if you ask fans and people at Kentucky, it's probably the team you hate the most just because of that shot and that moment."

In that game, Sean Woods made a running layup to give Kentucky a 104–103 lead with just 2.2 seconds remaining. Needing a miracle, Laettner caught a 70-foot pass from Grant Hill and nailed a turnaround jumper at the buzzer to send the Blue Devils to the Final Four. A spot in the Final Four was also on the line in the 1998 rematch, and it was every bit as epic.

Kentucky traded shots with Duke early on, and the Wildcats trailed only 21–20 midway through the half. Over the next four minutes, however, the Blue Devils played nearly perfect basketball, scoring on every possession and forcing Kentucky into a barrage of charges and turnovers. By the time Kentucky coach Tubby

Smith called a timeout with 7:21 left, his team faced a 38–20 deficit.

"There was an unspoken calmness, even though we were down and kind of up against being knocked out of the tournament, we just simply had the maturity to continue to play," senior Jeff Sheppard said. "I always had the belief that we could make a comeback."

The Wildcats did just that, as five different players scored in a three-minute stretch to bring them back within six. But after fighting through the whole half to stay within striking distance, the Blue Devils hit a couple of late shots, including one at the buzzer, to give them a double-digit lead heading into halftime.

Kentucky started to develop a little rhythm in the second half, but the Blue Devils just continued where they left off in the opening period. Back-to-back rebounds for Duke set up Chris Carrawell's easy putback to give his team a 71–54 lead with 9:38 on the scoreboard.

Unable to tolerate the tension anymore, Padgett's girlfriend, a volleyball player at UK, left her seat to stand by herself outside. What she missed was one of the most remarkable comebacks in NCAA history.

UK's Wayne Turner followed back-to-back Kentucky three-pointers with a three-point play of his own, and in just over a minute, the Wildcats had cut the lead to 71–63. Allen Edwards followed a Duke free throw with yet another three-pointer, and Sheppard's free throw eventually cut the lead to 72–71 with six minutes to go.

But the Blue Devils weren't done yet, and as the three-minute mark approached they still led by four. Just when it appeared the Wildcats were through, however, they made one final push. Turner hit a runner to bring the Cats to within two, and after another stop on the defensive side, Kentucky had a chance finally to take its first lead of the game. Wayne Turner brought up the ball and attacked the basket, floating a ball in the air that caromed off the back of the rim. UK's Heshimu Evans, sandwiched between two Blue Devils, got just enough of the ball to tip it near the three-point line, where Cameron Mills was standing by himself. Having missed all six of his shots during the tournament, Mills was faced with the decision of passing the ball or taking the biggest shot of his life.

"In every sport, you don't want to think, you want to react," Mills said. "In basketball, especially in that moment, there was no thinking at all."

Mills opted for the shot, and he drained it to put the Wildcats ahead 80–79, but Duke quickly answered with two free throws. Moments later the Blue Devils returned the favor by sending Padgett to the line for some free throws of his own. By this time, Padgett's future wife was back in her seat, watching as he stepped to the line. But Padgett, who had never missed an NCAA Tournament free throw in his life, missed the second to leave the score tied.

Padgett would get a chance to redeem himself a minute later. After Duke's Sean Avery missed a turnaround in the lane, Heshimu Evans cleared the board for Kentucky and tossed it over to Turner. Using a screen by Padgett, Turner drove to his left, taking his teammate's defender with him. When he threw the ball back to Padgett, there was nobody within seven feet of the shooter.

"If he threw that ball back to me a million times, I would shoot it a million—I would never pass that shot up," Padgett said. "As soon as I let it go, I knew it was good."

And Padgett was correct, nailing the shot to give Kentucky an 84–81 cushion. Although Mills and Padgett were roommates who had a knack for clutch shooting, that was the extent of their similarities. Mills had arrived in Lexington carrying a little excess weight, while Padgett had come in as a 6-foot-9 freshman weighing 205 pounds.

"They're having me eat a 10,000-calories-a-day kind of diet to gain weight, and he's on the not-allowed-to-eat diet," Padgett joked. "I'm sitting there every night stuffing my face with food, and he's sitting over in the room licking his chops wishing he could eat."

Fortunately by their senior years, both players were at ideal form, and thanks to their clutch shooting UK was now just 39 seconds from the Final Four. Turner added another free throw on their next possession to put the Wildcats up 85–81, but with eight seconds left Duke's Roshown McCleod hit a three-pointer, cutting the lead to just a point. After another free throw by Turner with four seconds remaining, Duke would once again be inbounding the ball at their baseline, looking for a miracle finish. The game was set up for an identical ending.

"I called my best friend after Sean Woods hit the running bank shot, and screamed into the phone, 'We're going to do it!'" Mills remembered of the 1992 game. "Laettner hit the shot and I laid down on the floor."

This time, however, the Wildcats made sure there was somebody guarding the inbounder, and instead of heaving the ball the length of the court, Duke had to settle for a five-foot pass. With only a few seconds to set up a shot, Avery was forced to fire a halfcourt prayer that hit the backboard and bounced away. And as the buzzer sounded, all the pains from six years earlier were gone. ●

1975: UCLA vs. LOUISVILLE

When the UCLA Bruins found themselves matched up against the University of Louisville in the 1975 Final Four, it felt as though they were looking in a mirror. At the helm for the Cardinals was Denny Crum, who had not only played for the Bruins but had also coached them as an assistant under John Wooden. As UCLA's primary recruiter for several years, he was actually the man responsible for bringing in most of the players he would now be facing. When Crum decided to take the coaching job at Louisville, he took Wooden's system and basketball philosophies with him. And while the Bruins knew what to expect from the Cardinals, that didn't necessarily mean it would be easy to stop them.

Louisville came out hitting eight of its first 10 shots, and eight minutes into the game the score was already 23–13. UCLA stormed back to tie the game at 29 on Richard Washington's layup, but a late burst from the Cardinals put them back in front 37–33 at halftime. The Bruins, who hadn't trailed at halftime of an NCAA Tournament game from 1963 to 1974, were now 20 minutes away from elimination. Wooden decided to keep that fact to himself to avoid any added pressure on his players. According to Bill Walton, who had won two championships with Wooden a few years before, UCLA was never out of a game as long as the coach still had faith.

"When Bill graduated in '74, he says, 'Now you guys have a really good chance of winning

next year. I predict that you guys can win it all. But this is what you do, Ralph, when you get insecure on the floor. Look over in coach Wooden's eyes, and he'll look into your eyes and he will impute confidence to you,'" senior Ralph Drollinger recalled. "So he says, 'Just make sure you always do that.'"

Despite the Bruins' feeling of invigoration, the Cardinals were able to match their intensity and continued to hold onto the lead. By the time Drollinger fouled out with more than six minutes remaining, the chances of a Bruin comeback appeared to be slim. Pete Trgovich tried to fill the void, but he also committed his fifth foul with 3:10 to go, forcing UCLA to mount a comeback without two of its key post players.

"I had never fouled out of a game in my life in college—I couldn't believe it," recalled Trgovich, who now had no control over the rest of the game. "I'm sitting there and I'm thinking to myself my college career might be over. And that's the worst feeling in the world, that you're going to finish your college career on the bench, not on the court. So you can understand how emotional I was at the end of that game."

Wooden brought in Wilbert Olinde and Jim Spillane, two freshmen who had seen only a handful of minutes the entire season, but the unnaturally poised duo helped UCLA tie the game at 61 in the final minutes. Unfortunately for the Bruins, UL's Allen Murphy responded with a shot from the baseline, and after Dave

Meyers was unable to connect at the other end for UCLA, the Cardinals went to their delay game. The Bruins were forced to foul Phil Bond, who sank both free throws with 1:06 left to give UL a 65–61 lead.

Louisville blocked two shots on UCLA's next possession, but both rejections went right back to the Bruins, and when Richard Washington went up for a third shot with 48 seconds remaining, he was rewarded with a foul call. His free throws cut the lead to 65–63, but UCLA still needed a miracle. They got one seconds later as Marques Johnson stole the inbounds pass and fed it to Spillane. His shot from the corner was off the mark, but Johnson was there for the follow-up to tie the game with just 35 seconds on the clock.

But Johnson was not done, as he deflected the ensuing inbounds off UL's Ulysses Bridgeman to give UCLA a chance to actually win the game in regulation. Andre McCarter missed a shot with seven seconds to go, and when the Cardinals missed an opportunity of their own in the final seconds, the teams were heading to overtime.

Louisville built a three-point lead with 1:18 to go, and even though Dave Meyers hit a pair of free throws with 57 seconds left to cut the

In what would turn out to be his second-to-last game, John Wooden looks on during his team's semifinal victory over Louisville. *Walter Iooss Jr./ Sports Illustrated/Getty Images*

lead to 74–73, the Cardinals still had the upper hand. With no shot clock at the time, they gave the ball to free throw specialist Terry Howard, who was instructed to dribble around until UCLA committed a foul. The Bruins applied the defensive pressure but were unable to come up with a steal, leaving them with no option but to send Howard to the line, where he was 28-of-28 on the year.

"I think we were pretty aware that this guy was their best free throw shooter," Trgovich said. "I mean, the guy sits at the end of the bench for the whole game and then all of a sudden they put him in at the end and keep giving him the ball."

But Howard's first attempt hit off the rim, and when the Bruins grabbed the rebound they called a timeout to set up the last shot.

"The plan was to get the ball in to Richard Washington," Trgovich said. "Richard was, in my opinion, the best shooter on the team."

Getting the ball to Washington, however, was easier said than done. Louisville's zone defense denied any early looks to the forward, and by the time UCLA did get Washington the ball, he had only four seconds to work with. Catching the ball with his back turned to the basket, Washington took one dribble to turn his body and rose up to fire a jumper from 10 feet away. The shot hit nothing but net with just two seconds to go, and when the clock struck zero the fans stormed the court. After missing the title game in 1974, the Bruins were back where they belonged. Little did the fans know that this was the moment that Wooden spontaneously decided to quit the game. When he reached the locker room, he explained his choice.

"He said, 'You know, alumni just told me, 'Thanks coach, you owed us that one from last year.' And he just had a guarded disgust in his voice that was somewhat the precursor of the motive for saying I'm bowing out," Drollinger said. "In other words, if that's what my spoiled alumni think, I don't need any more of this. And that was the somewhat underlying tenor of the retirement announcement, which turned out to be very motivational."

The Bruins were determined to win his last game, and when they defeated Kentucky two nights later, the dream was complete. John Wooden was going out a winner. ●

#36

N.C. STATE   **UCLA**

David Thompson, N.C. State: 28 points,
10 rebounds, 2 assists

1974: N.C. STATE
vs. UCLA

The last time UCLA had failed to win a national title, David Thompson was still attending middle school. During that time, the Bruins dominated college basketball like no team ever had before, and like no team ever has since. During a 12-year period in which the Bruins won 10 championships, John Wooden's club went 335–22 for a 93.8 winning percentage. Even though N.C. State had won 56 of its last 57 games, the sole loss had been an 84–66 thrashing at the hands of UCLA in December, a game that brought UCLA's winning streak to a ridiculous 79 games. The Wolfpack were certainly a talented team, but there was no question that history was on the side of UCLA.

"I don't know if athletes really get involved in as much of that as the media or coaches," N.C. State senior Tim Stoddard said. "Athletes that have a lot of success are playing day by day, game by game. I don't care what happened five years ago or 10 years ago—you're playing for now."

Even ignoring history, the Bruins were still an incredibly formidable opponent, featuring two-time national Player of the Year Bill Walton. And although the teams went into halftime tied, Walton's talent emerged when the Bruins made their first four shots of the second half, including his putback with 16:00 left that put UCLA up 49–38. The Bruins appeared ready to deliver the knockout punch after State missed its next shot and Walton cleared the rebound, but Wolfpack senior Tom

Burleson sent a message that neither he nor his teammates were going to be intimidated. The 7-foot-3 Burleson stripped Walton of the ball, put in the layup, and added two more baskets as the Wolfpack grabbed a 63–61 lead with just five minutes to play.

UCLA's Dave Meyers made a layup of his own, and Walton scored with 2:22 left to put the Bruins back in front 65–63, but thanks to a basket by Thompson, the teams were still locked at 65 as regulation ended. Overtime wouldn't be enough to settle the score either, as a steal by Stoddard prevented UCLA from holding for the last shot. Burleson's last-second turnaround rimmed out, leaving the score knotted at 67, but the longer the Wolfpack stuck around, the better chance they had. Going into the game, most had predicted that Walton would have a huge mismatch over Stoddard, but despite the four-inch height differential, the 6-foot-7 Stoddard was holding his own.

"I held and pushed and scratched. He was a tremendous ballplayer, extremely quick for a guy his size, but I knew some tricks of the trade on how to hold and block and get him out of the flow a little bit," he smiled. "I was fortunate enough not to get caught doing anything illegal."

For the lucky fans in attendance at the Greensboro Coliseum that night, there was little doubt they were getting their money's worth. Most were there to support N.C. State, which was located just 80 miles away in

Raleigh, but their cheers fell silent when UCLA came out swinging in double overtime. Walton sank a pair of free throws to start the onslaught, and his fadeaway jumper moments later gave UCLA a 71–67 advantage. UCLA forward Keith Wilkes followed it up with a three-point play to give the Bruins a seven-point advantage, one that seemed impossible to surrender in an era with no shot clock or three-point line.

Even with little chance of a victory, the Wolfpack continued to plug away. Monte Towe converted a pair of free throws to cut the lead to five, and after UCLA's Tommy Curtis made just one of two free throws, Thompson brought the team back to within four when he tipped in his own missed shot. Instead of holding the ball and forcing N.C. State to commit a foul, Walton tried to fire the ball to a streaking teammate, only to have Stoddard snatch the pass at the last second. Burleson tipped in

a shot at the other end of the court, and all of a sudden the lead was down to just two.

UCLA wised up and got fouled this time, but it made little difference, as Meyers bricked the front end of a one-and-one. Burleson had a chance to tie the game at the other end as he also went to the charity stripe, but his second shot rimmed out, giving Meyers a chance to redeem himself when he grabbed the rebound. With 1:16 to play, he stepped back to the line, knowing that a pair of free throws would extend the lead back to three points, but by now the crowd was buzzing. His first shot hit off the back of the rim and landed in the hands of Thompson, who connected on a pull-up jumper with 50 seconds to go, giving N.C. State its first lead in nearly 30 minutes.

Greg Lee couldn't connect on the other end, and with 34 seconds to play Thompson had a chance of his own to put the game away. Unlike Meyers, Thompson connected on both free throws to give State a 78–75 lead, and when Burleson intercepted the inbounds pass moments later, it was all over. N.C. State had conquered history, and the fans deservingly stormed the court to celebrate. Thompson, who had been held to 7-of-20 in the first contest, scored 28 points, including the four most important of the game. As for Walton, his torch was passed to Thompson.

"David Thompson was clearly the best player we ever played against in college," Walton admitted. "I now realize, after all the tears, sleepless nights, sadness, and inner turmoil, how wrong I have been for all this time. We lost that horrendous day not because we beat ourselves; we lost to a better player and ultimately a better person."

In the end, David had indeed beaten Goliath. And his last name was Thompson. ●

David Thompson rises up to sink a shot over UCLA's Bill Walton, proving to the world that the Bruins could be defeated. *Rich Clarkson/Sports Illustrated/Getty Images*

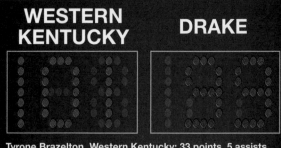

WESTERN KENTUCKY   DRAKE

Tyrone Brazelton, Western Kentucky: 33 points, 5 assists, 5 rebounds, 2 steals

2008: WESTERN KENTUCKY vs. DRAKE

Even before Ty Rogers' NCAA Tournament debut, he was already living his dream. Like most other boys growing up in Kentucky, Rogers had always wanted to play college basketball. And like only the most talented of youngsters, he actually got to play for the team he grew up watching. The only difference between him and his counterparts is that his aspirations had nothing to do with the University of Kentucky or Louisville, the state's premier programs.

Rogers was born and raised in Eddyville, a town of about 2,500 that featured only three stoplights but shared an enormous pride in Western Kentucky basketball. It should come as little surprise that Rogers became the first recruit to commit to the 2004–2005 Hilltoppers, a team that qualified for the NCAA Tournament as a 12 seed three years later.

But the day before the NCAA Tournament, Rogers was having a dream of a different sort.

"Growing up and watching the NCAA Tournament all those years, there's always so many big moments. I just had a feeling we were going to be a part of that," Rogers said. "I think all kids dream of having a moment like that, especially if you love the game of basketball."

Rogers wasn't the only one thinking something was in the air. The father of WKU coach Darrin Horn also mentioned that Ty was going to have a special night, and he made sure to tell his son about the premonition.

"I kind of pulled it off like, sure, Ty's an important component but, man, I didn't think a thing of it at the time," Horn said.

No one could blame him, as WKU point guard Tyrone Brazelton stole the show for most of their game against fifth-seeded Drake. Brazelton scored a career-high 33 points as the Hilltoppers grabbed a 16-point lead, and after his layup with 8:30 left, the team still led 74–59. But the Bulldogs, who won the Missouri Valley Conference after finishing in last place the year before, were not about to let their season end that easily.

Drake applied full-court pressure, and the lead started slipping in a hurry. After Josh Young's three-pointer with 1:24 to go, WKU's lead had dwindled to 86–85, and when his teammate Jonathan Cox nailed a three-pointer of his own with 30 seconds left, the game was tied. Thanks to a charging call on Western Kentucky, the score was still knotted at 88 as regulation ended.

"When we got up by 16, I never thought that the game was over by any means because I knew the kind of shooters and the kind of players that Drake had," Rogers said. "The biggest thing is you got to keep your composure and understand that basketball is a game of runs. That's going to happen, we had ours and they had theirs."

Drake's run did not stop once the buzzer sounded, as the Bulldogs raced off to a 96–92 lead in overtime. And thanks to a pair of free throws by Cox, the Bulldogs still led 99–98 with just 5.7 seconds remaining. Horn called a timeout and instructed Brazelton to drive in for a layup, but after watching the WKU senior burn their defense all night long, the Bulldogs were not about to let him take matters into his own hands. Immediately after Brazelton took the inbounds pass, Drake put two defenders on him, forcing him to shovel a pass to a trailing Rogers well behind the three-point line.

"Most kids would have taken more dribbles and forced a bad shot. What Tyrone did was he threw it to the open man, and that sounds really simple in a late-game situation but a lot of teams won't do that," Horn said. "It was the best play to make, and only the kind of play to make when you've got a team that really trusts and believes in each other."

Although Rogers had scored only eight points on the night, he was more than capable of taking the shot. As a high schooler, Rogers broke the state record for three-pointers, and before the final play he had advised Brazelton to kick it back out if the defense was tight.

Ty Rogers celebrates his game-winning basket against Drake as his fellow Hilltoppers prepare to mob him. *Doug Benc/Getty Images*

But now that he had gotten the chance he had asked for, his look at the basket was anything but clean. When he caught the ball nearly 25 feet from the hoop, an additional defender came over to help, forcing Rogers to fire over three defenders as the final second ticked by. It was hardly the scenario he had dreamed of, but after the ball sailed over the trio of defenders, it landed softly through the net to give WKU the impossible 101–99 victory.

"You look back on it and it's kind of like one of those surreal moments," Horn said. "It was the culmination of everything we wanted our program to be about going to fruition. We wanted our program to be about the team and not just an individual player."

The whole team ran over to join Rogers, who glided around the court with his arms out to the side, almost as if he were floating on cloud nine.

"As far as my celebration afterwards, I think I just kind of lost a little control," Rogers joked. "It was just an amazing feeling, and something still to this day I cannot describe."

Once Rogers had calmed down, he went to the locker room where he discovered hundreds of text messages awaiting him on his cell phone. Rogers didn't have any text messaging on his cell phone plan, but the hefty bill was certainly worth the price.

"I was laying on the bed just reading those text messages, and to be honest I just broke down in tears," Rogers said. "It's such an amazing feeling to be able to experience something like that and also have that kind of support behind you—that was definitely a pretty cool part of it all."

Not quite as sentimental but equally flattering was the student on campus who decided to try his own taste of the Ty Rogers lifestyle.

"He was younger than we were, and every time he would go out to a bar or go out to hang out with our friends or people out in town, he would tell everybody that he was Ty Rogers," the real Rogers said. "I think he got away with it a few times."

Fortunately, ESPN picked the authentic Ty Rogers when they handed him the ESPY for Play of the Year. That, unlike his cell phone bill, was free. ●

1982: NORTH CAROLINA vs. GEORGETOWN

CBS' had barely placed its foot in the door of the NCAA Tournament, and already the network had managed to insult the entire state of North Carolina. In 1982, the first year CBS was covering the tournament, basketball analyst Steve Grote lamented how unfortunate it was that Louisville and Georgetown were paired up in the semifinals, as they were the two best teams remaining in the field. That little comment didn't sit well with UNC fans, who felt the 33–2 Tar Heels were more than capable of competing with anybody. After dismantling the Houston Cougars, the Tar Heels found themselves lined up against the Hoyas, who had defeated Louisville 50–46 earlier in the day.

It was only fitting that the UNC would play the Hoyas, as it would be pairing fellow Gastonia natives James Worthy and Eric "Sleepy" Floyd. Most residents in the North Carolina town would be cheering for Worthy, who donned the Tar Heels jersey. The game would also be a matchup of Dean Smith and John Thompson, who had coached the USA Olympic team together six years earlier. Thompson was also the first African American coach in Final Four history, while Smith had been the coach responsible for integrating the ACC when he signed UNC's first African American player in 1966. Always a free thinker, Smith took the same approach to the national championship game.

"Going into the game, I thought we were pretty relaxed," senior Matt Doherty said.

"I remember coach Smith talking before the game, saying, 'Hey, there's a billion people in China that don't care who wins this game.' Basically, go out, be loose, and relax, and I think we were."

If Smith needed any confirmation that his strategy would work, it came when he ran into Danny Worthy, the brother of UNC's star forward. When Smith asked how his brother was feeling, Danny claimed, "I've never seen him so zeroed in. I'll be shocked if he doesn't have a great game."

The Tar Heels were certainly more at ease than Georgetown freshman Patrick Ewing, who goaltended UNC's first four baskets. In fact, North Carolina didn't even make a field goal for the first eight minutes of the game, but thanks to Ewing they were down just 12–10 when Doherty made the team's first shot.

"I think that Georgetown tried to intimidate us, by Patrick Ewing goaltending the first four shots, and we all looked at each other like this is ridiculous, you're just giving us these buckets," Doherty laughed.

Another goaltending violation by Ewing helped the cause, and when Worthy connected on a jumper late in the first half, UNC had tied the game at 22, with 16 of its points coming courtesy of Worthy. The junior would add 12 more points before the night was over, and his dunk late in the second half gave Carolina a 54–53 lead.

Despite Worthy's play, Carolina only led 61–60 with three minutes remaining when Smith called for the "four corners" play, designed to run out the remaining time. Although most coaches would only employ the strategy with a sizable lead, Smith's gamble paid off as the anxious Georgetown defense allowed freshman Michael Jordan to drive in for the layup. Ewing answered back with a long jumper with 2:37 remaining, but Smith went right back to the stall. This time Georgetown fouled Doherty with 1:16 to go, but his first free throw hit off the back of the rim and into the hands of Ewing. The Hoyas worked the ball to Floyd, who drove to the free throw line and leaned in between two defenders to clear some space. His shot banged off the rim but landed in, giving Georgetown a 62–61 lead with 55 seconds to go.

Smith, who almost never called a timeout, let his players decide who should take the last shot. But when the Tar Heels looked unsure of how to execute their final play, he reluctantly asked for time. His players had just squandered their lead and looked unprepared for the final

play, but they would never know by the way Smith addressed them.

"This is right where you want to be. This is just what we want," Smith declared. "I'd rather be in our position than theirs right now. Wouldn't you?"

He understandably called for a play that put the ball in Worthy's hands, but Smith knew that Thompson wasn't just going to let the best player on the floor get an easy look. As the team was breaking from the huddle, Smith whispered to Jordan, "If it comes to you, knock it in."

And sure enough, when the rest of the team was covered, point guard Jimmy Black threw it across the court to Jordan, who fired away. Before the game, the freshman said he had envisioned having a chance to make the game-winning shot, but now that the moment had come, he couldn't bear to look. But had he opened his eyes, he would have seen the shot hit nothing but net, putting North Carolina in front 63–62 with 17 seconds to play.

"He could have easily bobbled the ball, he could have faked the shot. Michael is wired a certain way, and I think we've all seen through the years the number of game-winning shots he has hit," Doherty said.

Georgetown had one last shot, as Fred Brown brought the ball up the court. Worthy thought Floyd would be the one to take it, and as the Georgetown senior motioned over toward Brown, Worthy darted in front. But it turned out to be a fake, leaving Worthy 40 feet from the hoop with nobody to defend. "When I saw it on tape . . . I realized how out of position he was," Doherty laughed. "He went for that steal and he was caught at halfcourt basically like out of the play."

But Floyd was so thrown off by the move that he tossed it right to him, giving Worthy the luckiest defensive mistake in NCAA history. It may not have been the prettiest steal, but it was the first of many great moments in his Hall of Fame career. As for Jordan, whose heroics that night were no accident, let's just say the shot was a sign of things to come. ●

A legend was born when a freshman named Michael Jordan hit this game-winner. *Manny Milan/Sports Illustrated/Getty Images*

#33

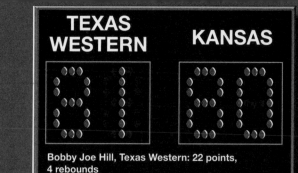

TEXAS WESTERN   **KANSAS**

Bobby Joe Hill, Texas Western: 22 points, 4 rebounds

1966: TEXAS WESTERN vs. KANSAS

When Texas Western coach Don Haskins finally got a chance to watch the team he had assembled for the 1966 season, he looked on in horror. As far as first impressions go, this was about as bad as they came.

"I can almost remember it like it was yesterday," said Nevil Shed, a junior on the team. He said, 'Just look at ya'all. You're far and none the worst bunch of athletes I ever had. I doubt if we'll even win half our games. Just a pitiful bunch of athletes.'"

At first glance, the Miners certainly did not look like a competitive team. Two of their best players were listed at 5-foot-6 and 5-foot-10, while the 6-foot-8 Shed—the team's biggest player—was rail thin. But deep down, Haskins knew his team was good. Really good. He just didn't want to let it get to their heads.

Unfortunately, his players could only ignore their results for so long. The Miners won their first game by 49 points, and by March Haskins' club had won all 23 of their games, 18 of them by double digits. And as much as their coach tried to prevent it, the inevitable occurred.

Before their first tournament game against Oklahoma City University, Haskins put a curfew on his players for the first time all season, which made little difference to point guard Bobby Joe Hill, who had already planned on partying that night. After his coach performed the bed check, Hill met with his teammates in the hotel lobby. But Haskins, who at 35 was still young enough to read their minds, quickly became aware of the plot and sat down Hill for the start of the upcoming game.

"He put a scare into us," senior Orsten Artis recalled. "He told us that he wasn't going to help us anymore."

Hill indeed watched from the sidelines as the Miners fell behind 11–2, a deficit that continued to grow as the half wore on. Finally, with their season falling apart, Haskins reluctantly put in his star, who scored 24 points en route to an 89–74 comeback win.

The Miners had advanced, but they were not going to be able to get away with such antics in the third round against fourth-ranked Kansas, which entered the game with a 23–3 record. Sure enough, midway through the second half it was the Jayhawks who led 55–53. Kansas coach Ted Owens instructed his players to slow the game down, which backfired as the Miners pulled ahead 69–64 with just 1:17 left, but thanks to a huge decision by the officials, the Jayhawks were not finished just yet.

After Kansas came up empty on the next possession, Texas Western senior David Lattin appeared to put an exclamation point on the victory when he delivered a dunk to put the Miners up 71–64. Before he came down, however, the referee blared his whistle. Lattin had hung on the rim too long—a technical foul that not only wiped out his two points but sent KU's Al Lopes to the free throw line. With no time expiring off the clock, TW's lead went from seven to three.

They still led 69–66 with 1:02 to play, but 30 seconds later Kansas guard Jo Jo White stole the ball and broke toward the other end of the court. The Miners tried to catch up with White, but to no avail. Not only did he make the layup, but he was fouled in the process, and his ensuing free throw tied the game at 69. Once Hill's last-second shot rimmed out, they were heading to overtime.

The score was still tied near the end of the extra period when White seemed to come up with yet another miracle. With just seven seconds left, White was standing near the left sideline when he felt some contact by Hill. The Kansas sophomore was standing nearly 35 feet away from the basket, but he instinctively rose up to fire a shot. White didn't get the call he was looking for, but it didn't seem to matter—his off-balance heave swished through the net to send the crowd into a frenzy.

But just like Lattin's dunk in regulation, the celebration was short-lived. Referee Rudy Marich, who had been right next to White as the final play transpired, blew his whistle and pointed to where White had taken the shot. His foot was on the end line.

"That was probably the most important moment in TW's history, right there," laughed sophomore Willie Worsley. "God bless Rudy Marich."

The call sent the game into double overtime, where the Miners worked a 77–71 lead. And although a late run by Kansas made things more interesting than they had to be, Texas Western hung on for an 81–80 victory. For all his worrying, Haskins' club was going to the Final Four after all. And although a party was now certainly due, the coach still had other things on his mind. In one week, his team would be playing in the most important game in basketball history (see page 60). ●

Don Haskins huddles the Miners during the 1966 tournament.
Rich Clarkson/Sports Illustrated/Getty Images

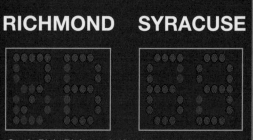

RICHMOND   SYRACUSE

Curtis Blair, Richmond: 18 points, 6 assists, 3 rebounds

1991: RICHMOND
vs. SYRACUSE

Long before Terry Connolly set his sights on becoming part of the first 15 seed ever to win an NCAA Tournament game, he had to find somebody to play for. After a high school career that yielded just one scholarship offer from a Division I school, an offer that was given under the premise that he would ride the bench for the duration of his career, Connolly ended up playing in the obscurity of the NAIA, a step below Division III. When his coach at Shepherd College left during the spring after his sophomore year, Connolly decided to transfer. But finding a new home wasn't exactly easy, and with just a few weeks to spare before the start of the fall semester, Connolly still didn't know where he would be playing.

"I started to look around and there weren't a lot of takers," said Connolly, whose high school coach decided to recommend him to Richmond coach Dick Tarrant. "I kind of fit the Richmond mold. I was a tough player. I wasn't the most athletic player by any stretch of the imagination or most skilled, but just tough, hard-nosed, and seemed to fit into coach Tarrant's coaching style."

More than anything, Connolly was a winner. After making the starting lineup in his first year at Richmond, he took a reserve role during his senior year, despite being the team's captain. The move helped the Spiders land an NCAA bid at Maryland's Cole Fieldhouse, where Connolly had gone 4–0 as a high school player. Win No. 5 looked like a possibility after

Connolly watched Syracuse practice the day before the game.

"They were laying on the scorer's table; they were shooting halfcourt shots," Connolly said. "We went our hour and we did drills the whole time. It wasn't going through the motions—we actually went through drills hard. That was in the back of my mind, and I let the guys know that this is what they think of us."

It would be hard to blame the second-seeded Orangemen for overlooking their opponent. After all, when Richmond played in the NCAA Tournament the previous year, Duke embarrassed them 81–46.

"We did get spanked pretty bad that tournament," point guard Curtis Blair said. "We just had to put that loss behind us because we knew we were playing a team that was much superior to us."

If the Spiders were going to lose, it was not going to be for lack of preparation. Tarrant tweaked their defensive schemes so that Syracuse would struggle to recognize them during the game, and he made sure his players did their homework on the Orangemen.

"We pretty much knew all of their offensive plays and their defensive schemes. And we had so many offensive plays back then that it's just hard for one team to scout us just in two or three days' time," Blair said. "So we knew if we could execute and rebound the ball and play good defense that we had a chance to beat them. And luckily, they had a hard time guarding us."

The Spiders shot almost 62 percent in the first half, and thanks in part to the new defense, took a 44–36 lead into the break. The team continued to fool the Syracuse defense, and by the time Kenny Woods made a layup with 4:48 remaining, the lead was still eight.

It took 35 minutes, but the Orangemen finally found their touch when they needed it most. Billy Owens sandwiched his three-pointer between a pair of long bombs from Michael Edwards, and the lead had suddenly shrunk to a 68–65 margin with three minutes to go. Owens added a layup a minute later to cut the lead to one, and after Gerald Jarmon missed the front end of a one-and-one at the other end, Syracuse actually had a chance to take the lead. This time the Richmond defense held firm, forcing a tough shot from Edwards that rimmed out. Connolly soared for the rebound and then fired an outlet pass to Jim Shields for a critical layup.

"Back then, we were a grit team," Blair said. "We had to pound everything out, we had to fight for everything, and I guess we probably did want it a little more than they did."

Now facing a three-point deficit, Owens hit another jumper with 32 seconds left to put Syracuse within a point. The shot clock was turned off, so the Orangemen had to foul. They chose Eugene Burroughs, a freshman who was fresh off the bench and hadn't scored all day. In fact, Burroughs had only attempted 14 free throws all year.

Syracuse coach Jim Boeheim called a timeout in an effort to ice the freshman, but Burroughs calmly sank both shots to put Richmond back up by three. Catching his dad sitting behind the basket, Burroughs put his fist in the air and gave him a wink. Tarrant teased the youngster that there must have been a pretty girl in the stands, but there would be plenty of time for celebration later. First, they would need a defense stop.

The Orangemen went back to Owens, but Jim Shields refused to let him get an open look. Owens forced up a shot that was off the mark, and although he got enough of the ball to tip it back to teammate Adrian Autry, the Richmond defense continued to hold strong. Moments later Autry tried to attack the basket, but before he could take a shot he was fouled by Blair, whose team had a foul to spare.

Owens received the inbounds, and swung the ball over to Edwards, who was stationed by himself in the corner. Kenny Woods desperately ran over to Edwards, waving his hands in the air. By the time Edwards launched the shot, Woods was right there, and the shot bounced off the rim and out of bounds with 2.6 seconds to go. All Richmond needed to do was inbound the ball, and when Curtis Blair broke free, his team had just pulled off the biggest upset ever seen in the NCAA Tournament.

The win was also a huge thrill for Connolly, who had come off the bench to score 14 points. The pressure wasn't off Connolly quite yet, as he had to be drug-tested after the game.

"I could not go to the bathroom to save my life. I was drinking Gatorade, water, and I remember being in where they did the drug test and it seemed like hours," Connolly laughed. "The rest of the team left back to the hotel."

Of course, the result came up negative, but that was about the only negative outcome of the entire evening. Waiting for him when he returned from the test was his family, still celebrating at the arena. Connolly was back home, but he had certainly come a long way. ●

#31

MICHIGAN **SETON HALL**

Glen Rice, Michigan: 31 points, 11 rebounds

1989: MICHIGAN vs. SETON HALL

As easily as basketball had come to Michigan guard Rumeal Robinson, life had been anything but simple off the court. Initially raised by his grandparents in Jamaica, Robinson later moved in with his biological mom in Cambridge, Massachusetts, where she had been saving money in order to move him in. What he encountered when he arrived, however, was a volatile relationship that resulted in him living on the streets.

Robinson, like many children, had threatened to run away, but unlike most parents, his mother simply let him. The 10-year-old spent his nights sleeping in apartment hallways and stairwells until he was discovered by Helen Ford, a generous woman who already had five kids of her own, in addition to numerous others that she had adopted. She didn't know it at the time, but she was taking in a young man who would become one of basketball's brightest stars.

Thanks to the play of Robinson, the Wolverines marched through the 1989 tournament to arrive at Seattle for the Final Four. Of the nearly 40,000 fans on hand, however, only two would come from the Ford household. His father, Louis, trying to support all those children on a postman's income, was unable to afford a ticket to the game, much less the plane ride to get there. But hearing of the father's plight was *Boston Globe* columnist Michael Madden, who brought it to attention the day before UM's semifinal game against Illinois.

Louis Ford wasn't aware of the article, but plenty of other people were, several of whom pitched in to buy him a ticket to the game, as well as travel accommodations. The only problem was that Ford only learned of his neighbors' generosity just a few hours before tip-off, when his supervisor stopped him midroute to share the news. There would be no time to change—Ford would have to dash to the airport in his postman's uniform. He encountered more generosity on the airplane, as the pilot, hearing of the story, put the game on the radio as the plane soared toward Seattle.

As soon as the plane landed, Ford raced to the Kingdome, landing merely seconds after the final score had been decided. But there was good news: Michigan had won on a buzzer-beater and would be playing Seton Hall two nights later for the national championship. This time, Ford would have a chance to be there in full force to cheer on his son— and what a game it would be.

This time Louis scrapped the postman outfit for some Michigan attire, but the Rumeal Robinson section was just as easy to identify, as Helen sported a "Rumeal's Mom" shirt. And just before halftime, it would be Robinson's free throws that gave the Wolverines a 37–32 lead going into the break. His dunk midway through the second half also gave Michigan its largest lead of the game at 51–39. Alas, it would be his last field goal of the half.

Robinson wasn't the only Wolverine turning cold. After starting the half 5-of-6 from the field, they would hit just five of their next 21 shots as Seton Hall cut the lead to just 64–61. The comeback came as little surprise to those who had watched the Pirates storm back from an 18-point deficit against Duke in the semifinals. Still, the Wolverines were clinging to the lead, and heading into their final defensive possession, the lead was still three. But with his twenty-second point of the half, Seton Hall's Johnny Morton nailed a clutch three-pointer with 25 seconds left to send the game into overtime. UM coach Steve Fisher knew his team had been one stop from the title, but now the responsibility was on him to reenergize the team for another five minutes of basketball.

"We talked about what we wanted to do, but I also remember at the end as we went into overtime, I talked about closing your eyes and envision cutting the nets down because that's what we're going to do," Fisher said. "And you try to get them in a mindset that they know they're going to be successful, especially when the other team makes their run the way they did."

Even after Morton hit another three-pointer in the extra session to give his team a 79–76 lead, Fisher still felt positive. After all, one of his close friends, who had accurately predicted the score to each of UM's earlier tournament wins—as well as how they would win—assured Fisher that forward Mark Hughes would be the star in a championship victory. The Wolverines still trailed by the same score with a minute to go, but forward Terry Mills brought the team to within 79–78 on a turnaround with 48 seconds to go.

Fisher instructed his players not to foul, a decision that paid huge dividends when the Wolverines forced Morton into an airball just before the shot clock expired. The Michigan players had gotten the result they were looking for, but they now had only 13 seconds left to travel the length of the court for the final shot. After rebounding the ball, Glen Rice tossed it to Robinson, who hurried his way down court. It was the biggest possession anybody on that court would ever face.

"I've been coming down and passing the ball and hiding a lot on last-second shots," said Robinson after the game. "This time I wanted it to be me."

By the time Robinson had reached the top of the key, only four seconds remained, and a trio of Seton Hall defenders awaited him. As badly as he wanted to take the final shot, Robinson knew he needed to pass the ball. The closest option, just a few feet away, was none other than Hughes. But before Hughes could take the game-winner, a whistle blared across the arena. Robinson had been fouled before the pass, with just three seconds to go. The foul sent Robinson to the free throw line, but the Pirates had escaped destiny. Not only would Hughes be unable to take the final shot as predicted, but the season now lay in the hands of Robinson, who was only a 64 percent shooter from the charity stripe.

"I got to the sideline and there was a kid, Marc Koenig, saying, 'Man, you got to make these free throws!'" Robinson laughed. "Yeah, I think I got to make the free throws. Tell me something else to calm me down!"

With the score at 80–79, one free throw would likely send the game into double overtime. Another would win it. Or, of course, Robinson could miss them both.

"Well, Rumeal was not a good free throw shooter, but I've said this before. We got beat at Wisconsin that year and Rumeal had a chance—we were down with seconds on the clock, not unlike the championship game—and Rumeal got fouled and had a two-shot foul and literally bricked both of them," Fisher recalled.

This time, and with all eyes focused on him, Robinson calmly knocked both shots down, making the score 81–80 Michigan.

"I had great confidence in him," Fisher said. "I could see by the look in his face and by his body language that he was not scared, that he was very comfortable that he was going to make the free throws. And he stepped up and shot it like there was nobody else in the gym."

And when Seton Hall's desperation shot missed at the buzzer, the saga was complete.

Rumeal Robinson was on top of the basketball world, but he had plenty of help, on and off the court, to help him get there. ●

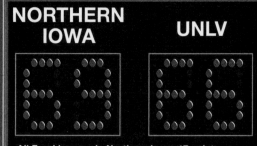

#30

2010: NORTHERN IOWA vs. UNLV

Ali Farokhmanesh was never supposed to pick up a basketball. The only son of a father who played on the Iranian Olympic volleyball team, and a mother who coached the sport, Farokhmanesh seemed destined to be diving for loose balls of the whiter, softer variety. But when he grew to only 5-foot-11, in a sport where many players were almost a foot taller, Farokhmanesh opted for the only sport with even more colossal adversaries. And the basketball world wasn't quite welcoming to his arrival.

After a high school career that yielded zero offers from Division I or II schools, Farokhmanesh opted for Indian Hills Community College, a decision that he assumed would at least allow him to earn some playing time. It wasn't long before he realized he was quite mistaken.

"I was the backup point guard, but I didn't back up anybody, I guess you'd say," Farokhmanesh joked. "So it was a pretty easy decision that I should leave because I wanted to play and I wasn't enjoying myself, so I decided to go."

Farokhmanesh called several college coaches to see if he could be a walk-on player, but he found no takers in that endeavor either. Refusing to give up, Ali settled on Kirkwood Community College, which was providing Ali with one last chance to reach his dream of playing basketball.

Farokhmanesh made the most of his opportunity, playing well enough at Kirkwood to land an offer from Northern Iowa. With no need to prove any doubters wrong, Farokhmanesh and the Panthers flourished, earning a 28–4 record and a spot in the NCAA Tournament. The only problem was that they were unfairly given a nine seed, putting them in a first-round matchup with UNLV, a team that was going to challenge the methodical Panthers.

"You know, UNLV was kind of a tough matchup for us just stylistically," senior Adam Koch said of the Rebels, who made it clear from the start they were going to push the ball. "I think part of what we struggled with at the beginning of the game was just getting the game played at our pace."

Midway through the first half, the Runnin' Rebels had already built up a 20–12 lead on a barrage of steals and layups. The Panthers, who refused to deviate from the game plan, were able to slow the pace down by getting to the free throw line. And once they got there, they were nearly automatic. By the time Koch made his seventh free throw in as many attempts, Northern Iowa had scored 11 of the last 12 points and led 58–49.

The team's 20-of-23 performance from the charity stripe was making it difficult for UNLV to mount any comeback, and the Rebels knew they would have to start taking some chances defensively. They implemented a full-court press, a strategy that worked to perfection.

Three critical steals by the Rebels brought them within a point with just three minutes to go. A layup by Kwadzo Ahelegbe pushed the lead back to three points, and heading into the last minute, all the Panthers had to do was get one more stop and the game would be theirs. But when Farokhmanesh left his man to provide extra help on UNLV's Tre'Von Willis, who was cutting to the hoop, the Rebels got the break they were looking for. Oscar Bellfield was camped out by himself on the right wing, and when Willis tossed him the ball, Bellfield drained the equalizer with 37 seconds left.

"It's kind of a joke—every time me and coach Ben Jacobson see that highlight video, they show Bellfield making a three on the side and coach looking at me because I was the one who helped over," laughed Farokhmanesh. "It was my responsibility for that guy making that three on that shot."

Never a stranger to adversity, Farokhmanesh looked to make up for the defensive lapse by tossing in the game-winner. But UNLV's full-court press had forced Jacobson to burn all of his timeouts earlier in the second half, leaving his players to fend for themselves. The first sign of trouble was when the Panthers couldn't find an open player to take the inbounds pass, nearly forcing a five-second violation. Ahelegbe took the inbounds just in time and fought through a double-team to bring the ball past halfcourt.

The Rebels continued to hound Ahelegbe, and with 10 seconds left he was still just in front of the midcourt logo. He passed off to Johnny Moran, who was standing almost as far away from the hoop on the right wing. Moran also faced heavy pressure under a double-team, and threw the ball to Farokhmanesh, who was standing directly across the court a good 30 feet away from the basket. With the clock winding down and the defense racing toward him from inside the arc, Farokhmanesh knew that was the best look he was going to get, and let it fly. And just seconds before the buzzer sounded, the ball dropped in to give the Panthers their first tournament win in 20 years. Ironically, their last NCAA Tournament victory, courtesy of another buzzer-beater (see page 242), was almost identical to the one made by Farokhmanesh.

"They showed some clips of it with the videos side by side and it looks exactly the same. I mean, the same spot, same everything," Koch said. "And it's kind of funny that that's how it would work out. Two victories that we had had at that time in the tournament ultimately came down to pretty much the same shot."

Thanks to the shot of a lifetime, Farokhmanesh was living his dream.

"That's probably the coolest thing that's come out of this for me is knowing that hopefully I gave some hope to some kid out there who maybe thought they weren't good enough or wouldn't be able to do whatever their dream is," Farokhmanesh said. "And hopefully through watching me and knowing what I went through, they think they can do that now because you truly can. If you want something bad enough, you can achieve it."

But his time was far from over. The best for Farokhmanesh was still to come (see page 334). ●

"Because of the amount of time Ali spends in the gym, there's nobody else they want taking that shot," UNI coach Ben Jacobson said of Ali Farokhmanesh, whose shot from well beyond the NBA line gave the Panthers a 69–66 victory. *Ronald Martinez/Getty Images*

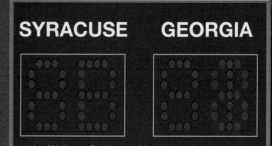

SYRACUSE   **GEORGIA**

John Wallace, Syracuse: 30 points, 15 rebounds, 2 assists

1996: SYRACUSE
vs. GEORGIA

Success had not always come so easy for John Wallace. The Rochester, New York, native was born with average basketball skills, but he happened to be blessed with an unparalleled appetite for making the most of his talent. During his high school days, Wallace would practice until three or four in the morning at the local park, much to the chagrin of his neighbors, but the extra hours paid off as he was offered a full-ride scholarship to play basketball at Syracuse.

Wallace brought his work ethic to college, and by the end of his junior year he was destined to become a high NBA draft pick. But that didn't necessarily mean he was ready to jump at the millions of dollars lying before him. Wallace, still looking for a piece of the March magic that had eluded the Orangemen, decided to stick around for his senior year.

The decision turned out to be a good one, as Syracuse earned a four seed in the 1996 NCAA Tournament and cruised into the Sweet 16 after a pair of easy wins. A spot in the Elite Eight also appeared to be theirs for the taking, as the Orangemen stormed out to a 35–22 lead over Georgia with five minutes to play in the first half. The team still enjoyed a sizable advantage at halftime, but Wallace picked up his third foul just before the break, and as soon as the second period started, Wallace committed another foul, forcing him to the bench. His absence was immediately noticeable, as the Bulldogs sank

four consecutive shots to grab their first lead at 42–40. Wallace watched in agony as the deficit ballooned to 52–42.

"It's like, what just happened? I'm just sitting on the bench, I'm furious," Wallace said. "Coach called timeout and he's in the middle of saying something and I just subbed myself in. He wasn't ready to put me in yet because it was at like the 13-minute mark. Coach looked at me like, 'What are you doing?' And I'm like, 'I'm going in the game.' I just looked at him and said, 'Who do you want me to take out?'"

Syracuse coach Jim Boeheim didn't always take kindly to players taking over his role, but Wallace was a special exception. The senior had carried the team on his back the whole season, and the team needed him. Desperately.

"I'm not going to let our season go away in my senior year sitting on the bench watching the game," Wallace said. "I huddled the guys in and said, 'We're about to make our run right now,' and we did."

The team still trailed 65–56 with less than 3:00 remaining, but a three-pointer by Lazarus Sims cut the lead to 65–59. And when he nailed another three moments later, the deficit was down to just three points.

"You could see the tide turning, you could feel it—so did Georgia, obviously," Wallace said. "We could look into Georgia's face and tell they weren't ready. You know, you can look into a player's eyes sometimes. You see the fear, and we saw the fear in their eyes."

The Orangemen went on to tie the game at 68 in the last minute, and they were one defensive stop from sending the game into overtime. They got the missed shot they were looking for, but with just 3.5 seconds to go UGA's Pertha Robinson grabbed the rebound and dropped in what appeared to be the game-winner. Syracuse called a timeout, and Boeheim instructed his players to throw the inbounds pass from the baseline to midcourt and call another timeout. His players executed the first play, but now with the ball at midcourt the team found it much more difficult to get the ball in. Guard Jason Cipolla ended up with the ball, but that was hardly what the plans had called for.

"Let's be honest—I was always the fifth option and I knew that," Cipolla laughed. "Basically the play was, I remember it, Otis Hill was supposed to come to the top of the key and grab the ball, but they denied him."

Wallace stood at the sideline ready to inbound the ball to Hill, but as the five-second mark approached he was forced to hurl the ball across the court toward Cipolla. The junior leaped up to catch the ball, and with just over two seconds remaining, he had no option but to take the shot himself. Standing just inside the three-point line at the left corner, Cipolla knocked down the fadeaway shot as time expired. His momentum carried him into the elated Syracuse bench, but just as the team started to celebrate the equalizer, Wallace brought them back to reality.

"He was the boss and we all knew that, and we all looked up to John. And it's basically that encouragement to go ahead, we got five more minutes. You know what? Great shot—let's go!" Cipolla recalled. "We fought back from 10 down and we got this far, so why give it away?"

The teams were still tied at 78 when Wallace caught a lob pass with 15 seconds left in overtime and banked in the shot to put Syracuse ahead. Georgia raced down the court and fired a pass in the corner to Robinson, who was being defended by Wallace. The senior assumed Robinson was going to drive to the basket, and he played several feet off his man, but Robinson decided to fire away from three-point land. And with 7.1 seconds left, the ball rang through the net to put Georgia back up 81–80.

"When he hit the shot, I felt like it was my fault," Wallace said. "So I remember when he hit the shot and the ball was bouncing around in back, and Todd Burgan's looking up and he's awestruck, like what just happened. I'm telling him, 'Hurry up—get the dang ball!'"

Now Wallace would have a chance to put those late-night practice sessions to use. He raced down and fired a shot from just inside the top of the key—a spot he had literally shot from a thousand times in the offseason. And just like he had done his whole career, Wallace buried the last shot to give his team one of the most unpredictable wins in tournament history.

"It's actually the only time I really ever cried in a game from joy—the only time I've ever felt so overwhelmed with joy, the whole emotional ride of it," Wallace said. "Just being at the pinnacle of feeling ecstatic about something. It's a great feeling and something you can't duplicate."

Emotions, unlike game-winners, are something you can't practice. ●

Jason Cipolla hugging Todd Burgan after their overtime victory over Georgia. *Ed Reinke/AP Photo*

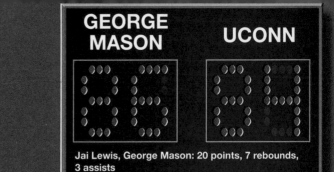

Jai Lewis, George Mason: 20 points, 7 rebounds, 3 assists

2006: GEORGE MASON vs. CONNECTICUT

Every basketball fan in America had fallen in love with George Mason. The eleventh-seeded Patriots had pulled off three consecutive upsets to land in the Elite Eight, but in the back of everyone's mind was just how long the run could last. The train that was George Mason appeared like it would be making its last stop against UConn. Not only were the Huskies the top seed in the tournament, many felt they were also about to become the first team in basketball history to have five players selected in the first round of the NBA draft. But by this point, the Patriots weren't going to be scared of anybody.

"They put their pants on just like I put my pants on," senior Lamar Butler said. "There's only one basketball, so it's not like they can all score at the same time."

Although this was true, any of UConn's players were more than capable of shooting the basketball. That level of balance and talent had earned the Huskies national acclaim, but George Mason coach Jim Larranaga realized that their opponent was held in such a high regard that it could actually benefit the Patriots. When Larranaga was relaxing in downtown Washington, D.C., before the game, he stumbled upon an article in the *Washington Post* that caught his eye.

"When they asked the Connecticut players about George Mason, they had no idea who the coach was, they had no idea what league they played in. One of them said, 'They're in that Missouri Valley League.' Another said, 'No,

they're in the Patriot League,'" Larranaga recalled.

As Larranaga addressed his team before tip-off, he made sure to remind his players just what they represented.

"They don't know that we belong to a secret organization called the CAA," Larranaga said. "Today CAA doesn't stand for Colonial Athletic Association, today CAA stands for Connecticut Assassins Association, and we need to go out and shoot these guys down."

The speech fired up the players, but the momentum appeared to be thrown off when the team bus got into an accident on their way to the stadium. The team finally arrived for the game, but Larranaga's players forgot the first rule of shooting down the Huskies—the element of surprise. Connecticut took a 6–0 lead almost as soon as the game began, and minutes later the gap had grown to 14–6. George Mason fought its way back to take a 29–28 lead with three minutes left before the break, but a 15–2 UConn run in the closing minutes appeared to spell the end for the Patriots.

"At halftime we basically told the team, hey, we've been here before, we've been behind at halftime against Carolina [see page 140]. We know that we're capable of coming back," Larranaga remembered. "I wanted it to be, hey, it's our ball, put the ball in the basket. It's their ball, stop them."

However simple the strategy was, it was clearly effective. George Mason went on a 10–2 run to cut the lead 47–46, and minutes later

Folarin Campbell tied the game at 49. Once Butler made a four-point play midway through the half to give the Patriots a 56–53 advantage, Larranaga took his faith in the team to a whole new level.

"It got to the point I didn't change one thing. We ran the same play 25 consecutive times, and I did not make a substitution from the 10-minute mark on all the way through," Larranaga said. "I did not change the lineup a single time. The same five guys, the starting five played the last 10 minutes of regulation."

The team was still up by two points with just 17.6 seconds to go when Butler converted two huge free throws to push the lead back to 74–70. UConn's Marcus Williams nailed a tough jumper in traffic to trim the lead in half, but only 5.5 seconds remained when Tony Skinn was sent to the line for George Mason. Skinn, who was an 81 percent free throw shooter, missed the front end of a one-and-one, and UConn grabbed the rebound.

The Patriots appeared to have the last play defended well when Huskies guard Denham Brown tried to go for a layup. Two defenders were there to meet him as he approached the basket, but the senior snuck along the baseline to reappear on the other side of the rim and rolled in a reverse layup as the buzzer sounded to send the game to overtime. It appeared that George Mason's chance at a miracle was shot, and the Washington, D.C., crowd, which had been cheering voraciously for the local Patriots, fell deathly silent.

"When the players came over, I could see the looks on their faces, and it was like, oh man, we could have won this. So it was very important to me to deliver a message that, hey, this game is still ours," Larranaga said. "When the players sat on the bench in front of me, I said, 'Hey, look it, we didn't play defense for five seconds. Now we got to play great defense for five minutes. But you know what? There isn't anywhere on earth I'd rather be than here with you guys playing the University of Connecticut for a chance to go to the Final Four.'"

The Patriots grabbed an early lead in the extra session, and when Campbell nailed a fadeaway jumper to beat the shot clock, the lead stood at 84–80 with just over a minute to go. Moments later, Thomas actually had a chance to push the lead to six, but he made

just one of two free throws to put George Mason up 86–81 with 25.4 seconds left. Williams responded by burying a three from well beyond the line with 10 seconds to go, giving UConn a glimpse of hope, and the Huskies applied full-court pressure on the inbounds pass. George Mason was able to inbound the ball to Jai Lewis, but as a 65.2 percent shooter from the line, he was hardly GMU's first option to take the free throws. With just 6.1 seconds to play, two free throws would have likely sealed the game, but like Skinn before him, Lewis missed his first free throw, giving UConn another shot to stay alive.

"I wasn't scared at all," said Butler. "I figured when we're in that situation again, we'll make the stop this time."

But Lewis followed it up by missing the second free throw as well, and when Brown grabbed the rebound, the Huskies needed only a two-point basket to tie. Brown once again drove toward the hoop, but when he dribbled just past the three-point line, he stepped back. There would be no second overtime—either his shot would go in, ruining the greatest story in recent memory, or the Patriots would make history. And as the clock struck zero, Brown's shot hit off the front of the rim, and George Mason had become the most improbable team ever to reach the Final Four. The players jumped on the scorer's table and held out their jerseys, just to make sure the world knew who they were.

"It makes me feel . . . there's a kind of emotional feeling that it's hard to put into words, this tremendous amount of pride and excitement and exhilaration," Larranaga said. "There's a tremendous amount of satisfaction and a feeling that we accomplished something, that we started the season believing something that we could do. With that in mind, we were able to accomplish it all in one split-second."

By this point, those in the crowd without high blood pressure were loving every second of it.

"It was an absolutely amazing environment," Larranaga said. "This was like there was lightning in a bottle. That arena was so unbelievably excited to have George Mason there, and we had become not only a local team or a regional team but a national team."

As announcer Gus Johnson put it, America had a new Cinderella, and her name was George. ●

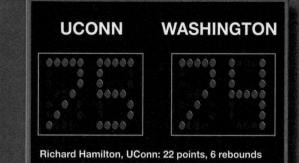

Richard Hamilton, UConn: 22 points, 6 rebounds

1998: CONNECTICUT vs. WASHINGTON

Richard Hamilton sat around with his teammates in front of the TV, trying to pass the time until their Sweet 16 match against Washington later that night. Tuning in to the West Virginia vs. Cincinnati game, the Huskies watched in disbelief as WVU guard Jarrod West banked in a desperation heave (see page 210) just before the buzzer to give the Mountaineers an improbable victory. Hamilton looked on as West was swarmed by teammates, wishing he could feel that sensation just once. Despite a career that included high school All-American honors and more than 1,200 points through just two seasons at UConn, Hamilton had never hit a buzzer-beater in his life, at any level. Fortunately for him, he would get that chance a few hours later.

If there was ever a time for Hamilton to get his first buzzer-beater, this certainly did not feel like the night. Not only had the sophomore been battling a cold and flu-like symptoms, but he was suffering from an upper-respiratory infection. Nevertheless, he decided to give it a go—after all, this was win or go home.

"I'm sure it's been not only that game, it's been a ton of games that people probably wouldn't believe the performance that he had. It's been a ton of games that he's been sick and performed at the highest level," guard Ricky Moore said. "Because you know, when you play at an elite school, nobody cares on the other end. Whoever you're competing against, they don't care that you're sick. So if you're not

down on the floor, you better be doing whatever you can in order to win the game."

But try as he would, Hamilton was unable to get in any rhythm in the first half, scoring just four points, well off pace of his 21.5 average. Washington took full advantage of his misfortune, going on a 14–6 run to tie the game at 31. Huskies point guard Khalid El-Amin tried to pick up the slack by tallying 16 points in the first half, but without Hamilton their 47–39 halftime lead was tenuous at best.

Fortunately for Connecticut, Hamilton picked up his confidence with a pair of layups to start the second half, and for the remainder of the game he was back to his old self. The junior scored 18 points over the final period as the Huskies took a 64–55 lead with 10 minutes to go. But just as Hamilton began to heat up, so did Washington, who ran off eight straight points to cut the lead to 64–63, and by the time Todd MacCullough hit a free throw with 1:27 left, UW had finally evened the score at 71.

"I mean, you just roll some tape from years past, you can see anything can happen in the tournament," Moore said. "And so when they go on a run, you're really worried. . . . You're up a certain amount of points, time is winding down, you're not making any shots, the other team is scoring it seems like every basket."

Now it was UConn's turn to answer, and all eyes were on Hamilton. But this time, he drove to the basket before dishing to Kevin Freeman at the last moment. MacCullough got a piece of Freeman's shot, but the ball ended up back in the hands of Hamilton, who quickly put it in with one minute remaining to give UConn a 73–71 lead. It would be a foreshadowing of what was to come. Washington coach Bob Bender called a timeout and instructed guard Donald Watts to toss the ball down low once play resumed, but the junior had an idea of his own.

"I kind of knew I wasn't going to throw it inside," Watts said. "I felt it wasn't the time to try to tie the thing up but to put them away."

He would indeed get the ball at the three-point line, and although the 6-foot-7 Freeman was right in his face, Watts decided to shoot it anyway. Bender may not have liked what he saw, but with 33 seconds left Watts' shot sailed in to give UW its first lead of the game at 74–73.

UConn put the ball in the hands of El-Amin, who waited for the clock to tick down to 11 seconds before making his move. Center

Jake Voskuhl came out to the top of the key to set a pick, and El-Amin drove to the basket and rose as if to take the game-winning shot. But when three defenders gathered around him, he thought better of it and tossed it back over to Voskuhl. Unfortunately, the senior was in no better position to take the shot, as UW's Patrick Femerling stood right before him, ready to block any shot that came his way.

Voskuhl leaned back and tossed up a fade-away, which seemed to hit every part of the basket except the bottom of the net. By the time the ball rolled off the tin, nearly every player on the court had converged toward the basket for the rebound. But so many players got their hands on the ball that nobody grabbed the rebound, and the ball was tipped right back to where Voskuhl had stood moments before. By this point, however, the UConn forward was nowhere near the ball. After taking the fade-away, he had kept on backing up, right toward the three-point line.

Voskuhl watched as Hamilton, now standing in his old spot, grabbed the board and fired a leaning baby hook. But Hamilton's shot was also off the mark, creating yet another swarm for the rebound. This time it was Freeman who redirected the ball back toward the hoop, but his shot flew off the backboard and into another crowd of players. UW's Jan Wooten got enough of the ball to tip it as far away from the basket as possible, but standing there to catch it yet again was Hamilton, who grabbed UConn's third offensive rebound in as many seconds.

"I think it's all about who wants it the most," Moore said. "I mean, Coach is going to tell you it's about boxing out, being technical, fundamental. And I think it's all about wanting the ball and going to get it. "Despite just two seconds remaining, Hamilton had the presence of mind to do a pump fake before fading back as far as possible to release the final shot of the game. Watching from his back as the ball sailed in the air, Hamilton saw the ball fall through just as the buzzer expired, giving the Huskies a 75–74 win and a spot in the Elite Eight. And although he could barely even see it, he finally had the first buzzer-beater of his career. ●

UConn teammates mob Richard Hamilton after his heroic game-winning shot. *Alal Marler/AP Photo*

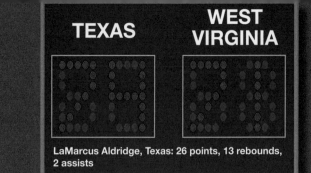

LaMarcus Aldridge, Texas: 26 points, 13 rebounds, 2 assists

2006: TEXAS vs. WEST VIRGINIA

Long before Kenton Paulino could set his sights on playing college basketball, he first had to set his sights on going to college. But as a first-generation American whose mother didn't know that one could earn a scholarship playing basketball, college seemed like a distant dream.

"In high school I kind of played basketball just to play ball, really not thinking about college or anything like that," said Paulino, who only started garnering interest from schools during his senior year. "But I still had no idea what went into it, what I was putting into it, because I didn't know the steps to take. I barely even knew about the SAT."

But before his final year, college coaches knew even less about Paulino than he knew about college. As a 6-foot-2, 130-pound guard, Paulino appeared to lack the strength to survive a season at the college level. Texas coach Rick Barnes, however, decided to give him a chance, and his faith in the recruit was rewarded. Paulino hit the weight room, and by the end of his senior year he had become one of the most accurate shooters in Longhorns history. Two victories in the 2006 NCAA Tournament set up a clash with the West Virginia Mountaineers, with a spot in the Elite Eight on the line. By this point, Paulino had nothing left to prove, but Barnes reminded his players that this was an opportunity to cement their legacy.

"He always preached toughness and, you know, this is what you live for. He gave one of those classic speeches to try to get us ready for that game," Paulino said. "So from the jump, we were ready to play and we knew what we were going up against and we knew what was at stake."

And early on it showed, as Texas raced out to a 6–0 lead. West Virginia fought back to score the next nine points, but the Longhorns soon realized they had a go-to player in LaMarcus Aldridge. The center couldn't miss, and by the time he recorded a dunk just before halftime, he was 8-of-8 from the field. Even better, the team was up 39–25 and West Virginia had yet to make a two-point field goal.

But before the game got out of hand, the Mountaineers recovered to make the next five shots, and forward Kevin Pittsnogle finally started to catch fire. His third shot of the half put West Virginia within 49–46, and when the big man nailed an open three-pointer from the corner, the game was tied at 58.

"You don't see a 6-foot-11 guy shoot like that, and he was arguably the best shooter on the team," WVU guard Mike Gansey said. "Guys would double me and leave him wide open, and then they'd go, what the heck are you doing leaving him wide open? And then the next play down, I'd be wide open."

Sure enough, Gansey swished a three-pointer on the next possession, and West Virginia had its first lead since the opening minutes of the first half. The Longhorns went back to Aldridge, and he put his team back in front 63–61 with 5:30 to go. Texas added another bucket to push the lead to four, and the margin was still the same when Gansey hit a layup with 2:26 left. That shot cut the lead to 67–65, and West Virginia looked poised to close the gap until Pittsnogle got tangled with Aldridge on a rebound with 1:29 left. Not only was Pittsnogle assessed with a foul, but he was on the receiving end of an elbow to the face. Aldridge's incidental contact caused a bloody nose, requiring Pittsnogle to leave the game until the bleeding stopped.

In the meantime, Aldridge added a free throw to push the lead to 68–65, and after WVU's J. D. Collins missed a layup at the other end, the Longhorns appeared ready to put the game away as the final minute approached. Moments later, the Mountaineers defense was able to knock the ball out of bounds, stopping the clock and allowing the refreshed Pittsnogle to return.

"We knew he was going to be back in the game, no doubt about it," Paulino said. "We knew that a bloody nose wasn't going to keep him out of that play."

When play resumed, Texas couldn't find an open shot, and Daniel Gibson had no choice but to launch a difficult three-pointer that clanged off the rim. Fortunately for the Longhorns, P. J. Tucker snatched the rebound, forcing WVU to foul. Tucker had the presence of mind to toss it to teammate A. J. Abrams, an 88 percent shooter, and the freshman sank both free throws to put UT up 70–65 with just 26.9 seconds to go.

Gansey connected on a deep three moments later to give the Mountaineers a chance, and this time they were smart enough to foul Aldridge, who was the worst free throw shooter on the court. His first attempt sailed long, and Texas called a timeout after Aldridge converted the second free throw. During the break, Barnes told his players not to foul, even though only 13.9 seconds remained. WVU forward Joe Herber tried to drive to the lane to draw defenders away from Pittsnogle, but by this point nobody was buying the routine.

When Herber fired it back to the three-point line, Pittsnogle was smothered by the defense. Using every inch of his 6-foot-11 frame, Pittsnogle faded away and sank the three-pointer with just five seconds left. "Without a doubt he was a folk hero. He is absolutely a folk hero," WVU coach John Beilein said of Pittsnogle. "Maybe the best shooting big man to ever play college basketball."

But Barnes had instructed the team not to call a timeout if the Mountaineers made a shot, hoping his players could score in transition. Abrams raced down the floor and fired a pass to Paulino that was almost out of his reach. But he corralled it in just before it sailed out of bounds and fired a shot from nearly 25 feet away. The buzzer rang as the ball sailed in the air, and a moment later Paulino's shot swished through the net.

"As soon as you hit that shot, it's like a rush of energy just goes through you and I had to let it out," Paulino said. "So I just yelled as loud as I can and I was kind of frozen there for a while, and then my teammates came and grabbed me."

But that was hardly the end of the celebration for Paulino. He asked for the videotape to be sent to his hotel room that night, where he watched it until three in the morning. Even after graduating, the shot still followed Paulino, who was playing in the NBA Developmental League when his team made a trade to bring in Pittsnogle.

"And guess whose roommate he was? He was my roommate in the D-League," Paulino laughed. "But he turned out to be a really nice guy, and we talked about it. I think he even called my shot a lucky shot to the media after the game, and I kept telling him that was no luck, that was a clean look."

Even after his playing days were over and he joined the Texas coaching staff, Paulino was still reminded of the shot every day. Before each home game, the Longhorns play the clip of his shot on the Jumbotron, where fans still cheer like they saw it for the first time. And deservedly so. ●

MICHIGAN STATE   **MARYLAND**

Durrell Summers, Michigan State: 26 points, 4 rebounds

2010: MICHIGAN STATE vs. MARYLAND

As Michigan State sophomore Korie Lucious watched the 2010 tournament unfold, he couldn't believe his eyes. During four consecutive days over the tournament's opening weekend, an unbelievable 17 games came down to the last minute of play, including the Spartans' first-round win over New Mexico State. For any fan of the game, this was the tournament at perfection.

"I mean, I watched every game throughout the whole tournament, and it was crazy the way the games went down to last-second shots and how many buzzer-beaters there were," Lucious said. "I felt like it was crazy—it was a different year that year."

Lucious had enjoyed his fill of incredible finishes, but when MSU coach Tom Izzo looked at the bracket, he knew the drama was far from over. In two days he would be facing Gary Williams, coach of a Maryland team that was one of the hottest in the country.

"Gary Williams is a good friend of mine, and we've had some epic battles," Izzo said. "They've all been one- or two-point games, and sure enough that's who we have to face in the second game."

This particular round, however, looked to be an easier win for the Spartans. Williams had to take a timeout when MSU raced out to a 15–7 lead, and just over two minutes later he had to burn a second timeout when the gap expanded to 22–10. The Spartans still led 44–35 after Kalin Lucas landed a teardrop late

in the first half, but when the All-American came back down, something felt wrong. Lucas hobbled to the ground, and the referees stopped play on the court. Although he didn't know it at the time, Lucas had just torn his ACL. If the Spartans were going to win this game, or any others for the rest of the tournament, it would be without their best player.

"When Kalin went down, the only thing I said to myself was it's time for me to step up. I mean, we really didn't have any other true point guards to come in and take control of the team and help us and lead us. So at that moment when he went down, I just knew it was the turning point of our tournament for our team," said Lucious, who was going to try to take the place of his teammate. "I was ready for the challenge. When he went down I was kind of sad, but at the same time I had to step up and be there to help my team try and get back to a Final Four and do whatever I could to help us win games."

Thanks to the play of Lucious and 5-of-6 shooting from behind the arc by teammate Durrell Summers, the Spartans continued to assert their will on offense. When center Derrick Nix slammed home a dunk with 12 minutes to play, the lead had grown to 67–51. MSU still led by 15 when Lucious drained a three-pointer from the corner with 8:40 left, and by 12 when Raymar Morgan scored with 4:46 to play, but the Terrapins were inching their way back. The lead shrunk all the way to 78–71 before Lucious converted a layup with two minutes to play, seemingly ending the comeback bid. And then Maryland senior Greivis Vasquez came alive.

The second-leading scorer in Maryland history, who by his standards had played a modest game with 17 points, converted a three-point play to bring the Terps within 80–74. Williams instructed his team to apply the full-court press, and the Terrapins lured Morgan into the corner, where they applied the trap. Maryland guard Sean Mosley came away with the steal and immediately laid it in, and when Morgan brought the ball past halfcourt, the Terrapins trapped him again. This time it was Cliff Tucker who swiped the ball away, and when Vasquez nailed a three from the left corner, his team was within 80–79 with 1:25 to play. Unbelievably, Tucker came up with yet another steal, and after Vasquez hit a bank shot with 38.7 seconds remaining, the Terrapins had taken their first lead in nearly 37 minutes.

"Vasquez almost single-handedly took the game with them, and it was an awesome

Korie Lucious watches his own shot sail toward the basket as the clock ticks down during Michigan State's second-round game against Maryland. Fortunately for Lucious and the Spartans, the shot hit nothing but net to send MSU into the Sweet Sixteen. *Gene Sweeney Jr/Baltimore Sun/MCT via Getty Images*

finish," Izzo said. "I think for Gary, that was a special team because he loved Vasquez."

Draymond Green answered back with a long jumper with 22 seconds left, only to have Vasquez drive to the lane and spin his way toward another basket with 6.6 seconds left. Michigan State, now down 83–82, would be inbounding the ball 90 feet away from the hoop.

"I knew, like everybody on the team knew, that we were going to win the game," Lucious said. "We all had extremely enormous confidence in each other and our abilities on the court and what we can do. So I think we had no doubt in our mind that we were going to win."

Green took the inbounds and raced toward the three-point line, where he was greeted by the Maryland defense. He faked the shot and threw it across toward the right side, where two Spartans stood. The first in line to receive the pass was sophomore Delvon Roe, who had the presence of mind to squat below the incoming ball, faking out the entire arena.

"And if Delvon Roe doesn't duck," Izzo pointed out, "if he puts his hands up, which 99 out of 100 kids will do, the game is over."

But now ready to receive the ball was a wide-open Lucious, who had been eying Green the entire time.

"Actually I didn't even know my teammate was there. I figured it was coming to me, but at the last second in the corner of my eye I saw him duck," Lucious said. "Thank God he did, because if he didn't, it probably would have hit him and we probably would have lost. I figured it was coming to me, but when he ducked I was like, oh man, that could have just ruined everything."

But there stood Lucious, just right of the top of the key, with the game in his hands. Lucious took one dribble and buried the three-pointer as time expired, prompting everyone on the team to tackle the hero of the game. A massive dogpile ensued, which of course saw Lucious at the bottom.

"I could breathe a little bit," Lucious smiled. "I found my ways."

The 2010 tournament, which would see more miracle finishes along the way, would go on to become the greatest NCAA Tournament of all time. But perhaps none was more thrilling than the game won by Korie Lucious. ●

1996: PRINCETON
VS. UCLA

After 29 years on the job, it had finally come to this. Just moments removed from clinching a spot in the NCAA Tournament, Princeton coach Pete Carril walked into a jubilant locker room and delivered a simple but tear-jerking message.

"I'm retiring," Carril wrote on the blackboard. "And I'm very happy."

The players, though happy as well, were going to miss their coach. His tell-it-like-it-is style of recruiting was truly one of a kind.

"He was the only guy who didn't say you're going to be great. He said, 'You're bad at this and this and this, but I can help you get better,'" center Steve Goodrich said. "He was an honest and direct communicator, which at the time kind of pisses you off, but he was right. He had credibility. He knew what he was talking about."

As freshman Gabe Lewullis would soon find out, nobody on the team was immune from Carril's rare honesty.

"He's in front of family members, and on the surface he can look like a really nice grandpa kind of figure—and then he sits you down," Lewullis laughed. "He told me I run like I have a piano on my back. He came to my house, and that's what he told me."

Fortunately, Lewullis had freed himself of the piano by the end of the year. But the Tigers didn't plan on doing much running against any team they faced in the tournament—especially when they found out they would be playing the UCLA Bruins, one of the quickest teams in the country—not to mention the defending national champions.

"The seeding came up and it was Princeton–UCLA, and I go, 'Who do we got in the second round?'—as a joke, to be honest with you," Lewullis said. "I honestly did not expect to win that game. I didn't pack enough underwear or socks, so I kind of had to reuse my underwear and socks for the games."

Not only would Carril refuse to run with the Bruins, he told his team to forget about rebounding. Literally.

"He told us that as soon as we shot the ball, he wanted all five guys to run back on defense, never to go for an offensive rebound," Lewullis said. "I never heard that before, and that goes against everything you're taught growing up."

Carril reasoned that the Bruins would be able to dominate any rebounding battles with their height and jumping ability, and his assumption was quickly affirmed when his team first encountered UCLA at practice the night before.

"A lot of people come to see UCLA. They are alley-ooping and doing 360s," said Goodrich, who was forced to follow up the dunk show with a layup drill. "The second time through the layup line, this one guy tried to do a dunk and we got one sarcastic clap."

The Tigers would concede the rebounds to the Bruins, but by running back on defense after every shot went up, Carril hoped his team would prevent any fast breaks. The plan sounded good on paper, but after UCLA had a quick 7–0 start, doubt started to set in.

"They won the Pac-10, they are defending national champions, they had four pros on the team. At some level we're not as good as them," Goodrich said. "The belief in yourself is something that has to evolve."

Belief finally came in the form of a Chris Doyle three-pointer. Doyle had played so poorly from the outset that he wanted to attempt at least one shot before his coach took him out. Instead, his three-pointer put the Tigers back in the game, and after another three by Lewullis, the deficit was just 7–6. Perhaps more importantly, the Tigers were able to slow the game down, and they found themselves down 19–16 just before halftime. With enough time for one more play, the team decided to run a play called "Center Forward," which—shockingly—calls for the center to pass the ball to a forward. Goodrich, who had been told that the play worked like clockwork when he came to Princeton, was disappointed to discover that the play hardly ever went according to plan. But on this night, Goodrich was able to find an open Lewullis cutting to the basket, and his layup just before the buzzer again put the Tigers within a point.

When the second half resumed, the now confident Tigers weren't going anywhere, as Sydney Johnson's three put Princeton back within a basket at 36–34. The team also realized it now had a rabid and growing crowd of support at the RCA Dome in Indianapolis. If there was any doubt as to whom the crowd was rooting for, one had to wait no further than a minute later when Reggie Miller appeared on the Jumbotron. Miller was an all-star for the hometown Indiana Pacers, but he was in attendance to support the Bruins, his alma mater. When his image flashed across the screen, Miller, who had been wearing his UCLA hat backwards, smiled and turned the cap around to a healthy chorus of boos.

"We knew we had to be in the game to make the crowd make a difference, but it was pretty cool to see the crowd get a lot of energy," Goodrich said of the noise, which was clearly affecting the Bruins. "They thought they're going to roll out the ball, we're going to roll over these guys by 25 points, and it's not happening."

But Princeton picked the wrong time to go cold from the field, and UCLA's lead eventually ballooned to 41–34—a pretty sizable margin to overcome considering the Tigers' slow pace and the shortage of time remaining. Johnson finally hit a much-needed three to cut the deficit to four points, and after a miss by UCLA's Toby Bailey, Goodrich grabbed a rebound to set up the offense. Moments later, he scored on a reverse layup to put Princeton within 41–39 with four minutes to go. After exchanging a pair of empty possessions, UCLA still had the ball with just over three minutes to go when Doyle came up with a steal, resulting in a three-on-one fast break. Johnson made the layup to tie the game, and three minutes remained.

The game was still tied at 41 with under a minute remaining when UCLA's Kris Johnson darted toward the hoop and attempted a floater. The shot hit off the front of the rim, and Goodrich grabbed the rebound. Princeton walked the ball up the floor and Carril called a timeout with 21 seconds left. There wasn't much of a debate as to which play to call. The Tigers were going to run "Center-Forward."

The UCLA coaches assumed the same, and they instructed their players to watch out for the backdoor pass. Anticipating exactly what was coming, UCLA's Charles O'Bannon was right with Lewullis when the freshman tried to cut to the basket. But time had not run out.

"At the end of the game I cut the first time, and just like Carill trained us to do, drilled in my head, you run back out to the three-point line and cut back again," Lewullis said. "Stevie threw a perfect pass, and anybody on the team would have done what I did."

Lewullis ran back to his original spot, as if to retrieve a pass there, and this time O'Bannon bit. As soon as his defender motioned away from the hoop, Lewullis cut right back, and Goodrich gave him the perfect pass. In one swift motion, Lewullis took the ball and banked in the shot with just under four seconds to go. And as UCLA's last-second shot rimmed off, Princeton had pulled off an upset for the ages.

"I still to this day will tell you that if we played them 100 times they would probably beat us 99 times," said Lewullis.

That might be true. But on that night, they did win. And that's all that matters. ●

Bryce Drew, Valpo: 22 points, 8 assists, 3 rebounds

1998: VALPARAISO vs. MISSISSIPPI

The most important recruiting visit Homer Drew ever took also turned out to be his shortest. The Valparaiso coach, hoping to land the player who could send his team to its first-ever NCAA Tournament, traveled to the home of a high school star who was being courted by major schools across the country. Fortunately for Drew, the visit didn't eat too much into the recruiting budget, as the house he was visiting also happened to be the one he owned. Waiting inside was his son Bryce, who was passing on several other offers to play for Homer. Although this was clearly a family affair, the NCAA required Homer Drew to make an official visit to his own home.

"You know, they were pretty much normal parents through the whole process. They really didn't do recruiting until basically the very end," said Bryce. "They kind of sat back as parents and wanted to see what were the best options for me and where I'd be happiest."

And Bryce was happiest at Valparaiso, where his older brother Scott was an assistant coach alongside his father. The new recruit made his presence known rather quickly, leading the Crusaders to 65 wins over his first three seasons. But none of those wins had come in the NCAA Tournament, and when the team was paired against Mississippi on Selection Sunday, Bryce knew it was his last chance to get that tournament victory. That is, if his team could get to the game.

The first obstacle to getting there came after the conference championship game, when the team bus ran out of gas. Some of the assistant coaches decided to trek to the nearest town, where a local policeman helped them get fuel and bring it back to the bus. It wasn't until 5 a.m. that the team arrived back home, where they were greeted with a massive snowstorm that knocked out power and made travel virtually impossible. By the time the Crusaders made it to Oklahoma City for their first-round game, they had less than 48 hours to prepare for tip-off.

"As a coach I was very concerned that we didn't get enough practice time, and of course hindsight is always great," Homer said. "As you look back, it was probably a blessing, because we were very well rested when we finally got to Oklahoma City for that game."

It didn't take the fourth-seeded Rebels long to get the message—Valpo wasn't just there to serve as a tune-up for the second round. The Crusaders held All-American Ansu Sesay to just four points, and despite allowing 17 first-half points from guard Keith Carter, Valparaiso trailed just 38–34 as the first half came to a close.

After battling through 13 ties or lead changes in the second half, it looked like the Crusaders finally gained the upper hand when they grabbed a 63–58 lead with just 6:23 to go—but Carter struck again. His three-pointer with just over four minutes left put the Rebels within a point, and when teammate Rahim Lockhart added three free throws moments later, the Rebels had taken a 69–67 lead.

Although Ole Miss failed to pad the lead, the Crusaders would miss their next three shots, the last of which occurred with just 45 seconds remaining, nearly allowing Mississippi to run out the clock. But Valpo responded by forcing freshman Jason Flanigan to take Mississippi's final shot with 16 seconds to go. Valparaiso came away with the rebound, and Drew brought the ball up the floor.

Drew spotted up to take the game-winning three-pointer, but when the defense closed in, he was forced to shovel a pass over to teammate Zoran Viskovic. The center immediately tossed it back to Drew, who had managed to find an open crease in the defense. But his shot bounced off the front of the rim, and by the time they fouled Sesay, just 4.1 seconds remained.

"You know, everything happened so quick there really wasn't time to think about it," Drew said. "I think we were all so focused and we still had faith and belief that we can still win."

After Sesay missed the first free throw, Homer called a timeout and reminded his team that the game was not over. The players looked at each other and decided to run "Pacer," a play that they had dreaded practicing the whole season. It was a desperation play designed to cover the length of the court in a matter of seconds, but it was also one that seemed like it would never be used. Well, now was their

chance, and Homer was more than on board with the call.

"All I did was say yes, so at that point I felt like we had already won the game because the players knew what to do—they didn't need me," Drew said. "I love for our players to make decisions on their own, and that's part of what we teach is to be a leader and know if we're behind what we're going to do to try and get a shot."

When the team returned, Sesay's second free throw again missed and fell out of bounds, but now only 2.5 seconds remained. On the inbounds, Jamie Sykes heaved the ball past midcourt, where in one motion Bill Jenkins caught the ball and threw it over to Bryce, who again was open at the three-point line. But this time, just as the clock struck zero, he buried the miraculous game-winner.

"It did feel a little short. And if you watch the replay, because we watched it in slow motion, it barely creeps over the front of the rim," Drew laughed. "It kind of skids it, so again, just a blessing it went in."

Bryce attempted to slide across the floor, but his body stuck to the court, resulting in an awkward celebration. Luckily his team piled on top of him, giving him back a few style points. Bryce went to his dad and simply said, "We did it!"—to which Homer replied even more simply, "I love you, Bryce." It was hardly a moment either will forget anytime soon.

"At Valpo it's kind of neat because they call it 'The Shot,' and it seems like it happened yesterday," said Homer, who shares the sentiment with every Crusaders fan. "I had one of our alums, he was driving from Detroit back to campus, he said he heard it on the radio. He pulled over on the side of the road and did a giant scream."

The miracle was a fitting end for Drew, who cherished a quote from LSU coach Dale Brown: "The impossible is what no one can do until someone does it."

Impossible? No. But the probability someone else will do it again? Not likely. ●

Bryce Drew had put the team on his back all season, but he took that theme to a whole new level after his buzzer-beater upset fourth-seeded Ole Miss. *Valparaiso Athletic Department*

CALIFORNIA WEST VIRGINIA

Denny Fitzpatrick, California: 20 points, 2 rebounds

1959: CALIFORNIA vs. WEST VIRGINIA

If there was ever a team that seemed like it didn't belong in an NCAA title game, it had to be the 1959 Cal Bears. It was not because they weren't talented, but because it didn't seem like any of their players would have ever ended up on Cal's basketball team.

Their leader was Pete Newell, who gave up an acting career to enter the coaching profession. Bob Dalton had originally come to Berkeley on a football scholarship, but with a body that Newell said looked like a picture from an X-ray, that dream quickly turned to basketball. Bill McClintock was considered out of shape, and center Darrall Imhoff was considered, even worse, a liability. With virtually no high school experience to gain recognition, Imhoff had little to show for his basketball skills. In fact, he had depended on the initiative of his aunt to join the basketball team.

"My aunt told Pete about a place for me to stay. And he said to her, 'Well, I'm not the housing director; I'm the basketball coach,'" recalled Imhoff, whose aunt replied that he was nearly 6-foot-9. "He said, 'Well, what's his name?' She told him, and it didn't mean much to him."

Having never seen the recruit play, Newell decided to call Imhoff's high school coach, who had seen little of Imhoff himself due to his uncanny knack for sustaining injuries. His own high school coach admitted that the center was injury prone, in addition to lacking ability. Nevertheless, Newell took a chance on Imhoff and allowed the youngster to join the team as a

walk-on, only to see him break his foot as soon as the season started. When Imhoff finally did earn a scholarship during his sophomore year, he was still relegated to third string.

By the next year, however, Imhoff's play had drastically improved, and Cal had all the pieces in place for a successful campaign. But that hardly meant the team was any sort of favorite to win the NCAA Tournament. Of the 16 teams that qualified for the tournament that year, *Sports Illustrated* ranked the Bears No. 15, giving them little chance of advancing very far. But somehow they reeled off three straight upsets, and as the field dwindled down to just two teams, they found themselves still alive.

As incredible as their run had been, however, it was supposed to come to a disappointing end against heavily favored West Virginia. The Mountaineers had actually thought so little of their opponent that they had almost no knowledge of the Golden Bears. Naturally assuming that Cincinnati would destroy Cal in the semifinals, West Virginia coach Fred Schaus spent nearly all of his time preparing for a showdown with the Bearcats. But with All-American Jerry West leading the team, most felt it didn't matter how much preparation the Mountaineers had.

"Athletes to a fault, no matter what they say, no matter what the context, always think they're equal to the challenge," said Bob Dalton, the senior responsible for guarding West. "You always got to go into the situation thinking you're going to win. You never can be intimidated by who you're playing, so you got to believe you can do it."

West paved the way early on as the Mountaineers grabbed a 23–13 lead, but the unfazed Bears stormed back. Dalton and teammate Jack Grout held West without a field goal for an eight-minute stretch as the Bears took a 39–33 lead into the break. Not long after play resumed, the Bears actually pushed the lead to 49–36.

"All of a sudden things started—we realized we could do anything we wanted offensively, and so I think it was just a manifestation of the guys saying, 'let's get going here,'" Dalton said. "Pete, at the point when we're up 13 points, of course he wanted to bring time off the clock, so he said slow it down."

Newell's decision turned out to be a costly one, as the cautious Bears killed their momentum. West Virginia started forcing turnovers, and with three minutes to go the lead had shrunk to 65–62. The lead was still just three points when Cal's Bill McClintock put back his own miss to give Cal a 69–64 cushion, and after a stop at the other end it appeared the Bears would survive after all. But their relief was short-lived, as Bernie Simpson was called for traveling and WVU's Marv Bolyard knocked down a pair of free throws to cut the lead to 69–66. Bolyard then intercepted the ensuing inbounds pass and dished it off to West, whose shot was blocked by Imhoff after it hit the backboard, resulting in a goaltending violation.

All of a sudden, the lead was down to 69–68 with 40 seconds to go. With no shot clock in effect at the time, Newell warned his players—unless a layup presented itself, do not shoot the ball. The goal, of course, was to run out the clock or force West Virginia to foul. But when Imhoff received a pass with 20 seconds left, the temptation was just too great.

"I can hear Pete yelling on the bench, 'No!'" laughed Imhoff. "It's kind of like the guy at the Augusta Masters with the putt that could cost you half a million dollars."

His hook shot was from only five feet away, but it was off the mark, giving West Virginia new life. But Imhoff made up for his lapse in judgment by tipping it back in a second later to put Cal back in front 71–68. Still, 17 seconds remained. WVU raced down the court and Willie Akers put in a shot to cut the lead back to one, but by the time they were able to foul Cal's Denny Fitzpatrick, only one second remained. His free throw rimmed out, but before West could fire the ball downcourt, the buzzer sounded. The Cal Bears were the new national champions.

For McClintock, a Milwaukee native who had been told by a Marquette scout that he would never be able to play college basketball, the win was extra sweet.

"No one gave us a chance," McClintock said. "We were definitely the underdogs. You kind of take that with you throughout life."

When McClintock ran into the same scout years later, he proudly displayed his national championship watch, earned in no small part to his clutch play in the final minutes. Needless to say, Bill McClintock had proven his doubters wrong. ●

Coach Pete Newell is carried off the court after Cal's 71–70 victory over West Virginia. *Charlie Kelly/AP Photo*

#21

1958: SEATTLE vs. SAN FRANCISCO

Long before he was even old enough to earn his first paycheck, John Castellani was certain of what the future held in store.

"When I was 14, I knew there were two things I wanted to do in life," Castellani said. "I wanted to coach and become a lawyer."

So eager was Castellani to check the first goal off the list that he accepted the head coaching job at Seattle University—before even visiting the campus. Little did the 29-year-old know, however, that he was taking over a program with some of the worst facilities in the country. The practice court was an old floor purchased from a nearby army base, and the arena was the equivalent of most high school gymnasiums.

The facilities could have used a little renovating, but the naive coach was also about to inherit something that would easily compensate for any playing surface they were using. The school officials hadn't wanted Castellani to take the job only because of the talent at his disposal, so they had avoided mentioning that the roster would also include Elgin Baylor, a future NBA Hall of Famer and recent transfer from the College of Idaho. Without the scouting tools available today, Castellani knew almost nothing about Baylor's potential until the new recruit started practicing with the team.

"The first time I saw him, he was playing with our players and they were playing pickup, and it was like our guys were in the eighth or ninth grade," senior Jim Harney laughed. "He

was further ahead of the game than any player has ever been ahead of the game. Baylor was in a class by himself for a long time."

Baylor quickly made a name for himself once the season started, and despite being just a sophomore he finished as the nation's third-leading scorer. The following year, Baylor finished second in scoring while leading the Chieftains to a berth in the NCAA Tournament. A first-round blowout of Wyoming set up a meeting with heavily favored San Francisco. The Dons were coming off three consecutive trips to the Final Four, including national championships in 1955 and 1956. With a 25–1 record heading into the 1958 tournament, San Francisco looked primed to win another NCAA title. It didn't help matters that the game would be played just five miles from USF's campus.

"We were used to situations that were tough," Harney said. "We had played tough teams that had beaten us."

Nevertheless, knowing that his team would need its best performance in order to have a chance, Castellani told his players that if they made more than seven mistakes, they would lose the game. But thanks to the brilliant tactics of USF coach Phil Woolpert, the first half was a disaster for Seattle. The Chieftains eclipsed the seven-turnover limit early in the game, and a double team on Baylor kept him scoreless for nearly the first eight minutes of play. Fortunately, Baylor started to develop a little rhythm, preventing the deficit from ever growing beyond four points. After he fired a pass the length of the floor to Jerry Frizzell for a buzzer-beating layup, the team trailed by only two, 33–31.

Time and again San Francisco tried to pull away, but the Chieftains answered each call, and they began to trade leads with USF as the final stretch approached. The turning point appeared to come when USF's Mike Farmer picked up his fifth foul with three minutes to play. Although the Dons had been double-teaming Baylor all night, it had primarily been the job of the 6-foot-7 Farmer to shut him down. Seattle started feeding the ball to Baylor, and when he sank two free throws with 1:27 remaining, the visitors went on top 67–66. USF decided to hold for the last shot, but Art Day was fouled with 15 seconds to go, and he stepped to the line to shoot two free throws. Day sank the first shot, but when his second hit off the rim, Seattle snatched the

board and called a timeout. Castellani called for Baylor to take the last shot, but the Dons also knew exactly who was getting the ball.

"When you got a guy with his talent, everybody is going to come to him," Castellani said. "And that's what happened."

Not willing to let the All-American beat them that easily, the Dons hounded Baylor before he could even get within 35 feet of the hoop. Baylor tried to fight through the crowd of defenders, but finally, with time winding down, he had no choice but to fire away. Blessed with unlimited range, Baylor was close enough where he could use his regular follow-through.

"It was just a regular jump shot," Harney said. "It wasn't like a cast-off. He went up in the air and shot it."

The 6-foot-7 Baylor rose above the trio of defenders, and just as the horn went off, the ball sailed through the net to win the game. The San Francisco crowd watched in shock as the team ran toward Baylor to celebrate.

The Chieftains then defeated Cal in the same arena, with the same partisan crowd, to land a trip to Louisville for the Final Four. But what they encountered on the plane ride there was much scarier than any road environment, as they battled enough turbulence to recognize that something was seriously wrong.

"It was like being a fighter pilot. We were sideways to the left; we were sideways to the right. We were flying straight; we were dropping," Harney said. "It was very harrowing, and I later found out we were flying between two tornadoes."

The team made it to Louisville, and Castellani suddenly realized he had become the hottest coaching commodity in the country.

"It's easy to be successful at that age if you have the best ballplayer that's playing in the country," Castellani joked.

Baylor was already primed for the NBA, but with the newfound recognition, Castellani landed the head coaching job for the Minneapolis Lakers, who had just taken Baylor with the top pick in the draft. College basketball's most exciting duo was reunited once again. ●

Seattle's Elgin Baylor goes in for a tip against USF's Art Day. *Robert H. Houston/AP Photo*

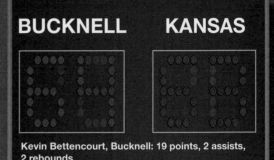

BUCKNELL   **KANSAS**

Kevin Bettencourt, Bucknell: 19 points, 2 assists, 2 rebounds

2005: BUCKNELL vs. KANSAS

When the NCAA selection committee paired Bucknell against Kansas in the 2005 NCAA Tournament, it could not have chosen two schools with less in common. Bucknell, a Patriot League team that had never won an NCAA Tournament game, was facing a school that was nearly 10 times larger and a team that was infinitely more talented. While the Bison would be taking their first chartered flight out to Oklahoma City for their opening-round matchup, this was just another day at the office for the Jayhawks, who had 73 tournament wins on their resume.

In the days leading up to the game, Bucknell coach Pat Flannery tried to convince his players that they were capable of playing with Kansas. After all, Flannery told his team, they had road victories against Pitt and Holy Cross, the regular-season champions of their conference. Nevertheless, it's hard to convince the school with the top graduation rate (they didn't even hand out athletic scholarships) that they are on par with the nation's No. 1 team in RPI, a team that had been to two Final Fours in the last three years.

"We knew that we *could* do it, but I don't think any of us knew we had a real chance against Kansas," said Chris McNaughton, Bucknell's 6-foot-11 center from Germany.

Even in the minutes leading up to the game, the Bison players joked about playing in the last game on Friday, stating that at least they were one of the final 33 teams in the country. But right before they took the court, the Bison watched fellow mid-major Vermont upset Syracuse.

"All of a sudden, it goes from maybe should've or could've to we all said, 'Hey, this could be us—we could do this,'" Flannery recalled.

But his team was greeted with a rude awakening as the game started. KU's Aaron Miles intercepted a pass and tossed the ball to Michael Lee for a three-point play. After 2:30 of action, the Bison already found themselves in a 5–0 deficit.

"There are people in press row that our kids recognize from TV," Flannery said. "First of all, you don't want to be shut out, because that makes news."

Luckily for Flannery, Bettencourt prevented any embarrassing headlines with a four-point play in front of the Kansas bench. Sensing the nervousness in his teammates, Bettencourt told everybody to calm down, reminding them that they were right in the game again. That play sparked the offense, as he and junior Charles Lee found the touch from beyond the three-point line to put Bucknell in front. Meanwhile, at the other end of the court, the Bison were completely throwing Kansas off their game. Using a 3-2 matchup zone that prevented any three-pointers in the first half, the Bison built up a 28–21 lead before KU reeled off the last 10 points of the half. It wasn't the ideal way to enter the locker room, but the run actually took a little pressure off Flannery's club, who didn't have to protect their lead.

"To go in there up 10, now you're pushing to be up 15 and you're correcting mistakes," Flannery said. "I can remember halftime being so positive, being such a great time, saying, 'Guys, we're right there—this is our ballgame!'"

The second half began as a seesaw affair, with neither team going up by more than two possessions. The Jayhawks trailed just 53–52 when they tried to implement a full-court press with 3:11 left. Although the Jayhawks nearly came up with a steal on two different occasions, the Bison were able to keep possession long enough to find a wide-open Chris Niesz behind the three-point line. His shot put the Bison up by four, and his team would eventually work the lead to 62–57 before the margin seemed to disappear before their eyes.

Kansas' Michael Lee hit a pair of free throws to cut the lead to 62–59 with 1:08 to play, and he followed it moments later with a steal. Bucknell's Charles Lee committed the foul to prevent an easy layup, but the officials ruled that he had committed the foul from behind—resulting in a "clear-path foul." Not only would Lee get two free throws, both of which he would hit, but the Jayhawks would also get to keep the ball. They would make the most of their extra possession as Keith Langford sank another pair of free throws to give Kansas a 63–62 lead with just 24 seconds left to play.

"We made some pretty big mistakes in that game in giving Kansas even a chance to win," McNaughton remembered. "We were a little nervous in the end because we realized, 'Oh my gosh, we might actually pull this off.'"

Instead of taking a timeout, Flannery actually showed confidence in his players, allowing them to create their own shot. The team decided to work the ball into McNaughton, who took a bounce pass about eight feet from the hoop. Spinning to his left, McNaughton unleashed a hook shot that bounced off the glass and into the net for a 64–63 lead with 10.5 seconds left. McNaughton took some chiding after the game for using the backboard—perhaps rightfully so.

"I don't know how many hook shots I've shot in my life from the front like that. I've never intended to bank one of them," McNaughton laughed.

Langford raced down the court for the pull-up jumper, but the shot failed to reach the iron and John Griffin—the smallest player on the court—came up with a huge rebound. Griffin stepped to the line with just 3.5 seconds remaining and had a chance to extend the lead to three, but he missed the front end of a one-and-one. Wayne Simien pulled in the rebound as the Jayhawks called a timeout with 2.4 seconds left. The plan was for Lee, standing at the baseline, to throw the ball the length of the floor to Simien.

When Simien caught the ball with his back to the basket and turned around for the jumper, it looked like Christian Laettner's shot would be relived all over again. But as the clock expired, Simien's shot bounced off the front iron, sparking a wild celebration for the Bison. The players gathered at center court, except for McNaughton, who initially ran to the opposite end of the court before realizing he was celebrating by himself. Luckily for McNaughton, he would have plenty of time to celebrate the win.

The players arrived back on campus to a parade celebrating their victory. Of course, being in Lewisburg, Pennsylvania, the parade didn't exactly last long.

"I don't think it even went three blocks," Bettencourt laughed. "I think we went down one road, took a right, took another right, and we were back at school."

As Bettencourt would soon discover, however, not all the notoriety was welcome.

"We arrived that night. I wake up, I go to my first class, and I'm running 10 minutes late," Bettencourt smiled. "My professor was my academic advisor—she'd be the first one to bust my chops if I was late. I walk into class, and I'm kind of nervous just trying to get in the back before no one notices. They all start clapping. I get a standing ovation."

Considering he had just delivered the biggest win in school history, perhaps Bettencourt deserved a pass just this once. ●

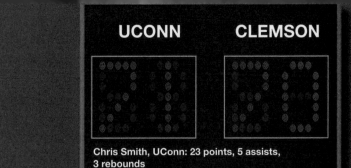

UCONN   CLEMSON

Chris Smith, UConn: 23 points, 5 assists, 3 rebounds

1990: CONNECTICUT vs. CLEMSON

Before the start of the 1989–90 season, many fans and analysts predicted that the UConn men's basketball team would carry on a tradition that had been going on for more than 30 years. A tradition, that is, of irrelevance in the basketball world. Since 1968, the Huskies had qualified for only two NCAA Tournaments, and 1990 looked to be no different. Connecticut was picked to finish near the bottom of the Big East yet again, despite the fact that new coach Jim Calhoun had the program turning in the right direction.

If the facilities were any indication of on-court success, 1990 would be the same as any other year. The team was playing in a 46-year-old venue that was home to five other sports. The fieldhouse sat only 4,600 people, but what it lacked in size it made up for in charm.

"Fans were fans because they loved UConn basketball—fans didn't expect us to win," forward Scott Burrell said. "There were no All-Americans, so everybody loved the effort we gave on the court."

So when the team actually got on a roll, the entire state was caught up in Huskymania, sensing they were a team of destiny. Their feelings were only more solidified on Selection Sunday, when the 31–5 Huskies earned a No. 1 seed, which meant they would get to play their first two games in Hartford. Two easy victories there meant that senior Tate George would get to face Clemson at the Meadowlands in

New Jersey, just minutes from his hometown of Newark.

"That really was the culmination of a perfect season for us and then the icing on the cake," George said. "When you grow up, you dream about playing on television and getting that kind of exposure, but to be playing on TV on a national level and to be close to home was really something."

With the George family out in full force, the Huskies attacked Clemson with a full-court press. The Tigers could barely get the ball past midcourt, and by the end of the first half UConn had forced 16 turnovers, and went into the locker room with a comfortable 38–29 lead.

"We knew one thing we could do well. We weren't a great scoring team, but we knew we had great athletes and we could play great defense," Burrell said. "And once we knew our defense was going to cause teams to fall over, we released that fuel every night in practice and every night we stepped on the court."

Calhoun warned his team that the game was far from over. Just a week earlier, the Tigers had come back from a 19-point deficit against La Salle for the right to face UConn. But Clemson's 79–75 victory that night was almost more of a norm than an exception.

"In our scouting report prior to playing them, they said, listen, they are a second-half team, they play better from behind," George said. "When you're young, you don't think it's going to happen to you. I remember when we were up by 15, 16 points and we thought we were walking away with it. I remember the coaches during the timeouts are saying, 'They are going to make a run.'"

Sure enough, as soon as John Gwynn's free throw pushed the gap to 59–40, Clemson went into comeback mode. The Tigers still had much of the second half remaining, and they slowly chipped away at the lead. Before long the margin was 63–48, and after Dale Davis tipped in a miss, Clemson's deficit was 65–53. Kirkland Howland's three-pointer put the Tigers within seven points, prompting Calhoun to call a timeout with 4:29 to go.

"When you have a big lead, it's hard to keep up the energy. That's for anybody, no matter what level or who you're playing against," Burrell said. "You get comfortable with your lead and you don't play with the same energy, the same enthusiasm, the same hunger, and that's what led them to come back."

Clemson continued to attack after the timeout, and after a layup with four minutes to go, the lead was down to just 67–65. The Huskies continued to hold onto their lead, however, and when Davis stepped out of bounds with just 21 seconds left and Clemson trailing 69–67, the game appeared to be over.

Now with the game looking desperate, the Tigers were back in their comfort zone. They hounded George after he received the inbounds pass, forcing him to get rid of the ball. His pass hit a teammate and sailed out of bounds, giving the Tigers one more chance. They inbounded the ball near midcourt, anticipating that they would run down the clock for the last shot. But when the Huskies left David Young all by himself in the corner of the floor, the Tigers opted for the easy scoring opportunity. Young sank the relatively uncontested three-pointer, and Clemson had come out with a miraculous 70–69 lead.

"We had a little lapse, a mental error, with about eleven seconds left when he hit that three-pointer," Burrell said. "A lot of times coaches would blast you for making a mental error, but we were just focused on what we had to do next and how we're going to get the ball in bounds, how we got to try and get the ball closer to the rim and get a bucket."

George took the ball near midcourt and drove hard toward the hoop. The defense assumed he was driving for a layup, and when he pulled up for a jumper near the top of the key, he was wide open. But his shot hit the front of the rim, and Clemson's Sean Tyson grabbed the rebound. The Huskies quickly fouled him, but with just 1.6 seconds remaining it appeared their fate was sealed.

Tyson's first free throw rattled in and out, and Burrell quickly snatched the rebound and called a timeout. One second still remained, and Calhoun knew exactly which play to run. Burrell, who years earlier had turned down a $100,000 contract from the Seattle Mariners, would use his strength and accuracy to fire a full-length pass down the court.

"We had always practiced that play, and different guys would take the shot at practice," George said. "But we never did it with one second. We always had five seconds, four seconds, and I think three was the lowest on the clock we played in practice."

Before the referees handed Burrell the ball, George could hear the Clemson players screaming to not foul. He jostled with Tyson to gauge how tightly he would be guarded, and after no pushback, George knew he would at least get a shot at the ball. Burrell heaved the ball 90 feet away, right into the hands of a leaping Tate George. As soon as he landed on the ground, George twisted his body and let the ball go just before the buzzer. And miraculously, it fell through.

"The interesting part about it—I was telling people when I caught it—there was a guy in front of me so I never even saw the basket. It was just a catch and turn and throw the ball up, and my delayed reaction was because I didn't think I got it off in time," George laughed. "Once I realized we got it off, it was bedlam."

The whole team ran over to the hero, while the Tate George section screamed from the stands. His shot not only put the Huskies in the Elite Eight, it also signified that Connecticut's days of losing were over.

"I'll always go back to the 1990 game as the game that got it all started. I went to Connecticut because I wanted to create history. I didn't want to be a part of history; I wanted to create it," George said.

And three national championships later, UConn is here to stay. ●

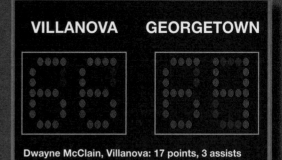

Dwayne McClain, Villanova: 17 points, 3 assists

#18

1985: VILLANOVA vs. GEORGETOWN

When the Villanova Wildcats arrived at the 1985 NCAA Tournament, a national championship was the last thing on their minds. After enduring a 20–10 season, they had little reason to believe their fortune would suddenly change while facing the best teams that college basketball had to offer. But five upsets later, the eighth-seeded Wildcats found themselves in the national championship game against Georgetown. The recent success did little to persuade fans, who gave the Wildcats almost no chance of winning. It was a position that they had become quite accustomed to over the previous three weeks.

"To actually have your family members and friends watch it, the biggest thing is many of them were feeling, okay, you guys got this far, but you may not beat Georgetown. It's just not going to happen," senior Ed Pinckney laughed. "They were just so dominant, so intimidating, so well coached, so experienced. They had talent. They just had everything you would want in a team."

The 35–2 Hoyas, coached by John Thompson, were winners of 16 straight games and appeared to be unbeatable. Not only had Georgetown already beaten Villanova twice that season, this was their third appearance in the championship game in the last four years. This would also mark the last game for Georgetown center Patrick Ewing, one of the best college basketball players of all time. But that didn't stop Pinckney from telling his team not to worry about Ewing—he would take care of guarding the big man.

"The key to the whole thing was Ed Pinckney because he loved to play against Patrick Ewing, and that was really very important," Villanova coach Rollie Massimino said. "And Eddie was sick for the championship game, but he still played terrific."

Thanks to some accurate shooting from Pinckney and his teammates, Villanova was keeping pace with the top-seeded Hoyas. When Dwayne McClain banked in a shot with just over seven minutes left in the first half, the score was tied at 20. Most remarkably, the Wildcats were shooting 90 percent from the field. While Georgetown's opponents had shot an average of less than 40 percent a game, the Wildcats were on pace to shatter the tournament's single-game field goal percentage record. As if that weren't aggravating enough for the Hoyas, forward Harold Pressley sank a shot just before the buzzer to give Villanova a 29–28 lead at halftime. Georgetown guard Reggie Williams responded by taking a swipe at Villanova's Chuck Everson, who mentioned the altercation to the officials before heading into their locker room.

Fans watching on television could see both teams going peacefully into their respective tunnels at opposite ends of the arena. What they did not see was that the locker rooms were actually situated next to each other, forcing the teams to cross paths behind the bleachers—a meeting that could have quickly turned ugly.

"He came in, he was going nuts. He was going crazy," Pinckney remembered as Massimino entered the locker room. "But after everyone settled down with the Chuck incident, he talked to us about going out in the second half and having a good time and just being real relaxed."

His players responded by playing a nearly perfect second half. Picking up right where they left off, the Wildcats shot 9-of-10 in the second half for a 22-of-28 performance on the night—shattering the previous mark for shooting percentage.

"You're just thinking where everybody's playing so well, I just don't know if we can lose a game. It wasn't any particular thing that happened or was said. I just think it started right at the beginning of the tournament, and fortunately for us we were able to just keep it going. I think that's the thing," Pinckney said. "We didn't say it, but we all just felt like we are playing so good, we might have a chance to win this game."

The Hoyas may not have been breaking any shooting records, but they weren't about to just hand Villanova the championship. When David Wingate banked in a jumper to give Georgetown a 54–53 lead, and after Villanova turned the ball over on the ensuing possession, the Hoyas went into a stall. It was an unusual move for the favored team to slow the pace down, but with just over two minutes remaining, it was a strategy that would force the Wildcats to play overly aggressive defense. It didn't take long for the plan to backfire, however, as Georgetown forward Bill Martin bounced a pass off a teammate's foot, right into the hands of the Villanova defense. The Wildcats had a second life.

Harold Jensen, who hadn't missed all day, decided he wasn't about to miss his first shot anytime soon. Jensen's long jumper put

Villanova back in front, and moments later his free throws gave the Wildcats a 59–54 lead with just 90 seconds to go.

"He always was a good shooter," Massimino said of Jensen. "And I had to convince him that he was a good shooter, and he got his confidence."

Jensen continued to deliver, as his free throws with 1:10 left put the Wildcats up 61–56, a lead they would not relinquish. Georgetown got within 66–64 with two seconds to play, but all the Wildcats had to do was inbound the ball and they would be crowned national champions. But with that much at stake, it's easier said than done.

"First of all, you always see the improbable happen in the tournament," Pinckney laughed. "It's sort of like you're almost literally holding your breath for that entire couple of seconds."

Dwayne McClain, the player meant to receive the inbounds pass, actually slipped down right before the ball was thrown, leaving the door open for a Georgetown miracle. But McClain caught the ball from his knees, and time ran out to give his team the biggest upset in championship history. It was a moment Villanova fans would never forget.

"Ten years later I'm walking around in Philadelphia and people are saying like, man, what a game—holy cow," Pinckney said. "I think over time it's given us great perspective on how special of a game it was for the university and for all of us."

Not even the most optimistic of Villanova fans could have predicted a national championship, which is why the players had to scramble to find suits for their upcoming visit to the White House. A simple wardrobe problem wasn't going to deny their shot to meet the president—that was certainly one shot they weren't going to miss. ●

NORTH CAROLINA · MICHIGAN STATE

Lennie Rosenbluth, UNC: 29 points, 3 rebounds

#17

1957: NORTH CAROLINA vs. MICHIGAN STATE

During the course of their undefeated season in 1956–57, UNC coach Frank McGuire had begun to make winning look routine. Time and again his Tar Heels had been on the verge of dropping their first game, only to come back from an impossible situation and escape with another victory. For his hard work and quick thinking, the 43-year-old was an easy choice for both the ACC Coach of the Year and national Coach of the Year awards from the media. Before his players took on Michigan State in the semifinals, however, McGuire made a mistake. It was one of the only errors he made all year, but it was almost enough to end their season.

As the 30–0 Tar Heels prepared to take the court against the Spartans, they were a clear favorite to advance to the championship game. The Spartans, who entered the game with a meager 16–8 record, were not even expected to keep the game close. But McGuire was determined to show his players just how big of a favorite they were by playing a tape full of MSU lowlights. It was a convincing reel of footage, but what it actually did was fool the players into a false sense of security. Lennie Rosenbluth, who took almost as many shots as the rest of his team combined, was a ghastly 11-of-42 from the field. His teammates, who shot 17-of-46, didn't fare much better.

"I didn't like the lighting. I thought it was the darkest place in the world, and we did not play two very good ballgames up there, to be honest with you," Rosenbluth said of the neutral arena in Kansas City. "We were terrible against Michigan State. I mean, we were absolutely terrible against them. The lighting was bad and of course they had Johnny Green, who was blocking everything that I shot up."

Thanks to the play of Green, the Spartans entered halftime tied at 29, and as the final minute of regulation approached, they had still managed to keep up with the Tar Heels. If they could just come up with more defensive stop, they would force the game into overtime. And not only did the MSU defense shut down the Tar Heels as they had all night, but when they snatched the ball in the final seconds, they had a chance of their own to win at the buzzer. They tossed the ball to Jack Quiggle, who despite standing a good 50 feet away, hoisted up a shot that appeared to be on line.

"They get the ball back with two seconds left to go and they take a wild shot past the midcourt line, and the ball goes in—the crowd goes crazy," Rosenbluth said. "We felt that the buzzer went off, but the referees could have just have said good basket."

In fact, that's exactly what the first referee did, before he was quickly overruled by his peers.

"People in the stands were cheering. We looked at each other and said that's no basket— I mean, that buzzer did go off while he was dribbling the ball," recalled junior Joe Quigg, who was right next to Quiggle as the final play developed. "We were watching that ball and it was heading toward the basket. There was no question about it. When it went in, we knew it was no good—we didn't pay attention to it. Coach was still talking to us and he didn't look up to see what the referee was going to do because we knew it was no good."

The Tar Heels had survived regulation by fractions of a second, but it was hardly a confidence booster heading into the extra session. Overtime passed and still they were unable to rid themselves of the Spartans. By the time the second overtime came to a close, it seemed UNC had let one too many chances slip by.

"With six seconds left to go, we were two points down and their best ballplayer, Johnny Green, is on the foul line with a one-and-one," Rosenbluth recalled. "All you got to do is make one foul shot and the game's over—there is no three-point play. The manager closed the books. The game's over; we lost."

In case that hadn't already been obvious to the players, Michigan State decided to do some clarifying of its own. Before Green took the clinching shot, one of his teammates walked over to UNC junior Tommy Kearns and whispered "30–1." But perhaps he had spoken too soon, as Green's free throw bounced off the rim and into the hands of Carolina forward Pete Brennan. The dream season was still alive.

And as bad as McGuire's mistake had been before the game, he certainly made up for it during the game's most crucial juncture. Knowing his team had adequately prepared for this situation, McGuire declined to use a time-out, instead letting his players take advantage of the fast-break opportunity.

As soon as Brennan snatched the ball, he raced down the floor, ignoring Kearns and Bob Cunningham, both of whom were open and closer to the basket. Still, McGuire watched faithfully as Brennan pulled up near the right elbow with three seconds to go.

"He had all the confidence in the world. He wanted to step up when that time came, and he had the greatest confidence in his ability, just like all of us did," Quigg said of Brennan. "He got that rebound and he wasn't looking for anybody. He was coming down to put the ball in the basket."

It was a bold move to say the least, but his shot rang through, sending the game into triple overtime with the score tied at 66. The Tar Heels carried that momentum all the way, as they grabbed a 74–68 lead with just 1:32 to play. And even though Quigg, Brennan, and Cunningham would all foul out before the 55-minute epic concluded, the Tar Heels hung on to survive yet again. Just one game remained between them and history (see page 342). ●

The Tar Heels had just endured one of the most exhausting games in NCAA history but still found the energy to celebrate their 74–70 win in triple overtime. *AP Photo*

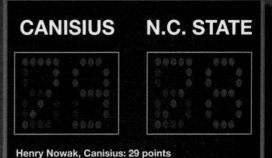

1956: CANISIUS vs. N.C. STATE

Heading into the 1956 NCAA Tournament, Canisius College had a good reason to feel overlooked. The school, whose enrollment consisted of only 3,000 students, played in a conference that included just two other teams. In fact, the school was so obscure that few could really blame N.C. State coach Everett Case when he made some less than flattering remarks about his opponent leading up to the game. When Case was pressed for his thoughts on Canisius, the coach responded that he didn't even know how to spell the school's name.

No team had a stranger journey to the tournament than the Golden Griffins, who four years earlier had recruited four Irishmen, all from Philadelphia, none of whom had ever played high school basketball. Following the path of one Philly native already on the team, the four recruits visited the campus together and were all offered scholarships that same day. By 1956, the group had matured into seniors and led the team to an NCAA Tournament berth. But with just a 17–6 record, the team was matched up against the 24–3 Wolfpack, the nation's second-ranked team. The ACC champions were led by 6-foot-8 All-American Ron Shavlik, yet the Griffins showed little fear of their heavily favored opponent.

"We had some insight into their type of play and what they used, so we had practices where we'd go over as the scouting team," Canisius captain John McCarthy said. "So it wasn't completely in the dark when we drew them."

The Griffins decided that if they were going to lose, they were going to make somebody other than Shavlik beat them. Double and triple-teaming him throughout the game, Canisius took a 43–34 lead in the second half. The Wolfpack, however, could only be contained for so long, and they started to chip away at the lead. By the time John Maglio hit a shot at the three-minute mark, N.C. State had finally pulled ahead 65–63. Dave Markey immediately responded for Canisius to tie the score, and they actually had a chance to win the game after a Wolfpack turnover, but McCarthy fell as he was driving to the hoop and regulation ended with the score tied at 65. Canisius also had multiple chances to put the game away in overtime. Bob Kelly and Markey both missed free throws with the Griffins clinging to a one-point lead, and State's Phil DiNardo responded by hitting a jump shot with 20 seconds left to put his team up 69–68. Hank Nowak tried to drive in for the winning layup and was fouled with just five seconds to play, but he also struggled from the line. Nowak converted his first free throw, but his second shot was off the mark, leaving the score tied once again as overtime came to a close. The second extra period was no different, as Kelly's last-second attempt also missed its target. Now a third overtime loomed on the horizon.

"When you're that age and you're that excited and it's that big of a game and that big of a tournament, I think the adrenaline pumps and you react to it," McCarthy said. "It's only after the game that you might feel spent."

The only problem was that after 50 minutes of play, the Griffins were starting to run into foul trouble. As the game was nearing its end, three of their best players, including McCarthy, had fouled out. Canisius, which normally relied on a six-man rotation and hardly ever used its bench, was now going to have to rely on its role players to pull the game out. And after Nowak again missed a game-winner at the end of the third overtime, it would be up to these role players to decide the longest game in NCAA Tournament history.

By this point in the game, Fran Corcoran's mom could not take the tension anymore. She went out into the hallway and started saying her rosary, looking for any sort of help from the powers that be. What she missed was one of the most miraculous finishes in the history of basketball.

Despite their lack of experience, the Canisius reserves seemed to compensate with fresh legs, and with less than a minute to go in the fourth overtime it was the Griffins who led 77–74. That lead appeared all the more secure because no three-point line existed at the time, but in one disastrous sequence, 55 minutes of work seemed to fall apart before their eyes. With half a minute to play, DiNardo hit a shot to bring the Wolfpack within a point, and Maglio followed by stealing the inbounds pass. He immediately scored to put N.C. State in front 78–77, and after Nowak missed at the other end with 20 seconds to go, the Griffins' upset bid seemed to be over. Shavlik grabbed the rebound for N.C. State and was sent to the line with a chance to put the game out of reach.

Shavlik was arguably the best player in the country, but the moment proved too much as he missed the front end of the one-and-one, giving Canisius one last chance. Markey snatched the rebound for Canisius and fed it to Corcoran, who raced down and pulled up at the top of the key with five seconds to go. Of all the players to take the last shot, Corcoran may have been one of the most unlikely. Although he had tallied a pair of free throws earlier, he hadn't made a shot all day. And unlike some of his teammates who had never attempted to play high school basketball, Corcoran had actually tried out for his high school team and didn't make the cut. As it stood, however, the season rested in his hands.

"Thinking back, it was like I had to get the shot up. I was a decent shooter—I had confidence in it," Corcoran said. "But I thought if I knew what it meant, if I really knew what it all meant, I probably would have thrown it airborne."

Fortunately for Corcoran, the shot sailed through the basket, and pandemonium ensued. While Fran's brother went to go and relay the good news to his mother, the Canisius fans stormed the floor at Madison Square Garden and lifted their hero on their shoulders. The latter part of the celebration, however, was completely unplanned.

"My brother-in-law, who was an ex-football player, was in the middle. And I couldn't breathe," Corcoran laughed. "He grabbed me and he pushed me up in the air."

Since he was already hoisted above the crowd, the students decided to carry him off the court like a king. That was just the beginning of the celebration for the overnight celebrity. After the game, Corcoran decided to go out and celebrate with Bob Kelly, one of the leading scorers on the team.

"They're not going to remember you, but they'll remember me for that one stinking shot," Corcoran said while teasing Kelly at the bar. "And honest, within 20 minutes, some older guy walks in the bar and he says, 'Corcoran, great shot! Hey partner, get him a beer and get his friend one.' And I turn around and said, 'It's just started, Kel.'"

"Fran got a lot of mileage out of that shot," McCarthy smiled. "And we love it."

The students at Canisius made sure that Case learned the spelling of their school, sending him a telegram with not only the final score, but with *Canisius* spelled in extra large letters. Case knew plenty about the team by the time he got the memo, but after the game the rest of college basketball did as well. ●

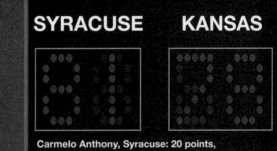

SYRACUSE   **KANSAS**

Carmelo Anthony, Syracuse: 20 points, 10 rebounds, 7 assists

#15

2003: SYRACUSE vs. KANSAS

Sixteen years earlier, on the exact same floor, Jim Boeheim watched his national championship dissolve before his eyes. His Syracuse team had been 38 seconds from winning a national title when, with a three-point lead, the dream turned into a nightmare. Even after Indiana guard Keith Smart had made a jumper that cut the lead to 73–72, all Syracuse forward Derrick Coleman had to do was make a pair of free throws to seal the game. But his first free throw hit off the front of the rim, and Smart stole the championship with a shot five seconds before the buzzer. Now, still looking for his first championship, Boeheim would have his shot at redemption.

Coaching on the other bench would be another man hungry for his first title. Kansas coach Roy Williams, like Boeheim, was a Hall of Fame coach regardless of whether he put six wins together in March. Fortunately, both had the perspective to realize it.

"I think you always want to win a championship—I don't think there's anybody that coaches in college that has a good team that doesn't feel that you want to win a national championship, and that's always there for everybody," Boeheim said. "But you know not everybody wins a national championship, and that doesn't mean you didn't have a good career."

If Boeheim was to win his first title, the phrase "and a child shall lead them" would never ring more true. The team's top players were a pair of freshmen in Gerry McNamara

and Carmelo Anthony, and early on it was McNamara who provided the bulk of the scoring. McNamara made a ridiculous six three-pointers in the first half, the last of which gave Syracuse a 50–37 lead.

"Gerry was very keyed up in the locker room. I kind of expected him to have a good first half, but I don't know if I expected *that*—I mean, he just went out and really. . . . You know, you don't make six threes in the first half too often—that's pretty hard to do," Boeheim smiled. "Gerry was one who overcame a lot of odds in high school to take his team to state championships, so you knew he had that in him."

But as well as the freshmen had played, they had let a great opportunity pass by. Instead of putting the game away when they were up 47–29, Boeheim's club had taken its foot off the accelerator. A 10–0 run by the Jayhawks to start the second half pulled KU within 55–52, and although Syracuse would push the margin to 76–64, Kansas clawed its way back once more. A dunk by Nick Collison brought KU within five points, and Michael Lee's layup at the one-minute mark made it a one-possession game. The Jayhawks called a timeout to set up their defense, and it looked as if 1987 was repeating itself all over again.

"We got off to such a great start, but you knew Kansas was a veteran team and they were going to come back," Boeheim said. "We missed a couple layups and missed obviously more than a couple of foul shots, and all of a sudden they're right back in the game."

Anthony was the first to miss from the line. The freshman had led the team in scoring, but with 58 seconds to go his front end of a one-and-one rattled out, right into the hands of Collison. Kansas worked the ball to Jeff Graves, who trimmed the lead to 80–78 with a free throw. And although the Jayhawks originally elected to play out the remaining 40 seconds, they knew they had to foul when the ball came to SU's Kueth Duany. The lone senior on Syracuse was just a 67.5-percent free throw shooter, and he predictably hit only one of his two free throws to keep the game within one possession. Kirk Hinrich missed the equalizer from the top of the key with 18 seconds left, but not all hope was lost.

The Jayhawks quickly fouled sophomore Hakim Warrick, who was now in the same position that Derrick Coleman had faced 16 years earlier. If Warrick could sink his free throws, the national championship would belong to Syracuse. Unlike his predecessor, Warrick needed to make only one shot and was guaranteed two chances from the line, but it didn't matter. Both rimmed out, and after

knocking on death's door twice, Kansas was still alive.

Boeheim knew exactly how the Jayhawks were going to approach the final possession of the game. Hinrich, despite missing his previous shot, was still one of the most dangerous three-point shooters in the country, and if he got an open look at the basket, Boeheim could consider the game tied. But first Hinrich would have to find an opening, something Syracuse wasn't intent on letting happen.

The Kansas senior circled around the court looking for an opening, but the Syracuse defense read the final play perfectly. By the time Hinrich finally received a pass with just over four seconds to go, he was standing nearly seven feet behind the three-point line. Hinrich nevertheless rose up to fire the shot, but at the last moment he wisely deferred to Lee. When the Syracuse defenders turned to where Lee was standing, they could not have found a more open player. As Lee prepared to hit the game-tying shot from the corner, the closest defender was Warrick, who was still standing in the middle of the paint. Warrick got only halfway there by the time Lee's feet left the floor, but the 6-foot-9 sophomore made up all the ground he needed.

As the ball made its way toward the basket, it was met by Warrick's outstretched hands and deflected out of bounds with just 1.5 seconds on the clock. And when Hinrich's desperation shot at the buzzer flew wide, Warrick had gone from goat to hero.

"I saw a guy open in the corner, and I knew they needed to hit a 3, so I just tried to fly at him," Warrick recalled. "I definitely wanted to go out there and make a play after missing those free throws. . . . I didn't want it to be another one of those Keith Smart shots."

And with one block, Smart's dagger was forever erased from Syracuse lore. In its place now stood an equally impressive play, one that was far more enjoyable. ●

All eyes were on Hakim Warrick as he made the biggest play in Syracuse history with his game-saving block against Michael Lee. *John W. McDonough/Sports Illustrated/Getty Images*

Kyle Singler, Duke: 19 points, 9 rebounds,
2 assists, 2 blocks, 1 steal

2010: DUKE vs. BUTLER

Butler coach Brad Stevens walked off the court feeling like a champion. More than 71,000 fans, nearly all of whom were there to pull for his team, had just watched the Bulldogs defeat Michigan State 52–50, despite scoring just one basket over the final 12 minutes. When Gordon Hayward snagged the rebound with two seconds left to secure the semifinal victory, Lucas Oil Stadium erupted in cheers for Butler, which was located just 5.7 miles away. Inside his hotel room, however, Stevens found a much more somber mood. When he walked in and opened the door, he found his wife staring at the wall, pondering the task ahead of them.

"You get right to work on Duke," Tracy Stevens remarked. Brad couldn't have agreed more. He had less than 48 hours to prepare for the Blue Devils, who were the top seed in the South Region and a perennial title contender. Duke was unlike any team Butler had faced all season in the Horizon League—and for that matter, unlike the Bulldogs themselves. Butler had never been past the Sweet 16 until two weeks earlier, while Duke's Mike Krzyzewski was trying to become only the second coach in history to win at least four championships. In fact, Coach K had started his career before the 33-year-old Stevens was even born. Stevens was actually so young that days earlier he was stopped by stadium security guards who didn't believe he was old enough to be a head coach.

In the 81 years since Butler's last title, nothing of note had really occurred, except when

the school almost abandoned the basketball program due to a shortage of money. And despite saving their program, the Bulldogs still spent less on their entire team than Duke spent on each of its 14 players.

But for all their disadvantages, the Bulldogs had something that nobody, not even the Blue Devils, could claim hold of—a 25-game winning streak. And while their coach slaved away to prepare for the biggest game of their lives, the players made sure to soak in every second of the madness they had created in Indianapolis. Eight players attended class the day of the game, and a day earlier Butler star Gordon Hayward signed autographs for well-wishers as he walked out of morning service at his local church. Indianapolis was nearly giddy about the school's run to the championship, but what fans had forgotten was that Matt Howard, their power forward and the 2009 Horizon League Player of the Year, was still suffering from a concussion he had incurred against Michigan State.

Stevens tried to test Howard early on, but it was clear the concussion was still taking its toll as he missed all four of his shots from the field and went just 1-of-4 from the free throw line. There to pick up the slack, however, were Shelvin Mack and little-known Shawn Vanzant, who had scored just 2.8 points per game during the season but chipped in with 10 in the first half. Thanks to an Avery Jukes three-pointer just before the end of the period, the Bulldogs went into the locker room down just 33–32, much to the delight of the Butler students who had camped outside the stadium overnight to support their team.

The Blue Devils would continue to hold their lead for much of the second half, but Butler never let the deficit grow beyond six points, and when Hayward sank a pair of free throws with five minutes to go, the lead was down to just 56–55. The fans rose to their feet, imploring the Bulldogs for one more run, but Duke's Kyle Singler answered back with a fadeaway jumper to extend the gap to 58–55. Nolan Smith added a pair of free throws moments later, and with just two minutes to play, the Bulldogs found themselves down 60–55 and without a field goal in nearly eight minutes.

Despite his concussion, Howard put in a layup with 1:42 to play, and added another with 54 seconds left to bring the Bulldogs within 60–59. Krzyzewski called a timeout to regather his players, but to no avail as Singler's jumper barely grazed the rim, and after a brief tussle for the rebound, rolled out of bounds. The officials ruled that Duke had touched it last, and with 33 seconds to go both teams began the biggest possession of their lives.

Ronald Nored brought the ball up and tried to work the ball into Jukes, but Singler knocked the ball out of bounds with 13.6

Gordon Hayward heaves up a half-court shot at the buzzer that misses by mere inches. *Butler University*

seconds to go. Butler called a timeout to set up the final play, and Coach K used the opportunity to give his players some final instructions.

"We're going to win a championship with our defense," Krzyzewski declared, and told senior Brian Zoubek to guard the inbounder, something he hadn't done all year long. It turned out to be the right decision as Hayward struggled to inbound the ball, resulting in another timeout. This time it was Howard who inbounded the ball to Hayward, and the sophomore took it upon himself to take the final shot. Standing near the top of the key, Hayward dropped Scheyer with a behind-the-back dribble, but before he could fire an open jumper from the baseline, Zoubek had raced over to throw his hands up. Instead of knocking in an easy 10-footer, Hayward was forced into a fadeaway from just inside the three-point line.

"It wasn't a great look. I thought they did a great job of defending it," Stevens said. "But it's a good look because of the player shooting it."

Hayward had carried the team all season long with his clutch play, but with 3.6 seconds remaining his high-arching prayer rimmed out of the hoop and back into the hands of Zoubek. For someone who had been chided his whole career for garnering one injury after another, Zoubek had just put together two of the biggest plays in Duke history.

Now with a chance to at least guarantee overtime, Krzyzewski took a huge gamble, telling his senior to make the first free throw and miss the second, knowing it would force Butler into a long-distance shot. The problem was that if Butler actually managed to put it in, the championship would be theirs. And as Hayward hauled in Zoubek's miss, he threw up a shot from beyond halfcourt that had everyone in Indianapolis holding their breath.

"From my angle, I felt like it was way off," Hayward said. "I thought I shot it too hard."

But to everyone else in the arena, it was obvious the shot had a chance to go in. As the clock stood frozen at zero, the ball clanged off the backboard and toward the rim. It would ultimately land softly back to the court, but the Bulldogs could take solace in the fact that they had played in one of the greatest games anybody had ever seen. They had done Indianapolis proud. ●

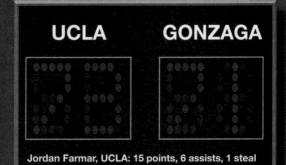

2006: UCLA vs. GONZAGA

As a 12-year-old picking up a basketball for the first time in Cameroon, Luc Richard Mbah A Moute knew little about the game, much less how it was being played over 8,000 miles away in California. Mbah a Moute's resources were limited—he started playing on a hoop attached to a street lamp—but it wasn't long before he realized he had quite a knack for this foreign sport. As his talents grew, so did his interest in the sport's history, and when Mbah a Moute stumbled across an old photo of Kareem Abdul-Jabbar bearing a UCLA jersey, he was hooked.

Jabbar was the greatest college basketball player of all time, but he was just part of the storied UCLA legacy. With 11 national championships under its belt, UCLA boasted the greatest program in the history of college basketball. Although he thought the school's name was "ooklah," Mbah a Moute knew that's where he needed to go. Not only would he eventually make it out to Westwood, but before his first year was complete, he would take part in the most exciting game that school had ever seen.

The game, versus Gonzaga, was for a spot in the tournament's Elite Eight. The Zags had been there once, as opposed to UCLA's 18 appearances, but early on it seemed to be the Bruins who were letting the pressure get to them. Despite shooting over 50 percent in each of their previous six games, they missed their first eight shots from the floor while also

making seven turnovers. Nearly nine minutes into the game, UCLA had yet to make a basket.

"Our team, we've been in those situations before. We knew we could come back," Mbah a Moute said. "Even though we were down, we were getting the shots we wanted, we were getting everything we wanted—we just weren't making shots. For some reason, everything just wasn't falling. But we were having our way, so we always felt like it was just time where we were going to start making shots and turning it around."

As cold as UCLA was, the Bulldogs had failed to take full advantage of their opponent's misfortune. When Arron Afflalo hit a leaning jump shot to give the Bruins their first basket, they trailed only 18–9. Ironically, it was only after UCLA started to heat up that the Bulldogs put some distance between their West Coast rivals. By the time Gonzaga star Adam Morrison made a layup with 3:17 left in the first half, the Zags—leading 37–20—were on the brink of doubling up their opponent. The Bruins eventually cut the lead to six points in the early minutes of the second half, but with 11:45 to go the Bulldogs pushed the margin back to 57–43. They still led 71–62 with just 3:27 to play when the Bruins gave it one final push.

A minute later, the Bruins had put two points into the comeback bid, and as another minute passed by, the lead had crept down to five—but it was hardly the pace needed to save their season. With just over a minute left, Gonzaga still enjoyed a 71–66 lead as well as possession of the ball. The Bulldogs smartly got the ball into the hands of Morrison, who had been selected as college basketball's Player of the Year. But for the hundreds of shots Morrison had delivered all season long, one of his rare misses couldn't have come at a worse time.

It took only 10 seconds for UCLA sophomore Jordan Farmar to race down court and hit a layup. The Zags once again got the ball to their All-American, who drove to the baseline to take a jump shot over Farmar. Morrison enjoyed a six-inch height advantage over his defender, but once more his shot was off the mark. Only this time the results were much more devastating.

The ball clanged off the back of the rim toward an empty space that would soon be occupied by Gonzaga forward J. P. Batista and UCLA center Ryan Hollins. While chasing after the ball, the referees whistled Batista for a foul, which not only sent Hollins to the line but kept the clock stopped at 19.7 seconds. Hollins converted both shots, and UCLA, which had trailed virtually the entire contest, was suddenly within a point. The Bruins needed a quick turnover, and coach Ben Howland knew just how to get it.

"It's crazy because we usually never pressed when I was at UCLA," Mbah A Moute recalled. "And then we were down and we had to press, and then I think Hollins made the free throw and I was on the ball."

Howland had originally put Hollins on the inbounder, but at the last second he took the center out and put Mbah a Moute in his place. The Bulldogs, still putting their faith in their leader, tossed it to Morrison near the left corner. Knowing that a defensive trap was coming, Morrison turned and fired a cross-court pass to Batista. Like Morrison before him, Batista also faced a double-team. But when he raised his arms to pass it over to point guard Derek Raivio, Batista realized that the ball was nowhere to be found.

"Jordan knocked the ball out of his hand, and I was right under the basket so I whipped my hand up," Mbah a Moute said. "Jordan threw a nice pass, kind of like a lob, and I just caught it and put it in."

The UCLA bench erupted as the Bruins took a 72–71 lead, but Raivio immediately took the inbounds ball and raced down court. With 8.6 seconds still remaining, the game was far from over. That is, until Mbah a Moute stepped up once again.

"As soon as I put it in, I saw Raivio taking off and all I could think of is just, man, you got to get that ball," he said. "And I was just running behind him, and [UCLA guard] Cedric Bozeman came in front of him, so Raivio tried to make a move and he kind of let the ball out, so I had no choice but just to dive."

And when Mbah a Moute sprawled out across the court, the ball popped loose and into a crowd of players who were desperately fighting for the ball. The whistle blew with 2.1 seconds left, and when the players glanced up to see the call, the referees raised their hands to signal a tie ball. Possession arrow? UCLA.

"It was crazy—it was one of the greatest games I've been a part of. Just the emotion at the end, everybody jumping, screaming— I mean, it was just draining," Mbah a Moute said. "It was just so emotional, man. I think that emotion carried us all the way to the championship game."

On the other end of that emotion, however, was Morrison, who could no longer contain the tears. For anybody who had seen the game, however, it was hard to blame him. Afflalo, sensing the kind of effort Morrison had just delivered, bent down to comfort him.

"He's a competitor. He wanted to win just as much as we did," Mbah A Moute said of Morrison. "He felt like they had, and they did have a chance to win. We're fortunate that we did and made plays."

And with a few big ones from Mbah A Moute, UCLA had added another chapter to its storied history. ●

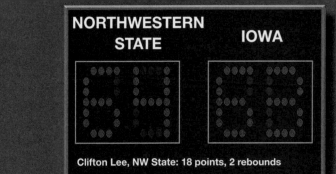

NORTHWESTERN
STATE   IOWA

Clifton Lee, NW State: 18 points, 2 rebounds

2006: NORTHWESTERN STATE vs. IOWA

Perhaps Mike McConathy should have stayed at junior college after all. For 16 years, he had made a habit out of winning games at a little school in northern Louisiana. Sure, he had to drive the team bus and do the team's laundry in addition to his coaching duties, but it was certainly a lot easier than the situation he found at the Division I level. Faced with the youngest team in the country, his Northwestern State club lost 30 games during a 38-game stretch, a trying time that brought out the true colors of his staff.

"That first year was a pretty tough year. In fact, one of my assistants walked into the office in January of that year and said, 'Coach, we need to fire eight of these guys that are coming back . . . . I can go get eight better players,'" McConathy recalled. "I said 'No, you *think* you can go and get eight better players. We know what we have. What you bring in here, you don't know if it's going to be as good, because when you're looking at kids, you think they might be better but in reality when they get here may not be.' And so my remark to him was to end the conversation was, 'You know what I think we probably need to do? We probably need to coach these kids and see where it takes us.'"

So McConathy stuck with the young, albeit underwhelming group of freshmen. And when his Demons matured into seniors and won the conference title in 2006, McConathy made sure to remind his assistant just what they had talked about years earlier.

"So on the Saturday morning when we're walking to play in the championship game, and I don't know if we'd won six or seven games in a row, I slapped him on the back of his shoulder," McConathy smiled. "And I said, 'Which one of them do you want to fire now?'"

The victory gave the Demons a matchup with third-seeded Iowa in the first round. McConathy still had his commercial driver's license, but he wasn't going to be driving a bus anytime soon. His team would be enjoying a nice plane ride out to Detroit for the game. But the fun looked like it was going to stop there, as the Hawkeyes grabbed an 18–4 lead less than seven minutes into the contest.

"I remember those guys were just nailing everything that they put up there at the time," McConathy said. "And it was just one of those things where they started off really solid and made shots, and we just had to hold the line and stay as positive as we could."

His team would indeed fight back to score the next 14 points, and when senior Jermaine Wallace nailed a three from the right corner with 2:48 remaining in the first half, the Demons had taken their first lead at 21–20. Northwestern State continued to hang tough, with the score tied at 28 early in the second half when the Hawkeyes slowly began to pull away. And with a 54–37 lead and just 8:29 remaining, the lead appeared to be for good.

But the Demons had overcome too much to fold that easily. Clifton Lee, another senior who had started his career on the 6–21 team in 2003, scored 16 points in the second half to bridge the gap to just 60–57. The lead was still at three, 62–59, before Northwestern State's Luke Rogers converted a pair of free throws with 40.2 seconds left.

McConathy told his team not to foul, that time remained to play a normal defensive possession, but the referees called a foul anyway—on what appeared to be a clean block with 14.6 seconds left. Going to the line would be Greg Brunner, who had already made five of his seven free throws on the day—and after his first attempt, six of his first eight. Now facing a 63–61 deficit, McConathy called his last timeout and decided to say something that had nothing to do with the situation at hand.

"Ya'll get in here, bus No. 2!" McConathy called, bringing a smile to each of his players. It had been their rallying cry all year, ever since the phrase was first used during an early-season tournament in Hawaii. When each of the eight teams at the tournament had arrived for a comedy show, the host wanted to see which of the squads, all of whom had arrived by bus, was most excited to be there. While all the other teams acted as if they had more interesting matters to attend to, the Demons from bus No. 2 decided to scream as loud as possible. And no, McConathy wasn't driving that bus, either. But the message still resonated with his players.

"It was almost like let's just play ball," McConathy said. "Instead of being uptight, they just relaxed and started playing."

And when Brunner's next free throw bounced off the front of the rim, Northwestern State now had the choice of playing for the win or a tie. To anyone who was familiar with the Demons' carefree demeanor, there was no question what they were going to do. They were going for the win.

Senior Kerwin Forges was the first to try, but his shot ricocheted off the side of the rim and deep into the left corner. Grabbing the rebound was Jermaine Wallace, who like so many others on the team was playing for more than himself. Wallace's girlfriend, ironically named Katrina, had her house swallowed up by the identically named hurricane just before the start of the year. The girlfriend of Forges, seven months pregnant with twins, had also been displaced when the hurricane struck.

Here Wallace stood, with a chance to provide a brief escape from all the troubles the people in his state had gone through. But if he was going to do so, it would have to be with a defender in his face. Wallace tried to throw off his opponent by taking even one step further toward the baseline, but the move just put him further out of position. Now shooting from behind the rim, Wallace fired up a prayer that seemed to have little chance of going in. But with 0.5 seconds on the clock, the ball swished through the net, giving many people in Louisiana a feeling they had not experienced in quite some time.

"That shot was a big deal for everybody—just not his girlfriend, not him, the team, but Louisiana in general," McConathy said. "Because truly, and I know LSU had a great year that year as well, but anything positive that happened in the state of Louisiana that year was enjoyed by everyone."

But perhaps none enjoyed it more than the folks from bus No. 2. ●

Jermaine Wallace never took a harder shot in his life, and his teammates took a little time to celebrate the moment. *Northwestern State Athletic Department. Photograph by Gary Hardamon*

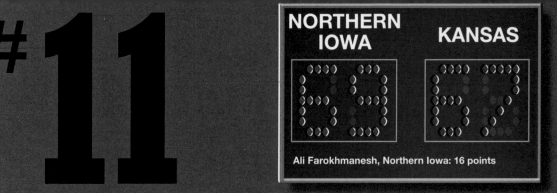

NORTHERN IOWA　　**KANSAS**

Ali Farokhmanesh, Northern Iowa: 16 points

2010: NORTHERN IOWA vs. KANSAS

Heading into their second-round bout with the Northern Iowa Panthers, the Kansas players had every reason to feel confident. Not only were they the most popular pick to win the entire tournament, many experts felt the Jayhawks had both the top offense and defense in the country. A team with truly no weakness, the players felt unbeatable. The only problem was they let the ninth-seeded Panthers know how they felt. Instead of scaring their opponent, the Jayhawks had just given them the ultimate pre-game speech.

"We got a guy on our team, Lucas O'Rear—who is kind of a tough guy, farm boy, who does all the little things, the dirty work, for our team—and he's one of the guys that they were talking to. And he's not a good guy to get pissed off at you," senior Adam Koch smiled. "He let everybody know that they were talking a little bit and we need to be ready to go out there right away and send a message."

The Panthers did exactly that, racing out to a 10–2 lead on the back of center Jordan Eglseder. The seven-footer, not normally known for his range, drained a three from the corner to put UNI on the board and followed it up with another long jumper. Before long the big man was draining turnarounds, and after his second three-pointer of the night—which was only his third of the season—the Panthers led 21–19.

Thanks to a perfect half by guard Ali Farokhmanesh, an 11-point performance in which he made every shot he took, the Panthers took a 36–28 lead into the break. Though it was normally a cause for celebration among the upset-happy fans, the majority of the Jayhawk-friendly crowd in Oklahoma City watched in silence as UNI pushed the lead to 47–35. After Johnny Moran sank a pair of free throws with less than seven minutes remaining, the Panthers still held a nine-point lead.

More importantly, the Panthers weren't beating themselves. They were in the midst of a 15-minute stretch without committing a turnover, a remarkable feat against the vaunted Jayhawk defense. But that all changed in a hurry, as Marcus Morris came away with two steals in less than 10 seconds, and when Xavier Henry's layup moments later cut the lead to 47–39, the crowd was back in the game.

The Panthers were clinging to a 59–53 lead with just over three minutes left when things began to unravel in a hurry. Following a Kansas free throw, the Panthers threw away the inbounds pass for an easy layup, and a few seconds later they threw it right back to the Jayhawks again. Northern Iowa, perhaps the most disciplined team in the country, was struggling to just get the ball to halfcourt.

Despite unraveling on the offensive end, UNI was holding strong on defense. And when Koch slammed down a thunderous dunk with 1:17 to go, giving the Panthers a 63–56 lead, the game looked to be theirs for the taking. But when you are facing the best team in the country, the lead is never safe. KU's Tyshawn Taylor converted a pair of free throws to cut the lead to five, and UNI again threw the ball away on the ensuing inbounds. That led to another pair of free throws, this time by Kansas forward Marcus Morris, and with 53 seconds still to play the lead was down to just three. UNI wasn't done quite yet, as Kwadzo Ahelegbe stepped on the baseline after receiving the inbounds pass. After appearing dead in the water just moments earlier, Kansas incredibly had a chance to tie. Sherron Collins elected for the quick two-pointer, and he scored a layup with 43 seconds left to put the Jayhawks within 63–62.

Kansas called a timeout, which actually gave UNI a chance to regroup, but on the ensuing possession the Panthers nearly turned it over again. Tyshawn Taylor anticipated the upcourt pass to Ahelegbe, but he arrived just a fraction of a second too late, leaving him as well as most of the aggressive Kansas defenders out of position.

Farokhmanesh received the ball on the right wing, just behind the three-point line, with teammate Johnny Moran lined up across the court near the left sideline. KU's Tyrell Reed, sandwiched between the two, was left with two distinct options. Going after Farokhmanesh would leave Moran wide open. Staying in the middle would give Farokhmanesh a wide-open look at the three-pointer. But considering Northern Iowa could have run the ball down to just seven seconds left, and was in no hurry to shoot, Reed decided to stay put and wait for his teammates to join him down court. Farokhmanesh, however, had no such interest in passing up the biggest shot of his life.

"When Reed backed off, I thought, oh boy, this is going to be interesting, because Ali is going to shoot it," coach Ben Jacobson said. "That adds to the fun of it. That goes against everything basketball common sense tells you."

The shot made even less sense considering that after his hot start, Farokhmanesh hadn't scored in the last 23 minutes of the game.

"My confidence was pretty much the same throughout the whole game, I didn't even realize that I had missed my last seven shots in a row leading up to that," Farokhmanesh smiled.

Koch, who was not exactly using the same logic, barely even saw the shot.

"To be honest, when they threw it ahead to Ali, it didn't occur to me that he would shoot it, so I put my head down and really tried to sprint up the floor to try and get in position where they had been pressuring and trapping and I could get a pass from him," Koch said. "I put my head down, took off, and then looked up all of a sudden and the ball is in the air."

A split-second later, that ball sailed through the net, giving UNI a huge four-point cushion with 35 seconds to go. To top it off, Koch's little brother, Jake—a freshman—sealed the upset moments later by drawing a charge.

"I don't think it hit me too much until the end of the year that I was playing with my brother because I was always playing basketball with him when I was growing up," Koch said. "I realized after my senior year that it's pretty special—not many guys get to do that."

The win was clearly the biggest in school history, but the players didn't miss the opportunity to pull a good prank, putting on their best acting faces as Jacobson entered the locker room.

"I walk in and the guys are all sitting in their chairs and they're not saying anything and they're not doing anything. Usually after a big win they're moving around a little bit and talking a little bit, and they're excited. And they're just sitting there," Jacobson laughed. "I'm standing there and I'm thinking, what in the world? And I didn't say anything, but I'm thinking to myself, you know, we just beat the No. 1 team in the country."

The players could only hold it in for so long, and moments later they were dancing and laughing in the celebration—a celebration that was only made possible by a gutsy decision and an even gutsier shot. ●

2005: ILLINOIS vs. ARIZONA

Bruce Weber stood in shock. This was not the way it was supposed to happen. Not after setting a goal 16 months earlier of reaching the 2005 Final Four, on the 100th anniversary of Illinois basketball. Not in front of their own fans in Chicago. But here the Illinois coach stood, watching as his dream season appeared to be slipping away before his eyes. His 35–1 Illini had blown a seven-point first-half lead, and as the second half began to unfold, Weber's team struggled to keep pace with a vastly underrated Arizona squad.

Illinois had managed to stay within 51–50 when the Wildcats made six of their next seven shots to break the game open at 64–58. By the time Channing Frye nailed a three-pointer near the top of the key to give Arizona a 70–58 lead, his team was shooting a ridiculous 64 percent from the floor, stunning the crowd of 17,500 spectators, nearly all of whom were clad in orange. Just six minutes remained.

Unfortunately for the Illini, the gap just continued to grow, and when Arizona's Jawaan McClellan sank a pair of free throws with only four minutes to go, the lead stood at 75–60. The Wildcats were certainly a strong team as a three seed, but hardly anybody predicted the kind of performance they put on against the Illini, the top-ranked team for nearly the entire season.

"We played as well we had played all year long," Arizona coach Lute Olson recalled. "It was a blowout."

Illinois guard Deron Williams, one of the few players on Weber's squad having a good game, nailed a three-pointer seconds later to cut the lead to 75–63. And when the game went to a TV timeout with 3:28 to go, Williams decided to speak up.

"Deron and a couple guys said some things and just talked about staying focused," Weber said. "Our goal was still to get to the Final Four, and they were very positive in the huddle. And I think that competitiveness and that will they had was probably the difference-maker as we went down the stretch."

Teammate Luther Head followed the example of Williams by making a three-pointer of his own, cutting the lead to 77–66 with 3:19 to go, and when UA guard Hassan Adams dribbled the ball out of bounds on the ensuing possession, the momentum had taken a drastic turn. Head would miss a three-pointer at the other end, but Dee Brown—the smallest player on the floor—came away with the rebound, and his putback trimmed the lead to 77–68 with 2:45 to go. Arizona's Salim Stoudamire missed a fadeaway on the other end, but it appeared that the Wildcats would survive after all when McClellan swatted away a shot by IU's Roger Powell. The lead was still at nine points, and now less than 90 seconds remained. But once again the Illini refused to cave in as Head, anticipating a pass to Adams, darted in to steal the ball. His dunk seconds later to brought the Illini within 77–70.

The emotions of the crowd are on display as Deron Williams downs a three to force overtime.
David E. Klutho/Sports Illustrated/Getty Images

"We had to have the ball bounce our way and things had to happen," Weber said. "My mom had passed away at the Big Ten Tournament, and we all kind of joked that she was sitting there knocking away the Arizona shots and tipping the ball our way because a lot of balls bounced our way. A lot of things happened that maybe shouldn't have happened."

Olson called a timeout to refocus his players, and McClellan hit a free throw with 1:14 left to extend the lead to eight, but Williams raced in for a layup just eight seconds later to cut the lead to 78–72. Brown quickly fouled Mustafa Shakur, and although the UA guard made both of his free throws, Head came right back down and drained a three-pointer from the left wing. One point at a time, the Illini were coming back.

Illinois was hardly done. Brown made a steal of his own, and his lay-in put the team within 80–77. Olson called another timeout, but Weber had something up his sleeve too. Sensing that Arizona would try to get the ball to Frye, who had played well all night, Weber instructed center Jack Ingram to switch players and guard him on the inbounds. Sure enough, the Wildcats tried to loft the ball up to Frye, but extending his hand just enough was

Ingram, who tipped the ball to Head. Head passed it off to Brown, who in turn swung the ball across the court to an open Williams. And with 38 seconds to go, Williams capped off the most improbable comeback in NCAA history by knocking down a three-pointer.

"You see a very cool and calm Deron jumping up to shoot it," Weber said. "Amidst all these fans with all these different emotions, sometimes guys get the ball and they rush things, and he just coolly and calmly jumped up and made that shot."

By this point the Illini fans were delirious, and after they watched their team get a defensive stop at the end of regulation, they would be sticking around a little while longer. Weber's club eventually worked the lead to 90–84 with two minutes left in overtime, but now it was Arizona's turn to come back. A three-point play by Adams brought the lead to 90–87, and his layup with 53 seconds to go brought the Wildcats within a point. Head proceeded to miss a jumper with 23 seconds to go, and after one of the most epic collapses Olson had ever seen, his team actually had a chance to steal the victory right back.

"We had the ball and called a timeout, and on defense Williams had done a great job on Salim Stoudamire. Salim was tiring, he was putting a lot of minutes in. Unbeknownst to me, Deron had told his coach *he too* was tired," Olson smiled. "We set it up for Hassan Adams, our second-most consistent scorer, to get the ball and for us to use Salim as a decoy. As fate would have it, we start the play and who's guarding Hassan except for Deron Williams."

Williams, who had pleaded with Weber to guard somebody besides Stoudamire, got what he had wished for. But now the Illinois dream season counted on him garnering enough energy for one more stop. And just as he had done all night, Williams delivered once again, preventing Adams from any decent look as the final shot hit off the backboard.

"People after the game said, man, what a great move!" Weber laughed. "How did you know they were going to go to this guy, to put Deron on him?"

He of course had no idea, but it didn't matter. After 16 months of waiting, the journey was now complete. The Illini were going to the Final Four. ●

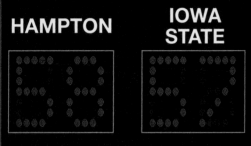

Tarvis Williams, Hampton: 16 points, 13 rebounds

2001: HAMPTON vs. IOWA STATE

The fans in Boise, Idaho, were not ready for the action to be over. They had already witnessed three dramatic games in the first two days, decided by a total of six points, and still it was not enough to fill their appetites for basketball. Late that night, the crowds gathered one last time to watch the finale of the opening round, a game that would actually pack more excitement than the rest of the days put together.

Feeding off the energy in the arena, Hampton was able to fight off a slow start and hang with the vastly quicker Iowa State Cyclones. Hampton found its rhythm late in the first half, going on a 14–5 run in the closing minutes to take a 31–25 lead at the break.

"We had a very confident group. They just believed that they were going to win," said coach Steve Merfeld. "At any level, at any game, any competition, if your players believe that and think that they are the better team, that's more than half the battle."

It took less than three minutes in the second half, however, for that momentum to evaporate. Hampton senior Tarvis Williams, the sixth-leading scorer in the country and the nation's leading shot-blocker, picked up his fourth foul, sending him to the bench. The Cyclones seized on the opportunity, as they went on an 11–0 run over the next 3:30 to grab a six-point lead. Even worse, Hampton missed all five of its shots to start the half, and by the time Merfeld knew he had to put Williams

back in, Iowa State had added a dunk and three straight layups to push the lead to 46–35.

The Cyclones were still enjoying a seven-point advantage when Martin Rancik followed his own miss to give Iowa State a 57–48 lead with 7:00 to go. Things were beginning to look desperate.

After Williams cut the lead back to seven, the Cyclones were bringing the ball up the court when Hampton guard Tommy Adams anticipated a pass and knocked it forward. Adams, who never dunked the ball during games, skied high for the slam to bring the crowd to its feet. Now the deficit stood at just 57–52. After two more Hampton layups brought the score to 57–56, the noise was almost deafening.

"I specifically remember Marseilles Brown telling the guys that if they hung in there long enough the crowd would come to the underdog's side, and they did," Merfeld said. "It was deafening in there."

The Hampton defense continued to shut down the Cyclones, and when Iowa State guard Jamaal Tinsley missed a shot with just over a minute to go, the fifteenth-seeded Pirates actually had a chance to take the lead. Brown looked to pass the ball inside, but when nothing opened up he opted to take the big shot himself. His three-pointer fell short, however, and Iowa State cleared the rebound with 39 seconds left to seemingly put the game away. But instead of dribbling out the rest of the clock or waiting to get fouled, Tinsley raced down the court and unleashed a layup. Williams, now unafraid of getting his fifth foul with just seconds remaining, rose up to throw Tinsley off guard, and when the ball rolled off the rim, the Pirates had a second life. Merfeld called a timeout with 21 seconds to go and knew exactly what to call.

"We had a play that we hadn't run all year that we had saved for that specific instance, and we called it 'Winner,'" Merfeld said. "We come to the bench and everyone is saying we're running 'Winner.' I don't have to tell them; they knew what we were going to do. And the bench was very calm, very matter of fact. They had practiced that thing forever and ever. We used our last timeout to set it up and make sure we were all on the same page."

But when the team went out to try and run it, the Cyclones kicked the ball away with just 11 seconds on the clock. The entire season's worth of preparation would now be substituted for improvisation. Brown received a pass to start the final play and decided to thread the needle to Williams, who was standing in triple coverage.

"There were guys all around him—the pass was kind of crazy," Brown laughed. "If you look at that pass again, that's not a pass you really want to throw. It was in traffic, the guy had his head turned for half a second, and Tarvis raised his hand so I just threw it."

And Williams delivered, sinking a hook shot with just 6.9 seconds to go to put Hampton up 58–57. Again, Merfeld felt his team was well prepared for the finish.

"If you watch the highlight, and we talked about this in the huddle prior to going out, was the fact that we had a foul to give," Merfeld said. "If you watch closely, I'm trying to get our guys to foul."

Apparently, the message didn't get through.

"Don't foul—that's what was going through my head," said Brown, who was supposed to guard Tinsley on the final play. "I'm running back; I'm like trying to get in front of him. He went right by me."

Tinsley raced straight toward the basket and fired a layup just before the buzzer sounded. Fortunately Williams was there to alter it again, and after the ball hit off the backboard, it bounced to the front of the rim and stood still. But luck was on Hampton's side, as the ball rimmed out to give the Pirates one of the most thrilling upsets in NCAA history. When junior David Johnson spotted Merfeld running around the court, a la Jim Valvano, he lifted his coach in the air, with Merfeld kicking his legs in elation.

"I don't know where I was going—I have no idea what I was doing," laughed Merfeld, whose kids still get a kick out of the celebration. "They laugh like crazy to this day that their dad would do something this crazy. But it is a great moment, and we tell the guys it's something that will never be taken from us. Just one of those deals that happened, and you live for those moments."

And for all those lucky fans in Boise, it was one they will never forget. ●

Hampton coach Steve Merfeld is hoisted into the air by a player after his team unseated the second-seeded Cyclones. *Robert Beck/Sports Illustrated/ Getty Images*

INDIANA   KANSAS

Don Schlundt, Indiana: 30 points

#8

1953: INDIANA vs. KANSAS

When Kansas coach Phog Allen and Indiana coach Branch McCracken met in the 1953 national championship game, the two adversaries had some unfinished business to settle. Allen was hoping to avenge his loss in the 1940 title game to McCracken, when Indiana defeated Kansas 60–42. McCracken also had revenge on his mind, as he had to watch the Jayhawks win the 1952 title with Indiana native Clyde Lovellette. Four years earlier, Lovellette had committed to the Hoosiers, but a last-minute change of heart to Kansas rose suspicion about Allen's recruiting methods. In the ultimate meeting between the two programs, Indiana entered as the No. 1 team in the country, but as defending national champions the Jayhawks were certainly a force to be reckoned with.

"The night before we played Kansas, we had just won our third game, and we're sitting in the stands and watching the Kansas game," forward Charlie Kraak said. "And they looked so good that night, it seemed that boy, when you went to sleep that night, you better get ready for tomorrow because they're not going to be easy."

Lovellette was gone now, but in his place was center B. H. Born, who had been more than a worthy successor. Born controlled the rebounding in the early going, and after he banked in a hook shot in the second quarter, the Jayhawks led 25–23. The junior eventually guided Kansas to a 39–33 lead, but thanks to some late shots by his counterpart, IU center

Don Schlundt, the teams went into the break knotted at 41. Kraak, who was normally a role player, had the game of his life with 12 points in the first half. The Hoosiers needed his performance, as All-American guard Bobby Leonard had tallied just two points.

Leonard would find his rhythm in the second half, but it appeared in vain as the Jayhawks continued to keep pace. Kansas grabbed a 53–49 lead in the third quarter and still enjoyed a 58–57 edge when Leonard took the ball in the closing moments of the period.

"We got the ball inbounds with just a second or two. You had to shoot it," Leonard said. "And I took a couple of dribbles across the midline and let it fly."

Unbelievably, the halfcourt toss went in, giving Indiana all the momentum as the teams entered the last 10 minutes of the contest. Kansas refused to cave in, but the Hoosiers finally got the break they were looking for when Schlundt broke a 65–65 tie with 2:25 remaining. His three-point play gave IU a two-possession lead because the three-point line had yet to be introduced, and when Kraak grabbed a KU miss at the other end, the game looked to be Indiana's for the taking.

With no shot clock in effect, the Hoosiers had the option of taking as much time off the clock as they desired, unless Kansas gave in and committed a foul. The team swung the ball around as the seconds ticked by, but when the ball came to Kraak, he decided to seal the game then and there with a layup. But as he was driving toward the hoop, KU's Gil Reich stepped in at the last moment, drawing a charge with 1:21 to play.

"That was a cheap-shot foul to begin with," Kraak said. "I was convinced that I did not charge that guy, and the films kind of proved it. But it was the ref's call."

Unfortunately, Kraak did not help the situation by heaving the ball in the air, and before the ball had even made its long descent down, he'd already been charged with a technical foul.

"Well, I just lost it at that point. That's where the whole season builds up in the matter of one play," Kraak admitted. "Branch probably would have been as kind as he could, but he was not a happy camper when I returned to the bench, I can assure you. I made sure I sat at the other end of the bench at that time."

Kraak knew his mistake, but the crime had already been committed. Not only would Kansas get to shoot free throws from the charge, they would also be shooting technical free throws and getting the ball back when all was said and done. Indiana lucked out when KU converted only one of the four free throws, but when Dean Kelley lofted in a shot with a minute to go, the game was tied at 68.

The Hoosiers again had the opportunity to hold for the last shot, but this time it was Leonard who attempted to drive in early for the winning score. The refs blew the whistle upon contact, but on this occasion the Hoosiers were on the better end of the call. Leonard was going to the line with 27 seconds left, with the national championship resting on his shots.

Although he was generally a solid free throw shooter, Leonard rarely took his time at the line, and this time was no different. He confidently stepped to the line and attempted his first shot, which bricked off the front of the rim. Before even contemplating the implications of the missed free throw, Leonard briskly attempted his second shot, which rang true. The shot gave the Hoosiers a 69–68, lead and created some interesting conversation among the press after the game.

"They came over to me and they said, 'Bobby, how did it feel standing on that free throw line with the national championship hanging in the balance?' They said, 'Coach McCracken just told us that you had ice water in your veins,'" Leonard laughed. "And I said, 'Hey, baby, if that was ice water, it sure as heck felt awful warm when it was running down my leg."

If the Hoosiers were to indeed hang on for the title, they would need to play the best 27 seconds of defense of their lives. As far as Leonard was concerned, all they needed to do was maintain the confidence that allowed him to sink the go-ahead free throw.

"You know, you can't let it get to you," Leonard said of the nerves. "The game is on the line, I mean you're either going to win the championship or you're going to lose it. So that's the type of defense you have to play. You don't want to be the goat of the whole thing and let your man score on you. So yeah, it's a tough deal. I mean there's pressure in those games, but you know it's an amazing thing."

The Jayhawks wasted no time in setting up their offense for the final shot. If the opportunity presented itself early, they were going to take it. But each pass was met with a stingier defense, and after seven passes in the final 27 seconds, the ball had landed in the hands of Jerry Alberts, who had to unleash a shot from the corner just before the buzzer. The Hoosiers had forced Kansas into a shot they didn't want to take, but history was not on their side. They had lost only three games all year, but each of them had come on buzzer-beaters, and the final game was set up for a similar finish.

"Sitting there and watching that guy shoot that last shot, you talk about being petrified, that was it, because as I remember the ball hit the rim and could have gone either way," Kraak recalled. "That's when it gets really nerve-racking because you know what you start thinking then."

But this time the Hoosiers were not to be denied. The ball bounced off the rim as time expired, and the mood instantly changed from anxiety to elation. The most relieved of anyone was Kraak, who could once again show his face in Bloomington.

"I don't think I'd have got on that plane and bus and gone back to school," Kraak laughed. "Because they would have hung me in effigy."

Thanks to Leonard's free throws, however, he would instead be returning as a hero. ●

1957: NORTH CAROLINA vs. KANSAS

To get a feel for just how "neutral" the 1957 championship site would be, all one needed to do was simply pull out a map. The North Carolina Tar Heels, hailing from Chapel Hill, would be traveling well over a thousand miles to get to Kansas City's Municipal Auditorium. For the Kansas Jayhawks, the arena was just over half an hour away.

"Not one parent came," laughed UNC center Lennie Rosenbluth. "They didn't have the money, they wouldn't come to the games, so we had very little fans in Kansas. What people forget is we only played eight homes games out of the 32 games. Everything else was on the road, so we didn't worry about going to someone's gym to play."

But to most experts, no amount of fan support was going to help UNC defeat the Jayhawks and their mighty center, Wilt Chamberlain. The Tar Heels arrived with a 31–0 record, compared with KU's 23–2 mark, but behind Chamberlain and his 29.6 points per game, it was not meant to be much of a contest.

The Jayhawks were listed as a 12-point favorite before the game, but UNC coach Frank McGuire had a completely different idea in mind, and he put any doubts to rest in the locker room moments before tip-off.

"Let's get down to it, we're a better team than Kansas," McGuire said. "They only got one player that can beat us. The rest of the Kansas team can't beat us, can't even come close." McGuire then turned to his big man. "Rosenbluth, are you afraid of Chamberlain?"

After receiving an emphatic no from the senior, McGuire went right down the line and repeated the same question to all his players. The responses were all identical, but to truly make his point, McGuire did something truly outrageous. He sent Tommy Kearns, the smallest player in UNC's rotation, to take the opening tip. McGuire said it was to prevent any fast-break opportunities if Kansas won the toss, but the move was perhaps more psychological than strategic.

"When Tommy went out there, the crowd was buzzing. All of a sudden the crowd is silent—like, what's going on here?" Rosenbluth said. "And Tommy is 5-foot-11 and he's crouching down like he's going to get the jump, and Chamberlain is looking down at him. I mean, there is a guy 7-foot-1, he's looking down at Tommy. So he must have been, 'What in the world is going on?'"

Chamberlain indeed won the tip, but the constant double-team by Quigg and a variety of teammates prevented KU's center from ever getting in rhythm. Carolina grabbed an early 9–2 lead, and thanks to 65-percent shooting from the field, it was the Tar Heels who led 29–22 as the half came to a close.

They still led 35–30 in the second half before Kansas finally went on the run everybody had been anticipating. The Jayhawks reeled off 10 of the next 12 points to grab a 40–37 lead with 10:20 to play, and when Rosenbluth committed his fifth foul with 1:45 to go, it appeared the Jayhawks were on their way to the national championship. The lead was still three points, but with Gene Elstun stepping to the line to make it a five-point game, several Kansas players walked over to Rosenbluth to commend him on a great season. Elstun, however, missed both shots, and Bob Young, Rosenbluth's little-known replacement, helped the Tar Heels tie the score at 46 before the end of regulation.

Five minutes of extra time wouldn't be enough to separate the teams. Neither was double overtime, as both teams walked back to their benches tied at 48.

Despite now playing their second triple-overtime game in as many days, the Tar Heels pulled enough energy to take a 52–48 lead with 3:47 to go before the Jayhawks made one final push. With the local crowd imploring him, Chamberlain converted a three-point play to bring the Jayhawks within a point, and after a missed free throw by UNC's Bob Cunningham, the Kansas guard tied the game on a free throw with 2:33 remaining. Ironically, the hero of the game appeared to be Elstun, who atoned for his miss near the end of regulation by converting a free throw to give Kansas a 53–52 lead with just 31 seconds to play.

The Tar Heels would normally have gone to Rosenbluth for the last shot, but with their best player out, they ended up relying to a player who had rarely wanted the ball in clutch moments during the season. But despite being guarded by Chamberlain, on this night Joe Quigg felt particularly confident. Catching the ball at the elbow with 13 seconds left, Quigg fooled Chamberlain with a pump fake and took two steps before firing a shot. Chamberlain tried to recover by blocking him from behind, but with six seconds to play the referees blew the whistle. Quigg would shoot free throws with the national championship on the line. But before he could take the shots, McGuire called a timeout.

"Joe, listen: After you make both shots, they're probably going to call timeout," McGuire predicted. "And if they don't, you guys got to sprint down and get in front of Chamberlain, because that's who they're looking for."

But just like his comments about the opening tip, there was maybe something else at work. He was guaranteeing that Quigg would make the free throws.

"I didn't feel nervous at all," Quigg said. "I felt just like it wasn't even a regular game or anything, I thought it was just like practice. I felt really good about it. Since I've been taking up golf, every once in a while you'll be over a six to eight-foot putt and you know you're going to make it. And I just did not have any doubts that I was going to make those shots."

Sure enough, Quigg not only made the free throws, but on KU's final possession, he made the most daring play of his life. The Jayhawks inbounded the ball to Ronald Loneski, who quickly tossed it toward Chamberlain. But as soon as he saw Loneski pass it off, Quigg went dashing for the ball. If he didn't get it, Chamberlain would be wide open for the winning score. But Quigg got just enough of the ball to knock it over toward Kearns, who threw it up into the rafters as time expired. Joe Quigg was a hero.

McGuire celebrated in style, going out with the media for an extravagant dinner, paying $48 alone for his dressing. Unfortunately for his less-wealthy players, they couldn't find anything affordable to eat.

"The manager, I think they usually gave us two, three, four, five dollars a man to get something to eat, but after 12 there was nothing open," Rosenbluth recalled. "And all the players were walking around town trying to find a place open to get something to eat and we never found anything."

After nearly giving up on eating at all, the team managed to find a few Tar Heels fans who had ventured out to Kansas City. All they had to share were some potato chips, which the players gladly wolfed down, but upon their return to Chapel Hill the team got the celebration they properly deserved. Fans were given no indication when the team would show up, but when they arrived at 3 o'clock the next morning, more than 3,000 fans were there to greet them. It was significantly later than their midnight cravings in Kansas City, but even at this hour, it was safe to say they could probably find a place or two willing to stay open. ●

Steve Alford, Indiana: 23 points, 5 assists, 3 rebounds

1987: INDIANA vs. SYRACUSE

When the Indiana Hoosiers punched their ticket to the Final Four in New Orleans, Keith Smart probably felt more mixed feelings than anybody else on the team. The Hoosiers were two wins away from a championship, but the Big Easy native was returning to his hometown. That would normally be cause for celebration, but the first time Smart played in front of his mother, just two weeks earlier on Senior Day, he hyperventilated under the pressure. And now back at home, he was going to be playing in front of *all* of his relatives.

To relieve the pressure, Smart sought the comfort of an old routine, and he invited his teammates out for some Cajun food the night before the game.

"I probably had a little too much; it was a little too rich for me. I got real sick, and I couldn't sleep that night," Smart said.

The junior recovered in time to play in the title game against Syracuse and even scored the first points of the game on a pair of free throws. After that, however, everything started to go downhill. Smart made only one shot in the first half, and it was only due to back-to-back threes by Steve Alford in the last minute that the Hoosiers went into the break with a 34–33 lead. But the team would only be able to survive so long without any production from its point guard.

"He was an integral part of the success that we had all season long," Alford said. "He was just an outstanding player."

Smart tried to turn things around in the second half, but after a missed shot and errant pass that sailed out of bounds, Indiana coach Bobby Knight had no choice but to sit him on the bench.

"I thought I was done for the night," Smart reasoned, until the assistant coaches assured him he would have one more chance. "That was something that kept me involved in the game, so when I went back in I could still focus on what was happening in the game, and what I could do, as opposed to being mad because I was out."

Meanwhile, Syracuse took full advantage of Smart's absence, turning a 41–40 deficit into a 52–44 lead with 13 minutes left. Knight walked to the end of the bench and reluctantly put Smart back in the game. Smart responded immediately by hitting a free throw to pull the team within five, and he then made an off-balance jumper to put the Hoosiers back in front. Minutes later, Smart banked in a jump shot that tied the game at 61. Little did he know it, but Smart had just entered the zone, a state of mind that few athletes ever experience in their careers.

"Everything that you're doing is slow motion; you have all the time in the world to make the right decision," Smart said. "You can hear your breathing, and you don't see anything else but whatever you're trying to accomplish."

Smart tied the game again at 63 on a layup, and he hit another bank shot to give IU a 67–66 lead. He then knotted the score at

70 on a reverse layup before Howard Triche's jumper put the Orangemen back in front with a minute to go. After a rare miss by Smart, Triche added another free throw to extend the lead to 73–70. Smart raced downcourt, firing a jumper from 10 feet away that narrowed the deficit back to 73–72.

The shot clock was turned off, leaving the Hoosiers with no choice but to intentionally foul, sending Derrick Coleman to the line with 28 seconds remaining. Coleman had played the game of his life with 19 rebounds, but with the national championship in the balance, the moment was too much for the freshman. His first shot hit off the front rim and right into the hands of IU's Darryl Thomas.

Indiana had the option of either getting the ball to Smart or Alford, who had already nailed seven three-pointers and whose eighth would break the Big Ten scoring record. But Syracuse switched into a special defense specifically designed to take away any looks from the two players.

"I think everybody on the court trusted that we could work the ball without panicking," said Alford, who was being hounded by Sherman Douglas. "Coach Knight does an amazing job of disciplining his team to make sure that they understand good shots and bad shots. The time and clock and those types of things didn't really matter."

But the clock started becoming more of an issue, as nobody on Indiana could get open. Smart took a pass with 13 seconds left, still 30 feet from the hoop. After a few dribbles, he dished off to Darryl Thomas, who was being guarded just as closely. Thomas passed it back to Smart at the three-point line. Now there were only seven seconds left, leaving no more time to work the ball around. Dribbling to the baseline, Smart rose up and let the ball fly as he drifted out of bounds.

"You always wanted to make a shot falling out of bounds into the arms of the cheerleaders,"

Smart joked. "We would literally practice that shot after we finished playing pickup five-on-five and just take turns shooting it and falling out of bounds. And here it is, a childhood game that we played ended up becoming an actual game-time situation for me."

Everyone on the court stood still as the ball sailed toward the hoop, and just seconds before the buzzer, the ball fell through the net. Syracuse tried to toss the ball in for a desperation shot, but it landed appropriately in the hands of Smart, who launched the ball into the air as his teammates surrounded him.

"You have no idea what you've done," Knight told the hero. "Sure you know you won a national championship, everything is great, but it won't really hit you until you're sitting with your kids."

Sure enough, Knight's premonition was as accurate as Smart's final shot.

"About five years later, I'm sitting with my son and the game is on," Smart said. "And the guy mentioned Keith Smart, you made the shot, and my little boy, Andre, my oldest son, he looked at it and said, 'Dad, that's you!'"

Andre wasn't the only youngster who relived the moment, as later on Smart walked to a playground where a group of kids, unaware that their idol was standing right next to them, were pretending to be Keith Smart, hitting the last shot to give Indiana the title.

The night of the title game was also the same day that the movie *Hoosiers* was being honored at the Academy Awards. The producers of the film skipped their own award show to watch the real team play in the national championship. What they saw was better than anything Hollywood could produce.

"Going through that entire season and that culminating in being able to play on the last day of the year was something very special," Alford said. "And ultimately winning a national championship? You couldn't write a better script." ●

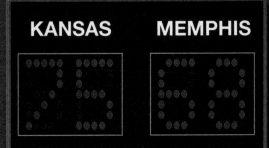

KANSAS   MEMPHIS

Darrell Arthur, Kansas: 20 points, 10 rebounds

2008: KANSAS vs. MEMPHIS

The Kansas locker room remained silent as coach Bill Self addressed his team for the biggest game of their lives. In moments, his players would be taking the floor in the national championship game. As the team circled around him, Self reminded his club that, with more wins than any other team in school in history, the Jayhawks had nothing to lose that night, but had so much to gain. But, he added at the end of his speech, "Most every day, if not every day for the rest of your life, you will be reminded of or think of this night."

That statement would have likely been true no matter what the final score read, but this wasn't just any championship game. This was a game for the ages.

It only took 3:21 for the Tigers to hand Kansas its biggest deficit of the tournament. Granted, it was only 9–3, but it sent a quick message that the Jayhawks could be in for a long night if they didn't elevate their game. But Kansas would do just that, returning the favor by handing the Tigers their own biggest deficit at 22–15. Memphis quickly knotted the game at 28 just before halftime, which was quite an accomplishment, considering the Tigers had only gotten three points from star freshman Derrick Rose. A day earlier, Rose was suffering from the flu, and although he claimed he was back up to speed by game time, the Tigers would need the point guard at his best if they were to take home the national title.

The teams continued to trade baskets in the second half until Rose came alive with 12 minutes to go. Trailing 43–40, Rose put the team on his back, scoring 14 of their next 16 points. His final points of the run, which came with 4:06 remaining, appeared to be the dagger. With the shot clock running out, Rose banked in a turnaround 20-footer to give the Tigers a 56–49 lead. Minutes later, Robert Dozier sank a pair of free throws to give Memphis a 60–51 lead. If the Jayhawks were going to make a comeback, they would have only 2:12 to do so.

"We were ready to cut the nets down," Memphis senior Joey Dorsey said.

Few could blame him. Not only did the Tigers have a seemingly insurmountable lead, their free throw shooting had become a sudden strength for the team. They had converted 75 percent of their opportunities against Michigan State in the Sweet 16, and two days later against Texas, the team shot 83 percent from the line.

If Kansas was going to mount a comeback, now was the time. Twenty years earlier, Danny Manning had led the Jayhawks to an unpredicted run to the national championship, on a team that became known as "Danny and the Miracles." Now it was time for the 2008 Jayhawks to produce a miracle of their own.

Kansas forward Darrell Arthur got the comeback bid started with a jump shot to cut the lead to 60–53 with 1:56 left, and senior Sherron Collins instantly changed the complexion of the game by stealing the inbounds pass.

Collins fed it to teammate Mario Chalmers, who drove to the hoop before kicking it back to his teammate, now open at the three-point line. Collins swished the shot to slice the lead to just 60–56, and the team immediately fouled Memphis on the inbounds pass. Following his team's recent trend, junior Chris Douglas-Roberts converted both free throws to bump the lead back to 62–56. For the night, the Tigers were now 9-of-12 from the line.

Chalmers responded by sinking a pair of free throws of his own to trim the lead to 62–58, and moments later he fouled Douglas-Roberts once more. This time the guard missed the front end of a one-and-one, and Arthur made him pay by burying a turnaround jumper with 1:00 remaining to bring the Jayhawks within 62–60. Douglas-Roberts was off target once again at the other end, this time on a jumper, and Collins snatched the rebound with 26 to seconds to go.

Collins could have held the ball in hopes of taking the last shot, but he wisely declined and instead looked to attack the basket with both teams in transition. He appeared to have the equalizing layup when Rose came in at the last second to swat the ball away. The ball wound up in the hands of Douglas-Roberts for yet a third time, and with just 16.8 seconds left he was sent to the free throw line. With two free throws, the game would likely be over.

But his first was well short and his second was off line, landing on the right side of the rim before bouncing away. It appeared the Tigers had squandered a golden opportunity, but there for the rebound was Memphis forward

Robert Dozier. The junior was smart enough to swing the ball over to Rose, who had not only shouldered the scoring burden in the second half, but had made his last 13 free throws going back to their semifinal game against UCLA. Although he had played extremely well as of late, Rose was still a freshman, and when his time came to put the game away, he too came up short. His first attempt hit all of the rim before bouncing away, and even though he would convert his second free throw, he had just given Kansas another chance.

Still, just 10 seconds remained for Kansas to get off a three-pointer, and the Tigers could commit a foul to put the Jayhawks in a real predicament. If they could foul before the Jayhawks attempted the game-tying three-pointer, Kansas would only shoot two free throws. But thanks to some out-of-control dribbling by Collins, the Memphis defense had trouble picking a right time to foul.

Just before Collins tumbled to the ground on the right wing, he shuffled the ball back to Chalmers, who was curling back from the corner over to the top of the key. Taking one dribble to set himself, Everyone stopped to watch as Chalmers turned and fired from beyond the arc. If the shot went in, the game would be heading to overtime. If it missed, the national championship would belong to Memphis.

As the ball continued on its way toward the hoop, it fell in with just two seconds left, giving Chalmers one of the biggest shots in basketball history.

"I had a good look at it," Chalmers said. "As soon as it left my hand it felt good, and I knew it was going in."

The Jayhawks would go on to score the first six points of overtime, and after holding off a late run from the Tigers, Kansas had pulled off the impossible.

More than 100,000 supporters, in a town of just 82,000 people, gathered to show their appreciation for the team's incredible comeback. As it turned out, Self had only forgotten one thing in his pre-game speech: It was a moment the fans would never forget, either. ●

Mario Chalmers takes the game-tying shot for KU just before the end of regulation. *Streeter Lecka/ Getty Images*

UTAH   DARTMOUTH

Arnie Ferrin, Utah: 22 points

1944: UTAH
vs. DARTMOUTH

Before Utah coach Vadal Peterson could ever worry about winning a national championship, he first needed a basketball team. And in 1944, when most young men had their minds on the war, that was no easy task. No other team in the conference even bothered to put a team together, but Peterson held an open tryout, hoping that the new NCAA rule allowing freshmen to play would result in more players to select from. His final roster wasn't pretty on paper—some of the members had never played high school basketball, and only two of the players had started on their high school teams. Even worse, the average age of the young men was just 18 years old.

"It was made up of a team of misfits. We didn't even have a clue that we would ever play on a winning team," sophomore Herb Wilkinson said. "But we were in there plugging away and wanting to do the best we could."

The team had managed a respectable 17–3 record, but the Utes weren't a household name. It was only because team manager Keith Brown sent newspaper clippings of the team to NIT organizer Ned Irish that they were able to snag the tournament's last bid. Utah took an early bow out of the NIT, but when the Arkansas team bus crashed, the Utes also received the last invitation to the NCAA Tournament. Utah found its way to the championship game against the Dartmouth Indians, who were considered by everyone to be the superior team. In fact, the Dartmouth players actually joked that they

should play against themselves to give the fans their money's worth. But Utah assistant coach Pete Crouch was at the same coffee shop when he overheard the remarks, and he made sure to tell his players just how their opponents felt.

"We knew we were underdogs, and we just wanted to leave it at that," guard Wat Misaka said. "We didn't try to dwell on the fact that the other team might be a lot better than us, and we always felt like our team play and our condition would be enough to win."

The Utes may have had confidence, but the Indians also had history on their side. Because the Navy was using the Dartmouth campus to train soldiers, their basketball team was a collection of former college stars now serving with the military. With the most talented lineup in the country, the Indians lost only one game all season, and once former St. John's standout Dick McGuire arrived on campus, they were undefeated.

Utah's task did not get any easier when center and leading scorer Fred Sheffield injured himself during a practice before the championship game.

"Sheffield went up for a rebound and came down on my foot. He turned his ankle, and oh, we were sick," Wilkinson said. "We just didn't know how we were going to make it."

Peterson's team was short-handed enough as it was. He gave Sheffield four minutes of playing time, but besides the short substitution for Misaka, his five starters played every second of the championship game—making it all the more imperative that the Utes win the game in regulation.

And for the first 39 minutes, everything went according to plan, as Utah held a 36–32 lead. Dartmouth's Bob Gale tipped in an errant shot to cut the lead to 36–34 with 40 seconds to go, but the Utes still had the ball—and during the sport's primitive years, that usually guaranteed a victory. The rules at the time stated that teams couldn't foul to get the ball back, as any team leading in the last two minutes would get to retain possession after a foul. So even if Dartmouth was to foul and Utah missed its free throws, the Utes would still have possession of the ball. The only option for the Indians was to come up with a steal to keep their season alive, and they got what they were looking for when they jarred the ball loose with 10 seconds left. They quickly fed the ball to McGuire, who had to cast off a long shot just before the buzzer.

The ball sailed through right before the buzzer, sending the game into overtime. As

Utah's Arnie Ferrin was responsible for nearly half of his team's points during the championship game against Dartmouth. *University of Utah Athletic Department*

tired as his players were, Peterson had little choice but to leave his starters in the game.

Arnie Ferrin paved the way for the Utes in overtime, hitting four clutch free throws to give his team a 40–38 lead. Aud Brindley answered back for Dartmouth to tie the game once again, but the Utes would at least have the final shot. The plan was to get the ball to Ferrin, who had scored almost half of his team's points, but the Indians would have none of it. If somebody was going to upset Dartmouth, it wasn't going to be him. The ball was still in the hands of Utah's Bob Lewis when only five seconds remained on the clock.

"He told me that 'I felt in my mind Herb could shoot better than I can on any given day,' and he passed it to me," Wilkinson said. "And I only had three seconds, so I just had no chance of getting it into Arnie.'

With no time to improvise, Wilkinson had little choice but to shoot from well beyond the top of the key, a place he rarely ventured as a post player. Long-range shots were not exactly his specialty, but when it mattered most, Wilkinson found the touch, and right as the clock struck zero the ball sailed through the net, giving the Utes one of the most improbable championships of all time.

"We all ran over and grabbed him and thought that was just great," Ferrin said. "I'm not sure we ever really realized the impact on our lives it would have to win an NCAA championship, and it's impacted all of us for our lives."

No one benefited more from the championship than Ferrin, who met his future wife, Pat, at the celebration back in Salt Lake City. The school had invited anybody with a convertible to take part in the ceremonies, and the young lady gladly accepted.

"She drove down to the train station hoping that she'd be getting one of the players in her car, and she ended up with the coach," Ferrin joked. "So we laugh about her effort to find a basketball player, but she found one later."

Not just any player. A national champion. ●

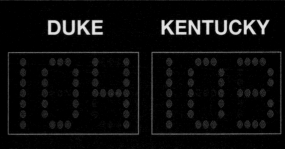

Christian Laettner, Duke: 31 points, 7 rebounds, 3 assists

1992: DUKE vs. KENTUCKY

Entering the East Regional Final against Kentucky, Duke forward Christian Laettner stood just nine points shy of the all-time record for career points in the NCAA Tournament. With a pair of game-winning shots (see pages 236 and 270) on his résumé, Laettner had already cemented his legacy as one of the game's greatest players. But on this night, with a chance to stand alone atop college basketball's scoring list, he put together arguably the greatest performance of all time. But that did not necessarily mean his team was moving on to the Final Four.

Laettner scored eight points in the early going, but six minutes into the game it was the Wildcats who found themselves in front 20–12. Even after the Blue Devils went on a 15–2 run to take a five-point lead, Kentucky came right back to tie the game at 27.

"They wouldn't go away. And usually with teams that we played against—and that year we were pretty dominant—we would go on a run and we'd extend the lead, and we'd put teams away," Duke point guard Bobby Hurley said. "We knew we were in a war at that point. Every possession meant so much, so just try and make the best of each one. They weren't going away, and it was going to take us beating them in order for us to move on."

Fortunately for the Blue Devils, Laettner was up to the task. With his layup late in the first half, Laettner surpassed Elvin Hayes as the tournament's most prolific scorer, and he gave

his team a 35–29 lead. When he sank a three-pointer early in the second half to put Duke up 62–53, Laettner still had yet to miss from the field. The Blue Devils would need each of those shots, as the Wildcats came storming right back.

As soon as Hurley buried a three-pointer to put his team up 67–55, Kentucky's Dale Brown connected on a layup to trim the lead to 10, and four seconds after UK forward Deron Feldhaus stole the inbounds pass, Jamal Mashburn drilled a three-pointer from the top of the key to bring the Wildcats within seven. Duke called a timeout, but Kentucky came up with yet another steal. This time it took only two seconds for Mashburn to bury another three, and in the blink of an eye, the lead was now down to 67–63.

Kentucky's resilience clearly took its toll on Laettner, who minutes later stomped on the chest of UK forward Aminu Timberlake. When Laettner caught a pass near the baseline and turned to face the basket, he knocked Timberlake to the floor, and once Laettner attempted his shot, he walked back toward his opponent. Looking down at Timberlake, Laettner stepped on him with his right foot.

"I thought he had pushed me at the other end of the court. It was just a stupid reaction type thing. Sure, I wanted to stomp a lot harder, but I knew that would be really, *really* dumb," Laettner admitted. "I wanted him to know that I wasn't going to take any crap, and there's nothing wrong with adding a little spice to the game."

There is something wrong, however, with compromising your team's chances at a victory. Timberlake jumped up with a big smile and started clapping. Laettner's intended message hadn't caused an injury, but it was enough to warrant a technical foul.

"Looking back on it, you know that it was not appropriate at all what he did. I don't really remember seeing Christian do something like that," Hurley said. "Christian at times could get under guys' skins as a player. I never saw Christian do anything like that as a player, so I was as surprised as heck."

The Wildcats were still smiling minutes later when they wiped away a 79–69 deficit to tie the game at 81 with just over five minutes to play. Both teams were still knotted at 91 with just over a minute left when Thomas Hill rattled in

a jumper just before the shot clock expired to put Duke on top. It was a lead that wouldn't last long, as Feldhaus put in a missed shot by teammate John Pelphrey to tie the score with only 38 seconds left. Hurley's last-second try hit off the back of the rim, and after 40 minutes of action a victor had yet to be determined.

Pelphrey got things started in the extra session with a three-pointer from the top of the key, but Hurley answered right back with a three of his own. Pelphrey responded with yet another basket, but now it was Laettner's turn to even the score. His seventh and eight free throws of the night, on eight attempts, left the score at 98–98 with 1:52 to play. The Duke junior followed it up by rebounding a Kentucky miss, and with the shot clock ready to expire, he made what appeared to be the play of the tournament. Sandwiched between two defenders as he went up for the shot, Laettner squeezed through to fire an off-balance shot at the backboard that managed to carom back in with 32 seconds remaining.

"You could tell the whole way through, especially late in the game, it came down to a contest of wills," Hurley recalled. "It was two teams continually one-upping the other team and continually making shots and making plays at critical moments, and it went on and on and on."

No sooner had Laettner put the Blue Devils ahead than Mashburn drove to the hoop to try and tie the game with 19.6 seconds left. Not only did he deliver on the shot, he also did so while being fouled, and his ensuing free throw gave the Wildcats a 101–100 lead. Considering Laettner was a perfect 9-of-9 from the field and 8-of-8 from the line, Hurley wisely got the ball to his teammate, and Laettner delivered once again. As soon as he caught the ball with 15 seconds to go, he turned toward the basket, only to be fouled by Mashburn. Laettner fittingly made both shots for yet another lead change.

This game, however, was too good to end like that. The Wildcats had made nearly 57 percent of their shots, while the Blue Devils

Christian Laettner sinks the game-winning shot over Deron Feldhaus in the final second of their regional final game. *Charles Arbogast/AP Photo* had shot over 65 percent from the floor. The game seemed destined to be won by the team with the last shot, and when Kentucky called a timeout with 7.8 seconds to go, that team appeared to be the Wildcats. The inbounds pass ended up in the hands of Sean Woods, who blew by Hurley before hoisting an awkward shot over Laettner. The half jumper, half hook shot flew way past its intended target, but the shot was on line, and as it bounced off the backboard it landed in the hoop with 2.1 seconds to go. As ugly as it was, the shot gave Kentucky a 103–102 advantage.

"In the playground when you bank it straight up, guys are like, 'That shouldn't count,'" Hurley said. "To see it go that way, it didn't feel real at that time. It was tough because we knew there was not a lot of time and we had to go the length of the floor. It did not look promising."

Sensing a dejected group, Duke coach Mike Krzyzewski snapped some life back into his players.

"We're going to win the game," declared Krzyzewski. "If you think we're not going to win this game, get up and leave the huddle because we're going to win."

Krzyzewski already had a plan for the last play—it was a play his team had run at the start of every practice. Grant Hill would hurl the ball nearly 70 feet from his own baseline to Laettner at the far three-point line. The last time they had tried the play at Wake Forest, Hill had tossed the ball out of bounds, but Krzyzewski was now going to give him a second chance.

"Grant, can you make the pass?" Krzyzewski asked. After Hill acknowledged that he could, Krzyzewski turned to Laettner.

"Christian, you're going to flash from the left corner to the top of the key," he said. "Can you do it?"

The senior nodded, and his team walked back out on the court for the most important play of their lives. This time, Hill's pass was indeed perfect, soaring right toward Laettner, who caught the ball and surprised everybody by taking a dribble as the clock ticked down. Then, with one second to go, he faked a move to the right before spinning left and firing away. He managed to get the shot off with 0.2 seconds left, and as the ball made its way toward the basket, the season hinged on his shot.

"It's one of those memories that's engrained in my mind that will never go away," Hurley said. "It just felt like time wasn't even moving. It was really crazy."

And in a fitting ending to his flawless performance, Laettner's shot swished through to give Duke a 104–103 victory. In one night, Laettner had not only claimed his stake as the best scorer in NCAA Tournament history, he also had its greatest play as well. ●

#2

1983: N.C. STATE vs. HOUSTON

Before his team's championship game against Houston, N.C. State coach Jim Valvano decided to pick up a copy of the *Washington Post*. "Trees will tap dance, elephants will drive in the Indy 500, and Orson Wells will skip lunch," columnist Dave Kindred predicted, "before N.C. State wins this game."

Kindred's assessment of Valvano's squad wasn't exactly flattering, but few had any reason to disagree. The Wolfpack were entering the game with 10 losses, more than any other championship team in history, and were lucky that number wasn't higher. In their last eight games following the end of the regular season, the Wolfpack had won six of them in the final minute, leaving fans wondering just how many miracles were left in store.

They had pulled off three of them just to get into the tournament (see page 94). Then they began the tournament by storming back from six points down in the final minute of overtime against Pepperdine (see page 262), followed it up with a last-second shot to beat UNLV (see page 172), beat Utah in Utah, defeated Virginia on a pair of free throws in the final seconds, and squeaked out a 67–60 victory over Georgia in the semifinals after nearly blowing an 18-point lead. But against Houston, there was no way they could play anything but their best game and expect to win. The Cougars were just too good.

Not only was Houston the top ranked-team in the country, with 26 consecutive wins to their résumé, they also featured two future Hall of Famers in Clyde Drexler and Hakeem Olajuwon. Along with Larry Micheaux and Michael Young, the group became known as "Phi Slama Jama," perhaps the most exclusive, as well as explosive, fraternity in the country. That lineup, combined with an ill N.C. State team, was a recipe for a blowout. N.C. State forward Dereck Whittenburg was sick, but he was actually better off than Valvano, who was suffering from a 104-degree fever the day of the game. Valvano got some IV fluids so he could make it out to the game, but it appeared he was marching to his own execution.

"Phi Slama Jama that year, they were a great team, there was no question about that," Wolfpack forward Thurl Bailey said. "So when you're facing a situation where the odds are tremendously against you, it takes something a little extra. It takes your mindset to be totally different."

Fortunately, Coach V knew just how to bring out the best in his players. Valvano, who had told the press all week that he was going to hold the ball the entire game, scrapped his plans at the last minute. As the team waited for his final instructions before tip-off, Valvano walked up to the chalkboard and erased everything he had written.

"If you think we're going to hold the ball against these guys, you got to be out of your mind," Valvano said with a smile, "because we're going to take it to them!"

As it turned out, N.C. State had a fraternity of its own—named "Phi Packa Attacka"—and early on it showed as Valvano's kids raced out to a 6–0 advantage. Thanks to four straight baskets from Bailey, the team still led 31–21 as halftime approached. The first half had been a considerable success, but Valvano knew that a victory was no guarantee. This locker room speech would be nothing like the one his team had heard before the game. If you let this lead slip away, he warned his players, it will haunt you for the rest of your lives.

The speech was intended to keep his players aggressive, but Valvano's worst fears came to pass. Houston scored the first 10 points coming out of the break, and midway through the half the Cougars had pushed the gap all the way to 42–35. The Wolfpack, who had been outscored 17–2 since play resumed, were shooting only 8 percent for the half. And with Houston outrebounding N.C. State 16–3, chances of a comeback appeared to be slim.

Houston's lead was still 52–46 late in the second half when the Wolfpack felt the adrenaline kick in one last time. Point guard Sidney Lowe sank a shot from the top of the key to cut the lead to four, and when he made a steal at midcourt moments later, he fired the ball down to Whittenburg, who was standing alone in the corner. The senior buried the shot, putting the Wolfpack within 52–50.

With just 2:20 remaining, Houston decided to work the ball to Olajuwon, rather than stall the game and risk missing a shot from the foul line. Olajuwon even got the look he wanted underneath the basket, but his turnaround bounced off the rim and into the hands of a streaking Lowe. The point guard wasted little time in firing another pass down to an open Whittenburg, this time at the right wing. When his shot rolled in with two minutes to go, the game was suddenly tied at 52.

The Cougars wisely decided to stall this time, knowing that they could hold for the last shot. N.C. State played a casual defense, appearing content to play for overtime, but when Houston tossed the ball over to freshman Alvin Franklin, Whittenburg raced over to commit the foul. Franklin was only a 63-percent shooter, and Whittenburg's quick thinking paid off when Franklin's free throw ricocheted off the rim and toward N.C. State's

Cozell McQueen. The Wolfpack proceeded to call a timeout of their own with 54 seconds to go. The next shot they took could very well decide the national championship.

"There's a lot of moments of nervousness and butterflies and anxiety and happiness. You feel special that you were able to be a character written into that story, regardless of the outcome," Bailey said. "It's very surreal because nobody knows what the ending is going to be. You know what you want the ending to be, but now you have the opportunity to write your own story, hoping it'll turn out like you're writing it."

But as the final possession began to unfold, it was obvious that the Wolfpack had waited too long to begin their final drive. With 12 seconds to go, the ball was still near midcourt, and as soon as they tried to advance the ball closer to the basket, they were turned back by the Houston defense. Desperation was setting in.

NINE SECONDS

Lowe managed to find Bailey in the corner, but when he hesitated, the defense swarmed in, forcing him to toss it back out.

SIX SECONDS

Now running critically low on time, Bailey tried to hurl it back Whittenburg, who was standing nearly 40 feet away near midcourt. But by the time the ball had arrived, Houston's Benny Anders had nearly caught up to Whittenburg, forcing the Wolfpack senior to twist his body while making the catch, so as to avoid the steal.

FOUR SECONDS

Whittenburg, who lost control of the ball while turning around, had no choice now. Reeling in the loose ball, he fired a shot from 15 feet behind the three-point line.

TWO SECONDS

As the ball made its long descent toward the basket, it began to fall well short of its intended target. Overtime appeared imminent, but there was one player Houston had forgotten to account for. Lorenzo Charles, the quiet sophomore on N.C. State, was standing all by himself underneath the basket. And just before the final second ticked by, Charles snatched the ball and redirected it into the basket. It was an

After Derrick Whittenburg's desperation shot missed, Lorenzo Charles slams home the winning dunk at the buzzer, giving N.C. State the most unbelievable championship in basketball history. *AP Photo*

improbable play to cap off an improbable game and an even more improbable season.

Whittenburg, who had been Valvano's go-to hugger all year long, was nowhere to be seen in the chaos that quickly consumed the court. The shot of Valvano running around the court by himself quickly became one of the most endearing images in tournament history. Fortunately, or perhaps not so fortunately, Valvano found some love anyway when Athletic Director Willis Casey caught up with

Valvano and gave him much more than V was looking for.

"Sixty million have watched me running around like a maniac . . . and then I fall into the arms of a fat old man who kisses me square on the mouth!" Valvano laughed. "I feel the thrill of victory and the agony of defeat all at the same time."

Valvano could have gone without the kiss, but if that was the cost for his first national championship, it was certainly worth the price. ●

1963: LOYOLA CHICAGO vs. CINCINNATI

When the Loyola Chicago Ramblers realized they would be facing the University of Cincinnati in the 1963 title game, they knew that they were going to need all the help they could get. With the winner of the last two championships on the horizon, the Ramblers decided they would need to take their motivational ploys a step further than they had for any other game. But what originally started as a simple tactic turned into every coach's nightmare.

"We stayed up all night," Loyola captain Jerry Harkness recalled, "yelling at each other, 'We've got to win!' We're hitting each other with pillows, acting crazy trying to psych ourselves up, and we stayed up too late. . . . We were dead tired the next day."

Needless to say, the Ramblers seemed sluggish at the start of the game. Midway through the first half, Loyola Chicago had missed 13 of its first 14 shots and trailed 19–9. Although the Ramblers cut the lead to 29–21 at halftime, they had shot just 8-of-34 in the first half and Harkness couldn't buy a basket.

Loyola coach George Ireland walked into the locker room, sensing that criticizing his team was the last thing they needed.

"We were all sitting there with our heads down," junior Ron Miller said. "We were thinking—no one was talking. He came down, looked around the room, and he kind of smiled."

With the team still in striking distance despite a poor performance, Ireland told his players that they could come back if they played their normal game in the second half. Unfortunately for the Ramblers, the halftime speech was about as effective as their pre-game antics. Cincinnati's Ron Bonham came out and hit three straight shots, and before long the Bearcats had pushed the lead to 45–30. With no shot clock to force Cincinnati to quicken the pace and the lead looking insurmountable, Harkness turned to a higher power.

"We went down 15 and it doesn't look like it's going to turn around," Harkness recalled. "So I'm saying, 'Dear Lord, if you need for us to lose, make it close.'"

Loyola managed to cut the lead to 45–33 with a little over 10 minutes remaining. It was at this time that the media made their final selections for the all-tournament team, which was to be announced after the final buzzer. Only one member of the group came from Loyola, while three Bearcats made the roster.

But right after the selections were finalized, Ireland's team started to turn the tide. Knowing that Cincinnati would turn down open shots to waste more time off the clock, Loyola started to take some chances defensively and looked to double-team the opposition at every opportunity. Combined with missed free throw attempts by the Bearcats, things started to change in a hurry.

With a little under five minutes remaining and Cincinnati's lead down to 48–41, Harkness made his first bucket of the game, and he scored again moments later off a steal.

Both teams battled until Loyola's Les Hunter cut the lead to 51–50 with one minute remaining in the game. Although Cincinnati could have held onto the ball to run off more time, the Bearcats had learned their lesson. Seeing a fast-break opportunity, Tom Thacker scored to put UC back up 53–50.

Needing a quick basket just to give Loyola a chance, Hunter delivered again with a tip-in to cut the lead back to one point with 17 seconds remaining. Cincinnati inbounded the ball to Larry Shingleton, and Harkness immediately decided to foul him. Unfortunately for Harkness, he had just unknowingly fouled one of the best free throw shooters in the country. Shingleton stepped to the line and made the first shot to push the lead to 54–52. He glanced at teammate Tony Yates and grinned, knowing that without a three-point line, the next free throw would seal the championship.

But the second free throw hit off the front of the rim and richocheted toward Hunter, who started the fast break. The junior tossed the ball over to guard Ron Miller, who found Harkness near the left sideline. Harkness was wide open as he took a jump shot with six seconds left, but with so much adrenaline coursing through his veins, Harkness struggled to put any touch on his shot. "To this day, I just didn't feel anything," Harkness said. "I didn't feel how much I had to shoot or anything. I just let it go."

The shot would indeed fall, and Cincinnati's desperate timeout plea was drowned out by the delirious crowd. The championship game was going to overtime.

After Harkness and Miller gave Loyola a 58–56 lead in the extra period, Shingleton redeemed himself by hitting the equalizer with over two minutes remaining. Ireland called a timeout with 1:49 left and told his team to hold for the last shot. However, while running the clock down, disaster nearly struck. A pass from Miller went off John Egan's foot and was headed for Shingleton, who quickly pounced on the ball. Egan recovered in time to force a jump ball, but Loyola would still have to win the ensuing toss to keep possession. Fortunately for the Ramblers, Egan did just that, tipping it back to Miller as the clock began to tick away once more.

Now with less than 10 seconds remaining, Harkness drove toward the left side of the basket and jumped for what looked to be the final shot. Standing in his way, however, was UC's Ron Bonham, forcing Harkness to pass the ball as the seconds continued to melt away. He found Hunter near the elbow, but with just three seconds remaining, Hunter had little choice but to force up a difficult fadeaway that rattled around the rim and bounced off. But before the last second could tick away, it landed in the hands of Vic Rouse, Loyola's toughest player, who had overcome Polio as a child to be in this spot.

With the season on the line, nothing was going to keep Rouse from tipping in the winning shot. As the ball went through the net and the buzzer sounded, Loyola's cheerleaders (including Ireland's daughter) ran out to center court to celebrate with the team. Rouse had just completed the most miraculous comeback in NCAA Tournament history.

"What Vic Rouse went though, man, I am so glad he got the winning basket," Harkness said. "He deserved it." ●

Loyola's Vic Rouse puts up the game-winning basket in the final second of overtime during the 1963 title game between Loyola Chicago and Cincinnati. *AP Photo*

Bibliography

BOOKS AND ARTICLES

Albom, Mitch. "The Human Side of a Sometimes Impersonal Hame." *Syracuse Herald Journal,* April 3, 1989.

Alford, Steve and John Garrity. *Playing for Knight: My Six Seasons with Coach Knight.* New York: Simon & Schuster, 1990.

Anderson, Dave. "Knight, Smith Hoop Philosophies Same." *Pacific Stars and Stripes*, April 2, 1981.

Berger, Dan. "Lew (Who Else?) Voted MVP Again." *Charleston Daily Mail*, March 25, 1968.

Black, Jimmy and Scott Fowler. *Jimmy Black's Tales from the Tar Heels.* Champaign, IL: Sports Publishing, 2006.

Boeck, Larry. "Hatton Fires Goal in Final 16 Seconds for 61–60 Win." *Louisville Courier-Journal*, March 21, 1958.

Brill, Bill. *An Illustrated History of Duke Basketball: A Legacy of Achievement.* Champaign, IL: Sports Publishing, 2012.

Brill, Bill and Mike Krzyzewski. *A Season Is a Lifetime: The Inside Story of the Duke Blue Devils and Their Championship Seasons.* New York: Simon & Schuster, 1993.

Bracy, Aaron. "Temple's Fernandez Hopes Confidence Heals." Philahoops.com, February 10, 2011.

Cave, Ray. "Cincinnati is No. 1, No. 1, No. 1!" *Sports Illustrated*, April 6, 1962.

———. "Jerry Lucas." *Sports Illustrated,* January 8, 1962.

Cohen, Stanley. *The Game They Played.* New York: Carrol & Graf, 2001.

Condotta, Bob. "UConn's Winning Shot 8 Years Ago Still Haunts Those UW Huskies." *Seattle Times*, March 22, 2006.

Davis, Seth. *When March Went Mad.* New York: Times Books, 2009.

Drehs, Wayne. "Magical Tournament Run Still Stuff of Dreams." ESPN.com, March 18, 2003.

Drew, Homer and Shawn Malayter. *Find a Way: Valpo's Sweet Dream.* Boulder, CO: Taylor Trade Publishing, 1998.

Einhorn, Eddie and Ron Rappoport. *How March Became Madness: How the NCAA Tournament Became the Greatest Sporting Event in America.* Chicago: Triumph Books, 2006.

ESPN College Basketball Encyclopedia: The Complete History of the Men's Game. Holmes, PA: ESPN Books; New York: Ballantine Books, 2009.

Fitzpatrick, Frank. *And the Walls Came Tumbling Down: The Basketball Game That Changed American Sports.* Lincoln, NE: Bison Books, 1999.

Forde, Pat. "Legacy of Rupp Slow to Recede Repercussions of 1966 Title Game Still Echo in Many Ears." *USA Today*, April 2, 1996.

"Freshmen Anthony, McNamara Lead Boeheim to First Title." Sportsline.com, April 7, 2003.

Fussman, Chet. "Sorry, Cinderella: Weber State's Dream Dashed by Fairy-Tale Ending." Scripps Howard News Service, March 20, 1995.

Grace, Kevin. *Cincinnati Hoops.* Mount Pleasant, SC: Arcadia Publishing, 2003.

Haller, Doug. "Recalling 'Danny and Miracles.'" *The Arizona Republic*, March 26, 2008.

Harrick, Jim. McGill, John. Wallace, Tom. *Embracing the Legend: Jim Harrick Revives the UCLA Mystique.* Bonus Books, 1995

Hiner, Jason. *Mac's Boys: Branch McCracken and the Legendary 1953 Hurryin' Hoosiers.* Bloomington, IN: Quarry Books, 2006.

Hohlfeld, Neil. "Georgia Tech Beats Oklahoma State, 67–65." *Houston Chronicle*, April 4, 2004.

Hummel, Bob. "1940 Introduction." *Bloomington Herald-Times,* January 3, 2006.

Jares, Joe. "A Wild Ride with Wooden, Alcindor and the 1968 UCLA Bruins." SportsIllustrated.com, July 20, 2011.

———. "Rematch for Elvin and Big Lew." *Sports Illustrated*, March 18, 1968.

Jenkins, Bruce. *A Good Man: The Pete Newell Story.* Lincoln, NE: Bison Books, 2010.

Johnson, James. *The Dandy Dons: Bill Russell, K. C. Jones, Phil Woolpert, and One of College Basketball's Greatest and Most Innovative Teams.* Lincoln, NE: Bison Books, 2009.

Juliano, Joe. "Clamps on Tar Heels for NCAA Toga." *Clearfield Progress*, March 31, 1981.

Keiderling, Kyle. *Heart of a Lion: The Life, Death and Legacy of Hank Gathers.* N.p.: Morning Star Books, 2010.

Keith, Larry. "They're a Fearsome Foursome." *Sports Illustrated*, March 27, 1978.

Kent, Milton. "Connolly Returns in Style." *Baltimore Sun*, March 15, 1991.

Kirkpatrick, Curry. "How King Rat Became the Big Cheese." *Sports Illustrated*, December 5, 1983.

———. "Mister Clutch." *Sports Illustrated*, April 10, 1989.

———. "Sweet 16 and the 32 Who Missed." *Sports Illustrated,* March 22, 1982.

Knight, Bob and Bob Hammel. *Knight: My Story.* New York: St. Martin's Griffin, 2003.

Krzyzewski, Mike and Donald Phillips. *Five-Point Play: The Story of Duke's Amazing 2000–2001 Championship Season.* New York: Grand Central Publishing, 2001.

Layden, Tim. "Heavenly Heels." *Sports Illustrated*, April 13, 2009.

———. "A Fling and a Prayer." *Sports Illustrated,* March 21, 2011.

"Legendary UCLA Basketball Coach John Wooden Dies at 99." *Los Angeles Times and Seattle Times news services,* June 4, 2010.

Lucas, Adam. *The Best Game Ever: How Frank McGuire's '57 Tar Heels Beat Wilt and Revolutionized College Basketball.* Guilford, CT: Lyons Press, 2011.

Lucas, Adam, Steve Kirschner, and Matt Bowers. *Led by Their Dreams: The Inside Story of Carolina's Journey to the 2005 National Championship.* Guilford, CT: Lyons Press, 2005.

———. *One Fantastic Ride: The Inside Story of Carolina Basketball's 2009 Championship Season.* Chapel Hill, NC: The University of North Carolina Press, 2009.

McDermott, Barry. "Al, You Went Out in Style." *Sports Illustrated,* April 4, 1977.

———. "Down and Out, Back Up and Ready." *Sports Illustrated,* March 25, 1974.

March Madness: Cinderellas, Superstars, and Champions from the Final Four. Chicago: Triumph Books, 2004.

"Mount's Shot Puts Purdue in Semis." *Beckley Post-Herald,* March 17, 1969.

"NCAA Men's Tournament: Lehigh Delivers Shocker." *Portland Press Herald,* March 17, 2012.

Newman, Bruce. "The Week (Feb. 13-19)." *Sports Illustrated,* February 21, 1978.

Nickel, Lori. "Milwaukee's Made the Most of NCAA Hosting." *Milwaukee Journal Sentinel,* March 18, 2010.

Olson, Lute and David Fisher. *Lute!: The Seasons of My Life.* New York: St. Martin's Griffin, 2007.

O'Neil, Dana. "Princeton's '96 Duo Take Different Paths." ESPN.com, September 24, 2009.

———. "Reed's Divine Shot Still Garners Attention." ESPN.com, September 25, 2009.

"Owens Inflicts His Pain on Tulsa." *Los Angeles Times,* March 23, 2003.

Packer, Billy and Roland Lazenby. *Fifty Years of the Final Four: Golden Moments of the NCAA Basketball Tournament.* Dallas, TX: Taylor Publishing, 1987.

Peeler, Tim. *When March Went Mad: A Celebration of NC State's 1983 National Championship.* Champaign, IL: Sports Publishing LLC, 2007.

Pitino, Rick. *Full-Court Pressure: A Year in Kentucky Basketball.* New York: Hyperion Books, 1993.

"Q&A: U.S. Reed, Part 1." Arkansas Expats/SB Nation, July 21, 2009.

Raleigh City Museum Staff. "Remembering the 1983 Cardiac Pack." *Raleigh Downtowner* 4, no. 2: 8.

Raley, Dan. "Where Are They Now? John Castellani, Seattle U Basketball Coach." *Seattle Post-Intelligencer,* March 27, 2007.

Rappoport, Ken. *The Classic: The History of the NCAA Basketball Championship.* Kansas City: National Collegiate Athletic Association, in cooperation with Lowell Press, 1979.

Reed, Billy. *The Final Four: Reliving America's Basketball Classic.* Lexington, KY: Host Communications, 1987.

Reed, William. "Scandal Branded Him, But His Charm Won People Back." SportsIllustrated.com, November 30, 2007.

———. "The Story of Ralph Beard." *Sports Illustrated,* November 30, 2007.

"Richmond Shocks Gamecocks." *Associated Press,* March 13, 1998.

Russell, Michael. "When Firs Stood Tall." *The Oregonian,* June 22, 2008.

Schrader, Loel. "Big Bad Bruins Huff, Puff Past Drake; Purdue Next." *Long Beach Press Telegram,* March 21, 1969.

Self, Bill and John Rhode. *Bill Self: At Home in the Phog.* Overland Park, KS: Ascend Media, 2008.

Schecter, B. J. "Harry Flournoy, Texas Western Forward." SportsIllustrated.com, April 6, 1998.

Smith, Dean, John Kilgo, and Sally Jenkins. *A Coach's Life.* New York: Random House, 2002.

Smith, Marcia. "Richmond Ousts South Carolina; Xavier is Upset." *Philadelphia Inquirer,* March 13, 1998.

Tarkanian, Jerry and Dan Wetzel. *Runnin' Rebel: Shark Tales of "Extra Benefits," Frank Sinatra and Winning It All.* Champaign, IL: Sports Publishing, 2006.

Terhune, Jim. *Tales from the 1980 Louisville Cardinals.* Champaign, IL: Sports Publishing, 2004.

Thompson, David, Sean Stormes, and Marshall Terrill. *David Thompson: Skywalker.* Champaign, IL: Sports Publishing, 2003.

"Thurman Buries Shot of a Lifetime." *Annapolis Capital,* April 5, 1994.

Tobitt, Bill. "Oregon, Texas Cages Clash in NCAA Tourney Tonight." *Oakland Tribune,* March 20, 1939.

Trease, Denny. *Tales from the Kentucky Hardwood.* Champaign, IL: Sports Publishing, 2002.

Turner, Landon and Stan Sutton. *Tales from the 1980–81 Indiana Hoosiers.* Champaign, IL: Sports Publishing, 2005.

"U.S. Reed: From Answering Prayers to Leading Them." Rivals.com, July 1, 2006.

Wahl, Grant. "Rock Chalk, Champions." *Sports Illustrated,* April 8, 2008.

Walker, Teresa. "Memphis Down After Defeat." *Associated Press,* April 8, 2008.

Walton, Bill and Gene Wojciechowski. *Nothing But Net: Just Give Me the Ball and Get Out of the Way.* New York: Hyperion Books, 1995.

Wilbon, Michael. "Led by Murray State, NCAA Tournament's Lower-Seeded Teams Make Their Presence Felt." *Washington Post,* March 19, 2010.

Woelfel, Gery. "Wood Recalls 'Game of Change.'" *Journal Times,* April 6, 2008.

Wolff, Alexander. "Ghosts of Mississippi." *Sports Illustrated,* March 10, 2003.

———. "State of Siege." *Sports Illustrated,* April 4, 2000.

———. "The Untouchables." *Sports Illustrated,* April 8, 1996.

Wolff, Alexander and Michael Atchison. "Utah the First Cinderella." *Sports Illustrated,* March 22, 2010.

Wooden, John. *They Call Me Coach.* New York: Contemporary Books, 1988.

VIDEO

"1992 East Regional Final Duke vs. Kentucky." *Battle Lines*. ESPN Classic. December 16, 2001. http://www.youtube.com/watch?v=KVLU94XTL4A.

"Top Tourney Performances." *Honor Roll*. ESPNU. Date unknown. http://www.youtube.com/watch?v=I2CE-SSkPJE&feature=related.

"UCLA Bruins-1969." *Honor Roll*. ESPNU. Date unknown. http://www.youtube.com/watch?v=Dt4UducROR4&feature=related.

"Greatest Sports Legends, Kareem Abdul-Jabbar." 1983. http://www.youtube.com/watch?v=4Qjthwn1_T4.

"Prelude to a Championship." CBS Sports. 2008. http://www.youtube.com/watch?v=KrG3BYQiI1Y.

NCAA Press Conference. Fox Sports. March 22, 2009. http://video.app.msn.com/watch/video/zags-beat-buzzer-top-hilltoppers/12z2fr4t.

NCAA Press Conference. Associated Press. March 22, 2009. http://www.blinkx.com/watch-video/gonzaga-wins-a-thriller/WuSpv569CMKKETzHHWZUZg.

"Gonzaga University: Demetri 'Meech' Goodson on Game-Winning." Gonzaga U News Service. March 21, 2009. http://www.youtube.com/watch?v=zEbsnyZKy8w&feature=related.

Marquette Washington NCAA Press Conference. http://www.ncaa.com/video/basketball-men/2010-12-15/ncaa-m-baskbl-pgpc-video-live-free-11-washington-vs-6-marquette-san-.

"From Glory Days TV Show w/ Terry Mills 1 of 3." From Glory Days. June 8, 2009. http://www.youtube.com/watch?v=uA0FDAAfWPk.

"Butler Punches Final Four Ticket, Defeats Kansas State 63–56." Horizon League Network. March 27, 2010. http://www.youtube.com/watch?v=nYjS1mtl_0E.

"Oral History Interview with Robert A. Kurland." O-State Stories. http://dc.library.okstate.edu/cdm4/document.php?CISOROOT=/ostate&CISOPTR=7169&CISOSHOW=7167.

"Rumeal Robinson." *E:60*. ESPN. October 12, 2010. http://www.youtube.com/watch?v=WdGe4-Migbc.

"Lions Drop Heartbreaker to Temple, 66–64." NCAA Press Conference. Blue White Illustrated. March 17, 2011. http://www.youtube.com/watch?v=I1n-GatvAH8&feature=endscreen&NR=1.

"Bobby Knight on the 35th Anniversary of His Undefeated Indiana Hoosiers." ESPN. March 29, 2011. http://www.youtube.com/watch?v=ERl9L3zQYoA.

"NSU Men's Basketball: Missouri Postgame Interviews pt.2." NSU Athletics. March 16, 2012. http://www.youtube.com/watch?v=JBzN_qjmLeU.

"Norfolk State Players: Mar. 16, 2012." GatorSports. March 16, 2012. http://www.youtube.com/watch?v=VHfNKI5yW4I.

"Brett Reed, Lehigh." *Sports Center Tonight*. ESPN Radio. March 16, 2012. http://espn.go.com/espnradio/play?id=7700807.

"Historic Defeat." *Sports Center*. ESPN. March 16, 2012. http://www.youtube.com/watch?v=fZmfNf5GJdA.

"McCollum Leads Lehigh Past Duke." ESPN. March 17, 2012. http://espn.go.com/video/clip?id=7700099

"Transcript of UK Press Conference After Title Game." April 3, 2012. http://johnclay.bloginky.com/2012/04/03/transcript-of-uk-press-conference-after-title-game/#.

"Video: Kentucky Press Conference Sunday at Final Four." April 1, 2012. http://johnclay.bloginky.com/2012/04/01/video-kentucky-press-conference-sunday-at-final-four/#.

"What's Next? Calipari Seeks Perfection." ESPN. April 3, 2012. http://espn.go.com/mens-college-basketball/blog/_/name/katz_andy/id/7768870/calipari-title-now-wants-undefeated-season.

Norfolk State vs. Missouri Live Postgame Press Conference. Recorded on March 16, 2012.

Lehigh vs. Duke Live Postgame Press Conference. Recorded on March 16, 2012.

AUTHOR INTERVIEWS

Steve Alford
Derek Anderson
Mike Anderson
Rick Anderson
Harold Arceneaux
Ronnie Arrow
Stanley Asumnu
Thurl Bailey
Greg Ballif
Lonny Baxter
John Beilein
Tony Bennett
Kevin Bettencourt
Curtis Blair
Frank Blatcher
Jim Boeheim
Matt Bouldin
Jim Boylan
Tom Brennan
Harry Broadnax
Marc Brown
Marseilles Brown
Scott Burrell
Lamar Butler
John Castellani
Jason Cipolla
Mateen Cleaves
Terry Connolly
Fran Corcoran
Dave Corzine
Bobby Cremins
Denny Crum
Bob Dalton
Dick Davey
Tom Davis
Matt Doherty
Bryce Drew
Homer Drew
Ralph Drollinger
Fran Dunphy
John Egan
Anthony Epps
Larry Farmer
Ali Farokhmanesh
Arnie Ferrin
Morris Finley
Steve Fisher

Pat Flannery
James Forrest
Richard Fox
Richie Frahm
Jeff Fryer
Kevin Gamble
Mike Gansey
Dino Gaudio
Tate George
Artis Gilmore
John Goldsberry
Steve Goodrich
A. J. Granger
Charlie Greenburg
Cliff Hagan
Billy Hahn
Jeff Hall
Jerry Harkness
Jim Harney
Vernon Hatton
Bob Heaton
Paul Hewitt
Bill Hodges
Al Horford
Darrin Horn
Tom Huerter
Bobby Hurley
Darrall Imhoff
Tom Izzo
Ben Jacobson
Jaren Jackson
Andy Jensen
Mike Jones
Popeye Jones
Wallace Jones
George Kaftan
Weldon Kearns
Brian Kellerman
Billy Kennedy
Bo Kimble
Toby Knight
Adam Koch
Charlie Kraak
Mike Krzyzewski
Matt Lapin
Jim Larranaga
Butch Lee

Bill Leinhard
Bobby Leonard
Junie Lewis
Gabe Lewullis
Michael Lindeman
Chris Lofton
Clyde Lovellette
Korie Lucious
Mark Madsen
Jeff Martin
Rollie Massimino
Luc Richard Mbah A Moute
Fran McCaffery
John McCarthy
Bill McClintock
Doug McIntosh
Mike McConathy
Chris McNaughton
Steve Merfeld
Joey Meyer
Eldon Miller
Ron Miller
Cameron Mills
Walt Misaka
Cameron Mills
Dan Monson
Don Monson
Mike Montgomery
Ricky Moore
Ronald Moore
Rex Morgan
Troy Muilenburg
Ford Mullen
Danny Nee
Drew Nicholas
Mel Nowell
Lute Olson
Freddie Owens
Scott Padgett
Kenton Paulino
Derrick Phelps
Ed Pinckney
Joe Quigg
Frank Ramsey
Randy Ramsey
Clinton Ransey

Fred Rehn, Jr.
Don Reid
Fred Roberts
Joey Rodriguez
Ty Rogers
Lorenzo Romar
Lennie Rosenbluth
Delaney Rudd
Kenny Sailors
Matt Santangelo
Bob Scrabis
Petey Sessoms
Jeff Sheppard
Larry Siegfried
Tony Skinn
Keith Smart
Shaka Smart
Ishmael Smith
T. J. Sorrentine
Terence Stansbury
Brad Stevens
Tim Stoddard
Dick Tarrant
Terrell Taylor
Tom Thacker
Danero Thomas
Isiah Thomas
Scotty Thurman
Pete Trgovich
Donnie Tyndall
John Vallely
Dean Vander Plas
John Wallace
Bobby Watson
Bruce Weber
Jarrod West
Paul Westhead
Herb Wilkinson
Donald Williams
Duck Williams
Gary Williams
Marvin Williams
Reggie Williams
Roy Williams
George Wilson
John Woolery

Index